Money, Financial Markets, and the Economy

Money, Financial Markets, and the Economy

J. C. Poindexter
North Carolina State University at Raleigh

Charles P. Jones
North Carolina State University at Raleigh

West Publishing Company
St. Paul • New York • Los Angeles • San Francisco

COPYRIGHT © 1980 By WEST PUBLISHING CO.
50 West Kellogg Boulevard
P.O. Box 3526
St. Paul, Minnesota 55165

Printed in the United States of America

Library of Congress Cataloging in Publication Data

Poindexter, Julius Carl, 1943–
    Money, financial markets, and the economy.

    Includes bibliographical references and index.
    1. Finance. 2. Financial institutions. 3. Money.
4. Banks and banking. I. Jones, Charles Parker,
1943– joint author. II. Title.
HG173.P64   332   79-10893
ISBN 0-8299-0225-2

To Carlyle, Katherine, and Kathryn

Preface

This textbook is designed for undergraduate courses in Money and Banking, Financial Institutions, and, in some cases, the courses offered under the Capital Markets designation. The introductory course in economics is adequate background for the courses which this volume is intended to serve. Undergraduates in economics and business often have only one of the three courses listed above for their complete formal exposure to the financial sector of the economy.

The importance of money and the banking system has long been recognized. Recently, however, the neglect of nonmonetary financial institutions and markets and of modern financial decision-making theory has become increasingly distasteful. Instructors in traditional money and banking courses have sought supplementary materials on the nonmonetary segments of financial markets and on portfolio management theory. At the same time, new entrants into the teaching of financial institution courses, which have traditionally been taught descriptively, have had no suitable text for analytically probing the financial market *within* the confines of a larger economic system.

Money, Financial Markets, and the Economy gives due regard to money and the banking system, but as prominent cogs in a broader, intergrated mechanism of financial markets, instruments, and institutions. The financial sector is, in turn, treated as an important part of the overall economic system, influencing that system and, in turn, being influenced by developments in the other parts of the economic system. In summary, the intention of this text is to provide comprehensive and integrated coverage of money and banking, financial system operation, money and capital markets, and real macroeconomy—a combination of topics that should serve the interests of a wide student audience.

As a beginning to a detailed consideration of the component parts of the financial system, the first section of the book provides a simple and largely descriptive overview of the overall economy and the financial sector of the economy. Money and the monetary role of the banking system are then treated comprehensively but compactly. Logically, attention is turned next to nonmonetary financial transactions. Under this broad heading, the functioning of the financial system as a conduit for transferring the savings of surplus units to those economic units that have high-priority uses for funds is probed. The analytical structure developed in this section provides a background for the more descriptive material on particular financial institutions and markets which follows.

The fourth section of the text explores the institutional structure of the financial system subdivided, first, by instruments, then by markets and financial institutions. The anatomies of intermediaries and other financial institutions, as well as of markets and methods of finance are discussed in the light of a previously developed financial market structure. After this section, attention is focused on developing the linkages between the financial system and the real macroeconomy. These linkages are exploited in assessing the causes and consequences of both inflations and excessive unemployment. Disagreements on the causes and appropriate cures for economic instability are discussed in this section of the text. The final chapter draws attention to the modern econometric efforts to construct models of the economy that integrate the financial sector. It also discusses international considerations.

While the issues treated in this text require an analytical approach, the descriptive material that is necessary for a broad understanding of the financial sector of the economy is provided as well. As much as possible the authors have tried to provide the most current economic and financial figures available so that this text is as up-to-date as it can be and an accurate statement of the present economic realities in the United States.

Contents

Money, Financial Markets, and the Economy

PART 1

An Introduction to Money, Financial Markets, and the Economy

Welcome to the world of money, financial markets, production, and employment! Of course, you already know of the existence of this world. Indeed, you are a participant in it, and some of you may have much more than a nodding acquaintance with various facets of this world. Your presence in this course, though, suggests that you don't know as much as you would like.

Perhaps you would like to know how banks as they currently exist came to be; why there is a Federal Reserve System; why the housing industry sometimes suffers from a "credit crunch" and, at other times, prospers while the rest of the economy is in the doldrums. You may want to know how unemployment and inflation occur and what money and financial markets have to do with these problems. You may be interested in the opportunities for enhancing your wealth that the purchase of stocks, bonds, or other financial assets provides. These and many other related issues are dealt with in this text. With a diligent effort on your part, you should know a great deal more about money, financial markets, and the economy by the time you complete this course.

This text is divided into five parts, of which the first and shortest contains just two chapters. The first chapter provides a broad overview of the financial system. By tracing the possible path of evolution of a hypothetical economy, from a primitive barter system to one that has the basic attributes of a modern-day economy, chapter 1 illustrates the functions that are performed by money, financial assets other than money, markets for financial assets and agents who serve those markets, and various other component parts of a modern financial

1

system. This exercise also serves to define, in terms of participants and functions, what constitutes a financial system.

Chapter 2 presents the conceptual framework necessary for understanding the measures that allow us to monitor financial activity and to identify emerging problems in today's financial, product, and labor markets. This chapter also provides some familiarity with the actual aggregate output and financial flow data that are of foremost interest to macroeconomists and financial analysts.

1

An Introduction to the Financial System in a Market Economy

"Money Supply Spurts Upward at a 9% Rate," "GNP Declines for Third Consecutive Quarter," "Inflation Slows as Year Ends." "Housing Starts Quicken," "Stock Market Hits New High for Year"—such signals receive widespread and close attention as indicators of current and future economic vigor. The importance of a healthy economy and of the roles of money and the financial marketplace in nurturing economic vitality are clearly indicated by the headline prominence of observations like these.

In the process of working through this book, you will develop a framework for analysis of the forces that influence the economy, and the causes of changes in the economy's vital signs will be probed within that framework. But the bulk of your attention will be focused on a portion of the economy that is commonly referred to as the *financial system*, an entity that is often ill defined, as it must remain for us at this time. To develop a comprehensive understanding of the financial system and its functions, it must be viewed as an integral part of a complete economic system, which influences and in turn is influenced by the rest of the economy. In light of that requirement, our first order of business is the provision of a brief overview of the basic functions of a complete economy.

AN OVERVIEW

Most beginning texts introduce students to economics by suggesting that people's material wants are insatiable while the resources available to accommodate those wants are limited. The recent popularization of inter-

3

est in environmental issues, energy resource depletion, and related concerns has led people to denigrate mere material possessions, but it is still the case that, for society at large, the amount of material goods and services that people want vastly exceeds the production capabilities of even the most advanced economic system. Economic utopia has not been achieved; every economic system must pursue the practical goal of providing for society's wants as well as possible, given the limits on its productive capacity.

All economic systems, then, must provide for the production, distribution, and consumption of material goods and services. An *efficient* economic system allocates resources to productive use in a pattern that maximizes society's material well-being, consistent with the prevailing state of technology and the endowment of resources available to that economy. The task is demanding, for the proper quantities of land, labor, capital, and entrepreneurial skill must be allocated to the production of thousands of different goods and services, and a proper division of production between goods for consumption and investment in new plants, equipment, and inventories must be accomplished. Moreover, the goals of full employment, price stability, balance-of-payments equilibrium, equity in the distribution of income, and political freedom are all accorded high priorities (but not necessarily equal priorities) by modern societies.

Needless to say, money and financial markets play a crucial role in every advanced economic system. Ask any participant in the business world how important the nation's financial system is, and the immediate response will be that it is fundamental. Indeed, the respondent might rightly claim that most of the industries that now serve us could not exist as we know them and that the standard of living we now enjoy would not be possible without an efficient financial system. Yet, he or she would likely be hard pressed if asked to provide a comprehensive and lucid explanation of what constitutes the financial system and why it is so fundamentally important.

Most of us are active participants in the financial system who take advantage of a number of the services it provides. Yet few of us have a coherent understanding of the great diversity of these services, both for individual economic units and for the economy at large. As you proceed through this book, the array of functions the financial system performs will be illuminated and the importance of financial institutions will be assessed. This chapter will record in some detail the basic functions of the financial system within the structure of the whole economy.

Since a modern financial system and its links to the rest of the economy are complex, efforts to understand them necessarily require substantial exertion. However, there are methods of extending our understanding of this intricate system that are more productive than a frontal assault on it. The remainder of this chapter will proceed simply to illustrate the most fundamental functions of a financial system. Yet the lessons conveyed must be learned, as they will be applicable to the complex real world with which we must deal.

MONEY AND FINANCIAL MARKETS IN THE EVOLUTION OF ECONOMIC SYSTEMS

Alternative forms of economic systems, even alternative forms of basically market-dominated capitalistic systems, provide for society's material needs with different degrees of success. Of course, the modern, sophisticated, western capitalistic economy and its financial system is our ultimate concern. But a broad view of the fundamental functions of a financial system can best be achieved by an indirect route, which involves a comparison of the performance of economies at different stages of historical development.

A Primitive Barter Economy

Let our evolutionary journey begin with a look at a relatively primitive economic system that lacks two entities of crucial concern to us, money and a financial system. (We shall see that it is highly unlikely that you would want to live in such an economy). For the population to survive in this primitive economy, there must be production of real goods and services—of food, clothing, shelter, and so on—and there must also be exchange. Corn growers who have a surplus might exchange corn with weavers who have surplus cloth, with cobblers who have surplus shoes, and so on. Such specialization in production is possible only if the fruits of each individual's efforts can be exchanged for other goods and services. Specialization and exchange permit each sort of commodity to be produced by the individuals and groups that are relatively most efficient in that commodity's production, and this vastly increases society's productive capacity over what would be possible without specialization (e.g., in a Robinson Crusoe world of self-sufficiency).

Unfortunately, arranging exchanges in a barter economy is a costly task, since it absorbs productive time and effort that have alternative uses. A corn grower with a three-bushel surplus must find a weaver willing to swap surplus cloth for corn at an exchange rate acceptable to the grower. A cattle raiser who wishes to swap one steer for two pairs of shoes, a haircut, a coil of rope, and a pig generally has to search out several producers who are willing to involve themselves in a complex set of direct and indirect barter transactions that will provide each participant with beef, shoes, haircuts, rope, and pork at acceptable exchange rates. Imagine the productive energy expended as this group bargains over who gets what, for what, and from whom, even after the cattle raiser has located suppliers who are willing to get involved in such a tangle. And the cattle raiser faces a relatively simple task. The difficulties that would confront any of the commercial enterprises that you deal with daily, enterprises that provide a large variety of products, clearly would be insurmountable. Few enterprises as we know them could survive in a barter system.

The fundamental deficiencies of a barter system for exchanging goods and services should be vividly apparent. The need for a *double coincidence of wants*—finding someone who has what I want and wants what I have—before barter exchanges can take place requires every producer to store and to transport surplus products, until a suitable exchange can be arranged, and meanwhile to expend resources in a search for trading partners. With time, human energy, and other productive factors devoured during the quest for exchanges, the volume of resources left for producing commodities and services is reduced. Considerable effort must also be expended to ascertain the rates at which each commodity can be exchanged for every other—information that is essential for one to make the most favorable (direct or indirect) exchanges possible. Moreover, a cumbersome, inefficient exchange system acts to offset the efficiencies gained by specialization in production, so that it discourages such specialization and hence further limits the economy's productive capacity.

The barter system also penalizes frugality; it inhibits the accumulation of productive resources, which would improve the nation's material well-being. In the barter economy, an individual household that wishes to save for future needs, such as a car, a home, or retirement income, must store its savings in commodities—in bins of corn or wheat, in cloth, in barrels of oil or wine, and so on. Storing accumulated savings in the form of commodities is clearly a costly and somewhat risky venture. And, without a financial system, producing units that wish to invest in new productive facilities are apt to be frustrated in their efforts to accumulate the necessary real resources. With no efficient mechanism to enable potential investors to acquire at once an enlarged volume of real resources from other savers, investment can take place only if individual producing units accumulate resources through their own saving. Many worthwhile opportunities for investment in expanded facilities, in technologically improved production processes, and in facilities to produce new products have to be postponed or even foregone under such a system. Moreover, the saving that takes place in such a system is not allocated to investment outlets that provide the greatest benefits to society. Savers who lack highly profitable investment outlets invest in low-yielding production facilities or simply hold idle stocks of commodities. At the same time, many of those with rewarding investment opportunities—(whose relatively attractive yields reflect the value society places on the potential production of those facilities) would be powerless to exploit those opportunities.

In our primitive system, improvement in society's well-being is severely restrained: investment is discouraged in total, and much of the investment that does take place is directed toward economically inferior projects. Quite obviously, this primitive barter economy is in need of some innovations that can (1) bring together the buyers and sellers of goods and services in a more efficient, less costly manner and (2) efficiently channel the financial surpluses of savers into uses that contribute most to society's material well-being.

The Miracle of Money

Although the guardians of morality in our barter economy might consider such an innovation threatening (after all, some consider money the root of all evil!), the introduction of a *money*—some item that is commonly accepted as a means of payment and in terms of which exchangeable goods and services can be valued—can vastly improve the performance of that system. After this innovation is introduced, the cattle rancher can sell his surplus production for money, then selectively purchase with money the goods and services he demands from other producers. Since money is readily accepted by all, no longer must a producer search for a group of cotraders willing to engage in a complex set of exchanges. Individuals can hold their accumulated savings in money—a form that enjoys lower storage costs and greater durability—rather than in commodities. Moreover, the amount of information needed by market participants is greatly reduced, since, in a money economy, there is no need to keep track of the exchange value of every salable item relative to every other salable item. Every item has a market price in money, and, by knowing these market prices, one has complete information on the relative values of any two items.[1]

Of course, with money providing an efficient means of exchanging commodities and services, resources that previously were absorbed in the arrangement of exchanges and in the storage and transportation of commodities while exchanges were sought are freed for alternative uses. By the same token, the volume of productive resources needed to keep track of the exchange values of different commodities is reduced. With lower costs of exchanging goods and services, specialization in production is encouraged, which further raises the economy's productive capacity. It is also worth noting that, since savings can be held in the form of money, a form more durable and less costly to store than commodities, saving and the attendant accumulation of productive resources are stimulated, which also contributes to an enlargement of the economy's productive capacity.

It is no mere coincidence that every known society, past and present, has had a money. The advantages that money bestows are so compelling that a society without a money would have to create one. In 1978, the

---

[1]Chapter 3, which focuses on money and the functions it performs, will illustrate the dramatic reduction in the volume of price information that is relevant in a money economy.

economy of the United States was served by a money supply of $360 billion. With a gross national product of over $2,100 billion, each dollar of the money supply was used on the average nearly six times during 1978 to buy final goods and services.

While the existence of money vastly improves the functioning of an exchange economy, its introduction into the primitive economy still does not provide for the allocation of the saving to the most desirable of ends. An individual household or producer still cannot spend for a new house, a new factory, an improved assembly line, or the development of new products until sufficient savings (in money or commodity form) have been accumulated to cover the cost of the project under consideration. Savings are still inefficiently deployed in low-yield ventures, while many more rewarding opportunities are postponed or abandoned. Once again, with no mechanism for those with financial surpluses to channel their saving to high-priority outlets and be rewarded for doing so, saving (and capital accumulation) still would not receive the encouragement that would be provided by an efficient mechanism for channeling saving into its most productive uses. The simple money economy remains fertile ground for further innovation, even though the introduction of money has vastly increased the system's productive performance.

A Market for Nonmonetary Financial Claims

Envision, for a moment, the plight of a producer who has an investment opportunity that is expected to return a handsome profit but who lacks the accumulated savings necessary to exploit it. If only a method could be devised for spending some of the income expected from that project *before* its receipt, the investment could be undertaken immediately. An innovative producer faced with this problem might invent a *nonmonetary financial claim*—a legal agreement that, in return for the provision of monetary purchasing power in the present, obligates the issuer to the supplier of funds. The nonmonetary financial asset could take the form of a *debt issue* (a bond or similar security that calls for the payment of interest and the repayment of borrowed principle) or, in the case of an incorporated business, an *equity issue* (a security, such as a common stock, that gives the buyer an ownership interest in the issuing firm).

Of course, the possessor of surplus funds will not willingly swap money for an alternative financial *asset* (the claim against the issuer of that asset) unless he expects a return that is superior to what is available through his own more direct use of the funds. But high-priority outlets for accumulated funds can provide compensation both for the financial surplus units (which provide saving) and for the financial deficit units (which spend more than current income). To illustrate, someone like Henry Ford, with a novel method of producing autos, might realize a 30 percent rate of return on investments in facilities for producing those autos—a return that could easily support the payment of an attractive interest yield on securities sold to obtain financing for that investment.

With the development of *financial markets*—institutions and mechanisms through which the savings of economic units with financial surpluses are exchanged for the financial obligations of units with financial deficits —the saving that accrues to units with financial surpluses can be allocated to preferred investment outlets. In this manner, real resources (labor, land, plants, and so on) are made available to those with uses that enjoy a high social (and hence a high private) priority. In a complex modern economy, a system in which demands, production techniques, and the accessibility of various sorts of raw materials can change dramatically over time, a system of financial markets to facilitate the transfer of resources from financial surplus units to financial deficit units is essential to the common welfare.

Clearly, financial markets are productive. Without them, Edwin Rand, who sought several hundred thousand dollars in the 1940s to finance the Polaroid Corporation, and Chester Carlson, who had no personal wealth to launch Xerox Corporation, would have been unable to convert their innovative ideas into products that meet society's needs. Likewise, existing economic units, large and small, need access to funds through the financial marketplace—funds for expanding facilities, for financing inventories, for maintaining adequate cash reserves in periods when sales revenues are depressed, and so on.

The invention of nonmonetary financial claims and the associated development of financial markets also serves the function of providing financial surplus units with access to earning assets without requiring them to purchase *real* (physical) *assets.* The availability of financial assets that yield a return on accumulated savings, which therefore allow financial surplus units to enjoy an enhanced standard of living in the future, is likely to stimulate the generation of saving-surpluses and their transfer to deficit units. If saving is increased by the availability of income-generating financial claims, the accumulation of the plants, equipment, and materials that contribute to growth in the economy's productive capacity is also stimulated. We must remember, too, that a household can experience deficits in the financing of a home, an automobile, or a similar big-ticket purchase. Nonmonetary financial claims make it possible to acquire consumer goods and services when they are wanted, so that households need not postpone their consumption for lack of savings. As a reflection of the expected mutual benefits to surplus and deficit units, approximately $485 billion passed through the U.S. financial marketplace in 1978. Of this total, around $55 billion was borrowed by households for consumption purposes, over $145 flowed into mortgages, just over $110 billion was borrowed by governmental units, and the bulk of the rest went to business firms.

Specialization in the Exchange of Financial Instruments

An economic unit (household, business firm, or governmental unit), to the extent that it has accumulated savings, can finance current expenditures greater than its current income by dissaving. An economic unit that wishes to incur a deficit that it cannot or will not cover with accumulated savings can do so by issuing *primary securities*—contracts, generally evidenced by pieces of paper, that represent debt or equity claims against the issuer. A borrower who issues a primary security and exchanges it with a saver in return for funds is involved in *direct finance.* For example, General Motors might negotiate a direct loan from a Rockefeller and provide Rockefeller with an IOU in return for the immediate use of money. The financing needs of large business firms, however, are often so massive that they would exhaust the savings of the richest of households. And think of the effort General Motors would have to expend to finance a large retooling program (say, to convert to small-car production) if it had to negotiate direct loans or direct sales of stock, presumably with a large number of lenders or investors. The need for large producing units like General Motors to borrow from many different lenders, each of which provides only a small part of the firm's financing needs, is made more complicated by the needs of financial surplus units, each with different wishes for the amount they wish to lend, the time periods over which they wish to lend, the risk they are willing to assume, and so on. While the mere creation of nonmonetary financial claims—of debt and equity securities—facilitates the direct flow of saving from financial surplus units to financial deficit units, restrictions on that flow still remain. These restrictions demand the emergence of specialized agents, institutions, and mechanisms for bringing surplus and deficit units together more efficiently than is possible with direct loans or equity purchases negotiated directly between the savers and the deficit unit that ultimately uses the savings.

Brokers and the Benefit of Improved Information. We might expect the appearance, at first, of loan *brokers,* who seek to match borrowers and lenders for a fee. As a specialist, continuously involved in the pairing of borrowers and lenders, the broker can be expected to arrange flows of savings from surplus to deficit units more efficiently than the ultimate lenders and borrowers could themselves. That is, brokers reduce the high information costs of getting surplus and deficit units together. Moreover, with access to numerous financial surplus units, the broker permits the issuer of primary securities to partition its borrowings into small lots, which are more acceptable to the lenders. With small-denomination financial assets available, savers can hold a *diversified portfolio* of financial assets issued by different borrowers (not put all their eggs in one basket). If primary securities are available in convenient sizes, small enough to allow lenders to reduce their risk through holding a diversified portfolio, the flow of saving to the ultimate users of that saving is encouraged.

Underwriters. Operating exclusively as a broker, the agent who pairs borrowers and lenders for a fee offers only search services and never acquires ownership of the securities being exchanged. Hence a broker bears no risk for the failure of an issue of primary securities to sell at a desirable price. However, since this risk of depressed security prices is disagreeable to the issuers of primary securities, it is likely that some specialists in the financial marketplace will find it advantageous to operate as *investment bankers,* underwriting the issuance of primary securities. An *underwriter* buys the primary securities directly from the issuer for an agreed purchase price and assumes the risk of selling them to financial surplus units, with the hope of gaining a profit from the spread between the purchase price and the resale price. The earnings the underwriter acquires through the resale of a primary security issue constitute a reward, not only for pairing the financial deficit unit with savers, but also for bearing a risk that the primary security issuer prefers to avoid—the risk that the issue's price will have to be reduced for it to sell.

Secondary markets. The direct flow of savings from economic units with accumulated financial surpluses to the ultimate users of savings is augmented further by the development of *secondary markets* for securities. In effect, secondary markets are "second-hand," or resale, markets in which existing securities can be bought and sold. With such markets, savers who hold financial claims acquire the ability to exchange those claims for money whenever the need arises. This possibility encourages financial surplus units to make their savings available to those with high-priority outlets rather than to hoard them.

Financial Intermediaries and Asset Transformation. Even after the emergence of brokers and underwriters, differences are apt to remain between the terms on which the issuers of primary securities wish to provide those securities and the terms on which savers want to offer their savings. The typical deficit unit wishes to obtain financing in large blocks for extended time periods. Savers, however, particularly small savers, prefer (ceteris paribus) to provide funds in small lots for limited periods and to outlets that expose their savings to minimum risk. Institutions called *financial intermediaries* can provide valuable services to overcome these differences.

Financial intermediaries purchase the primary securities issued by the ultimate users and, in turn, acquire funds by issuing their own securities, which are tailored to be more attractive to ultimate savers, especially to relatively small-scale savers. Hence these institutions occupy an intermediate position between savers and the ultimate users of savings; they help to channel saving to high-priority uses indirectly. Commercial banks, mutual savings banks, savings and loan associations, credit unions, insurance companies, and a number of other institutions, including some government agencies, act as financial intermediaries, transforming primary securities into *indirect securities*. Savings and loan associations, for example, acquire funds from savers by offering interest-paying *savings accounts* (called *share accounts*) and *certificates of deposit*. They use these funds mainly to purchase mortgages (primary securities issued by building contractors, households, and business firms). The objective of financial intermediaries is to profit from the purchase of primary securities that yield more than what they must pay on the indirect securities they issue. Of course, to merit employment as a conduit of funds from savers to users, financial intermediaries must provide funds to the issuers of primary securities on more attractive terms than those that would be available if the primary securities were sold directly to the ultimate savers: without more attractive terms, the primary securities would be directly placed. In addition, intermediaries must provide indirect securities to savers that are more attractive than the available primary securities: without this attraction, savers would opt to exchange their funds for primary securities. With the sizable accumulation of savings that it collects from numerous financial surplus units, an intermediary is able to acquire a portfolio of primary securities that differ in size, time to maturity, and identity of the issuer. Holding financial claims against a number of issuers of those claims insulates the intermediary from catastrophe, if, say, one or two of those primary security issuers go bankrupt and default on their financial obligations. The indirect securities that the intermediary issues typically are available for small and variable cash outlays and, in many cases, can readily be converted to money when the saver chooses. Such characteristics are highly attractive to small savers. Moreover, the intermediary provides the opportunity for small savers to enjoy the default-risk-reducing benefits of diversification, an opportunity that would be far less accessible to them if primary securities were the only earning financial assets available.

The benefits to the economy at large from the emergence of financial intermediaries fit what is now a familiar mold. Attractive income-yielding indirect securities, issued by intermediaries, promote saving, particularly on the part of small savers, who previously were unable to use savings except perhaps to purchase low-risk, low-yield primary securities or to invest directly in physical assets. Investment is also encouraged, since total investment is not limited to what can be financed directly. Moreover, investment can be directed toward potentially higher-yield, more innovative outlets, since the risk-reducing potential of diversification in the portfolios held (directly and indirectly) by savers encourages risk-taking by individual users of savings. Highlighting the importance of financial intermediaries, data for 1978 show that around 80 percent of the total funds supplied to the nonfinancial sectors of the U.S. economy flowed through intermediaries, while the rest flowed directly from surplus to deficit units. In contrast, as recently as the 1920s, more than half of the funds advanced in the financial market were directly placed. In 1978, commercial banks, savings institutions, and insurance and pension funds provided 93 percent of all funds advanced by private financial intermediaries in the United States, out of a total of $290.0 billion.

A visual overview of the channels through which funds can be transferred from surplus to deficit units is given in Figure 1–1.

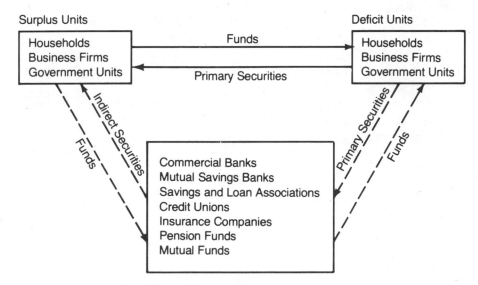

Figure 1–1. An Overview of Financial Flows. *Direct Finance* is indicated by solid lines. *Indirect Finance* is indicated by broken lines.

Any economy that enjoys the advanced degree of financial market specialization represented in the figure contains a large number of routes by which funds can be transferred. The direct and indirect routes by which funds can flow and the economic units that are involved in these flows will receive detailed attention in the chapters ahead.

SUMMARY

Every economic system must provide for the production, distribution, and consumption of material goods and services. In primitive economies, with no money and no financial system, economic trade is difficult, and consequently family units are largely self-sufficient. But the emergence of money encourages trade and, with it, the specialization and division of labor. These results improve the economic system's efficiency and hence promote an enlarged volume of current output for the system's members to enjoy, while saving and investment are encouraged and productive capacity is further enlarged by the ability to hold savings in money form. The creation of nonmonetary financial claims, which permit the transfer of funds and real resources from surplus to deficit units, provides additional improvement in the efficiency with which an emerging market economy can allocate resources, particularly between use for current consumption and use for investment, as nonmonetary financial claims permit the transfer of resources from surplus units to those with high-priority needs. But imperfect information, an aversion to risk, the preferences of surplus and deficit units for different sizes and maturity periods of financial claims, and a host of other impediments to the ideal flow of funds from surplus to deficit units have required the emergence of specialized financial agents and institutions, including brokers, underwriters, and a variety of financial intermediaries.

By tracing the development of a hypothetical primitive economy and following the improvement of its functioning, this chapter has provided a bareboned summary of what constitutes a modern-day financial system. The financial system, as outlined in this chapter, is comprised of the following:

1. money and nonmonetary claims (debt and equity securities)

2. places, institutions, or communication systems that provide a market in which financial claims can be bought and sold

3. specialists, such as brokers and underwriters, who aid in the direct transfer of funds from surplus to deficit units

4. a wide array of intermediaries that provide attractive indirect routes for the transfer of funds from surplus to deficit units

5. households, business firms, and government units that generate financial surpluses and deficits

The nature of each of these component parts and the services they bestow on an economy were described briefly in this chapter. The chapters ahead will provide a much deeper understanding of each of the major segments of the financial system in the U.S. economy and will explore the interactions between that system and the rest of the economy. In the next chapter, attention is focused on the flows of saving, investment, and credit financing in the U.S. economy of the 1970s. Chapter 3 will then initiate an intensive look at the financial assets and institutions that serve that economic system.

2

Descriptive Measures for a
Modern Economy

The overview of a market economy in chapter 1 drew attention to the
benefits generated by saving when that saving can be allocated to individuals or institutions that operate as deficit units. Historically, business
firms as a group have been the dominant deficit unit, using the saving
generated by the rest of the economy for investment purposes. In an
economy like ours, the flow of saving into investment outlets must pass
through a maze of financial institutions and markets, as saving and investment are carried out mostly by separate groups of individuals and institutions.

　　Because saving and investing are important factors in business fluctuations, economic growth, and financial market developments, we need
a clear understanding of (1) the processes that generate saving and investment and (2) the channels through which the flow of saving is allocated
to the use of deficit units. This chapter will provide a strong foundation
for that understanding and will furnish familiarity with some of the descriptive measures that are most useful to financial analysts. To address
these objectives, the first part of this chapter traces the aggregate flows
of output, saving, consumption, and investment that every economy
experiences. These flows can be visualized as streams of real goods and
services to which there correspond financial flows. The linkages between
these flows are described, and the requirements for maintaining a particular level of output and income (as the equilibrium level) from period to
period are explained.

　　With the aggregate real and financial flows in mind, the second part of this chapter provides a detailed view of the major sources of saving, the channels through which funds are transferred to deficit units, and the end uses of the funds advanced. The flow-of-funds account that is compiled for the U.S. economy is introduced and employed for tracing the paths of the funds advanced in the financial marketplace.

SURPLUS UNITS, DEFICIT UNITS, AND FINANCIAL INTERMEDIARIES

Savers are individuals or institutions that are spending less than their current income on current consumption. They can choose to directly invest some or all of their savings in real assets. In general, though, savers as a group can be expected to save more than they invest directly in real assets, which leaves a saving surplus. As was indicated in chapter 1, units whose investment in real assets is less than their current saving can conveniently be labelled *financial surplus* or *saving surplus units*. The ultimate users of saving—*financial deficit units*—are individuals or institutions that are spending more than their current income on consumption or investment.

Financial deficit units, to the extent that they possess accumulated savings in the form of money or other assets, can spend more than their current income by drawing down their money balances or selling their assets. Without accumulated savings, a deficit unit must sell new claims on itself to acquire current purchasing power greater than its current income. Financial surplus units can accumulate their surplus savings in money balances, use those savings to repurchase (and retire) existing financial claims on themselves (which they sold when operating as deficit units), or use those savings to buy other assets—notably, financial claims issued by deficit units in exchange for money.

Intermediation Everywhere

Of course, not every deficit unit restricts its financial transactions to the issuance of financial claims. For example, a business firm planning a major expansion of its production facilities may market a long-term bond (debt) or stock (equity) issue this period. In the same time period, if the funds acquired are not all used immediately for capital expenditures (and generally they are not), the firm is apt to use some of these funds to buy income-yielding securities such as short-lived U.S. Treasury securities. Conversely, economic units that generally operate as financial surplus units may also issue financial claims. For example, a household, which may have a savings account "claim" on a bank or may own U.S. Savings Bonds or stock as evidence of its role as a financial surplus unit, may also owe a large mortgage debt on its home; the mortgage is a financial claim issued by the household.

Not only is it possible for economic units of all types (households, businesses, or governments) both to issue and to acquire financial claims, but one class of economic units, the financial intermediaries, continually does both in a roughly balanced fashion. Intermediaries issue claims against themselves in order to attract funds, which they use to acquire financial claims issued by others. The very essence of intermediation is the acquisition of financial claims together with the issuance of claims against the acquiring unit; this combination allows an intermediary to raise funds from savers and pass them along to deficit units.

Any economic unit that both issues claims against itself and acquires claims against others is engaged in intermediation—in raising funds and passing them on to others. If Acme Plastic, a manufacturing firm, issues $200,000 of bonds, then turns around and extends a like amount of *trade credit* to buyers of its plastic products, it is functioning as an intermediary. All types of economic units engage in intermediation to some degree. Financial intermediaries as a class are distinguished, however, in that their assets consist predominantly of financial claims. In fact, financial claims are the quantitatively dominant entry on both sides of their balance sheets. In contrast, a quick glance at the balance sheet of Acme Plastics is likely to show that its plant and equipment assets have a value of tens of millions of dollars, while the company's financial assets (mainly in the form of trade credit) are worth a few hundred thousand dollars. In chapters 12–14, the functioning of financial intermediaries will be investigated in detail. In the meantime, attention is focused on units that, even though they may engage in some intermediation, do so in a limited fashion (so that their assets are not mainly financial).

In spite of the fact that economic units that do not qualify as intermediaries may, to some extent, both issue and acquire financial claims, it is useful to view groups of such units either as saving surplus units (engaged in the acquisition of financial claims) or as financial deficit units (engaged in the issuance of claims, which they exchange for funds). The classification as a surplus or deficit group is dictated by the net flows of funds and claims to and from that group.

The financial claims that are created to facilitate the transfer of current purchasing power from savers to the ultimate users of saving take many particular forms, but all represent future claims on real resources. A saver who purchases a financial claim exchanges money now for a future payoff that is expected to be more valuable because of *interest, dividends,* or *capital appreciation.* Of course, the issuer of financial claims incurs a liability—an obligation for a payoff in the future—in return for current purchasing power. It is apparent that the sum total of financial liabilities incurred by deficit units cannot expand or contract without a corresponding change in the total of financial assets held by saving surplus units. Indeed, every financial claim has two faces, for *the financial claims (assets) held by surplus units are obligations of the issuers.* However, this does not mean that the holder of a financial claim has to wait for its issuer to repurchase and retire it in order to *liquidate* the claim. As we already know, many financial claims can readily be sold (and resold) in secondary markets before any scheduled maturity date for their retirement.

Grouping Surplus and Deficit Units

The aggregate amount of saving that the economy generates is of fundamental importance. In addition, financial analysts benefit greatly from knowing the identities of the providers and the users of saving. This is not to say that the distribution of saving or of uses of saving across individual economic units is important for financial analysis, and fortunately so, for to monitor the transactions of every individual and institution would be an awesome task. But the roles of large cohesive groups of economic units in the generation and use of saving are a crucial concern.

Surplus and deficit units can be grouped in many ways: by region, by income class, by age group, and so on. The choice of particular groups whose actions we wish to monitor is made on the basis of its usefulness in dealing with specific problems. For several decades now, since the publication of John Maynard Keynes's *General Theory of Employment, Interest, and Money,* (1936) analyses of business fluctuations and economic growth have focused on the saving and spending activities of four groups—households, business firms, governments, and the foreign (export-import) sector. Since to understand what causes changes in economic activity is one of our major objectives, our first major task in this chapter is to describe the basic activities of the most important of these groups and to provide an introduction to the descriptive measures that capture those activities.

A Simple Two-Sector Economy

A very useful view of the functioning of a market economy can be developed by an analysis of the simplest imaginable economy—one that consists of households and business firms with no government and no foreign sector. With no government, there are no taxes and no government expenditures to complicate our task. With no foreign sector, there are no exports or imports to contend with. With all production located in the business sector of the economy and all consumption and saving occurring in the household sector, the important flows that take place in our simple two-sector economy can be represented as in Figure 2–1.

In our rudimentary economy, households, which are the ultimate owners of all factors of production, exchange productive services for money: they receive incomes in the form of wages for labor services, interest for the use of money capital, rent for the use of land, and they also

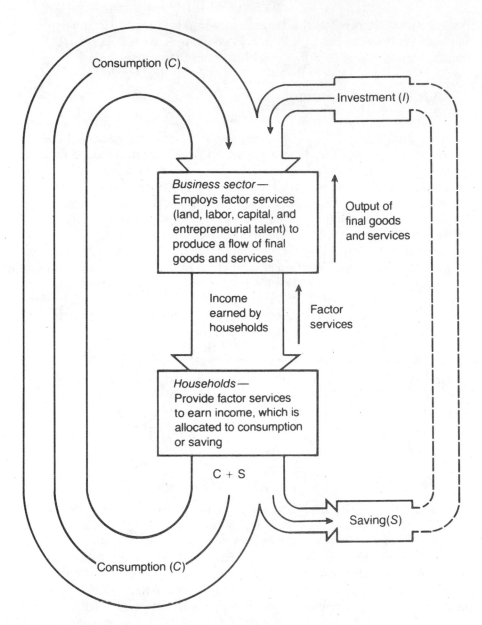

Figure 2-1. A Simple Two-Sector Economy.

receive the residual profits. The factors of production provided by households are combined in the business sector to supply a flow of goods and services for the economy's use. Some of the flow of current production is purchased for consumption as households spend a portion of their incomes. All other output in this two-sector world is "bought" as investment by business firms, which adds to the economy's accumulated stock of plants, equipment, inventories, and residential structures.

Output and Income

Valued in money terms, the total output of our rudimentary economy could be measured by adding consumption expenditures by households to investment in plants, equipment, inventories, and residential structures. That is, the value of output (Y) is $Y = C + I$, where C is consumption purchases and I is investment. This *expenditures approach* to measuring an economy's production is representative of a very limited number of techniques that are actually used for valuing output. A comparable measure of the value of output can be obtained by summing factor earnings—wages, interest, rent, and profit. Of the total revenue received by business firms in the sale of consumption and investment products in our rudimentary economy, part is allocated to the payment of wages, part goes for interest returns, and part is absorbed in rent for the use of property. Any difference between the value of total output and sum of these three factor rewards is, by definition, profit—another factor reward. Hence, in our simple economy, the income earned by the factors of production must exhaust and be identical in value to total output. Clearly, an *income approach*—a summation of wages, interest, rent, and profit—can be used to provide measures of output comparable to those offered by the expenditures approach. Expenditures and income receipts are both reflections of the same transactions, as expenditures are also, ultimately, income receipts.

Actual Saving and Actual Investment

Recall that, in reality, the bulk of saving is done by households and the bulk of investing is done by businesses (1n our model, all saving is by households and all investment by business). Since different groups are responsible for deciding how much to save and how much to invest, the amount of saving that society chooses to generate can differ markedly from the volume of investment that firms want to undertake. The flow of saving into investment is therefore shown somewhat tentatively, with broken lines, in Figure 2–1. However, the link between *actual saving* and *actual investment* in real capital goods is quite direct and unambiguous. For the two-sector economy as a whole, saving is simply the flow of current output of real goods and services that are not currently consumed. While individuals, by spending less than their current earnings on current consumption, can save and build up their money balances, their stock of nonmonetary financial claims, or their real assets, the economy at large can save only in the form of accumulated real commodities.

The part of output that is not consumed but saved is an addition to society's accumulated stock of real wealth and, presumably, is available for future use. Moreover, such additions to society's accumulated stock of physical wealth (in the form of plants, equipment, residences, and inventories) constitute the nation's investment in real commodities, and therefore all saving (nonconsumption) of current output in our simple economy is properly viewed as investment. That is, for actual measured values of saving (S) and investment (I) in our rudimentary economy, it is always the case that $I = S$.

Planned Saving and Planned Investment

While the actual flows of saving and investment in a simple, two-sector economy are identical, it remains true that *planned saving* and *planned investment*, the volumes of saving and investing that households and businesses respectively would voluntarily choose to provide under prevailing conditions, can differ markedly. Indeed, we can generally expect that the amount that people plan to save out of their income during any period will differ from the amount which businesses plan to invest during that period. And any discrepancies between planned saving and planned investment are of crucial importance, for it is precisely those discrepancies that lead to expansions and contractions of the economy's output.

With Figure 2–1 in mind, consider for a moment what basic requirement must be met for the business sector to continue to produce at the current level of output with the current volume of factor inputs. Whatever the value of current output happens to be, an identical amount of income is generated in the form of wages, rent, interest, and the residual profit. If exactly all of that income is spent on final goods and services, the business sector will be happy to maintain its current production rate, for its output has matched demand. But, as Figure 2–1 shows, some of the income generated each period is saved—some "leaks" out of the pipeline that returns (through the purchase of goods and services) the dollar outlays that the business sector provided for income payments. Clearly, for planned spending on goods and services to clear the market of current output at current prices, there must be an injection of planned investment expenditures that just offsets the leakage of saving out of the income/expenditure stream. Thus, planned investment and planned saving must be equal if the market for goods and services is to be in equilibrium.

With an injection of planned investment that just matches the leakage of saving, the sum of planned consumption and investment purchases equals the value of current output, so that businesses will be satisfied to maintain their current production rates. But what happens if, say, households decide to save more, so that planned saving comes to exceed planned investment? If planned saving increases, planned consumption spending decreases, so that the volume of total planned spending is less than current output. To illustrate such a disturbance, suppose that an economy currently produces $100 billion of goods and services, that this period's planned investment is $20 billion and planned saving is $30 billion, and that total planned purchases total $90 billion ($70 billion consumption plus $20 billion investment). Now, products that are not willingly purchased don't magically disappear; they are merely absorbed in an unintended, unplanned addition to inventories. Inventory additions are measured as investment, whether planned or not. In our example, these amount to $10 billion so that the actual observed investment is $30 billion which matches saving (observed investment = planned investment + unplanned inventory changes = $20 billion + $10 billion). But an unplanned addition to inventories causes business firms to be dissatisfied with their current production rates: it serves as a signal that the demand for their products is weaker than was expected. Firms will not continue to produce more than they can expect to sell, so that if planned saving becomes greater than planned investment, a contraction in output and employment can be expected until planned saving and planned investment are equalized.

Like an increase in planned saving, a decline in planned investment also leaves planned saving greater than planned investment (planned spending less than the value of current output) and results in a contraction in output and employment. In contrast, if planned saving falls or planned investment rises, so that planned investment exceeds planned saving (planned spending exceeds the value of current output), an unplanned shrinkage in inventories occurs. This shrinkage serves as a signal to business that demand for its production is unexpectedly strong, so that we can expect an increase in output, employment, and/or prices until planned saving and planned investment are once again equal.

Financial Flows

The saving and investment totals that we have described represent flows of real, physical products—current production that is not currently consumed, but which accumulates in an enlarged stock of material wealth available for future use. Of course, there are purely financial flows that correspond to these physical flows. Households, which provide factor inputs for the production process, are paid in money for the services they render, as shown in Figure 2–1. If households as a group spend less than their current income on real output, the surplus money receipts must be (1) hoarded, adding to households' money balances, or (2) used to acquire other, nonmonetary financial claims or real assets from the other group in the economy (i.e., from business, in our simple model). Conversely, by exchanging nonmonetary financial claims for money, the business sector can operate at a deficit and invest, and hence it can add to its accumulated stock of real assets. In our simple economy, in which business does no saving, all investment must be financed externally, through the exchange of nonmonetary financial claims for money. Hence, there is a flow of money from households to business in exchange for a return flow of non-monetary financial claims. The value of the flow of financing extended to the business sector is equal to the value of investment, and, unless new money is created, it is equal to the value of saving. In the previous example, if output and income in our rudimentary economy were at equilibrium at $100 billion, with saving and investment of $20 billion each, households would have to be purchasing $20 billion of financial claims from business firms.

Generalizing Our Analysis

The preceding analysis can be broadened considerably to take account of a number of real-world complications without altering the basic conclusions developed for the two-sector model. To begin with, some business firms don't, in fact, pay out all of their profits in dividends to their owners. Instead, they accumulate *retained earnings*, and, out of the funds accumulated, they can expand their physical facilities, add to their inventories, or acquire financial claims. Also, not all households are savers: some are always operating as deficit units, buying houses, taking "go now-pay later" vacations, and so on. Of course, it is still true that the flow of production that deficit units purchase in excess of their current incomes must have the same value as the income that savers do not consume. And the financing of the deficit incurred by businesses and households together must involve the exchange of an equivalent value of financial claims for current purchasing power. Moreover, households as a group are savers and businesses as a group operate at a deficit, so that it is still appropriate to assume that household saving provides for investment, the accumulation of capital for future productive use.

The rudimentary model can be further generalized by the addition of a government which taxes and spends. The government can save (in standard terms, operate at a surplus) if it spends less than it currently receives in taxes. Alternatively, as all of us are acutely aware, the government can operate at a deficit and spend more than it currently receives, covering the gap with the issuance of financial claims (bonds or newly created money). Government saving, like other varieties, results in investment—the accumulation of physical capital—and a government deficit is apt to result in a reduction in investment.

With a government added to our model, the money value of the economy's output (Y) is given by $Y = C + I + G$, where G is government spending and, as before, C and I are consumption and investment purchases respectively. In this more comprehensive model, total saving leakages consist of private saving (S) and government saving (the budget surplus $T - G$, where T is taxes). Hence the relevant equality between saving and investment (which always holds in an economy represented by this model) is:

$$I = S + (T - G).$$

In the more comprehensive model, equilibrium occurs only if planned spending $(C + I + G)$ is equal to output and planned investment is equal to planned saving $(S + T - G)$.

A Glimpse at the Data

Data for the United States on the most important variables confronted so far in this chapter—annual economywide flows of consumption and saving, investment, output, and income—are updated quarterly and published in the National Income and Product Accounts provided by the U.S. Department of Commerce. Illustrating the kind of measures available in those accounts, Table 2–1 shows measures of actual aggregate saving and investment for 1976.

Before attempting to digest Table 2–1, note that until now the term *investment* has been used to designate an addition to the accumulated stock of real capital. At this point, this measure of additions to capital can be more formally identified as *net investment*, with the recognition that, even as firms purchase capital goods and add to their capital stock, some of the existing stock of capital is being consumed—wearing out, becoming obsolete, or being accidentally destroyed. To have a net addition to the stock of capital, the total value of investment outlays, designated *gross investment*, must exceed the value of capital being used up, which is labelled *depreciation*. Hence, net investment is the difference between gross investment and the replacement investment necessary to offset capital depreciation. The National Income and Product Accounts provide an output measure, called *net national product*, which is the value of consumption purchases, net investment, government purchases, and (to account for sales of domestic production to foreign purchasers) net exports. Gross national product, which everyone recognizes as a popularly cited measure of the economy's output, is the corresponding sum that includes gross (instead of net) investment.

The summary measures of investment that are maintained in the United States are compiled on the basis of gross investments: they measure total outlays on investment goods, both for replacement of and for net additions to the existing capital stock. For consistency, saving must also have a "gross" measure, combining household saving, government saving, and two forms of business saving—retained earnings and the allowances firms provide for depreciation.

As Table 2–1 illustrates, gross investment and gross saving are identical, totalling $242.5 billion in 1976. Measures of net saving and net invest-

TABLE 2–1. Gross Saving and Investment, 1976 (in billions of dollars)

Gross private domestic investment		243.3
Fixed investment	230.0	
Change in business inventories	13.3	
Net foreign investment		– 0.8
Gross investment		242.5
Personal saving		65.9
Gross business saving		212.2
Undistributed profits (retained earnings)	27.6	
Capital consumption (depreciation) allowances	179.0	
Adjustment for statistical error	5.6	
Government surplus or deficit (–)		– 35.6
Gross saving		242.5

Source: *Survey of Current Business,* January 1978.

ment must be identical too; they can be obtained simply by subtracting the actual value of capital depreciation from gross saving and from gross investment. This adjustment is generally not made, because accurate measures of capital depreciation are very difficult to obtain.

Within the investment totals in Table 2–1, it is worth noting that the bulk of expenditures, $230.0 billion, are for *fixed* investment—plant, equipment, and residential structures. Inventory investment was $13.3 billion, reflecting a swelling of inventories during 1976. (Had inventories been reduced during 1976, this figure would be negative). Note that there is an entry in the table for net foreign investment. U.S. import purchases, transfers to foreigners, and government interest payments to foreigners exceeded exports in 1976, so that foreign-held dollar claims against the U.S. economy increased by $0.8 billion.

Within the saving totals in Table 2–1, business saving appears to be the main source of investable funds. This reflects the inclusion of depreciation allowances in measured saving.[1] Removing those depreciation allowances to show net saving would make the important role of household saving as a source of net investment more apparent. Note, too, that government saving (in 1976, dissaving), which reflects the combined budget balances of federal, state, and local governments, was a sizable

---

[1] It should be noted that depreciation charges are not cash outlays. They are simply accounting charges against gross revenues. The cost of assets with useful lives of several years may not be charged against firms revenues in the year of asset purchases, but must be charged against operations over the full, multi-year useful life of the assets. Depreciation allowances do represent funds available out of gross revenues for investment and other uses. Hence the usual measure of net cash flow for business firms is net income after tax plus depreciation.

$-35.6 billion. While it is still large, this deficit is significantly smaller than the $64.4 billion deficit in 1975, which was due in large part to a shortfall in federal tax receipts, as the U.S. economy in 1975 was experiencing its deepest recession since the Great Depression of the 1930s.

By providing summary measures of the economy's output—notably gross national product and net national product—the National Income and Product Accounts allow us to monitor the aggregate economy's production performance. Perhaps even more significantly, the summary measures of saving and investment that appear in those accounts are of particular importance in assessing the causes of economic fluctuations, for changes in saving or investment are the direct causes of those fluctuations. But financial analysis can benefit from more detailed information about the sources of saved funds, the channels through which they can be transferred to deficit units, and the nature of the ultimate uses of those funds. We will next focus our attention on a set of measures that provide such information, after a brief look backward to review some basic concepts and introduce some distinctions that have tacitly been assumed in the discussion to this point.

A Review of Basic Concepts

Our discussion requires a careful distinction between *stock* and *flow variables*. Flow variables must be measured across time and hence must be expressed in terms of time. In contrast, stock variables are measurable at an instant and involve no time dimension. The 11 gallons of gas in a motorboat's gas tank is a stock. The 4 gallons of gas per hour that the boat consumes at waterskiing speed is a flow. Of course, there is a close link between the flow rate of gas usage and the stock of gas in the boat's tank, as the flow rate of usage is just the rate of change in the stock over time.

A number of the economic variables confronted in this chapter can be usefully cataloged as stocks or flows. Without fail, the terms *saving* and *investment* have been used to refer to flows. Of course, the act of saving results in the accumulation of a stock—which are labelled *savings*—so that the flow rate of saving represents the rate of change of the stock of savings. Likewise, investment results in the accumulation of a stock of capital. As noted earlier, individual economic units, which save by spending less than their current incomes, can hold their accumulated savings in the form of money, nonmonetary financial claims, or real assets. In contrast, society at large, which saves by consuming less than the current production of real goods and services, can accumulate savings only in commodity form. Such net additions to the accumulated stock of real assets, in the form of new plants, equipment, residential structures, or inventory additions, constitute net investment. Hence aggregate saving and investment must be identical, as has already been demonstrated.

It should also be noted at this point that society's aggregate wealth, which consists of a stock of real assets, can be increased only by a growth of that stock. An increase or decrease in the volume of financial claims against a nation's real wealth can neither enrich nor impoverish that nation directly.

Our discussion has also maintained a clear distinction between *investment in real assets* and *financial investment.* Individual economic units refer to purchases of financial claims (stocks and bonds) as investments. Of course, acquisitions of such claims are investments for individuals, and they provide the sellers of claims with funds, which, now or in the future, can be invested in real assets. With a large secondary market for claims, however, there is no necessary close correspondence between total current financial investment (the purchase of nonmonetary financial claims) and the real investment flow that is of crucial importance in national income determination. Hence macroeconomists and financial analysts draw a clear distinction between investment (i.e., real investment, as measured in the National Income and Product Accounts) and financial investment.

SAVING SOURCES, USES, AND TRANSFER CHANNELS

In a modern industrialized economy, the sources of saving and the ultimate uses of saving are diverse. Individual households, individual business firms, and individual government units can in any period operate either as saving (surplus) or dissaving (deficit) units. To tap the diverse sources of saving efficiently and to transfer that saving to deficit units that have the highest-priority needs for funds, a sophisticated financial system is required. Just as the demands of efficiency require the manufacturing sector of a modern industrialized economy to exhibit extensive specialization, so they have required modern financial marketplaces to develop into complex systems of specialized channels for matching suppliers of saved funds with demanders of those funds.

The modern financial system offers savers a variety of alternatives to money and physical capital in which to hold their savings. Correspondingly, deficit units are provided with an array of means to acquire needed funds. Numerous specialized agents and institutions are involved in channeling funds from savers to deficit units. As a refinement of the financial flow diagram in Figure 1-1 (page 13), Figure 2-2 provides a detailed overview of the array of routes through which saving can be transferred to deficit units. Commercial banks are kept separate from other financial institutions in the figure, to reflect the distinctive role of banks in providing money—a role we will explore in the next chapter. In time, each of the routes illustrated in Figure 2–2 will receive individual attention. For now, however, our task is to acquire familiarity with a summary data set

Figure 2-2. Saving Sources, Uses, and Transfer Channels

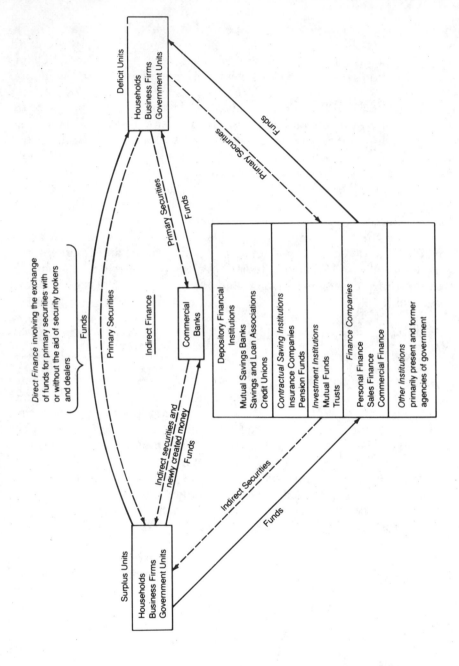

that provides financial analysts with the most comprehensive available measures of the sources of saving, its ultimate uses, and the main channels through which funds flow from savers to deficit units.

The Flow of Funds Account

Over two decades ago, the *flow of funds account* was developed as a social accounting system to provide a comprehensive compilation of sources and uses of saving in the U.S. economy. Flow of funds data first became available for the U.S. in 1955, and quarterly measures have been compiled by the Federal Reserve Board since 1959.

Like the National Income and Product Accounts, the flow of funds account provides measures of economywide saving and investment. However, it also provides measures that indicate how saving is converted into capital investment, so that it bridges the gap between financial and real transactions. In particular, the flow of funds account provides measures of the gross and net saving of each of a number of sectors into which the economy is subdivided, the gross level of real investment by each sector, and the changes in the value of financial assets owned and financial obligations owed by each sector. These measures permit inferences about the flow of funds among sectors.

The Flow of Funds Identity

Construction of a flow of funds account requires the application of a simple accounting identity. By conventional accounting practice, an economic unit in any accounting period can be conceived to be acquiring spendable funds by saving out of current income, by incurring additional financial obligations, or (in the case of some distinctive economic units) by issuing money itself. In turn, whatever their source, all funds that an economic unit acquires must be allocated to some use—to acquiring real commodities, to increasing its money balances, or to acquiring financial assets other than money. The equivalance of the sources and the uses of funds is highlighted in the following identity:

$$\overbrace{S + \Delta MS + \Delta FI}^{\text{sources}} \equiv \overbrace{\Delta K + \Delta M + \Delta FA}^{\text{uses}}$$

Here S is saving, ΔMS is the change in the money stock through new money issue, ΔFI is the change in the economic unit's financial obligations, ΔK is the change in real asset holdings, ΔM is the change in money holdings, and ΔFA is the change in financial assets other than money. If money issuance is ignored (it is not legally permissible for most economic units), this identity shows that any unit that saves more than it invests ($S > \Delta K$) must hold more money, hold more financial assets other than money, or reduce its financial obligations. The latter two options involve the unit in an exchange of funds for nonmonetary financial claims.

Clearly, the simple identity expressed above can be rearranged into a number of other forms. The particular form above was chosen for its consistency with prevailing accounting conventions, as reflected in the balance sheets from which flow of funds data are drawn.

To compile a list of sources and uses of funds for an economic unit, its balance sheet must be compared at two different points in time to see what changes have occurred. From the left side of a unit's balance sheet, we can observe changes in the assets (amount of money, nonmonetary financial assets, and real assets) held by the unit. From the right side, we can observe changes in financial liabilities and in net worth.

Since the acquisition of assets shows what an economic unit does with its spendable funds, net increases in assets constitute uses of funds. Funds are acquired as economic units incur financial obligations or enjoy an increase in net worth; hence increases in liabilities and net worth represent sources of funds. Saving is what increases an economic unit's net worth: it permits a unit to increase its holdings of money or other assets, to reduce its obligations, or both. By the same token, a unit that experiences a deficit (dissaving) must reduce its holdings of money or other assets, increase its liabilities, or both.[2]

A Simple Flow of Funds Account

To construct a flow of funds account for the economy as a whole, the economy must be subdivided. As always, the division of the economy into units or sectors must provide measures that are useful for descriptive and analytical purposes. The flow of funds data compiled for the United States are generally based on a division of the economy into nine sectors. Changes in the balance sheets are compiled for these sectors and are recorded at quarterly intervals to provide measures of the sources and uses of funds in each sector. The data are displayed in a table, or *matrix*, designed to allow the main flows of funds between sectors to be traced easily.

To avoid getting bogged down in the detail of an actual 9-sector matrix for the U.S. economy, we can illustrate the principles of flow of funds accounting with an economy subdivided into four sectors, consisting of households, business firms (other than financial intermediaries), financial intermediaries, and government. The measures of sources of funds (S)

---

[2]As a matter of accounting convention in flow of funds data, disinvestment (financial or real) is counted, not as a source of funds, but as a negative use of funds. Similarly, the repayment of financial liabilities is counted as a negative source, although it can be reasonably conceived to be a use of funds. The result of these conventions is that all flows of funds are measured on a net basis.

and uses of funds (U) for each sector provide the simplified flow of funds account presented in Table 2–2.[1]

TABLE 2–2. A Flow of Funds Account for a Four-Sector Economy (in billions of dollars)

	Households		Business		Financial Institutions		Government		All Sectors	
	U	S	U	S	U	S	U	S	U	S
Saving (net worth)		230		112		9		−8		343
Investment (real assets)	175		160		8				343	
Money	13		0			11	−2		11	11
Financial assets (other than money)	112		57		224		19		412	
Financial liabilities		70		105		212		25		412
Total	300	300	217	217	232	232	17	17	766	766
Sector surplus (+) or deficit (−)	+55		−48		+1		−8		0	

Accounting Properties of the Flow of Funds Matrix

A brief glance at Table 2–2 shows that the flow of funds measures reflect the accounting relationships explored in this chapter. For each sector, the total of sources of funds is equal to the total of uses of funds. Hence, for any combination of sectors, including all sectors combined, the overall sources must match the overall uses of funds. Of more interest to economists and financial analysts, total (gross) saving is equal to investment in real capital during the accounting period.

Note too that, for all sectors combined, the changes in financial assets and in financial liabilities are the same. For the economy as a whole, any increase (or decrease) in financial obligations is matched by an offsetting increase (or decrease) in financial assets. This observation corroborates the principle that the economy as a whole can neither save (increase its wealth) nor dissave (diminish its wealth) through a change in the volume of financial claims in existence. Of course, it remains true that individual

---

[1]For a more complete treatment of flow-of-funds accounts, see A. D. Bain, "Surveys in Applied Economics: Flow of Funds Analysis," *Economic Journal* 83 (December 1973): 1055–1093 and Jacob Cohen, "Copeland's Moneyflows after Twenty-five Years," *Journal of Economic Literature* 10 (March 1972).

sectors and individual economic units within sectors can accrue savings in the form of financial assets, altering their net worth in the process.

The Information Content of the Flow of Funds Account

The most immediately obvious use of the flow of funds account is to identify which sectors are the providers of saving and which are the saving deficit sectors. The measures in Table 2–2 were derived from the actual 1973 flow of funds account, with the nine sectors in that account collapsed into four. Hence they give a realistic view of the roles of the basic component sectors of the economy in providing or absorbing saving. To determine whether a sector is operating as a surplus unit or as a deficit unit, its saving (net worth) must be compared to its investment (real assets). Of course, if a sector saves more than it invests, it generates a saving surplus, but, if it invests more than it saves, it operates as a deficit sector.

The entries in the first two columns of Table 2–2 are consistent with the expectation that households as a group always operate as providers of saving and that businesses as a group always operate with a deficit. Household saving of $230 billion exceeds household investment (basically, the sum of expenditures on houses and consumer durables) of $175 billion by $55 billion, which is shown as a sector surplus at the bottom of the table.[3] Businesses which as a group wish to invest more than their current saving ($160 billion versus $112 billion), must finance the saving deficit ($48 billion) with funds acquired from other sectors.

The government sector can operate as a surplus unit or as a deficit unit. It incurs deficits far more often than surpluses, as it did to the tune of $8 billion in 1973, according to the figures in the table.

It appears that the household sector is the basic source of a net supply of saving, which flows from it to business and, in most years, to government. A large proportion of this flow of funds goes through the financial-institutions sector as it performs its intermediary role. Financial institutions appear in the table as a saving surplus sector, but this role is of very modest significance, reflected in the very small size ($1 billion) of the measured surplus.

A more accurate indication of the significance of the financial sector is reflected in the third, fourth, and fifth rows of the table. The third row—money—shows that financial institutions serve as a source of newly created money for the rest of the economy. Additions to money balances are classified as uses of funds: households are shown to have added $13

---

[3]Over the period from 1960 to 1970, annual surpluses of the household sector ranged from about $4 billion to about $47 billion. From 1965 to 1970, the average value of household saving surpluses was roughly $35 billion yearly. As shown in Table 2A–1 (in the appendix to this chapter), the household saving surplus in 1975 was $77 billion.

billion to their money balances, government reduced its money balances by $2 billion, and business money balances were unchanged. The net increase of $11 billion in money held by those three sectors was supplied by the financial sector. This sector includes the nation's providers of money—commercial banks and governmental monetary authorities, which supply currency and demand deposits (checkbook money) to the rest of the economy.

The fourth and fifth rows—financial assets other than money and financial liabilities—clearly illustrate the intermediary role of the financial sector. As intermediaries issue their own financial obligations (indirect securities) to acquire financial assets (primary securities) issued by others, changes in the financial assets and obligations of the financial sector should approximately offset each other. According to the table, the financial sector raised $212 billion in funds by the issuance of financial obligations. In turn, it acquired financial assets worth $224 billion, providing that amount in spendable funds to other sectors of the economy. Most of the difference between the measures of its financial assets and its financial obligations ($12 billion) is accounted for by money issued by commercial banks and governmental monetary authorities. Note, too, the financial sector's very small total of real investment in relation to the volume of spendable funds raised from and transferred to other sectors of the economy. The low value of real investment is simply a reflection of the specialized role this sector performs: modest physical facilities are sufficient for the processing of an enormous dollar total of financial transactions.

The fourth and fifth rows of the table also show that the business sector acquires a substantial volume of funds through the issuance of financial obligations—$105 billion. That source of funds, combined with $112 billion of business saving—retained earnings and depreciation allowances—permitted businesses, not only to invest $160 billion in real assets, but also to acquire $57 billion worth of financial assets other than money. A full explanation of why some business firms are always acquiring financial assets is the province of a course in corporate finance and cannot be pursued here. But it is instructive to note that the need for liquidity, combined with a desire for earnings on money capital, prompts firms to hold short-term, interest-bearing financial claims, such as U.S. Treasury bills and certificates of deposit offered by commercial banks. (These financial instruments will be examined in detail in subsequent chapters.)

Even though households collectively are savers, the fifth row shows clearly that not all households are savers in any accounting period: as a group, they incurred $70 billion of financial obligations to banks, savings and loan institutions, and so on. Still, the dominant role of households as providers of funds to other sectors is apparent: after adding $13 billion to their money balances, they swapped spendable funds for $112 billion of the financial obligations of other sectors.

Finally, the fourth and fifth rows of the table show that to finance its saving deficit, the government sector is required to issue financial obligations in excess of its acquisition of financial assets.

Uses of Flow of Funds Data

For our purposes, the most important uses of the flow of funds data, as measures of flows that have already occurred, are to identify the financial roles played by different sectors of the economy and to show the relative importance of the various sources and uses of funds. By representing nine sectors of the economy with a detailed breakdown of these sources and uses for each sector, the actual flow of funds accounts compiled by the Federal Reserve System offer the best available description of the financial flows our economy enjoys.

Financial analysts generally are interested more in what will happen in the future than they are in what occurred in the past. Hence the most important use of flow of funds data for financial analysts is to provide the data base for attempts to forecast emerging changes in the supply of and demand for funds. Such changes will alter interest rates and (to the extent that interest rates and credit flows affect expenditures on final goods and services) levels of production, employment, and prices. If the demands for funds by the saving deficit sectors of the economy are expected to exceed the supply provided by savers, interest rates can be expected to rise; conversely, a surplus of saving depresses interest rates. Moreover, changes in the supply of or demand for funds in particular segments of the market can also result in changes in *relative* values of yields on different sorts of financial claims. Thus an increased demand by corporations for bank loans can be expected to raise the interest rate on those loans. In time, this may result in a rise in other interest yields, but, at least for a time, interest rates on bank loans to business will have increased in relation to yields on other financial claims.

Monitoring the flow of funds data provided by the Federal Reserve System over time helps financial analysts project swings in the supplies of and demands for funds that will result in significant changes in interest rates and credit flows. In addition, a number of institutions that have an important stake in the financial sector—Salomon Brothers, Bankers Trust Company and the Life Insurance Association of America—regularly publish flow of funds data. Bankers Trust Company, in its annual *Investment Outlook*, provides projections of future flows of funds, as does Salomon Brothers.

The Federal Reserve System itself uses flow of funds data to assess the impact of money supply changes on various sectors of the economy. When analysis of flow of funds data indicates that some sectors of the economy are being too strongly affected by a money supply change, or that they will be in the future, the Federal Reserve can be expected to take policy actions to soften that impact.

The flow of funds accounts are also rich sources of data for research in economics and finance. Studies of the selection of assets to be incorporated in portfolios often employ flow of funds data, and an effort is now underway to incorporate that data in broadened measures of the nation's economic and social performance.

Problems with Flow of Funds Data

While the flow of funds accounts obviously provide useful data for financial analysis, they are not without shortcomings. To begin with, the very choice of sectors for which data will be compiled limits the portion of credit flows that can be directly observed. Only credit flows between sectors can be directly observed, so that the direct flow of credit between saving and deficit households is obscured. Of course, the indirect flow of credit, from household savers to financial institutions to deficit households, is observable. Quantitatively, the most serious information loss takes place in the (nonfinancial) business sector, as firms provide a substantial volume of trade credit directly to other firms.

A second problem arises from the difficulty of attaching correct values to some assets. This is not too surprising, since the quest for an accurate valuation of assets is at the very heart of the discipline of finance. To compile a flow of funds account, the financial assets and obligations of each sector can be valued at either *book value* (original cost adjusted for depreciation) or *market value* (current value). For the most part, market values are used in compiling an actual flow of funds account, so that measured fund flows are changes in the total market value of financial assets held and financial obligations owed by each sector. But market values of financial assets and obligations change, not only through the acquisition or issuance of additional financial claims, but also through changes in the market price of existing claims, and the latter change reflects no current flow of saving from surplus to deficit units. With no method of adequately distinguishing between changes in the value of assets and obligations that correspond to credit flows and changes that merely reflect capital gains or losses on existing assets, the measures of saving and credit flows in flow of funds accounts are distorted by changes in asset prices. The larger and more frequent are changes in the market price of financial assets, the greater is the potential distortion in flow of funds measures.

Additional problems arise from a number of sources. For example, the measurement of flows between sectors on a net rather than a gross basis and inconsistencies in the valuation of claims (due to the lack of a ready market, some must be appraised at book value) lead to information losses and biases that have already been reviewed. Without a detailed discussion of these or any additional problems, it is clear that the flow of funds accounts do have shortcomings. Still, while the distortions present in the flow of funds measures cannot be ignored, those measures offer the financial analyst the most comprehensive available view of the credit flows that are of crucial importance in a modern market economy.

A NOTE ON REAL AND NOMINAL VALUES

At the beginning of this chapter, you were asked to visualize aggregate output, saving, consumption, and investment as flows of real goods and services. To measure those flows, however, we employed a technique (viz., an expenditures approach) that values them in terms of money, which focuses on the flows of money that accompany the flows of goods and services. This is ncessary in any economy that produces more than one commodity. The millions of products manufactured in a modern economy must be valued in terms of a common dominator, such as the dollar, if the volumes of aggregate flows of those variables are to be measured. Adding the values of roller skates, oranges, skateboards, and so on is simply not possible except in terms of money.

Unfortunately, unlike a yardstick, the dollar is not constant in (purchasing power) size over time. As a consequence, economic and financial analysis must clearly distinguish between nominal values and real (or constant-price) values of variables.

The *nominal value* of a variable is its current money value with no adjustment for price-level changes, i.e., for changes in the value of money. If the general price level changes over time, measures of output, consumption, saving, investment, and many other variables will change, even if there has been no change in the underlying flows of real goods and services. For example, if prices had risen by 10 percent in 1977 while the physical flow of output of goods and services had not changed at all, measured output would have shown a 10 percent increase.

Price Indexes

Fortunately, there are devices, called *price indexes*, which permit nominal values of commodity and money flows to be converted into their *price-deflated* counterparts, *real values.* Price indexes measure changes over time in the cost of a selected "market basket" of goods and services. Of course, the larger the set of goods and services included in the market basket, the more accurate is the index which serves as a measure of changes in the economywide, or *general*, price level.

A price index for capital goods measures changes over time in the cost of a selected mix of factory, office, and sales buildings in combination with the machinery and office equipment that those structures would house. With the cost of such a basket of capital goods rising by 12% during 1978, a capital goods price index for that year has a value of 1.12, or 112% of its 1977 value. To compare the real, physical accumulation of plant and equipment in 1978 to the 1977 total, the 1978 purchases must be *deflated* by the value of that price index; this converts them into terms of 1977 prices.

Suppose that capital investment outlays on plant and equipment were a nominal $280 billion in 1978. In this case, real capital outlays in 1978, valued in terms of constant purchasing power 1977 dollars, would be:

$$\frac{\text{Real 1978 investment}}{\text{in 1977 Dollars}} = \frac{\text{Nominal 1978 Investment}}{\text{Capital assets price index, 1977 base}}$$

$$= \frac{\$280 \text{ billion}}{1.12} = \$250 \text{ billion}$$

This $250 billion total can be compared to the actual capital outlays that took place in 1977, or to capital outlays in any other period that have been expressed in 1977 dollars by the use of the capital assets price index. Such comparisons show how the volume of real capital accumulation has changed over time.

In similar fashion, by measuring changes over time in the market basket of goods and services bought by households, a consumer price index (CPI) can be constructed. In fact, such an index is maintained for the U.S. economy, as you probably already know, since the monthly updates of that index make headline-winning news. With a properly measured consumer price index, the current dollar (nominal) flows of consumption and saving can be converted into their real counterparts.

There is no need to review all the possible price index measures that could be constructed for different categories of flows in a modern economy. It should be noted, however, that a price index representing changes in the costs of all categories of goods and services has broad use in economic analysis. For example, it can be applied to determine the real value (the command over goods and services) of society's money stock or of its total wealth, and both of these are thought to play important roles in the functioning of the aggregate economy.

SUMMARY

This chapter has concentrated on the flows of saving, investment, and financing that occur in a modern, market economy. The levels of saving and investment that households and business firms would voluntarily provide were recognized as important determinants of the economy's vigor. In the economy as a whole, saving is current output that is not currently consumed, which adds to the stock of capital. Hence a larger flow volume of saving today means a bigger productive capacity in the future through the accumulation of capital goods.

While actual saving and actual investment are always equal, planned saving and planned investment can generally be expected to differ. An excess of planned saving over planned investment results in a contraction in the value of output and employment; an excess of planned investment over saving is expansionary.

The National Income and Product Accounts were introduced as a source of data on saving, investment, and a number of other flows, such as aggregate consumption and income, which are of concern to macroeconomic analysts. These accounts, however, do not provide a view of the credit flows that permit financial deficit units to spend more than their current earnings by tapping the savings of others. For information on the financial flows that take place between different sectors of the economy, it is necessary to refer to the flow of funds accounts, which provide a detailed listing of the sources and uses of funds for each sector of the economy.

A simple, four-sector flow of funds account was presented to illustrate the construction and use of the actual accounts compiled for the U.S. economy by the Federal Reserve System. Containing numerical entries that were drawn from the actual 1973 flow of funds account, that flow of funds example lent credence to the assertion that households collectively are savers, freeing current production and providing financing for business investment and, often, government purchases that exceed the "earnings" accruing to those saving-deficit sectors. Our flow of funds account also showed the sizable and approximately equal volumes of financial assets issued and acquired by the financial institutions sector. which illustrates the intermediary role of that sector.

The review of national income accounts and flow of funds accounts in this chapter showed that many of the variables that economic and financial analysis must deal with are measured in terms of money, or nominal value. Hence, these variables, can change either because of a change in prices or because of a change in the underlying real quantities. Price indexes permit changes in nominal values to be separated into real and price-change components.

In spite of some limitations, the descriptive measures reviewed in this chapter offer a relatively clear view of the real and financial flows that are of fundamental interest to financial analysts. Our next task, confronted in chapter 3, is to explore in detail the forms and functions of money. In the meantime, the appendix to this chapter provides a recent, actual flow of funds account, which you can review to deepen your perception of the financing needs of a modern economy and the channel's through which these needs can be met.

Appendix 2A
The Flow of Funds Account
for 1975

Table 2A–1 presents the actual flow of funds account for the U.S. economy in 1975, as compiled by the Federal Reserve System.[1] It is immediately apparent that this table offers much more detail than the simple account used in chapter 2 for our explanation of flow of funds data. To begin with, the financial sector of the economy is subdivided into four subsectors—commercial banks, private nonbank financial institutions, monetary authorities, and federally sponsored credit agencies. There are also separate sector accounts for the U.S. government and for state and local governments. With the addition of a "rest-of-the-world" sector for international credit flows, there are nine individual sectors in the matrix.

With nine individual sectors, subtotal columns, and 42 rows for listing sources and uses of funds, Table 2A–1 may appear a bit formidable. However, the principles involved in constructing that table are the same as those employed in the simple example developed in the text. You should be well equipped by now to understand and use the entries in that table. Line 1 provides measures of gross saving for each sector. Line 5 lists expenditures on real capital. Comparison of line 1 and line 5 shows which sectors are saving surplus and which are saving deficit sectors. For example, households saved $256.5 billion and invested $179.2 billion, so that they accrued a saving surplus of $77.3 billion. Lines 6 through 9 show the

---

[1] Full statements for sectors and transaction types quarterly, and annually for flows and for amounts outstanding, can be obtained from the Flow of Funds Section, Division of Research and Statistics, Board of Governors of the Federal Reserve System, Washington, D.C.

TABLE 2A–1. Summary of flow of funds accounts for the year 1975 (Annual rates in billions of dollars)

	Total		Financial Sectors								All Sectors		Natl. Svg. & Inv.	
			Fed. Spons Agencies & Mtg. Pools		Monetary Authority		Commercial Banking		Nonbank Finance					
	U	S	U	S	U	S	U	S	U	S	U	S	U	S
1 Gross saving		6.8		0.6		0.2		2.2		3.8		311.0		323.0
2 Capital consumption		4.3						2.2		2.1		285.0		285.0
3 Net saving (1 − 2)		2.4		0.6		0.2		0.0		1.6		26.0		37.9
4 Gross investment (5 + 11)	9.4		0.3		0.2		6.5		2.4		317.6		−6.6	331.6
5 Pvt. capital expenditures	9.9						4.6		5.3		315.4		−4.4	315.4
6 Consumer durables											131.7			131.7
7 Residential construction	1.0								1.0		51.2			51.2
8 Plant and equipment	8.9						4.6		4.3		147.1			147.1
9 Inventory change											−14.6			−14.6
10 Mineral rights														
11 Net financial investment (12 − 13)	−0.5		0.3		0.2		1.9		−2.9		2.2		−2.2	16.2
12 Financial uses	171.0		15.5		11.2		34.0		110.3		406.7		−2.2	31.3
13 Financial sources		171.5		15.2		11.0		32.1		113.2		404.4		15.1
14 Gold & official fgn. exchange	0.3				0.3						0.5	0.5	0.0	
15 Treasury currency	1.0				1.0						1.0	0.9		1.8
16 Demand deposits & currency	1.3	16.1	0.0			10.6	0.1	5.4	1.2		14.3	16.1		

	1	2	3	4	5	6	7	8	9	10	11	12	13
17 Private domestic	1.3	13.2	0.0	...	...	6.2	0.1	7.0	1.2	...	11.3	13.2	1.9
18 Foreign	...	0.1	...	...	...	0.0	...	0.2	...	...	0.1	0.1	...
19 U.S. government	2.8	2.8	...	...	...	4.5	...	-1.7	...	...	2.9	2.8	-0.1
20 Time and savings accounts	4.3	90.0	...	...	...	...	...	30.1	4.3	59.8	89.9	89.9	...
21 at commercial banks	3.7	30.1	...	...	...	...	...	30.1	3.7	...	30.1	30.1	...
22 at savings institutions	0.6	59.8	...	...	...	...	...	...	0.6	59.8	59.8	59.8	...
23 Life insurance reserves	...	7.6	...	...	...	...	...	...	...	7.6	7.6	7.6	...
24 Pension fund reserves	...	32.4	...	...	...	...	...	...	...	32.4	36.1	36.1	...
25 Interbank claims	-3.3	-3.3	...	...	1.6	0.8	-4.9	-4.1	...	...	-3.3	-3.3	...
26 Corporate equities	8.3	1.2	...	...	...	...	0.0	1.0	8.3	0.2	11.2	11.2	...
27 Credit mkt. instruments	139.1	13.7	14.5	13.5	8.5	...	27.6	0.7	88.5	-0.5	214.0	214.0	...
28 U.S. Treasury securities	52.0	12.7	1.5	...	7.4	...	28.8	...	14.3	...	85.8	85.8	...
29 Federal agency securities	10.4	-0.0	-0.0	...	1.0	...	1.4	...	8.1	...	12.1	12.1	...
30 State & local govt. secur.	7.3	...	...	...	...	...	1.7	...	5.6	...	17.3	17.3	...
31 Corporate & foreign bonds	25.3	2.9	...	...	...	...	1.8	0.2	23.5	2.7	36.3	36.3	...
32 Mortgages	49.8	2.3	15.7	...	...	...	4.3	...	29.8	2.3	59.0	59.0	...
33 Consumer credit	7.2	...	...	...	...	...	2.9	...	4.3	...	8.5	8.5	...
34 Bank loans	-14.4	-3.9	...	...	0.0	...	-14.4	-0.3	...	-3.6	-14.4	-14.4	...
35 Pvt. Short-term paper	0.0	2.8	-0.2	...	0.1	...	1.1	0.8	-1.0	2.0	0.5	0.5	...
36 Other loans	1.4	-3.1	-2.4	...	...	...	0.0	...	3.8	-4.0	8.7	8.7	...
37 Security credit	4.4	2.2	0.9	...	...	...	1.9	...	2.5	2.2	4.5	4.5	...
38 Trade credit	0.6	...	...	...	...	...	...	...	0.6	...	11.5	10.1	-1.4
39 Taxes payable	...	-0.1	...	...	...	...	...	-0.3	...	0.2	-3.4	-3.4	0.0
40 Equity in noncorp. bus.	...	...	...	...	-0.2	-0.4	...	-0.7	...	...	-9.9	-9.9	...
41 Miscellaneous	15.0	12.0	0.9	...	1.6	...	9.4	-0.7	4.9	11.4	32.6	30.0	-2.6
42 Sector discrepancies (1 – 4)	-2.6	...	0.3	...	0.0	...	-4.3	...	1.4	...	-6.6	-6.6	-8.7

TABLE 2A–1. Summary of funds accounts for the year 1975 (Annual rates in billions of dollars)

	Private Domestic Nonfinancial Sectors								Rest of the World		U.S. Government	
	Households		Business		State & Local Govts.		Total					
	U	S	U	S	U	S	U	S	U	S	U	S
1 Gross saving		256.5		138.7		−4.1		391.1		−12.0		−75.0
2 Capital consumption		149.6		131.1				280.7				
3 Net saving (1 − 2)		106.9		7.6		−4.1		110.4		−12.0		−75.0
4 Gross investment (5 + 11)	280.9		124.2		−5.4		399.7		−16.2		−75.2	
5 Pvt. capital expenditures	179.2		127.6				306.9				−1.3	
6 Consumer durables	131.7						131.7					
7 Residential Construction	42.4		7.8				50.2					
8 Plant and equipment	5.1		133.2				138.3					
9 Inventory change			−14.6				−14.6					
10 Mineral rights			1.3				1.3				−1.3	
11 Net financial investment (12 − 13)	101.6		−3.4		−5.4		92.8		−16.2		−73.9	
12 Financial uses	154.8		38.4		10.4		203.6		15.1		17.0	
13 Financial sources		53.1		41.9		15.8		110.8		31.3		90.9
14 Gold & official fgn. exchange									−0.0	0.5	0.3	0.3
15 Treasury currency												0.9
16 Demand deposits & Currency	6.7		2.9		0.3		10.0		0.1		2.9	

17 Private domestic	6.7			2.9	0.3		10.0		0.1		
18 Foreign										2.9	
19 U.S. government									0.7	0.1	0.1
20 Time and savings accounts	84.9	1.9		-2.0			84.8		0.7	0.1	
21 at commercial banks	25.7	1.9		-2.0			25.7		0.7	0.1	
22 at savings institutions	59.2						59.2				
23 Life insurance reserves	7.6						7.6				0.1
24 Pension fund reserves	36.1						36.1				3.6
25 Interbank claims											
26 Corporate equities	-1.8	9.9		9.9			-1.8		4.7	0.1	0.1
27 Credit mkt. instruments	27.2	49.7	14.4	37.7	12.1	14.9	53.7	102.3	6.1	12.8	85.2
28 U.S. Treasury securities	10.5	9.0		6.3			25.8		8.1		85.8
29 Federal agency securities	-4.8	-0.7		2.7			-2.8			4.5	-0.6
30 State & local govt. secur.	8.7	-0.2		2.6	1.5		9.9	17.3			
31 Corporate & foreign bonds	10.4			2.6	27.2		10.4	27.2	0.6	6.2	
32 Mortgages	4.4	40.5		16.4			6.0	56.8		3.2	
33 Consumer credit		8.5		1.6			1.3	8.5			
34 Bank loans		-1.5		-13.0				-14.5		4.0	
35 Pvt. Short-term Paper	-1.9	5.0		-2.2			3.1	-2.2	-2.6	-0.1	
36 Other loans		2.2		6.7		0.2	9.1			2.8	7.3
37 Security credit	0.1	2.2					0.1	2.2	0.1	0.1	
38 Trade credit		0.6	7.9	4.8		0.9	7.9	6.3	1.6	2.1	1.7
39 Taxes payable				-3.2	-0.1		-0.1	-3.2			-3.3
40 Equity in noncorp bus.	-9.9		-9.9				-9.9	-9.9			
41 Miscellaneous	3.7	0.7		11.3	2.4		15.1	3.1	1.8	15.6	0.7
42 Sector discrepancies (1 − 4)	-24.3			14.5	1.3		-8.5		4.3	0.3	-0.7

kinds of real capital that each sector invests in. It is readily apparent that real investment by households is mostly in consumer durables and residential construction. A look across all of the sectors in Table 2A–1 shows that households were the dominant saving surplus sector in 1975. Business was experiencing an unusual saving surplus in 1975 and the federal government was experiencing a not-so unusual substantial deficit.

Line 12 shows the change in financial assets (a use of funds) for each sector, and line 13 shows the change in each sector's financial obligations. The difference between lines 12 and 13, which appears in line 11, is the difference between gross saving and expenditures on real capital. Once more, these measures reflect the identity between sources of funds (saving + financial obligations issued) and uses of funds (real investment + financial assets acquired for the "gross investment" total in line 4).

As in our simplified example, the total sources and uses of funds must be equal for every individual sector and for all sectors combined. Any discrepancy between observed values of sources and uses of funds is attributed to measurement errors and is recorded in line 42 of the table. It also remains true, subject to some statistical error, that gross saving for the entire economy is equal to private capital expenditures (compare lines 1 and 5 of the last column).

Lines 14 through 41 of the flow of funds account are of particular interest to financial analysts. These lines provide measures of the changes in the volume of specific types of financial claims outstanding as deficit units acquire funds from surplus units. Moreover, the types of financial instruments employed by each sector and the claims acquired by each sector are identified in these rows. Note that by far the largest source of financing in 1975 for the household sector was mortgage credit ($40.5 billion), with consumer credit a distant second ($8.5 billion). Line 32 shows that the nonbank financial sector, containing savings and loan associations, insurance companies, and a number of other intermediaries, provided the bulk of mortgage funds ($29.8 billion); federally sponsored agencies and mortgage pools were the next largest group of suppliers, and commercial banks were third. Note too that, for all sectors combined, the total sources and uses of mortgage funds are equal.

The entries in lines 14 through 42 for the business sector column show that the issuance of bonds was the primary source of funds for nonfinancial business firms in 1975 ($27.2 billion). Mortgage loans, equity issues, and the trade credit extended by other firms were also important sources of funds. Bank loans to businesses are usually an important source of financing, but in 1975 there were net repayments of $13 billion of such loans. Line 31 shows that households and nonbank financial firms were important providers of funds through the purchase of corporate securities ($10.4 billion and $23.5 billion respectively). A review of lines 26, 32, 34, 35, 36, and 38 will illuminate the importance of different sectors in providing funds to business firms through the acquisition of other claims.

Entries in Table 2A–1 for the government sector indicate that both the federal government and state and local governments collectively experienced deficits in 1975. The deficit in state and local government budgets was financed almost exclusively by the issuance of securities, most of which were purchased by households ($8.7 billion) and nonbank financial enterprises ($5.6 billion). To finance the sizable federal budget deficit, heavy reliance was placed on the issuance of U.S. Treasury securities. Commercial banks constituted the largest provider of funds to the federal government in 1975 (purchasing $28.8 billion of Treasury securities) with nonbank financial institutions serving as the second largest provider of funds ($14.3 billion). The Treasury also obtained substantial funds through the sale of securities to households ($10.5 billion), business ($9.0 billion), state and local governments ($6.3 billion), the rest of the world ($8.1 billion), and the U.S. monetary authority ($7.4 billion).

You can review the flow of funds account in Table 2A–1 further on your own. You should be concerned with identifying the major sources of credit for each sector, the types of financial instruments employed by each sector to obtain funds, the changes in the stock of money held by each sector, and the role of the monetary authority in acquiring financial assets.

To complete our brief review of the full flow of funds account, note that the matrix in Table 2A–1 portrays financial transactions with sufficient generality to accommodate the appearance of new financial instruments, new channels for financial flows, and changes in the patterns of financial activities of different sectors. Moreover, the accounting constraints on flow of funds data insure that interactions among major sectors of the economy are incorporated in the analysis of financial disturbances.

To illustrate the discipline imposed on analysis by the flow of funds matrix, suppose that some major financial development occurs, such as a sharp rise in government borrowing. That disturbance, entered in the appropriate cell of the flow of funds matrix, calls forth a limited array of possible adjustments of financial flows in other sectors. The borrowing undertaken by government must be matched by equal lending elsewhere, and there must be a source of funds available for this use by the sector(s) that lend them. Economic analysis is required to predict likely responses to financial developments, but the flow of funds framework requires a consistent appraisal of economywide interactions in the analytical process.

PART 2

Money and Banking

As indicated in the discussion of an evolving economy (chapter 1), the most fundamental innovation that benefits a primitive economy is the creation of money. Hence it is appropriate that we begin our detailed probe of the component parts of the financial system by focusing on money. To that end, chapter 3 describes money's functions and discusses what has served as money in the past and what it consists of today. There is less than complete agreement over what should be counted as money; indeed, controversy over the appropriate definition of money is one of the major issues confronting economists and financial analysts today. Chapter 3 describes the components of the money supply as it is most popularly defined and identifies the suppliers of those components.

In pinning down what serves as money, chapter 3 shows that commercial banks are the source of the largest part of our money supply. Hence to know how the quantity of money in circulation is determined requires an understanding of the crucial role that commercial banks play in the creation and destruction of money. Chapter 4 explains how the commercial banking system can affect the money supply and develops a formal model to account for changes in the quantity of money in circulation.

The model constructed in chapter 4 shows that some of the important factors that influence the money supply can be controlled by a central bank—in the U.S. economy, by the Federal Reserve System. In recognition of this fact, chapter 5 provides a comprehensive introduction to the structure and functioning of the Federal Reserve System.

3

Money and Its Origins

In chapter 1, a brief assessment of the performance of alternative forms of economic systems indicated that the role of money is so important that any economic system without a money might be expected to create one. Historical facts corroborate that assertion, for every known civilization, past and present, has used some form of money. From the dawn of recorded history, uncoined precious metals (gold, silver, and bronze), jewelry, and utensils were employed as money in the Mediterranean countries. Primitive cultures in the South Pacific and in North and South America also created monies. In the sixth and seventh centuries B.C., monetary systems based on coined metals flourished in Greece, Persia, Babylonia, and China. Of course, all economies today, whether capitalistic or socialistic, whether advanced or underdeveloped, rely on elaborate monetary systems.

Obviously, the monies and monetary systems employed by different economies and in different time periods have varied widely. In addition to uncoined precious metals, jewelry, and utensils, primitive economies have employed stones, shells, fish, cattle, and an array of other items as money.[1] In contrast, as a participant in a highly developed economy with a sophisticated financial system, you are accustomed to holding command over goods and services in the form of coins and paper money, checking

---

[1]See Paul Einzig, *Primitive Money in Its Ethnological, Historical and Economic Aspects* (London: Eyre and Spottiswood, Ltd., 1949). Also see R. A. Radford, "The Economic Organization of a P.O.W. Camp," *Economica* 12 (1945): 189–201.

deposits at banks, or, as substitutes for these, interest-bearing deposits in financial institutions and credit cards.

Since money is of such apparent importance, the first section of this chapter presents a fairly detailed probe of the functions money performs and of the traits different items display when they are used as money. Next, as an aid in understanding the monetary system that serves our economy and prospective changes in that system, the historical evolution of money is traced. As that discussion returns us to the current monetary system, some modern controversies over the measurement of the supply of money in circulation require attention. Finally, the closing section of this chapter identifies the suppliers of the component parts of the money supply as it is most often defined.

THE FUNCTIONS OF MONEY

Money has traditionally been characterized as an asset that performs four basic functions: it provides an economy with a *unit of account*, a *medium of exchange*, a *store of value*, and a *unit of contract*.

Money as a Unit of Account

As a *unit of account*, or a *standard of value* or a *numeraire*, money functions as a measure of value, comparable to physical measures of length or weight. Just as it is highly convenient to employ standard measures of length, such as feet, yards, or meters, so it is compellingly convenient to employ standard measures of value, which permit the values of different items to be compared. Of course, comparisons of relative values could be made in terms of the value of wheat, dried fish, skateboards, or virtually anything. In practice, however, the dollar is employed as the unit of account in the United States, the franc in France, the pound in England, and so on. Since the unit-of-account function is closely related to the other functions money performs, as we will see a bit later, there are good reasons for these familiar currency units to serve as the basic monetary measures in these countries.

The particular convenience of employing a standard unit of account in an exchange economy is a vast reduction in information costs. Consider an economy in which 10,000 different goods and services are produced and exchanged; a product can be swapped for any one of the other 9,999. With no single unit of account, a pair of shoes would have 9,999 prices, expressed in terms of apples, haircuts, skateboards, and all the other products of the economy. Likewise, haircuts, skateboards, and all other goods and services would have prices expressed in terms of the other 9,999 products. In this economy, there would be a total of 49,995,000 (nearly 50 million!) unique barter exchange rates—a mind-numbing total. In general, for an economy that produces n different goods and services, the number of unique exchange values is $N = \dfrac{n(n-1)}{2}$. Since developed economies provide many tens of thousands of different products, an informed participant in the marketplace would need to know far more exchange values than the 50 million in the example—a taxing if not impossible task.

Fortunately, as soon as one thing is selected as the unit of account, be it wheat, skateboards, gold or what-have-you, the amount of information an informed trader needs is vastly reduced. If all goods and services are valued in terms of one item (and, historically, the one item most often employed has been a specified weight of a precious metal), the number of exchange rates that a fully informed trader must keep up with is just $(n - 1)$, or 9,999 in our example. If the value of apples, haircuts, skateboards, wheat, cattle, shoes, and so on are known in terms of any one item (e.g., in terms of units of gold), the relative exchange values of each of those items, one for another, are also known. Thus the presence of a unit of account lowers the real resource cost of acquiring and maintaining price information, which is needed for rational exchanges in a market economy. With the reduced cost of information (one component of the total cost of transactions), specialization and trade are encouraged.

Money as a Medium of Exchange

A second function of money, by which it makes its greatest contribution to specialization in production, is to provide a readily accepted *medium of exchange*. In every modern economy, commodities and services (including labor) are sold for money, and money is *sold for* (used to buy) goods and services. Chapter 1 pointed out how high the costs of transactions would be if there were no commonly accepted medium of exchange, so that producers (of corn, cloth, shoes, cattle, and so on) had to arrange barter exchanges of the goods and services they produce for the things they desire. With the high costs of arranging trades and storing and transporting exchangeable items, and with the loss of trading power through deterioration and disappearance of their stock or through adverse changes in the exchange value of those products, participants in a barter exchange system cannot rationally exploit available opportunities for improved production through specialization. But these opportunities are so rewarding that any system, facing the exaggerated transaction costs a barter economy imposes, quickly develops a medium of exchange to reduce those costs.

Very little experience in a barter market is sufficient to teach traders that some items are far better suited for exchange purposes than others. In general, the things that serve best as *trading goods* are widely recognized and desired, homogeneous, divisible into small units, durable, easily stored and transported, and stable in value. An ice cream maker or a lettuce grower would choose to quickly exchange those products for an inventory of widely accepted goods that are more durable and more stable in value, rather than to permit such perishable products to deteriorate during a search for trading partners. Also, a cattle raiser would likely benefit by swapping his periodic production of market-ready cattle for trading goods that are more divisible and less costly to store and transport. Hence there naturally evolved the practice of holding trading power in the form of a limited number of widely known and accepted trading goods. The more extensively these selected goods are used for trading purposes, the more acceptable they become as media of exchange. Therefore the costs of transactions fall as trading goods are adopted for exchange purposes.

Traders naturally seek trading goods that most reduce the cost of transactions. Hence our economy, in its natural evolutionary process, can be expected to place a strict limit on the number of items that circulate as media of exchange. Historically, gold and silver were settled upon as preferred exchange media, superior to other metals, jewels, shells, and so on, because of the widespread desire for them and because of their homogeneity, divisibility, durability, storability, and portability. Also, these precious metals naturally assumed the role of money as a unit of account (e.g., expressing value in terms of a weight of gold), and this further simplified the process of exchange and lowered transactions costs. Notably, the attributes of gold and silver that resulted in their common use as money within nations also resulted in their use in exchanges between nations.

While it constituted a major advance in facilitating the exchange of goods and services, the adoption of gold and silver as media of exchange did not end the evolution of money. Later we will see how, from bullion to coins, to paper and checkbook money, to electronic means of transferring purchasing power from one person to another, the continuing quest for reduced inconvenience, cost, and risk has created the modern system of payments we enjoy today.

Money as a Store of Value

Since it is durable, stable in value over time, and generally acceptable as a means of payment of debt, money serves a third function as a *store of value*. This means that one can accumulate purchasing power and hold it over time in the form of money. With confidence that the money they receive today will still be money in the future, individuals are willing to accept weekly or monthly payments for goods and services and are happy to accumulate savings in money form to provide for future purchases.

Of course, other things besides money, including land, jewels, rare coins and stamps, paintings, and other durable assets, can serve as stores of value (and, of course, lettuce, fresh fish, and other perishable things cannot perform this function). Things that serve as money, however, have greater *liquidity* than other stores of value. For our purposes, the more liquid an asset is, the more easily it can be converted into generalized purchasing power and the less likely it is that it will lose value by the time we dispose of it. Anything that serves as money must be highly liquid. Indeed, many analysts place so much emphasis on money's function as a medium of exchange that they identify as money only things that confer generalized purchasing power, whose values are fixed in nominal terms. Of course, nothing could be more liquid. But, by any commonly accepted definition, the things that serve as money are the most liquid of society's assets.

Money as a Unit of Contract

In its fourth function, money serves as a *unit of contract*, or a standard of *deferred payment*. This means that debts can be contracted for future payment in money. When a household borrows money to buy a home, the mortgage debt it incurs is expressed in dollars and requires specified periodic payments of money (typically monthly) over the life of the mortgage. When a business borrows to finance a plant expansion or an inventory investment, it incurs a debt, which is expressed in money terms. Of course, in principle (as well as occasionally in practice), debts can be incurred in terms of cattle, haircuts, skateboards, or some combination of such goods and services. But, to decide the terms on which they would voluntarily enter into a debt contract, lenders and borrowers must estimate the value of the future payments involved. If debts are contracted in money form, only an estimate of the future value (purchasing power) of the money is required. Contracting a debt in terms of one or more products typically involves an exposure to considerably more uncertainty with regard to the value of future debt payments, since it requires predictions of individual product prices.

THE FURTHER EVOLUTION OF MONIES

As indicated already, attempts to reduce inconvenience, cost, and risk in the exchange process have historically resulted in the emergence of a highly restricted set of assets serving as money. We have already recognized the distinct natural advantages of gold and silver for employment as money. To better understand modern monetary systems and their continuing development, it is worthwhile to trace the highlights of the evolutionary steps money has traversed since the widespread adoption of gold and silver as trading media.

Although they were originally employed in bulk form, with exchange values determined by weight (three ounces of gold being worth three times as much as one ounce of gold), the need to weigh and assess the purity of precious metals in every exchange was costly. To reduce these costs, coins, which can be made uniform in weight and purity, were created. This innovation cut costs and therefore encouraged trade. Of course, it is possible to *debase* coins (lower their precious-metal content, and hence their value); this allows the issuer to mint additional coins and therefore to enjoy increased purchasing power until the prices of goods and services are fully adjusted to the debasement. Since coinage is generally monopolized by governments, rulers have frequently engaged in this practice, particularly in war periods. Unfortunately, the recognition that an issuer might debase the coinage diminishes confidence in coins: traders are still required to establish the values of coins from countries where the threat of debasement is significant. This raises transactions costs and therefore reduces specialization and exchange. Hence, in spite of their potential for lowering transactions costs, gold and silver coins are not free of shortcomings.

Indeed, gold and silver suffer from a number of handicaps that we now judge serious, and some of these handicaps plague bullion money as well as coins. Precious-metal monies suffer from wear and tear, gradually lose weight as they circulate, and hence lose value. They also subject the user to the risk of robbery, and, for large transactions, they are bulky and hard to transport. Moreover, since gold and silver are valued for use as commodities independently of their role as monies, and since they can be mined and refined only through the employment of productive resources that have alternative uses, it is wasteful to rely on those metals for a money supply if something that is less costly to produce or less valued in alternative uses can serve as well.

As governments emerged in developing countries and assumed the responsibility for providing a money supply, they naturally have looked to the use of *token monies*, consisting of items that have a higher value in their role as money than as a commodity, such as paper monies and coins containing small quantities of precious metals. Token monies can be produced substantially cheaper than commodity monies, so that they free the bulk of the available stocks of gold and silver for their commodity uses. Public confidence in token monies can be instilled if, initially, they are redeemable in gold and silver. Ultimately, it might be possible even to eliminate this redemption privilege and thus to free all of the supply of precious metals for commodity uses.[2]

Although the creation of token monies was a distinct movement toward more efficiency in monetary systems, it was a minor development in comparison to the emergence of *bank credit* as a means of clearing

---

[2]The last vestige of redeemability of monetary claims in precious metals ended, in the United States, on June 30, 1968. At the close of that day, the U.S. Treasury ended the exchange of silver for paper "silver certificates," which had previously been issued by the Treasury, but which had been in the process of retirement since the early 1960s.

debts in the exchange process. Since hoards of gold and silver are subject to loss through theft, it became common practice, in the Middle Ages, for those who had accumulated gold and silver to deposit their hoards with prominent and reputable merchants and goldsmiths. These business operations had found it necessary to provide vaults for protecting their own hoards, so that they were able to provide safekeeping services for others at low cost. Initially, deposits of gold and silver were held with the owner's name attached, and each deposit was redeemable only by its owner. At this stage, the practice of offering safekeeping services had no notable monetary significance. The adoption of homogeneous metals and coins, however, soon made it apparent that deposits could be kept in a common pool, with depositors holding receipts for specified volumes of gold, silver, or coins. These receipts, being effective claims against commodity monies, gradually came to be accepted as a means of paying debts; with general acceptance, these paper claims themselves became money.

Thus a set of institutions came into being, which accepted deposits and issued in return a paper claim that circulated as money. In the meantime, these institutions profited from lending a portion of the metallic monies that were deposited with them for safekeeping. This was possible because only a small fraction of their depositors would be redeeming their metallic money deposits at any one time, and new deposits tended to appear even as old ones were withdrawn. Of course, to maintain a reputation for reliability, these depositories had to have on hand at all times enough metallic monies to meet all demands for withdrawals.

At this point, these depository institutions had only one major hurdle left to clear before they could function like modern banks. It had to be recognized that, with paper claims against deposits in circulation as money, depositories could lend merely by printing additional receipts, in which process they would be *creating* money. Again, printed bank notes could be issued in amounts that exceeded the metallic money on deposit because only a portion of the notes would be presented for redemption at any one time. Today's demand deposits are the counterpart to these bank notes. Hence, when depositories began to issue bank notes in amounts greater than the metallic money deposits they held, they were truly operating as modern banks—accepting deposits, making loans, and creating money in the lending process. It was a small step from printing notes for loans to making bookkeeping entries to credit borrowers with spendable funds, which the borrowers could spend by writing checks.

With this refinement, and with the emergence of a government that prints money that cannot be redeemed for a commodity of comparable intrinsic value, we have the essential core of today's monetary system—a system that has evolved as the natural consequence of the quest for economy in the exchange process. Money has evolved from commodity forms to redeemable claims; to nonredeemable, or pure claim, forms (sometimes referred to as *fiat money*, since it is money by government decree or fiat).

This evolution has freed resources from the mining and refining of precious metals and has provided for a spread of specialization in production and exchange that could not have been dreamed of when economies emerged from the barter stage.

MODERN FORMS OF MONEY

We will soon want to focus detailed attention on the institutions that provide our modern economy with money. First, however, since we know that many things have served as money in different places and times, we need to carefully identify what now serves as money. This identification is crucial, because the amount of money in existence plays an important role in determining the levels of production, employment, and prices that prevail in an economy. Moreover, the government has the ability to control the money supply and hence wields some degree of control over the functioning of the economy.

The task of identifying what serves as money is complex and controversial. Among reputable monetary experts, there are clearcut disputes over how money ought to be defined. Our own discussion early in this chapter may have suggested that anything is money if it performs the functions of money—if it serves as a unit of account, as a medium of exchange, as a store of value, and as a unit of contract. If we should formally adopt the procedure of identifying as money only items that perform these four functions, we would be in good company, for this is the traditional approach, and it results in the definition of money that continues to be favored by most economists. In this procedure, money in its role as the medium of exchange occupies center stage, for, although many things can perform one or more of the remaining monetary functions, the list of items that are generally accepted as media of exchange is quite limited. To begin with, currency (coins and paper money) is generally accepted as a medium of exchange and also serves as a store of value, as a standard of value, and as a standard of deferred payment: currency is money. So are demand deposits (checkbook money) in commercial banks. Denominated in dollar amounts, these deposits perform all four monetary functions, including serving as a generally accepted means of clearing debts.

Some savings and loan associations and mutual savings banks in the northeastern United States have recently begun offering accounts that, like savings accounts in banks, pay interest; unlike savings accounts, however, these accounts can be used to draw drafts for the payment of debts, just as drafts (checks) for debt-clearing are drawn on demand deposit accounts in commercial banks. Drafts drawn on these recently created accounts are called *Negotiable Orders of Withdrawal*, so that the accounts are called *NOW accounts*. Recognizing that NOW accounts comprise additions to the checkbook component of the money supply, our measures of the assets that perform all the functions traditionally associated with money need not be substantively altered to accommodate NOW deposits since, at present, their use is limited. The chapters ahead will have a good deal to say about NOW accounts.

No other items that are quantitatively significant perform all four monetary functions.[3] For example, one familiar asset, passbook savings accounts in commercial banks, which are denominated in dollars just as demand deposits are, serve as a store of value, as a standard of value, and as a standard of deferred payment; to finance the purchase of goods and services, however, those savings deposits must be converted into currency or demand deposits. Similarly, the holders of savings-type deposits (other than NOW accounts) in mutual savings banks and in savings and loan associations, the holders of readily salable U.S. Treasury securities, and the holders of all other financial assets besides currency and demand deposits must exchange those assets for currency or demand deposits before they can clear their debts. Hence, with emphasis on its medium-of-exchange function, money consists basically of the currency and demand deposit balances of the non-bank public.

Money as Liquid Wealth

Although most economists in the United States prefer the narrow definition of money, a sizable minority has argued that, in defining money, they have placed too much emphasis on its function as a medium of exchange, especially since even currency and checks are not always acceptable as means of payment.[4] This minority contends that money should instead be thought of as just one of many forms in which wealth can be held, including stocks and bonds, jewelry, antiques, stamps, land, and so on. According to this view, the important distinguishing characteristic of assets, which determines whether they should or should not be counted as money, is their liquidity—their capacity to be converted into spendable form without risk of loss. Of course, different assets possess this quality in different degrees. Currency and demand deposits are certainly the most liquid of all assets: they are already in spendable form, requiring no conversion before use. Other assets, such as passbook savings deposits, are nearly as liquid. In practice, they are readily and immediately convertible into spendable form with no risk of loss, since their value is fixed in nominal terms. Short-term government securities and large negotiable

---

[3]Some other items, such as American Express Travelers Cheques and postal money orders, meet the four-function requirement for serving as money, but the quantity of these is negligible in comparison to the volume of currency and demand deposits in existence.

[4]Those who lack safe storage facilities for currency or who fear counterfeit payments often try to avoid the receipt of currency. All of us know the difficulty of getting checks accepted where the identity of the check-writer and the status of the account are unknown.

certificates of deposit are also highly liquid, since they can be exchanged easily for cash with only a small risk of loss in value. Longer-term government securities are only slightly less liquid.

Clearly, there is a wide spectrum of liquidity characterizing different assets, and, if a degree of liquidity must be selected to distinguish between money and other assets, there is likely to be an element of arbitrariness in that selection. Reflecting the difficulty of determining how much liquidity is necessary, different advocates of a broader definition of money propose competing definitions of it, and the U.S. central bank—the Federal Reserve System—now officially keeps track of four different measures of the U.S. money stock in addition to money in the narrow (currency plus demand deposits) definition. The narrowly defined measure of money is labelled M_1, and the successively broader measures of money reported monthly by the Federal Reserve System are

$M_2 \equiv M_1 +$ savings and time deposits at commercial banks other than large negotiable certificates of deposits (CDs)

$M_3 \equiv M_2 +$ mutual savings bank deposits, savings and loan shares, and credit union shares (deposits in nonbank thrift institutions)

$M_4 \equiv M_2 +$ large negotiable CDs

$M_5 \equiv M_3 +$ large negotiable CDs

Science or Mysticism?

At this point, you may be wondering whether different analysts choose a definition of money on the basis of pure whimsey or on other, defensible, grounds. In spite of the element of arbitrariness in the selection of a line of division between money and other assets that are almost as liquid (near-monies), there is a logical motivation for the choices that are made. Behind the choices of which function(s) of money should be emphasized and which specific definition of money is best lie judgments on the causal links between money and the economy's vigor. Analysts focus attention on the measures of money that they judge, on the basis of theory and empirical evidence, to have the strongest and most reliable links to production and prices. Hence those who favor the narrow definition of money typically believe that currency and demand deposits, as the items that serve for the ultimate clearing of debt, are uniquely important. If there were an increase in the quantity of these media of exchange held by the nonbank public, they would expect more spending on goods and services and an expansion of economic activity. Those who favor a broader definition of money believe that society's spending plans depend, not so much on the amount of the medium of exchange that is in circulation, but rather on the total liquid wealth that society possesses. Hence advocates of the M_2 definition argue that spending units think of time deposits in commercial banks as "money in the bank," comparable to demand deposits, when they make spending decisions. In turn, advocates of the M_3 definition believe that deposits in nonbank thrift institutions are comparable to bank deposits in their influence on spending decisions.

Current concepts of money are scientific constructions based on theoretical and empirical judgments. Their status is clearly revealed in the assertion by Milton Friedman and Anna J. Schwartz that

> the definition of money is to be sought ... on the grounds of usefulness in organizing our knowledge of economic relationships. "Money" is that to which we choose to assign a number by specified operations; it is not something in existence to be discovered, like the American continent; it is a tentative scientific construct to be invented, like "length" or "temperature" or "force" in physics.[5]

The Inconclusive Empirical Evidence on Money

With general agreement that money is important—that the quantity of it in existence has an important influence on economic activity—a great deal of research effort has been expended in recent years on attempts to identify the best measure of money. One method of identifying the best measure of money follows directly from the belief that the quantity of money in existence is closely related to the value of output the economy provides—in particular, that a change in the stock of money *causes* a change in the value of output. In application, this approach seeks to identify the set of financial assets that enjoys the strongest statistical link, or *correlation*, with the value of output.[6] That is, the preferred definition of money is the measure that is most highly correlated with the value of income, in the hope that observed changes in that measure will provide the most reliable predictions of resulting changes in money income.

In 1963, Milton Friedman and David Meiselman published a report on their efforts to identify statistically the best measure of money supply. The measure they found to be most closely correlated with the value of income was the M_2 definition of money—the sum total of currency, de-

---

[5]Milton Friedman and Anna J. Schwartz, *Monetary Statistics of the United States* (New York: National Bureau of Economic Research, 1970), p. 137.

[6]The degree to which two variables *covary*—change values together—can be represented by a *correlation coefficient*. If, for example, the variables y and x were linked, in a manner represented by the expression $y = a + bx$, every change in x would be accompanied by a predictable change in y. Hence y and x are perfectly correlated, and the correlation coefficient between y and x would be 1. If y and x were not correlated at all, the correlation coefficient would be 0. The closer the correlation between any two variables, the closer to 1 is the correlation coefficient for those two variables; and the weaker the correlation, the closer to 0 is the correlation coefficient.

mand deposits, and time deposits at commercial banks.[7] Other studies, however, have revealed different results. An investigation by Richard Timberlake and James Fortson concluded that the narrow (M_1) definition of money is most highly correlated with money income and that the inclusion of time deposits added nothing to the money/nominal income correlation.[8] More recently, with explicit recognition that money supply changes in any one time period might be most closely associated with money income changes in some other period, George Kaufman investigated the correlation between money and the value of income with different lead-lag patterns. His results did not permit the identification of any one measure of money that consistently performed best; rather, they indicated that different definitions perform best depending on the lead-lag relationships employed. According to Kaufman, "A definition that includes demand and time deposits at commercial banks appears best at explaining income two or more quarters later. Demand deposits and currency are best at explaining income observed concurrently and one quarter later.... [The] broader the concept of money, the later are the corresponding income periods yielding the highest correlations."[9]

These and other studies that have provided conflicting conclusions have not been able to settle the question of what definition of money is best, though they have contributed to a more complete understanding of the nature of the link between money measures and money income. On the basis of these studies, it is clear that the important relationship between money and income is relatively stable over extended time horizons. Unfortunately, these studies have not been able to distinguish one measure of money that enjoys the closest and most reliable link with income. Moreover, none of the definitions of money provides a means of predicting income changes that is sufficiently reliable for short-run forecasting purposes, although few forecasters are willing to ignore money supply changes in compiling their estimates of forthcoming economic developments.

An alternative approach that has been employed in the effort to provide an empirical basis for choosing a definition of money focuses on the degree of substitutability between narrowly defined money and other financial assets. One argument to include time deposits at commercial banks in the definition of money rests on the proposition that time deposits

---

[7]Milton Friedman and David Meiselman, "The Relative Stability of Monetary Velocity and the Investment Multiplier in the United States, 1897–1958," Research Study Two in *Stabilization Policy* (Englewood Cliffs, N.J.: Prentice-Hall, for the Commission on Money and Credit, 1963).

[8]Richard H. Timberlake, Jr. and James Fortson, "Time Deposits in the Definition of Money," *American Economic Review* 47 (March 1967): 190–94.

[9]George G. Kaufman, "More on an Empirical Definition of Money," *American Economic Review* 49 (March 1969): 78–87.

are so much like money narrowly defined—hence so substitutable for it in the portfolios of wealthholders—that they cannot be distinguished, statistically, from the assets encompassed by the traditional definition of money. Similarly, an argument to adopt the M_3 definition of money rests on the proposition that deposits in nonbank thrift institutions are virtually indistinguishable from (that is, are highly substitutable for) the assets that comprise M_1 and M_2 monies.

To measure the degree of substitutability among various financial assets, so that the appropriate cutoff point between money and other assets can be identified, researchers have employed measures called *cross-elasticities of demand.* As applied by economists, cross-elasticities measure the responsiveness of the demand for one product to changes in the price of another product, with both price and quantity changes measured in percentages. The greater the degree of substitutability between two products, the larger is the cross-elasticity of demand between those products. Hence, if one of two bookstores that serve a college community raises the price of math texts, even by a small percentage, the demand for the identical math texts sold by the second bookstore is likely to increase by a sizable percentage: the high degree of substitutability between texts bought at the two stores would be reflected in a large numerical value for the cross-elasticity of demand between texts from the two stores. In contrast, the increase in math textbook prices is likely to have no perceptible influence on the quantity of ice cream demanded in that college community, so that the measured cross-elasticity of demand between math texts and ice cream would be zero. Numerically, the cross-elasticity of demand between two products that are independent is zero; values between zero and infinity indicate less than perfect substitutability. It is also possible to find a negative cross-elasticity, indicating that the two products are complements—things that are used together, like, say, movies and popcorn. If a cut in movie prices results in an increase in popcorn purchases at movies, complementarity is indicated. The negative change in movie prices resulted in a positive change in popcorn demand, and hence the calculated cross-elasticity of demand has a negative value.

To evaluate the degree of substitutability that characterizes different financial assets, we must accommodate a reversal in the signs on our cross-elasticity measures if we are to use the percentage interest yields those assets provide as measures of their attractiveness. This necessity is easy to visualize. U.S. government bonds and bonds issued by corporations are certainly substitutes (not necessarily perfect substitutes). An increase in percentage interest yields on corporate bonds, while yields on government bonds remain unchanged, would cause a reduction in the demand for government bonds in wealthholders' portfolios of liquid assets. But an increase in yields on corporate bonds occurs with a decline in the prices of those bonds (bought at a lower price, they offer a higher percentage yield on investment). Since an increase in corporate-bond yields is part and parcel of a decline in corporate-bond prices, the demand for government bonds exhibits a negative cross-elasticity if the attractiveness of bonds is measured by percentage yields, while it retains a positive cross-elasticity if bond prices are the measure of attractiveness. In either case, a larger absolute value for our measure of elasticity implies a greater degree of substitutability.

Now, as an aid in determining whether to include commercial-bank time deposits in the definition of money, we should take note of the cross-elasticity of demand between those time deposits and demand deposits. If they are close substitutes, there is a strong case for including time deposits in the definition of money. This argument applies equally to the consideration of deposits in the nonbank thrift institutions and to any other financial assets that are candidates for inclusion in measures of the money stock.

TABLE 3–1. Average Cross-Elasticities between Money and Other Assets, 1964–1976

	Bank Time Deposits	Savings and Loan Deposits	Treasury Bills
Mean	−0.129	−0.312	−0.057
Range			
Low value	−0.632	−1.050	−0.150
High value	0.113	0.423	−0.006

Source: Adapted from E. L. Feige and D. K. Pearce, "The Substitutability of Money and Near-Monies: A survey of the Time-Series Evidence," *The Journal of Economic Literature* 15 June 1977: pp. 439–469.

In recent years, a large number of studies have been conducted that provide evidence on the cross-elasticities of demand between money and other assets. In 1977, Edgar Feige and Douglas Pearce published a survey article summarizing the evidence on cross-elasticities generated by studies that took place between 1964 and 1976. Table 3–1 presents average or mean measures and high and low estimates of the cross-elasticities found in those studies. According to the first cross-elasticity value in that table, a 10 percent increase in the interest rate paid on bank time deposits (as from 5 to 5½ percent) would reduce the demand for money by just 1.3 percent. The responses to changes in yields on savings and loan deposits and on Treasury bills appear to be just over twice that strong and just under one-half that strong, respectively. The ranges of cross-elasticity values appear fairly wide, but, on the basis of the overall evidence available, Feige and Pearce conclude that the "estimates of cross-elasticities between money and near-monies are surprisingly consistent and display relatively weak substitution relationships." Accordingly, "it is difficult to escape the conclusion that there does indeed exist an unacknowledged empirical consensus on the inelasticity of responses of the demand for money to changes in the rates of return on 'money substitutes.' "[10] Feige and Pearce clearly believe that available evidence on cross-elasticities supports a narrow definition of money.

Of course, in testing for the degree of substitutability between financial assets as an aid in identifying the best definition of money, a decision must be made on what elasticity magnitudes are large, indicating close substitutes. Even with a liberal interpretation of what elasticities imply close substitutability, however, the cross-elasticities revealed by the studies incorporated in the Feige and Pearce survey provide no compelling justification for a broader definition of money than the conventional one, M_1.

In light of the mixed results provided by efforts to establish a definition of money on an empirical basis, the burden of justifying abandonment of the narrow definition rests squarely on the shoulders of those who advocate broader ones. In the meantime, the majority of economists and financial analysts continue to pay most of their attention to money narrowly defined, on the basis of the judgment that currency and demand deposits, in their role as exchange media, are clearly distinguishable from other financial assets. Moreover, as will be shown in the near future, the stock of narrowly defined money is subject to control by the nation's central bank, so that, if money is measured narrowly, the central bank's monetary actions can be closely monitored. Where it is essential for analytical purposes to pay heed to alternative measures of money, we will do so as our exploration of financial markets and institutions proceeds. In the meantime, we will accept the conventional definition of money, mindful that (1) the view that money should be defined and measured on the narrow (M_1) basis is not unanimous and (2) with the emergence of NOW accounts, telephone transfers of funds from savings to checking accounts, and other innovations, the clear distinction between demand deposits and savings-type deposits is eroding, so that our working definition of money will have to be broadened in the relatively near future.

---

[10]E. L. Feige and D. K. Pearce, "The Substitutability of Money and Near-monies: A Survey of the Time-Series Evidence," *The Journal of Economic Literature* 15 (June 1977): 463. It is worth noting that some of the studies reviewed by Feige and Pearce, although not stressed in this paper, also measured the cross-elasticity of demand between money and consumer durables and found no evidence of substantial substitutability.

THE THREE COMPONENTS OF NARROWLY DEFINED MONEY AND ITS THREE SUPPLIERS

Defined narrowly, the money supply consists of three quantitatively significant components—the coin, paper currency, and demand deposits held by the nonbank public. Also, there are three suppliers of money in the United States. They are the U.S. Treasury, the Federal Reserve System, and commercial banks. The volumes of each of the three component parts of the narrowly defined money stock that was in circulation (i.e., in the possession of the nonbank public) as of October 30, 1978, are shown in Table 3–2.

Coins, which are token monies in the United States, are issued by the

TABLE 3–2. Money in Circulation (Narrowly Defined), October 30, 1978

Form of Money	Amount (in millions of dollars)	Percentage of Coin & Paper Currency	Approximate Percentage of Total Money in Circulation
Coin and paper currency			
... Coins:*			
Dollars	$ 1,096	1.0	
Fractional coin	9,493	8.7	
... Paper currency:			
United States notes*	313	.3	
Federal Reserve notes†	98,146	89.8	
Various notes no longer issued*	279	.3	
... Total coin and paper currency outside of the Treasury and Federal Reserve banks	$109,307	100.0	
... Coin and paper currency held by commercial banks	$ 11,100		
Total coin and paper currency in circulation (line 3 minus line 4)	$ 98,207		20.5
Demand deposits‡	$380,500		79.5
Total money supply in circulation	$478,707		100.0

Source: *Federal Reserve Bulletin* and *Statistical Appendix to the Annual Report of the Secretary of the Treasury on the State of the Finances,* 1978.

*Obligation of the United States Treasury.
†Obligation of the Federal Reserve System.
‡Obligation of commercial banks.

Treasury. They make it possible to pay and receive exact change and permit purchases from coin-operated machines. However, the bulkiness of coins limits the extent of their usage. Paper money, while not available in units smaller than $1, permits sizable sums of money to be carried with little bulk. Of course, paper currency is pure token money in the United States. The intrinsic value of the paper employed as money is negligible, and no government agency will redeem paper money in gold, silver, or anything else that has a commodity value comparable to the paper's value as money. As the data in Table 3-2 suggest, paper currency is roughly 20 percent of the money supply, with the bulk of outstanding paper currency (nearly 90 percent) consisting of notes issued by the Federal Reserve System. The remaining paper currency essentially consists of remnants of paper currency issues that were more important in the past, such as silver certificates and Treasury notes. Hence a small part of our paper money is an obligation of the Treasury.

Whatever their historical origins, paper currencies are subject to theft and to accidental loss, limiting their desirability, particularly for financing large transactions. Coin and paper currency together constitute just under 21 percent of the money supply. Hence demand deposits, or checkbook money, making up about four-fifths of the money in circulation, are the quantitatively dominant form in the United States. Demand deposit money is held in and (as will be demonstrated in the next chapter) is created by the nearly 15,000 commercial banks that serve the U.S. economy. Since it is the demand deposits that are money, not the checks we draw on those deposits, this form of money is not so subject to accidental loss and theft as is currency. The loss of a check does not result in the loss of our deposits. This safety feature, combined with the convenience of paying exact amounts to designated parties by check, accounts for the popularity of demand deposits (even though information problems sometimes make it difficult to get checks accepted).

The nonbank public—the collection of household, business firms other than banks, and state and local governments—has freedom to choose the form in which it holds its money. In comparing the advantages offered by alternative forms of money, if the public decides, say, it wants more of its money in currency form and less in demand deposits, it need only cash checks to make the desired change. Hence the composition of the money supply is determined by the nonbank public. Yet, while the actions of the nonbank public have an influence on the amount of money in circulation, the central bank possesses and uses the power to control the total amount of money available for the public's use. Chapter 4 begins an exploration of the processes through which the economy's money supply is provided, shedding light on the roles that the Treasury, the Federal Reserve System, and the commercial banking system play in those processes.

SUMMARY

By any acceptable definition, money must be ranked among the foremost inventions of mankind for its contributions to a rational allocation of resources and efficiency in the processes of production and exchange.

Money is a dynamic organism that through history has evolved into different forms, dictated by the prevailing economic environment and by the quest for safety and economy in the exchange process. At the present point in this evolution, there exists a significant disagreement with regard to just what should be counted as money. Advocates of the narrow definition of money (M_1), which encompasses currency and demand deposits, emphasize the medium-of-exchange function as the distinguishing characteristic of money. Most economists and financial analysts currently favor this view, but a number of prominent monetary experts emphasize the role of money as a liquid store of value and hence advocate a broader definition of it.

Unfortunately, available empirical evidence does not permit a full resolution of this disagreement. It does, however, reinforce the belief that money has a profound influence on the economy's vitality, so that economic forecasters dare not ignore changes in money stock measures as they attempt to predict the future.

In view of the failure of available evidence to support a broader definition of money, we may for now adopt the conventional narrow definition. Then, mindful of the participation of the Treasury, the Federal Reserve System, and commercial banks in the supplying of coins, paper currency, and demand deposit money, we can proceed with an analysis of the forces that influence the amount of money in circulation. Where our arguments are affected by the definition of money employed, we will endeavor to reveal how the lessons we learn would be altered by changing the money measure.

4

Commercial Banking and the Money Supply Process

With an awareness of what serves as money in modern economies and of the functions money performs, our next major task is to develop an understanding of how the amount of money in circulation is determined. To that end, this chapter focuses first on the crucial role of the commercial banking system in the money supply process. The banking transactions that influence the money supply are described and the mechanics of demand deposit money creation are explained. A formal money supply model is then constructed, which shows just what factors influence the quantity of money in circulation. This model shows clearly that households, commercial banks, and the Federal Reserve System are jointly involved in determining the size of the money stock.

To get started on the immediate task of analyzing the functioning of the commercial banking system, it is helpful to distinguish commercial banks from other financial institutions. A bank is a privately owned, profit-seeking business that holds money deposits for customers and extends credit through negotiated loans and security purchases. Of course, there are several other financial intermediaries—mutual savings banks, savings and loan associations, and credit unions are examples—that perform these same functions, but commercial banks are the largest single source of loanable funds for business, households, and government. Moreover, banks have in the past been clearly distinguished from other intermediaries in that a substantial part of their obligations—their demand deposit debt—has been generally accepted as a means of payment. No institution that does not meet this criterion can be classified as a commercial bank. As other institutions acquire methods of issuing claims that circulate as money, this distinction between commercial banks and those other institutions will erode (along with the dichotomy between narrowly defined money and a broader monetary aggregate).

In addition, commercial banks are distinguished in that they offer a broader array of financial services than any other type of financial institution, so that they merit the label "department stores of finance." Another distinctive feature of banks is the volatility of their obligations. Their checking-account (demand deposit) obligations, comprising nearly half of all claims against banks, are indeed payable on demand, legally and in practice. The bulk of banks' remaining obligations (mostly time deposits) are in principle payable after short notice, but, in practice, prior notice is not required for withdrawals.

Banks are further distinguished by their slim margin of equity claims by owners in relation to their obligations to others. The typical bank's net worth is well under 10% of the total claims against it, a fraction far smaller than that which characterizes most other business firms. Finally, banks are distinguished by the extent to which their activities are regulated by governmental bodies.

As of June 30, 1978, there were 14,698 banking firms operating a total of more than 40,000 headquarters banks, branches, and allied banking offices, to provide financial services for the U.S. economy.[1]

BASIC BANKING OPERATIONS

A firm understanding of the forces that influence the stock of money cannot be acquired unless the basic principles of commercial bank transactions are familiar. Hence this section provides a brief review of basic banking operations, beginning with the organization of a local commercial bank.

Envision a group of businessmen in Burbank, California, who, in anticipation of a growing local economy, decide to establish a new commercial bank. They may petition the U.S. Comptroller of the Currency or their state banking authority for a corporate charter. A bank chartered federally is a national bank, easily recognized by the presence of the word *national* in its name. A national bank is required to be a member of the Federal Reserve System (the Fed) and to adhere to the regulations im-

---

[1]The number of banking corporations in the United States has grown very slowly in recent decades, from 14,278 banks at the end of 1941 to the current total. At the same time, the number of bank branches and associated offices and facilities has increased substantially, reflecting the migration of population to the suburbs, the relaxation of laws limiting branching, and other developments. From a total of 3,564 units at the end of 1941, the number of bank branches and bank-related offices and facilities has grown to a current total of around 30,000 units.

posed by the Fed, including the requirement of insuring its depositors' accounts with the Federal Deposit Insurance Corporation (FDIC).

A state-chartered bank is not required to be a member of the Federal Reserve System, but those that qualify and agree to abide by Fed regulations can be members. As we will see, there are benefits associated with Federal Reserve membership, but there are also costs—in particular, Federal Reserve restrictions on bank operations can reduce bank profits. As a consequence, only about one state-chartered bank in ten is a member bank.

TABLE 4–1. Class Composition and Assets of U.S. Commercial Banks, December 31, 1977

Class of Banks	Number of Banks	Percentage of all Banks	Assets in Bank Class (in billions of dollars)	Percentage of all Banks
Insured banks:				
Federal Reserve members				
State member banks	1,014	7	210	18
National banks	4,654	32	651	56
Total member banks	5,658	39	861	74
Insured nonmember banks	8,729	59	268	23
	14,397	98	1129	97
Noninsured, nonmember banks	310	2	36	3
...Total banks	14,707	100	1166	100

Source: *Federal Reserve Bulletin,* June 1978, p. A-17.

As Table 4–1 shows, only about 32 percent of all commercial banks are national banks and only some 39 percent of all commercial banks, state and national, are members of the Federal Reserve System. It is equally apparent, however, that member banks are larger than nonmembers, collectively possessing some 74 percent of all commercial bank assets as of December 31, 1977. Finally, Table 4–1 shows that the overwhelming majority of state banks, even those that are not members of the Federal Reserve System, have acquired FDIC insurance coverage on their deposit obligations.

To represent the prominence (as indicated by assets) of federally-chartered member banks, suppose that our business consortium obtains a federal bank charter. It may then obtain investment funds through the sale of stock.[2] The bulk of the funds obtained are likely to be absorbed in procuring a bank building and office equipment and supplies. The rest, it can be assumed, will be held as *vault cash* (till money) to serve the coin and currency needs of the new bank's customers as it opens for business. With $500,000 acquired through stock sales, a $360,000 bank building constructed, and $120,000 of office equipment and supplies obtained, the new bank's assets and liabilities appear as in Balance Sheet 4–1.

BALANCE SHEET 4–1.

Assets		Claims	
Vault cash	$ 20,000	Capital stock	$500,000
Property	480,000		
	$500,000		

This bank is now ready to open for business, accepting deposits and extending credit.

Acquiring Deposits

Because of its convenient location or some other attraction, a number of Burbank's citizens decide to deposit their funds in this new bank. Suppose that, after a brief period, the new bank has enjoyed deposit inflows of $800,000. For the sake of simplicity, assume that all of these funds are deposited in checking (demand deposit) accounts rather than in time deposits. Some of our new bank's customers will have opened their checking accounts by exchanging coin and paper currency for demand deposit credit. But the bulk of the deposits in this new bank will come in the form of checks drawn on accounts in other commercial banks, and it is essential to understand how money transfers of this sort take place.

Suppose that we observe the deposit in this new bank (Bank B) of a $1,000 check drawn on an account in another bank (Bank A). Bank B, having received this check, credits the depositor's demand deposit account for $1,000. With both banks being members of the Fed, Bank B may exercise the $1,000 claim that it now has against Bank A by sending the $1,000 check to its Federal Reserve district bank for collection or *clearing*. Now, as members of the Federal Reserve System, both Banks A and B are required to maintain *reserves* against their deposit obligations, and the

---

[2]Funds may be raised also through the sale of a class of long-term bonds called *subordinated debentures.* The sources of bank funds will be discussed in more detail in the future.

TRACE 4–1.

Bank B

Assets		Claims	
Reserve deposits	+ $1000	Demand deposits	+ $1000

Bank A

Assets		Claims	
Reserve deposits	– $1000	Demand deposits	– $1000

Federal Reserve System

Assets		Claims	
		Bank A reserves	– $1000
		Bank B reserves	+ $1000

---

bulk of these reserves are held as *reserve deposit* credit in accounts maintained for member banks at the Fed. Consequently, to clear this check, transferring money credit from Bank A to Bank B, the Fed has to adjust the reserve deposit entries of the two banks in its balance sheet; it then sends the check to Bank A to inform it that both its deposit obligations and its reserve deposits at the Fed have been reduced by $1,000. The changes that take place in the balance sheets of Bank A, Bank B, and the Fed are recorded in trace statements, as shown in Trace 4–1. At the completion of this transaction, both Bank B's deposit obligations (to the depositor of the check) and its reserve deposits at the Fed have increased by $1,000, and Bank A's deposit obligations and reserve deposits have been reduced by a corresponding $1,000. The Fed has experienced no change in the total volume of its assets or liabilities, but $1,000 of reserve debt to member banks has been shifted from Bank A to Bank B.

Of the $800,000 total of deposits the new bank in Burbank has acquired, if $50,000 were in the form of coin and currency, which has been added to the cash held in its vault, and $750,000 were in the form of checks drawn on other banks, these sums would appear as in Balance Sheet 4–2. With demand deposits representing claims that depositors have against the bank, the new bank's obligations have increased by $800,000. Of course, its assets have increased by a like amount, since vault cash and reserve deposit claims against the Fed together have increased by $800,000.

BALANCE SHEET 4–2.

Assets		Claims	
Vault cash	$ 70,000	Demand deposits	$ 800,000
Reserve deposits	750,000	Capital stock	500,000
Property	480,000		
	$1,300,000		$1,300,000

The Reserve Account

As we indicated earlier, banks that are members of the Federal Reserve System are required to hold reserves against their deposit obligations. Under current regulations, both member-bank deposits at the Fed and vault cash are counted as reserves. Hence the vault cash and reserve deposit entries for our new bank can be consolidated as in Balance Sheet 4–3, permitting attention to be focused on the overall status of the bank's reserve account. The volume of reserves that member banks maintain is a fraction of their deposit obligations, the value of that fractional *reserve ratio* being set by the Fed, within a range of values established by Congress. If the current reserve ratio is 20 percent, the new bank would have to hold 0.20 × $800,000, or $160,000, in reserves (vault cash, deposits at the Fed, or both forms). Since the bank's actual reserves are $820,000, it has $660,000 of *excess reserves.* It is on the basis of these excess reserves that the bank can lend or invest.

BALANCE SHEET 4–3.

Assets		Claims	
Reserves	$ 820,000	Demand deposits	$ 800,000
Property	480,000	Capital stock	500,000
	$1,300,000		$1,300,000

A Transaction That Creates Money

To complete our review of the simple mechanics of basic banking transactions, suppose that our new bank is confronted by a dependable, credit-worthy local business requesting a loan of $660,000. If it chooses to meet this request, in return for a promissory note signed by the borrower, the bank will extend $660,000 of demand deposit credit in an account maintained by the borrower.[3] All that is required is a set of pen-and-ink bookkeeping entries (or the computer-controlled electronic-image equivalent) to credit the loan applicant's demand deposit account with a full $660,000 of spendable demand deposit money. The bank adds $660,000 to its demand deposit obligations and an offsetting $660,000 of loans to its assets, as shown in Balance Sheet 4–4. This transaction illustrates clearly that, as has often been said, "with the mere stroke of a pen" commercial banks create money as they extend credit.

BALANCE SHEET 4–4.

Assets		Claims	
Reserves	$ 820,000	Demand deposits	$1,460,000
Property	480,000	Capital stock	500,000
			$1,960,000
Loans	660,000		
	$1,960,000		

    The capacity of commercial banks to extend credit in a form that can be directly spent by check—that is, in a form of money—is of substantial importance. Yet we must not exaggerate the capacity of any one particular bank nor, for that matter, of all banks combined to create money. In particular, we cannot conclude that, if only bookkeeping entries are necessary to provide money to any credit applicant, commercial banks have unlimited capacity for the creation of money, individually or collectively. In fact, the particular set of transactions described above has only minor monetary significance, as can be readily demonstrated.

    A loan applicant generally cannot be expected to accept the burden of interest charges on borrowed funds that sit idle in an unused checking account. Hence a commercial bank can expect its loan recipients to draw checks on their borrowed deposits as they pay their accrued debts. With many thousands of banks serving the public, the probability is extremely small that checks drawn on a single commercial bank will be redeposited by the recipients in accounts in that same bank. As a consequence, to be certain that it can meet its reserve requirement after loaned funds have been withdrawn, a single commercial bank like the one we have been observing can extend at most an amount of credit equal to its excess

---

[3]In reality, banks are legally restrained from extending to a single customer loans that exceed a minor fraction of the bank's capital and surplus. For purposes of understanding the mechanics of basic banking transactions, this legal restriction can be ignored.

reserves. If the customer who borrowed $660,000 from the bank in Burbank spends it (by drawing checks on that account), in all likelihood those funds will not be redeposited there. If the recipients of $660,000 in checks drawn on that account deposit them in their own banks, our Burbank bank will have a reduction of $660,000 in both its demand deposit obligations and its reserves when all checks have been cleared, as shown in Balance Sheet 4–5. Having exchanged its $660,000 of excess reserves for $660,000 of interest-earning loans, it has exactly the volume of reserves necessary to meet its legal reserve requirement. If it had extended loans in an amount greater than $660,000, it would suffer an unallowable reserve deficiency when those loaned funds were spent and redeposited elsewhere.

BALANCE SHEET 4–5.

Assets		Claims	
Reserves	$ 160,000	Demand deposits	$ 800,000
Property	480,000	Capital stock	500,000
			$1,300,000
Loans	660,000		
	$1,300,000		

Moreover, the amount of money and credit provided by our bank in Burbank in this set of transactions is not likely to involve a net increase in the total volume of money and credit outstanding. Remember that the credit that it can extend is based on the $660,000 of excess reserves it accrued as it attracted deposits. If those deposits were attracted from other banks that previously were fully loaned (just meeting their reserve requirements), those other banks collectively would have suffered an offsetting $660,000 reserve deficiency, requiring them to contract the volume of money and credit available for public use. With the total volume of reserves available to commercial banks being an important determinant of their ability to provide credit, and with currency serving as reserve money when held in bank vaults, the loans extended by our new bank in Burbank would result in a net increase in the supply of money and credit only if, with that bank's appearance, society had decided to hold less of its money in currency form, which would have provided more vault-cash reserves to the banking system. Since there is no reason to expect the opening of one new bank to prompt society to alter the mix of currency and demand deposits it holds, there is no reason to expect our new bank's operations to measurably alter the money and credit totals provided by the banking system. However, there are many transactions that, through the commercial banking system, very powerfully affect the supply of money and credit. The potential of one such transaction is demonstrated in the next section of this chapter—a section that will be easy to follow if you have mastered the mechanics of the basic banking operations reviewed up to this point.

THE DEMAND DEPOSIT CREATION PROCESS

Our immediate goal is to demonstrate the commercial banking system's potential for creating demand deposit money. With a handful of simplifying assumptions, the explanation of this is straightforward. Moreover, while the discussion immediately ahead will ignore some complications that tend to impose narrower limits on this capacity to expand or contract the money supply, the banking system's maximum potential for doing so will be clearly revealed. Any necessary refinements to our probe of the money supply process can be added later.

Assumptions of a Rudimentary Money Supply Model

Our review of the deposit creation process assumes the following:

1. All banks are members of the Federal Reserve System and face the same reserve requirements.

2. Banks offer only demand deposit accounts (time deposits are ignored for now) and must hold reserves.

3. Recognizing the opportunity cost of holding excess reserves, all banks attempt to stay fully loaned, just meeting their reserve requirements. At the same time, all banks have credit applicants available for any volume of funds they choose to lend.

4. The expansion (or contraction) of the volume of demand deposits does not result in a change in the volume of currency held by the nonbank public.

Initiating an Expansion of Deposits

With all banks fully loaned in the beginning, let the Federal Reserve Bank of New York purchase $100,000 of U.S. government securities from one of the several New York City securities dealers with which it deals regularly. In exchange, the securities dealer receives a check for $100,000, drawn on the Federal Reserve System. The securities dealer deposits that check (consistent with our simplifying assumptions) in a checking account in a commercial bank that is a member of the Federal Reserve System. In turn, the member commercial bank credits the security dealer's account for $100,000 of demand deposits and returns the check to the Fed for reserve deposit credit. The changes in the balance sheets of the commercial bank (Bank 1) and the Fed are presented in Trace 4–2.

TRACE 4–2.

Bank 1

Assets	Claims
Reserves + $100,000	Demand deposits + $100,000
⎡Required reserves + $ 20,000 Excess reserves + $ 80,000⎤	

Federal Reserve System

Assets	Claims
U.S. government securities + $100,000	Member bank reserves + $100,000

Notably, these trace statements show that, with the financing of the transfer of $100,000 of securities from the dealer to the Fed, two important claims were created. The securities dealer has a new $100,000 demand deposit claim against the commercial bank (created by the commercial bank with a set of bookkeeping entries), and the commercial bank has a new $100,000 reserve deposit claim against the Fed (created when the Fed drew a check against itself, then transferred it by deposit to the commercial bank). The $100,000 of new demand deposits is money that previously did not exist. Moreover, the reserve deposit claim acquired by Bank 1 represents an increase in the total volume of reserves available to the entire banking system, and this increase relaxes the constraint against a further extension of credit in the form of demand deposit money. Since, with a 20 percent reserve ratio, $100,000 of new reserves can meet the legal reserve requirement on $500,000 of demand deposits, the banking system should now be able to extend $400,000 of new credit in the form of demand deposits. The existence of available excess reserves, which can serve as the basis for the extension of loans, is reflected in the entries in brackets in Trace 4–2. The terms in brackets do not reflect balance sheet entries but just a division of the posted $100,000 of reserve credit. Bank 1 now has $80,000 of excess reserves, permitting it to lend or invest that amount.

Deposit Creation by Commercial Banks

Now suppose that Bank 1 just happens to have available a credit-worthy loan applicant who wishes to borrow, say, $80,000 to construct additional storage facilities for a thriving carpet business. The borrower signs a promissory note, acknowledging the bank's claim for repayment of the loan. In turn, since the borrower is not likely to choose to leave the bank with $80,000 in currency, the loan is turned over in the form of $80,000 of demand deposits credited to the borrower's account. The changes that this loan transaction produces in the balance sheet of Bank 1 and the overall banking system are shown in Trace 4–3.

TRACE 4–3.

Bank 1

Assets	Claims
Loans	Demand deposits
+ $80,000	+ $80,000

Consolidated Banking System

Assets	Claims
Loans	Demand deposits
+ $80,000	+ $80,000

With the extension of this loan, Bank 1 has created $80,000 of new money with nothing but a set of bookkeeping entries. This is not $80,000 that some depositor previously left with the bank, and which has now been loaned to our credit applicant, for all other depositors still possess their money claims against the bank. The commercial bank has created new money simply by creating a deposit obligation against itself, for which it receives an interest-earning loan. The basic results would have been the same, of course, had the bank extended loans totaling $80,000 to any number of credit applicants.

At this point, it is good to remind ourselves that borrowers generally do not pay interest only to let borrowed funds sit idle. Hence we can expect our borrower to spend his $80,000 by drawing checks on his deposit, which the recipients are apt to deposit in other banks. When those checks are cleared, Bank 1 will have lost both demand deposit obligations and reserves in the amount of $80,000. Of course, the banking system will lose neither reserves nor deposits: the existing total will simply be distributed differently among banks. With all transactions complete, balance-sheet traces, showing the overall changes in deposit liabilities and cash and earning assets that have accrued following the Fed's purchase of $100,000 of securities, first for Bank 1 and then for other banks (Banks 2) combined, appear as in Trace 4–4.

TRACE 4–4.

Bank 1

Assets	Claims
Reserves + $ 20,000 Loans + $ 80,000 + $100,000	Demand deposits + $100,000

Banks 2

Assets	Claims
Reserves + $80,000 ⎡Required reserves⎤ ⎢ + $16,000 ⎥ ⎢Excess reserves ⎥ ⎣ + $64,000 ⎦	Demand deposits + $80,000

Having lost its $80,000 of excess reserves, Bank 1 is now fully loaned and can extend no more credit. The $100,000 of new demand deposit money that was provided when the Fed bought securities still exists as a deposit obligation of Bank 1, and the $80,000 of demand deposits created when Bank 1 extended loans continues to exist as obligations of Banks 2. In addition, as the entries in brackets show, Banks 2 now have excess reserves on the basis of which they can extend $64,000 of loans. In the process, they will create $64,000 of new money through the creation of demand deposit claims against themselves. And, as the borrowers spend these newly created funds, the recipients of their spending will deposit the checks received in a third set of banks, so that the deposit obligations and reserves of that third set of banks will be raised by $64,000. In turn, these banks will find themselves blessed with excess reserves, in the amount of $51,200, permitting them to extend loans by the creation of $51,200 of new deposit obligations. And so the process of deposit expansion can continue until the full $100,000 of reserves injected into the banking system when the Fed bought securities is absorbed as reserves against deposit obligations created by the commercial banking system.

Several rounds of the balance-sheet changes that reflect these transactions are summarized in Table 4–2. From the discussion above, as well

TABLE 4–2. A Summary of Demand-Deposit Credit Creation

Round 1. Bank 1 accepts and clears a check drawn on the Fed for $100,000.

Bank 1		
Assets	Claims	Additions to Demand deposits
Reserves 　+ $100,000 ┌Required reserves┐ 　+ 　　20,000 Excess reserves └　+ 　　80,000┘	Demand Deposits 　+ 　$100,000	$100,000

Bank 1 lends $80,000.

Bank 1		
Assets	Claims	
Loans 　+ 　$　80,000	Demand deposits 　+ 　$　80,000	$　80,000

Round 2. Checks for $80,000 are deposited in Banks 2.

Banks 2		
Assets	Claims	
Reserves 　+ 　$　80,000 ┌Required reserves┐ 　+ 　　16,000 Excess reserves └　+ 　　64,000┘	Demand deposits 　+ 　$　80,000	

Banks 2 lend $64,000.

Banks 2		
Assets	Claims	
Loans 　+ 　$　64,000	Demand deposits 　+ 　$　64,000	$　64,000

Round 3. Checks for $64,000 are deposited in Banks 3.

Banks 3		
Assets	Claims	
Reserves 　+ 　$　64,000 ┌Required reserves┐ 　+ 　　12,800 Excess reserves └　+ 　　51,200┘	Demand deposits 　+ 　$　64,000	

Banks 3 lend $51,200.

Banks 3		
Assets	Claims	
Loans 　+ 　$　51,200	Demand deposits 　+ 　$　51,200	$　51,200

Round 4: In the fourth round, banks will be able to lend $40,960 (80% of $51,200), in the fifth round $32,768 (80% of $40,960), and so on. With the deposit creation process completed, the total volume of new demand deposits stemming from the Fed's purchase of $100,000 of securities will be

$$D = \$100,000 + \$80,000 + \$64,000 + \$51,200 + \$40,960 + \$32,768 + \ldots$$
$$= \$100,000 \, [1.00 + 0.80 + (0.80)^2 + (0.80)^3 + \ldots + (0.80)^n + \ldots]$$

$$= \$100,000 \, \frac{1}{1.00 - 0.080}$$

$$= \$100,000 \, \frac{1}{0.20}$$

$$D = \$500,000$$

as from this table, it is apparent that the injection of $100,000 of new reserves into the banking system initiates an infinite geometric process of demand-deposit credit expansion of the form

$$\Delta D = \Delta R \, (1 + b + b^2 + b^3 + \cdots + b^n + \cdots)$$

where ΔR is the change in reserves available to the banking system ($100,000, in the example), b is one minus the reserve ratio ($b = 1 - r = 1.0 - 0.2 = 0.8$, in the example), and ΔD is the resulting change in demand deposits when the expansion process is completed ($500,000, in the example). It is well known that the sum of the geometric series in parentheses is

$$1 + b + b^2 + b^3 + \cdots + b^n + \cdots = \frac{1}{1 - b}$$

and, since $(1 - b)$ is the reserve ratio, r, the impact on demand deposits of a change in the volume of reserves in amount ΔR is

$$\Delta D = (1/r) \, \Delta R$$

A balance sheet trace statement for the consolidated banking system, showing the balance sheet changes that have taken place in the system as a whole when the expansion process we have been following is completed, appears in Trace 4–5.

Note again that, with the expansion process completed, the $100,000 of new reserves provided by the Fed's purchase of securities are fully absorbed as required reserves for the $500,000 of new demand deposit obligations of the commercial banking system. The system is once again fully loaned after member banks, by issuing deposit claims against themselves, have created money in an amount equal to a multiple of five times

---

TRACE 4–5.

Consolidated Banking System

Assets	Claims
Reserves	Demand deposits
+ $100,000	+ $500,000
Loans	
+ $400,000	
$\left[\begin{array}{l}\text{Required reserves}\\ +\quad\$100,000\end{array}\right]$	

---

the original injection of reserves.[4] No wonder reserve funds are sometimes referred to as *high-powered money.* This multiplicative response is possible only because of the dominant role of checkbook money in our economy, which causes the reserves lost by one bank to end up with other banks in the system. A leakage of reserves out of the banking system as deposit expansion takes place reduces the size of that expansion. By the same token, an increase in the required reserve ratio diminishes the multiple by which a change in reserves alters the stock of demand deposits. Apparently, the volume of reserves and the reserve ratio are crucial determinants of the money supply.

Investments and Deposit Creation

During our review of the mechanics of banking operations, it was noted that, when banks have excess reserves, they can either lend or invest in the amount of their excess. In the subsequent description of the deposit creation process, the role of negotiated loans in the creation of demand deposit money was illustrated repeatedly. But no heed was paid to the effect on the deposit creation process of banks' financial investments. To remedy that omission, we can look back at the deposit creation process at any stage and substitute bank investments for extensions of negotiated loans.

In Round 2 of the deposit expansion process, banks had $80,000 of excess reserves. Suppose, instead of lending $80,000, they purchased $80,000 of securities in Round 2. The banks can pay for their security acquisitions by issuing cashier's checks drawn on themselves. The security sellers deposit those checks in accounts in their own banks and receive demand deposit credit for $80,000. Once the cashier's checks are cleared,

---

[4]In summary, the complex deposit creation process traced above rests on (1) the reserve requirement relationship—(required reserves) = (required reserve ratio) × (demand deposits); and (2) the "loaned-up" assumption—(reserves) = (required reserves). Together, these imply that $\Delta R = r\Delta D$. Solving for the change in demand deposits (ΔD) yields $\Delta D = (1/r)\ \Delta R$.

the issuing banks will have lost $80,000 of reserves (matching their excess reserves), and the sellers of securities will have $80,000 of newly created demand deposit claims against the banking system.

The balance-sheet changes reflecting this set of transactions are provided in Trace 4–6. Note that, just as in the case of extension of negotiated loans, banks have created $80,000 of additional demand deposit money through investment in securities. Moreover, having accrued the $80,000 of new deposit obligations, banks also have $80,000 of additional reserves, leaving them with $64,000 of excess reserves, which can serve as the basis for a new round of deposit-creating loans or investments. With an increase in available reserves, the banking system can be expected to increase both its loans and its investments. In both cases, demand deposit money expands, ultimately to a multiple of the injection of reserves; the value of that multiple is the reciprocal of the reserve ratio (i.e., $1/r$).

TRACE 4–6.

Banks Purchasing Securities

Assets	Claims
Investments	
+ $80,000	
Reserves	
− $80,000	
[Excess reserves	
− $80,000]	

Security Sellers' Banks

Assets	Claims
Reserves	Demand deposits
+ $80,000	+ $80,000
Required reserves	
+ $16,000	
[Excess reserves	
+ $64,000]	

Deposit Contraction

Just as an addition to reserves available to the banking system provides the basis for deposit expansion, a loss of reserves serves to contract the stock of demand deposit money. To reverse the transaction that resulted in our deposit expansion process, let the Fed sell a $100,000 security to a government securities dealer. In exchange for the security, the Fed receives a check drawn on a commercial bank (Bank 1). Clearing the check will reduce Bank 1's reserves (and the banking system's reserves) by $100,-000. Meanwhile, its demand deposit obligations are also reduced by $100,-000, which constitutes a decline in the money stock.

With Bank 1's deposit obligations reduced by $100,000, its required reserves will be $20,000 less, but its actual reserves are reduced a full $100,000, leaving a reserve deficiency of $80,000. Some of Bank 1's reserve deficiency may be relieved by inflows of deposits from other banks, but, even so, the banking system is left with the $80,000 reserve deficiency. Banks as a group may temporarily relieve this deficiency by borrowing reserves from the Fed (individual banks could also increase reserves by selling securities to other banks or by borrowing reserves from other banks, so that the reserve deficiency is shifted elsewhere). But with reserves reduced by $100,000, only a contraction of the deposit obligations of the commercial banking system can restore the required relationship between reserves and deposits.

As in the case of deposit expansion, a demand deposit contraction can take place either through sales of investments to the nonbank public or by reductions in loans. If a set of banks that are suffering an $80,000 reserve deficiency sells securities to the nonbank public, they will receive checks, providing for the transfer of $80,000 of reserves. At the same time, in exchange for securities, the nonbank public will have given up $80,000 of demand deposit money. At this point, deposits have shrunk by a total of $180,000, but there remains a reserve deficiency of $64,000 at banks whose depositors drew down their accounts to purchase securities. Alternatively, if reserve-deficient banks cease making new loans or refuse to renew outstanding loans as they come due, demand deposit money will be extinguished as the deposits built up by borrowers are drawn upon for loan retirement.

At each stage of the deposit contraction process, as reserve-deficient banks make up their deficits by selling securities or reducing loans, further deposit contraction takes place. Once again, within the confines of our simple representation of the banking system, the change in demand deposits brought on by a change in reserves is given by the rudimentary expression $\Delta D = (1/r) \Delta R$. With a reserve ratio of 0.2, the eradication of deposit obligations of individual banks must proceed until the banking system's obligations are reduced by five times the loss in reserves.

A MORE REALISTIC MONEY SUPPLY MODEL

Without a thorough grasp of the rudiments of deposit expansion and contraction, a full understanding of the forces that influence the money stock is not possible. But the money supply model we deduced from reviewing the deposit expansion process is not an adequate representation of reality, as the list of simplifying assumptions provided at the beginning of that review surely suggested. At this point, it is not possible to offer one model of the money supply process that would satisfy all monetary experts. It is possible, however, to provide a simple money supply model that eliminates the most glaring deficiencies of the rudimentary expression for predicting changes in the volume of demand deposits. Recognizing that the narrowly defined money supply consists of the sum of demand deposits and currency, that society can hold time deposit claims against banks on which reserves are required, that banks can choose to hold some cushion of reserves in excess of legal requirements, and that the required reserve ratio is different for different kinds of deposits and for different banks, a money supply model can be constructed that is widely accepted as a rough approximation of the real-world money supply process. To develop that more realistic money supply model requires the following definitions and assumptions.[5]

I. Definitions

A. Narrowly defined *money* (M_1) is the sum of currency (C) and demand deposits (D) held by the nonbank public. This total excludes currency held by banks and the federal government, demand deposits held by the federal government, and interbank deposits, since it is not "money" held by these institutions but money held by the nonbank public that is thought to influence economic activity. Algebraically, the narrowly defined money supply is

$$M_1 = D + C$$

B. The *monetary base* (B) is the sum of all reserves (R) held by member banks (we will continue to ignore the existence of nonmember banks) and the currency (C) held by the nonbank public. Remember that currency serves as reserves if held as vault cash by member banks. Algebraically,

$$B = R + C$$

C. The total *deposit obligations* of commercial banks consist of private demand deposits (D), private time deposits (T), and federal government or Treasury deposits in commercial banks (G).

---

[5]For a more complete treatment of this form of a money supply model see Jerry Jordan, "Elements of Money Stock Determination," *Review—Federal Reserve Bank of St. Louis*, October 1969, pp. 10–19.

II. Assumptions

A. Member banks are required to hold reserves against all of their deposit obligations; the percentage reserve requirement is dictated by the kind of deposit obligation and the class of the depository bank as designated by the Fed. As such, the overall required reserve ratio (r) against all deposit obligations is a weighted average of the ratios for different categories of deposit obligations.[6] The value of the overall required reserve ratio is total required reserves (RR) divided by total deposit obligations or, algebraically,

$$r = \frac{RR}{D + T + G}$$

Thus, with the overall reserve ratio given, the total volume of required reserves is

$$RR = r(D + T + G)$$

B. To guard against the possibility of a reserve deficiency due to deposit withdrawals exceeding deposit inflows, banks can hold a safety cushion of excess reserves (E). As the total demand deposit obligations of commercial banks expand, it is reasonable to suppose that the risk of net deposit losses increases proportionately. To protect against this risk, banks can hold additional excess reserves. Assuming that excess reserves increase in proportion to demand deposits, total excess reserves are given by the expression

$$E = e \cdot D$$

in which e is a proportionality constant.

C. The non-bank public decides what proportion of its liquid wealth it prefers to hold in the form of demand deposits, time deposits, and currency. Assuming that these proportions are constant, the volumes of currency and time deposits held are proportional to the volume of demand deposits. Algebraically, the volume of time deposits is

$$T = t \cdot D$$

and the volume of currency is

$$C = c \cdot D$$

where t and c are proportionality constants.

---

[6]For example, if Bank X has two kinds of deposit obligations, demand deposits and time deposits, with required reserve ratios of 0.20 and 0.05 respectively, and if its time deposit obligations are 1.5 times its demand deposit obligations, its overall required reserve ratio would be $[(1 \times 0.20) + (1.5 \times 0.05)]/2.5 = 0.11$.

D. As they accrue to the U.S. Treasury, income tax revenues, revenues from bond sales, etc. are deposited in commercial bank accounts. Funds from these deposits are shifted to accounts kept with Federal Reserve Banks as the treasury faces approaching obligations. The volume of government deposits in commercial banks may be expressed as a fraction of demand deposits. Algebraically,

$$G = g \cdot D$$

where g is a proportionality constant.

We now have the building blocks for our more realistic money supply model. To construct that model, it must be recognized that there are three absorbers of the monetary base. They are required reserves, excess reserves, and privately held currency. Together, they exhaust the available monetary base, so that it is definitionally true that

$$B = \underbrace{r(D + T + G)}_{\substack{\text{required} \\ \text{reserves}}} + \underbrace{E}_{\substack{\text{excess} \\ \text{reserves}}} + \underbrace{C}_{\substack{\text{privately held} \\ \text{currency}}}$$

Substituting the simple behavioral functions proposed above for T, G, E, and C yields

$$B = r[D + (t \cdot D) + (g \cdot D)] + (e \cdot D) + (c \cdot D)]$$

or, expanded,

$$B = D[r(1 + t + g) + e + c]$$

Solving for D yields

$$D = \frac{1}{r(1 + t + g) + e + c} \cdot B$$

which is the equilibrium volume of demand deposits that can exist when the entire available monetary base is absorbed in private currency hoards, in required reserves, and in excess reserves voluntarily held by commercial banks. The total money stock is

$$M_1 = D + C$$
$$= D + (c \cdot D)$$
$$= D(1 + c)$$

or, by plugging in the known equilibrium value of D,

$$M_1 = \left[\frac{1 + c}{r(1 + t + g) + e + c} \right] \cdot B \tag{4-1}$$

The term in brackets can be thought of as a *money multiplier,* like the one identified in our rudimentary discussion of the link between reserves and demand deposit money; if its value is known, the multiplier can be used to predict the change in the money supply that results from a specified change in the money base. That is, if the quantity in brackets above is designated m, the absolute value of the narrow money stock is

$$M_1 = mB$$

For a given value of the money multiplier (m), changes in the monetary base provide changes in the money stock in the amount

$$\Delta M_1 = m \ \Delta B$$

and the value of m, by definition, is $m = \dfrac{\Delta M_1}{\Delta B}$.

As of July, 1977, the value of m was 2.435, indicating that each dollar of monetary base was supporting just over $2.43 of money. With part of the monetary base absorbed in private currency hoards, and with the base that is absorbed in currency, in required reserves against time deposits and government deposits, and in excess reserves, swelling with the expansion of demand deposits (and hence draining reserves from stocks available to support the deposit expansion), we should have expected a money multiplier that is smaller than the 5:1 ratio between checkbook money and reserves deduced from the rudimentary money-supply model.

The money supply model above appears to provide a means of predicting the money supply response to a change in the monetary base. More importantly for us, the model permits an easy assessment of the changes in the money multiplier that are wrought by (1) changes in the reserve ratio, (2) shifts in the demand for currency, time deposits, or demand deposits, (3) changes in the proportion of deposits that banks choose to hold as excess reserves, and (4) changes in the magnitude of Treasury deposits in commercial banks. For example, with just a glance at the money-multiplier expression, it is apparent that an increase in the required reserve ratio reduces the value of the money multiplier, which limits the volume of monetary base to providing for a reduced money stock.

Remaining Qualifications

It may be noted that the model above has not provided systematically for commercial banks that are not members of the Fed. This is a very minor omission, however, for nonmember banks do adhere to reserve ratios (determined by state regulations or by the banks themselves) and hence can be readily accommodated in the model developed above. That model is on shakier ground as a consequence of the assumption that the ratios c, t,

g, and e are fixed, remaining constant as the central bank endeavors to alter the money stock, say, by altering required reserves or changing the monetary base. Both theoretical considerations and empirical evidence suggest that these ratios change systematically in response to a number of variables that are influenced by money supply changes.

Suppose that the Fed reduces the supply of money. This action to make money more scarce is apt to increase the interest cost of money. In turn, with higher interest rates on financial instruments, society may try to shift into interest-bearing securities and out of currency and demand deposits (and out of time deposits, too, since ceilings on allowable interest payments often keep banks from raising time-deposit yields in step with market interest rates). If interest-bearing, nonspendable time deposits are closer substitutes for other interest-bearing securities than are checking deposits and currency, the shift from time deposits to other assets may far outweigh shifts out of currency and demand deposits, so that we can reasonably restrict our present focus to the variable t, the ratio of time deposits to demand deposits. The arguments above suggest that this variable shrinks as interest rates rise; such a decrease enlarges the money multiplier.

The volume of excess reserves that banks choose to hold is also widely regarded as sensitive to interest rates. Excess reserves are held to insure banks that they will be able to meet their reserve requirements, even if there are unexpected deposit and reserve outflows. The volume of the excess reserve cushion that a bank chooses to hold depends on the variability of its deposits, the level of interest yields on loans and security purchases (which the bank foregoes by holding excess reserves), and the cost of suffering a reserve deficiency. Given the variability of deposits and the costs of covering a reserve deficiency, as interest rates rise it becomes profitable for banks to economize on excess reserves and to face a higher risk of a reserve deficiency in pursuit of more profitable loans and investments. As excess reserves are squeezed (the ratio e reduced), the money supply expands.

A monetary policy action, to the extent that it influences the economy's output level, can have an additional impact on the currency ratio (c) because the income elasticities of demands for currency and checkbook money differ. For example, if purchases of big-ticket items (which are typically financed by check) become a larger proportion of total purchases as output expands, the currency ratio falls. Any decline in the currency ratio constitutes a greater proportionate change in the denominator of the money multiplier than in the numerator, and therefore the currency ratio decline increases the money supply.

Without further effort in this regard, it is apparent that opportunities for additional refinements in our money supply model persist. Yet, the model we have constructed is adequate for our purpose. It focuses attention on the most important intricacies inherent in the money supply pro-

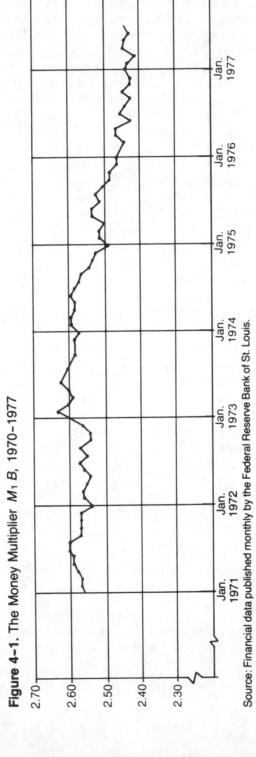

Figure 4-1. The Money Multiplier $M_1 B$, 1970–1977

Source: Financial data published monthly by the Federal Reserve Bank of St. Louis.

cess. In addition, a number of financial analysts would argue that the systematic changes in the behavioral ratios built into that model are of a low order of magnitude, so that the money multiplier is sufficiently stable for practical use in predicting money supply changes. Monthly observations on the ratio of the narrowly defined money stock to the monetary base are plotted in Figure 4–1 for the period from January 1971 through July 1977.[7] That plot shows that there are monthly variations in the value of m around its average or trend value. These short-run variations around the trend value of m suggest that the ability of a simple money multiplier to predict changes in M_1 is greater for time horizons longer than a month. For a time horizon of several months, the value of m appears to have followed a sufficiently stable path to permit reasonably accurate predictions of money supply changes to be made by multiplying changes in the monetary base by trend values of the money multiplier. Of course, the observed variations in m argue persuasively that the determination of the money stock is not a simple, mechanical process to be easily represented by a single equation. Indeed, our one-equation money supply model is best suited to drawing attention to the factors that crucially influence the money supply.

FACTORS THAT INFLUENCE THE MONEY SUPPLY

Any event that enlarges the monetary base (B) or the money multiplier (m) produces an increase in the stock of money; a shrinkage of the monetary base or the money multiplier reduces the supply of money. Some important factors that influence the money supply do so by altering the money multiplier, some do so by changing the monetary base, and some alter both the base and the money multiplier. A student of the financial system needs to know how changes in the money supply come about, so that attention is devoted next to particular factors that expand or contract it, beginning with those that impinge directly on the money multiplier—the composition of the public's portfolio of liquid assets, bank demand for excess reserves, the Treasury's allocation of funds to commercial bank deposits, and reserve requirements.

Shifts Between Demand Deposits and Currency

Suppose that the nonbank public decides to hold a larger fraction of its money in currency and a smaller fraction in demand deposits. To implement this portfolio revision, the owners of demand deposit accounts draw checks on those accounts, draining currency out of the vault-cash

---

[7]By way of comparison, during the 1960s the value of the money multiplier ranged from 2.52 to 2.72.

reserves of commercial banks. If member commercial banks' vault-cash inventories shrink below desired levels, they can replenish them with currency shipments requested from the Federal Reserve System. The recipient bank's reserve account at the Fed is reduced by the amount of the currency shipped.

From the point of view of the nonbank public, a shift from demand deposits to currency is simply a change in the composition of its money stock. But that conversion drains reserves (vault cash or reserve deposits) out of the possession of banks, where they can support a multiple volume of demand deposit money. Hence a given monetary base provides a reduced money stock if the nonbank public absorbs a larger proportion of that base in currency.

In terms of the money supply equation (4–1), an increase in the currency ratio (c) increases both the numerator and denominator. But since, in terms of absolute values, the numerator of the money multiplier is larger than the denominator (by a factor of about 2.4 to 1 at present), any increase in c raises the value of the denominator by a larger proportion than it raises the numerator. Hence the value of the money multiplier is reduced by a rise in the currency ratio.

Symmetrically, a reduction in the currency ratio increases the money multiplier, permitting any monetary base to support an increased stock of money, as a larger proportion of the monetary base is available for commercial banks to use as reserves.

Shifts Between Demand Deposits and Time Deposits

Since time deposits are not included in the narrowly defined money stock, any exchange of demand deposits for time deposits directly eradicates an amount of M_1 money equal to the number of dollars shifted. This shrinkage of the money supply is partly offset by excess reserves that are available because the required reserve ratio on time deposits is lower than that on demand deposits. Overall, however, the shift in favor of time deposits must reduce the narrowly defined money stock, for, with more of the monetary base absorbed in required reserves against time deposits, less is available for private currency stocks and reserves against demand deposits.

In terms of the money supply equation, a shift from demand deposits into time deposits raises the time deposit ratio (t); it also lowers the required reserve ratio (r), since that ratio is an average of percentage requirements on both demand and savings-type accounts. These conflicting changes are reflections of those discussed in the preceding paragraph, so that, overall, the denominator of the money multiplier must rise (the increase in t outweighs the decline in r), limiting a given monetary base to providing a reduced money stock.

Conversely, if the nonbank public decides to hold more funds in demand deposits and fewer in time deposits, the money stock increases, since, with less of the monetary base required as reserves against time deposits, more is available for private currency stocks and reserves against demand deposits.[8]

Excess Reserves

By retiring maturing loans without issuing a comparable volume of new loans, or by selling securities to the nonbank public, the commercial banking system can enlarge its stock of excess reserves, and it simultaneously reduces the money stock as some of its demand deposit obligations are eradicated. Conversely, the banking system reduces its excess reserves as it extends additional loans and makes investments, and it creates demand deposit money in the process. As suggested earlier, an increase in available interest yields on loans and investments can be expected to cause banks to draw down their excess reserves, enlarging the stock of money provided by any volume of monetary base. In the algebraic model developed above, changes in the demand for excess reserves alter the ratio e: an increase in demand raises e and reduces the size of the money multiplier; a decrease in demand (e.g., in response to rising interest rates) lowers e and increases the size of the money multiplier.

Moreover, as was noted earlier, efforts to economize on excess reserves as interest yields rise are not the only possible source of systematic changes in the money stock induced by changes in interest rates. Shifts from currency to time deposits as interest yields become more attractive and any change in the monetary base itself as interest rates change serve to alter the money stock. A number of empirical studies have attempted to measure the responsiveness of the money stock to interest-rate changes. The reported elasticities of money supply to changes in interest yields cover a range from 0.12 to 0.25.[9] These measures indicate that the money

---

[8]Changing the definition of money would change these conclusions. For example, by the M_2 definition of money (incorporating currency, demand deposits, and time deposits at commercial banks), a shift from demand deposits to time deposits increases the money stock, since the accompanying reduction in the required reserve ratio permits a given monetary base to support an enlarged volume of currency, demand deposits, *and time deposits*.

[9]If the money supply's interest-elasticity is 0.15, a 10 percent increase in the interest rate (as from a rate of 8 percent to a rate of 8.8 percent) increases the money supply by 1.5 percent. Empirical evidence on the money stock's response to interest-rate changes appears in a number of sources, including R. L. Teigen, "The Demand for and Supply of Money," in W. L. Smith and R. L. Teigen (eds.), *Readings in Money, National Income, and Stabilization Policy* (Homewood, Ill.: Richard D. Irwin, 1974), pp. 68–103; P. H. Hendershott and F. DeLeeuw, "Free Reserves, Interest Rates, and Deposits: A Synthesis," *Journal of Finance* 25 (June 1970): 599–613; and Thomas D. Thompson and James L. Pierce, "A Multiperiod Econometric Model of the Financial Sector," paper presented at the meeting of the Federal Reserve System, Committee on Financial Analysis, May 1971. The evidence from these and

multiplier increases with the level of interest rates, or that there is a positive response in the money stock to interest-rate changes. However, the magnitude of this response appears to be small enough that, as suggested earlier, the money multiplier can be used to make useful predictions of money stock changes for known changes in the monetary base.

Shifts in U.S. Treasury Deposits

While member-bank reserve accounts make up the bulk of the deposit liabilities of the Federal Reserve System, other institutions—mainly the U.S. Treasury, foreign central banks, and international financial institutions—also maintain balances at the Fed. These balances are usually increased by the deposit of drafts drawn on accounts in commercial banks, so that an increase in these balances generally reduces the monetary base. In turn, checks written against these balances are usually deposited in commercial banks, so that the accrual of reserve credit generally raises the monetary base.

The U.S. Treasury is the most important nonbank depositor in the Fed, as it maintains part of its working balances in deposits at the Federal Reserve banks. The rest of the Treasury's working balances are held in commercial banks throughout the country in *tax and loan accounts,* so called because the funds in those accounts stem from accruals of tax revenues and revenues from the sale of Treasury securities (which are exchanged for loans to the Treasury by the purchasers). The Treasury pays the bulk of the obligations it incurs by drawing checks on its deposits in Federal Reserve bank accounts. To replenish those accounts, the Treasury calls funds from tax and loan accounts in commercial banks.

To illustrate the channels through which Treasury transactions affect the money supply, suppose that the Treasury (1) collects tax revenues and places them in tax and loan accounts, (2) calls deposits from member-bank accounts for deposit in Fed banks, and (3) makes payments to the public. As the Treasury collects taxes, the stock of money in circulation shrinks (remember that federal government balances are not counted as part of money in circulation). Commercial banks are required to hold reserves against government deposits, just as they are on other deposit obligations. Hence the larger the portion of the monetary base absorbed in reserves against government deposits, the smaller the money stock that that base can support. In our algebraic money supply model, an accumulation of government deposits raises the value of g and reduces the size of the money multiplier.

---

other papers is reviewed in Robert H. Rasche, "A Review of Empirical Studies of the Money Supply Mechanism," *Review—Federal Reserve Bank of St. Louis,* July 1972, pp. 11–18.

As the Treasury calls funds out of tax and loan accounts, the deposit obligations of commercial banks are reduced, so that the reserves that were held against Treasury deposits are freed. This is reflected in a decline in the government deposit ratio (g), which increases the money multiplier. At the same time, however, member-bank reserves shrink in step with their loss of Treasury deposits. Hence the banking system, which previously was holding what was viewed as an optimal volume of reserves, attempts to replenish its reserve balances. A contraction in the money stock follows from such efforts of the banking system, since they cause a reduction in the monetary base.

Finally, as the Treasury pays its financial obligations with checks drawn on accounts in Federal Reserve banks, the monetary base is increased, providing an expanded money stock. And, as this money supply increase takes place, the government deposit ratio falls, so that the value of the money multiplier is raised.

Clearly, Treasury operations can have a potent influence on the money stock, by altering both the monetary base and the money multiplier. But why does the Treasury involve itself in the roundabout set of transactions described above, maintaining accounts in both commercial banks and Federal Reserve banks? The answer is that this arrangement limits the influence that Treasury activities have on the money stock. Rather than collecting revenues at a uniform rate throughout the year, the Treasury enjoys large inflows of revenues as tax due-dates approach. If these funds were directly deposited in Fed banks, the monetary base would shrink precipitously, constricting the money supply and the flow of credit through the financial market. In turn, commercial bank reserves would be increased in spurts as Treasury outlays occur. By coordinating the transfer of funds from commercial banks to Fed accounts with Treasury outlays, the volatile ebb and flow of money and credit that could accompany Treasury activities is avoided. Even so, fluctuations in the Treasury's balances at Federal Reserve banks can have significant effects on the monetary base. For example, during March 1975, week-to-week changes in the daily averages of Treasury deposits in Fed banks averaged $1.5 billion, corresponding to roughly 4½ percent of member-bank reserves.

Gold Transactions

In the past, gold enjoyed far more important roles in national and international monetary systems than it does today, and therefore, until August 1971, the Treasury bought and sold gold at a fixed dollar price. As gold was acquired, in the main through the settling of debts across national boundaries, it was added to the *monetary gold stock.* Historically, acquisitions of gold were an important source of the monetary base, and, even in mid-1977, the monetary gold stock was equivalent to about 10 percent of the monetary base. The monetary effects of Treasury gold transactions are first in our treatment of factors that affect the money supply by altering just the monetary base.

To visualize the impact of gold acquisitions, suppose that the Treasury purchases $1,000 of gold from a domestic mine. Payment for this purchase is made with a check drawn on the Treasury's deposits in the Fed. The recipient of this check takes it to a bank and exchanges it for deposit credit, currency, or a mix of both. Then, with this check cleared through the Fed, the monetary base is increased by $1,000. In the meantime, the Treasury has drawn down its deposits at the Fed by the amount of the gold purchase. To replenish those deposit balances, the Treasury issues $1,000 of *gold certificates* and tenders those claims against the acquired gold to the Fed in return for deposit credit. At this stage, the gold purchase has been *monetized*—the monetary base has increased by the amount of the gold purchase, and the Treasury's spendable deposits have been restored to their previous level with the acquired gold added to the monetary gold stock.

Interestingly, in the early 1970s, the official dollar price of gold increased, raising the monetary value of the existing monetary gold stock. The Treasury was able to issue gold certificates against the increased value of gold hoards, and, when the Treasury spent the deposit balances credited to its accounts at the Fed, the monetary base was increased.

Should the Treasury sell gold at the official gold price, the monetary base is reduced.[10] Buyers would pay for their gold purchases with checks drawn on deposits in commercial banks. The Treasury would send those checks to Federal Reserve banks for clearing, providing a reduction in the monetary base as deposit credit is shifted from reserve accounts of commercial banks to Treasury deposits. The Treasury could then draw on this deposit credit to retire gold certificates in an amount equal to the official value of gold that was sold. Of course, if sales should take place at actual prices above the official gold price-level, the Treasury can enjoy profits, which, when spent, raise the monetary base. In recent years, a sizable fraction of the monetary gold stock has been auctioned off at prices considerably above the official level, so that the Treasury has received substantial windfall profits. In the meantime, with free-market prices of gold well above the last posted official price, the U.S. government has remained committed to ending gold's historical monetary role, so that the Treasury has not been a gold purchaser.

---

[10]From 1939 to December 1971, by international agreement, gold used for clearing international debts was valued at $35 per ounce. In December, the dollar was devalued to an official $38 per ounce; in February 1973, to $42.22 per ounce; shortly thereafter, efforts to control the market price of gold were abandoned.

Special Drawing Rights

The rapid expansion of world trade after World War II aroused concerns that the stock of gold available worldwide would be inadequate to meet the growing needs for a means of settling debts across boundaries. This concern led to the creation by the International Monetary Fund (IMF) of paper claims, called *Special Drawing Rights* (SDRs). These claims, sometimes referred to as *paper gold*, can be used to clear debts between countries that are members of the IMF, in much the same fashion that gold has been used. To provide a growing international trading medium, the IMF allocated SDRs to member countries in 1970, 1971, and 1972. The acquisition of these units of paper gold increases the recipient country's monetary base, much as the acquisition of actual gold does.[11]

When the U.S. Treasury acquires SDRs, it tenders them to the Fed and receives deposit credit in return. As the Treasury spends those deposits, reducing its deposit balances to their original level, the monetary base is increased by the amount of the SDR allocation.

Treasury Currency Outstanding and Treasury Cash Holdings

Treasury currency consists of coins, silver certificates, and a small volume of other currency that was originally issued by commercial banks but for which the Treasury now has redemption responsibility. New currency issued by the Treasury (now mainly coin) is shipped to the Federal Reserve banks for credit to Treasury deposits there. These deposits are drawn down again, however, as the Treasury makes expenditures. Checks issued against these deposits are paid out to the public. As individuals deposit these checks in commercial banks, the monetary base is increased.

When Treasury currency is retired, the monetary base declines. Payment for currency turned in for redemption is made with checks drawn on the Treasury's deposits in the Reserve banks, and the immediate effect is a reduction in these balances. Transfers from the Treasury's deposits in commercial banks to the Reserve banks replenish these deposits and simultaneously reduce the monetary base.

In addition to deposit balances in commercial and Federal Reserve banks, the Treasury holds some currency in its own vaults. Changes in these holdings affect the monetary base just like changes in the Treasury's deposit account at the Reserve banks. If Treasury holdings of currency

---

[11]For reasons to be explained in chapter 18, the arrangements by which international transactions are financed are much different from those that prevailed when SDRs were created. As a consequence, SDRs have never assumed the major role as an international payments reserve asset for which they were intended, and there has been no allocation of SDRs since 1972.

increase, they do so at the expense of publicly held currency and reserves of commercial banks, and hence the monetary base is reduced. If cash holdings of the Treasury decline, however, these funds move into commercial bank reserves and publicly held currency, and hence the monetary base is increased.

Foreign and Other Deposits in Reserve Banks

Besides member banks and the U.S. Treasury, foreign central banks, international institutions, and a few nonmember banks keep funds on deposit in the Federal Reserve banks. In general, these balances are built up by the transfer of deposits from member banks. Such transfers can take place either directly, if these groups also have deposits in U.S. commercial banks, or indirectly, by the deposit of funds acquired from others who have commercial bank balances—the Treasury, other foreign banks, or the general public. In either case, member-bank reserves and the monetary base are reduced.

When foreign institutions draw on their Federal Reserve balances (say, to purchase securities), these funds are paid to the public and deposited in commercial banks; thus reserves and the monetary base are increased.

Federal Reserve Security Transactions

There are an additional number of Federal Reserve operations that influence the money stock by altering the monetary base. One such operation, as we already know, is the purchase (or sale) of securities by the Fed. It was such purchases that initiated the deposit expansion process reviewed at the beginning of this chapter. The Fed draws checks on itself to pay for its security purchases; when the checks are cleared against the Fed, the monetary base is increased by the amount of security purchases. Of course, Federal Reserve sales of securities have the opposite effect: the monetary base is reduced as checks drawn on commercial banks to pay for those securities are cleared.

The Fed is authorized to buy and sell U.S. government securities, government agency securities, and banker's acceptances. (*Banker's acceptances* are drafts, drawn by one party, which order a second party, a bank, to pay a specified sum to a third party on a particular date or on demand. When the bank signifies its willingness to be liable for the payment specified in the draft, that claim becomes a banker's acceptance.) In practice, the Fed engages in relatively few transactions involving banker's acceptances and concentrates its security transactions in the market for U.S. government and government agency securities.

In addition to outright purchases, the Fed acquires a small portion of the securities it holds through *repurchase agreements:* it buys securities that the seller agrees to buy back within a few days. These purchases provide funds to government securities dealers for a short time period and hence raise the monetary base temporarily.

Reserve Loans

When deposit and reserve inflows accrue too slowly, or when deposit and reserve outflows occur too rapidly, banks are left with reserve deficiencies, which must be covered. The Fed provides one route by which member banks can cover their reserve deficiencies, as Federal Reserve banks stand ready to extend reserve loans to banks in their district. Of course, any reserves that are credited to member-banks' reserve accounts entail additions to the monetary base, providing for the sustenance of an enlarged money stock. Conversely, when member banks pay off their debts for reserves borrowed from the Fed, their reserve accounts (as well as bills payable to the Fed) are reduced, so that the monetary base shrinks.

The interest charge levied on Federal Reserve loans, called the *discount rate,* is an administered rate set by the Fed. If this interest cost of reserves is held constant while market interest yields on loans and investments rise, rational bank managers can be expected to extend credit more aggressively. By economizing on idle, excess reserves, such banks expose themselves to greater risks of reserve deficiencies, but the cost of such deficiencies is reduced as the gap between the discount rate and market interest yields widens. Clearly, reserve loans can serve as a safety valve to relieve strains on the reserve positions of individual banks. But, unless the discount rate is adjusted as market interest yields change, member banks' usage of their borrowing privilege can be expected to measurably alter the monetary base.

Federal Reserve Bank Float

A large proportion of the checks drawn on one bank and deposited (or cashed) in another bank is cleared through the Federal Reserve System. Some of these checks—those passing between banks that are near each other—are credited immediately to the reserve accounts of the depositing banks and are collected the same day by debiting the reserve accounts of the banks on which the checks are drawn. But, when checks are deposited in banks that are far from those on which they were drawn—e.g., checks drawn on banks in the South and deposited in New York during the Christmas season—it is often impossible to shuttle them through the Federal Reserve system before a lapse of several days. Nonetheless, after a maximum of two days, the Fed grants reserve credit for any check a member bank has presented for collection, even if that check has not completed the clearing process. During the two-day waiting period, the Fed is obligated to the recipient bank for *deferred availability cash items.*

The reserve credit extended for checks not yet collected is called Federal Reserve *float*. On the books of the Federal Reserve banks, float is the difference between the asset item "cash items in process of collection" and the liability item "deferred availability cash items". This difference is always positive, because there are always checks that cannot be collected within the prescribed time interval.

Since float represents the extension of reserve credit to the banking system, an increase in float raises the monetary base, and a fall in float reduces the monetary base. On an annual average basis, the volume of float is fairly stable, but there can be sharp fluctuations over short periods. Some fluctuations (like those that accompany major holidays, when the volume of checks to be cleared rises and then drops sharply) occur in a repetitive yearly pattern, so that they are predictable. But widespread snowstorms, postal strikes, and other events that slow the transmission of checks in the clearing process can produce unexpected temporary increases in float and hence in the monetary base.

Other Factors

The discussion a few pages back considered how the monetary base increases when the Fed buys securities and declines when it sells them. The same results follow from any Federal Reserve expenditure or receipt. Every payment made by the Federal Reserve banks, in meeting expenses or acquiring assets, affects bank deposits and reserves in the same way as the payment to a dealer for government securities. Similarly, Reserve bank receipts—interest paid on loans and securities and increases in the capital paid by member banks to be "owner-participants" in the Federal Reserve System—absorb reserves and reduce the monetary base.

A Summary of Factors Affecting the Monetary Base

The monetary base consists of currency held by the nonbank public plus reserve deposits held by member banks in their district Federal Reserve banks. All currency is either Treasury issue or Federal Reserve notes, and all member-bank reserves are currency or reserve deposits at the Fed. Hence all member-bank reserves and all of the monetary base consist of obligations of the Federal Reserve or the Treasury. As shown in our discussion of particular factors affecting the monetary base, the Fed incurs obligations by acquiring assets. Therefore its balance sheet should reflect factors affecting bank reserves and the monetary base. In particular, we can examine its balance sheet to isolate potential sources of reserves and base money plus any potential absorbers of those items. The same inspection of the Treasury balance sheet is necessary to assess its role in providing and absorbing reserves and base money.

The principal balance sheet entries for the Federal Reserve System appear in Balance Sheet 4–6.

BALANCE SHEET 4–6.

Federal Reserve System

Assets	Claims

1. Federal Reserve credit
  a) U.S. government securities
  b) Loans to member banks
  c) Float
2. Gold certificates
3. Special Drawing Rights
4. Treasury currency
5. Other Federal Reserve assets net of minor obligations and capital.
	1. Federal Reserve notes
	  a) Held by the nonbank public
	  b) Held by member banks
	2. Deposit obligations
	  a) Member bank reserves
	  b) U.S. Treasury deposits
	  c) Foreign and other deposits

A statement of the Treasury's "monetary" assets and liabilities appears in Balance Sheet 4–7.

BALANCE SHEET 4–7.

Treasury

Assets	Claims

1. Gold stock
2. Treasury currency issued
	1. Gold certificates held by the Federal Reserve
	2. Treasury currency except that held by the Treasury
	  a) Held by the public
	  b) Held by member banks
	  c) Held by the Fed‡

Each month, the relevant balance sheet entries of the Federal Reserve System and the Treasury are consolidated to provide a summary statement of factors supplying reserve funds and factors absorbing reserve funds, which is printed in the monthly *Federal Reserve Bulletin.*[12] Adding Federal Reserve and Treasury assets, then adding their liabilities, and cancelling entries that appear on both sides of the resulting statement (gold certificates and Treasury currency held by the Fed) provide the entries shown in Balance Sheet 4–8, using figures for July 1977.

It is apparent that not all the obligations incurred in the acquisition of assets constitute member-bank reserves or publicly held currency. But the principal entries in that statement can be readily rearranged to show

---

[12]Weekly figures are available from the Federal Reserve System.

BALANCE SHEET 4–8.

Consolidated Monetary Accounts of the Federal Reserve and the Treasury, July 1977
(in millions of dollars)

Assets		Claims	
1. Federal Reserve credit		1. Currency (Federal Reserve notes	
a) U.S. government and federal		and Treasury currency)	
agencies securies	106,479	a) Held by the public	88,218
b) Loans to member banks	788	b) Held by member banks	8,829
c) Float	2,543	c) Held by the Treasury	426
d) Other Fed assets net			
of minor liabilities			
and capital	472	2. Deposit obligations	
2. Gold stock	11,620	a) Member bank reserves	26,912
3. Special Drawing Rights	1,200	b) U.S. Treasury deposits	8,789
4. Treasury currency issued	11,119	c) Foreign and other deposits	1.047
	134,221		134,221

member-bank reserves as a residual—the difference between the total sources of reserve funds and total uses for purposes other than bank reserves. Hence, member-bank reserves are given by the *reserve equation.*[13]

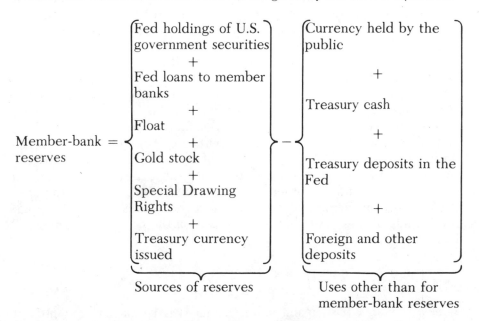

---

[13]Summary measures of weekly changes in member-bank reserves, recorded in a reserve equation format, are reported in the *Wall Street Journal* at the end of each week.

The monetary base, consisting of member-bank reserves plus public currency holdings, is obtained by adding currency held by the public to both sides of the reserve equation. Hence the monetary base is

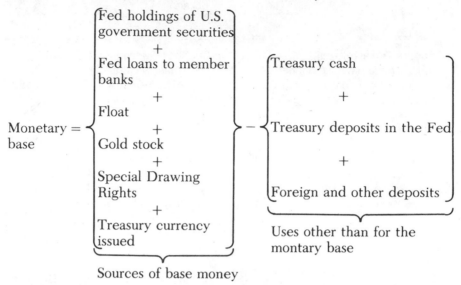

$$\text{Monetary base} = \left\{ \begin{array}{c} \text{Fed holdings of U.S.} \\ \text{government securities} \\ + \\ \text{Fed loans to member} \\ \text{banks} \\ + \\ \text{Float} \\ + \\ \text{Gold stock} \\ + \\ \text{Special Drawing} \\ \text{Rights} \\ + \\ \text{Treasury currency} \\ \text{issued} \end{array} \right\} - \left\{ \begin{array}{c} \text{Treasury cash} \\ + \\ \text{Treasury deposits in the Fed} \\ + \\ \text{Foreign and other deposits} \end{array} \right\}$$

Sources of base money — Uses other than for the montary base

These equations indicate that, in July 1977, member-bank reserves and the monetary base were $35,741 million and $123,959 million respectively. Far more importantly, these equations provide a summary view of the factors that determine the size of the monetary base and of the bulk of the factors that influence the stock of bank reserves (shifts by the public between currency and bank deposits change the volume of member bank reserves while leaving the monetary base unaltered). As an illustration of their usefulness, the monetary-base equation permits us to corroborate, with a brief glance, our earlier arguments that the monetary base is increased (or decreased) with a rise (or a decline) in the volume of Federal Reserve credit extended, government purchases (or sales) of gold, and so on. Those equations also show that some of the factors that influence bank reserves and the monetary base are under the control of the Federal Reserve System and that others reflect actions by the Treasury, the nonbank public, and member commercial banks themselves to the extent that the lending of reserves to banks takes place at the behest of commercial banks.

SUMMARY

Banks are unique participants in the financial marketplace in a number of respects, but, most importantly, they are unique because their demand deposit obligations serve as money. Indeed, those obligations constitute the dominant portion of the narrowly defined money supply. And, since their demand deposit obligations are widely employed as money (so that reserves lost by one bank are likely to reappear elsewhere within the banking system), banks collectively have the capacity to create money, through the extension of credit, in an amount equal to a multiple of the reserve base available to them.

The volume of money that can be sustained by a particular volume of monetary base differs depending on the cushion of excess reserves that banks choose to hold, the allocation of Treasury deposits between commercial banks and the Fed, the required reserve ratio that banks face, and the mix of liquid assets that the nonbank public chooses to hold. There are systematic changes in these factors, which cause the money multiplier to vary somewhat as the central bank seeks to change the money supply. Historical evidence suggests, however, that the money multiplier is sufficiently stable to be useful in forecasting the money supply response to known changes in the monetary base.

The monetary base is affected in turn by an extended list of factors, including Treasury transfers of funds between commercial banks and accounts at the Fed, gold transactions, Special Drawing Rights allocations, Treasury currency issue and cash holdings, Federal Reserve Security transactions, changes in Federal Reserve loans to member banks, and float. The Federal Reserve and Treasury activities that influence the monetary base are reflected, in summary terms, in a modified form of the reserve equation.

Through the development of a fairly sophisticated money supply model, this chapter was able to illustrate the means by which the Federal Reserve is able to influence the money stock by altering the monetary base, the money multiplier, or both. At the same time, it was shown that the central bank is not the only source of changes in the money supply. The Treasury, commercial banks, and the nonbank public also exert important influences on the amount of money in circulation. Still, the Fed has ultimate control over the money supply since, with adequate time, it can offset any unwanted changes in the money stock.

To anticipate the adjustments in financial markets and in the goods-and-services sector of the economy, economists and financial analysts keep a close watch on the factors that cause money supply changes. In this regard, many forecasters can be classified as avid "Fed-watchers," as they keep close tabs on week-by-week changes in the financial variables that the Fed's policy actions directly impinge upon.

5

The Federal Reserve System and Monetary Control

A central bank is an integral part of any modern financial system. It facilitates the orderly and efficient functioning of both the private sector of the economy (by control of the money supply, collection and clearance of checks, etc.) and the public sector (by action as fiscal agent for the Treasury). A central bank has as its primary function the control of the monetary system, with the goal of promoting national economic objectives. In this role it serves as a "banker's bank"—it provides services to the commercial banking system, which in turn provides services to individuals and firms. The central bank also acts as the federal government's banker.

As a result of performing so many functions and rendering so many services, the central bank directly or indirectly affects every individual in the country. A simple chain of events can be used to show how the central bank ultimately affects everyone. GNP, prices, employment, etc., which are variables affecting every individual, are significantly influenced by the money supply and credit conditions, which are in turn influenced by the volume of commercial bank reserves. The central bank acts to control commercial bank reserves. Thus the central bank is of prime importance because monetary policy—implemented by the central bank through commercial banks—is among the most important, if not the most important, government tool in influencing aggregate economic activity.

Given the influence of the central bank and its broad impact, it is important to understand what it tries to do, what it can reasonably expect to do, and what it cannot do. Only with this understanding can efforts be made both to improve its operations and to prevent the unwise interference with its activities by those (particularly in politics) who fail to grasp the importance of the central bank and its role in the economy or who wish to use it for some poorly thought-out cause.

Accordingly, this chapter is designed to outline the nature, functions, and effects of the Federal Reserve System. The first topic discussed is the structure of the system. Each of the five parts of the system are examined, with particular emphasis given to the Federal Open Market Committee and the commercial banks. Next, the functions of the system are examined. This will aid the reader in understanding what the system does in terms of the services it performs. More important to the functioning of the economy, from a macroeconomic standpoint, is the Fed's influence on the money supply. This process must be clearly understood to fully appreciate the many controversies that have arisen about monetary policy.

In addition, this chapter examines the defensive and dynamic operations of the Fed, dealing with the questions of what actions are initiated by the Fed and what independent elements affect reserves. Finally, problems encountered in applying monetary control are considered: how successful can the Fed expect to be, and how successful has it been?

A BRIEF HISTORY

Although the concept of a central bank is hundreds of years old, central banks as they exist today are a relatively recent creation. Our central bank, the Federal Reserve System, was created by Congress in late 1913 and began operations in 1914.

The U.S. banking system in the 1800s and even the early 1900s consisted of many independent, privately owned commercial banks. Each bank sought to maximize its own welfare, and there were no controls on credit expansion other than those provided by the market itself. Little wonder, then, that the U.S. economy suffered frequent booms and busts, as sharp changes in the money supply caused sharp changes in income. Crises occurred rather regularly during the nineteenth and early twentieth centuries—1819, 1837, 1857, 1873, 1884, 1907, 1921, and 1929.

Banks in this period accentuated the volatility of the economic system. During expansions, banks significantly increased new loans, and, during contractions, they permitted the amount of loans outstanding to decline; respectively, such actions increased and decreased the money supply and therefore contributed to both the expansions and the contractions. Bank failures were widespread during contractions. Many people were ruined financially. These were ripe conditions for bank runs, in which individuals tried to convert bank notes into gold specie or bank deposits into currency. Obviously, bank failures caused a loss of confidence in both the banking system and the economy.

Precedents for the Federal Reserve Banks can be traced back to the first Bank of the United States, which was chartered in 1791 and lasted twenty years. This bank did several tasks that the Fed does today, such as the issuance of notes that circulated as currency. The second Bank of the United States was chartered by Congress in 1816 in response to a shrunken money supply and a multitude of notes issued by various banks. This bank did control the money supply, just as the Fed attempts to do today. As was the case with its predecessor, politics finally destroyed the second Bank. The National Bank Act was passed in 1863 to permit the chartering of national banks and to reintroduce a national currency, but problems persisted.

The Panic of 1907 resulted in a large number of bank failures, which served as a stimulus to do something about unrestricted private banking. A National Monetary Commission, established to study such panics and failures, issued its findings in 1912 and recommended that a central bank be created. The Federal Reserve Act became law in late 1913.

STRUCTURE OF THE FEDERAL RESERVE SYSTEM

The structure of the Federal Reserve System is a result of political compromise forged in the Federal Reserve Act of 1913. Both the public and the banks had to be satisfied. For example, populist feelings prevented the establishment of a system having a single central bank. Also, emphasis on states' rights meant that membership in the system could be required only for national banks.

The Federal Reserve System is divided into twelve Federal Reserve districts, each with its own district bank or banks, and the commercial banks that are members of the system. Additionally, there are a board of governors, the Federal Open Market Committee, and the Federal Advisory Council. Figure 5–1 depicts the total structure of the Federal Reserve System and shows the relationships between its parts.

The Board of Governors of the Federal Reserve System

The Board of Governors is at the top of the system. Directly or indirectly (through veto), it makes most of the significant decisions for the System.

The Board of Governors consists of seven members, appointed by the president (and ratified by the Senate) for fourteen-year terms, which are staggered so that one member's term expires every other year. No more than one member can come from any single Federal Reserve district. Although the President can remove a member "for cause," this has never occurred. Within the Board are a chairman and a vice-chairman, selected by the President for four-year renewable terms.

The Board of Governors is an independent entity, reporting directly

Figure 5–1. Organization of the Federal Reserve System.

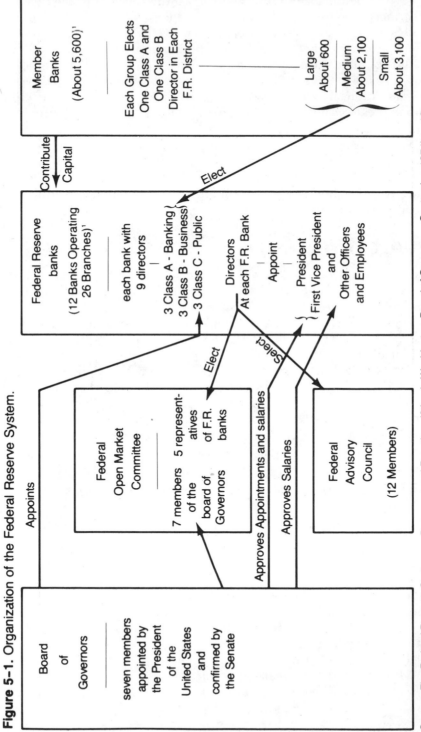

Source: *The Federal Reserve System — Purposes and Functions* (6th ed.; Washington: Board of Governors, September 1974), p. 18.

¹Updated figures.

to Congress.[1] Its overall responsibility is to formulate monetary policy and to see that it is executed properly.

Powers of the Board of Governors include the following:

1. Formulation of monetary policy. The board constitutes seven of the twelve members of the Federal Open Market Committee, which formulates open-market operations policy.

2. Specification of reserve requirements for member banks within limits set by Congress, and approval of the discount rates (which determine member-bank borrowing costs) set by individual Federal Reserve banks.

3. Setting of interest-rate ceilings for time-deposit accounts of member banks.

4. Examination of Reserve banks and member banks and action on applications for membership in the system, member-bank merger requests, branching requests, etc.

5. Control over the international operations of the Federal Reserve banks.

6. Regulation of a variety of financial activities, such as the extension of consumer credit and margin trading for securities.

7. Appointment of Class C directors to Federal Reserve bank boards.

Federal Open Market Committee (FOMC)

This committee consists of the seven-member Board of Governors and five Reserve Bank representatives (who in practice are the presidents of those five banks). One of the district bank representatives is always the president of the Federal Reserve Bank of New York. The other four are rotated among the remaining eleven presidents. Structurally, the Federal Open Market Committee is second only to the Board of Governors in terms of importance in the system. In fact, it has in practice become the dominant force in formulating major monetary decisions. Many monetary policies are discussed and courses of action are developed by the committee.[2]

---

[1] For many years, the board was dominated by the Treasury, which persuaded the Fed to buy government securities during new debt offerings, in order to put downward pressure on the interest rate. The Federal Reserve–Treasury Accord of 1951 ended this support program and made the Fed independent.

[2] Technically, the board's monetary policy plans could be outvoted in this committee if two of the board's members voted with the five bank presidents for a course different from that desired by the board.

Open-market operations are the primary vehicle for carrying out U.S. monetary policy. These operations consist of the buying and selling of government securities in the open market, which directly affects member-bank reserves and therefore the money supply. Since the quantity of money is a key variable in the economy, the ability of the FOMC to affect that monetary aggregate directly is obviously important.

The FOMC passes its policy decisions to the manager of the Federal Open Market Account, who executes the committee's directives through private dealers. These decisions have typically been made about every three or four weeks. The open-market trading desk of the Federal Reserve Bank of New York conducts all purchases and sales to carry out the monetary policy directives of the FOMC.

Figure 5-2 summarizes the organization and the procedures of the FOMC in 1976. This summary can be generalized for any year. In 1978, Arthur Burns was replaced as Chairman of the Board of Governors by William Miller who, in turn, was replaced by Paul Volcker in 1979.

The Federal Advisory Council

This council has no real power and little influence. It acts as advisor to the Board of Governors. As such, it meets in Washington several times a year to make recommendations to the Board. The council consists of one member—typically a commercial banker—from each Federal Reserve District, appointed by the district bank's board of directors.

The Federal Reserve Banks

A prominent part of the Federal Reserve System is, of course, the twelve district banks, which are really the intermediary between the Board of Governors at the top and the member commercial banks at the bottom. These twelve banks serve geographic areas that purport to comprise economically similar regions of the country.[3] The banks clearly differ according to the size of their assets and the size of the geographical areas they serve. The New York bank occupies a prominent position because of its location in the center of the country's money market and because it handles the open-market operations for the entire system.[4] All but two of the banks have at least one branch to facilitate transactions.[5]

The twelve banks are actually federally chartered corporations that are owned by the member banks in each district. Each commercial bank,

---

[3]The bank in each of the twelve districts is named after the city in which it is located. The twelve are, in order of district number: Boston, New York, Philadelphia, Cleveland, Richmond, Atlanta, Chicago, St. Louis, Minneapolis, Kansas City, Dallas, and San Francisco.

[4]The New York Bank owns about one-fourth of all Federal Reserve bank assets.

[5]There are twenty-six branch banks in total.

FIGURE 5–2. Organization of the Federal Open Market Committee in 1976.

The Federal Open Market Committee (FOMC) consists of the seven members of the Federal Reserve Board of governors and five of the twelve Federal Reserve Presidents. The Chairman of the Board of Governors is also, by tradition, Chairman of the Committee. The President of the New York Federal Reserve Bank is a permanent member of the Committee and, also by tradition, its Vice Chairman. All other Federal Reserve Bank Presidents attend the meetings and present their views, but only the four Presidents who are members of the Committee may cast votes. These four memberships rotate among the Bank Presidents and are held for one-year terms beginning March 1.

The Committee met regularly once each month during 1976 to discuss, among other things, economic trends and to decide upon the future course of open market operations.[1] During each regularly scheduled meeting, a directive was issued to the Federal Reserve Bank of New York stating the general economic goals of the Committee and providing general guidelines as to how the Manager of the System Open Market Account at the New York Federal Reserve Bank should conduct open market operations to achieve these goals. Each directive contained a short review of economic developments and the general economic goals sought by the Committee. The last paragraph gave operating instructions to the Account Manager. These instructions were stated in terms of bank reserve and money market conditions which were considered consistent with the achievement of desired growth rates of monetary aggregates. Special factors, such as Treasury financing operations, were also taken into account.

Decisions regarding the exact timing and amount of daily buying and selling of securities in fulfilling the Committee's directive are the responsibility of the System Open Market Account Manager at the Trading Desk of the New York Bank. Each morning, the Account Manager and his staff decide on a plan for open market operations to be undertaken that day. In developing this plan, money and credit market conditions and aggregate targets desired by the Committee are considered, as well as other factors which may be of concern at the time. Each morning, the Account Manager, in a conference call, informs one voting President and staff members of the Board of Governors about present market conditions and open market operations which he proposes to execute that day. Other members of the Committee are informed of the daily program by wire summary.

A summary of the Committee's actions is presented to the public in the "Record of Policy Actions of the Federal Open Market Committee." Following the Committee's decision at the May 18, 1976 meeting, the "Record" was released approximately 30 days after each meeting, beginning with the "Record" of the April 20, 1976 meeting. Soon after it is released, the "Record" appears in the Federal Reserve Bulletin and, in addition, "Records" for the entire year are published in the Annual Report of the Board of Governors. The "Record" for each meeting during 1976 generally included:

1) a staff summary of recent economic developments, such as prices, employment, industrial production, and components of the national income accounts; projections concerning real output growth for two or three quarters ahead: and prospective financial developments;
2) a discussion of recent international financial developments and the U.S. foreign trade balance;
3) a discussion of credit market conditions and recent interest rate movements;
4) a discussion of open market operations, the growth of monetary aggregates, and bank reserve and money market conditions since the previous meeting;

5) a discussion of current policy considerations, including money market conditions and the movements of monetary aggregates;
6) conclusions of the FOMC;
7) a policy directive issued by the Committee to the Federal Reserve Bank of New York;
8) a list of the members' voting positions and any dissenting comments;
9) a description of any actions and consultations that may have occured between the regularly scheduled meetings.

Source: A. Burger and D. Mudd, "The FOMC in 1976: Progress against inflation," *Review– Federal Reserve Bank of St. Louis,* March 1977, p. 9.

[1]The Committee held a special meeting on March 29, 1976 for the purpose of reappraising the methods employed in formulating and implementing the directives issued to the Manager of the System Open Market Account.

[2]On November 8, 1976 the Committee held a telephone meeting for the purpose of establishing monetary aggregate growth ranges over the year ending third quarter 1977.

as a condition of joining the Federal Reserve System, is required to subscribe to the district bank's capital in an amount equal to 3 percent of each commercial bank's own capital and surplus. The commercial banks receive annual dividends on this investment, limited to a maximum of 6 percent of the stock's par value. The system's net earnings in recent years have been large enough to pay many times this amount (a large percentage of earnings is returned to the Treasury).

The Federal Reserve Banks earn money through their operations. This is used to pay expenses for themselves and the Board of Governors, to pay dividends, and to increase their surplus accounts. Excesses beyond this amount are returned to the Treasury, and this has often amounted to serveral billion dollars per year—for example, about $7.4 billion in 1978.

Each district bank has a president, chosen by the bank's board of directors for a five-year term (subject to approval of the Board of Governors). The president basically formulates policy decisions and management procedures for the bank. A nine-member board of directors sets general operating policy for each bank.[6] Six of these are elected by the bank, and three are chosen by the Board of Governors, all for three-year terms. The nine are divided into three classes: Class A directors are bankers and represent the member banks; Class B directors are private individuals in business or industry and represent the borrowers; Class C directors, chosen by the Board of Governors, represent the general public. One of the Class C directors is chosen by the Board of Governors to be Federal Reserve agent and chairman of the board of directors.

---

[6]The composition of the board of directors was established in the Federal Reserve Act of 1913 and has never changed.

The Member Banks

The remaining component of the System comprises approximately 5,600 commercial banks, which are its members. They are the vital cogs in the day-to-day implementation of Federal Reserve policy, even as they pursue their own self-interests.

Banks become members of the Federal Reserve System by purchasing stock in their district Federal Reserve bank and by agreeing to the rules and regulations of the System. An important part of this requirement is adherence to the reserve requirements set by the Board of Governors. The reserves held by member banks to meet this requirement can consist only of vault cash or, more importantly, of deposits with the Federal Reserve banks.

Membership in the System allows participants to utilize the services of the Federal Reserve Banks, such as check-clearing and borrowing from the Federal Reserve Banks. Banks do not receive interest on their deposits at the district banks. The Fed provides at least five services to member banks; these are discussed in the next section, and Table 5–1 lists them and shows their cost in 1976.

It is difficult to balance all the advantages and disadvantages of membership in the system. We can note simply that about 40 percent of all commercial banks are members and that most of the larger banks belong, as shown in Table 5–2. Approximately 72 percent of all bank deposits are within the System, since the larger banks dwarf the nonmember banks with regard to deposits. It is interesting to note that membership has declined in recent years. From 1942 to 1976, about 950 banks dropped out of the System. Table 5–3 shows clearly that the recent withdrawals are mostly small banks. These banks presumably felt that the costs of belonging to the System outweighed the benefits of membership. This trend is alarming to officials of the Fed, who have often argued that the Fed's ability to carry out monetary policy is weakened by the existence of nonmember banks, holding about one-fourth of all deposits, over which the Fed has no control.

By law, all national banks must belong to the System.[7] State banks can join if they meet the requirements. Because these are demanding, many banks apparently choose to be regulated by state authorities, who are in general less stringent.[8] Some are automatically excluded by capital requirements imposed by the Board of Governors. Others are against centralized bank regulation in principal. Finally, a number of

---

[7]A national bank has a charter from the federal government.

[8]For example, reserve requirements for nonmembers as established by the states are generally less stringent than those for member banks in that some items that cannot be counted as reserves by member banks can be counted as reserves by nonmember banks. This is the reason most often cited for withdrawing from Federal Reserve membership.

TABLE 5–1. Costs of providing selected services to member banks in 1976

Service	Total Federal Reserve System		Federal Reserve Bank of St. Louis[1]	
	Cost of Providing Services	Percent of Total Cost of These Services	Cost of Providing Services	Percent of Total Cost of These Services
Check Collection	$124,566,969	65.6%	$3,714,454	73.1%
Coin and Currency Pickup and Delivery	50,220,644	26.4	946,111	18.6
Wire Transfers	5,672,666	3.0	124,695	2.5
Safekeeping of Securities	7,224,907[2]	3.8	199,439[1]	3.9
Discounts and Credits	2,303,490	1.2	99,908	2.0
Total	$189,988,676	100.0%	$5,084,607	100.0%

Source: R. Gilbert, "Utilization of Federal Reserve Bank Services by Member Banks: Implications for the Costs and Benefits of Membership," *Review — Federal Reserve Bank of St. Louis (August 1977), p. 5.*

[1]Cost data pertain only to head office operations.
[2]These figures include the cost of providing some safekeeping services for nonmember banks.

TABLE 5–2. Percent of insured commercial banks in each size group that are members of the federal reserve system as of December 31, 1976

Asset Size (in millions)	Percent
$ 5 or less	18.7%
5–9.99	25.5
10–24.9	38.0
25–49.9	48.9
50–99.9	58.5
100–299.9	66.3
300–499.9	78.6
500 or more	86.7

Source: Gilbert, p. 4.

TABLE 5–3. Size distributions of insured banks in the U.S. that withdrew from federal reserve membership, January 1971–March 1977, and all member banks, December 31, 1976

Range of Total Deposits† (millions of dollars)	Banks that Withdrew from Membership			All Member Banks	
	Number	Percentage	Cumulative Percentage	Percentage	Cumulative Percentage
up to 5	15	5.0%	5.0%	6.6%	6.6%
5 to 10	42	14.1	19.1	14.1	20.7
10 to 20	77	25.8	44.9	24.8	45.5
20 to 30	46	15.4	60.3	15.9	61.4
30 to 40	30	10.1	70.4	8.9	70.3
40 to 50	17	5.7	76.1	5.6	76.9
50 to 60	14	4.7	80.8	3.6	79.5
60 to 75	7	2.4	83.2	4.5	84.0
75 to 100	12	4.0	87.2	3.6	87.6
100 to 150	16	5.4	92.6	4.0	91.6
150 to 250	7	2.4	95.0	2.8	94.4
250 to 500	12	4.0	99.0	2.7	97.1
500 to 1000	3	1.0	100.0	1.4	98.5
1,000 and over	0	0.0	100.00	1.5	100.0
Total	298	100.0%		100.0%	

Source: Gilbert, p. 4.

†Measured as of December 31, 1976, except in 8 cases in which recent data were not available. In those cases total deposits were measured around the time banks withdrew from membership.

state-chartered banks apparently feel they have nothing to gain by joining since they can satisfy their demands alternatively. For example, correspondent banks can provide many of the same services that direct membership does.[9] The Federal Deposit Insurance Corporation is available to all.

FUNCTIONS OF THE FEDERAL RESERVE SYSTEM

Besides acting to control the money supply, the Federal Reserve performs a number of important service functions. These might be thought of as the daily tasks of the System, and, in fact, they involve the bulk of its employees. These activities are very important to the orderly operation of our financial system and deserve some consideration. Some major functions are discussed below.[10] The first five are services provided to the banking system, as were mentioned above.

Check Collection

In terms of our financial system's everyday functioning, which affects virtually everyone in the United States, probably nothing the Federal Reserve System does is more important than check collection. It is much more efficient for the Federal Reserve System to handle this than for each bank to maintain balances with other banks for this purpose, which was done before the System was created. The Fed provides the only national system of check collection.[11]

We will consider the check collection process in steps.

Local Check Collection. This step does not directly involve the Federal Reserve, but it is a part of the overall system and should be considered first. Banks within a city form a clearinghouse, which is simply a designated focal point for the purposes of settlement with each other. Here the net claims of each bank can be settled very quickly: if Bank A owes Bank B $20,000 and B owes A $19,000, A can settle both claims with a net payment of $1,000. Settlement is typically handled through the Federal Reserve Banks, which simply debit or credit each commercial bank's account by the indicated amount needed to settle its claims. The particular procedures of clearinghouse mechanics vary from place to place, depending

---

[9]Traditionally, many banks developed *correspondent relations* with other banks—for example, small banks with large banks or rural banks with city banks. By keeping funds on deposit at the correspondent bank, the smaller or the rural bank receives services such as the processing of their checks.

[10]Part of this discussion is drawn from R. Gilbert, "Utilization of Federal Reserve Bank Services by Member Banks: Implications for the Costs and Benefits of Membership," *Review —Federal Reserve Bank of St. Louis,* August 1977, pp. 2–15.

[11]In 1976, over 13 billlon checks were cleared by the Fed, which amounts to about 45 percent of all checks written that year.

upon how many banks are involved. The important point is that the clearinghouse facilitates the transfer of local claims by banks.

Single-District Check Collection. When banks within the same Federal Reserve district—but not within the same city—receive checks on each other, the district bank is used as the collection mechanism. The district bank debits and credits member-bank reserve accounts as necessary to settle the claims. Nonmember banks may make partial use of the clearing facilities of the Federal Reserve as long as they maintain small clearing balances at the district bank.

A deferred availability schedule is established at each district bank to facilitate the clearing of checks. This schedule indicates the number of days that must elapse before a bank actually receives credit for checks it presents for collection. Hence a check can be credited to the collecting bank before it is debited to the paying bank; the consequent overlapping creates float. That is, one bank can have its reserves increased before another bank has its reserves decreased in connection with a particular check, because the System operates on this deferred availability schedule. This extension of credit by the Federal Reserve, or float, is a part of the monetary base.

Multi-District Check Collection. The clearing process involving banks in different districts is essentially the same as the previous step. Assume that an individual writes a check on a bank in New York and sends it to Chicago to pay for purchases made there. The recipient of the check deposits it at a Chicago bank, which in turn sends it to the Federal Reserve Bank of Chicago. This district bank sends the check to the New York district bank, which collects from the commercial bank in New York. The New York district bank now owes the Chicago district bank. This claim is settled through the Interdistrict Settlement Fund which settles accounts among Federal Reserve district banks.

Additional Check Collection Procedure. Nonmember banks may also use the Fed's collection system if they are located in zones served by Regional Check Processing Centers and if the paying banks are in the same region (out-of-region checks are collected by these banks through their correspondents). Credit for the nonmember-bank checks presented for collection is made to the reserve accounts of member banks serving as correspondents. Nonmember banks are not charged for this service.

Coin and Currency Service

The Federal Reserve Banks issue new currency and coins to all banks and thereby provide a very important functional service to the economy.[12] In the metropolitan areas of the Federal Reserve Banks, such service can

---

[12]Nonmember banks are charged fees to cover costs.

be provided daily, through the use of armored cars. Other banks receive their currency through the mail. Member banks pay for (or receive credit for) the currency they obtain or deposit at the Reserve banks through debits or credits to their reserve accounts or those of their correspondent banks.

Wire Transfers

A wire transfer is an electronic transfer from the reserve account of one member bank to the reserve account of any other member bank. Such transfers are available to member banks, at no charge.[13] Transactions in the federal funds market (explained in chapter 10) and payments for large business customers are typically handled via wire transfers. The largest banks are the heaviest users of this service. Mechanics of the service involve either telephoning the Reserve bank or using on-line electronic equipment between the commercial bank and the Reserve bank.

Safekeeping of Securities

Member banks can keep securities at Reserve Banks at no cost. Such securities can be the normal type (i.e., pieces of paper to evidence the claim), or they can simply be bookkeeping entries to evidence ownership. In the latter case, a commercial bank can hold certain federal government obligations at the Reserve Bank where the evidence of ownership is not a physical debt certificate but rather a book entry. Such securities can even change ownership through wire transfers.[14] Although all sizes of banks use this particular service more than some others provided by the Fed, a greater percentage of the large banks use it.

Borrowing From Reserve Banks

Member banks can borrow from Reserve Banks for various reasons. Typically, such loans are used to adjust a bank's reserve position as a result of unanticipated events, in which case they are of short duration—a few days. Other reasons include seasonal borrowing privileges and emergency credit, and loans for these are often extended for longer periods such as months.

The rate members pay to borrow, which is set by the Fed, is called the *discount rate*. When the discount rate is low in relation to other money market rates (e.g., as it was in 1974), banks have an incentive to borrow from the Fed. Such funds can be used directly or indirectly to earn returns.

---

[13]Nonmember banks can initiate these transactions through member banks.
[14]Also, customers of member banks can hold securities in this form.

In 1975 and 1976, when the discount rate exceeded the federal funds rate, member banks borrowed from the Fed mostly to make short-term adjustments in their reserve positions.

Regulation and Supervision of Commercial Banks

The Federal Reserve has an obvious interest in promoting good banking and maintaining the integrity of the banking system. The Fed has considerable influence over banks, although it is not the only supervisory agent.

The Comptroller of the Currency examines the operations of the national banks. The Federal Reserve examines all other member banks, with each Reserve Bank having a staff of bank examiners. The primary emphasis is on soundness of lending policy and an evaluation of bank assets. Various reports are required from the banks. Hundreds of member banks submit a weekly statement of condition, which is used by the Board of Governors in a publicized report summarizing bank conditions.

Fiscal Activity for the United States Treasury

The Federal Reserve serves as the bank for the U.S. government—i.e., for the Treasury. The Treasury maintains an account at the Fed, against which it writes checks, just as any individual writes checks on his or her checking account. Most of the Treasury's funds are actually held in commercial banks, because it deposits its tax receipts and loan revenues into tax and loan accounts at most of the commercial banks in the country. When the Treasury receives a check for taxes or employees' withholding, etc., it deposits the check into its tax and loan account at the commercial bank on which the check is written. These funds are transferred to the Fed as needed to pay bills, so that the amount on deposit at the Fed at any one time is quite small.

The Treasury initiated a new Tax and Loan Investment Program in late 1978 whereby tax and loan funds can be used to purchase interest-bearing notes from the banks. Funds not placed in this program must be counted as regular demand deposits by banks.

The Federal Reserve assists the Treasury in the job of debt-management. This involves helping the Treasury sell new issues of government debt. When government securities mature, the Fed acts as the agent for redemption. It also pays the interest on the debt instruments.

THE TOOLS OF MONETARY CONTROL AND THEIR INFLUENCES ON THE MONEY SUPPLY

In this section we consider the various Federal Reserve activities that affect the money supply. Of the three principal techniques that exist, the

Fed relies almost exclusively on open-market operations for general monetary control.

Open-Market Operations

Open-market operations constitute the most important method by which the Federal Reserve conducts monetary policy. This importance is attributable to the tremendous flexibility that open-market operations give the Fed. Adjustments to the monetary base can be made daily or weekly in virtually any amounts.

As noted, the Manager of the System Open-Market Account at the Federal Reserve Bank of New York, acting as agent, carries out these operations on behalf of the Federal Open Market Committee. Operations are conducted in Federal agency and U.S. government securities bought from or sold to dealers in the private market. The Federal Reserve acquires these securities by purchasing them in the open market and, when it sells to others, it does so out of its portfolio (i.e., its inventory of securities).

The Manager is in frequent contact with the government securities dealers to execute orders according to the System's needs. Many millions of dollars worth of securities can be traded in minutes. Most Federal Reserve open-market operations are conducted in short-term securities— generally in Treasury bills, which have maturities of less than one year. Treasury bills have a stable and deep market, which permits a large volume of transactions to be executed in a short period of time. Since the Treasury bill market is so stable, the Fed is, in a sense, like any other participant in the market, while it simultaneously carries out desired changes in monetary policy.

Most open-market operations cannot be correlated with a specific change in monetary policy. They are carried out to offset the numerous forces that affect bank reserves. They do occur frequently. Because many financial transactions outside of the control of the Fed change bank reserves, the Fed can implement a policy simply by refusing to counteract these changes.

In 1978, outright transactions amounted to about $25 billion in purchases and $14 billion in sales. Matched sale-purchase transactions (involving a simultaneous sale to, and repurchase from, dealers) amounted to $511 billion of sales and $510.8 billion of purchases.

The Federal Reserve actively uses repurchase agreements to purchase government securities. It is understood by the market that these transactions are only temporary and that the dealer from whom the securities are purchased will repurchase them (for the same price plus interest) on a particular date. For all practical purposes, repurchase agreements constitute a source of financing extended to government securities dealers (repurchase agreements amounted to about $150 billion in 1978).

Although open-market operations are initiated by the central bank, they are not executed independently of what is going on in the economy. They affect the market price and the yield on government securities; that is, other things being equal, the purchase of securities by the Federal Reserve raises prices and reduces yields, and the sale of securities has the opposite effects. Portfolio adjustments on the part of individuals or institutions (explained in Chapter 6), which continuously take place in response to changes in financial parameters, transmit the change in government securities yields to a change in the general level of interest rates. Thus, the Federal Reserve has to consider the repercussions, in their effect on interest rates, of the open-market operations that it initiates. And interest rates have become a sensitive political issue.

Reserve Requirements

The reserve requirement stipulates that member banks keep some minimum ratio of reserves to deposits. The required amount is calculated as a percentage of the average level of deposits held by banks two weeks earlier.[15] Although the Fed may impose supplementary requirements on certain liabilities, the basic ranges are specified by law. In 1978, for example, the legal lower and upper limits on demand deposits were 10 percent and 22 percent for reserve city banks and 7 percent and 14 percent for other banks.[16]

A change in the reserve ratio alters the required reserves of banks for any volume of deposits and therefore changes their excess reserves. With roughly $40 billion of required reserves in early 1979, changes in reserve requirements are potentially significant. In fact, such changes are quite strong and nondiscriminating in nature, and are less useful for precise changes than are the other actions discussed here. Only a small change in reserve requirements—for example, one-half of one percent—is needed to have a significant, widely felt effect.

By changing the excess reserves of member banks, a change in reserve requirements is likely to change both their asset portfolios and their deposit obligations. Also, as noted in the previous chapter, an increase in reserve requirements reduces the money multiplier, which predicts the change in the money supply that results from a change in the monetary base. A supplementary two percent reserve requirement imposed on large time deposits in 1978 increased required reserves $3 billion.

---

[15]A 2 percent surplus or deficit can be carried to the next week.

[16]In January 1979, the actual requirement for all banks was a percentage of deposits, starting at 7 percent for the first $2 million and rising to 16¼ percent for all amounts over $400 million. A reserve city bank is defined as a bank having more that $400 million in net demand deposits.

Federal Reserve Discount Rates

The interest rate charged on member-bank loans from the Fed is called the Federal Reserve *discount rate*. When the System was created, the discount rate was intended to be the primary monetary policy instrument. Today, it is primarily used, not as a method of influencing bank reserves, but as a method of increasing the liquidity of the monetary system by allowing member banks to borrow from the Fed.

Loans to member banks from the Fed are technically of two types—discounts and advances. *Discounts* involve a commercial bank's own notes from its customers, which are endorsed by the borrowing banks. The Fed lends an amount equal to the face value of the notes minus a discount, reflecting the going discount rate. This discounted amount is credited to the borrowing bank's account at the Fed. An *advance* is a direct loan to the bank on the basis of its own note (promise to pay). Collateral is normally required—typically, government securities—and the prevailing discount rate is the interest rate charged for this advance.[17] Advances are more prevalent than are discounts.

Setting the Federal Reserve discount rate is a district bank chore. Technically, each of the 12 district banks set their own; however, the Board of Governors must ultimately approve any rates that are set.[18] It is reasonable to infer that the Board of Governors influences the rates as they are set. Between December 31, 1970 and January 31, 1979, the discount rate at the New York Federal Reserve Bank changed 30 times. Each change was typically one-fourth or one-half of a percentage point, but the last change (in late 1978) involved a raise to 9½%, which was a change of a full percentage point. One problem with the discount rate is that it often lags changes in other money market rates which are constantly adjusting to current market conditions.

The Federal Reserve has traditionally discouraged member banks from borrowing except for emergency purposes, such as temporary and unanticipated fluctuations in deposits and loans. The borrowing bank is supposed to be carefully examined. Loans are for approved purposes only, and borrowing for extended periods is discouraged unless advance arrangements have been made. However, it appears to be true that the member banks have usually been granted their loan requests.

In order to modernize the process of discounting, the Federal Re-

---

[17]Advances secured with other collateral, such as mortgages and special advances, carry higher rates than the normal advance rate. For example, effective January 1979, the discount-normal advance rate was 9½ percent, whereas other advance rates ranged from 10½ to 12½ percent, depending on the collateral, the borrower, etc.

[18]This mechanism results in a uniform discount rate for the system as a whole, which contributes to a consistent monetary policy.

serve has standardized the procedures. Current procedures essentially permit a member bank to borrow for one of the three reasons: (1) seasonal borrowing privileges; (2) adjustment credit, which permits borrowing to meet unanticipated withdrawals or loan demands; and (3) emergency borrowing. The discount rate for emergency credit is higher than the normal discount rate, which by mid-1979 had risen to 10%.

The discount rate, according to the Fed, is useful because of its announcement effect; that is, changes in the discount rate are said to influence market expectations. These changes supposedly provide financial market participants with an indication of the current direction of monetary policy. This idea has been heavily criticized by economists who point out that most changes in the discount rate are made for technical reasons, to prevent the differential between the discount rate and the Treasury bill rate from becoming too large, and therefore that it cannot convey accurate information.

Selective Credit Controls

In addition to the three major controls of bank reserves (and ultimately money supply) discussed above, the Federal Reserve has other controls known as *selective credit controls*. The rationale for them is that general monetary policy can be made more effective by impacting in certain areas that may not be fully affected by the major controls.

Regulation A is a selective control that defines what types of claims are eligible for discounting at the Fed. Obviously, a broader interpretation makes borrowing easier, since it makes more kinds of paper eligible to be discounted, other things equal.

Regulations T, U, and G are concerned specifically with the minimum margin requirements that brokers, banks, and other lenders must demand in allowing purchasers of securities to make transactions with less than 100 percent of the purchase price. These regulations apply to stocks on national security exchanges and to convertible securities of these same stocks. Margin requirements are changed from time to time as the Fed alternately wishes to encourage or to discourage market activity. A lower margin requirement, other things being equal, encourages the purchase of stocks, since the term designates the amount the purchaser must put up to buy the securities with the remainder to be borrowed from the broker at a rate of interest perhaps ¾ of one percent above the prime rate.

Regulation Q. The primary selective control is Regulation Q, which allows the Fed to regulate the maximum rate of interest on time deposits and savings accounts in banks and nonbank savings institutions. The Federal Reserve has had this authority since 1933, when it was instituted for the purpose of preventing an increase in the risk of financial difficulties for banks that were offering high interest rates in an effort to compete for

TABLE 5–4. Maximum interest rates payable on time and savings deposits at federally insured institutions.

	Commercial banks				Savings and loan associations and mutual savings banks			
	In effect Aug. 31, 1978		Previous maximum		In effect Aug. 31, 1978		Previous maximum	
Type and maturity of deposit	Percent	Effective date	Percent	Effective date	Percent	Effective date	Percent	Effective date
1 Savings	5	7/1/73	4½	1/21/70	5¼	(6)	5	(7)
2 Negotiable order of withdrawals (NOW) accounts[1]	5	1/1/74	(8)	......	5	1/1/74	(8)	......
3 Money market time deposits of less than $100,000	(2)	(2)	(2)	(2)	(2)	(2)	(2)	(2)
Other time (multiple and single maturity unless otherwise indicated)								
30–89 days:								
4 Multiple maturity	5	7/1/73	4¼	1/21/70	(8)	......	(6)	......
5 Single maturity			5	9/26/66				
90 days to 1 year:								
6 Multiple maturity	5½	7/1/73	5	7/20/66	[5]5¾	(6)	5¼	1/21/70
7 Single maturity	6	7/1/73	5	9/26/66	6½	(6)	5¾	1/21/70
8 1 to 2 years[3]	6	7/1/73	5½	1/21/70	6¾	(6)	6	1/21/70
9 2 to 2½ years[3]	6½	7/1/73	5¾	1/21/70	6¾	(6)	6	1/21/70
10 2½ to 4 years[3]	6½	7/1/73	5¾	1/21/70	7½	(6)	(9)	......
11 4 to 6 years[4]	7¼	11/1/73	(9)	......	7½	11/1/73	7½	11/1/73
12 6 to 8 years[4]	7½	12/23/74	7¼	11/1/73	7¾	12/23/74	7½	11/1/73

13	8 years or more[4]	7¾	6/1/78	(8)	....	8	6/1/78	(8)	....
14	Governmental units (all maturities)	8	6/1/78	7¾	12/23/74	8	6/1/78	7¾	12/23/74
15	Individual retirement accounts and Keogh (H.R. 10) plans[5]	8	6/1/78	7¾	7/6/77	8	6/1/78	7¾	7/6/77

Source: Adapted from the *Federal Reserve Bulletin*, February 1978, p. A10 and October 1978, p. A10.

[1]For authorized States only. Federally insured commercial banks, savings and loan associations, cooperative banks, and mutual savings banks were first permitted to offer NOW accounts on Jan. 1, 1974. Authorization to issue NOW accounts was extended to similar institutions throughout New England on Feb. 27, 1976.

[2]Effective June 1, 1978. The ceiling rate for commercial banks is the discount rate on most recently issued 6-month U.S. Treasury bills; for savings and loan associations and mutual savings banks, ¼ percent higher. Maturity is exactly 26 weeks; minimum denomination, $10,000.

[3]a minimum of $1,000 is required for savings and loan associations, except in areas where mutual savings banks permit lower minimum denominations. This restriction was removed for deposits maturing in less than 1 year, effective Nov. 1, 1973.

[4]$1,000 minimum except for deposits representing funds contributed to an Individual Retirement Account (IRA) or a Keogh (H.R. 10) Plan established pursuant to the Internal Revenue Code. The $1,000 minimum requirement was removed for such accounts in December 1975 and November 1976, respectively.

[5]3-year minimum maturity.

[6]July 1, 1973, for mutual savings banks; July 6, 1973, for savings and loan associations.

[7]Oct. 1, 1966, for mutual savings banks; Jan 21, 1970, for savings and loan associations.

[8]No separate account category.

[9]Between July 1, 1973, and Oct. 31, 1973, there was no ceiling for certificates maturing in 4 years or more with minimum denominations of $1,000; however, the amount of such certificates that an institution could issue was limited to 5 per cent of its total time and savings deposits. Sales in excess of that amount, as well as certificates of less than $1,000, were limited to the 6½ per cent ceiling on the deposits maturing in 2½ years or more.
Effective Nov. 1, 1973, the present ceilings were imposed on certificates maturing in 4 years or more with minimum denominations of $1,000. There is no limitation on the amount of these certificates that banks can issue.

NOTE — Maximum rates that can be paid by Federally insured commercial banks, mutual savings banks, and savings and loan associations are established by the Board of Governors of the Federal Reserve System, the Board of Directors of the Federal Deposit Insurance Corporation, and the Federal Home Loan Bank Board under the provisions of 12 CFR 217, 329, and 526, respectively. The maximum rates on time deposits in denominations of $100,000 or more were suspended in mid 1973. For information regarding previous interest rate ceilings on all types of accounts, see earlier issues of the Federal Reserve *BULLETIN*, the Federal Home Loan Bank Board Journal, and the Annual Report of the Federal Deposit Insurance Corporation.

deposits.[19] Interest rates on virtually all savings held in banks and in nonbank savings institutions are now under control, because (1) the Fed has control over member banks; (2) the Federal Deposit Insurance Corporation has authority over nonmembers—banks and mutual savings banks—that are insured; and (3) the Federal Home Loan Bank Board sets rates on savings and loans accounts. The Fed is the leader in this threesome. Rates have changed frequently since 1962; maximum rates payable on time deposits and savings deposits are shown in Table 5–4.

Regulation Q does not affect total member-bank reserves, but it does affect the money supply. For example, if the maximum rate payable is increased, the actual rate paid on time deposits may rise, and individuals may be induced to hold more time deposits, so that the money supply (M_1) decreases. A decrease in the maximum rate may result in an increase in the money supply (M_1).[20]

Regulation Q is quite important as a selective tool of monetary control. In fact, to some extent, it can be considered along with the three major tools of monetary control. It is not yet, however, universally accepted as a general tool, as are the other three. And it is not without its critics. When market rates rise, Regulation Q may prevent small savers from enjoying the benefits of the higher rates. It does not affect large savers in the same way; for example, deposits over $100,000 and with a certain maturity have no maximum rate. Thus Regulation Q has the potential for inequities.

Moral Suasion

The Fed has another policy tool in the form of moral suasion, which used to be referred to as *jawboning*. In effect, this is pressure applied to banks to move along lines desired by the Fed. For example, the prime rate is a national focal point for attention in the financial markets. The Fed can exert some influence on banks to maintain a certain prime rate rather than to raise it, because of the adverse implications such raises are often thought to have. Since banks are reluctant to be on the "wrong side" of the Fed, this can have an effect. Moral suasion is sometimes formalized, particularly in times of severe economic stress, when each district bank sends to each commercial bank a letter outlining what the Fed believes is appropriate at the time.

---

[19]At the same time, the Fed was given the authority to prevent banks from paying interest on demand deposits.

[20]If money stock is defined as the product of the base-money multiplier and the monetary base, and if M_2 is used as the measure of money stock, the impact is reversed. That is, a reduction in the rate paid on time deposits reduces M_2, and vice versa.

DEFENSIVE AND DYNAMIC OPERATIONS

Because the most important component of money is demand deposits, and because these deposits must be supported by reserves, the central bank's influence over money hinges on its control over the aggregate volume of reserves and the conditions under which banks can obtain and employ them.[21] However, it is apparent that member-bank reserves are affected in several ways that are independent of the control of the central bank. Most of these independent elements are changing more or less continually. Sometimes their effects may last only a day or two before they are reversed automatically. This happens, for instance, when bad weather slows up the check collection process, giving rise to an automatic increase in Federal Reserve credit in the form of float. Other influences, such as changes in the public's currency holdings, may persist for longer periods of time.

Still other variations in bank reserves result solely from the mechanics of institutional arrangements among the Treasury, the Federal Reserve banks, and the commercial banks. The Treasury, for example, keeps part of its working balance on deposit with commercial banks, against which fractional reserve requirements apply. But disbursements are made only from its balance in the Reserve banks. The transfer of these deposits to the Reserve banks prior to expenditure by the Treasury causes a dollar-for-dollar drain on member bank reserves. The independent elements affecting bank reserves are shown in Table 5–5.

In contrast to these independent elements that affect reserves are the policy actions taken by the Federal Reserve System. The way in which purchases and sales of securities (open-market operations) affect reserves has already been described as have the two other ways by which the System can directly affect bank reserves and potential deposit volume— loans to member banks and changes in reserve requirements. A change in the required reserve ratio, of course, does not directly alter the total volume of reserves but does change the amount of deposits that a given amount of reserves can support. These policy actions are also shown in Table 5–5.

Defensive operations protect a particular monetary policy from outside forces. *Dynamic operations* attempt to change the monetary base in a certain direction in response to a change in monetary policy. Perhaps the Fed wants to counterbalance a decrease in cash holdings by the Treasury. This could be done by selling government securities (see Table 5–5). Thus the Fed can significantly influence the total amount of the monetary base

---

[21]In chapter 4, we talked in terms of the monetary base and the money multiplier, which together determine the money supply. Here we talk in terms of the factors affecting bank reserves, which in turn affect deposits, which in turn are the predominant part of the money supply (demand deposits in the case of M_1 and demand deposits and time deposits in the case of M_2).

TABLE 5–5. Factors affecting bank reserves

	Member bank reserves
Public Operations	
Increase in currency holdings	−
Decrease in currency holdings	+
Treasury and Foreign Operations	
Increase in Treasury deposits in F.R. banks	−
Decrease in Treasury deposits in F.R. banks	+
Gold purchases (inflow)	+
Gold sales (outflow)	−
Increase in Treasury currency outstanding	+
Decrease in Treasury currency outstanding	−
Decrease in Treasury cash holdings	+
Increase in foreign and other deposits in F.R. banks	−
Decrease in foreign and other deposits in F.R. banks	+
Federal Reserve Operations	
Purchases of securities	+
Sales of securities	−
Loans to member banks	+
Repayment of loans to member banks	−
Increase in Federal Reserve float	+
Decrease in Federal Reserve float	−
Increase in other assets*	+
Decrease in other assets*	−
Increase in other liabilities*	−
Decrease in other liabilities*	+
Increase in capital accounts*	−
Decrease in capital accounts*	+
Increase in reserve requirements	−†
Decrease in reserve requirements	+†

Source: *Modern Money Mechanics*, Federal Reserve Bank of Chicago, page 15.

*Included in "Other Federal Reserve accounts."
†Effect on excess reserves. Total reserves are unchanged.
Note: To the extent reserve changes are in the form of vault cash, Federal Reserve accounts are not affected.

and bank reserves, even though it does not control all of the factors that affects banks reserves (as can be seen in Table 5–5).

As noted, the trading "desk" at the Federal Reserve Bank of New York conducts the System's open market operations. Working within the general guidelines of the Federal Open-Market Committee, the manager of the open-market account interprets daily data on money supply, etc., and makes decisions. The objective is to affect bank reserves and the monetary base in order to achieve monetary policy goals. Forecasts are made of pertinent factors, but open market operations are clearly an inexact science because of such factors as a buildup of float. Any change in reserves has the same potential effect on deposits regardless of its origin. Therefore, in order to achieve net reserve effects that are consistent with its cyclical and long-run monetary objectives, the Federal Reserve System must continuously take account of what the independent factors are doing to reserves and then, through its policy actions, must offset or supplement them as the situation may require.

By far the largest amount of the System's gross open-market transactions are undertaken to offset drains from or additions to bank reserves from other sources, which, if unchecked, might cause abrupt changes in the availability of credit. That is, defensive actions are the most important in terms of activity. However, dynamic actions (such as purchases made to effect a gradual net increase in reserves and hence to support money growth needed in a growing economy) are extremely important in meeting economic objectives, promoting national goals, etc.

A GLIMPSE AT PRACTICAL PROBLEMS IN THE APPLICATION OF MONETARY CONTROL

Chapter 4 developed the concept of the monetary base and identified factors affecting bank reserves. We also know that the money supply, which is a function of these variables, is an important determinant of economic activity. And we have just considered how the Fed exercises monetary control and how it conducts defensive and dynamic operations.

In theory, money supply can be adequately controlled by the Fed over time, in the sense of matching the actual money supply quite closely with that desired by the Fed, using quarterly or six-month periods as check points. This is because the Fed can control the monetary base to a large extent and can make reasonable estimates of the base money multiplier. These two factors determine money supply. That is, money supply (M_1) is equal to the monetary base times the base money multiplier. Also, as we have noted, the Fed can control member-bank reserves.

In practice, there are many problems in carrying out monetary policy. First of all, the transmission mechanism through which monetary policy reaches the economy is not completely understood. The Fed needs an indicator of the current status of the economy as well as a means by which it can judge the effects of its actions. The former includes the money supply, long-term interest rates, etc.; the latter includes bank reserves, interest rates in the money market, etc. There is no universal agreement on which factor should be used for either purpose.

TABLE 5–6. Federal open market committee operating ranges, 1975–76

| Date of Meeting | Federal Funds Rate | Short-Run Tolerance Ranges[1] | | Ranges Specified | | Actual Growth Rates | |
		RPD[2]	Period to which M₁ & M₂ Ranges Apply	M_1	M_2	M_1	M_2
December 16, 1975	4½–5½%	4–7%	Dec.–Jan.	4–7%	7–10%	6.8%	11.0%
January 20, 1976	4¼–5	2–7	Jan.–Feb.	4–9	7–11½	4.1	12.6
February 17-18, 1976	4¼–5¼	(−½)–(−4½)	Feb.–Mar.	5–9	9–13	5.7	11.0
March 15-16, 1976	4¼–5¼	(−2)–(+2)	Mar.–Apr.	4–8	7–11	10.1	11.0
April 20, 1976	4½–5¾		Apr.–May.	4½–8½	8–12	10.9	11.5
May 18, 1976	5–5¾		May–June	4–7½	5–9	2.8	6.6
June 22, 1976	5¼–5¾		June–July	3½–7½	6–10	3.0	8.2
July 19-20, 1976	4¾–5¾		July–Aug.	4–8	7½–11½	6.1	10.6
August 17, 1976	5–5½		Aug.–Sept.	4–8	7½–11½	3.1	9.6
September 21, 1976	4¾–5½		Sept.–Oct.	4–8	8–12	7.4	13.0
October 19, 1976	4½–5¼		Oct.–Nov.	5–9	9–13	6.8	13.0
November 16, 1976	4½–5¼		Nov.–Dec.	3–7	9½–13½	4.1	11.4
December 20-21, 1976	4¼–5		Dec.–Jan.	2½–6½	9–13	6.8	11.0

Longer-Run Tolerance Ranges[3]

Date Announced	Target Period	M_1	M_2	M_3	Credit Proxy[4]
November 4, 1975	III/75–III/76	5–7½%	7–10½%	9–12%	6–9%
February 3, 1976	IV/75–IV/76	4½–7½	7½–10½	9–12	6–9
May 3, 1976	I/76–I/77	4½–7	7½–10	9–12	6–9
July 27, 1976	II/76–II/77	4½–7	7½–9½	9–11	5–8
November 11, 1976	III/76–III/77	4½–6½	7½–10	9–11½	5–8

Source: A. Burger and D. Mudd, "The FOMC in 1976: Progress against Inflation," *Review–Federal Reserve Bank of St. Louis*, March 1977, p. 3.

[1]Short-run tolerance ranges were adopted at each of the FOMC's regularly scheduled meetings. The ranges for the monetary and reserve aggregates were specified in terms of two-month simple annual rates of change from the month prior to the meeting at which the the ranges were established to the month following the meeting. The ranges for the Federal funds rate were specified to cover the period from the meeting at which the ranges were adopted to the following regularly scheduled meeting. Short-run ranges were made available in the "Record of Policy Actions of the Federal Open Market Committee" approximately 30 days after each meeting.

[2]At a special meeting held on March 19, 1976, the Committee reached the understanding that several reserve aggregates (including nonborrowed reserves, total reserves, and "monetary base" — total reserves plus currency) should be considered in formulating their instructions to the Manager of the System Open Market Account. Hence, the Committee agreed to no longer specify expected growth rates for reserves available to support private nonbank deposits (RPD's).

[3]Chairman of the Federal Reserve Board Arthur F. Burns announced intended growth rates of monetary aggregates over the indicated one year periods in statements presented before Congressional Committees at intervals of approximately 90 days.

[4]Daily average member bank deposits, adjusted to include funds from nondeposit sources.

Another problem for the Fed in carrying out monetary policy is that the money supply itself is difficult to measure accurately. Revised figures often show significant differences between what actually happened and what was believed to be happening at the time.

A good example of the difficulty of measuring the money stock is given by the impact of NOW accounts on the financial economy. Since 1972, individuals in the New England states have been able to withdraw funds from financial institutions by writing a negotiable order of withdrawal (NOW). These funds, which can be in mutual savings banks, savings and loan associations, or even commercial banks, earn interest at a maximum rate of 5 percent.[22] The NOW functions exactly like a check and therefore is a draft on an interest-bearing checking account. Currently, NOW accounts are not included in M_1. This means that M_1 figures underestimate the growth of money to the extent that funds have been switched from demand deposits into NOW accounts.[23] Although the total NOW accounts are not yet large enough to create a significant problem ($2.8 billion in early 1978), they could be in the future. New regulations which became operational on November 1, 1978 (and were challenged during 1978 by a savings and loan association trade group) permit commercial bank customers to earn, in effect, interest on their checking accounts by having funds automatically switched from their savings accounts to their checking accounts.

On a short-run basis, it can be very difficult to control the monetary base. There are always unanticipated changes in such variables as member-bank borrowings and float. These changes can be caused by random, seasonal, cyclical, and other factors. Any control of the monetary base more frequent than quarterly is probably not possible.

In actually carrying out monetary policy, the FOMC decides upon long-run and short-run ranges for the monetary aggregates. The long-run (one-year) ranges were initiated in 1975 at the request of Congress. Previous to 1975, there was about a ninety-day delay in the release of the record of each FOMC meeting. This was shortened in 1976, so that the short-run operating targets for the monetary aggregates could be seen about one month after each FOMC meeting. Table 5–6 shows FOMC operating ranges for 1976 for both M_1 and M_2. Both the specified ranges and the actual growth rates are indicated.

The difficulty of actually carrying out monetary policy according to plan was illustrated nicely in 1977. As a result of recent changes in operating procedures, the Federal Reserve is required to disclose its monetary

---

[22]NOW accounts in commercial banks are included in M_2, and NOW accounts at the thrift institutions are included in M_3.

[23]This information is based on C. Gambs, "Money—A Changing Concept in a Changing World," *Monthly Review—Federal Reserve Bank of Kansas City*, January 1977, pp. 6–7.

targets—for example, what rate of growth in M_1 and M_2 it is trying to achieve over the year. This is a radical departure from the past, when the Fed's intentions were known only with a lag—that is, the Fed's monetary policy for any period was disclosed only after some months had passed.

For 1977, the Fed's intended annual growth rate for M_1 was between 4.0 and 6.5 percent. Over much of that period, the actual growth rate was about 9.5 percent. For M_2, the target was a growth between 7.0 and 9.5 percent versus an actual growth of 9.5 percent. Why this occurred is not clear. One Fed explanation was that there may have been a shift in seasonal factors affecting the demand for money. At least one well-known economist attributed the growth to the fact that the Fed was trying to hold down short-term interest rates.[24]

There are some factors that are said to significantly affect the U.S. money supply (M_1) that in fact do not have a real impact—at least if the Fed chooses to take action. A prominent recent example of this is Eurodollars, which have been said to cause monetary disturbances that the Fed cannot offset.[25] Eurodollars (described in chapter 11) are dollar-dominated deposits owned by U.S. citizens as well as foreigners and held in banks outside the United States. These dollar-denominated deposit liabilities of banks can be loaned on a fractional basis; therefore, Eurodollar deposits can be created exactly as bank deposits in this country are created. The Eurobanks doing this (dealing in dollars) become, in effect, a part of the U.S. banking system. On this basis, some observers claim that M_1 is expanded by transactions in the Eurodollar market, which causes adverse effects on the dollar in foreign exchange markets.

In fact, although Eurodollar assets are acquired by supplying U.S. dollars, there is no change in total dollars. Therefore, a multiple expansion of Eurodollar deposits does not affect the total level of demand deposit liabilities held by the banking system. If a time deposit is shifted to a demand deposit, which then becomes a Eurodollar deposit, M_1 increases, just as it does in the case of any time deposit that becomes a demand deposit. This increase in M_1 could easily and fully be offset by open-market operations.

SUMMARY

The Federal Reserve, the central bank for the United States, is a very important part of our financial system. Its primary function is to control

---

[24]See Lindley H. Clark, Jr., "Fed's Failure to Keep Money Supply in Line Draws Wide Criticism," *The Wall Street Journal*, October 7, 1977, p. 1.

[25]This discussion is based on G. E. Wood and D. R. Mudd, "Do Foreigners Control the U.S. Money Supply?" *Review—Federal Reserve Bank of St. Louis* December 1977, pp. 8–11.

the monetary system in order to promote national economic goals. The Fed exercises its control by affecting the volume of commercial bank reserves.

The Federal Reserve System consists of a Board of Governors, a Federal Advisory Council, the Federal Open Market Committee, the twelve Federal Reserve District banks, and the commercial banks that are members of the system. The Board of Governors exercises overall control, while the Federal Open Market Committee is the dominant force in actually formulating major monetary decisions. The twelve district banks are federally chartered corporations, each with its own board of directors and each owned by the member banks in that district. The roughly 5,600 member banks, in turn, are privately owned, profit-seeking institutions, which have the ability to create money in the course of their activities. The number of member banks has declined over the years because of the costs of system membership—primarily, the cost of more stringent reserve requirements.

Functions of the Federal Reserve System include check collecting, providing coins and currency, making electronic transfers among member banks, safekeeping of securities, lending to member banks, regulating and supervising commercial banks, and acting as the fiscal agent for the U.S. Treasury. These activities are essentially the daily tasks of the Fed. They provide for the orderly functioning of the financial system. More interesting to economists and politicians are the activities by the Fed that affect the money supply. Of the three principal techniques that exist, open-market operations—involving the purchase and sale of government securities—are relied on almost exclusively. This reliance is a result of the flexibility that open-market operations give the Fed. Changes in reserve requirements, in contrast, are viewed by the Fed as harsh, indiscriminating, and less useful for effecting precise changes. Changes in reserve requirements alter, not total reserves, but required, and therefore excess, reserves. The third technique, a change in the Federal Reserve discount rate (the interest rate charged on member-bank loans from the Fed), is not really used as a primary method of influencing bank reserves but rather as a means of increasing the liquidity of the monetary system. The Fed can also use selective credit controls in attempts to influence certain areas of the economy that may not be fully affected by the three principal techniques.

Member-bank reserves are affected by several factors that are independent of control by the central bank. The Fed can undertake defensive operations to offset these factors so as to maintain a particular monetary policy. Alternatively, it can undertake dynamic operations, designed to alter the monetary base to conform to a change in monetary policy.

The chapter concluded with a brief examination of the practical problems that the Fed faces in the application of monetary control. Although the Fed can control the monetary base reasonably well, there are many problems in actually carrying out monetary policy. There is not an agreed-upon indicator of current conditions. Furthermore, the money supply itself is difficult to measure accurately, because of such innovations as NOW accounts. Other factors felt by some to be important in affecting the money supply—Eurodollars are a prime example—are in fact of little significance.

PART 3

Saving, Investment, and Interest Rates

The first major innovation that led toward the modernization of the primitive barter economy described in chapter 1 was the introduction of money. That innovation vastly reduced the information costs associated with trade, encouraged specialization and exchange, and hence expanded the economy's productive potential. To a lesser extent, the emergence of money as a durable and relatively low-cost means of storing purchasing power encouraged saving and investment and hence enlarged the economy's future productive capacity. But the greatest contributions toward saving and capital accumulation stemmed from the enhanced income levels achievable in a money economy.

Chapters 3 through 5 have concentrated on money—on defining what it is, explaining how it gets into circulation, describing the institutions that create and control the supply of it, and explaining how the amount of money in existence is determined.

Since the bulk of the narrowly defined money supply consists of demand deposit credit extended by banks, the preceding discussion necessarily touched on the second major innovation that elevated the efficiency of the barter economy in meeting society's economic needs. That was the emergence of nonmonetary financial claims—by which savings could be transferred to the use of financial deficit units (i.e., credit could be extended)—and markets where those claims could be bought and sold. The next three chapters will concentrate on the functioning of savers (sources of funds) and users of funds, on the flow of funds between source and user, and on the general level of the interest price of such funds in financial markets. Chapter 6 looks at household saving as an important source of loanable funds and explores the decisions households must make on allocating their savings to alternative assets. Chapter 7 focuses primarily on the demand for loanable funds, with concentration on business demand for investment funds, household demand for funds to invest in houses and durable goods, and government demand for funds to provide government services. Chapter 8 examines the combined supply of and demand for loanable funds to identify the factors that influence the interest cost of funds, then looks at an alternative view of the interest-rate determination process.

To complete this part of the text, chapter 9 explains the patterns of different interest yields that can be observed at any time on different financial claims.

6

Saving and the Supply of Loanable Funds

Saving occurs when an economic unit's current consumption is less than its current income. The level of aggregate saving is a crucial determinant of the economy's performance. In the short run, changes in the rate of saving can contribute to cyclical fluctuations in the level of production. Also, since it is through saving (as opposed to consuming current production) that the stock of productive capital grows, the level of current saving is an important determinant of the economy's productive capacity in the near and the distant future. Finally, current saving is an important source of funds flowing into the financial marketplace, and financial analysts therefore keep a close watch on the saving rate as they attempt to predict financial market developments.

In chapter 2, it was noted that the household sector of the economy is the principal provider of saving. This is not to say that business saving (retained earnings and depreciation allowances) and government saving (government budget surpluses) are unimportant, and we will have more to say about them in the chapters ahead. This chapter, however, in recognition of the crucial role played by the household sector, pays special attention to factors that determine its level of saving and the uses of that saving. As part of that discussion, the modern theories that provide the underpinnings for macroeconomic forecasts of consumption and saving will be introduced.

A second major concern of this chapter is the use to which households apply their savings. Household savings can be invested in real assets (primarily consumer durables and houses). In practice, the household sector always enjoys a level of saving in excess of its investment in real assets. Hence there is a flow of saving that the household sector can exchange for financial assets, providing funds to other sectors of the economy. The most important considerations that determine the allocation of funds to financial assets are the concerns of *investment portfolio analysis*, the rudiments of which are introduced in this chapter.

As a background for the explanations of household saving and its allocation to competing uses, Table 6–1 offers a quantitative perspective on the significance of saving and investing decisions. The column entries in that table show the disposable income available to households, the volume of their saving (after investing in houses and consumer durables), and the percentage of disposable income saved each year over the period from 1965 to 1977. It is apparent that, as income has grown, the ability of the household sector to provide funds to other segments of the economy has increased sharply. At the same time, the fraction of disposable income allocated to saving has varied from year to year, with a recent tendency to decline markedly. It is worth noting that, in an economy generating $1,000 billion in disposable income (a threshold passed in 1975), a change of one percentage point in the saving ratio translates into a $10 billion change in the flow of saving. It is little wonder that financial market analysts pay close heed to predictions of household saving and its uses.

TABLE 6–1. Income and Savings, 1965–77

Year	Disposable Personal Income	Personal Saving	Saving Ratio
	(in billions)		
1965 . . .	$ 472.2	$30.3	6.4%
1966 . . .	510.4	33.0	6.5
1967 . . .	544.5	40.9	7.5
1968 . . .	588.1	38.1	6.5
1969 . . .	630.4	35.1	5.6
1970 . . .	685.9	50.6	7.4
1971 . . .	742.8	57.3	7.7
1972 . . .	801.3	49.4	6.2
1973 . . .	503.1	72.7	8.0
1974 . . .	983.6	74.0	7.5
1975 . . .	1,014.4	80.2	7.4
1976 . . .	1,185.8	65.9	5.6
1977 . . .	1,309.2	67.3	5.1

Source: *Economic Report of the President and Survey of Current Business*

EXPLAINING THE LEVEL OF HOUSEHOLD SAVING

Concern among economists for factors that influence the level and the rate of saving has a long history. Prior to the Great Depression (which began in 1929) and the publication of Keynes's *General Theory* (1936), economists focused attention on the saving rate as the primary determinant of the economy's long-run growth path: the greater the rate of saving, the larger the addition to the capital stock in any period, and hence the greater the increase in the economy's capacity to produce. These pre-Keynesian (often labelled *classical*) economists believed that income set the limit on what can be consumed or saved and that the interest rate exerted an important influence, affecting the division of income between consumption and saving. The classical theorists assumed that, with a higher interest yield on saving, more income would be saved and less would be consumed.

In the *General Theory*, Keynes emphasized the role of income in determining both consumption spending and saving, but he left the role of interest rates open to question. Statistical tests of consumption models, conducted in the 1940s, reinforced the Keynesian view that income wielded the dominant influence. They revealed strong correlations between consumption or saving and income, while changes in interest rates appeared to have little connection with changes in consumption or saving levels.

Unfortunately, a Keynesian saving and consumption schedule, in which only current income influences consumption and saving, leaves some significant variations in those flows unaccounted for. Such schedules have also provided misleading predictions at times. Most notably, at the close of World War II, many economists forecast a severe contraction, as Keynesian analysis predicted depressed levels of consumer spending and high saving rates. In actuality, there was a consumer spending spree after the war, and a boom period inflation, rather than recession, turned out to be the major macroeconomic problem facing the United States.

In recognition of the shortcomings of the simple Keynesian model of household behavior, a number of alternative explanations of consumption and saving have been developed in the postwar period. The most widely accepted of these modern explanations are developed from the standard microeconomic theory of utility-maximizing households, to which our attention now turns.

UTILITY-MAXIMIZING CONSUMPTION AND SAVING

By borrowing or drawing down accumulated savings, households can spend more in any period than they receive as income in that period. Alternatively, households can spend less than their current income and accumulate funds for possible future uses. Every household strives to take advantage of opportunities to borrow and to lend so as to achieve an optimal pattern of consumption and saving over time.

To envision how different households, with different tastes and different income flows, allocate their incomes, consider a single household unit that wants the maximum possible pleasure or *utility* from the stream of income accruing to it over its lifetime. Presumably, utility is derived from consumption. If utility is designated U and the real value of goods and services in general consumed in time period t is c_t, the unit's objective is to maximize

$$U = U(c_0, c_1, c_2, \ldots, c_t, \ldots)$$

with utility increased by an increase in consumption during any time period (i.e., $\Delta U/\Delta c_t > 0$).

Obviously, any unit would like to enjoy unlimited consumption in every period, but households, as well as whole economies, are constrained by scarcity. Consumption spending is limited by the finite stock of wealth and the flow of income that a unit enjoys. Given current and future income flows, a household can consume more in any period only if it sacrifices consumption in one or more other periods. Fortunately, in a modern economy, a household can in any period borrow against future income, so that consumption in any period need not be limited to an amount equal to current income. Alternatively, a household can save and lend, so that it can enjoy enhanced consumption levels in the future.

Possible Consumption and Saving Patterns

Figure 6–1 illustrates the range of values by which a household's consumption level can differ from its income level. Because textbook pages are only two-dimensional, the figure can show patterns only over a two-period time horizon, but the principles illustrated are applicable to a time horizon of any number of periods. (Note, too, that our time periods can be of any length in calendar units, so that the two-period analysis is not unduly restrictive.) The household represented in the figure has an income stream of y_0 in period 0 and y_1 in period 1 (plotted as point A). By saving all of its income in period 0 and lending it at interest rate r, this household could enjoy a maximum possible consumption level in period 1 of $y_1 + y_0(1 + r)$. On the other hand, consumption in period 0 can be lifted well above income in that period by borrowing against future (period 1) income. With interest charges at rate r, the maximum amount the household can borrow and repay with period 1 income is amount B such that $B(1 + r) = y_1$. If it borrows the maximum amount $B = y_1/(1 + r)$, consumption in period 0 could be $y_0 + y_1/(1 + r)$, with no consumption spending (only debt repayment) in period 1. Of course, less extreme mixes of consumption and saving are possible, as the schedule plotted in Figure 6–1 shows. The slope of this schedule, which represents the rate at which our household can exchange current for future consumption, is

$$\frac{y_1 - [y_1 + y_0(1 + r)]}{y_0 - 0} = -(1 + r)$$

That is, for each \$1 reduction in consumption (increase in saving) in period 0, our household can enjoy additional period 1 consumption of \$1(1 + r).

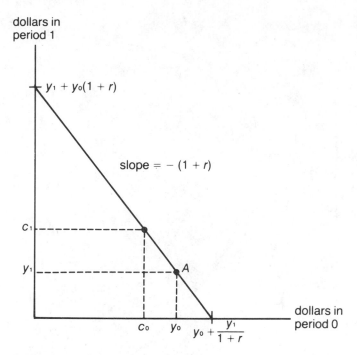

FIGURE 6–1. Consumption Possibilities

Saving and lending are clearly rewarding as, with prices constant, the current cost of each dollar of next period's consumption is $1/(1 + r)$. For example, with an interest rate of 10 percent, the current price of period 1 consumption is 90¢ on the dollar.

Preferred Time Patterns of Consumption and Saving

Our household can place itself anywhere along the tradeoff schedule plotted in Figure 6–1. For example, it might strive to balance its consumption pattern over the two-period time horizon by consuming amounts c_0 and c_1 in periods 0 and 1 respectively. With consumption of c_0, period 0 saving is $s_0 = y_0 - c_0$. Earning interest at rate r, this saving permits period 1 consumption to be $c_1 = y_1 + (y_0 - c_0)(1 + r)$—that is, the sum of period 1 income and the saving with interest from period 0. A household's selection of one particular pattern of consumption and saving depends on its tastes or preferences, reflected in the utility function $U = U(c_0, c_1)$. One possible set of preferences is represented in the form of a set of indifference curves (U_0, U_1, U_2) in Figure 6–2. Any *indifference curve* in that figure shows combinations of period 0 and period 1 consumption that provide equal levels of utility; for any one such curve, a household is

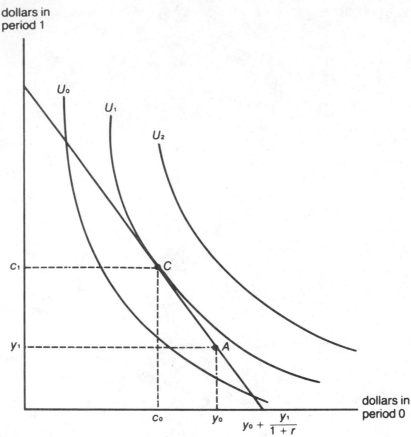

FIGURE 6–2. Optimal Consumption-Saving, Current-Period Saving

indifferent to which of the combinations it should choose. Of course, to enjoy an undiminished level of satisfaction even though its consumption in period 0 is reduced, the household's consumption in period 1 must be increased. Likewise, with less period 1 consumption, its utility level would be unchanged if it received adequate compensation in the form of enlarged period 0 consumption. The upward concavity of the indifference schedules indicates that the *marginal rate of substitution*—the marginal rate at which the household is willing to substitute consumption in one period for consumption in the other period—changes with the consumption pattern. With a relatively high level of period 0 consumption, the household is willing to forego a relatively large amount of consumption in period 0 to enhance its period 1 consumption. On the other hand, with a relatively low consumption level in period 0, the household is willing to give up a relatively large volume of consumption in period 1 in exchange for increased consumption in period 0.

While the household enjoys the same level of utility at any point along a given indifference curve, a movement northeastward in Figure 6–2 to a higher indifference curve provides an increase in utility, as the household can enjoy (1) more consumption in one period with no less in the other period or (2) more consumption in both periods. Hence indifference curve U_1 is preferable to U_0, and U_2 is preferable to U_1. Figure 6–2 could be covered with indifference curves for all conceivable utility levels. What our household would surely like to do is to pick the consumption-saving pattern that places it on the highest attainable indifference curve.

Given the budget constraint facing the household represented in Figure 6–2, the highest attainable indifference curve is U_1, which is tangent to the budget constraint at point C. This utility-maximizing position is attained by our hypothetical household consuming c_0 in period 0 (say, $2,000), saving $s_0 = y_0 - c_0$ (say, $1,000), and consuming c_1 in period 1 (say, $2,000, consisting of $800 of period 1 income and $1200 of principal and accrued interest from period 0 saving). For period 0, this household is a saver and a potential provider of loanable funds for some other units in the economic system.

Factors Influencing Consumption and Saving

The factors that influence the amount of saving that the household provides in period 0 are the household's tastes; the level and the timing of the lifetime stream of income the household can expect to receive—in this case, (y_0, y_1); and the interest rate, which dictates the rate at which current consumption can be exchanged for future consumption.

Illustrating the importance of the timing of income receipts, Figure 6–3 shows a household whose consumption preferences are just like those of the one in the preceding example and whose budget constraint has the same slope as the one in that example but whose income endowments are timed differently. In this case, the utility-maximizing household would be a dissaver in period 0 (in the amount $c_0 - y_0$), borrowing the amount $(y_1 - c_1)/(1 + r)$ against future income to provide an enlarged level of current consumption. The financial marketplace, where lending and borrowing are conducted, permits this household to divorce its consumption level from its income level in any period. A much more even pattern of consumption is thus made possible.[1]

---

[1]Needless to say, households select patterns of consumption that differ from their income streams only because doing so enhances their material well-being. The extent to which financial markets contribute to the well-being of individual households is easily demonstrated with the apparatus developed above.

Consider an individual operating in an economy without financial markets. Producing outputs y_0 and y_1 in periods 0 and 1, that individual is apt to consume in amounts roughly equal to current income. (It is possible to save in period 0 and use the saving to raise period

Shifting attention from the timing of income receipts to the level of income, Figure 6–4 shows how an increase in the level of income, in this case only in period 0 income, influences consumption and saving over the household's remaining time horizon. With no change in the interest rate, a change in the level of income simply shifts the household's budget constraint in parallel fashion. With the assumption that consumption in any period is a normal good,[2] the income change incorporated into Figure

---

1 consumption, but this is unlikely, since period 1 purchasing power is already much greater than period 0 purchasing power.)

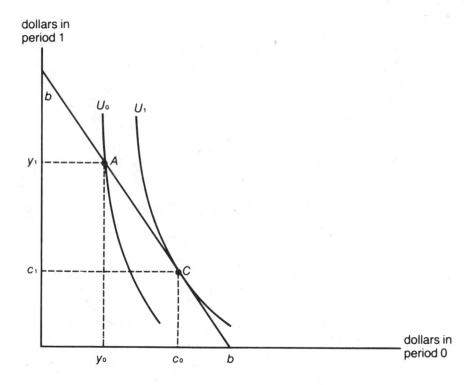

There are, of course, many other combinations of period 0 and period 1 consumption that yield an amount of utility equal to that from consuming at A, and indifference curve U_0 shows those combinations. In addition, by introducing the possibility of borrowing and lending, along the budget constraint bb, a vast array of alternative time patterns of consumption become available. The individual in the figure here can maximize utility by exploiting the opportunity to borrow, so as to move to point C. The existence of a financial market allows a move from indifference curve U_0 to the higher-utility indifference curve U_1. With the general availability of financial markets to provide more pleasing time patterns of consumption, society's welfare is clearly enhanced by financial claims and markets for them.

[2]For a normal good, the quantity consumed changes in the same direction as income.

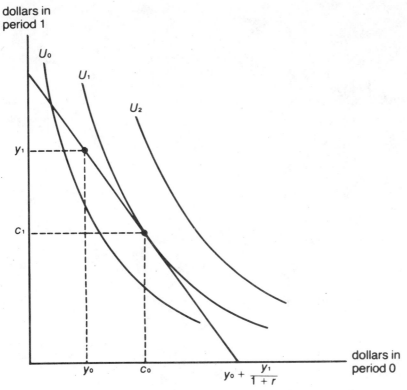

dollars in
period 1

U_0

U_1

U_2

y_1

c_1

y_0 c_0 $y_0 + \dfrac{y_1}{1+r}$

dollars in
period 0

FIGURE 6–3. Optimal Consumption-Saving, Current-Period Dissaving

6–4 results in an increase in both period 0 and period 1 consumption. Consumption in period 0 does not rise by the full amount of the increase in income of $y_0' - y_0$ in that period, but only by some fraction of it; the extra income is spread over the full time horizon of the household, so that it raises the consumption level in each period. Comparably, a decline in income in one period (a shift leftward of the budget constraint) is spread over the household's time horizon, with consumption reduced by a portion of the income decline in both period 0 and period 1. This requires a reduced flow of current saving, since current consumption is reduced by less than current income.

Finally, the indifference-curve apparatus can be applied to explore the influence of a change in the interest rate at which the household can borrow and lend. Consider a household with income endowments (y_0, y_1), which is initially in equilibrium with consumption pattern (c_0, c_1), as shown in Figure 6–5. With an increase in the interest rate, the budget constraint facing this household is rotated clockwise about point (y_0, y_1). The household can now acquire future consumption at a lower cost in terms of current saving by lending at the higher interest rate r'. In the same vein,

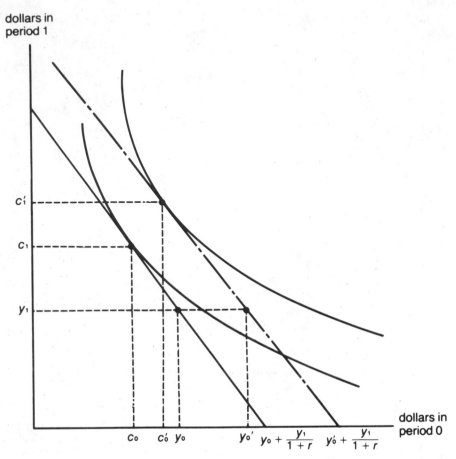

FIGURE 6–4. Income and Optimal Consumption-Saving

with borrowing costs increased, the maximum amount our household can consume currently, borrowing to the hilt against future income, is the reduced amount $y_0 + y_1/(1 + r')$.

For the household unit represented in Figure 6–5, an interest-rate increase reduces current consumption and hence stimulates current saving; an interest-rate decline raises current consumption and lowers saving. Thus the classical view that an increase in the reward for saving (the interest rate) raises the saving rate appears to be supported.

However, other patterns of response are possible. An alternative, involving an increase in current consumption (a decline in saving) in response to a rise in the interest rate, is illustrated in Figure 6–6. To generate the contrasting responses to interest-rate changes shown in Figures 6–5 and 6–6, it is necessary only to alter the shape of the indifference curves that are employed to reflect the preferences of a hypothetical consumer. Since different preference patterns are permissible, we cannot rule out the

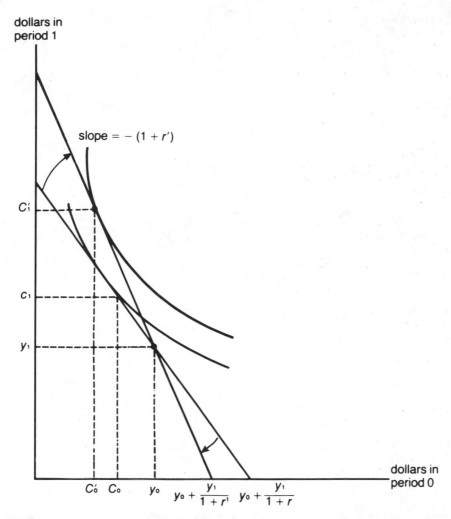

FIGURE 6–5. Interest Rate and Optimal Consumption-Saving, Positive Saving Response (Substitution Effect)

possibility that consumption responds positively (and saving negatively) to interest-rate changes, as illustrated in Figure 6–6.[3]

---

[3]The contradictory response patterns illustrated in Figures 6–5 and 6–6 reflect the fact that an interest-rate change generates a response that can be decomposed into two components—a *substitution effect* and an *income effect.* An interest-rate increase alters the relative price of current versus future consumption, with future consumption becoming relatively cheaper as interest rates rise. This relative price change, which involves a clockwise rotation of the budget constraint facing our consumer, induces a substitution of future for current consumption, so that current consumption is lowered and saving is increased. At the same time, the interest-rate increase provides an income effect, which can be viewed as a parallel outward shift of the budget constraint. A consumer can be expected to respond to an income

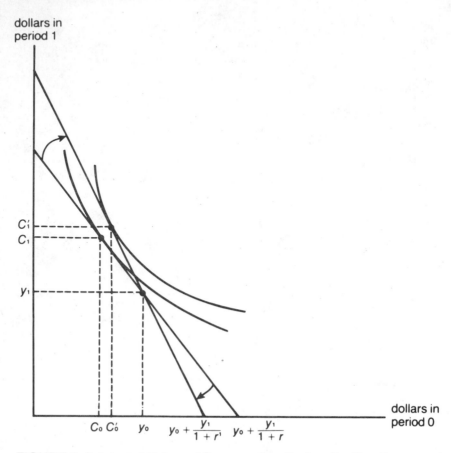

FIGURE 6–6. Interest Rate and Consumption-Saving, Positive Consumption Response (Income Effect)

THE MODERN CONSUMPTION THEORIES

The most prominent modern theories of aggregate consumption and saving behavior have been developed on the basis of the preceding microeconomic theory. Understanding these modern models, which play crucial roles in macroeconomic forecasts of consumption and saving flows, is easy if the analysis of individual consumption and saving choices is kept in mind. Most importantly, remember that consumers base each period's consumption and saving, not only on the income they receive in that period, but also on the stream of receipts they expect to receive over an extended time horizon.

increase (a shift outward of the budget constraint) by consuming more. If this response is sufficiently strong, it can override the substitution effect and produce an overall increase in current consumption in response to an interest-rate increase.

The Life-Cycle Hypothesis

According to the *life-cycle hypothesis* a typical individual has an income that is low in the early and late years of life and relatively high in the middle years, which are the prime earning years. With time on the horizontal axis and dollars on the vertical axis, a typical individual with an expected lifetime of T years is represented in Figure 6–7. The humped income schedule assumed in the life-cycle hypothesis is represented by schedule Y, and schedule C represents consumption. The individual represented in this figure is spreading the lifetime income stream over the expected lifetime, dissaving in the early years (borrowing against future income) and in the final years (using up accumulated savings), so that the consumption standard in any one year is not tied uniquely to income in that year.

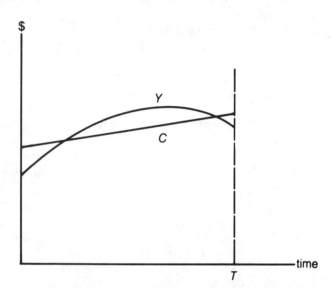

FIGURE 6–7. Income and Consumption over the Life Cycle

The Formal Hypothesis. In the two-period model developed in this chapter, the maximum consumption a household can enjoy in the current period is the full amount of its current income plus the maximum amount it can borrow against future income and repay with interest at rate r. This sum can be thought of as the household's total current *wealth*, or as the value in the present of a stock of wealth that, at interest rate r, will provide the household's expected lifetime stream of income.[4]

---

[4]For an individual household, this total wealth can consist of financial claims, but the aggregate wealth (W), for all participants in the economic system, which generates the income flow (Y), must consist of property wealth and human wealth (skills, talents, and

The fraction of its wealth (that is, of the *present value* of its lifetime income stream) that a household chooses to consume in any one period depends on its preferences, on the household member's stage in the life cycle (i.e., the remaining expected lifetime), and perhaps on interest rates. Should some event occur that raises (or lowers) the present value of the typical consumer's income stream, consumption can be expected to be increased (or reduced) in every period roughly in proportion to that increase (or decrease) in wealth, unless there is some specific reason to favor consumption in one period over another.

To provide an aggregate consumption function for an entire economy, it must be possible to add together all the individual consumption functions for the economy's population. The resulting aggregate consumption function can be expected to be a stable function, and hence useful for prediction purposes, if society's preferences for current as opposed to future consumption are stable through time and if the age and income distributions in the population are roughly constant. In this case, the aggregate consumption function implied by the life-cycle theory takes the form

$$C_t = k \cdot PV_t$$

where C_t is aggregate consumption in the current period, PV_t is current wealth, and k is the fraction of wealth to be consumed.

Unfortunately for the statistical application of the life-cycle hypothesis, the total value of society's wealth, composed partly of real, property assets and partly of *human capital,* or *human wealth* (the value of the skills, talents, and human energy that provide a stream of earnings), is not directly observable. Estimates are available for the value of property wealth, but the value of future labor earnings and the corresponding value of the *human capital* or *human wealth* that generates those earnings cannot be directly observed but must be represented indirectly in statistical consumption functions by a proxy variable—for example, by current labor earnings—which serves as a predictor of future labor income.[5] If we

---

energy). The nation's income flow, then, is the yield (at rate r) on wealth, or $W \cdot r = Y$. This link between the stock of wealth and the flow of income is also at the heart of a second modern consumption theory, the permanent income hypothesis, which will be discussed shortly.

[5] Using current labor income as a predictor of future labor earnings and hence as a proxy for human capital, R. Ando and F. Modigliani fitted a consumption function for the U.S., which took the form

$$C_t = (0.7)Y_t + (.06)A_t$$

where Y_t is current labor income, A_t is the value of property wealth, and C_1 is consumption. This equation says that consumption is a positive function of both current income and property wealth. See R. Ando and F. Modigliani, "The 'Life-Cycle' Hypothesis of Saving," *American Economic Review* 53 (March 1963), pp. 55–84.

dismiss the need to determine what the best proxy variable for expected future income is—that is a concern we can leave for professional business forecasters—the most enlightening conceptual representation of the life-cycle consumption theory recognizes that an individual's total wealth in period t depends on the value of property wealth and income in that period and on income receipts expected to be earned by working in the future. With Y_t representing current labor income, Y_t^e the stream of income receipts expected from labor services in the future, and A_t the value of property wealth, consumption in period t, according to the life-cycle hypothesis, is

$$C_t = C(Y_t, Y_t^e, A_t)$$

Implications for Consumption and Saving. The life-cycle model, as represented in the preceding equation, provides a number of important predictions on the pattern of society's consumption and saving. Most fundamentally, it indicates that the response of consumption and saving to changes in current income depends crucially on whether society perceives those changes to be temporary, leaving wealth unaltered, or whether it sees them as a portent of a permanently altered earnings level and hence a changed volume of wealth. Of course, rather than growing at a steady rate, income in capitalistic economies fluctuates as it expands. According to the life-cycle hypothesis, if income rises briskly in a cyclical expansion, society (not willing to believe that such rapid growth can persist) consumes only a small proportion of the increase (i.e., $\Delta C_t / \Delta Y_t$ is small) and saves the bulk of the increase to provide a higher consumption standard later. In this case, only current income (Y_t in the consumption function) changes to provide a consumption and saving response; expected future labor earnings (Y_t^e) and property wealth (A_t) are unaffected. Comparably, in cyclical contractions or recessions, saving is reduced as society tries to maintain its consumption standard in the face of a decline in income, which is interpreted as being temporary, and which hence leaves wealth (property wealth and the present value of future labor earnings) unaltered. The flow of saving should therefore exhibit a strong cyclical pattern, according to the life-cycle theory: it should expand in the recovery phase of the business cycle and contract as the economy's vigor wanes. Of course, the flow of funds to the financial marketplace mirrors these fluctuations in saving.

In a comparable vein, the life-cycle theory argues that society's response to changes in the tax revenues that government collects is crucially dependent on whether the change is viewed as temporary or permanent. A tax increase designed to slow down economic activity reduces current disposable income. But the more temporary society perceives that loss of income to be, the less the effect on wealth and hence the smaller the resulting cutback in consumption spending, as household saving (and the supply of that saving to financial markets) is allowed to shrink instead. Comparably, a tax cut, which raises current disposable income, has a smaller impact on consumption spending and adds more to saving (and to the supply of loanable funds) to the extent that the cut is perceived to be temporary.

It is also interesting to note that, according to the life-cycle hypothesis, the proportion of income that households consume and save depends on the household's stage in the life cycle, so that the fraction of total income that is consumed in the whole economy can be altered by systematic changes in the age distribution of the population. A baby boom of the sort the U.S. experienced after World War II initially lowers the average age of the population, then raises that average as the war babies mature. With the average age of the population lowered, a larger fraction of society's income is consumed (a smaller fraction is saved). But, with the postwar bulge in the population entering the middle years of life, during which saving is greatest, the fraction that is consumed will fall. Clearly, over the long haul, changes in the age distribution of the population can have important effects on both the overall levels of consumption and saving and on the mix of products purchased. (Would you favor entering the baby-food manufacturing business after a marked decline in a country's birth rate?)

The Permanent Income Hypothesis

The *permanent income hypothesis*, most frequently associated with economist Milton Friedman, bears a close relation to the life-cycle hypothesis. Once again, consumption in any period is not strictly constrained by income in that period but depends on the entire stream of income the consumer expects to receive. That is, it is the consumer's total resources that constrains consumption.

In the formal permanent income theory, Friedman breaks down the observed values of income and consumption into two components, a *permanent component* and a *transitory component*. That is, he lets

$$Y = Y_p + Y_t$$

where Y is observed income, Y_p is permanent income, and Y_t transitory income, and

$$C = C_p + C_t$$

where C is observed consumption, C_p = permanent consumption, and C_t = transitory consumption.

According to Friedman, "The permanent component [of income] is to be interpreted as reflecting the effect of those factors that the unit regards as determining its capital value or wealth."[6] If a consumer unit's total wealth (human and property) in period t is PV_t and the prevailing percentage yield available on wealth is r, permanent income is the income that unit could consume each period without reducing its wealth. That is, permanent income is

$$Y_p = r \cdot PV_t$$

Permanent consumption is consumption that is deliberately and systematically engaged in, based on what the consumer views as permanent income, which in turn depends on the consumer's total wealth.

Transitory income and consumption (Y_t and C_t) are unexpected, chance movements in income and consumption. Microeconomic examples include, on the one hand, income losses due to an unforeseen illness and gains due to an unanticipated inheritance and, on the other hand, unplanned consumption stimulated by unexpectedly good opportunities to make purchases and expenses due to unforeseen illness.

The Aggregate Consumption Function. At the aggregate level, our concern is to explain the response of consumption and saving to income changes; those responses differ according to whether the income change is perceived as permanent or transitory. Cyclical deviations of income from its long-run expansion path can be viewed as transitory and hence may have little effect on consumption.

According to the permanent income hypothesis, aggregate consumption in the current period is

$$C = K(i, z) \cdot Y_p$$

where Y_p is the value of permanent income, i is the interest rate, and z is a catchall variable representing any other factor (such as the age distribution of the population) that influences aggregate consumption. Changes in current income cause changes in consumption only through altering permanent income. The response in consumption per unit of change in current income is given by the expression

$$\Delta C / \Delta Y = (\Delta C / \Delta Y_p) \cdot (\Delta Y_p / \Delta Y)$$

in which the crucial term is $\Delta Y_p / \Delta Y$. A change in current income (ΔY) that is perceived as transitory has no substantive effect on permanent income, so that $\Delta Y_p / \Delta Y$ has a small or null value and consumption is not altered; only saving is affected. In contrast, with a change in current income that is perceived as a reflection of a permanently altered income level, $\Delta Y_p / \Delta Y$ has a value of 1, so that a substantial change in consumption results.

Implications for Consumption and Saving. As did the life-cycle hy-

---

[6]Milton Friedman, *A Theory of the Consumption Function* (Princeton: Princeton University Press for the National Bureau of Economic Research, 1957), p. 21.

pothesis, the permanent income hypothesis indicates that consumption, based on permanent income rather than just current income, is more stable than observed income. Faced with a decline in current income during recessions, consumers save less without reducing consumption (which is based on permanent income). In boom periods, with income rising more briskly than historical experience suggests is normal, households continue to base their consumption on what they perceive as normal or permanent income and save an unusually large fraction of the transitory increase in earnings. Again, we should expect procyclical swings over time in saving and in the flow supply of funds that saving provides to the financial marketplace.

Moreover, government policy actions can be expected to prompt consumption and saving responses that vary with society's perception of the permanence of those actions. A change in received income stemming from a government policy action that is temporary (transitory) has at most only a weak effect on consumption, according to the permanent income hypothesis. Hence, for example, supporters of this hypothesis would argue that the one-time 10 percent rebate on personal income tax liabilities that Congress provided in 1975 was added mostly to saving in 1975 and generated little additional consumption.

The Stock Market's Influence on Consumption and Saving

Among the most prominent efforts to construct statistical models of the U.S. economy is the *MIT–University of Pennsylvania–Social Science Research Council (MPS) model.* Its consumption function is based on the life-cycle hypothesis, and the property-wealth measures employed in that function include the value of corporate stocks (which are equity claims on real assets) owned by the U.S. population. Changes in stock prices, by altering the perceived wealth of stockholders, appear to significantly influence consumption and saving. An increase in stock prices, which increase society's perceived wealth, raises consumption and lowers saving—a result that makes sense, since the need to save to accumulate wealth is relaxed by a rise in stock prices. The size of the response of consumption to changes in the price of stock is the subject of continuing research, but the existence of the response is one of the exciting revelations of modern research on the consumption function. It suggests that accurate predictions of saving flows may require consideration of changes in the values and yields on a wider array of existing assets.

An Overview of Household Consumption and Saving Patterns

Our analysis has suggested that economywide consumption should be more stable than income, as consumers try to spread their wealth over an extended time horizon. It may be argued that the hypotheses examined above exaggerate the extent to which consumers can rationally foresee and plan for the future. But even if the time horizon over which households plan is of relatively short duration, say, only a few years, it is still rational to spread temporary income changes over that planning horizon, to allow saving to increase when the economy expands and to shrink when it contracts. A shorter planning horizon only alters the size of the response to temporary income changes. For example, with a three-year horizon, an increment in income is spread over three years, with roughly one-third of the temporary increment in income consumed each year and two-thirds of it saved in the year in which it is received. Of course, the bulk of any increase in income that is perceived as permanent is consumed in the year in which it is received so that relatively little is added to saving.

Our microeconomic analysis of consumer behavior suggested that the level of interest rates might also influence consumption and saving. Yet such an influence was not mentioned in the discussion of the aggregate consumption function. That omission reflects the fact that statistical tests of aggregate consumption functions have failed to provide evidence that interest rates play any significant role in changes in the levels of consumption and saving.

Our discussion has noted that changes in financial market values (in particular, changes in corporate stock prices) influence consumption and saving. A rise in stock prices stimulates consumption (reduces saving). Indexes of stock prices are often watched closely as indicators of future spending levels.

Finally, our analysis has indicated that, for purposes of forecasting consumption and saving flows, it is necessary to determine whether society interprets income changes as temporary or permanent. Whether they result from cyclical swings in economic activity, from government policy actions, or from some other source, income changes that are viewed as temporary, or transitory, have the bulk of their effect on saving and influence consumption relatively little, but permanent changes are reflected for the most part in consumption changes.

THE ALLOCATION OF SAVING

To enjoy the most pleasing possible consumption pattern over time, households must sometimes operate as borrowers (deficit units) while at other times they can consume less than their current income and operate as savers (surplus units). It must be remembered that some proportion of the consuming population is always operating as a demander of loanable funds, but the household sector collectively always operates as a net saver and provider of loanable funds.

In the remainder of this chapter, households that provide loanable funds will be referred to simply as investors; that is, households with net savings can "invest"[7] them in a wide variety of assets. Subsequent chapters will show in detail that financial intermediaries also act as "financial investors" by reallocating household saving that has flowed to them from purchasers of indirect claims. The remainder of this chapter, however, focuses on a theory of asset choice—of *portfolio management*—that identifies the important factors that determine how households allocate their savings to alternative uses. Happily, the analysis developed here has general applicability; it is a useful approach to decisions on the allocation of accumulated funds, not just for households, but also for other units.

Allocation Decisions

The basic investment problem facing economic units is to regulate consumption over time so as to maximize utility, or satisfaction, given the constraints of wealth and opportunity. By forgoing current consumption and allocating saving to assets that yield financial returns, individuals can enjoy additional future consumption. Hence an individual saver-investor must evaluate the opportunities available, select some combination of assets to hold, allocate wealth between consumption and these assets, and manage the chosen package of assets.

A basic premise of the process of selecting and holding assets, i.e., of portfolio management, is that optimal investment decisions cannot be made in isolation; they are dependent on each other and on other factors, such as constraints on investors. Portfolio management should be thought of as a careful blending of various assets within a unified framework. Indeed, the very essence of portfolio theory is that the whole is not equal to the sum of the parts: the performance characteristics of the portfolio are not equal to the sum of the characteristics of the individual securities.

All individuals make portfolio decisions sooner or later. Even if no discretionary saving exists for an individual at a certain point in time, such decisions are relevant in that the individual still has a portfolio of claims—e.g., through social security contributions, life insurance, and other retirement benefits. Thus a grasp of the rudiments of portfolio management analysis has virtually universal relevance.

Returns

The obvious goal for investors in allocating their saving would seem to be maximum (or optimal) consumption and thus maximum utility. Since more consumption always raises utility, why can't investors simply invest in the financial asset with the largest return?

---

[7]Note that purchases of financial claims constitute financial investment and do not count as investment in the national income-accounting or macroeconomic sense.

The problem with this operating rule is that the future is uncertain. We do not know with certainty what the payoffs on various financial assets will be for the forthcoming period (e.g., this year). Just because XYZ stock returned 30 percent last year does not mean it will do the same this year: XYZ Company could have a bad year or could even go bankrupt.

To deal with uncertainty, investors think in terms of probabilities. A probability is the likelihood of a particular outcome, expressed as a fraction or as a decimal. For example, the probability of heads landing on top when a fair coin is flipped is 0.5, regardless of the preceding outcomes. A group of probabilities reflecting estimates of unknown future events is called a *probability distribution*. For a particular group, the sum of the probabilities must be 1.0. As an example of a probability distribution for a financial asset, consider the following possible yields on XYZ common stock and the associated probability of each.

Possible Outcome	Probability of Outcome
11%	0.25
13%	0.25
17%	0.25
19%	0.25
	1.00

Notice that XYZ is expected to return either 11 percent, 13 percent, 17 percent, or 19 percent and that the four outcomes are equally likely. Also notice that the probabilities sum to 1.0, as they must if the probability distribution is to be valid: this indicates that all possible outcomes have been accounted for. Although in the final analysis any estimates of future probabilities are subjective, known past events can be used to assign values to them.[8] Knowing the possible outcomes and their respective probabilities of occurrence, one can calculate the arithmetic mean of the probability distribution. This is usually called the *expected value* of the distribution; it is found by summing the products of outcomes and probabilities. For XYZ stock, the expected value (expected percentage yield) is $0.25 (0.11) + 0.25 (0.13) + 0.25 (0.17) + 0.25 (0.19) = 15$ percent. The expected value of the return, therefore, is the weighted sum of the possible outcomes, with the weights corresponding to probabilities of occurrence. It represents the best single-point expression of the value of the possible outcomes over a large number of trials. In other words, an investor owning XYZ stock realizes one of those four returns in any period (if the probability distribution does not change); over many periods, the

---

[8]A group of numbers depicting known past events is called a *frequency distribution*, because the frequency of each outcome is known.

average return approaches 15 percent, or the weighted mean of this particular probability distribution. In effect, the very good returns of 17 percent and 19 percent balance out the smaller returns of 11 percent and 13 percent.

With the uncertainty of returns, but also with the ability to deal with uncertainty by the calculation of expected values based on probabilities, should investors make portfolio decisions by maximizing expected returns? If so, it would appear that savers-investors need only select the investment with the highest expected value. The problem with this approach is that it fails to take into account the risks that investors are willing to assume. Investment alternatives are not always equal, even if their expected values are the same. Therefore, one cannot state categorically that investment D dominates investment E in every period. Both may have the same expected value of return (say, 25 percent), but we would not expect them both to return exactly 25 percent in any given period. Investment E may have no probability of a negative return, while investment D may have some probability of one or more negative returns. Under these circumstances, since not all investors are willing to take the same chances, the principle of maximum expected return becomes unsatisfactory. Investor A may be unwilling to accept the chance of a negative return in any period; such an investor would not be indifferent to choosing between investments D and E, even though their expected values are the same. The risk of the investment is therefore an important consideration.

Risk

The reason that the principle of maximum expected return is unsatisfactory is that not all investors are indifferent to risk. Most are averse to it. Not only must expected values of returns be calculated, but an investor's aversion to assuming risk must also be considered. To understand why, we need to understand what risk is.

Risk is the chance that the actual outcome of an event will differ from the expected outcome. In the case of a Treasury bill held to maturity, only one outcome is possible (the probability is 1.0). When two or more outcomes are possible, risk is involved.

The easiest way to think about risk is to consider how the possible outcomes in a particular distribution are dispersed around the expected value (which is their mean value). The greater the dispersion, the greater the risk. For example, consider stock UVW with a 0.5 probability of a 14 percent return and a 0.5 probability of a 16 percent return. Although the expected value is 15 percent, just as it is for stock XYZ, UVW involves less risk because it involves less dispersion: the lowest the return can be for UVW is 14 percent, but for XYZ it could be 11 percent.

The most often used measure of dispersion in modern investment analysis is the variance or standard deviation of returns. This is an absolute measure of the dispersion of possible returns around the mean return. The greater the standard deviation, the greater the risk.[9]

Rational investors are risk-averse: they will not assume risk for its own sake, and they will incur a given level of risk only if they expect to be adequately compensated for doing so. Since risk involves the chance of a smaller return than expected, or loss, investors must expect to be compensated by higher expected returns; they will not otherwise invest in risky assets. Hence, large (or small) potential risks accompany large (or small) potential returns; that is, the greater the risk, the greater the expected return must be. It follows, then, that investors have to assume larger risks if they want a chance to earn larger returns.

Expected returns and risk go together so completely that making investment decisions amounts to making a tradeoff between expected return and risk. Treasury bills provide very safe, but relatively low, returns. Since common stocks are more risky than Treasury bills, their expected returns have to be larger to induce investment. Investors making portfolio decisions must decide whether the additional return is adequate compensation for the additional risk, and they must decide individually, according to their own degrees of risk aversion. Thus maximizing expected yields is inadequate as a basis for making portfolio decisions, since the tradeoff between expected returns and risk must also be considered.

Utility Functions

To obtain a workable operating rule for financial investments, we turn to utility theory, which has been refined in the last few decades in an attempt to describe how individuals can make decisions under uncertainty. An *expected* utility hypothesis can be utilized by investors to express an order of preference for risky assets that involve probability distributions. If we can determine an investor's utility function, we have a method of determining reactions to probability distributions and therefore a way to explain the decisions the investor would make under conditions of uncertainty.

To determine an investor's utility function, we could examine how the investor responds when presented with some alternatives. One method often advanced is to offer a set of lotteries and to determine what price the investor is willing to pay to play them. Arbitrary numbers called *utiles* can be used to assess the values of the various dollar payoffs and the entry prices of the lotteries. Since ordinal (relative) utility is being measured

---

[9]The standard deviation is the square root of the variance. For variable X, the formula for variance is

$$\text{variance} = \frac{\Sigma X^2}{n} - \left(\frac{\Sigma X}{n}\right)^2$$

where n is the number of observations.

here, and not cardinal (absolute) utility, the size of the numbers used for various money amounts are not important. For example, assume that an investor would pay $4,000 to enter a lottery with a fifty-fifty chance of uinning either $0 or $10,000. The utile value assigned to $4000 would be 0.5. Based on this, other dollar amounts can be assigned utile values until a relation between wealth and utility has been established for this investor. Such values, plotted in utility-wealth space, form curves from which a utility function emerges. This function can predict the investor's behavior in other circumstances.

Although the utility function specified for an investor is somewhat arbitrary, when such a function is represented graphically (in utility-wealth space), it will slope upward (i.e., marginal utility is positive) because investors prefer more wealth to less. In addition, risk-averse investors' utility curves slope upward at a decreasing rate,[10] and therefore their marginal utility decreases as their wealth increases. This form of utility function is represented by a curve concave from below, as shown in Figure 6–8.

FIGURE 6–8. A Utility-Wealth Curve with Diminishing Marginal Utility

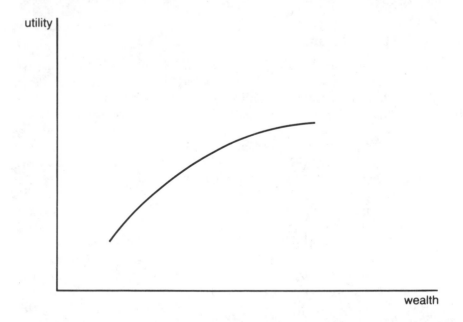

---

[10]Technically, a risk averter is an individual who, for a given level of expected return, prefers a less risky portfolio to a more risky one.

Risk-Return Tradeoffs

Investors are apt to think directly in terms of risk and expected return, rather than in terms of utility. That is, they want their portfolios to yield the maximum possible return for a given level of risk. Assuming that we use a utility function of the shape illustrated in Figure 6–8, investment decisions can be based on only these two parameters. Therefore, the discussion below is in terms of risk-return space instead of utility-wealth space.

Many alternative opportunities in risk-return space offer the same utility, so that investors are indifferent to choosing among them. In other words, different combinations that provide equal utility lie on a single indifference curve. Therefore, it is possible to condense three dimensions (return, risk, and utility) into two dimensions (risk and return). Each indifference curve in Figure 6–9 describes the risk-return tradeoff—which, as we have seen, is the essence of the investment decision—that permits a saver-investor to maintain a constant level of utility. Every point on a particular curve represents the same utility. Every point on an indifference curve that is higher (lower) than another curve represents a utility that is greater (less) than that represented by the other curve. Since every investor has an unlimited number of indifference curves, each corresponding to a set of equally valued combinations of return and risk, the indifference curves in the figure are only examples.

Curves U_1, U_2, and U_3 in Figure 6–9 represent the indifference curves for a highly risk-averse investor. In risk-return space, such curves are positively sloped and concave from below. Since each investor attempts to obtain the greatest expected utility, U_3 is preferable to U_2, which is preferable to U_1, and so forth. In contrast to a highly risk-averse investor, an aggressive investor has indifference curves of the type illustrated by U_6, U_5, and U_4 in the figure. These curves are flatter than the first three and represent a smaller tradeoff between return and risk. For example, an increase in risk from A to B requires an increase in return from R_1 to R_2 for an aggressive investor with indifference curve U_4, but it requires a larger increase, from R_3 to R_4, for a highly risk-averse investor with indifference curve U_1.

Portfolio Theory

Basic Assumptions. Portfolio theory (a theory of asset choice) can be derived from the preceding analysis and is closely related to the theory of consumer choice, which is fundamental in economics; in fact, portfolio theory can be directly derived from consumer-choice theory. The basic assumption is that individuals receive utility from two principal characteristics of investments—return and safety of return. In making optimal asset choices, an investor maximizes utility in terms of these two desirable

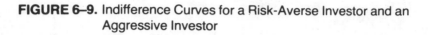

FIGURE 6–9. Indifference Curves for a Risk-Averse Investor and an Aggressive Investor

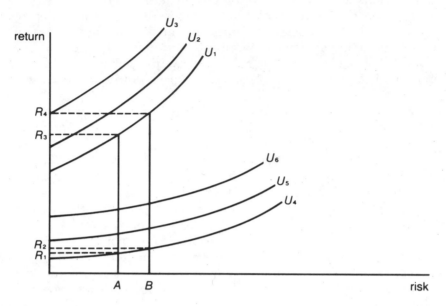

characteristics. Conventional finance literature, however, refers to the negative characteristic, risk, rather than the positive characteristic, safety. Therefore, the following discussion will be conducted in terms of the two characteristics most commonly associated with investing in financial assets —return and risk.

Figure 6–10 is a graphical representation of the economic theory underlying portfolio discussions, which is based on just these two parameters. The curve AB represents the possibility locus of attainable combinations of return and risk. The optimal choice of assets is determined by the point (X) at which the possibility curve just touches the highest attainable indifference curve (assumed here to be U_3). Any other point on the possibility curve is sub-optimal in that a less preferred combination of assets results. The figure, then, shows how portfolio choices can be explained in terms of investor preferences (indifference curves) and available portfolios (the possibility locus).

The Markowitz Model. The principles of portfolio theory are contained in the Markowitz model for the selection of efficient portfolios.[11]

---

[11]See Harry M. Markowitz, "Portfolio Selection," *Journal of Finance* 7 (March 1952): 77–91 and *Portfolio Selection: Efficient Diversification of Investments* (New York: John Wiley & Sons, 1959). Markowitz is considered to be the father of portfolio theory.

FIGURE 6–10. The Basis of Portfolio Theory

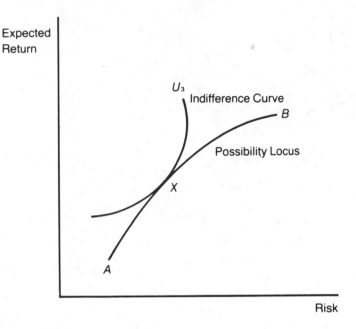

For simplicity, we will talk in terms of portfolios of common stocks. The Markowitz procedure gives investors a way to determine the *efficient set* of portfolios. An efficient portfolio is one that has the smallest risk for a specified level of return or the largest expected return for a specified amount of risk. In this analysis, risk is measured by the standard deviation of returns, which is the common procedure referred to earlier.

The Markowitz analysis can be illustrated by a figure similar to Figure 6–11. The enclosed area of Figure 6–11 represents the attainable set of portfolio combinations from some population of securities. Each point in this attainable set represents a possible portfolio, with its own risk and expected return. The efficient set, given by the arc *AB*, is a boundary of the attainable set. Any point inside the enclosed area is less efficient than a corresponding point on the efficient set; that is, the efficient set dominates the attainable set. The portfolios on the efficient set can be said to dominate those represented by the enclosed area (i.e., representing all other possible portfolios) in that they offer higher yields at a given level of risk or lower risks at a specified rate of return than portfolios not on arc *AB*. After the efficient set is defined, an investor can maximize the expected return or minimize the risk by selecting a portfolio from that set.

In order to select one portfolio from the efficient set, an investor's utility function must be specified. As we have seen, indifference curves depict return-risk opportunities with the same utility. The point of tangen-

FIGURE 6–11. The Markowitz Model of Efficient Portfolios.

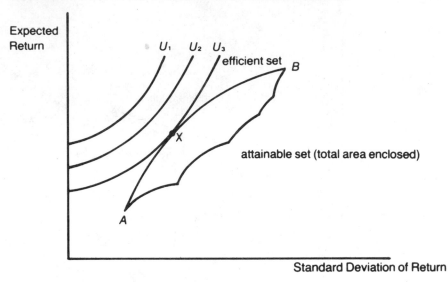

cy between the investor's indifference curves and the efficient set designates the efficient portfolio that is optimal for the investor. In Figure 6–11, the portfolio at point X is the most satisfactory available portfolio for the particular investor represented in the diagram. Different investors have different optimal portfolios, depending upon their preferences, as reflected in their own indifference curves. For example, for an investor that is more averse to risk, the point of tangency is between X and A on the efficient set.

Portfolio theory has been developed considerably beyond the Markowitz analysis presented above. Theoretically, all investors can hold the same portfolio of risky assets. By varying how much of their wealth they invest in the same portfolio, investors can achieve different risk-return portfolios. For example, an investor who places half of his or her wealth in a portfolio of risk assets and the other half in Treasury bills assumes a less risky position than another investor who places the whole sum in the portfolio of risky assets. Furthermore, both of these investors are assuming less risk, and have expectations of a smaller return, than a third investor who not only invests 100 percent of his or her wealth in the portfolio of risky assets, but also borrows an equal amount to invest in them. These more advanced concepts of portfolio theory are beyond the scope of this discussion.

One of the most important results to emerge from modern portfolio theory is a proper understanding of the nature and importance of diversification. Before Markowitz's work in the 1950s, investors believed in diversification, but they did not know exactly what constituted proper diversification. The feeling was that, if funds were distributed among a number of securities, losses on some would be offset by gains on others. Markowitz's real contribution was to show that proper diversification depends upon the relation between returns patterns on individual securities. Portfolio risk can be reduced, without a loss in return, if securities are combined "correctly," that is, with regard to their covariances. *Covariance* is a statistical term that is used to reflect the extent to which stock returns move together. Markowitz's work demonstrated that a portfolio's securities should not have high positive covariances among themselves. As an example, stocks in the same industry often have high covariance. It is preferable to put together a portfolio from assets whose covariance is zero (in which case their returns move independently of each other) or whose covariance is negative (in which case they move inversely to each other).

Using modern approaches to portfolio building, diversification is considered very carefully in terms of relevant relations among securities. Part of the risk of individual securities can be eliminated if they are correctly combined into a portfolio whose risk is *not* equal to the weighted sum of the risks of the individual securities in the portfolio (as measured, for example, by each security's variance or standard deviation). Nor does it take many securities to provide adequate diversification. Roughly twenty or thirty stocks provide virtually all the risk reduction that can be gained from diversification. Since investors like returns and dislike risk, and since some portfolio risk can be eliminated by proper diversification, it is clearly sensible for investors to diversify their portfolios.

Allocation Decisions in Perspective

We started out seeking a way for investors to make allocation decisions; that is, we wanted to determine how saver-investors allocate their saving to alternative uses. Our analysis has shown an operating approach to the asset-choice decision in which both risk and return have to be considered.

One problem remains. Although portfolio analysis has been generalized to include several assets such as cash, bonds, riskless assets, etc., most of the literature on portfolio theory has been devoted to the allocation of saving (or wealth) to specific categories of assets—most particularly, to common stocks.[12] The literature has been very well developed in this regard, but little has been said about the operational allocation of wealth to other available assets—bonds, real estate, commodities, liquid assets, etc. Although theoretical means have been developed that allow us to

---

[12]See James Tobin, "Liquidity Preference as Behavior Towards Risk," *Review of Economic Studies* 25 (February 1958): 65–87.

discuss various assets together, practical procedures are not as readily available.

It is important to realize that individuals ultimately have to make multiasset portfolio choices, even if they do not think directly in portfolio terms: they still must make decisions about the allocation of wealth to available alternatives. Such decisions, in their total effect, greatly influence individuals' future consumption patterns. A brief scenario for making multiasset portfolio choices is presented below; however, better implementation procedures are needed.[13]

Investors need to gather all the information that they can reasonably obtain about possible investment alternatives. Then, they need to consider these assets according to the attributes that are most important in portfolio theory, namely, return and risk (i.e., safety of return). Other characteristics of assets, such as tax status, liquidity, marketability, etc., could also be considered.

Whatever attributes are chosen, each individual investor needs to derive a scheme for weighting their relative importance. For example, perhaps an individual views income return as being twice as important as appreciation return; suppose that this individual is also very conservative and therefore weights safety equally with appreciation return. This amounts to weights of 25 percent, 25 percent, and 50 percent on appreciation, safety, and income return respectively. Investors then must choose which categories of assets they are willing to consider, such as savings accounts or stocks, because most individuals cannot reasonably consider all available alternatives. Having chosen the alternatives that they consider reasonably accessible, investors must examine each of these assets with respect to the weighted attributes. Finally, the appropriateness of the assets considered must be judged according to the individual's preferences by means of some type of measurement scheme.

The important point here is simply that investors must make multiasset choices and that these choices should be made in a portfolio context. Investors should choose, from among the available alternatives, those meeting their specifications, and saving should be allocated on the basis of these characteristics. Changes in the portfolio should be made as conditions indicate. Investor preferences change over time, primarily depending upon one's stage in the life cycle. Also, environmental factors change, as in the case of inflation, which has become a much more important part of the economic scene since 1966.

In the final analysis, applying a multiasset portfolio approach is dif-

---

[13]This analysis is indebted to Keith Smith, "The Major Asset Mix Problem of the Individual Investor," *Journal of Contemporary Business* 6 (Winter 1974): 49–62.

ficult at best. There is little in the way of a formal model to go by. And, yet, investors must—and do—allocate their savings over a wide range of alternatives. We next consider their actual allocation decisions concerning financial assets only.

HOUSEHOLD INVESTMENTS IN THE PAST

One small bit of information on the allocation decision of individuals can be obtained by examining their ex-post investment decisions; that is, what have they done with their wealth in the past. Although we cannot decide if they have made good decisions (because we do not know the aggregate utility functions for this group), we can learn some interesting facts about how individuals allocate saving to liquid vs. nonliquid investments, to debt vs. equity, etc. It is reasonable to believe that individuals have acted to maximize their utility in an uncertain world—and the financial market-place (and environment) has changed dramatically over the years. It is also reasonable to believe that individuals have responded to conditions as they perceived them and have changed to meet new conditions as the situation warranted.

Table 6–2 shows the year-end outstanding amounts of financial assets and liabilities for the household sector for the years 1966 through 1975.[14] Our analysis is somewhat limited here, in that investment in real assets is not shown. However, data on real-asset investment is sketchy at best, and (as pointed out) portfolio theory has until now had a somewhat narrow focus, with little attention devoted to areas other than common stocks and, perhaps, bonds.

Table 6–2 shows that, by 1975, deposits plus debt market instruments were twice the size of corporate equities in household portfolios. We might think of all of these as direct financial investments by households: i.e., they owned in 1975 $114 billion of Treasury securities, $776 billion of time and savings deposits, etc. However, households also owned over $500 billion in indirect assets in the form of just two intermediary holdings—$165 billion in insurance reserves and $369 billion in pension fund reserves. These two indirect investments, particularly the latter, have grown rapidly in the past and probably will continue to grow rapidly in the future; for example, by the end of 1978 these figures were $180 billion and $539 billion respectively.

We can see from the table that households did not increase their

---

[14]In particular, this sector is comprised of households, personal trusts, and nonprofit organizations.

TABLE 6–2. Financial Assets and Liabilities for Households, 1966–75 (in billions of dollars)

	1966	1967	1968	1969	1970	1971	1972	1973	1974	1975	
Total financial assets	1458.057	1691.414	1913.981	1859.843	1922.796	2150.066	2389.561	2254.243	2149.852	2496.852	1
Dep. & cr. mkt. instr.¹	586.841	634.210	688.106	732.025	784.680	860.843	958.279	1069.784	1170.778	1288.634	2
Demand deposits & currency	85.812	95.663	106.551	109.102	117.887	126.877	141.440	153.935	158.915	165.649	3
Time & savings accounts	307.716	342.881	373.887	383.102	426.747	494.617	565.571	633.429	691.308	776.230	4
at commercial banks	130.743	149.430	167.555	168.402	195.357	223.605	249.178	288.649	324.912	350.661	5
at savings institutions	176.973	193.451	206.332	214.700	231.390	271.012	316.393	344.780	366.396	425.569	6
Credit market instruments	193.313	195.666	207.668	239.821	240.046	239.349	251.268	282.420	320.555	346.755	7
U.S. govt. securities	94.635	96.282	102.561	113.338	105.186	94.625	94.125	110.447	117.718	123.414	8
Treasury	83.850	85.011	89.896	95.664	82.873	74.571	77.583	94.565	103.882	114.345	9
Savings bonds	50.249	51.219	51.866	51.770	52.089	54.416	57.667	60.354	63.338	67.363	10
Other Treasury	33.601	33.792	38.030	43.894	30.784	20.155	19.916	34.211	40.544	46.982	11
Agency issues	10.785	11.271	12.665	17.674	22.313	20.054	16.542	15.882	13.836	9.069	12
St. & loc. obligations	39.835	37.562	36.890	46.033	45.248	44.984	47.148	54.371	65.538	74.196	13
Corporate & fgn. bonds	11.870	15.118	19.418	25.189	35.941	44.508	48.417	49.063	56.648	65.928	14
Mortgages	44.216	46.114	48.668	51.290	52.896	54.114	60.459	64.034	68.257	72.748	15
Open-market paper	2.757	0.590	0.131	3.971	0.775	1.118	1.119	4.505	10.015	6.824	16
Money-market fund shrs.	0.000	0.000	0.000	0.000	0.000	0.000	0.000	0.000	2.379	3.645	17
Corporate equities	575.418	730.586	869.040	755.132	737.527	843.036	928.992	683.389	477.118	630.509	18

19	Investment company shares	34.829	44.701	52.677	48.289	47.618	56.694	59.831	46.519	34.061	42.178	19
20	Other corporate equities	540.589	685.885	816.363	706.843	689.909	786.342	869.161	636.870	443.057	588.331	20
21	Life insurance reserves	110.570	115.424	120.045	125.023	130.265	136.437	142.997	150.274	156.699	164.591	21
22	Pension fund reserves	164.299	186.403	208.106	218.679	239.623	276.213	322.952	311.806	304.564	368.593	22
23	Security credit	2.730	4.943	7.039	5.221	4.354	4.886	5.022	4.866	3.891	3.985	23
24	Miscellaneous assets	18.199	19.848	21.645	23.763	26.347	28.651	31.319	34.124	36.802	40.540	24
25	Total liabilities	380.133	406.726	442.813	474.017	498.497	544.484	614.987	685.275	729.758	782.815	25
26	Credit market instruments	364.126	386.341	418.666	452.397	477.727	520.387	585.280	658.914	703.907	753.510	26
27	Home mortgages	228.431	241.700	258.358	276.555	291.260	318.387	359.864	406.822	441.959	481.245	27
28	Other mortgages	15.485	16.679	17.814	19.090	20.348	21.658	23.077	24.519	25.881	26.972	28
29	Installment cons. credit	76.245	79.428	87.745	97.105	101.898	111.195	126.756	146.434	155.384	162.237	29
30	Other consumer credit	19.994	21.355	23.025	24.041	25.099	27.445	30.491	32.530	33.356	35.039	30
31	Bank loans N.E.C.	12.030	13.917	16.409	17.307	18.222	19.429	21.484	22.435	17.943	16.474	31
32	Other loans	11.941	13.262	15.315	18.299	20.900	22.273	23.608	26.174	29.384	31.543	32
33	Security credit	9.025	12.709	15.627	12.225	10.445	13.109	17.571	13.218	11.416	13.660	33
34	Trade credit	3.323	3.729	4.218	4.707	5.207	5.552	6.160	6.767	7.349	7.901	34
35	Deferred and unpaid life insurance premiums	3.659	3.947	4.302	4.688	5.118	5.436	5.976	6.376	7.086	7.744	35

Source: Board of Governors of the Federal Reserve System, *Flow of Funds Accounts 1946–75*, December 1976, p. 100.

Note: Includes personal trusts and nonprofit organizations.
¹Excludes corporate equities.

holdings of U.S. government securities very much (from $95 billion to $123 billion) over this decade. Perhaps this reflects a growing disenchantment with the lower yields offered by such securities and a willingness to assume more risk in an attempt to earn a larger return. Corporate bonds, for example, grew almost sixfold over the period, and they certainly offer better returns than government bonds, but with greater risk. Corporate equities are reported at market value, and thus the amounts shown fluctuate widely depending upon the state of the stock market; for example, 1966, 1970, and 1974 were very bad years for the market. Individuals have actually been net sellers of stock for several years, which perhaps reflects a growing disenchantment with the stock market and an increasing indirect stake in equity securities in the form of pension fund reserves, which are quite heavily invested in common stocks.

Taken together, the allocation of savings to the financial assets shown in Table 6–2 reflects individuals' efforts to maximize utility, given their possibilities and their preferences, with wealth as the constraint. In choosing among alternatives, individuals have had to balance the possibilities available with a set of conflicting criteria—the desires for maximum return and for minimum risk, the need for liquidity, the desire to insure against death, the desire (or mandate) to provide for retirement, etc.

SUMMARY

To achieve the most satisfaction possible from its income stream, a household can (1) borrow against future income to raise current spending or (2) save and exchange its savings for income-yielding assets in order to enhance future consumption. According to the modern consumption function theories—the life-cycle hypothesis and the permanent income hypothesis—aggregate saving can generally be expected to vary systematically as the economy fluctuates. Both of those models predict that the fraction of income saved rises during economic booms and falls during recessions, as society tries to maintain a consumption path (based on permanent income, or wealth) that is smoother than the time-path of received income. The modern consumption theories interpret this tendency to smooth the consumption path as an effort to alter consumption only in response to income changes that are permanent, with temporary (transitory) income changes absorbed by saving. It follows that consumption and saving respond differently to government economic policy actions, depending on whether the actions are interpreted as causes of temporary or of permanent alterations in income.

It was also noted that modern research on the consumption function, which employs the value of common stocks as an indicator of a portion of society's perceived wealth, shows an increase in consumption (reduction in saving) as the stock market rises. Hence efforts to explain and predict changes in saving flows may have to pay heed to changes in the market's valuation of financial claims.

The choice of a saving rate also depends on the nature of the income-earning opportunities that saving makes available. The availability of a broad array of income-yielding financial claims encourages saving and the exchange of accumulated savings for those claims.

Of course, to achieve the most satisfying consumption path, savers must allocate their savings to income-earning claims in an optimal fashion. The optimal choice of income-earning assets is the subject of investment portfolio management, which was introduced in the final section of this chapter.

All saver-investors make portfolio decisions sooner or later. They should do so by thinking of their portfolios as a careful blending of various assets. Investors need an operating rule to make allocation decisions. Maximization of returns, or expected returns, is not a suitable criterion. To earn larger returns, larger risks must be assumed. Investors, however, are risk-averse; hence they must also consider the risk of investment opportunities, as well as the expected return. Utility theory provides an approach to making decisions about risky assets. Given a utility function, investment decisions can be based on only two parameters, expected return and risk. Indifference curves describe risk-return tradeoffs for individual investors.

Portfolio theory has been developed to allow investors to choose an optimal portfolio based on individual preferences. Portfolio theory asserts that a possibility locus of attainable combinations of returns and risks, at the point at which it is tangent to an investor's highest attainable indifference curves, indicates the optimal portfolio of assets. The Markowitz procedure determines the efficient set of portfolios—efficient in the sense that they provide the most utility in terms of risk and return. A key concept to emerge from this analysis is diversification. Some portfolio risk can (and should) be eliminated by proper diversification. To properly diversify, the interrelationships among security returns must be considered. Finally, the problem of allocating wealth to the full array of available assets was considered and a brief description of a process for making multiasset portfolio choices was presented. Much work remains to be done in this area.

The chapter concluded by examining the actual allocation decisions of households in the past. Such decisions reflect investors' efforts to maximize utility, given their possibilities and preferences, with wealth as the constraint.

7

Investment and the Demand for Loanable Funds

After our discussion of household saving as an important source of loanable funds, it is logical now to concentrate on the demand for loanable funds (though we will mention some additional sources of loanable funds as we proceed). The demand for loanable funds reflects the composite need of the sectors requiring funds to finance their activities (primarily business, households, and government), and it is evidenced by their issuance of primary (new) securities. These sectors are affected by various factors in the economy that induce them to alter their positions by seeking loanable funds.

As a starting point, this chapter examines the total demand for loanable funds for several recent years. This allows the magnitude of the demand to be placed in perspective. Next, business demand for loanable funds is considered. How do business firms decide to invest in real assets? How can they finance such investments? In what types of assets do they invest? Such questions are of prime importance to the economy as a whole and have been examined in great detail in the corporate finance literature. The second major topic in this chapter is household demand for loanable funds. Although households are not the primary demanders of funds for investment in real assets, their desires in this regard are significant, particularly for specific markets such as the mortgage market. Government— federal, state, and local—demand for funds is analyzed next. Finally, foreign demand is considered, since international transactions are of major importance in today's world.

AN OVERALL VIEW

For the sake of simplicity, the financial sector will be ignored in this discussion. Thus, although financial institutions do lend to each other in the normal course of their business, this discussion will concentrate on the primary securities issued by nonfinancial sectors to obtain loanable funds.

The upper part of Table 7–1 shows the total credit market debt owed by nonfinancial sectors for the years 1966 through 1975. By careful examination of this table, the demand for loanable funds can be described in terms of both the absolute amounts involved and the relative relationships between the sectors. The business sector is shown to have been a substantial borrower of loanable funds. In 1975, for example, the corporate nonfinancial business sector showed a total indebtedness of $630 billion (line 9). This took various forms, such as corporate bonds, bank loans, mortgages, and open-market paper. The household sector, although it is a net supplier of funds on balance, also borrows a great volume of funds. Its total indebtedness at the end of 1975 amounted to $754 billion (line 6). This debt took several forms, which, in order of importance, were mortgages, consumer installment credit, other loans, and bank loans. The government sector has also borrowed substantially. The federal government showed a marketable debt outstanding of $446 billion (line 3) at the end of 1975, and state and local governments had $230 billion (line 10) in debt outstanding. Finally, note that there is a sizable foreign demand for loanable funds, which resulted in an outstanding debt of $94 billion (line 4) by the end of 1975. Each of these borrowers will be considered in turn in the following sections of this chapter.

The amounts in the table are, of course, stock figures, representing the total amounts owed by sectors at particular points in time. The corresponding flow figures—which represent changes in the stock measures above—will be examined below on a sector-by-sector basis.

Although some of the numbers used in the following discussion are for 1975, the principles demonstrated for analyzing the demand for loanable funds are applicable to any year. Data for other years can be obtained from the *Flow of Funds Accounts* issued by the Federal Reserve System.

NONFINANCIAL BUSINESS DEMAND

The nonfinancial business sector—often referred to as the corporate sector —is a major demander of funds in our economy. It is the center of attention in the private sector in many respects. For example, one individual firm can raise millions of dollars (even hundreds of millions) in one securities offering. This is a spectacular accomplishment even for the U.S. financial system, which evolved for the primary purpose of allocating saving from surplus units to deficit units.

Why Businesses Demand Funds

The purpose of nonfinancial business firms is to acquire and to hold real assets, which are the basis for the creation of additional wealth. In finance, the operating objective of business firms is assumed to be the maximization of shareholder wealth. Shareholders, after all, are the owners of business firms, and it seems appropriate that firms should operate toward a goal of enhancing the welfare of the owners. Maximization of shareholder wealth is equivalent to maximizing the equity interest of the firm, i.e., maximizing the price of its stock.

Given this objective, business firms attempt to earn returns through investment in real assets. These returns must be considered in relation to the risk taken to earn them, since, *ceteris paribus,* expected returns and risk are positively related. In effect, then, firms utilize funds (financing) for the benefit of the owners of the firm: they invest these funds in an attempt to earn the maximum returns possible, given a level of risk assumed.

Every dollar of a firm's assets must be financed by a dollar of liabilities or by a dollar of net worth. Each firm strives to hold the best combination of assets possible at a point in time, given the constraints imposed by technology, financial conditions, government regulations, etc. The net returns earned by these assets accrue to the holders of the liabilities and to the owners of the firm. Obviously, the larger the net returns earned, the larger the benefits to the owners, who are entitled to all net earnings after creditor claims are satisfied. Again, the risk attached to these earnings must be considered.

Thus firms demand loanable funds because they believe they can earn a return in excess of their cost and thereby enhance stockholder wealth. Business demand for funds, then, is based upon the expected net returns from assets to be financed with the additional funds. These assets are primarily real assets, such as plant, equipment, etc. (Note, however, that sizable amounts of current assets, which also must be financed, are required in order to carry on the operations of a business. For example, credit sales generate accounts receivable, a current asset that must be financed just as machines or equipment must be financed.)

Sources of Funds

Table 7–2 shows a statement of saving and investment for nonfinancial corporate business for the years 1966 through 1975. It contains detailed information on how businesses use funds (an increase in their assets) and their sources of funds (increases in their liabilities plus their net worth). Focusing on 1975, let us examine how firms obtain funds and what they do with them.

The total amount of funds available to corporate business in any year is the sum of their internal and external financing. Internal financing is

TABLE 7–1. Total Financial Assets and Liabilities, 1966–75 (in billions of dollars)

	1966	1967	1968	1969	1970	1971	1972	1973	1974	1975	
					Credit Market Debt Claims*						
1 Total credit mkt. liabilities owned by:	1182.141	1261.351	1369.749	1487.833	1595.322	1748.296	1941.855	2186.988	2411.079	2626.713	1
2 Nonfinancial sectors	1114.039	1194.336	1292.036	1380.688	1477.176	1616.632	1783.552	1973.470	2156.020	2357.994	2
3 U.S. government	266.063	279.063	292.631	288.967	300.818	325.565	340.779	349.051	361.048	446.254	3
4 Foreign	39.900	42.849	45.309	47.500	51.881	57.080	62.267	68.444	81.433	94.215	4
5 Private domestic	808.076	872.424	954.096	1044.221	1124.477	1233.987	1380.506	1555.975	1713.539	1817.525	5
6 Households	364.126	386.341	418.666	452.397	477.727	520.387	585.280	658.914	703.907	753.510	6
7 Farm business	35.504	38.815	41.565	44.617	46.922	51.390	57.218	67.208	75.079	84.483	7
8 Nonfarm noncorp. bus.	52.475	56.869	62.200	69.676	75.323	85.676	98.783	111.801	118.554	119.864	8
9 Corporate business	246.642	273.117	304.453	339.647	375.319	409.558	457.051	521.968	601.266	630.065	9
10 St. & loc. governments	109.329	117.282	127.212	137.884	149.186	166.976	182.174	196.084	214.733	229.603	10
11 Financial sectors	68.102	67.015	77.713	107.145	118.146	131.664	158.303	213.518	255.059	268.719	11
12 Sponsored credit agencies	19.007	18.386	21.862	30.645	38.879	40.021	43.542	59.837	77.134	80.340	12
13 Mortgage pools	1.314	1.988	2.526	3.204	4.755	9.526	14.404	18.040	23.799	34.138	13
14 Commercial banks	2.638	2.633	3.461	5.877	3.777	5.587	9.234	16.139	14.051	14.722	14
15 Bank affiliates	0.000	0.000	0.000	4.294	2.349	1.973	2.637	4.881	8.332	8.654	15
16 Foreign banking agencies	0.134	0.106	0.191	0.349	0.429	2.070	2.914	7.998	10.870	10.533	16
17 Savings & loan assns.	8.737	7.035	8.167	12.271	14.116	14.050	16.010	22.035	28.320	26.217	17
18 Finance companies	36.272	36.867	40.740	49.025	51.662	54.326	60.802	70.238	74.354	75.011	18
19 Real est. invest. trusts	0.000	0.000	0.766	1.480	2.179	4.111	8.760	14.350	15.820	15.459	19
20 Money mkt. fund shares	0.000	0.000	0.000	0.000	0.000	0.000	0.000	0.000	2.379	3.645	20
21 Total credit market assets held by:	1182.141	1261.351	1369.749	1487.833	1595.322	1748.296	1941.855	2186.988	2411.079	2626.713	21
22 Private dom. nonfin. sectors	258.345	262.284	282.558	328.016	328.852	328.946	352.260	399.165	449.649	502.372	22
23 Households	193.313	195.666	207.668	239.821	240.046	239.349	251.268	282.420	320.555	346.755	23

24	Nonfarm noncorp. business	7.768	7.999	8.361	8.730	9.223	9.689	10.192	10.959	11.707	12.576
25	Nonfin. corporate business	31.628	33.158	39.262	46.927	47.132	49.468	51.905	57.959	59.387	72.902
26	State & local governments	25.636	25.461	27.267	32.538	32.451	30.440	38.895	47.827	58.000	70.139
27	Rest of the world	14.281	16.078	16.112	14.850	25.705	52.456	61.273	61.994	70.444	77.492
28	U.S. government	42.442	47.055	51.951	55.081	57.768	59.918	62.391	65.462	73.059	88.226
29	Financial institutions	867.073	935.934	1019.128	1089.886	1182.997	1306.976	1465.931	1660.367	1817.927	1958.623
30	Sponsored credit agencies	23.382	23.289	26.530	35.300	44.878	45.343	49.712	67.493	87.305	91.515
31	Mortgage pools	1.314	1.988	2.526	3.204	4.755	9.526	14.404	18.040	23.799	34.138
32	Federal Reserve System	44.509	49.314	52.995	57.218	62.199	71.065	71.336	80.563	86.713	95.250
33	Commercial banking	317.533	353.374	392.083	410.422	445.457	496.009	566.501	653.050	717.816	745.370
34	Commercial banks	314.409	349.727	387.950	400.781	434.001	484.240	553.013	633.857	692.552	721.760
35	Bank affiliates	0.000	0.000	0.000	3.946	2.954	2.840	2.598	4.300	4.901	4.375
36	Foreign banking agencies	2.396	2.771	3.172	4.504	7.176	7.292	8.966	12.860	17.865	16.372
37	Banks in U.S. poss.	0.728	0.876	0.961	1.191	1.326	1.637	1.924	2.033	2.498	2.863
38	Private nonbank finance	480.335	507.969	544.994	583.742	625.708	685.033	763.978	841.221	902.294	992.350
30	Savings institutions	191.397	206.366	221.973	236.611	253.969	293.215	340.521	376.520	403.006	453.745
40	Savings & loan assoc.	124.362	133.419	143.120	152.704	164.894	192.518	227.263	254.718	275.522	310.524
41	Mutual savings banks	57.681	62.728	67.135	70.121	73.919	83.494	93.238	98.281	100.610	111.227
42	Credit unions	9.354	10.219	11.718	13.786	15.156	17.203	20.020	23.521	26.874	31.994
43	Insurance	235.415	248.422	262.250	275.584	292.708	306.900	324.724	348.557	378.647	417.954
44	Life insurance companies	145.941	153.341	160.687	167.625	174.605	182.759	192.463	204.767	217.713	234.839
45	Private pension funds	31.893	32.762	33.823	34.621	36.866	35.403	34.624	37.114	42.934	50.956
46	St. & loc. govt. rtr. fund	34.948	38.280	41.640	45.468	49.602	52.876	57.614	63.299	69.766	78.451
47	Other insurance cos.	22.633	24.039	26.100	27.870	31.635	35.862	40.023	43.377	48.234	53.708
48	Finance n.e.c.	53.523	53.181	60.771	71.547	79.031	84.918	98.733	116.144	120.641	120.651
49	Finance companies	44.937	45.455	50.622	59.182	61.924	66.875	76.196	87.670	92.655	94.473
50	Real est. invest. trusts	0.000	0.000	0.000	2.007	3.904	6.203	10.396	15.956	16.145	13.178
51	Open-end invest. cos.	5.355	4.843	5.791	6.695	7.208	7.207	7.190	6.988	6.668	7.343
52	Money market funds	0.000	0.000	0.000	0.000	0.000	0.000	0.000	0.000	0.757	1.451
53	Security bkrs. & dealers	3.231	2.883	3.528	3.663	5.995	4.633	4.951	5.530	4.416	4.206

(continued from pages 178 and 179)

TABLE 7-1. Total Financial Assets and Liabilities, 1966-75 (in billions of dollars)

	1966	1967	1968	1969	1970	1971	1972	1973	1974	1975	
					Total Claims and Their Relation to Total Financial Assets						
1 Total credit mkt. liabilities	1182.141	1261.351	1369.749	1487.833	1595.322	1748.296	1941.855	2186.988	2411.079	2626.713	1
Other liabilities:											
2 Official foreign exchange	1.647	2.765	4.818	5.105	2.564	0.861	0.706	0.560	1.857	2.292	2
3 Treasury curr. & SDR ctfs.	3.963	4.646	5.062	5.334	5.956	6.446	6.979	7.401	7.733	8.670	3
4 Deposits at financial insts.	530.531	586.110	634.379	640.865	708.310	807.733	920.887	1017.445	1103.598	1209.587	4
5 Banking system	351.485	390.393	425.942	424.501	474.840	533.737	600.884	669.618	734.420	780.623	5
6 Demand dep. & currency	191.651	206.645	221.473	229.376	241.750	259.284	284.088	301.888	308.925	325.006	6
7 Time & savings deposits	159.834	183.748	204.469	195.125	233.090	274.453	316.796	367.730	425.495	455.617	7
8 Savings institutions	179.046	195.717	208.437	216.364	233.470	273.996	320.003	347.827	369.178	428.964	8
9 Insurance & pension reserves	274.869	301.827	328.151	343.702	369.888	412.650	465.949	462.080	461.263	533.184	9
10 U.S. government	28.097	29.492	30.814	32.399	34.886	37.800	40.862	43.065	45.872	49.586	10
11 Insurance sector	246.772	272.335	297.337	311.303	335.002	374.850	425.087	419.015	415.391	483.598	11
12 Security credit	18.729	25.752	32.334	25.676	24.877	28.722	37.391	29.470	24.460	28.986	12
13 Trade debt	124.893	133.925	151.693	175.132	184.655	196.131	213.504	239.146	262.646	272.757	13
14 Profit taxes payable	22.115	17.195	20.216	17.096	13.951	15.788	15.703	18.239	19.410	16.049	14
15 Miscellaneous	152.173	165.978	185.707	215.122	228.282	242.503	268.099	315.251	366.983	406.888	15
16 Interbank claims	28.856	31.528	35.305	37.228	41.685	47.267	49.252	57.116	61.901	58.610	16

17	Investment company shares	34.829	44.701	52.677	48.289	47.618	56.694	59.831	46.519	34.061	42.178	17
18	Total liabilities above	2374.746	2575.778	2820.091	3001.382	3223.108	3563.091	3980.156	4380.215	4754.991	5205.914	18
	+ Financial assets not included in borrowing											
19	Other corporate equities	647.824	823.938	981.352	866.353	859.373	1003.741	1142.237	864.526	608.911	812.482	19
20	Gold & SDR's	43.185	41.600	40.905	41.015	44.689	48.069	55.870	61.088	61.028	60.978	20
	− Floats not incl. in assets											
21	Demand deposits — U.S. govt.	−0.232	−0.565	−0.178	−0.706	−0.656	−0.838	−0.261	0.078	−0.152	−0.271	21
22	Other	13.936	13.434	14.647	17.439	19.343	21.371	25.182	26.753	33.055	34.964	22
23	Trade credit	−16.946	−18.292	−20.728	−22.833	−22.907	−24.869	−30.760	−32.276	−34.810	−36.168	23
	− Liabilities not allocated as assets											
24	Treasury currency	−2.198	−1.982	−1.733	−1.514	−1.593	−1.581	−1.734	−1.715	−1.920	−1.942	24
25	Profit taxes payable	4.184	4.161	5.237	4.800	4.021	3.780	3.669	4.150	4.035	4.077	25
26	Miscellaneous	15.114	16.201	20.654	29.459	27.243	29.988	33.089	38.965	38.358	36.593	26
27	Totals allocated to sectors as assets	3051.897	3428.359	3824.449	3882.105	4101.719	4587.050	5149.078	5269.874	5386.364	6042.121	27

Source: Board of Governors of the Federal Reserve System, *Flow of Funds Accounts 1946–75*, December 1976, p. 169.

Note: Year-end outstanding amounts.

*Excludes corporate equities.

TABLE 7-2. Saving and Investment, Nonfinancial Corporate Business, Year-Total Flows, 1966–75 (in billions of dollars)

		1966	1967	1968	1969	1970	1971	1972	1973	1974	1975
1	Profits before tax	69.341	65.288	71.781	68.308	55.145	63.182	75.563	91.990	102.074	95.274
2	− Profits tax accruals	29.417	27.638	33.542	33.232	27.229	29.826	33.360	39.377	42.370	39.576
3	− Net dividends paid	18.061	18.844	20.688	20.629	19.848	19.952	21.626	23.791	30.228	28.907
4	= Undistributed profits	21.863	18.806	17.551	14.447	8.068	13.404	20.577	28.822	29.476	26.791
5	+ Foreign branch profits	1.446	1.574	1.821	1.783	1.564	1.854	1.906	3.661	10.833	3.861
6	+ Inv. valuation adjustment	−2.098	−1.744	−3.447	−5.526	−5.067	−5.029	−6.597	−18.584	−39.782	−11.415
7	+ Cap. consumption adjustment	3.790	3.621	3.693	3.544	1.551	0.500	2.695	1.846	−2.957	−11.554
8	+ Capital consumption allow.	35.497	39.009	42.726	47.421	52.737	57.853	62.195	68.090	80.020	45.672
9	= Gross internal funds	60.498	61.266	62.344	61.669	58.853	68.582	80.776	83.835	77.590	103.355
10	Gross investment	52.171	57.401	54.236	56.464	49.831	54.665	64.332	67.687	64.489	88.856
11	Capital expenditures	76.006	72.558	77.614	85.047	80.627	86.221	101.004	124.398	134.577	95.740
12	Fixed investment	62.801	63.758	69.419	76.676	76.902	81.886	92.531	107.913	116.094	110.803
13	Plant & equipment	59.964	60.881	65.912	72.785	73.278	77.103	87.048	102.197	111.885	107.934
14	Home construction	−0.201	0.019	0.319	−0.044	−0.205	0.928	0.671	−0.326	−0.414	0.895
15	Multi-family residential	3.038	2.858	3.188	3.935	3.829	3.855	4.812	6.042	4.623	1.974
16	Change in inventories	13.205	8.800	6.865	8.327	3.396	3.618	7.561	13.317	11.993	−16.386
17	Mineral rights from U.S. govt.	0.000	0.000	1.330	0.044	0.329	0.717	0.912	3.168	6.490	1.323
18	Net financial investment	−23.835	−15.157	−23.378	−28.583	−30.796	−31.556	−36.672	−56.711	−70.088	−6.884
19	Net acq. of financial assets	12.607	16.833	28.790	28.359	15.441	28.847	36.506	41.107	35.285	35.223
20	Liquid assets	−3.661	4.763	7.960	2.346	2.272	7.749	9.017	6.659	2.079	17.713
21	Demand dep. & currency	−0.682	2.532	2.714	0.591	0.937	1.568	1.418	0.373	−2.560	2.746
22	Time deposits	−0.390	1.079	−0.626	−5.404	1.695	4.162	5.981	1.133	3.841	1.887
23	U.S. govt. securities	−1.705	−2.462	0.774	1.929	2.170	2.476	−2.430	−3.805	3.513	8.230
24	St. & loc. obligations	−0.961	−0.339	0.482	−0.982	−0.625	1.000	1.000	−0.137	0.616	−0.173

25	Commercial paper	-0.225	4.178	4.165	4.022	1.172	-2.300	1.437	6.521	-0.554	2.777
26	Security r.p.'s	0.302	-0.225	0.451	2.190	-3.077	0.843	1.611	2.574	-2.777	2.246
27	Consumer credit	0.560	0.377	0.233	0.505	0.565	0.317	0.819	0.901	0.630	0.436
28	Trade credit	11.987	8.237	18.407	22.549	8.513	14.747	21.489	25.255	22.967	7.943
29	Miscellaneous assets	3.721	3.456	2.190	2.959	4.091	6.034	5.181	8.292	9.609	9.131
30	Foreign dir. invest.*	3.029	2.690	0.843	2.161	3.459	3.577	1.528	3.745	7.665	6.081
31	Foreign currencies	0.104	0.084	0.532	-0.414	-0.375	1.387	1.784	2.568	-0.200	0.826
32	Insurance receivables	0.565	0.668	0.789	1.147	0.896	1.047	1.851	1.960	2.127	2.214
33	Equity in sponsored ags.	0.023	0.014	0.026	0.065	0.111	0.023	0.018	0.019	0.017	0.010
34	Net increase in liabilities	36.442	31.990	52.168	56.942	46.237	60.403	73.178	97.818	105.373	42.107
35	Net funds raised in mkts.	25.582	28.877	31.915	38.440	41.469	46.358	58.768	72.855	83.130	37.059
36	Net new equity issues	1.259	2.397	-0.159	3.406	5.694	11.435	10.922	7.883	4.097	9.908
37	Debt instruments	24.323	26.480	32.074	35.034	35.775	34.923	47.846	64.972	79.033	27.151
38	Tax-exempt bonds†	0.000	0.000	0.000	0.000	0.000	0.086	0.548	1.796	1.648	2.600
39	Corporate bonds*	10.224	14.658	12.893	11.975	19.756	18.807	12.187	9.159	19.670	27.204
40	Mortgages	4.546	3.959	6.173	5.398	7.169	11.311	17.782	18.524	14.189	10.095
41	Home mortgages	-0.161	0.015	0.254	-0.035	-0.163	0.742	0.537	-0.262	-0.330	0.716
42	Multi-family	0.725	0.803	1.033	1.469	2.086	2.904	3.733	3.086	2.149	0.569
43	Commercial	3.982	3.141	4.886	3.964	5.246	7.665	13.512	15.700	12.370	8.810
44	Bank loans Natl. Inc. Acc.	8.297	6.431	9.748	11.746	5.564	3.789	13.168	29.735	30.759	-12.883
45	Commercial paper	0.825	1.412	1.215	1.107	1.777	-0.886	0.721	1.414	4.312	-2.519
46	Acceptances	0.130	0.119	0.134	0.353	0.403	0.265	0.025	0.532	1.255	0.174
47	Finance company loans	-0.065	-0.290	1.747	4.338	0.813	1.325	3.174	3.464	5.671	2.274
48	U.S. government loans	0.366	0.191	0.164	0.117	0.293	0.226	0.241	0.348	1.529	0.206
49	Profit taxes payable	0.205	-4.727	2.861	-3.306	-3.706	1.991	-0.092	2.323	1.010	-3.214
50	Trade debt	10.568	7.582	17.072	20.976	7.444	12.229	14.122	19.985	18.488	5.825
51	Miscellaneous liabilities	0.087	0.258	0.320	0.832	1.030	-0.175	0.380	2.655	2.745	2.437
52	Discrepancy	8.327	3.865	8.108	5.205	9.022	13.917	16.444	16.148	13.101	14.499

(continued from pages 182 and 183)

					Memorandum items:						
Excess of capital expenditures											
53 Over gross internal funds	15.508	11.292	15.270	23.378	21.774	17.639	20.228	40.563	56.987	−7.615	53
54 Trade credit net of trade debt	1.419	0.655	1.335	1.573	1.069	2.518	7.367	5.270	4.479	2.118	54
55 Profits tax payments	30.484	32.342	31.757	36.101	30.156	27.594	33.341	37.535	41.245	42.832	55
Debt subtotals:‡											
56 Long-term debt	18.251	21.174	22.711	22.107	29.313	30.977	35.248	41.636	48.141	34.030	56
57 Short-term debt	6.072	5.306	9.363	12.927	6.462	3.946	12.598	23.337	30.892	−6.879	57
58 Total s-t liabilities	16.845	8.161	29.296	30.597	10.200	18.166	26.628	45.645	50.390	−4.268	58
Percent ratios:											
59 Effective tax rate	42.423	42.332	46.728	48.650	49.377	47.206	44.148	42.805	41.509	41.539	59
60 Capital outlays/internal funds	125.633	118.431	124.493	137.908	136.997	125.719	125.042	148.384	173.446	92.632	60
61 Cr. mkt. borrowing/cap. exp.	32.001	36.494	41.325	41.193	44.370	40.504	47.370	52.229	58.726	28.359	61
Cash flor and capital expenditures on book basis											
62 Cap. cons. allowance, Natl. Inc. Acc.	35.497	39.009	42.726	47.421	52.737	57.853	62.195	68.090	80.020	95.672	62
63 + Cap. cons adjustment	3.790	3.621	3.693	3.544	1.551	0.500	2.695	1.846	−2.957	−11.554	63
64 = Book depreciation	39.287	42.630	46.419	50.965	54.285	58.353	64.890	69.936	77.063	84.118	64
65 Inventory change, Natl. Inc. Acc.	13.205	8.800	6.865	8.327	3.396	3.618	7.561	13.317	11.993	−16.386	65
66 − Inv. val. adjustment	−2.098	−1.744	−3.447	−5.526	−5.067	−5.029	−6.597	−18.584	−39.782	−11.415	66
67 = Inventory chg., book	15.303	10.544	10.312	13.853	8.463	8.647	14.158	31.901	51.775	−4.971	67
68 Undistributed profits	21.863	18.806	17.551	14.447	8.068	13.404	20.577	28.822	29.476	26.791	68
69 + Foreign branch profits	1.446	1.574	1.821	1.783	1.564	1.854	1.906	3.661	10.833	3.861	69
70 + Book depreciation	39.287	42.630	46.419	50.965	54.288	58.353	64.890	69.936	77.063	84.118	70
71 = Gross internal funds, book	62.596	63.010	65.791	67.195	63.920	73.611	87.373	102.419	117.372	114.770	71
72 Gross investment, book	54.269	59.145	57.683	61.990	54.898	59.694	70.929	86.271	104.271	100.271	72
73 Capital expenditures	78.104	74.302	81.061	90.573	85.694	91.250	107.601	142.982	174.359	107.155	73
74 Fixed investment	62.801	63.758	69.419	76.676	76.902	81.866	92.531	107.913	116.094	110.803	74
75 Inventory chg., book	15.303	10.544	10.312	13.853	8.463	8.647	14.158	31.901	51.775	−4.971	75
76 Mineral rights	0.000	0.000	1.330	0.044	0.329	0.717	0.912	3.168	6.490	1.323	76

Source: Board of Governors of the Federal Reserve System, *Flow of Funds Accounts 1946–75*, December 1976, p. 18.

*Foreign investment is net of bond issued abroad, and bond issues outside the U.S. are excluded from sources of funds above.

†Industrial pollution control revenue bonds. Issued by state and local governments to finance private investment and secured in interest and principal by the industrial user of the funds.

‡Maturity split on debt is approximate: l-t is bonds, m-f & commercial mortgages, and 40% of bank loans. S-t debt is other credit market borrowing. Total s-t liabilities is s-t borrowing + tax liabilities + trade debt.

equal to retained earnings (undistributed profits) plus foreign branch profits and adjusted depreciation (adjusted capital consumption allowance) minus inventory valuation adjustment. In 1975, this amounted to (in billions) $27 + 4 + 84 − 11 = $103 billion (rounding accounts for the difference of $1 billion).

External financing (shown in the table as net increase in liabilities) involves money and capital market funds. These sources include new equity and preferred stock financing, debt instruments, trade debt, and miscellaneous liabilities, minus profit taxes payable. Debt instruments include bonds, mortgages, bank loans, and other short-term debts of various types. In 1975, external financing amounted to the following sum (in billions):

Net funds raised in markets	$37
Profit taxes payable	−3
Trade debt	6
Miscellaneous liabilities	2
Total external financing	$42 billion

Thus total financing available in 1975 was $145 billion, or the sum of $103 billion from internal sources and $42 billion from external sources.[1]

Uses of Funds

We are concerned here with the use of funds in order to explain why firms demand loanable funds. Gross business firm outlays for assets can be divided into two major parts—financial investment and capital expenditures, or acquisition of real assets.

The real earning power of a business firm is in its capital budget, i.e., its real assets. It is new equipment, new products, more efficient computers, modern plants, etc., that provide firms with the means to enhance returns for their stockholders. As can be seen from Table 7–2, the business sector spent $96 billion on capital expenditures (line 11) in 1975, consisting of fixed investment (line 12) and inventory changes (line 16).[2] It just happens that the change in inventories for that year was a negative $16 billion, so that capital expenditures approximated $96 billion, even though fixed investment amounted to about $111 billion. It is interesting to note

---

[1]This $145 billion must be adjusted downward by the discrepancy (shown as line 52 of Table 7–2) of $14 billion to equal the total uses of funds in 1975.

[2]Mineral rights from the U.S. government, a very minor factor, are ignored here.

that 1975 was the only year listed in which the investment in inventory was negative; the business sector was liquidating rather than accumulating inventories that year.

The net financial investment in 1975 amounted to about −$7 billion. As Table 7–2 shows, this represents the difference between the net acquisition of financial assets ($35 billion) and the net increase in liabilities ($42 billion) referred to earlier.

Each of the two major components of gross business firm outlays for assets will be discussed in detail, beginning with the latter.

Net Financial Investment

Net financial investment has been negative for every year shown in Table 7–2. Business firms increase their financial liabilities more than their financial assets because they are ultimately trying to finance real asset acquisitions; i.e., they are investing in real assets, and they need funds to finance these assets. The major liability items—funds raised in markets, taxes payable, trade debt, and miscellaneous liabilities—were considered above. However, it is worthwhile to consider the acquisition of financial assets by firms. Why do they invest in such assets, if their primary function is investment in real assets?

Business firms must maintain a certain percentage of their total assets in the form of current assets—cash, marketable securities, and accounts receivable. These are held as a part of doing business; they must be financed, and this gives rise to a need for loanable funds as part of the total financing required by business firms.

All firms need cash to carry on their operations. Cash, however, has an opportunity cost associated with it, since idle cash earns no return. Firms try to optimize their cash holdings because of this opportunity cost. They hold marketable securities as a substitute for cash, because these securities provide liquidity while they earn a return. As Table 7–2 shows, business firms hold small amounts in demand and time deposits and a considerable amount in U.S. government securities, primarily Treasury bills.

Most firms generate accounts receivables in the ordinary course of business, since they typically sell on credit. Thus trade credit (line 28) is a significant financial asset which firms have to finance. The new amount acquired each year can fluctuate sharply; it decreased greatly in 1975 in relation to the preceding four years.

Miscellaneous assets, consisting primarily of foreign direct investment, constitute the remainder of financial assets acquired by business firms.

The prevailing belief in financial theory is that earning assets are probably best financed by a combination of permanent and short-term sources of capital. Although all firms must maintain some level of cash and accounts receivable to carry on business, the optimum amount varies from firm to firm. On average, such current assets constitute a very substantial percentage of total assets. Financial assets that are permanently needed by a firm should probably be financed by permanent liabilities and net worth to insure that they will always be financed. Short-term financing is typically less costly than permanent financing, but it is more risky, because it may not be renewable.[3] Financial needs that fluctuate within a year—for example, as inventory builds to a peak in a particular season—should be financed with short-term sources because of their cheaper cost and their greater flexibility.

In summary, corporate businesses require both permanent financing, in the form of stock and bond sales, and temporary financing, in the form of, say, bank loans and the sale of commercial paper (a form of short-term IOU) to finance their ongoing operations. This gives rise to part of their total demand for loanable funds. In 1975, total demand for loanable funds from external sources amounted to $42 billion, of which $37 billion was in the form of net funds raised in markets (debt or equity). An unknown part of this $37 billion went to finance permanent increases in financial assets.[4] The remaining portion of the $42 billion came from trade credit, miscellaneous liabilities, and finance-company loans.

Capital Expenditures

The nonfinancial corporate business sector has as its primary function the buying, holding, operating, and disposing of real assets. Because real assets, not financial assets, contribute to the creation of additional wealth, this function is obviously important for society. How do these firms decide to invest, and how do they choose projects in which to invest?

The Time Value of Money. To understand investment decisions, it is necessary first to understand the *time value of money.* The simple proposition that always applies in financial decisions is that a dollar received today is more valuable than a dollar received at some future time. The reason for this is that money received today can be invested at compound interest to earn additional future returns. Thus, $1,000 can earn, say, 5 percent in a bank; at the end of one year, the owner would have $1050. Obviously, this is more advantageous than receiving the same $1,000 one year from now, other things equal. To account for the differences in the timing of cash receipts, future dollars must be discounted back to their

---

[3]Or, if it is renewable, the cost may rise sharply, as a reflection of conditions, and exceed the cost of long-term financing.

[4]Most of this $37 billion ($27 billion, to be exact) was in the form of debt instruments, the composition of which is given on lines 38–48 of Table 7–2. Interestingly, bank loans were reduced by about $13 billion during 1975, as was commercial paper (by about $2½ billion).

value in the present (often called *time period zero*). The farther out in time that dollars are to be received, the less valuable they are today.

Equation 7–1 expresses the present value of a dollar to be received in the future:

$$PV = FV \left[\frac{1}{(1+r)^n} \right] = \left[\frac{FV}{(1+r)^n} \right] \qquad (7\text{--}1)$$

where PV is the present value, FV is the future value, r is the rate at which future dollars are to be discounted, and n is the number of periods involved.

For example, if $1,000 is to be received two years from now, and if the opportunity cost of money is 8 percent, the present value is

$$PV = \$1000 \left[\frac{1}{(1+0.08)^2} \right] \text{ since } r = 0.08 \text{ and } n = 2$$

$$= \$1000 \left[\frac{1}{1.1664} \right]$$

$$= \$857.34$$

If the $1,000 were to be received three years from now rather than two, its present value would be less because of the additional time involved, that is,

$$PV = \$1000 \left[\frac{1}{(1+0.08)^3} \right]$$

$$= \$1000 \left[\frac{1}{1.2597} \right]$$

$$= \$793.84$$

As the interest rate or opportunity cost increases, the present value decreases. This is because the higher the interest rate, the higher the terminal value at any point in the future if the funds were available today to be invested. In a similar manner, the longer the time period, the smaller the present value. The value of $1,000 to be received 5 years from now is greater than that of $1,000 to be received 6 years from now, at any positive interest rate. It does not take a large number of years to reduce the present value of future dollars to a very small amount. For example, if the opportunity cost is 17 percent, a dollar to be received 25 years from now is worth less than two cents today.

There are standard tables available for the computation of present values, so that equation 7–1 need not be used. These tables show the present value factors for various combinations of time periods and interest rates. These factors can be multiplied by whatever dollar amount is being considered to obtain its present value.

Cash Flow Patterns. Investment projects consist of outflows (typically at time period zero, although future outflows can occur) and one or more inflows. To evaluate any proposed investment project, the exact sequence of flows must be identified. For example, assume that XYZ Corporation can invest in a widget machine today by purchasing the machine for $5,000. Installation costs $300. Assume also that the machine will generate profits after tax plus depreciation (called *cash flow*) of $2,000 a year for four years and that the widget machine can be sold for scrap for $1,000 at the end of the four-year period. The pattern of cash flows will be as follows:

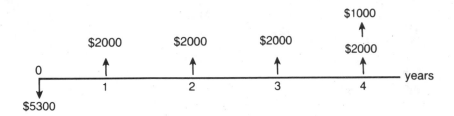

Knowing the complete sequence of cash flows, XYZ could decide whether this project is profitable and worth undertaking. Note that all cash flows relevant to the investment project must be identified and designated by their timing.

The investment decision really amounts to an assessment of the inflows and the outflows—on the basis of present values. The four annual receipts of $2,000 each and the $1,000 receipt for the scrap are not worth $9,000 today because of the time value of money. Each of the receipts is worth less than its stated amount, by a factor that depends on the rate used to discount it. As the discount rate increases, the total value of these payments declines. As long as the discounted value of the receipts exceeds the discounted cost (typically, the total amount at time period zero, which needs no discounting), the investment is favorable and should be undertaken.

Criteria for Investment Decisions. Two criteria, often used by business firms to make investment decisions, involve matching the discounted benefits with the discounted cost. It should be noted that, although other criteria are still used to make such decisions, any that do not take account of the time value of money are inappropriate and can easily lead to incorrect or suboptimal decisions. For example, one criterion is based on the *payback period,* which is the number of years it will take to recover the outlays from a project. A standard (in years) is initially set; if the calculated payback is less than the standard, the project is accepted; if not, it is rejected. Such a procedure is inadequate, not only because it ignores the time value of money, but also because it ignores cash flows occurring beyond the payback period.

A capital asset entitles the buyer to a stream of future benefits. The rate of return on such an investment is sometimes called the *internal rate of return (IRR)*, a concept explained in more detail below. Keynes referred to this as the *marginal efficiency of capital (MEC)*. As in our initial example of $1,000 deposited at 5 percent interest for one year, if investment opportunities of similar nature yield 5 percent, $1,000 today is exactly equivalent to the receipt of $1,050 one year from today. The MEC is the discount rate at which the present value of receipts expected in the future is equal to the present cost.

In particular, the marginal efficiency of capital, or the internal rate of return, is the discount rate k such that

$$C_0 = \frac{R_1}{(1 + k)} + \frac{R_2}{(1 + k)^2} + \frac{R_3}{(1 + k)^3} + \cdots + \frac{R_n}{(1 + k)^n} \qquad \textbf{(7–2)}$$

where C_0 is the cost of the project today and R is the return from the project in a given year. With estimates of C_0 and of the expected receipts $R_1, R_2, \ldots R_n$, the value of k can be found by trial and error. The analyst refers to the present value table and, by repetitive testing, determines the value of k at which the right-hand side of the equation is equal to the left-hand side. The values of R can vary or can be identical. If they vary, such that $R_1 \neq R_2$, etc., the only solution is a trial-and-error procedure. If R is the same for each year, however, the solution is much simpler.[5]

The internal rate of return has intuitive appeal, because it is stated as a percentage and can be compared to the cost of funds for a firm undertaking investment projects. If the internal rate of return exceeds the cost of funds, the project is acceptable; if it is less, the project is unacceptable. One problem with the internal rate of return is that there can be more than one rate that will equate the present value of the inflows with the present value of the outflows. Such multiple rates of return can occur if there are net outflows in more than one period and if the outflows are separated by inflows.

An alternative procedure that firms can use involves the *net present value (NPV)*, which is the sum of the discounted benefits less the discounted costs, expressed in dollars. The discount rate used to calculate the NPV is the cost of capital to the firm. Mathematically,

---

[5]In the latter case, C_0 is divided by the constant R, and this factor is looked for as a present value in an annuity table (an *annuity* is a stream of payments of specified and equal size for a stated number of periods). Since the factors in the table represent the intersection of years and rates, one can look across the row of years until the factor is found, which indicates the value of k that will solve the equation.

In the particularly simple case of a perpetual stream in which R is the same for each year, equation $C \cdot k = R$ allows any variable (C, k, or R) to be solved for if the other two are known.

$$NPV = \frac{R_1}{(1 + k)} + \frac{R_2}{(1 + k)^2} + \frac{R_3}{(1 + k)^3} + \cdots + \frac{R_n}{(1 + k)^n} - C_0$$

If a firm uses this method, it will accept all projects with a positive net present value, because undertaking any projects on which the discounted benefits exceed the discounted costs adds to the firm's worth. Projects with a negative NPV are, of course, unacceptable.

Fixed Investment Decisions. To enhance stockholder wealth, firms must invest in profitable projects. Those that enhance a firm's profitability or make the value of a share worth more than it was previously should be undertaken, in line with the assumed objective of maximizing stockholder wealth. Indeed, the very survival of a firm, much less its continuing attractiveness, depends upon its efforts to find, develop, and select profitable investment opportunities.

As a starting point, assume that a firm has unlimited access to loanable funds and that the cost of these funds is constant. A firm seeking to invest funds optimally should rank projects by a proper criterion, such as one of those discussed above. The criterion should reflect the discounted benefits from the project in relation to its discounted cost.

If the internal rate of return method is used, firms rank projects in descending order of IRR and accept all projects for which the IRR exceeds the cost of funds. As the firm invests an increasing amount of funds, it accepts projects with lower and lower IRRs until it reaches the constant cost of funds, as shown by the line in Figure 7–1.

FIGURE 7–1. Ranking Projects by IRR with a Constant Cost of Funds

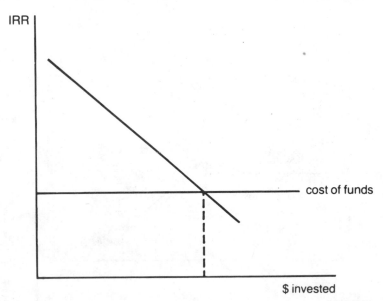

It is unrealistic, however, to assume a constant cost of funds. Creditors demand higher returns as firms raise more and more funds. As a firm increases the amount of debt financing it uses, it raises the probability that it will fail to meet its debt obligations, with bankruptcy as a possible result. Lenders require a higher yield to compensate for such an increase in risk. Also, owners of equity shares become increasingly averse to the additional risk and demand higher returns on equity funds. The result is a rising cost of funds curve, like the one depicted in Figure 7–2.

The firm will still accept all projects with IRRs in excess of the cost of funds, but the rising curve in Figure 7–2 gives a different cutoff point than the one given by the constant cost line in Figure 7–1.

In terms of aggregate business investment, the preceding discussion can be related to the Keynesian aggregate demand schedule that slopes downward from left to right. Such a schedule is shown in Figure 7–3. This schedule indicates the rate of return that can be expected during any period on new investment, given the level of investment expenditure. In effect, it is a demand curve. If the cost of funds (c) is just equal to the internal rate of return (k), investment in the aggregate should be I_o. If k exceeds c, there is an incentive for investment to be increased. If the two rates are equal, there is no further incentive to invest. If returns decline below the cost of capital, there is an incentive to contract investment expenditures until equality between the two rates is again achieved.

FIGURE 7–2. Ranking Projects by IRR with a Rising Cost of Funds Curve

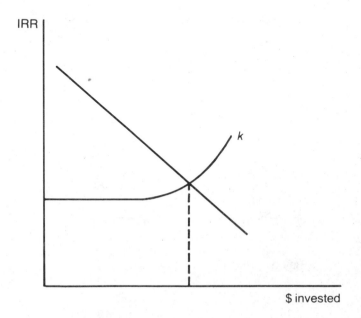

FIGURE 7–3. Aggregate Investment Demand.

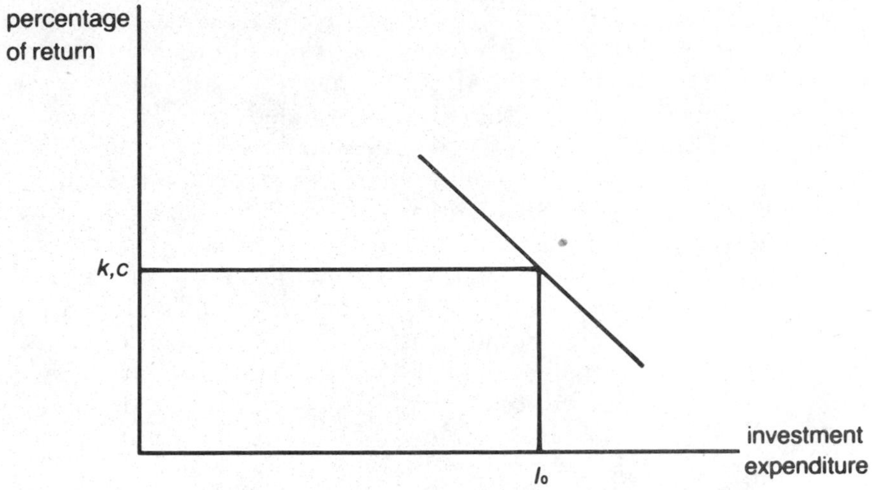

Inventory Change Decisions. Besides fixed investment, the other part of capital expenditures is change in inventories. As we can see from Table 7–2, this change was negative in 1975, although it was positive in every other year back to 1966, and usually it has been substantial. Thus corporate businesses typically demand loanable funds to finance an increase in inventories.

As mentioned previously, some amount of current assets—of which inventory is one—must be maintained continuously as a part of the ongoing nature of a business firm. Furthermore, assets such as inventory build up during a part of the year, and this increase must also be financed. Firms demand both permanent funds and temporary funds to finance the total inventory held; various short-term liabilities, such as bank loans, are used to finance temporary increases.

Inventory fluctuations can be quite sharp from year to year. The stage of the business cycle is a dominating factor; other factors include expectations about the future, fear of shortages, fear of strikes, etc. Although inventories generally fluctuate in a stable relation to sales, deviations from this relationship do occur in some cases.

HOUSEHOLD DEMAND

Although households are the principal saving surplus sector in the economy and the major source of loanable funds, they simultaneously borrow significant amounts of loanable funds. It is essential to recognize household demand as an important part of the total demand for loanable funds.

Table 7–3 shows the year-total flows for credit market instruments issued by the household sector for the years 1966 through 1975. Although demands for loanable funds fluctuate widely, the trend has been upward over this period. The small amount of funds raised in 1970 reflects the credit crunch that existed then. Mortgage money, for example, was scarce and very expensive. The total more than doubled by 1972 as economic conditions improved, but 1974 was a recession period, and the total obtained in that year was down considerably from 1972 and 1973. (Both 1976 and 1977 showed sharp increases over 1975, and 1978 showed a moderate increase—with a total flow of $161 billion).

It can be readily seen from the table that home mortgages (line 40) constitute the bulk of credit market funds raised by the household sector. Installment consumer credit (line 42) is the second largest use of funds, but it was only one-sixth the size of mortgage funds in 1975. Miscellaneous loans (line 45), which constitute the third largest category, are relatively quite small. Clearly, the household demand for loanable funds in any one year is primarily a demand for mortgage funds.

The Mortgage Market

Mortgages are simply claims on real assets—namely, on real estate. They are used to finance various types of real estate—houses, commercial structures, multi-family residences, and farms; therefore, the total demand for mortgage funds comes from several groups. Attention here is focused on residential construction, however.

Mortgages are by definition long-term instruments, since maturities are usually long (up to 40 years). Mortgages today are based on the amortization principal whereby the borrower pays a monthly lump sum that usually includes principal repayment, interest, property taxes, and insurance. This periodic repayment (in the case of residential mortgages) provides a continuous inflow for the lender and gradually builds an equity for the borrower.

Because of modern features such as amortization, long maturity, low downpayment, etc., mortgages as a method of financing have grown rapidly; in fact, they have shown the largest expansion of all debt instruments since World War II. The net change in all mortgages averaged about $97 billion per year for the five years 1974 through 1978; home mortgages averaged about $68 billion per year. Total mortgages outstanding at year-end 1978 amounted to $1169 billion, an enormous amount indeed in comparison to the amount for year-end 1946—$42 billion. (Comparable home mortgage figures are $758 and $23 billion respectively.)

Mortgage Characteristics. Mortgages have some characteristics that differentiate them from virtually all other financial claims. In the first place, collateral is in the form of claims on specific real assets—land and buildings. Second, mortgage debt is quite varied in nature. There is no uniform mortgage dollar amount, and the collateral varies in each case, since each piece of real estate is different. This means that mortgages cannot be traded as easily as, say, corporate bonds. Secondary markets for mortgages have traditionally not been well developed.

Demand for Household Mortgage Credit. As noted, home mortgages are the largest single category of mortgages. Increasing population, rising incomes, and the American dream of home ownership have all contributed to the sharp increase in home construction since World War II. Housing starts and the availability and cost of mortgage funds are clearly related; for example, housing starts declined sharply in 1974 because of very high interest rates and a scarcity of mortgage funds. Savings and loan associations and mutual savings banks, the principal suppliers of mortgage funds, have been quite vulnerable to sharp swings in saving flows. In some years, large amounts of savings have been channeled to these institutions, because the rates they pay on deposits are attractive in relation to alternatives. In other years, the rates paid on savings, which are regulated, have not been competitive with alternative investment opportunities. Treasury bills, for example, reflect current market forces and yield the going rate, whatever it may be. *Disintermediation* is the process by which individuals withdraw funds from financial institutions and invest them directly in alternatives with higher yields. One result is a lack of mortgage funds, so that the amounts that are available carry a higher interest rate. Disintermediation occurred during the credit crunches of 1966, 1969, and 1973, as the difference between market rates and rates on time deposits widened.

Other factors also affect the demand for mortgage credit. Obviously, land and building costs are a significant influence on individual decisions to purchase. In the 1970s, average house prices rose sharply. The effects of this rise are not clear-cut. On the one hand, some families may be discouraged from trying to purchase a house because of the sharp increase in price, and many may simply be priced out because they cannot raise enough for the down payment or cannot qualify with the lender for the now higher monthly payments. On the other hand, rising prices may encourage families to purchase, whatever the sacrifice, in expectation of even higher prices in the future. Thus houses have come to be viewed by many as hedges against inflation. After all, land suitable for building is limited in many localities and cannot readily be increased. Building codes have become much stricter, so that, in some areas (California is a good example), it may take years for builders to secure all the approvals needed for a new housing development.

Lenders' requirements for down payments and loan-to-value ratios also affect demand. Conventional loans made by financial institutions may require higher down payments (have lower loan-to-value ratios) than loans

TABLE 7–3. Credit Market Instruments, Household Sector, Year-Total Flows, 1966–75 (in billions of dollars)

	1966	1967	1968	1969	1970	1971	1972	1973	1974	1975	
1 Personal income	584.873	626.624	685.218	745.825	801.270	859.091	942.535	1052.438	1153.292	1249.671	1
2 − Personal taxes + nontaxes	74.477	82.078	97.082	115.400	115.336	116.281	141.237	150.777	170.367	168.816	2
3 = Disposable personal income	510.396	544.546	588.136	630.425	685.934	742.810	801.298	901.661	982.925	1080.855	3
4 − Personal outlays	477.398	503.679	550.067	595.318	635.361	685.475	751.929	831.339	910.717	996.893	4
5 = Personal saving, NIA basis	32.998	40.867	38.069	35.107	50.573	57.335	49.369	70.322	72.206	83.962	5
6 + Credits from govt. insurance	5.586	5.488	6.142	7.073	8.880	9.468	11.553	11.683	12.504	14.669	6
7 + Capital gains dividends	1.318	1.690	2.458	2.536	0.923	0.776	1.420	0.944	0.485	0.219	7
8 + Net durables in consumption	12.914	10.212	14.368	13.657	7.917	13.901	21.507	25.408	11.081	8.068	8
9 = Net saving	52.816	58.257	61.037	58.373	68.293	81.480	83.849	108.357	96.278	106.918	9
10 + Capital consumption	65.043	70.305	77.913	85.956	92.178	99.440	107.238	118.502	133.582	149.595	10
11 = Gross saving	117.859	128.562	138.950	144.329	160.471	180.920	191.087	226.859	229.860	256.513	11
12 Gross investment	127.952	134.528	145.588	143.929	167.001	191.064	209.155	239.812	248.936	280.857	12
13 Capital expend. — net of sales	92.633	94.885	108.588	116.033	114.957	134.805	157.408	173.913	169.618	179.212	13
14 Residential construction	20.809	21.184	24.369	25.860	25.201	32.584	40.626	44.993	42.745	42.410	14
15 Consumer durable goods	67.663	69.646	79.995	85.478	84.931	97.087	111.241	123.714	121.634	131.726	15
16 Nonprofit plant & equip.	4.161	4.055	4.224	4.695	4.825	5.134	5.541	5.206	5.239	5.076	16
17 Net financial investment	35.319	39.643	37.000	27.896	52.044	56.259	51.747	65.899	79.318	101.645	17
18 Net acq. of financial assets	59.194	66.376	72.859	59.207	76.524	101.730	122.152	136.059	123.969	154.775	18
19 Dep. & cr. mkt. instr*	38.604	48.407	54.176	42.830	51.541	76.019	97.750	111.803	98.556	118.851	19
20 Demand dep. & currency	2.370	9.750	10.883	2.428	8.785	9.004	14.563	12.495	4.980	6.734	20
21 Time & saving accounts	19.096	35.300	31.088	9.094	43.585	67.764	70.954	67.858	57.879	84.922	21
22 at commercial banks	11.919	18.687	18.125	0.726	26.955	28.142	25.573	39.471	35.497	25.749	22
23 at savings inst.	7.177	16.613	12.963	8.368	16.630	39.622	45.381	28.387	22.382	59.173	23

24	Credit mkt. instruments	17.138	3.357	12.205	31.308	-0.829	-0.749	12.233	31.450	35.697	27.195	24
25	U.S. govt. securities	7.583	1.647	6.280	10.777	-8.151	-10.469	-0.499	16.322	7.160	5.696	25
26	St. & loc. obligations	3.423	-2.218	-0.672	9.136	-0.785	-0.264	2.164	7.223	11.167	8.658	26
27	Corporate & fgn. bonds	1.356	4.040	4.215	5.364	9.532	8.316	4.154	0.944	5.258	10.396	27
28	Mortgages	2.040	2.055	2.841	2.222	1.771	1.325	6.413	3.575	4.223	4.370	28
29	Open-market paper	2.736	-2.167	-0.459	3.809	-3.196	0.343	0.001	3.386	5.510	-3.191	29
30	Money market fund shrs.	0.000	0.000	0.000	0.000	0.000	0.000	0.000	0.000	2.379	1.266	30
31	Investment company shares	3.722	3.036	5.907	4.929	2.770	1.287	-0.529	-1.211	-0.540	0.790	31
32	Other corporate equities	-4.408	-7.261	-12.390	-9.379	-3.539	-4.989	-3.985	-5.668	-0.689	-2.554	32
33	Life insurance reserves	4.694	5.063	4.621	4.978	5.242	6.172	6.560	7.277	6.425	7.618	33
34	Pension fund reserves	14.478	13.970	15.590	16.274	19.185	21.127	22.613	25.570	29.570	36.088	34
35	Net inv. in noncorp. bus.	0.691	-0.517	1.062	-0.725	-0.392	-0.722	-3.061	-4.361	-11.056	-9.850	35
36	Security credit	0.197	2.213	2.096	-1.818	-0.867	0.532	0.136	-0.156	-0.975	0.094	36
37	Miscellaneous assets	1.216	1.465	1.797	2.118	2.584	2.304	2.668	2.803	2.678	3.738	37
38	Net increase in liabilities	23.875	26.733	35.859	31.311	24.480	45.471	70.405	70.160	44.651	53.130	38
39	Credit market instruments	23.313	22.354	32.097	33.838	25.330	42.142	64.788	73.499	45.161	49.676	39
40	Home mortgages	13.350	13.395	16.766	18.197	14.705	27.142	41.477	46.958	35.305	39.359	40
41	Other mortgages	1.257	1.194	1.135	1.276	1.258	1.310	1.419	1.442	1.362	1.091	41
42	Installment cons. credit	5.352	3.183	8.317	9.360	4.793	9.297	15.561	19.678	8.950	6.853	42
43	Other consumer credit	1.004	1.361	1.670	1.016	1.058	2.346	3.046	2.039	0.826	1.683	43
44	Bank loans N.E.C.	0.307	1.900	2.492	1.005	0.915	0.674	1.950	0.951	-4.492	-1.469	44
45	Other loans	2.043	1.321	1.717	2.984	2.601	1.373	1.335	2.431	3.210	2.159	45
46	Security credit	-0.073	3.684	2.918	-3.402	-1.780	2.666	4.469	-4.346	-1.802	2.244	46
47	Trade debt	0.279	0.407	0.489	0.489	0.500	0.345	0.608	0.607	0.582	0.552	47
48	Miscellaneous	0.356	0.288	0.355	0.386	0.430	0.318	0.540	0.400	0.710	0.658	48
49	Discrepancy	-10.093	-5.966	-6.638	0.400	-6.530	-10.144	-18.068	-12.953	-19.076	-24.344	49

(continued from pages 196 and 197)

MEMORANDA:

Net physical investments

(A) Residential construction

Line												
50	Expenditures	20.809	21.184	24.369	25.860	25.201	32.584	40.626	44.993	42.745	42.410	50
51	Mobile homes	1.056	1.180	1.674	2.308	2.469	3.274	4.049	4.391	3.181	2.415	51
52	Other	19.753	20.004	22.695	23.552	22.732	29.310	36.577	40.602	39.564	39.995	52
53	– Capital consumption	8.790	9.206	10.478	12.056	12.833	13.685	14.717	17.068	19.534	22.001	53
54	– Home mortgages	13.350	13.395	16.766	18.197	14.705	27.142	41.477	46.958	35.305	39.359	54
55	= Excess net investment	-1.331	-1.417	-2.875	-4.393	-2.337	-8.243	-15.568	-19.033	-12.094	-18.950	55

(B) consumer durables

Line												
56	Expenditures	67.663	69.646	79.995	85.478	84.931	97.087	111.241	123.714	121.634	131.726	56
57	Capital consumption	54.749	59.434	65.627	71.821	77.014	83.186	89.734	98.306	110.553	123.658	57
58	Net investment	12.914	10.212	14.368	13.657	7.917	13.901	21.507	25.408	11.081	8.068	58
59	– Consumer credit	6.356	4.544	9.987	10.376	5.851	11.643	18.607	21.717	9.776	8.536	59
60	= Excess net investment	6.558	5.668	4.381	3.281	2.066	2.258	2.900	3.691	1.305	-0.468	60

(C) Nonprofit plant + equip.

Line												
61	Expenditures	4.161	4.055	4.224	4.695	4.825	5.134	5.541	5.206	5.239	5.076	61
62	– Capital consumption	1.504	1.665	1.808	2.079	2.331	2.569	2.787	3.128	3.495	3.936	62
63	– Nonprofit mortgages	1.257	1.194	1.135	1.276	1.258	1.310	1.419	1.442	1.362	1.091	63
64	= Excess net investment	1.400	1.196	1.281	1.340	1.236	1.255	1.335	0.636	0.382	0.049	64

Per cent ratios:

Line												
65	Effective tax rate	12.733	13.098	14.168	15.472	14.394	13.535	14.984	14.326	14.772	13.508	65
66	Saving rate. NIA basis	6.465	7.504	6.472	5.568	7.372	7.718	6.161	7.799	7.346	7.768	66

Per cent of disposable income adj. †:

Line												
67	Gross saving	22.783	23.301	23.285	22.550	23.064	24.024	23.467	24.812	23.080	23.409	67
68	Capital expenditures	17.907	17.197	18.196	18.129	16.523	17.901	19.331	19.021	17.031	16.355	68
69	Acquisition of finan. assets	11.442	12.030	12.209	9.250	10.998	13.508	15.001	14.881	12.447	14.125	69
70	Net increase in liabilities	4.615	4.845	6.009	4.892	3.518	6.038	8.646	7.673	4.483	4.848	70
71	Credit market borrowing	4.506	4.051	5.378	5.286	3.640	5.596	7.956	8.038	4.534	4.533	71
72	Disposable income adj.†	517.300	551.724	596.736	640.034	695.737	753.054	814.271	914.288	995.914	1095.743	72

Source: Board of Governors of the Federal Reserve System, *Flow of Funds Accounts 1946–75*, December 1976, p. 12.

Note: Includes personal trusts and nonprofit organizations.

*Excludes corporate equities.

†Disposable income adjustment (line 72) = NIA disposable income + govt. insurance credits + capital gains dividends.

guaranteed by the Federal Housing Administration (FHA) or the Veterans' Administration (VA). Loans backed by these two organizations are, in effect, guaranteed by the government.[6] The lenders who make such guaranteed loans are protected against loss of principal and interest in the event of foreclosure. Conventional loans involve less paperwork and typically yield higher returns.

Mortgage Money Flows. Mortgage funds flow to various geographical areas, depending upon demand. For example, in the past, California savings and loan associations were very aggressive in pursuing savings deposits from individuals all over the United States. Institutions in areas of surplus funds send funds to deficit areas where yields are high.

Government agencies augment the mortgage market by purchases and sales as needed. For example, the Federal National Mortgage Association (FNMA) provides a marketplace for the trading of existing mortgages. If loan demand is high and money is scarce, FNMA purchases mortgages. It sells on balance if mortgage money is more plentiful. The Government National Mortgage Association is another organization designed to operate in the mortgage market and to facilitate mortgage financing. Finally, the Federal Home Loan Mortgage Corporation was established in 1970 to buy and sell mortgages. All of these government agencies contribute to the flow of mortgage funds, since they obtain funds themselves and purchase mortgages. If an agency purchases existing mortgages from a financial institution, the latter gains additional funds with which to purchase new mortgages.

Installment Consumer Credit

Installment consumer credit is the second largest source of household demand for loanable funds. This type of demand has increased substantially in the postwar period. For example, in 1951, only $591 million was borrowed in this form; in 1975, the figure was almost $7 billion. In 1976, 1977, and 1978 installment consumer credit leaped dramatically to $21 billion, $31 billion, and $45 billion respectively.

Households demand installment credit primarily to finance automobiles, appliances, and other consumer durables. Since these real assets are expected to provide useful services for a period of years, households reasonably expect to pay for them over similar periods. Lending institutions, responding to this demand, have developed financing plans that are desirable to households. New institutions have developed over the years to service this demand and have grown rapidly as a result of their ability to meet it. Credit unions are a good example of an institution developed to

---

[6]Technically, FHA loans are insured and VA loans are guaranteed.

meet this need. Lenders have also changed their installment financing plans to reflect new conditions. For example, the higher cost of new automobiles in the 1970s has resulted in repayment periods beyond the traditional maximum of 36 months, to 42 months or even 48 months.

GOVERNMENT DEMAND

The total government demand for loanable funds is a very significant part of the overall demand. In 1975, for example, the total funds raised in the credit markets by the government sector amounted to approximately $100 billion—$85 billion by the federal government and $15 billion by state and local governments. Perhaps as important as the size of the demand is the wide fluctuation in yearly demand. Thus, in 1974, only $31 billion was raised in the credit markets by the government sector, while in 1978 $93 billion was raised. Such fluctuations are important because of their potential impact on interest rates and on the allocation of loanable funds. Interest rates, of course, reflect the joint impact of the demand for and the supply of loanable funds: other things equal, smaller (or greater) demands are associated with lower (or higher) interest rates. An increase in government use of loanable funds leaves a smaller supply for nongovernmental uses, so that interest rates rise to ration the available funds among competing uses. Because the federal government differs from state and local governments in many important respects, we will consider them separately.

Federal Demand

The federal government borrows enough each year to cover any deficit and to maintain a satisfactory cash balance. Just as any other sector in the economy, the federal government has revenues (from taxes) and expenditures. The latter are determined by Congress on the basis of a budget prepared by the executive branch. Until the mid-1970s, there was no coordination between the spending plans designed by Congress and the amount of funds available to be spent in any one year. After the total appropriation had been approved, the government had to determine the total spending designated, assess revenues for that year, and finance any deficit. Even now, with Congress more attuned to thinking about both revenues and expenditures so that the budget process is on a better financial planning basis, deficits still occur. When they do, the government becomes a demander of loanable funds.

Federal government borrowing is assumed to be interest-inelastic; that is, the government will borrow the amount needed in any one year, whatever the going interest rate. The position taken is simply that any shortage between receipts and spending plans must be met at the time of occurrence. The federal government feels that it can service the new debt, because it always has the power to increase taxes to raise additional revenues. Also, as we know, the federal government can create money.

The record shows that, in fact, the government as a borrower has paid the going rate for funds. For example, an issue of six-month treasury bills in 1974 was sold to yield slightly over 9 percent (on an annual basis).

A Look at Deficits. A deficit financed by government borrowing results in an increased demand by the government for credit. Since the total demand for credit is composed of private demand plus government demand, a deficit results in an increase in the total demand for credit.

It is important to determine if the deficit results from active or passive budget factors.[7] *Active factors* are discretionary changes in spending and taxes caused by executive or congressional actions such as attempts to stimulate the economy through tax reduction or through increases in spending. Thus changes in receipts and spending that result from current congressional legislation and executive action, and which are generally designed to influence national economic goals of full employment, price stability, and economic growth, are active factors in the federal budget. *Passive (nondiscretionary,* or *automatic) factors* are changes in expenditures or receipts that occur automatically by previous legislation, and which reflect changes in the level of economic activity. For example, unemployment benefits respond automatically to changes in economic activity. As another example, tax receipts depend on levels of income, profits, and spending. In both cases, there is a feedback of economic activity into the budget. The increase in the total demand for credit is larger if the deficit is associated with active rather than passive factors. Passive factors are associated with a decline in economic activity, with which there is typically a decline in the private demand for credit.

Interest rates usually rise as the deficit-induced total demand for credit rises (whether the deficit is due to active or passive factors). However, the supply of credit also rises, as lenders are induced to supply more of it at the higher rates. Since government borrowing is interest-inelastic, the presumed effect of higher interest rates is on the private sector. The private sector may wish to borrow less at the higher rate. Whether, in fact, government borrowing crowds out private borrowing is a question to be considered below. First, however, it is necessary to consider the actual figures on government financing for the last few years.

Some Figures on Government Financing. Table 7–4 shows the fiscal year surpluses and deficits for the period 1965 through 1976. There were record deficits in 1975 and 1976, which easily surpassed the previous record for this period, set in 1968 (−$25.2 billion).

Table 7–5 shows the funds raised by the government sector and the

---

[7]See R. W. Lang, "The 1965–76 Federal Deficits and the Credit Market," *Review—Federal Reserve Bank of St. Louis* 59 (January 1977): 6–19.

TABLE 7–4. Fiscal Year Surpluses and Deficits, 1965–76

Fiscal Year	Surplus (+) or Deficit (−) (In Billions of Dollars)
1965	− 1.6
1966	− 3.8
1967	− 8.7
1968	−25.2
1969	+ 3.2
1970	− 2.8
1971	−23.0
1972	−23.2
1973	−14.3
1974	− 3.5
1975	−43.6
1976	−65.6

Source: R. W. Lang, "The 1965–76 Federal Deficits and the Credit Market, "*Review — Federal Reserve Bank of St. Louis* 59 (January 1977), p. 9.

nonfinancial sectors for the period 1965 through 1976. The year-to-year changes are quite dramatic. For example, the government raised $50.7 billion in 1975, in comparison to $3.3 billion in 1974. The nonfinancial sectors raised $55.5 billion less in 1975 than in 1974—the largest year-to-year decrease since World War II.

One of the principal buyers of federal debt is the Federal Reserve. The percentage held rose fairly steadily, from 12 percent in 1962 to about 24 percent in 1974, and then declined. The part of the new debt issued each year that is purchased by the Fed is often referred to as debt that is *monetized.* The Fed writes checks on itself to pay for the debt (it must purchase securities in the open market and not directly from the Treasury itself), and these checks affect the money supply, and thus the debt is monetized. For the years 1970 through 1976, the Fed purchased, i.e., monetized, the following percentages of new federal debt issued in each of those years: 53, 40, 29, 19, 150, 8, and 12. In 1975 and 1976, there was no large increase in the growth of the monetary base. Although a surge in the money stock had been expected to finance purchases of the massive changes in federal debt in those years ($51 billion and $83 billion respectively), it did not take place.

Table 7–6 shows the federal debt and its owners by year from 1965 through 1976. Since 1972, the Fed and individuals have been the two largest owners and have been about equal each year in the dollar amount owned.

The Support of Government Borrowing: A Case in Point. Given the

TABLE 7–5. Funds Raised by Nonfinancial Sectors, 1965–76 (in billions of dollars)

Fiscal Year	Total*	U.S. Government	All Other Nonfinancial
1965	$ 71.2	$3.8	$ 67.5
1966	76.0	1.6	74.4
1967	60.8	1.8	59.1
1968	97.0	20.7	76.3
1969	96.7	−0.4	97.1
1970	93.6	3.8	89.8
1971	124.4	19.5	105.0
1972	161.5	19.4	142.1
1973	202.1	19.5	182.6
1974	191.5	3.3	188.1
1975	183.3	50.7	132.6
1976	241.0	82.8	158.2

Source: R. W. Lang, "The 1965–76 Federal Deficits and the Credit Market, "*Review — Federal Reserve of St. Louis* 59 (January 1977), p. 11.
Note: Based on the sum of unadjusted quarterly flows for each fiscal year, series updated as of November 1976.
*Columns may not sum to total due to rounding.

record deficits of 1975 and 1976, what was the impact on credit markets? Did the increased government demand for credit more than offset a decrease in the private demand as well as any increase in the supply of credit?

As noted, government demand for credit rose sharply in 1975, and the government raised $50.7 billion. All other nonfinancial sectors' demand fell very sharply, and these sectors raised $55.5 billion less in 1975 than in 1974. The general explanation for this decline is the recession of 1974.[8] Short-term interest rates did not exceed mid-1974 peaks but declined instead. Long-term rates also generally declined from 1974 levels, but not as much.

In 1976, the private sector raised more funds, but the increase was not substantial—the amount raised was $30 billion less than in 1974. Private demand for credit did not increase substantially in 1976. The total demand for credit did increase because of increased government demand. Business firms were acquiring financial claims in this period. Rather than increasing, interest rates were actually lower than in 1975. Hence the

[8]The particular factors are more complex: the end of wage and price controls, the oil embargo, crop failures, etc.

TABLE 7-6. Ownership of Federal Debt (in billions)

Period Ending June:	Federal Debt	Federal Reserve Banks	Commercial Banks	Federal Debt Held By: Individuals	Insurance Companies	Mutual Savings Banks	Corporations	State and Local Governments	Foreign and International	Other Investors
1965	$253.9	$39.1	$58.2	$70.7	$10.7	$5.6	$15.3	$24.1	$15.7	$16.8
1966	253.2	42.2	54.8	72.8	10.0	5.0	14.2	24.5	15.4	16.9
1967	250.9	46.7	55.5	70.4	9.0	4.2	11.0	23.6	14.7	19.3
1968	271.6	52.2	59.7	74.2	8.5	4.0	12.0	25.1	12.9	22.7
1969	268.9	54.1	55.3	77.3	8.1	3.5	11.1	26.4	11.1	22.0
1970	275.7	57.7	52.6	81.8	7.2	3.2	8.5	29.0	14.8	21.0
1971	295.2	65.5	61.0	75.4	7.0	3.3	7.4	25.9	32.7	17.2
1972	315.8	71.4	60.9	73.2	6.7	3.5	9.3	26.9	50.0	14.0
1973	334.7	75.0	58.8	75.9	6.3	3.3	9.8	28.8	60.2	16.6
1974	336.9	80.5	53.2	80.7	5.9	2.6	10.8	28.3	57.7	17.3
1975	387.9	84.7	69.0	87.1	7.1	3.5	13.2	29.6	66.0	27.6
1976	470.8	94.4	91.8	96.4	10.5	5.1	25.0	39.5	69.8	38.2

Source: R. W. Lang, "The 1965–76 Federal Deficits and the Credit Market," *Review — Federal Reserve Bank of St. Louis,* (January 1977), p. 15.

supply of credit must have increased both absolutely and in relation to total demand.

In summary, a large decline in private demand for credit in 1975 and an increased supply of credit in 1976 prevented the very large deficits from forcing interest rates upward. Although a larger proportion of the total funds raised went to the government in 1975 and 1976, compared to the previous ten years, no crowding out occurred.[9] The deficits were primarily the result of passive factors. They were financed mostly by the private sector. The percentages of the federal debt owned by the Federal Reserve Banks for 1974, 1975, and 1976 were respectively 23.9, 21.8, and 20.0. Banks, corporations, and some nonbank financial institutions picked up a larger proportion of the debt during 1975 and 1976.

It should be noted that a series of large deficits could be a problem. Private demand for credit could increase strongly, or the supply of credit could fail to increase correspondingly to demand. In either case, heavy government borrowing could exert upward pressures on interest rates.

State and Local Demand

State and local government expenditures have been growing more rapidly than those of the federal government (the average annual rate is now over 10 percent). To help meet this spending, state and local government securities have increased rapidly. In 1967, these securities totaled $114 billion; by 1979, however, the total was roughly $300 billion.

One can think of state and local government expenditures as consisting primarily of the purchase of goods and services of all types. Such purchases now amount to about 14 percent of GNP, compared to 8 percent for federal purchases. The reason for this rapid growth is the increasing demand by citizens for services supplied by state and local governments—roads, schools, water and sewage, airports, recreation facilities, trash collection, etc. Virtually everyone is aware of the suburban phenomenon that has occurred in the United States: the population increased and people left the city for various reasons. This explosion brought with it the need to finance many new activities in all the various communities, each with its own schools, water systems, etc., with the state taking responsibility for roads to link all the communities together, for schools to meet the growing demand for education, etc. Also, it seems safe to assert that the population in general simply demands more services today than

---

[9]*Crowding out* refers to an absolute decrease in the amount of credit available to the private sector as a result of government borrowing to finance an increased government deficit. Federal government borrowing is relatively insensitive to a rise in borrowing costs, while private borrowers desire to borrow less at a higher interest rate. Thus, although the total quantity of credit supplied increases, the proportion of credit going to the government rises.

it did 50 or even 25 years ago. At any rate, one has only to examine the explosive growth of the labor force in state and local government to see the impact that this sector can have on the economy.

Some Facts About Borrowing

As noted, the growth of state and local government debt has been spectacular, at least in the postwar period. We need not concern ourselves with pre-1945 conditions, except to note that the state and local government sector has defaulted on its debts a number of times, such as in the 1890s and in the 1930s.

Starting at the end of the war, when state and local government securities totaled only $15 billion, debt issuance became significant as these units strove to meet the new demands they encountered. Patterns have changed over time, however. For example, population growth is now slowing down, and ecological considerations present a different operating environment than was previously the case. Some states have been running surpluses in the 1970s. Also, federal aid has increased greatly, changing the situation significantly.

The primary form of borrowing by state and local governments is bonds that are sold publicly. These are typically issued in *serial maturities*, meaning that a specified portion of the issue matures each year. Maturities have lengthened over the years. These bonds are supported by the "full faith and credit" of the issuer except in the case of revenue bonds, which are supported by income from the project for which they were issued (e.g., by income from the Chesapeake Bay Bridge Tunnel). State and local government bonds are also quite often rated by Moody's Investor's Service or Standard and Poor's Corporation rating as to default risk.

An important point is that state and local governments as demanders of funds usually raise all the funds needed for a particular project before they initiate it. Thus, if the officials responsible decide to undertake a project and current revenues are insufficient, they recommend borrowing. However, the legislature or the citizens as a whole may have to approve the issuance of securities, and the whole process of formal paperwork and negotiations must then be undertaken, which may be very time-consuming. Even if all this has been completed, there often remains an effective check on potential borrowing, which is discussed below.

State and Local Debt Securities

Securities issued by state and local governments have a unique feature: the interest received by the holders of the bonds is exempt from federal taxation (and usually from state taxation for holders residing in the state of origin of issuance). Hence the interest rates at which these securities are issued are lower than the rates of comparable instruments whose interest is subject to federal taxes. The historical justification for the tax exemption was that it would lower the cost of state and local government financing so as to encourage these units to provide facilities and services for their constituents. The chief purchasers of these securities have been commercial banks (which are often in high marginal tax brackets), households, and property and casualty insurance companies (holding, at year-end 1978, $124 billion, $89 billion, and $60 billion, respectively).

The problem that state and local governments have faced is that, as interest rates in general rise, which happens during credit crunches or periods of tight money, the going rate (which they would have to pay to issue securities) may exceed a legal limitation imposed on the issuer. For example, a state's legislature may have imposed a limit of 6% on the long-term bonds it issues. If the going rate is 7%, no bonds can be issued. In addition, their largest purchasers, commercial banks, typically find that, in times of strong loan demand (which generally means high interest rates overall), they have few funds left to invest in such securities. Thus the state and local government sector may find itself unable to raise substantial funds at certain times.

FOREIGN DEMAND

Barring controls imposed by governments, foreigners seek loanable funds, just as do domestic sectors of our economy. Thus, foreign governments, business firms, and individuals need funds to finance various activities, and they seek the funds that are available (again, in the absence of government restrictions) subject to the same conditions that other demandees face.

Foreign borrowers can include firms or government agencies, and United States lenders can include individual investors and financial institutions. For our purposes, the foreign demand for loanable funds is represented by American purchases of foreign bonds and by bank loans; equity issues constitute only a tiny part of the total funds raised. The total funds raised in credit markets by the foreign sector in 1975 amounted to almost $13 billion—$6 billion in bonds, $4 billion in bank loans, and almost $3 billion in U.S. government loans. Actually, this total is large in relation to the amounts raised in each of the previous years, except for 1974, when $15 billion was raised. The average for the eight previous years was only about $4 billion.

It is interesting to note that a record $26 billion was raised by the foreign sector in 1978—a potentially significant demand on loanable funds. Furthermore, almost half of this amount was in the form of bank loans—a record in recent years. Open market paper was also relied on heavily in 1978 (about $7 billion). Direct investment in the United States by the foreign sector amounted to only about $4 billion in 1978.

In the last two decades, our government has undertaken considerable activity concerning the role of foreign financial activity. Foreigners have acquired very large dollar holdings in the past. The U.S. balance of payments deficit finally resulted in restrictions intended to reduce foreign demand for loanable funds. These restrictions have included such measures as an interest-equalization tax, which was applied to the purchase of foreign securities in an attempt to reduce such investments. Restrictions were eliminated in early 1974, making possible an unrestricted two-way flow of funds between the United States and foreign countries—U.S. citizens and institutions could lend to foreigners through purchases of bonds, bank loans, etc., and foreigners could invest in this country. Consequently, as noted, credit market funds raised by foreigners increased dramatically in 1974 and 1975. Furthermore, this trend continued in 1976 and 1977, and, in particular, 1978.

SUMMARY

Investment, giving rise to a demand for loanable funds, interacts with saving and the supply of loanable funds to influence interest rates. It is a significant factor in our financial system. Much of the activity that takes place in our economy—including that of the financial institutions sector, which is discussed in Part IV—involves the making and the financing of capital expenditures.

The total demand for loanable funds is a composite of business, household, government, and foreign demand. These funds are raised through the issuance of various instruments including bonds, stocks, mortgages, and short-term liabilities.

Business demand for investment funds was considered in some detail, both because of its importance and because it is the best demonstration of the theory of the demand for capital. Firms invest loanable funds in an attempt to enhance their stockholders' welfare. They make rational investment decisions based on a comparsion of the costs and the benefits of such investments. The time value of money is an important part of this process, because dollars to be received in the future are not as valuable as dollars received today. After an assessment of their sources of funds and the cost of funds, expected receipts from investment projects can be discounted back to time period zero, with the cost of funds applied as a discount rate.

Households, as noted in chapter 6, are the principal saving surplus sector in the economy and are therefore the major source of loanable funds. Simultaneously, however, households demand loanable funds, primarily for mortgages and secondarily for installment consumer credit. Mortgages are used by the household sector to finance real estate (e.g., houses).

Government demand for loanable funds is a very significant part of total demand. Its importance is related to both the total funds raised in some years and the potential wide fluctuations from year to year. Federal government demand is a function of political decisions concerning expenditures: if revenues are inadequate and deficits occur, they must be financed. Federal government borrowing is assumed to be interest-inelastic. State and local government borrowing is a function of the services a particular government body opts to provide. The major form of such borrowing is publicly sold bonds, which are exempt from federal taxes. Rates that can be paid are often limited by law, so that state and local borrowing is not interest-inelastic.

Finally, foreigners seek loanable funds, just as domestic users do. Such borrowers include governments and business firms. Foreign demand is typically met with bank loans and purchases of foreign bonds. The role of foreign financial activity is continually debated, and various regulatory actions are periodically taken, such as restrictions designed to reduce foreign demand for loanable funds. Large U.S. balance of payments deficits and the role of the dollar in the international financial system will probably continue to be topics of widespread interest and discussion.

8

Financial Market Equilibrium— Determination of Interest Rates

From the very beginning, this text has been concerned with the flow of funds from surplus units to deficit units. Through a review of the flow of funds accounts compiled for the U.S. economy, chapter 2 presented a descriptive introduction to the roles of various sectors in providing and absorbing funds. The household sector as a whole was seen to be the major source of loanable funds; business investment and, often, government deficits absorb the funds provided.

The forces that account for the saving/lending (financial investing) activities of household suppliers of loanable funds were analyzed in chapter 6. The demand for loanable funds for business, household, government, and foreign use was probed in chapter 7. To accommodate the wishes of surplus and deficit units, funds flow through the financial marketplace directly (with or without the aid of brokers, underwriters, etc.) and indirectly (through the intermediary system, which includes commercial banks, thrift institutions, life insurance companies and pension funds, brokers, and others). The objective of this chapter is to combine what we know about the supply of loanable funds (from household saving, the creation of new money, and the dishoarding of existing money balances) with what we know about the demand for funds (for business, government, or foreign use) to explain how the price of financing is determined and what the volume of financing will be. Of course, the price that prevails for the borrowing, or "renting," of money—the price of the extension of credit—is an interest rate, expressed as a percentage. Hence this chapter's title, which draws attention to the determination of interest rates.

It should be recognized that, in the actual financial marketplace,

211

there coexist many different interest rates on different financial claims. The reasons for this variation according to the type of financial instrument will be provided in chapter 9. The immediate concern of this chapter, however, is to isolate the broad forces that cause interest yields in general to rise or decline. Hence it will be permissible for us to conceive of a financial claim that is virtually free of the risk of default by the issuer, that enjoys no special tax status, and that, in general, is free of any other unique features that might influence the interest yield it offers. The yield on this instrument could well be labelled the *pure* rate of interest (or just *the* interest rate).[1] The observed yield on any other financial claim comprises this pure rate charge along with adjustments for any distinctive features that the claim enjoys.

The *equilibrium value* of the interest rate equates the supply of and the demand for a flow of loanable funds over a specified time period.[2] The *loanable funds theory* analyzes the forces that influence the flow supply of and demand for loanable funds (and hence the interest rate). Alternatively, the forces that influence the interest rate can be analyzed in stock terms, focusing attention on the supply of and demand for a stock of money at any instant in time; this approach to explaining the behavior of the interest rate is called the *liquidity preference theory*.

As will be shown shortly, the loanable funds theory and the liquidity preference theory are not separate and independent explanations of interest-rate behavior. However, their different foci provide each with advantages in particular applications. For example, business forecasters generally couch their predictions of short- and medium-term financial market developments in terms of loanable funds. The liquidity preference theory, however, is most easily integrated into macroeconomic models. We will need to be familiar with both approaches.

LOANABLE FUNDS

In the loanable funds theory, the level of prevailing interest rates can be viewed as being determined by the overall supply of and demand for a flow of funds (credit) in the financial marketplace or, since the demand for funds is met by the creation of financial claims, while funds are supplied by demanders of financial claims, by the overall flow supply of and demand for financial claims. Our discussion will concentrate on the flow of funds.

---

[1]The three-month rate on U.S. Treasury bills is often viewed as a good measure of the pure rate of interest.

[2]Since the extension of credit involves the creation of a financial claim issued by the borrower and acquired by the lender, the equilibrium interest rate also equates the flow supply of and demand for financial claims.

Supply of Funds

The major source of loanable funds is household saving, which, as we noted in chapter 6, may or may not exhibit a significant sensitivity to interest rates. Unquestionably, however, household saving is closely associated with changes in income. Business firms also provide saving, in the form of depreciation allowances and retained earnings. Finally, government units can generate saving if they operate at a surplus (collect more in tax revenue than their current expenditures). The saving schedule S_1, plotted in Figure 8–1, exhibits some positive response to interest rates, to reflect the possibility that households may save more as the yield on saving rises. A change in income would shift this schedule, as a higher income level generates more saving at any interest rate and a lower income level generates less.

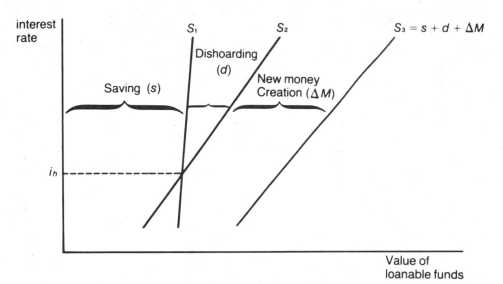

FIGURE 8–1. Supply of Loanable Funds

A second source of loanable funds is the *dishoarding* of money balances, which all economic units tend to engage in as yields on nonmonetary financial claims rise. That is, if yields are increased, economic units tend to reduce their money balances and swap funds for income-yielding claims. Assuming that a rise in interest yields does lead economic units to dishoard money in exchange for bonds and other financial claims, the supply of loanable funds is then the sum of saving (S) and dishoarding (D), represented by schedule S_2 in Figure 8–1. (Note that, at interest rates below i_h, money balances are hoarded, so that the supply of funds in the credit market is reduced.)

Finally, the supply of loanable funds is altered by every change in the money stock, the size of which is jointly determined by the Fed, commercial banks, and the nonbank public. For example, a Federal Reserve open-market purchase of securities, which expands the monetary base and raises the money supply by amount ΔM, shifts the loanable funds supply schedule to S_3. Note that S_3 has a slightly flatter slope than S_2; this reflects the extension of more demand deposit credit (which is money) by commercial banks as banks' attempt to economize on their excess reserves as interest rates rise.

Demand for Funds

Business firms demand funds to meet their investment and liquidity needs, as discussed in chapter 7. Schedule D_1 in Figure 8–2 represents business demand (B) for loanable funds. It slopes downward from left to right to reflect the negative response of business borrowing (and fund use) to interest-rate changes. Changes in the level of national income, by altering the intensity of utilization of capital and by influencing businessmen's expectations of future demand for goods and services, would shift this demand schedule, rightward as income expands and leftward as it contracts.

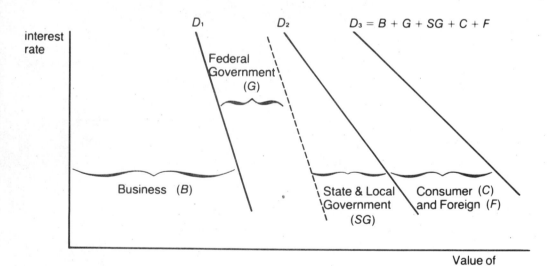

FIGURE 8–2. Demand for Loanable Funds

Government, both at the federal level and at the state and local levels, is a major demander of loanable funds. The federal government, issuing securities to cover its budget deficit, does not alter its borrowing in response to interest-rate changes. In contrast, many state and local government units face legal ceilings on the interest rates they may offer for borrowed funds, so that they must curtail their borrowing if financing costs rise above acceptable levels. Adding both federal demand and state and local demand to business demand provides schedule D_2.

Finally, in any period, some households are borrowing, by and large to finance purchases of homes and consumer durables. There may also be a foreign demand that exceeds the foreign supply of funds in the U.S. financial market. Both household borrowing (C) and net foreign demand (F) are likely to respond negatively to interest-rate changes, so that the addition of these components to those already represented provides the slightly flatter schedule D_3, which represents the total demand for loanable funds—the sum of business, federal government, state and local government, consumer, and net foreign demand.

The Equilibrium Interest Rate

Figure 8–3 combines the loanable funds supply and demand schedules from Figures 8–1 and 8–2 to indicate that the equilibrium interest rate that prevails for these particular flow supply and demand schedules is i_0. This rate is not likely to persist, in particular because the dishoarding and

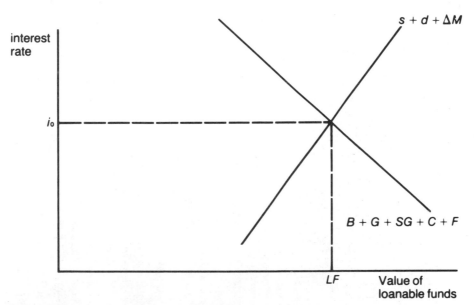

FIGURE 8–3. Equilibrium in the loanable funds market

TABLE 8-1. Summary of Supply and Demand for Credit ($ Billions)

	Annual Net Increases in Amounts Outstanding							Amounts Outstanding 12/31/77
	1972	1973	1974	1975	1976	1977e[1]	1978p[2]	
Net Demand								
Privately Held Mortgages	68.8	68.7	42.8	40.2	72.0	94.0	97.0	866.4
Corporate Bonds	18.9	13.2	26.9	32.9	30.7	29.5	32.2	366.2
Domestically Held Foreign Bonds	1.0	1.0	2.2	6.2	8.4	4.3	4.0	37.5
Subtotal Long-Term Private	88.7	82.9	71.9	79.3	111.1	127.8	133.2	1,270.1
Business Loans	26.2	41.0	35.6	-12.4	5.4	34.1	43.5	277.0
Consumer Installment Credit	14.8	21.4	9.3	7.5	20.5	32.0	36.5	217.5
All Other Bank Loans	9.4	6.8	3.6	2.7	12.1	13.2	14.0	114.3
Open Market Paper	1.6	8.3	17.7	-1.3	8.1	13.7	15.5	88.2
Subtotal Short-Term Private	52.0	77.5	66.2	-3.5	46.1	93.0	109.5	697.0
Privately Held Treasury Debt	16.0	-0.6	9.7	76.3	58.6	48.2	54.2	453.8
Privately Held Federal Agency Debt	11.5	22.2	19.7	11.5	16.9	24.4	30.0	163.5
Subtotal Federal	27.5	21.6	29.4	87.8	75.5	72.6	84.2	617.3
State & Local Tax-Exempt Bonds	14.1	13.3	11.9	17.5	21.7	30.4	23.2	260.9
State & Local Tax-Exempt Notes	-1.3	0.8	2.6	-1.2	-4.6	-0.7	-2.0	12.6
Subtotal Tax-Exempt	12.8	14.1	14.5	16.3	17.1	29.7	21.2	273.5
Total Net Demand for Credit	181.0	196.1	182.0	179.9	249.8	323.1	348.1	2,857.9

Net Supply¹

Mutual Savings Banks	8.8	5.3	3.2	10.6	12.5	11.8	10.8	134.5
Savings & Loan Associations	35.3	27.1	19.6	37.4	50.5	60.5	57.4	410.8
Credit Unions	3.0	3.6	2.8	5.4	5.8	7.5	7.6	45.1
Life Insurance Companies	8.8	10.0	10.3	15.3	22.3	23.6	24.2	256.1
Fire & Casualty Companies	3.8	3.5	4.6	8.2	8.8	10.5	11.0	74.3
Private Non-Insured Pension Funds	-0.7	2.0	5.8	7.9	5.3	10.2	11.4	67.0
State & Local Retirement Funds	3.1	3.4	8.0	8.3	9.6	10.9	11.2	95.1
Foundations & Endowments	-0.1	0.6	0.9	1.1	0.9	0.7	1.0	16.8
Closed-End Corporate Bond Funds	1.2	1.1	0.2	0.0	0.0	0.0	0.0	2.8
Money Market Funds	0.0	0.0	1.0	0.7	0.4	-0.3	0.5	1.9
Municipal Bond Funds	0.4	0.7	1.1	2.2	3.1	4.5	5.0	13.8
Open-End Taxable Investment Funds	0.0	-0.2	-0.4	0.8	1.1	1.1	0.3	9.6
Real Estate Investment Trusts	4.1	5.6	0.2	-4.9	-3.7	-1.5	-1.2	7.8
Finance Companies	9.4	11.6	4.9	1.3	8.7	19.9	20.0	122.5
Total Non-Bank Institutions	77.1	74.3	62.2	94.3	125.3	159.4	159.2	1,258.1
Commercial Banks²	73.3	77.6	59.8	31.0	64.0	78.4	93.3	883.8
Business Corporations	-2.7	0.9	8.8	9.5	11.9	7.7	5.3	74.3
State & Local Governments	5.5	3.3	1.2	3.4	4.9	15.5	13.1	58.7
Foreigners	8.4	0.6	11.2	6.1	15.2	30.2	31.8	126.9
Subtotal	161.6	156.7	143.2	144.3	221.3	291.2	302.7	2,401.8
Residual: Households Direct	19.4	39.4	38.8	35.6	28.5	31.9	45.4	456.1
Total Net Supply of Credit	181.0	196.1	182.0	179.9	249.8	323.1	348.1	2,857.9

Note: Adapted from *Prospects for the Credit Markets in 1978* by Salomon Brothers. Reprinted with the permission of Salomon Brothers.

¹e = estimated

²p = projected

³Excludes funds for equities, cash and miscellaneous demands not tabulated above.

⁴Includes loans transferred to books of non-operating holding and other bank-related companies.

the sizable increase in the money supply incorporated into the supply curve are unlikely to persist. A slowdown in money supply growth or a cessation of dishoarding would shift the supply schedule leftward, calling for a rise in interest rates. As this possibility illustrates, some of the factors that influence interest rates in the loanable funds model are transitory and short-lived. Since those factors are prominent in our analysis, this model is best suited for explaining the current state of the financial marketplace and for predicting near-term changes in the interest rate.

Table 8–1 provides detailed summary measures of the supplies of and the demands for funds over the period 1971 through 1977, as compiled by Salomon Brothers, one of the country's prominent investment banking firms. Business analysts make use of such detailed measures, combined with predictions of Federal Reserve policy actions, of general economic developments, and of sectoral responses to these developments, to provide forecasts of movements in interest rates in general and to predict sectoral changes in the flow of funds and the cost of credit. A somewhat different summary of flows of fund supplies and demands will be provided a bit later to illustrate the practice of real-world forecasting in the loanable funds framework. After reviewing that forecast, you should return to Table 8–1 and, with special attention to year-to-year changes in credit flows (in the economy as a whole and in individual sectors), apply loanable funds reasoning to see what predictions of credit flows and interest-yield changes you would make each year.

Applying the Loanable Funds Theory

The detailed list of participating sectors provided in the loanable funds framework makes it possible to predict the impact on interest rates of a broad array of disturbances, even those that have only a brief influence. For example, if the U.S. Treasury offers a larger volume of securities than expected in one of its frequent sales, this increase in the demand for funds (supply of securities) is apt to temporarily depress security prices, which raises interest yields. Figure 8–4 provides a graphical demonstration of the impact of this increment in Treasury security sales. Initially, at the interest rate i_0, the total volume of loanable funds advanced and acquired is LF_0. Of this total, the quantity G_0 is procured by government, and the rest ($F_0 = LF_0 - G_0$) goes to business or foreign use. If the government's borrowing is increased by ΔG (to a total of G_1), the interest yield on financial claims rises to i_1. More saving and/or more dishoarding then occurs in response to the enticement of this higher yield, to provide the larger total flow of loanable funds LF_1. Government's use of loanable funds increases by the full ΔG increment in its spending, but private use of funds is squeezed from level F_0 to level F_1. That is, the increased government borrowing crowds out some private borrowing as the interest rate is driven up.

To prevent an unexpectedly large Treasury issue from failing to sell quickly on the terms set by the Treasury, the Fed can generally be expected to follow an "even-keel" policy, purchasing Treasury securities to prop up their prices and to prevent the interest-rate increase described above. In this case, the loanable funds supply curve would be shifted rightward in step with the loanable funds demand schedule, which would leave the interest rate and the private use of funds unchanged (at i_0 and F_0 respectively) but which would raise the government's use of funds by an amount equal to the money supply increase provided by the Fed's open-market purchase of securities.

Changes in Federal Reserve float also tend to produce some temporary changes in financial market conditions. For example, an increase in float, which provides additional reserves to the commercial banking system, is quickly reflected in a decline in the federal funds rate. In return, this might allow commercial banks that face the prospect of a reserve deficiency to postpone moves toward a more restrictive credit policy, so that they can temporarily hold the supply of loanable funds higher than it otherwise would be.

Over the course of several months, developments that have more pronounced and more persistent effects on interest rates occupy center stage. In the recovery stage of the business cycle, financial analysts who are concerned with forecasting interest rates pay close heed to changes in household and business saving, the rate of money supply growth, the projected federal budget deficit (or surplus), the level of business inventory investment (much of which is debt-financed), and the demand for mortgage funds.

The demand for housing (and hence for mortgage credit) is usually strong during the recovery stage of a business cycle, and, as sales expand, business firms increase their demand for loanable funds to finance inventory additions. Whether these demand pressures result in a rise in interest rates depends on a number of other factors. As incomes rise, household saving becomes greater (increasing the supply of loanable funds), while, with tax revenues growing, the business recovery reduces the government demand for funds in the financial market. At the same time, if the Fed is trying to encourage the business recovery, the money supply grows, providing a further increase in the supply of loanable funds. Whether interest rates rise or fall during this period depends on the sizes of these changes in supply and demand.

Experience suggests that, in the past, business expansions could proceed for an extended period while interest rates remained fairly stable.[3] However, in a continuing expansion, production rates impinge ever more

---

[3]In the inflationary era in which we now live, this may no longer be the case. This issue will be addressed later in this chapter.

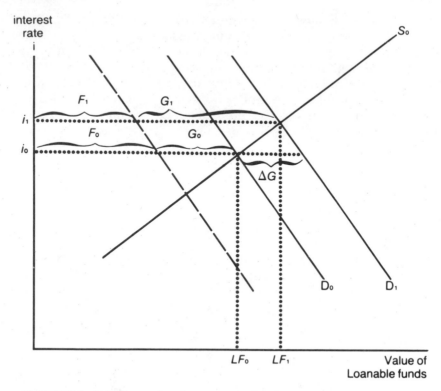

FIGURE 8–4. Effects of an Increase in Government Demand for
Loanable Funds

strongly on existing production facilities, which prompts firms to
undertake increasing volumes of costly plant and equipment investment.
The financing of this investment shifts the loanable funds demand
schedule rightward, which tends to increase interest rates. The
inflationary pressures that have emerged in past booms have also tended
to raise interest rates, since inflation has directly increased the demand for
loanable funds, has prompted the Fed to reduce the rate of monetary
expansion, and, as we will explain shortly, has altered society's
expectations of future inflation rates.

Once an expansion has ended and the economy is contracting, the
investment demand for funds is sharply curtailed, which permits interest
rates to decline. The future comes to be viewed as more uncertain, so that
society can be expected to save more out of any prevailing income level.
This by itself would further depress interest rates. However, society can
also be expected to hoard more money, and, as income declines, household
and business saving are depressed. Interest rates consequently fall less

than they otherwise would. The Fed, should it increase the money supply in an attempt to revitalize the economy, would reinforce the decline in interest rates.

The following discussion clearly illustrates the use of the loanable funds model applied to real-world interest-rate forecasting. It traces the supply of funds through the channels it follows to the financial marketplace and provides entries for sources and uses of funds.

FINANCIAL MARKETS: PROSPECTS FOR 1978[4]

The consensus among macroeconomic analysts is that "real" economic growth will range between 4% and 5% in 1978, with a gradual slowing as the year progresses. Inflation rates are expected to remain in the 5.5 to 6% range.

Against this backdrop, the expected flows of funds in 1978—both the demand for credit and where the money might come from—are set forth in the tables below.

U.S. financial markets next year will handle a record net volume of funds estimated at $370 billion. That record amount of financing is in prospect primarily because of a new high in short-term credit demand by the nation's businesses to a total of $65 billion—$10 billion more than in 1977.

The Demand for Funds

The continuing expansion in economic activity will fuel a growing corporate need for funds. Capital outlays, expected to rise next year by 13%, and a continued slowing in the growth of internally generated funds—after-tax profits are expected to increase by 11% next year as against an estimated 12.5% this year—are important reasons to expect a widening in the corporate financing "gap" and enlarged borrowing. Financing a larger stock of inventories will also add to the need for short-term funds.

The pick-up in short-term credit demands by business is expected to be enhanced, too, by a continued decline in the volume of new corporate bond offerings. For 1978, net corporate bond floatations are expected to be down to $23 billion from $26 billion in 1977. This would mark the third consecutive year of shrinkage in corporate

---

[4]Extracted with minor modifications from "Financial Markets: Prospects for 1978," *The Morgan Guaranty Survey*, December 1977, pp. 8–12.

bond calendars and would bring new bond issues far below the huge volumes of 1975 and 1976, when corporations made massive efforts to improve their liquidity positions by using bond sale proceeds to pay off short-term liabilities.

Analysis of U.S. government financing needs for the coming year has, of course, been made more difficult by uncertainties about the timing and magnitude of the Administration's energy, tax reform, and fiscal-stimulus proposals. The energy legislation is assumed to be neutral in terms of the deficit—i.e., it will give back in rebates just about what it takes in—and, therefore, will have no impact on government financing requirements next year. And assuming that the revenue-reduction/reform package takes time passing Congress and does not take effect until late 1978, it now appears that Treasury borrowing in 1978 will rise only modestly to $55 billion from an estimated $50 billion for 1977. That pattern would mean that the budget deficit will be shrinking gradually through the end of 1978. This dovetails with the widening of the corporate financing gap.

Federal agency borrowing is estimated to decline in 1978 from 1977's huge volume. Much of recent borrowing has been for the purpose of refunding and pre-refunding older, higher-rate debt, a process which is becoming less attractive as interest rates rise. Also, state and local government budgets have moved strongly into surplus, reflecting restrained expenditures and rapidly growing receipts from taxes and federal grants. Moreover, these governments have added a huge volume of U.S. government securities to their portfolios over the past two years. All these factors should operate to restrain state and local borrowing in 1978.

The mortgage market, booming recently, is estimated this year to have net flows of $115 billion—up a third over last year. The turnover of existing homes has been running at a rapid pace, but is expected to slow. Housing starts next year, especially in single-family homes, are also forecast to decline from their recent peak. These developments indicate a less brisk demand for home-mortgage loans. But an increase in the net extension of multifamily and commercial mortgages is expected to offset any drop in home-mortgage credit extended. Thus, the net flow in total mortgage credit is estimated at $115 billion, the same as in 1977.

Finally, there's the consumer's need for credit to pay for mounting purchases all across the board. So far this year consumer expenditures have generally been strong and consumer credit is estimated to rise by a record $33 billion—almost $10 billion more than in 1976. Recently, however, consumer plans to buy homes, cars, and appliances and their confidence in future economic conditions have begun to ebb. Consumption spending for autos and durable goods will continue to grow next year, but at a much reduced pace from that of the past two years. Thus, the use of consumer credit in 1978 is estimated at $35 billion, only a modest increase over 1977.

TABLE 1. The Demand for Funds (in billions of dollars)	1977	1978
Federal government issues	50.0	55.0
Federal agency issues	25.0	30.0
State and local issues	25.0	20.0
Corporate bonds	26.0	23.0
Corporate stocks	9.0	8.0
Foreign securities	6.5	7.0
Mortgages	115.0	115.0
Consumer credit	33.0	35.0
Other business credit	55.0	65.0
All other credit	13.0	12.0
Total uses	357.5	370.0

TABLE 2. Sources of Funds (in billions of dollars)	1977	1978
Commercial banking	85.0	90.0
Savings institutions	79.0	72.0
Insurance and pension sector	54.0	60.0
Other finance	18.0	20.0
Nonfinancial corporations	20.0	18.0
Government, including Federal Reserve	55.0	58.0
Foreign investors	27.0	27.0
Individuals and others	19.5	25.0
Total funds supplied	357.5	370.0

Sources of Funds

So much for the demand for funds, represented by the estimates in Table 1. Where will the funds come from? The largest volume of funds this year and next is expected to come through the commercial banking sector. Official monetary policy, quite obviously, will play a key role in banks' ability to accommodate credit demands but, all told, commercial banks are expected to supply a record $90 billion to the money and capital markets in 1978, up a bit from this year's $85 billion.

With the economy's expansion fueling a growth in saving, thrift institutions have been experiencing a surge in deposit inflows. However, with short-term interest rates now on the rise, some diminution in savings flows must be expected. Savings institutions are currently estimated to provide $72 billion to credit markets, down modestly from 1977's record pace. As usual, the mortgage markets will be the main outlet for these funds.

The insurance and pension sector as a source of funds is expected to continue transmitting a growing volume of households' contractual saving to credit markets. Life insurance companies, in particular, have enjoyed hefty inflows of funds, reflecting strong sales of life insurance in recent years and healthy increases in pension fund business. Next year a somewhat greater volume of the life insurance industry's investments may be directed toward nonresidential mortgages than has been the case in recent years as credit demands from this sector are increasing. And, with the rise in interest rates, policy-loan outflows are likely to be more of a problem than in recent years. Still, the bulk of this industry's funds will once again be directed toward corporate bonds; interest in corporate stocks is likely to remain relatively subdued.

State and local retirement systems and private pension funds are also showing more interest in bonds than equities. When these factors are set against a backdrop of an expected smaller bond supply next year, the balance of supply and demand in this market appears to be tilting sharply toward an adequate supply of funds in the bond market.

A major uncertainty always overhanging the credit market in any year is the behavior of foreign investors. The figure for this sector shown in Table 2 is difficult to project since it results from a combination of factors such as international interest rate differences, balance-of-payments developments, and the degree of intervention by central banks in foreign exchange markets. In recent years, for example, the flow of foreign-sources funds has ranged from $3.4 billion in 1973 to an estimated $27 billion in 1977. Recognizing these imponderables, the best guess is that foreign investors will supply approximately the same amount of funds to U.S. markets next year—largely in purchases of U.S. government securities. This chiefly reflects the expectation that the U.S. trade deficit in 1978 will be about the same as the estimated $18 billion this year.

Conclusions

The estimates of credit demands and supplies presented in this analysis suggest that fears expressed by some analysts that financial market developments next year may threaten economic expansion probably have been exaggerated.

What seems reasonable at this juncture is that short-term interest rates will continue to rise a bit into early 1978 as the Fed maintains a credit stance restrictive enough to contain inflationary pressures. In the longer-term credit markets, though, the estimates presented above, coupled with the assumption that rates of inflation will not accelerate, suggest that any rise in long-term interest rates will be relatively modest.

Limitations on Loanable Funds Analysis

While loanable funds analysis accommodates a detailed collection of forces that can influence interest rates, some of the events that play prominent roles in that analysis are inconsistent with an economywide, or general, equilibrium. For example, hoarding and dishoarding influence the current flow of loanable funds and hence affect the interest rates that can clear the financial marketplace, but they can occur only when society's demand for money differs from the available stock of money—a disequilibrium situation. Hence the loanable funds model as it is normally developed, in which transitory influences on interest rates play a prominent role, cannot be conveniently integrated into standard models of the macroeconomy, for those models seek to explain how different events will alter the properties of an economy that *begins* and *ends* in full, general equilibrium.

In a similar vein, interest-rate changes that might be forecast by the loanable funds theory have effects on the real sectors of the economy, which in turn feed back into the financial marketplace. For example, increases in the money stock, (which, according to this theory, lower interest rates) also stimulate spending on real goods and services and are apt to result in an expansion of output and prices, and higher output and prices tend to produce further adjustments in the financial marketplace that usually are not systematically accounted for by the loanable funds model.

LIQUIDITY PREFERENCE

An alternative, which avoids the limitations on the loanable funds theory, is the liquidity preference theory. For example, it explains the existence of hoarding and dishoarding as disequilibrium phenomena. This alternative therefore serves as an integral component of modern analysis of the macroeconomy.

In the loanable funds theory, the interest rate is the price paid for borrowed funds and received by those who extend credit. But this rate is also the opportunity cost of holding money, which (narrowly defined) pays no interest. Hence the interest-rate level that provides financial market equilibrium must not only balance borrowers' demands for credit with lenders' supplies, but it must also equate society's demand for money balances with the available money stock. The forces that determine the interest-rate level can therefore be analyzed in terms of the supply of and the demand for a stock of money. This is the approach embodied in the liquidity preference theory, developed by Keynes in the *General Theory*.

While recognizing the disagreements that exist with regard to the best definition of money, our development of the liquidity preference model will employ the narrow definition (currency and demand deposits). In addition, to facilitate the integration of money's role in our future discussions of economywide adjustments, the liquidity preference model will be developed in real terms: the money supply function will represent the real purchasing power that is provided to the economy in the form of money, and the money demand function will represent the command over real goods and services that society chooses to hold in money form.

Money Supply Again

In chapter 4, a money supply model was developed in which the nominal stock of money (the number of dollars of currency and demand deposits) is jointly determined by the Fed, commercial banks, and the nonbank public. The Fed can influence the money supply by alterations in the monetary base or by changes in reserve requirements; the commercial banking system can influence it by alterations in the volume of excess reserves it chooses to hold, extending demand deposit credit as it puts idle reserves to work; and the nonbank public can influence it by the composition of the portfolio of liquid assets (currency, demand deposits, and time deposits) it chooses to hold.

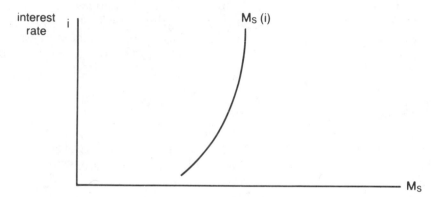

FIGURE 8–5. The Nominal Money Supply

According to our money supply model, with a given monetary base, the size of the money stock is apt to expand a bit as interest rates rise. This response reflects the efforts of banks to extend loans so as to economize on excess reserves as interest yields on loans become more attractive; it also accommodates a possible shift by the nonbank public from currency to time deposits (providing banks with more reserves) as yields become more attractive. With the interest rate (i) on the vertical axis and the nominal quantity of money (M_S) on the horizontal axis, the money supply schedule in Figure 8–5 illustrates the money supply response to interest-rate changes. This schedule would be shifted by actions taken by the Fed to alter the monetary base or to change reserve requirements; it would shift rightward with an increase in the monetary base or a cut in reserve requirements and leftward with a shrinkage of the monetary base or an increase in reserve requirements.

To formulate the money supply model in real, or price-deflated, terms, we need only to divide the nominal money stock (M_S) by an appropriate general price index (P). Thus the real money stock is just M_S/P. If the general price level is constant, a change in the interest rate prompts a change in the real money supply that is proportional to the change in the nominal money supply described earlier. Figure 8–6 shows this link between the interest rate and the real money supply, as the supply schedule in that chart has the same appearance as the schedule in Figure 8–5. Also, by prompting a change in the nominal money stock, a Fed action that changes the monetary base or alters reserve requirements would shift the real money supply schedule, in the directions described before. In addition, the real money supply function is shifted by a change in the general price level. A rise in prices reduces the real purchasing power embodied in the nominal stock of money (the real money supply schedule is shifted leftward), and a decline in prices increases the real value of the existing nominal money stock (the real money supply schedule is shifted rightward).

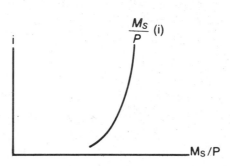

FIGURE 8–6. The Real Money Supply

Money Demand

Money demand in the liquidity preference model is broken down into three components: transactions demand, precautionary demand, and speculative demand. *Transactions demand* is demand for money balances to bridge the gap between the receipt and the disbursement of income. If all income receipts were instantaneously spent, the value of transactions balances would always be zero. Such a coincidence of receipts and disbursements is, of course, not achieved in reality, so that, on average, some positive volume of cash balances must be held to avoid the difficulties that arise from running out of money. To take a simple example, think of an individual who receives a monthly income of $300, which is spent at the uniform rate of $10 per day during the 30-day month. On average, this individual holds $150 of money balances ($300 at the beginning of the month and $0 at the end) for transactions purposes.

Like households, business firms are continually receiving and making money payments. They, too, need positive transactions money balances during the interval between the receipt of income (sales revenue) and its disbursement for wages, rent, interest, raw materials, and so on.

What determines the volume of real purchasing power that society demands to hold in the form of transactions money balances? Generally, the volume of real income has been viewed as the primary determinant of transactions demand in the liquidity preference model. With an increase (or a decrease) in output and income, the real volume of transactions that must be financed is increased (or reduced), calling for greater (or lesser) money balances for transactions purposes. In addition, although Keynes's original analysis exhibited little concern for this, the interest rate is an opportunity cost of holding money for transactions purposes, so that an increase (or a decline) in the interest rate can reduce (or raise) the quantity of money demanded for transactions purposes. Algebraically, the transactions demand for money takes the form

$$\frac{M_t}{P} = M_t(i,\, y) \qquad\qquad (8\text{--}1)$$

where M_t/P is the volume of real money balances demanded for transactions, which is a function of the interest rate i and real income y, such that

$$\frac{\Delta(M_t/P)}{\Delta i} < 0$$

and

$$\frac{\Delta(M_t/P)}{\Delta y} > 0$$

Note that, as long as i and y are unchanged, the real purchasing power of money demanded for transactions stays constant. Hence a change in the general price level, other things being the same, requires a proportional change in the nominal quantity of money held.

The *precautionary demand* for money balances exists because there is uncertainty with respect to the timing and the size of future income receipts and necessary expenditures. An individual never knows with certainty what future income will be. One may unexpectedly become disabled or be laid off from work. One never knows with certainty what expenditures will be necessary in the future. There may be unforeseen medical bills, unexpectedly favorable opportunities to make purchases, and so on.

Similarly, business firms never know with certainty what future receipts and production costs will be. Revenues may fall temporarily or permanently as a result of shifts in demand (for example, demand for lawn sprinklers may melt away during an unusually rainy summer). Costs may rise, for example, because of unexpectedly successful wage-bargaining efforts by labor unions. To avoid the pecuniary and nonpecuniary (for example, embarrassment) costs of running out of money as a result of unforeseen events, both individuals and firms are likely to maintain some precautionary balances.

The demand for precautionary balances is likely to be a positive function of the level of real income: the higher an individual's income, the larger the safety margin that individual can afford to hold, and the larger unexpected transactions needs tend to be. In addition, precautionary demand tends to respond to the interest rate. As in the case of transactions balances, an increase in this opportunity cost of holding noninterest-bearing money balances induces an effort to economize on the size of those balances. With i and y respectively representing the interest rate and real income, as before, the real volume of money demanded for precautionary purposes is

$$\frac{M_p}{P} = M_p(i, y) \tag{8-2}$$

such that

$$\frac{\Delta(M_p/P)}{\Delta i} < 0$$

and

$$\frac{\Delta(M_p/P)}{\Delta y} > 0$$

Once again, a change in the general price level, other things being equal, results in a proportional change in the nominal quantity of money demanded for precautionary purposes, so that the real demand for precautionary balances is left unchanged.

A glance at equations 8–1 and 8–2 shows that the demand functions for transactions and precautionary balances have exactly the same form. As such, we can readily combine the transactions and precautionary demands for money to provide a transactions-precautionary demand schedule of the form

$$\frac{M_{t+p}}{P} = M_{tp}(i, y) \tag{8-3}$$

This demand schedule is illustrated in Figure 8–7 for a given prevailing income level. An increase in the level of real output and income, which increases the transactions-precautionary demand, would shift this schedule rightward, and a contraction, which reduces that demand, would shift it leftward. Once again, a change in the price level leaves the real quantity of purchasing power that society demands to hold in money form unchanged, while it alters the nominal quantity of money demanded, in proportion to the change in prices.

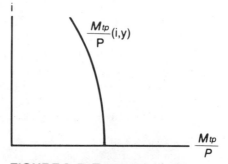

FIGURE 8–7. Transactions — Precautionary Demand

The third component of the demand for money balances is the demand for money to be held as an asset. This *speculative demand* clearly distinguishes the Keynesian theory of interest-rate determination from that of his precursors, who emphasized the role of money as a medium of exchange and therefore dealt only with transactions or transactions-precautionary demand for money. Keynes emphasized the proposition that an individual must decide, not only how much to spend and how much to save, but also what form to hold savings in—whether to use it to buy interest-yielding securities (in Keynes's terminology, "bonds") or whether to hold it in the form of idle, noninterest-yielding money balances. Presumably, one chooses to hold the asset (money or bonds) that maximizes one's economic well-being. Since bonds pay a positive interest yield and money does not, savings are held in cash form only if bond prices are expected to fall. As such, speculative demand can be characterized as the demand for money to be held as an asset in order to avoid capital losses on bonds.

Suppose that an individual has $100 of savings and is trying to choose the best form in which to hold it. Like Keynes, we can simplify our discussion of this portfolio decision by the assumption that there are only two financial assets available, money and long-term bonds—contractual agreements that obligate a borrower (the bond-issuer) to pay fixed sums of money at stated intervals. Typically, the issuer is obligated to make semiannual interest payments over the life of a bond and to pay its face value, or maturity value, upon maturity of the bond. For example, a 3 percent, $1,000 bond due in 20 years pays $15 semiannually (or $30 annually) for 20 years, plus $1000 at the end of the 20 years.

Some bonds, less common than those with specified maturity dates, are designed never to mature but to provide a perpetual stream of equal semiannual or annual interest payments. Such perpetual bonds, or *perpetuities*, are particularly simple for computational purposes, and hence they can conveniently be employed to examine the speculative demand for money. In the example of the individual with $100 of savings, suppose that the alternative forms in which it can be held are money and a $100 perpetual bond currently paying a 10 percent annual coupon yield ($10 per year in interest payments). Whether this individual chooses to hold speculative money balances or the bond depends on what he or she expects to happen to the market rate of interest in the future. If it is expected to rise, say, to 12 percent in the next year, the individual will keep the $100 in money form rather than buy the bond, for, with this increase in the market interest rate, the market price of a perpetual bond paying $10 yearly would fall from $100 to $83.33.[4] The loss in capital (market) value

---

[4]At a price of $83.33, our saver's perpetual bond yields a 12 percent rate of return, like all other comparable securities in the bond market. Of course, this equilibrium market price is just the present value of the bond, obtained by the application of the 12 percent

of $16.67 on the bond more than offsets the $10 coupon payment our saver would receive in one year as a bondholder, so that, clearly, it is less profitable to hold the bond than to keep the savings in idle, money form. An individual who expects a substantial rise in the market interest rate, which means a corresponding fall in bond prices, should therefore hold savings in money rather than in bonds so as to avoid capital losses.[5] On the other hand, an individual who expects the interest rate to fall (bond prices to rise) should hold savings in the form of bonds, since they are expected to provide a capital gain in addition to the coupon interest payment. Thus it is the individual's expectation of future interest-rate movements that governs the choice between speculative money balances and bonds.

To explain these expectations of interest-rate changes, Keynes suggested that every individual has some notion of what the normal rate of interest is (for example, from historical experience, one might think that the normal rate of interest for the United States is close to 7 percent). If the currently observed market rate exceeds the normal rate, according to an individual's notion of it, that person would expect to see market rates fall (bond prices rise) in the future and would prefer to hold bonds instead of money. Conversely, if the market rate is below the perceived normal rate, an individual would expect market rates to rise (bond prices to fall) and would choose to hold speculative money balances instead of bonds. Of course, an individual's notion of what the normal interest rate level is can change with experience, but that possibility in no way alters our conclusions about the portfolio choice a wealth-holder makes at one point in time. We now must explore the aggregate speculative money demand schedule that results from individual portfolio decisions.

If, among the millions of participants in the money (bond) market, there is a diversity of opinion with regard to what the normal rate of interest is, then, given typical market interest rates, some individuals ex-

---

market interest rate (as the discount rate) to future income receipts generated by the bond. From the section on present value calculations in chapter 7, you may recall that the present value of an asset that yields a perpetual stream of uniform payments (as this bond does) is $V = R/i$.

[5]In more detail, the total yield from bond holdings consists of the interest yield plus any capital gain (or loss) from a change in bond prices. The percentage yield is

$$\% \text{ yield } = i + \left(\frac{1}{B}\right)\left(\frac{\Delta B}{\Delta t}\right)$$

where i is the interest yield at the price at which the buyer purchases the bond and B is the bond price, so that $(1/B)(\Delta B/\Delta t)$ is the percentage rate of capital gain yield. As long as wealth-holders expect the overall yield to be positive $[i > -(1/B)(\Delta B/\Delta t)]$, they prefer to hold bonds rather than money, according to the Keynesian analysis. But, if bond prices are expected to fall (interest rates to rise) at a rate that exceeds the interest yield on bonds, wealth-holders would be better off holding their savings in money form.

pect rates to rise and some expect them to fall.[6] Thus, for interest rate i_0 in Figure 8–8, we should find some positive demand for purchasing power held in the form of speculative money balances (say, $[M_{sp}/P]_0$), since those who expect a substantial interest-rate rise prefer to hold their savings in money balances rather than in bonds.

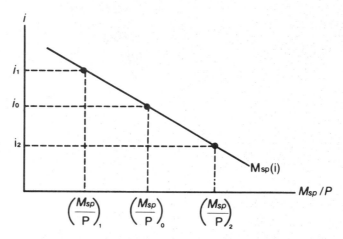

FIGURE 8–8. Speculative Money Demand

If the market interest rate were higher (say, i_1), fewer individuals would expect the interest rate to rise and more would expect it to fall. Thus the real value of idle speculative balances demanded would be less (say, $[M_{sp}/P]_1$) than demanded at interest rate i_0.

Analogously, for an interest rate below i_0 (say, i_2), more individuals would expect the interest rate to rise and fewer would expect it to fall. Thus more individuals would choose to hold their savings in the form of money balances, and fewer would choose bonds, so that the quantity of money balances demanded would be greater (say, $[M_{sp}/P]_2$). As shown in Figure 8–8, then, the aggregate demand for speculative balances is an inverse function of the interest rate, or

$$\frac{M_{sp}}{P} = M_{sp}(i) \qquad (8-4)$$

such that

$$\frac{\Delta(M_{sp}/P)}{\Delta i} < 0$$

---

[6]In popular investment jargon, an individual who expects interest rates to fall (bond prices to rise) is a *bull* and one who expects interest rates to rise (bond prices to fall) is a *bear*.

The total demand for money is simply the sum of the transactions-precautionary demand and speculative demand. Since speculative demand is definitely an inverse function of the interest rate, and since transactions-precautionary demand for money also tends to exhibit some negative interest-sensitivity, the total money demand function, plotted against the interest rate, slopes downward from left to right, as shown in part (c) of Figure 8–9.

In graphic terms, the total money demand schedule is obtained simply by the horizontal summation of the transactions-precautionary demand schedule and the speculative demand schedule. Algebraically, this sum is (from equations 8–3 and 8–4)

$$\frac{M_D}{P} = \frac{M_{tp}}{P} + \frac{M_{sp}}{P} \tag{8–5}$$

or, to plug in the schedules for transactions-precautionary and speculative demand,

$$\frac{M_D}{P} = M_{tp}(i,\ y) + M_{sp}(i) \tag{8–6}$$

or

$$\frac{M_D}{P} = M_D(i,\ y) \tag{8–7}$$

The resulting total demand for money is an inverse function of the interest rate, as shown in part (c) of Figure 8–9, and a positive function of real income, so that the total money demand function shifts rightward (or leftward) with an increase (or a decrease) in real income. A price change leaves the real value of the demand for money balances unchanged, with the nominal quantity of money demanded varying in the same proportion as prices.

The Equilibrium Interest Rate

The money supply schedule and the money demand schedule developed above are combined to form a hypothetical money market in part (a) of Figure 8–10. The equilibrium interest rate in this market is i_{eq}, the rate that just exactly equates the supply of and the demand for money. The nature of the financial market adjustments that insure that i_{eq} is the equilibrium rate can readily be visualized if, like Keynes, we treat all income-yielding financial assets as perpetual bonds. The participants in the money market are restricted to the substitution of money for bonds (or vice versa) when the interest rate is not at level i_{eq}. If savers have only the financial assets money and perpetual bonds in which they can hold their savings, the interest rate that makes wealth-holders just satisfied to hold the exist-

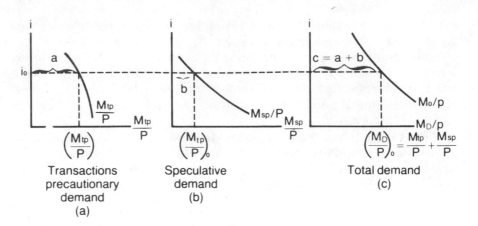

FIGURE 8–9. Total Demand for Money

ing stock of money in their portfolios must also make them just satisfied to hold the available supply of bonds. To illustrate that point, the market for bonds is depicted in part (b) of Figure 8–10, with bond supply and bond demand equated at interest rate i_{eq}.

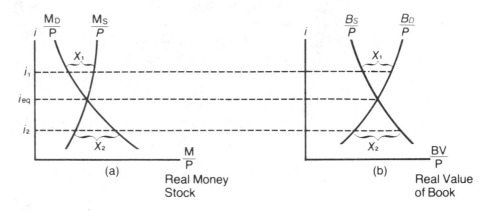

FIGURE 8–10. The Equilibrium Interest Rate

Notice that the schedules in part (b) of Figure 8–10 have an unusual appearance—the bond supply schedule (B_S) slopes downward from left to right and the bond demand schedule (B_D) slopes upward. The apparent reversal of the normal slopes of those schedules is the result of our plotting of supply and demand against the interest rate instead of against bond prices (remember that bond prices are inversely related to the interest rate). Also, for consistency with part (a) of Figure 8–10, the horizontal axis of the bond market diagram shows the real value of bonds supplied and demanded. Since the bonds in our analysis have been assumed to be perpetuities, the real value of every bond is $V = (1/P) \cdot (R/i) = (R/iP)$ and, if there are B bonds in existence, the total market value of the supply of bonds is $B \cdot V = B \cdot R/iP$. An increase in the interest rate decreases the market value of every bond, and hence of the entire existing supply of bonds. In addition, since an increase in the interest rate means a higher cost of funds to borrowers, the flow supply of newly issued bonds can be expected to decline. Thus our bond supply schedule slopes downward from left to right, with a higher (or a lower) interest rate resulting in a smaller (or a larger) real value of bonds supplied.[7] On the other hand, an interest rate increase convinces more wealth-holders that they should dishoard money, which pays no interest, and exchange money for bonds. Hence a higher (or a lower) interest rate results in an increased (or a decreased) demand for bonds, which results in the upward slope of the bond demand schedule.

We can now corroborate the claim that i_{eq} is the equilibrium interest rate. Suppose that the actual market interest rate rises to level i_1. With more wealth-holders wanting to hold their accumulated savings in bonds and fewer wanting them in money form at this elevated interest rate, there is now an excess supply of money (dishoarding) and an excess demand for bonds. Further, since our wealth-holders are confined to placing their wealth either in money or in bonds, the real value of the excess supply of money must be equal to the real value of the excess demand for bonds (X_1 in both the money market and the bond market). This excess demand for bonds drives bond prices upward. As bond prices rise (the interest rate falls), the quantity of money demanded increases and the quantity supplied shrinks, which closes the gap between money demand and money supply. Likewise, this fall in the interest rate (increase in bond prices) closes the gap between bond supply and bond demand. Clearly, any excess supply of money (excess demand for bonds) sets in motion forces that depress the interest rate toward the equilibrium rate—a rate at which society is willing to hold the available supply of money and, simultaneously, at which bond supply equals bond demand.

Should the interest rate fall below the equilibrium level, say, to level i_2, the result is an excess demand for money (hoarding) and, correspondingly, an excess supply of bonds. The consequent effort by society to build up its money balances by the sale of the alternative asset, bonds, raises the

---

[7]If we are interested in the forces that influence interest rates in the short run, flow changes in bond supply are negligible compared to changes in the value of the existing stock of bonds and hence can be ignored without a change in our arguments.

rate of interest (lowers the price of bonds), so that the supply of money increases and the demand for money is reduced until no gap remains between the two. This rise in the interest rate must also raise the demand for bonds and reduce the bond supply until these two are equal. Quite apparently, the adjustments that restore equilibrium in our bond market also restore equilibrium in our hypothetical money market: hoarding is eliminated when the interest rate has reached its equilibrium level.

Applying the Liquidity Preference Theory

To see how the liquidity preference model can be applied in analyzing financial market developments, suppose that the Fed decides to increase the monetary base through an open-market purchase of government bonds. Of course, with a larger reserve base, commercial banks will be induced to extend more credit, expanding the money supply. Figure 8–11 shows money and bond markets originally in equilibrium at interest rate i_0. With an increase in the reserve base available to commercial banks, the money supply is increased, as is indicated by schedule $(M_S/P)'$. At the original interest rate (i_0), there is now an excess demand for bonds, as wealth-holders attempt to exchange surplus money balances for the alternative financial asset, bonds. Therefore bond prices must rise (interest rates decline) until both the money and bond markets are cleared at interest rate i_1. In contrast, a reduction in the monetary base reduces the money supply and consequently raises the interest rate.

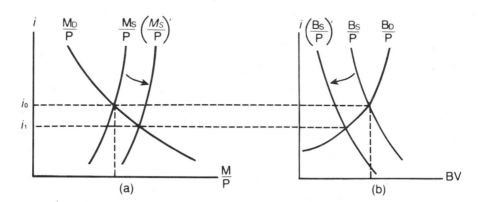

FIGURE 8–11. An Increase in the Monetary Base

Our analysis of the effects of a change in the monetary base has shown again that the forces that influence the interest rate and provide equilibrium in the bond market do so in the market for money as well. As such, our discussion of those forces can be conducted by focusing on either market and ignoring the other. By convention, the liquidity preference model has generally been employed and the bond market suppressed, and we will follow that convention as we consider another example of a financial market adjustment.

Consider, next, the impact on interest rates of an expansion in the economy's output. With an increase in output, the transactions demand for money is increased, raising the overall demand for money. Figure 8–12 shows the resulting excess demand for money (X) at interest rate i_0 as the money demand schedule has shifted outward to position $(M_D/P)'$. In an effort to increase its money balances, society will then offer to sell increased volumes of bonds (the excess demand for money is matched by an excess supply of bonds), so that bond prices fall and the interest rate rises to level i_1. At this point, the markets for bonds and for money are again in equilibrium, with a higher interest rate equating both money supply with money demand and bond supply with bond demand. In contrast, a contraction in the economy's output reduces the demand for money, which results in some decline in the amount of money available and a fall in the interest rate. Like the loanable funds theory, then, the liquidity preference theory predicts systematic changes in interest rates as economic activity fluctuates.

Using the liquidity preference model to describe the pattern of adjustments that might take place over a business cycle requires us to employ the arguments developed above on the impact of output and money supply changes and also allows us to deal with some additional factors that influence interest rates. Output and the demand for money rise in the early stages of a business expansion. At the same time, monetary policy is apt to be expansionary, so that the growing demand for money may be satisfied with an increased money supply, without much change in interest rates. But, as the expansion proceeds and exerts increasing pressure on productive capacity, prices typically rise, reducing the real value of the money supply. In addition, by this stage of the business cycle, the Fed is apt to have begun to tighten the reins on credit out of fear of accelerating inflation. Hence interest rates can be expected to rise by the latter stages of a business expansion, a tendency which, we will soon see, may be reinforced if society expects the prevailing inflation rate to rise during the expansion.

Once an expansion has ended and the economy is contracting, money demand is reduced, as the transactions need for money shrinks and interest rates decline. However, if the contraction contributes to an increase in the uncertainty with which society perceives the economy's future, the precautionary demand for money increases, preventing interest rates from falling as far as they otherwise would. Finally, as the contrac-

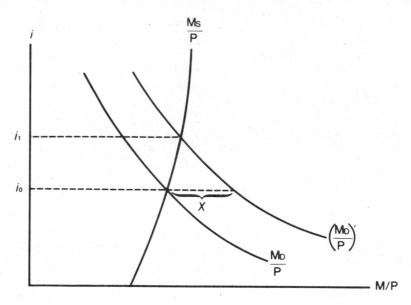

FIGURE 8–12. The Effects of a Change in Output

tion proceeds, attempts by the Fed to revitalize the economy by increasing the money supply produce a further decline in interest rates.

Loanable Funds or Liquidity Preference?

In our development of the liquidity preference theory, we saw that, if money and bonds are the only alternatives in which savers can hold their wealth, the bond market and our hypothetical market for money are mirror images of one another, with the same forces influencing interest rates in each market. A moment's reflection will permit you to realize that activities in the bond market (in the liquidity preference theory) correspond to activities in the credit market (in the loanable funds theory). The *flow* demand for bonds in any period is the supply of credit (loanable funds), and the *flow* supply of bonds to the bond market is the demand for credit (loanable funds). At equilibrium, according to the liquidity preference model, the *stock* of money matches the demand for a money stock, and the *stock* of bonds matches the demand for a stock of bonds. For this latter condition to hold, it is also necessary for the flow supply of bonds to equal the flow demand for bonds. Hence the liquidity preference model and the loanable funds model should not be viewed as completely separate and independent explanations of the interest-rate determination process. The interest rate that equates money supply and demand (so that no hoarding and no dishoarding occur) must also provide for a full equilibrium in the market for loanable funds, so that loanable funds supply (flow demand for bonds) equals loanable funds demand (flow supply of bonds). It remains true, of course, that, when hoarding or dishoarding does occur, the loanable funds model provides a temporary, market-clearing interest rate, which does not correspond to equilibrium in the money market. This simply reflects the focus of loanable funds analysis on forces that produce week-to-week and month-to-month changes in the interest rate. When events that temporarily influence interest rates have run their course, there can be only one interest rate that provides equilibrium in both the market for money and the market for loanable funds.

It may be objected, however, that in reality wealth-holders are not limited to just money and securities as assets in which they can hold their wealth. For instance, they might switch out of money into consumer durables in anticipation of an increase in the price of consumer goods. That is, an excess supply of money might be a reflection, not of an excess demand for bonds, which reduces interest rates, but of an excess demand for hard goods. Similarly, an excess supply of bonds, which raises interest rates, might reflect an accompanying excess demand for goods as society tries to revise its wealth portfolio to hold more in hard goods and less in securities. Hence wealth-holders engage in spending, in lending or borrowing, and in hoarding or dishoarding money balances as they strive for more pleasing portfolios of assets. These activities take place in the markets for goods and services, for loanable funds, and for money, respectively. For a general, or economywide, equilibrium, all three markets must be cleared —planned spending on goods and services must match the supply of goods and services, the volume of funds made available for loans must match borrowers' demand for funds, and the supply of money must match the demand for money. Of course, if any two of the markets are in equilibrium, the third must also be cleared: an excess supply or demand condition cannot prevail in one market alone. The interest rate that provides equilibrium in both the commodities market and the money market must also clear the market for loanable funds. Likewise, an interest rate that clears the goods market and the loanable funds market must also clear the money market. Whether models focus on the loanable funds market or on the money market, they must yield comparable explanations of interest-rate movements from one position of general equilibrium to another.

Price Expectations and the Market Interest Rate

In analyzing the determination of an equilibrium value of the interest rate, we have allowed for once-and-for-all changes in the general price level by adjusting the real value of the money supply in the liquidity preference theory or by adjusting the demand for loanable funds in the loanable funds model. However, we have not entertained the possibility of a continuing, nonzero rate of price change. Hence we have tacitly assumed that the general price level is *expected* to remain unchanged in the future.

When no change in the general price level is anticipated, the *nominal* interest rate, which is observed in both the money market and the loanable funds market, measures the expected *real* interest yield on bonds. But, when the general price level is expected to change, the real (price-adjusted) yield on bonds can differ substantially from the observed interest rate, so that we are required to distinguish between the nominal and real rates of interest.

Without attempting here to explain how those expectations are generated, suppose that borrowers and lenders have come to expect an increase in the price level. If prices rise, the purchasing power of money shrinks. Hence lenders (bond-holders), whose financial claims for interest and principal payments are fixed in dollar terms, suffer capital losses while borrowers (bond issuers) enjoy equivalent capital gains. Of course, instead of lending, savers could exchange their savings for real property (land and commodities), the dollar value of which rises with the general price level. With this option available, savers who anticipate inflation would be willing to lend their savings (buy bonds) only if the nominal interest yield is sufficient (1) to compensate for the loss of purchasing power of the dollar repayments they receive and (2) to provide the reward (real interest) they require to forego the current use of funds. By the same token, borrowers who anticipate inflation would be willing to pay a higher nominal interest rate since they expect their future interest and principal payments to be made in depreciated dollars.

If lenders and borrowers both expect the same rate of change in the general price level, the nominal interest rate differs from the real rate by that expected rate of price change. In algebraic terms, with prices expected to change at the rate of $\Delta P^e/P$ each period (e indicates an expected change in P), the nominal interest rate is

$$i = \rho + \frac{\Delta P^e}{P}$$

where ρ is the real rate of interest—the rate that would prevail if no change in the price level were expected.[8] With the price level expected

---

[8]To be mathematically complete, our expression for the nominal interest rate should be written as

$$i = \rho + \frac{\Delta P^e}{P} + \rho \frac{\Delta P^e}{P}$$

where the last term, $\rho(\Delta P^e/P)$, measures the expected change in the real value of interest payments. Since this term is quantitatively negligible, it is normally ignored in attempts to explain movements in the nominal interest rate.

to remain unchanged, if the equilibrium interest rate (nominal and real) were 4 percent and prices were expected to rise by 4 percent per period, the nominal interest rate would be 8 percent; if prices were expected to rise 6 percent per period, the market interest rate would be 10 percent; and so on. If the substantial inflation that the United States began to experience in the mid-1960s produced expectations of continuing inflation, the record high interest rates witnessed in the United States in recent years may largely reflect these expectations instead of a rise in the real rate of interest. What portion of observed interest yields does, in fact, represent an inflation premium must remain to some extent a matter of conjecture, since we cannot directly observe either the real interest rate or the value of expected price changes.[9]

To complete our current discussion of the role of expected changes in the price level, we must determine whether it is the nominal or the real rate of interest that our previous analytical efforts have identified as an important determinant of both money demand and planned investment spending. First, for the holders of money balances, the nominal interest rate is relevant, for this is the rate that must be sacrificed if one holds money instead of bonds. In contrast, it is the real interest rate that determines the level of investment spending. To justify that claim, consider an inflationary period—a period in which the prices business firms receive for the goods and services they produce are rising. During a generalized inflation, the production costs firms face are also rising, in the same proportion as prices. Hence the net revenue firms can expect to flow from any investment they undertake is increased by just the expected rate of inflation. Since the nominal interest cost of investment is also increased by just the expected inflation rate, the same investment decisions would be made no matter what the size of the inflation premium built into the nominal interest rate. That is, the level of investment must depend on the real interest rate.

A Look Back

Our objective in this chapter has been to isolate the forces that determine the level of interest rates in general. Two models were devel-

---

[9]For the most part, existing investigations of the formation of price expectations conclude that expectations are modified only very slowly in response to experienced price-level movements. For example, see T. J. Sargent, "Commodity Price Expectations and the Interest Rate," *Quarterly Journal of Economics 83* (February 1969) 127–40; and W. E. Gibson, "Price Expectations Effects on Interest Rates," *Journal of Finance 25* (March 1970) 19–34. A shorter adjustment period is found in W. P. Yohe and D. S. Karnosky, "Interest Rates and Price Level Changes," *Review—Federal Reserve Bank of St. Louis*, Vol. 51, December 1969, pp. 19–36.

oped to attain that objective, the loanable funds model and the Keynesian liquidity preference model. The former focuses attention on the flow supply of and demand for credit, and the latter concentrates on the demand for and the supply of a stock of money.

For general equilibrium, all markets in our economic system—including the goods market, the money market, and the loanable funds market—must be cleared. Thus the interest rate that provides general equilibrium must equate planned spending on final goods and services with their supply, the supply of loanable funds with the demand for them, and the supply of money with the demand for it. As such, the forces that influence the interest rate can be analyzed and explained in terms of the loanable funds model or the liquidity preference model, the choice between those two generally being made on the basis of convenience.

Liquidity preference models can be more conveniently integrated into analyses of the functioning of the economy as a whole, so that those models have been the focus of a great deal of attention from economists and financial analysts. That attention has resulted in a number of refinements in the treatment of the demand for money, to remedy some apparent shortcomings in the original Keynesian analysis. A review of the resulting modern money demand models will complete this chapter.

POST-KEYNESIAN MONEY DEMAND MODELS

The Keynesian liquidity preference theory of interest-rate determination provides an aggregate demand function for money balances, which involves an inverse relation between the interest rate and money demand. However, a smooth, continuous, functional relation between the interest rate and money demand is possible only if, among the millions of individual demanders of money, there is a diversity of opinion about the value of the normal rate of interest. That is, there is no comparably smooth, continuous response to interest in individual money demand, since, in Keynes's analysis, every individual wants to hold *all* of his or her speculative wealth either in money (if bond prices are expected to fall) or in bonds (if bond prices are expected to rise), never part in each. This kind of behavior is reasonable if individuals feel certain they know the future path of changes in the interest rate (or of changes in bond prices). However, the real world rarely allows expectations about the future to be held with certainty, and, as we know, the existence of uncertainty or risk is likely to prompt an individual to hold wealth in both money and securities, that is, to hold a diversified portfolio. The arguments below show that, in a world characterized by uncertainty or risk, an individual's speculative money demand can be a continuous inverse function of the interest rate. As a consequence, a smooth aggregate relation between the interest rate and money demand is possible without an appeal to a diversity of opinion, which would gradually erode as the interest rate rests at a near-constant level for substantial time periods.

Risk and Money Demand

We know that individuals hold diversified portfolios (for example, one might simultaneously hold money, stocks, bonds, and savings deposits). This would not be the case if there were certainty with respect to yields on various assets, for then individuals would hold only one asset—the one that offers the highest yield. In a Keynesian world, where there are only two liquid assets, money and long-term bonds, one can increase the expected yield on one's portfolio only by increasing the proportion of wealth held in the form of interest-yielding bonds. However, since interest rates (and hence bond prices) are subject to unexpected movements, an individual who increases the proportion held in bonds faces a greater risk of capital loss. James Tobin has developed a model that takes into account the risk that wealth-holders associate with bonds, to analyze its influence on speculative money demand.[10]

Assuming all bonds are identical, we can use Figure 8–13 to graphically describe the risk-yield tradeoff available to an individual. In that figure, the expected percentage yield on the individual's total portfolio of liquid assets is measured on the vertical axis, and the risk of the total portfolio is measured on the horizontal axis. The linear tradeoff schedule indicates that (since all bonds are assumed to be identical) both expected yield and risk increase in direct proportion to the allocation of speculative wealth to bond holdings. If an individual's entire portfolio is held in the form of money (point A in Figure 8–13), there is zero yield and zero risk. In contrast, for any given total stock of liquid wealth in the portfolio, both expected yield and risk attain their maximum values (i_{max} and R_{max} respectively) if the entire portfolio is held in the form of bonds (point B in the figure).

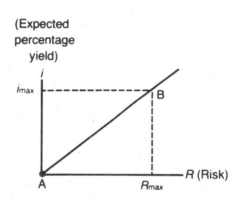

FIGURE 8–13. Risk-Yield Tradeoff Available to a Wealth-holder

[10]See James Tobin, "Liquidity Preference as Behavior Toward Risk," *Review of Economic Studies* 25 (February 1958) 65–68.

If a typical wealth-holder finds risk unpleasant, i.e., is risk-averse,[11] this individual would be willing to hold a higher-risk portfolio of assets only if it had a higher expected yield, as compensation for the additional risk. We can represent this willingness to trade yield for risk by a set of indifference curves, as shown in Figure 8–14. As was noted in chapter 6, an individual is indifferent to choosing between alternative portfolios represented by points on any one indifference curve. For example, an individual would feel equally well off at position A or at position A' on indifference curve II. However, movement to a higher indifference curve provides an unequivocal improvement in the individual's well-being (in our figure, movement to a higher indifference curve provides a higher expected yield with no increase in risk or an equal yield with lower risk).

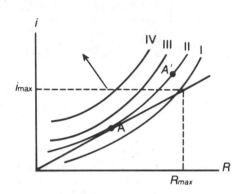

FIGURE 8–14. Portfolio Equilibrium

As was indicated earlier, a risk-averse individual would accept a riskier portfolio only if it had a higher expected rate of return, to compensate for the accompanying disutility. Further, it is usually assumed that the higher the level of risk, the larger must be the compensatory addition to the expected yield. These assumptions dictate the shape of the indifference curves in Figure 8–14. Given the initial endowment of wealth (which constrains the size of the portfolio), the interest rate, and the degree of uncertainty with respect to future interest rates (bond prices), our utility-maximizing individual would choose to hold the one determinate mix of money and bonds that lay on the highest attainable indifference curve (point A on curve II).

Now, suppose that the market interest rate (i.e., the expected percentage yield on bonds) rises with no change in the perceived risk of bonds. This change in the expected percentage yield would rotate the available risk-yield tradeoff schedule counterclockwise, as shown in Figure 8–15. As a consequence, our utility-maximizing individual would change holdings to move from point A to point B. The new portfolio (point B) could be subject to more risk (R_1 instead of R_0) only if the proportion of the portfolio held in bonds were to increase and, therefore, only if the

---

[11]Individuals who are risk-averse would choose to receive $100 with certainty, in preference to an expected return of $100 (e.g., an opportunity to receive either $0 or $200 with a 50 percent probability of each outcome).

proportion held in money were to decrease. Thus we have shown that, for the individual represented by the figure, an increase in the interest rate can reduce the speculative demand for money.[12] Direct aggregation of such individual speculative demand schedules generates a market speculative demand function exhibiting the same property of inverse interest-sensitivity, but which need not rely on the assumption of a diversity of opinion about the normal interest rate. Other indifference map patterns, which support different conclusions about the response of money demand to interest-rate changes, can be constructed. But if the Tobin analysis is a correct explanation of speculative money demand, then the widespread empirical support for an inverse interest-sensitivity in aggregate money demand suggests that the behavioral response illustrated in Figure 8–15 is the dominant pattern.

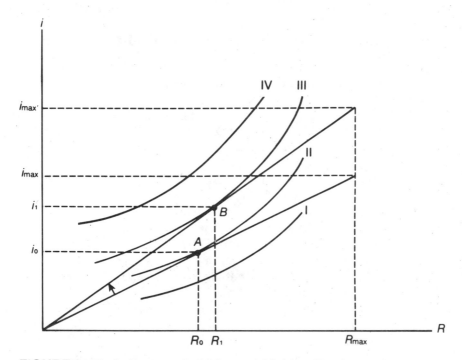

FIGURE 8–15. An Increase in the Interest Yield on Bonds

---

[12]We have not shown that the speculative demand for money is an inverse function of the interest rate for every individual in every range of possible interest rates. In fact, you can and should construct sets of indifference curves that show a positive response of speculative demand to interest-rate changes.

In the Tobin model, the degree of risk that wealth-holders associate with bonds also influences bond demand, as well as money demand. Should events (such as energy crises, strikes, bank failures) cause society to perceive bonds as more risky, the budget constraint facing wealth-holders would be rotated clockwise: portfolio risk would be greater at every conceivable interest rate. For the individual represented in Figure 8–15, and for society at large if this response is typical, an increase in the risk associated with bond-holding reduces the demand for bonds as it raises the demand for money.

The two-asset analysis conducted above can be generalized to n assets, including real business capital and other financial claims in addition to money and bonds. Hence Tobin's analysis represents a generalization of the liquidity preference theory, which introduces uncertainty as a reason for holding money in a portfolio of assets that may also contain a number of alternatives to money.

Interest-Sensitive Transactions Demand for Money

Both the Keynesian version and Tobin's version of the liquidity preference theory rationalize the existence of a strong interest-sensitivity in the aggregate money demand function by demonstrating an interest-sensitivity of speculative demand. They do so, however, in an artificial world that has only two assets—money, the value of which is constant, and long-term bonds, the value of which varies with changes in the interest rate.

In the real world, wealth can also be held in stocks, short-term bonds, savings bonds, savings accounts, and so on. The existence of a significant speculative demand for money in such a world has been seriously questioned, since individuals who fear declines in bond prices can still hold their wealth in an interest-bearing form, instead of money, with little or no fear of capital losses—for example, in a savings account or in 90-day Treasury bills, both assets being essentially risk-free and virtually instantly convertible into money or other assets.

If interest-rate changes do not induce a shift in speculative wealth between bond holdings and money, total money demand can be interest-sensitive only if transactions demand is interest-sensitive. A number of analysts have demonstrated that a significant interest-sensitivity in transactions demand should be expected, on the basis of simple cash management models provided by both William Baumol and James Tobin.[13]

Baumol's analysis suggests that transactions money holdings should

---

[13]William Baumol, "The Transactions Demand for Cash: An Inventory Theoretic Approach," *Quarterly Journal of Economics* 66 (November 1952), 545–46; and J. Tobin, "The Interest-Elasticity of Transactions Demand for Cash," *Review of Economics and Statistics* 38 (August 1956), 241–47.

be treated as an inventory, from which gradual drains occur as transactions needs are met. There are costs involved in maintaining this inventory (as is the case with every inventory), and it is in the interest of any individual or business firm to minimize these costs.

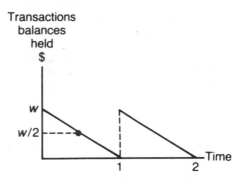

FIGURE 8–16. The Time Path of Transactions Balances

Let us look at an individual's inventory control task and assume, for simplicity, that purchase transactions are perfectly foreseen and occur in a steady stream. If money balances in amount w are acquired at the beginning of each time period and are steadily expended through the period until they are exhausted at its end, the average transactions balance held is $w/2$. Such a flow pattern is graphed in Figure 8–16.

There are two components of the total cost of maintaining an inventory of money balances. First, the value of foregone interest income, on an average volume of money inventory of $w/2$, is simply $i \cdot w/2$ if i is the available market interest rate. Second, noninterest transactions costs are incurred each time a cash acquisition occurs: for example, there are brokerage fees for converting securities into cash, postage, bookkeeping expenses, and transportation costs of going to a bank or broker. If T is the value of transactions that must be financed in our selected time period and w is the size of withdrawals, then T/w is the number of cash acquisitions (withdrawals) required. If the dollar transactions cost of making one cash acquisition or withdrawal is n, then the noninterest cost of money inventory management in our selected period is $n \cdot T/w$.

Thus the total cost of money inventory management is

$$tc = (i \cdot w/2) + (n \cdot T/w),$$

the interest cost plus transactions (withdrawals) cost. An individual who holds large cash balances will make few withdrawals, and $n \cdot T/w$ will be small; foregone interest costs will be large, however. Conversely, small average cash balances will result in relatively high transactions costs and low interest costs. Only one size of withdrawal (and hence only one value of average cash balances) will minimize the total cost of maintaining an adequate cash inventory.

Figure 8–17 shows how the interest cost and the transactions cost of maintaining an inventory of transactions balances vary with the size of withdrawal. Vertically summing these two cost components yields the total cost schedule plotted in that figure. The size of withdrawal that

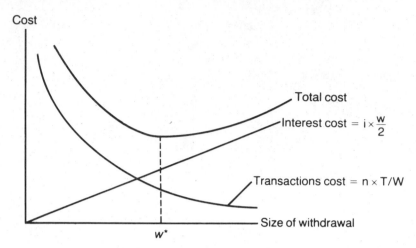

FIGURE 8–17. The Costs of a Cash Inventory for a Specified Volume of Transactions per Period

minimizes the total cost of maintaining an inventory of cash balances sufficient to finance our T dollars of transactions per period is w^*. In this example then, average money balances would be $w^*/2$.

An increase in the interest rate would rotate the interest-cost schedule counterclockwise, which would shift the total cost curve upward and leftward. The leftward shift would reduce the cost-minimizing size of cash withdrawal and would thus reduce the average volume of desired transactions balances. Quite simply, a rise in the interest cost of holding an inventory of transactions balances induces a reduction in the quantity of dollars demanded for that purpose.

An increase in the volume of transactions to be financed during our observation period would shift the transactions cost schedule upward, since more withdrawals of any selected size would be required to meet transactions needs. As a result, the total cost schedule would be shifted rightward, which would increase the optimal size of withdrawal and the average size of transactions balances.[14]

Thus the inventory model argues that transactions demand for

---

[14]The formula for the optimal size of withdrawal is $w = \sqrt{2nT/i}$. This formula makes it clear that this optimum and the corresponding average cash inventory ($w/2$) vary inversely with the interest rate. It also suggests that transactions demand for money is proportional to the square root of the volume of transactions, which implies that there are some scale economies in cash-holding. Empirical evidence that there are such scale economies is provided in Stephen Goldfeld, "The Demand for Money Revisited," *Brookings Papers on Economic Activity* 3 (1973), 602.

money is positively related to the volume of transactions and inversely related to the interest rate. These conclusions have general applicability, since this model was developed to analyze either individual or business behavior. That is not to say, however, that we should expect to see the average individual investing a fraction of his or her monthly salary in interest-yielding securities, to be exchanged for cash during the following month in order to meet transactions needs. For most individuals, the fixed cost of converting cash into securities and then back into cash exceeds the interest income that could be earned during the period between income receipts. On the other hand, a large business firm that must accumulate sizable cash balances to pay annual employee bonuses or to meet quarterly tax liabilities profits from temporarily investing those funds in interest-earning securities. The broad array of highly liquid, low-risk assets available, as well as the ease with which those assets can be acquired and disposed of, makes such investments irresistible.

It should be apparent that the inventory model provides an aggregate money demand function that is qualitatively equivalent to the Keynesian model. According to either model, aggregate money demand is a positive function of the income level and an inverse function of the interest rate. Significantly, though, the inventory model can explain the empirically observed interest-sensitivity of money demand without resort to a speculative demand for money.

The thrust of the Keynesian analysis and of the modern refinements just reviewed, is that the demand for money is the result of rational choice, taking account of the yields on assets that are substitutes for money, the risk associated with those assets, and the level of income. Money demand is inversely related to the interest yield on money-substitutes and to the perceived riskiness of income-yielding assets; it is directly related to income (transactions). This Keynesian *portfolio balance approach* to explaining the demand for money contrasts sharply with the treatment of

---

The derivation of the optimal withdrawal formula is a straightforward application of the classical calculus of maximization. If the total cost of maintaining the cash inventory is

$$tc = \left(\frac{i}{2} \cdot w \right) + \left(n \cdot \frac{T}{w} \right)$$

the rate of change (first derivative) of total cost with respect to withdrawal size is

$$\frac{d(tc)}{dw} = \frac{i}{2} - n\frac{T}{w^2}$$

Setting the rate of change equal to zero (an extreme value of the total cost function) and solving for the withdrawal size yields the formula above. The second derivative of the total cost function is positive, which indicates that the extreme value for total cost is a minimum value.

money demand by most of Keynes's predecessors, who considered only a transactions demand for money, and who mechanically linked nominal money demand to the value of output.

Friedman's Modern Quantity Theory of Money

In the 1950s, Milton Friedman reformulated the quantity theory of the demand for money to make it more acceptable to modern-day analysts.[15] Like Keynesians, Friedman treats the demand for money as a result of asset choice. However, he draws no distinctions among money balances that are held for different purposes (transactions, etc.) but simply regards all money holdings as an asset that yields a stream of services to the holder.

To Friedman, money is just one of many assets in which an individual's total wealth can be held, and total wealth (both human and property wealth) is the proper budget constraint for all asset demands. Of course, *permanent income* is just the yield on total wealth, which rises and falls with wealth, so that it can be employed as a proxy for wealth in the money demand function. Friedman argues further that money is a luxury good—one that has an income-elasticity greater than one—so that a change in income calls forth a proportionally greater change in money demand in the same direction.

As is the case with any asset, the quantity of money demanded is also influenced by the opportunity cost of holding it, and that cost is determined by the rate of interest and the rate of change in the general price level. By holding money, an individual forgoes the interest earnings that would be provided by securities (e.g., bonds). The higher the interest rate, the greater the loss of earnings and, presumably, the smaller the demand for money. Hence money demand is an inverse function of the interest rate.

The real purchasing power of money shrinks as prices rise. By holding real assets (such as land), which increase in nominal value as prices rise, one can avoid this loss of purchasing power. In this case, money has, in effect, a negative yield. The higher the rate at which prices are expected to rise, the greater the shrinkage in command over real goods and services and, presumably, the smaller the demand for money. Conversely, a decline in the general price level produces an effective positive yield on money balances. The faster the rate at which prices are expected to decline, the

---

[15]Milton Friedman, "A Theoretical Framework for Monetary Analysis," *Journal of Political Economy* 78 (March/April 1970), 193–238.

larger the demand for money, according to Friedman. (Other factors, such as anticipated wars, instability in capital markets, and the ratio of human to nonhuman wealth, may also influence money demand, according to Friedman, but our discussion will ignore these less crucial determinants.)

Friedman's modern quantity theory of the demand for money takes the form

$$M_D = f(W, i, \Delta P^e/P)$$

such that

$$\frac{\Delta M_D}{\Delta W} > 0$$

$$\frac{\Delta M_D}{\Delta i} < 0$$

$$\frac{\Delta M_D}{\Delta P^e/P} < 0$$

Where W is an individual's total wealth, i is the interest rate, $\Delta P^e/P$ is the expected inflation rate, and M_D is money demand. Without reliable data on wealth (measures of human wealth are very hard to acquire), this equation can be reformulated as

$$M_D = f(Y_P, i, \Delta P^e/P)$$

In this equation, permanent income (Y_P) is employed as a proxy for wealth; in turn, estimates of Y_p can be obtained from observed measures of income. The aggregate demand for money is obtained by summing all the individual money demand schedules for the wealth-holders in our economy.

Alternatively, since the modern quantity theory assumes that the demand for money is a demand for real purchasing power—that nominal money demand varies in proportion to changes in the general price level if no change occurs in the anticipated inflation rate—Friedman's money demand function can be rewritten as

$$M_D = P \cdot f(y_p, i, \Delta P^e/P)$$

or

$$\frac{M_D}{P} = f(y_p, i, \Delta P^e/P)$$

In these equations, y_p is the real value of permanent income, and P is the general price level.

In a static world in which income stayed the same period after period, observed income would be viewed as permanent income. If, in addition, no changes in the general price level were anticipated ($\Delta P^e / P = 0$), the money demand function could be rewritten as

$$\frac{M_D}{P} = f(y, i)$$

This equation says that real money demand depends on current real income and the interest rate, just as in the simple Keynesian model. But this is a prediction for a special case in Friedman's analysis, which requires very restrictive assumptions.

Clearly, the Friedman formulation of the modern quantity theory of money is a portfolio balance model (like the Keynesian model) which has been generalized to take account of nonzero rates of expected inflation and extended income horizons. Friedman's analysis is also distinctive in that he views money and bonds as poor substitutes for one another, so that, in his model, interest rate changes have only a weak effect on money demand.

Conclusions on Money Demand

Our brief review of the modern evolution of money demand analysis has revealed that portfolio balance models, involving the application of standard asset choice techniques, have provided the common framework for each extension or refinement of money demand theory. Various forms of the portfolio balance model have indicated that money demand tends to be influenced by wealth, income, the interest rate, the general price level and its expected rate of change, and some other, more esoteric factors, such as transaction costs of conversions between money and securities and perceived risk on income-yielding securities. Numerous statistical investigations have been conducted to test the reasonableness of our money demand models and to measure the responsiveness of money demand to changes in the variables upon which it depends.[16]

Many of the empirical investigations of money demand simply assume that nominal money demand varies in proportion to the general price level. Others have tested this assumption and have generally supported this proportional relation.

To avoid statistical problems, empirical money demand models must

---

[16]For more detailed summaries of the empirical evidence on money demand functions, see J. Carl Poindexter, *Macroeconomics* (Hinsdale, Illinois: The Dryden Press, 1976), pp. 196–97; and David Laidler, *The Demand for Money: Theories and Evidence* (New York: Dun-Donnelley, 1977), chaps. 6–8.

employ a single interest rate (such as the rate on short-term treasury securities) as an indicator of movements in interest rates in general. But different securities experience differing magnitudes of interest-rate variations over time, so that statistical measures of money demand changes that result from interest-rate changes vary with the security chosen. Variations in long-term interest rates are smaller than in short-term rates, so that measured responses in money demand to unit changes in long-term rates are larger.

The measured response of money demand to interest-rate changes also varies with the definition of money, the narrow definition exhibits more interest-responsiveness than do broader measures. With an increase in interest rates in general, the yield on time deposits may rise, which would prompt a significant shift of funds from narrowly defined money (M_1, or currency plus demand deposits), which pays no interest, into time deposits at commercial banks. At the same time, a broader monetary aggregate (say, M_2, consisting of M_1 plus time deposits at commercial banks) may be changed very little if any. In this case, the interest-elasticity of demand for M_1 is much greater than that on the broader measure of money. With different definitions of money, different interest rates, and different time periods from which data are drawn, the many empirical tests of money demand models have uncovered a fairly wide range of measured values of interest-elasticity. Most measures, however, indicate that money demand is definitely an inverse function of the interest rate, with an elasticity considerably less than unity.

In most of the empirical tests of money demand models, changes in either income or wealth have been associated with roughly proportional changes in money demand. Milton Friedman's tests, in contrast, found an income-elasticity factor of 1.8 (i.e., a 1% increase in income resulted in a 1.8% increase in money demand). This greater-than-proportional response in money demand is just what is required to classify money as a luxury good. It is worth noting that this result was obtained with money defined broadly. With the narrow definition of money, which most analysts prefer, the response of money demand is more nearly proportional to permanent income changes. It is also worth noting that the most recent studies have found evidence of economies of scale in the demand for money, such that money demand rose by a smaller proportion than output. Stephen Goldfeld, for example, found that money demand had an income-elasticity of 0.68, using quarterly data for the post–World War II era.[17]

---

[17]S. Goldfeld, "The Demand for Money Revisited," *Brookings Papers on Economic Activity* 3 (1973) 602.

SUMMARY

Continuing our focus on the generation and use of loanable funds, this chapter examined the supply of loanable funds (from saving, dishoarding, and new money creation) and the demand for loanable funds (for business, government, or consumer and foreign use). The combination of these supply and demand schedules, known as the loanable funds model, illustrated the process that determines the volume of financing and the interest price of financing. This model was then applied to explain how a number of events might influence the volume and the interest cost of credit flows in an economy.

Our applications of loanable funds analysis showed it to be a useful device for explaining and forecasting financial market developments. However, it has traditionally been thought that the loanable funds format did not conveniently fit in the more comprehensive models of the economy that are used for macroeconomic forecasting. Those models, instead, have employed the Keynesian liquidity preference theory of interest-rate determination, in which interest rates are determined by money supply and money demand. The liquidity preference theory was developed and employed in this chapter to explain interest-rate responses to a number of possible real-world events. We have also reviewed, in light of its prominence in modern monetary analysis, the major refinements that Keynes's successors have introduced into portfolio balance models of money demand.

The core objective in developing both the loanable funds model and the money market models was to explain the forces that influence interest rates. Both models meet that objective, as they must, for they are not independent explanations of the functioning of independent parts of the financial marketplace. The markets for money, bonds, loanable funds (and, indeed, for real goods and services and for labor) are not independent, and only one interest rate level can simultaneously equate (1) the demand for and the supply of money, (2) the demand for and the supply of bonds, and (3) the demand for and the supply of loanable funds.

With the forces that influence interest rates and the models used to predict the impact of those forces now in mind, our next chapter will explain why, at one point in time, there are distinctively different interest yields on different financial claims, such that, instead of seeing one rate in the financial marketplace, we see an entire structure of rates. In this more complicated and more realistic framework, the forces identified here as influences on interest rates cause increases or decreases in the entire structure of existing interest yields.

9

Accounting for Interest Rate Differentials

In chapter 8, we discussed financial market equilibrium. By considering both the demand for and the supply of funds (or money), we examined the broad forces that influence interest rates. However, in order to focus on the forces that influence these rates in general—i.e., *the* interest rate or *the* level of interest rates—we ignored a number of factors that distinguish among the many interest rates that exist. To complete our analysis of interest yields, we must consider the factors that cause observed differences in yields on various financial instruments. This chapter goes beyond the determination of interest rates in general and considers the differences among particular interest rates.

At any point in time, interest rates vary across a range depending on the type and characteristics of different instruments. The question is, why? Explanations lie in the following factors: time to maturity, risk differences, tax status, ability of the creditor to retire the issue, taxes, marketability, and other miscellaneous factors. Each of these factors will be considered in turn, although this chapter directs a disproportionate share of the attention to variation in time to maturity as a source of interest-rate differentials. This involves the so-called term structure of interest rates, to which we now turn.

THE TERM STRUCTURE OF INTEREST RATES

The *term structure of interest rates* refers to the systematic relationship between the time to maturity and the interest rate on debt instruments. In order to focus only on this relationship, other factors (such as risk or tax considerations) that can also cause interest-rate differentials will be held constant. (These other factors will be considered later in the chapter).

Yield Curves

A yield curve is a graphical depiction of the relation between yields and time for bonds that are equivalent in all respects except maturity.[1] Typically, Treasury securities are chosen for the construction of yield curves because they represent a unique class of debt instruments—they have only one issuer, are default-free (for all practical purposes), and, with minor exceptions such as "flower bonds," are taxable in a uniform manner.[2]

To plot a yield curve, percentage yield is measured on the vertical axis and years to maturity on the horizontal axis. Each point plotted on such a graph depicts a particular Treasury security's yield on a particular date. Yield curves plotted at different times have different shapes. In fact, they change a little every day. Figure 9–1 shows yield curves for U. S. government (Treasury) securities for four different dates during a recent 11-month period.

It is possible to draw a yield curve for any class of debt securities, such as corporates or federal agency securities. Each type has a different curve: the greater the risk (in comparison to Treasury bonds) of each class of securities, the higher the level of its curve. These differences in levels reflect the additional riskiness of these other types of bonds; i.e., the risk premiums demanded by lenders to compensate for the risk of default. These alternative yield curves are not as stable as the yield curve for Treasury bonds. To avoid these complications, we will concentrate on the latter in explaining the term structure of interest rates.

The Shapes of Yield Curves. Yield curves either slope upward, slope downward, or are horizontal (flat). Each of these shapes has implications about the future movements of interest rates. We are ultimately interested in explaining the shape of the yield curve, for which purpose there are hypotheses about the term structure of interest rates, which we will examine shortly.

Typically, yield curves slope upward, as do all four shown in Figure 9–1. Those curves show the rising pattern of interest rates over the period from November 1976 to October 1977. A comparison of the curves in the

---

[1]Yield here refers to *yield to maturity*, which is defined as the percentage yield earned or to be earned on a bond from purchase date to maturity date.

[2]Flower bonds (so called because they are designated for the payment of estate taxes due from the bondholder at death) can provide tax breaks to holders in the settlement of estate taxes. The IRS values such bonds at market value to determine the value of an estate; however, the IRS accepts them at face value for the payment of estate taxes. Therefore flower bonds can save estate taxes if they are selling below par value.

FIGURE 9–1. Yield Curves for U.S. Government Securities for Four Periods During 1976–1977

Source: "U.S. *Financial Data,*" Federal Reserve Bank of St. Louis, October 21, 1977, p. 1.

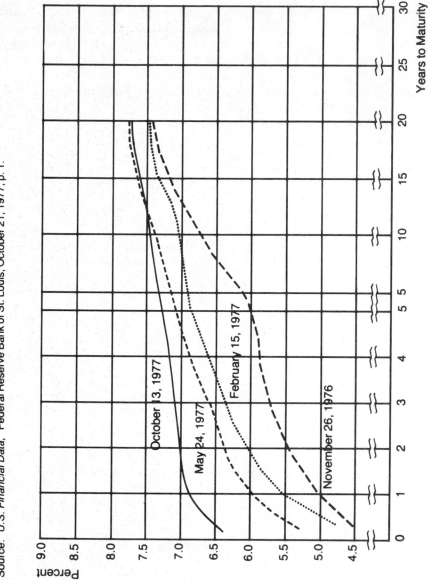

figure demonstrates an important point about interest rates in relation to maturity, namely, general interest-rate fluctuations (upward and downward) result in sharper fluctuations for short-term rates relative to long-term rates. For example, the top two yield curves in the figure show that yields on Treasury securities with maturities in excess of 10 years remained about the same while yields on short-term Treasury securities rose sharply from May to October.[3]

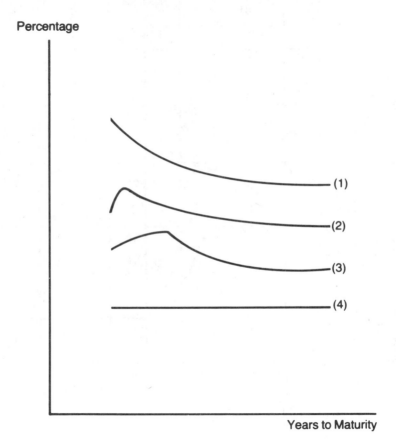

FIGURE 9–2. Downward-Sloping and Flat Yield Curves

Yield curves sometimes slope downward, for example, curves that are plotted when rates are at a peak. Such a curve is (1) in Figure 9–2. Yield curves can also be "humped," with a peak somewhere in the short or

---

[3]A second important point about bonds is that long-term bond prices fluctuate much more than do short-term bond prices for a given percentage change in yield.

intermediate maturity part of the curve. Such curves are respectively (2) and (3) in the figure. Finally, yield curves can be flat, as is (4) of the figure, or flat except for a hump. All of the shapes illustrated in Figure 9–2 are typically associated with periods close to business cycle tops and/or periods of quite high interest rates.

Considering the various shapes of yield curves that have been observed in the past, we can state the following generalizations about interest rates and yield curves:

1. In the early years of the twentieth century—1900 to about 1930—yield curves typically sloped downward.

2. Since the early 1930s, upward-sloping curves have predominated and are now considered normal.

3. Yield curves still slope downward at times, particularly during periods of high interest rates, such as the late 1960s and the mid-1970s. At these times, investors expect short-term rates to fall more sharply than long-term rates.

4. The shape of the yield curve appears to change systematically as the economy expands and contracts over time.

Theories About the Term Structure

The task of a theory of the term structure of interest rates is to explain both the shape and the slope of the yield curve and, correspondingly, to explain why the yield curve shifts into different forms over time. There are three hypotheses commonly advanced to explain the term structure of interest rates: the expectations theory, the liquidity premium theory, and the market segmentation theory. Actually, the liquidity premium theory can be incorporated into either of the other two, so that we really have two major theories. For purposes of exposition, however, we will outline each of the three separately.

The Pure, or Unbiased, Expectations Theory

The pure, or unbiased, expectations theory of the term structure of interest rates holds that the long-term rate of interest is equal to the average of the short-term rates expected to prevail over that long-term period.[4] This equivalence is usually derived from the assumptions that

---

[4]This theory is attributed to Irving Fisher. It was elaborated upon by Friedrich Lutz. See Irving Fisher, *The Theory of Interest Rate.* (New York: Macmillan, 1930) and Friedrich A. Lutz, "The Structure of Interest Rates," *Quarterly Journal of Economics* 55 (November 1940), 36–63.

there are no transactions costs, no market imperfections, and many profit-maximizing investors with identical expectations about future short-term interest rates.[5] If these conditions hold, the term structure at any point in time is, in effect, a set of forward rates (i.e., rates expected to prevail in the future) and a current known rate. For example, a three-year commitment (loan) consists of a one-year current commitment plus two forward one-year commitments, which renew the loan at the beginning of the second and the third years.

Investors desiring a three-year commitment can purchase a three-year security, or, alternatively, they can purchase a one-year security, use its proceeds at the end of the year to purchase another, and repeat the process for the third year. Investors who are rational maximizers choose the alternative with the highest expected return. Forward rates for any period are a function of actual current interest rates in the marketplace. The implicit assumption here is that expected future rates are equal to computed forward rates; investors acting on their expectations will invest in securities in such a way as to equilibrate future rates with their expectations. Whether their expectations are realized or not, the assumption here is that investors hold them today and act upon them.

The expectations theory states that long rates must be an average of present and future short-term rates. For purposes of exposition, let $_tR_n$ be the current yield (i.e., at time t) on a security with n periods to maturity. For example, the yield today on a one-year security is designated $_tR_1$ and the yield today on a five-year security is $_tR_5$. Let $_{t+1}r_n$ be the yield expected to prevail a year from today (i.e., at time $t + 1$) with n periods to maturity. Thus R represents a current rate, and r represents a forward rate.

As an example of the theory, the rate for a three-year bond must be an average of the current rate for one year and the expected forward rate for the next two years. Technically, this average is a geometric, not an arithmetic, mean.[6] Thus

$$(1 + {}_tR_3) = \sqrt[3]{(1 + {}_tR_1)(1 + {}_{t+1}r_1)(1 + {}_{t+2}r_1)} \qquad (9\text{–}1)$$

Likewise, the current two-year rate today is a function of the current one-year rate and the expected one-year rate for period 2. For example, if $_tR_1 = 0.06$ and $_{t+1}r_1 = 0.08$ then $_tR_2 = \sqrt{(1 + 0.06)(1 + 0.08)} = \sqrt{1.1448} = 1.06995$.

---

[5]Market imperfections, as used here, are impediments that prevent interest rates from moving to their competitive level. Examples include governmental regulations and inadequate communications.

[6]The geometric mean is the nth root of the product of n numbers: the geometric mean of 8 and 5 is $\sqrt{8 \cdot 5} = \sqrt{40}$; the geometric mean of 8, 5, 6, and 9 is $\sqrt[4]{8 \cdot 5 \cdot 6 \cdot 9} = \sqrt[4]{2160}$.

Regardless of the number of periods involved, the principle is the same. The market rate for any time to maturity is reducible to a function of the current rate and the applicable forward rates. The formula for any number of periods n is

$$(1 + {}_tR_n) = \sqrt[n]{(1 + {}_tR_1)(1 + {}_{t+1}r_1) \cdots (1 + {}_{t+n-1}r_1)} \qquad (9\text{--}2)$$

Since long rates are averages of current and future short-term rates, an investor can receive the same rate of return regardless of the choice of investment: a five-year bond bought today provides the same return as a four-year bond held to maturity plus a one-year bond bought at the beginning of the fifth year; or the same as a three-year bond held to maturity plus a two-year bond bought at the beginning of the fourth year; or the same as a succession of five one-year bonds; or even the same as a ten-year bond bought today and sold at the end of the fifth year.

The implied forward rate for one-year periods for any future period can be found from

$$_n r_1 = \frac{(1 + {}_tR_n)^n}{(1 + {}_tR_{n-1})^{n-1}} - 1 \qquad (9\text{--}3)$$

For example, assume that the actual rate today on a five-year Treasury bond is 6 percent and, on a six-year Treasury bond, 6½ percent. The implied (forward) rate on a one-year bond five years from now can be derived from equation 9–3 as follows:

$$\frac{(1 + 0.065)^6}{(1 + 0.06)^5} - 1 = 9 \text{ percent}$$

In summary, an existing long-term interest rate is a geometric average of consecutive forward one-period rates. If this hypothesis depicts the interest rate formation process, investors can purchase and hold any combination of securities for a specified period—regardless of the combination, the expected return for a specified period is the same. It is important to note the word *expected* in the preceding statement; that is, the expected return at the time of the transaction is the same; however, expectations need not be realized.

It is also important to realize that the rationale for this hypothesis is that profit-seeking individuals will exploit profit opportunities in the marketplace. If a difference exists between forward rates and expected rates, investors have an incentive to act until the discrepancy disappears. In the final analysis, according to the unbiased expectations theory, forward rates are unbiased estimates of expected future rates.

Implications for the Yield Curve. The expectations theory maintains that the term structure of interest rates is a function of expectations about future interest rates. Hence the shape of the yield curve at any particular time has implications about what market participants are expecting for the future.

1. A rising curve implies that future short rates are expected to rise. If short rates are expected to exceed the current long-term rate, investors are unwilling to buy long-terms unless their yield is greater than the short-term yield.

2. A horizontal curve implies that future short rates are expected to equal the current short rate. Such expectations are unusual; they reflect a state of transition.

3. The implication of a downward-sloping yield curve is that future short rates are expected to fall.

The important point here is that yield differentials with respect to maturity exist because market participants expect interest rates to change, not because they expect different returns on bonds with different maturities.

The Liquidity Premium Theory

As we have just seen, the pure expectations theory states that investor expectations determine future short-term interest rates. Forward rates would in fact be perfect forecasters of future short-term interest rates if complete certainty prevailed. If there is uncertainty, however, the situation is different: forward rates are biased estimates of expected future rates, and a new hypothesis, the liquidity premium theory (sometimes called the biased expectations theory), is needed to explain the term structure.

We can reasonably expect uncertainty to increase with time; that is, we can be more sure today of the state of the world next year than of its state thirty years from now. It is also a fact that long-term bond prices fluctuate more than short-term bond prices for any given change in interest rates. Because of this uncertainty, risks associated with long-term securities are greater, and investors are said to prefer to lend for the short term. Borrowers, however, prefer to borrow for the long term in order to insure themselves of funds that do not have to be refinanced for a long period of time. The result of these forces is that investors pay a price premium (i.e., receive lower yields) for short-term securities; conversely, they receive a liquidity (risk) premium to induce them to lend for the long term. As a consequence, according to the liquidity premium theory, interest rates reflect (i.e., are the geometric average of) the sum of current and expected short rates and their liquidity premiums.

This hypothesis, therefore, differs from the unbiased expectations theory in its recognition that savers and lenders respond to uncertainty rather than acting strictly on the basis of their interest-rate expectations as though they were certain. Market participants are risk-averse and seek adjustments for greater risk—lenders require more, borrowers are willing to pay less. Liquidity premiums arise to make up the differences between forward rates and estimated future rates.

The argument that a liquidity premium must be incorporated into the expectations theory is consistent with the argument that short- and long-term securities are not perfect substitutes. It is clear that, if a positive bias exists in forward rates, different maturities are not perfect substitutes for each other: long-term securities should return higher yields than successive reinvestments in short-term securities.

Implications for the Yield Curve. The liquidity premium theory implies that upward-sloping yield curves are normal, i.e., that they should predominate. And, as noted earlier, this has been true historically since the 1930s. A downward-sloping yield curve could exist only when expected future short rates are lower than the current short-term rate by an amount that exceeds the liquidity premium.[7] Holding expectations constant, the liquidity premium theory is associated with a yield curve higher (by the amount of the liquidity premiums) than that associated with the unbiased expectations theory. With both the unbiased expectations theory and the liquidity premium theory, the yield curve shifts as expectations about future rates change.

The Market Segmentation Theory

The third hypothesis for explaining the term structure of interest rates regards rates on different maturities as, in effect, being determined separately by demand and supply conditions that prevail in the different segments of the market. Securities with varying maturities are treated as imperfect substitutes for one another. Hence a change in the supply of or the demand for securities in one maturity range will alter the term structure of interest rates (change the slope of the yield curve), but changes in the interest rate in any one maturity range have little effect on interest rates in other maturity ranges.

As an illustration, assume that there is an increase in the supply of short-term securities to finance business investment in inventories during an economic boom. According to the segmented market theory, such an increase would depress short-term security prices (raise short-term yields) without eliciting portfolio revisions that would result in interest yields increasing throughout the maturity structure of securities. By the same token, a reduced supply of short-term securities, reflecting a decline in inventory investment as the economy contracts, would raise short-term

---

[7]George G. Kaufman, *Money, The Financial System and the Economy* (Chicago: Rand McNally Publishing Company, 1977), pp. 210–211.

security prices (lower their yields) with little effect on the yields offered by longer-term securities.

This theory is also referred to as the hedging theory. *Hedging* involves the offsetting of liabilities with identical maturity assets. For example, a financial institution may arrange its portfolio of financial assets to roughly match the maturity of the liabilities to which it is committed. Widespread application of this approach would force investors to be restricted to particular segments of the maturity spectrum according to the maturity of their liabilities.

Why should lenders and borrowers limit themselves to one particular maturity range of the securities market? One appealing rationale suggests that they do so to minimize risk. An investor-lender who has funds to lend for a specific period, say, five years, could (1) sequentially purchase five one-year securities, (2) purchase a five-year security, or (3) purchase a security with a longer maturity time, which can be sold at the end of the five years. In the first case, the yields to be earned on investments from the second year through the fifth year are uncertain—they may be lower or higher than those currently available. In the third case, the level of future interest rates in general and hence the price at which the long-term security will sell are unknown. The investor can avoid the risk of uncertain future yields (case 1) and of an uncertain future security price (case 3) by the purchase of a security whose maturity time is equal to the time over which the investment is to be made, as in case 2. Analogously, a borrower can minimize the risk of injurious changes in the cost of borrowing by the issuance of securities whose lives coincide with the time horizon over which borrowed funds are to be employed.

A view of a segmented market would find market participants operating within certain maturity ranges. As will be seen in chapter 13, banks prefer short- to medium-term assets, because their liabilities (primarily demand and time deposits) are short-term. They also have traditionally stressed liquidity, because of the unique nature of banking—to maintain confidence in a fractional reserve system, they must be prepared to meet withdrawals of any size at any time. In contrast, life insurance companies can forecast their obligations with a high degree of confidence many years into the future, because mortality rates for large populations can be predicted actuarially. These companies can accommodate long maturities, and, in fact, they prefer them because long-term securities enable them to insure themselves of (i.e., "lock in") the returns needed to meet known obligations. Thus these two institutions typically operate at different ends of the maturity spectrum.

From these differences in the maturity preferences of lenders (and the same reasoning applies to borrowers), segmented markets are said to result. Supply and demand conditions in one part of such a market may differ from the conditions existing in another part. Participants come to specialize in particular segments and are not likely to be attracted to others even though yields there are attractive. This situation could result in a failure to shift among maturities such that the expectations theory would not be valid. In a market dominated by hedgers, forward rates may diverge from expected future short rates.

In actuality, institutional investors are not too rigid with respect to maturity composition, with the exception of banks' emphasis on liquidity. In the late 1960s and the early 1970s, institutions placed a strong emphasis on "performance," which lead them to seek out the highest expected yields, regardless of maturity. Such an emphasis on yields by enough participants in various maturity segments should prevent segmentation. However, the hypothesis is not invalidated by the recognition that participants have more than one maturity position and are willing to make some shifts. If institutions have a preferred maturity position and require compensation (in the form of premiums) to shift to another position, the hypothesis would have validity. Furthermore, we can distinguish between short- and long-term securities on the basis of characteristics that tend to affect investment choices. Short-term securities reduce the risk of capital loss; long-term securities provide an income stream of guaranteed size for a long specified period (barring default, of course).

Implications for the Yield Curve. Under the market segmentation theory, the shape of the yield curve is a function of supply and demand forces applicable for various maturity segments at a particular time. Thus, the shape will change as the demand for or supply of securities in any part of the maturity spectrum changes; furthermore, such changes may have little or no effect on the other parts of the yield curve.

Conclusions about the Three Theories

Each of the three theories postulates different behavioral assumptions about investors. The unbiased expectations theory assumes that investors attempt to maximize expected returns. This leads them to act on their expectations. The market segmentation theory, in contrast, assumes that investors wish to minimize risk. One way to do so is to hedge—to buy securities with the maturities that the investor wants rather than having to reinvest or to sell securities with time remaining to maturity. Finally, the liquidity premium hypothesis assumes that investors balance returns and risk, since expectations of both are important. A preference for liquidity implies a preference for stability of principal over stability of income; therefore long-term securities are seen as more risky and must accordingly be priced to yield more.

It is worthwhile to note the implications concerning the expected holding-period yields (i.e., total returns) from securities under each of these hypotheses. The unbiased expectations theory indicates that the expected holding-period yields for alternative maturity positions are equivalent. The liquidity premium hypothesis indicates that the longer maturity positions yield larger expected returns than shorter maturity positions (although, in equilibrium, the extra yield just compensates for the additional risk assumed). The market segmentation hypothesis indicates that holding-period yields are a function of maturity composition and that such yields are determined by the unique supply and demand factors that exist in each of the separate markets.

What does the empirical evidence indicate about these theories? Many studies have been done, but the results are somewhat conflicting. Support has been found for both expectations and hedging, with expectations having the stronger impact, although market segmentation studies indicate only a mild role for this activity in the determination of the term structure of interest rates. However, modern (i.e., post–World War II) data indicate nonetheless that liquidity premiums do exist; that is, that forward rates are biased estimates of expected future rates. The problem here is that the studies are conflicting and therefore inconclusive with regard to the dimensions of these premiums.

The only safe conclusion that can be drawn from this analysis is that the issue has not been resolved: there is no universal agreement on what theory best explains the term structure of interest rates.

One could argue that the liquidity premium hypothesis comes closest to doing the job. There is strong empirical support for the existence of liquidity premiums over the last 30 years. The upward-sloping yield curves that have predominated during this period are consistent with this hypothesis. Also, the idea that investors balance returns with risk is generally consistent with modern portfolio theory, as was explained in chapter 6. It is much more reasonable to consider investors' attempts to balance returns and risk than to categorize them as strict return-maximizers (the pure expectations theory) or as strict risk-minimizers (the market segmentation theory). Modern portfolio theory emphasizes that investors should be concerned with total risk-adjusted returns.

Empirical Evidence on Bond Maturity Premiums

Regardless of which of these three theories is correct, it is possible to obtain some historical evidence on differences in returns that can be attributed to differences in maturity. To do this, it is necessary to calculate so-called bond maturity premiums, which reflect the differences between returns on U.S. Treasury bills and on U.S. government bonds. This comparison abstracts from default, a subject considered in the next section of this chapter, because federal government securities have no practical risk of default. The difference between returns from these two series reflects only a decision to hold long-maturity or short-maturity issues.

Maturity premiums (sometimes called liquidity premiums) can be calculated as

bond maturity premiums = returns on long-term government bonds
                         − returns on Treasury bills

In a comprehensive study of the historical returns on several financial assets, Roger Ibbotson and Rex Sinquefield have calculated year-by-year bond maturity premiums for the 51-year period from 1926 through 1976.[8] The average annual maturity premium for this period was 1.1 percent. Not surprisingly, these premiums varied quite widely over that period; the low was −0.11 in 1969 and the high was 0.1574 in 1932. The standard deviation, a measure of dispersion around the mean, was 5.9 percent.

In summary, the historical evidence indicates that an annual maturity premium of 1.1 percent, on average, has prevailed over a long period of time. Thus, 1.1 percent annually has been the average additional return to lenders for holding long-maturity instead of short-maturity government securities.

RISK DIFFERENCES

A second major factor that causes differences in interest rates is risk. Although the term *risk* is used in various ways, securities risk is properly thought of as the possibility that the actual outcome from an investment will differ from what is expected. In the case of common stocks, for example, investors are guaranteed neither dividends nor capital gains—the only two ways a common-stock investor profits from ownership of stock. The risk element is obviously large for stocks. As for bonds, both the annual interest payments and the repayment of the principal are specified and represent a contractual obligation. The timing and amount of the payments are known with certainty but failure to meet either obligation on time can result in default and bankruptcy. The only question here is, will the issuer default?

Default Risk

Theoretically, all bonds are risky in that the issuer could fail to meet the specified contractual (i.e., legal) obligations incurred when a bond is issued. As a practical matter, Treasury securities have no risk of default because of the unique taxing and money-creating abilities of the federal government. It is possible, therefore, to use Treasury securities as a benchmark against which to measure the default risk of other types of bonds. Lenders will demand a risk premium to compensate them for the additional risk of holding a non-Treasury bond; the greater the perceived risk, the

---

[8]Roger Ibbotson and Rex Sinquefield, *Stocks, Bonds, Bills, and Inflation: The Past (1926–1976) and the Future (1977–2000)* (Charlottesville, Virginia: Financial Analysts Research Foundation, 1977), pp. 19–20.

greater the risk premium demanded. Of course, to assess this premium in the market, all other factors, such as time to maturity, must be held constant. Before considering the risk premiums on debt securities, let us examine some basic information on default risk.

Defining Default Risk. *Default risk* is the risk that the issuer of bonds will be unable to pay the annual interest premiums or to repay the principal when it is due. Theoretically, all corporations, state and local governments, and issuers of mortgages face some degree of default risk. As a practical matter, the chance of a default on, for example, IBM's bond obligations is so small as to be negligible.

If an issuer does fail to meet any of the contractual obligations on its bond issue, severe consequences, such as exchange of securities or reorganization, are possible. At the extreme, the issuer can be declared in default, placed in bankruptcy, and liquidated (in the case of a corporation). Bond-holders are then paid in order of seniority (e.g., mortgage bonds ahead of debentures), but, in all cases, they are paid ahead of those who hold preferred or common stock.

Rating Services. An investor interested in the relative default risk of a bond issue can obtain a rating of its quality from Moody's Investors Service or Standard & Poor's Corporation (S & P). Their ratings are viewed as indicators of the likelihood of default.[9] S & P uses the ratings AAA, AA, A, BBB, etc.; Moody's uses Aaa, Aa, A, Baa, etc. Both use nine categories.[10] Bonds rated AAA (Aaa) are of the highest quality—the probability of default is nil; BBB (Baa) bonds are of medium quality. For most bond analysts, the first four grades represent reasonable-quality securities. Ninety per cent of all corporate bonds fall within the top four categories.[11]

The first four categories of bonds are very strongly affected by shifts in interest rates. Although the other categories are also affected by such shifts, they are affected even more strongly by shifts in general business and economic conditions.

These bond ratings are well respected and widely used by investors. They have been refined over a long period of time and are considered to be very accurate. Although a few mistakes have been made, the investment community believes that these two rating agencies do their job very well.

Both agencies also rate many municipal bonds. Such ratings can be

---

[9]These ratings are based on numerous qualitative and quantitative factors such as the ratio of debt to assets, liquidity, the stability of sales and earnings, mortgage provisions and other restrictions, pension liabilities, and regulatory constraints. The rating agencies claim that no exact formula is used for a particular company but rather that there is considerable subjective judgement exercised by those who conduct the ratings.

[10]Standard and Poor ratings also include + and − signs to indicate relative standings within the major categories, AA, A, and BBB.

[11]This figure is based on the par value outstanding of all corporate bonds rated by Moody's.

very important, because investors are unfamiliar with most issuers and because individuals find it difficult to assess the likelihood of default by a state or local government. Many thousands of such units issue these bonds. Several well-known issuers have defaulted and the continuous financing problems of New York City are now famous (or infamous).

Ratings are even available for commercial paper, a short-term money market instrument explained in chapter 10.[12] Ratings for other money market instruments are either not necessary (Treasury bills, which have no default risk) or not available (federal agency issues).

Risk Premiums

The risk premiums associated with default risk are referred to simply as *default-risk premiums*. They represent the difference between investing in long-term government securities, which are default-free, and corporate bonds, which carry some risk of default. Note that maturity must be held constant in any such comparison (as we have seen maturity premiums can also be calculated). The default-risk premium is therefore

Bond Default-Risk Premium = Returns on Corporate Bonds
                            − Returns on Government Bonds.

Ibbotson and Sinquefield have studied default premiums as well as maturity premiums. They used 20-year bonds with no special tax or call features to measure corporate bond returns. Since the two series have almost identical maturities, the net difference between their rates of return is basically due to the risk of default. Thus the bond default-risk premium is the net differential return from holding high-grade corporate bonds instead of government bonds.

For the period 1926 to 1976, Ibbotson and Sinquefield calculated the annual default-risk premiums on corporate bonds to be 0.6 percent on average.[13] The standard deviation was 3.2%. This means that the distribution of default-risk premiums was closely packed around the mean value. The default-risk premiums varied substantially over this period, ranging from a low of −0.0610 in 1945 to a high of 0.1065 in 1933.

RETIREMENT PROVISIONS

Bonds can be retired before maturity. If the amount outstanding of a particular issue is systematically reduced, the risk of the bonds that remain outstanding at maturity should be lower, other things being equal. For

---

[12]The lettering system for commercial paper differs from that for bonds. Standard and Poor, for example, uses A-1 to designate the highest investment grade and D to designate commercial paper that is expected to default.

[13]Ibbotson and Sinquefield, *Stocks, Bonds, Bills, and Inflation,* pp. 19–20.

example, a firm that borrows $100 million for 30 years has an obligation that involves some risk. However, if $2 million of the issue is retired each year for 30 years, only $40 million is outstanding in the thirtieth year—a considerably smaller obligation for the firm and a considerably smaller risk to the remaining bondholders.

Sinking Funds

Bonds can be systematically retired through the establishment of a sinking fund. Bonds with this provision for early retirement should yield a lower return than bonds without such a provision, other things being equal, because of the reduction in risk to the remaining bondholders. For example, suppose that a corporation agrees to establish a sinking fund for the systematic retirement of its bonds. This means that it agrees to contribute x dollars each year for this purpose. In principle, the money could be set aside annually, for example, in a savings account, so that it would definitely be available to pay off the bondholders at the maturity of the bonds. In practice, the trustee for the bond issue, who is a representative designated to protect the bondholders, buys the bonds on the open market or conducts a random lottery by which certain bonds are chosen to be retired each year. The numbers of such bonds are published in the financial press to inform the holders. Alternatively, to retire bonds, the issuers can call them in and retire them.

Call Features

In most cases today, issuers can *call in* corporate bonds and retire them prior to maturity. Issuers find such actions attractive when interest rates have dropped low enough. Such a decision is made on a cost-benefit basis. The overall cost of calling in an issue reflects the paperwork, the notification process, the call premium, and related costs attached to the retiring of the old bonds plus the costs of issuing new ones—legal fees, flotation costs, registration costs, etc. The benefits stem from the difference between the old (higher) interest rate and the new (lower) interest rate, expressed in dollars per year multiplied by the number of years to maturity and then discounted back to the present to take account of the time value of money. If the benefits exceed the costs, it is financially favorable to call in the bonds.

Obviously, the call feature is an advantage to the issuer and a disadvantage to the buyer-holder, who may have to give up a higher-yielding bond for a lower-yielding one. To compensate for this disadvantage, the issuer typically pays a *call premium*, amounting to one year's interest, when the bonds are called. However, this hardly makes up for giving up a 30-year, 8 percent bond for a 6 percent bond a few years after purchase.

Call provisions vary from no protection (the bonds are immediately callable) to a deferred call provision (for example, the bond is not callable for the first five years). It might be expected that bonds without a call provision would provide a lower yield than bonds with a call provision, since the call feature is solely a benefit to the issuer, and that this feature would therefore affect interest-rate differentials. Most corporate bonds carry a call feature. It does seem reasonable to believe that a call feature would be more important, so that a callable bond would carry a higher yield, in times when interest rates are at relative highs.

Some treasury issues are also callable. Most municipal bonds are not callable.

TAXES

Taxes are an inescapable fact of financial life. It is indisputable that governmental policies regarding taxes affect investors' actions and the characteristics of financial instruments. Therefore, yield differentials on these instruments can be explained, in part, by tax considerations; that is, two instruments otherwise identical can have different yields because of taxes. Several aspects of their role are considered below.

Probably the most prominent aspect of taxes as they affect financial instruments stems from the distinction between capital gains and ordinary income. Financial assets held for one year (before 1977, those held for 6 months) qualify for favorable long-term capital gains treatment.[14] The tax applicable on long-term gains is 40 percent of that for short-term gains, with a maximum of 28 percent. For individuals in high tax brackets, this favorable treatment is obviously an important consideration. An investor in the 50 percent marginal tax bracket who buys a bond for $1,000, holds it 6 months, and sells it for $1,100 has a $100 short-term capital gain. Although the actual computation of the total tax due can be complicated, the investor would in general have a tax obligation of $50 on the transaction; if it had been held for, say, 15 months, the tax obligation would probably be $20.

To understand how the capital gains tax treatment can affect rate differentials on securities that are otherwise identical, we must consider the phenomenon of interest-rate risk.[15] If interest rates rise, bond prices decline; if interest rates fall, bond prices rise. Thus, a 30-year, 5 percent corporate bond sold 15 years ago for $1,000 (which is the face value of all corporate bonds) may have a current market price of only $800 because interest rates have subsequently risen. This bond (call it A) would not be

---

[14]Net long-term capital losses, however, are not as favorable as short-term capital losses. Two dollars of long-term loss offset one dollar of income; within limits, short-term losses offset ordinary income dollar for dollar.

[15]See Charles P. Jones, Donald L. Tuttle, and Cherrill P. Heaton, *Essentials of Modern Investments* (New York: The Ronald Press Company, 1977), pp. 20, 172–174.

identical to a 15-year bond newly issued by the same corporation (call this one B) and sold for $1,000 at the prevailing (higher) market rate. That is, these two bonds of the same firm, which have the same rating and the same remaining time to maturity, and which are otherwise identical, would carry different yields. The reason is that a bond purchaser could buy A, hold it to maturity, receive $1,000 and realize a capital gain of $200. The buyer of B who holds it to maturity realizes no capital gain—all of this buyer's return is in the form of interest income. Thus A is preferred to B, other things being equal, because of the tax advantage of A.

Tax considerations are of paramount importance in the consideration of state and local securities, i.e., municipal securities. The income from them is exempt from federal taxes and, in some cases (such as state bonds held by residents) from state taxes. Obviously, then, a comparison of a municipal security and, say, a Treasury issue with identical characteristics (even with equal default risk) would nonetheless show rate differentials. Treasury securities are fully taxable and are sold to yield a return reflecting that fact. Thus a 5% municipal may be equivalent to a 7% Treasury, all other factors being equal, because their after-tax rates of return are the same.

As an actual example, consider the beginning of 1979. Aaa municipal securities were yielding 6.05 percent. The average yield on 20 and 30 year Treasury bonds was 8.97 percent. Assuming that other factors are roughly constant, the yields are considerably different in part because of the tax factor (in this case, the difference is equivalent to the taxes that would be paid on the Treasury issues by a holder in the 33 percent marginal tax bracket).

Looking at it in the reverse manner, the marketplace adjusts for the tax advantage of municipals by adjustments in the yield spreads between them and all other securities. Other things being equal, if the adjustment were exact, a bondholder would be indifferent to the choice between a municipal security and a Treasury security. However, the market-adjusted yield spread that exists does not have the same value for all holders. Some holders apparently benefit, particularly those in the highest tax brackets. For example, it may be that some purchasers of municipals receive more after-tax income than they could from a comparable alternative taxable security. Clearly, a 5 percent nominal tax-free return does not mean the same to an individual in the 20 percent marginal tax bracket as it does to one in the 50 percent marginal tax bracket. The latter individual would have to earn 10 percent before taxes to keep 5 percent after taxes.

As is true of other factors affecting the return differentials among securities, the spread between municipals and other securities changes across time. Compared to the almost three percentage point differential at the start of 1979, the corresponding differential for 1975 was only 1¾ percentage points. Since banks are the major purchaser of municipals, bank actions involving municipals are important in the determination of yields and yield spreads. Bank demand for municipals varies in relation to their efforts to accommodate their loan customers. Increased demand can result in upward pressures on prices and corresponding downward movements on yields.

MARKETABILITY

Marketability refers to liquidity, or the ease with which an investor can sell a particular security.[16] Bonds privately placed with insurance companies have no marketability while Treasury bills have virtually instant marketability. As a general rule, long-maturity issues have less marketability than do short-maturity issues, because risk is expressed by an increasing function of time, other things being equal.

Low marketability is equated with high risk, so that investors demand higher yields on debt securities that may be difficult to sell. Where an issue is traded affects marketability, as do price and quantity. In particular, marketability involves such considerations as how long it takes to transact, how easy it is to transact, how many securities can be bought or sold together without affecting the price, the transactions cost, and where the security is traded. A less marketable, or less liquid, issue is one that involves considerable time to transact in any reasonable quantity and/or one where a significantly different price than market price is involved, or where it is simply difficult to liquidate the position.

Private placements—issues sold directly to institutional investors—typically carry higher yields than comparable securities traded publicly. One reason is liquidity, since the resale of such issues are rare. Purchasers almost always plan to hold such issues until maturity.

Some corporate bonds are traded on the New York Stock Exchange, and marketability in this case is reasonable—even for small transactions involving only a few bonds. Most corporate bonds, however, are traded over-the-counter where small transactions are less likely. As for municipal bonds, small transactions of five and ten bonds are quite common.

MISCELLANEOUS FACTORS

In addition to the principal factors discussed above, there are several miscellaneous factors that also tend to cause differences in interest rates. Two of these are discussed below.

---

[16]This discussion has benefitted from David Darst, *The Complete Bond Book* (New York: McGraw-Hill Book Company, 1975), pp. 41–42.

Seasoned Issues and New Issues

Seasoned issues (ones that have been traded in the market for some time) often yield less than new issues of bonds even if other factors are similar. This is particularly true for higher absolute levels of interest rates. The variance in spreads due to "seasoning" can be quite wide, or, as is often the case for AAA utility bonds, it can be zero or very close to it.

The explanations for seasoning differentials lie in the underwriting process, which involves the distribution of an issue from the borrower to the lenders (i.e., to the public).[17] Underwriters may lower the price of a new offering to make it more attractive than older issues; this facilitates its sale and reduces their risk. Such underpricing is particularly likely to appear when interest rates are high and when there is a strong probability that they will go higher. Also, since underwriters must finance their inventories with more expensive borrowed funds during periods of high interest rates, they have an extra incentive to lower the price of the new issue (and thus raise its yield) in order to be sure that it will sell quickly.

Convertibility

Some bonds are convertible, at the holder's option, into the underlying common stock of the issuing firm. The holder of such securities can simply turn it in to the company and receive a predetermined number of common shares. Convertible securities therefore have features of both debt and equity, and this hybrid nature makes it difficult to evaluate them.

This factor can produce very significant yield differentials between convertible and comparable nonconvertible (*straight*) issues: it is possible for the difference to be as much as one perent or more. The difference results from investors' willingness to accept a lower interest rate on the convertible issue in exchange for an option on the common stock of the issuing firm. In effect, the investor engages in a tradeoff, giving up some interest income in exchange for the opportunity to speculate on a rising stock price. It follows, therefore, that the greater the perceived prospects of the common stock, the lower the interest rate on a convertible debt issue in relation to a similar straight debt issue.

There are a number of other complicating factors that involve convertibles and the yields they offer. Almost all convertible securities are issued with the call feature, which has an effect in its own right. Also, convertible debentures have lower ratings than straight debts of the same company. Finally, the right to convert to common stock is typically extended for a fixed time period, so that the longer the time period, the more valuable the conversion feature (other things being equal).

---

[17]Darst, p. 43.

SUMMARY

This chapter has focused on the factors that cause observed differences in yields on various financial instruments. It complements chapter 8, which focused on the determination of interest rates in general.

The factors that cause differences in interest rates include time to maturity, risk, retirement provisions, taxes, marketability, and miscellaneous items. Each of these factors was considered in turn.

Time to maturity is formally related to yield to maturity in the concept of the term structure of interest rates. Yield curves are drawn to depict this relationship for securities that are equivalent except for their maturity. Yield curves can slope upward or downward or can be flat. Upward-sloping curves have predominated since the early 1930s and are now considered normal.

A term structure theory should explain both the shape and the slope of the yield curve, as well as why the curve shifts into different forms over time. Three popular theories have been advanced to explain the term structure: the pure, or unbiased, expectations theory; the liquidity premium theory; and the market segmentation theory.

The unbiased expectations theory holds that securities that are similar in all respects except maturity are perfect substitutes for each other. Thus rates of return on such securities are expected to be equivalent for a particular time period. Such rates reflect the expectations of profit-maximizing investors. Long-term rates are the geometric average of the short-term rates that are expected to exist for that particular long-term period. Forward rates—those expected to exist at some point in the future —for any future period can be computed from actual current market rates. Forward rates equal expected future rates. In effect, investors, acting on their expectations, cause the maturity pattern of rates to conform to their expectations. Yield differentials for various maturities exist, not because yields are expected to vary with maturity, but because the market expects interest rates to change over the future.

The liquidity premium theory holds that, because of uncertainty, forward rates are biased estimates of expected future rates. Longer-term securities are more risky than short-term securities, so that investors prefer the latter. They pay a price premium for short-terms and receive a liquidity (risk) premium for long-terms. Therefore interest rates reflect the sum of current and expected short rates and their associated liquidity premiums. This hypothesis implies that upward-sloping yield curves should predominate.

The market segmentation theory holds that securities with different maturities are imperfect substitutes for one another. Market participants may specialize in different maturities and therefore operate in different segments such that supply and demand conditions differ across parts of the total market. Investors may hedge to reduce risk by borrowing or lending for particular time periods to meet particular needs. In such a market, forward rates may diverge from expected future short rates. The shape of the yield curve according to this hypothesis is a function of the different supply and demand forces applicable for the various sectors at a point in time.

Available empirical evidence on bond maturity premiums (the difference between returns on long-term government bonds and returns on Treasury bills) reveals an average annual maturity premium of 1.1 percent.

Risk differences are a second major factor causing differences in interest rates. For bonds, default risk is of primary importance. Relative default risk can be assessed from bond ratings. Default-risk premiums (the difference between returns on corporate bonds and returns on government bonds) have averaged 0.6 percent on an annual period over a span of 50 years.

Retirement provisions can reduce the risk of bonds that remain outstanding and therefore result in lower yields for such bonds. Methods of retirement include sinking funds and call features.

Taxes are a pervasive influence. Capital gains are a significant factor for investors and can result in yield differentials. Municipal securities are exempt from federal taxation, so that the market adjusts for the tax advantage of municipals, although the adjustment may not be complete for all market participants.

Marketability is the ease with which securities can be sold. Low marketability results in higher risk and therefore in higher yields.

Miscellaneous factors include the difference between seasoned issues and new issues and the convertibility feature of some bonds. Seasoned issues often yield less than a new issue of similar securities. Convertible issues yield less than similar nonconvertible securities, because the conversion feature has potential value for which investors forego some interest income.

PART 4

The Structure of the Financial System

We have examined the financial system from a broad perspective and have focused particularly on money and banking considerations and on the saving-investment process. We have identified the factors that determine interest rates, both in general and on specific instruments. It is now time to turn our attention to the instruments and the institutions that constitute our financial system. Our discussion in this part includes a close examination of why these institutions exist; it gives the rationale for their activities.

Chapter 10 describes financial instruments in general. Since these claims are at the very foundation of the economy, our discussion provides necessary background to an understanding of financial institutions and financial markets. This chapter also describes the organization of financial instruments by markets.

With this background, chapter 11 proceeds to characterize the major financial claims, classified as short-term and long-term. These are the types of claims held by saving surplus units, and they simultaneously represent the means by which economic units that need funds obtain them.

Chapter 12 explains the nature of intermediation, so that the intermediaries themselves can be intelligently examined in the subsequent two chapters. Intermediation refers to the practice of economic units that simultaneously obtain and issue claims, but the exact details of this process must be understood if the intermediaries themselves are to be comprehended.

Chapters 13 and 14 concern, respectively, banks and nonbanks as intermediaries. Banks deserve considerable attention because of their role in the money supply process, which was described earlier, and because they are the largest and most commonly used intermediary. Nonbank intermediaries include a wide range of institutions, each with particular features characterizing its assets and liabilities. All the major types of nonbank financial intermediaries are examined in chapter 14.

10

Financial Instruments and Financial Markets

Financial instruments are created as claims on the borrowers in the flow of funds between surplus units and deficit units.[1] These funds help to finance borrowers' investment in real assets, augmenting our wealth.

This chapter presents some basic facts about financial instruments. Since they are claims on the resources of the issuer, they have four important characteristics, which need to be examined first: the certainty, timing, duration, and amount of the payments to be received.

Next, the principal types of financial instruments are considered. Claims are classified here by whether they involve positions of creditorship or of ownership. It is then useful to examine the existing stocks of all financial assets, to obtain an idea of the amount of financial instruments outstanding, both on an absolute and on a relative basis.

Given the emphasis in chapter 6 on returns and risk, this chapter briefly analyzes these variables for major financial instruments over the last 50 years. In the final analysis, these are the two most important characteristics of financial instruments.

Financial instruments are bought and sold in various markets, collectively known as the financial markets, or the securities markets. This chap-

---

[1]The term *financial instrument* is used here to represent any money-denominated direct claim on an issuer (other than an individual), as opposed to an indirect claim on a financial institution. For example, Treasury bills and savings deposits are both financial assets, but only the Treasury bill is a financial instrument. Thus financial instruments are a subset of financial assets.

ter concludes with an analysis of the purpose and the organization of these markets.

CHARACTERISTICS OF FINANCIAL INSTRUMENTS

Although all financial instruments represent a claim on a future stream of payments, they can vary in many ways. The following parameters need to be specified:

1. How certain is it that the actual return will equal the expected return? This question reflects the element of risk, which, along with its twin parameter, return, dominates any discussion of financial instruments. Holders and prospective buyers (investors at the margin) of such claims must always carefully assess the potential risk, because the future is uncertain.

2. If the expected return is in fact likely to be received, when will it be paid? Money has a time value: the sooner payments are received, the more valuable they are, because they can be reinvested to earn compound interest.

3. If it is known when the future stream of payments will be received, how long will they continue at that rate? Both common and preferred stocks can pay dividends forever, whatever the amount, but these payments can change in amount or stop completely. In contrast, a corporate bond with two years to maturity pays interest only four times—every six months for two years.

4. Finally, how large will the returns be? Obviously, rational investors prefer more to less per dollar of investment, but financial instruments vary widely in expected returns offered.

The most basic distinction among financial instruments is that between *debt instruments* (or *fixed dollar instruments*) and *equity instruments*. The former represents a loan. The face amount of the loan is clearly specified, as is the date at which it will be repaid (the maturity date). The timing and the amount of fixed interest payments are clearly stated, unless the instrument is sold on a discount basis, as Treasury bills are. Holders of fixed dollar assets are assured of priority over holders of equity instruments with respect to payment and in case of liquidation. Buyers of fixed dollar assets have, in effect, a contract with the borrower, which is strict, binding, and legally enforceable.

In contrast, equity securities (and related equity accounts, such as retained earnings) represent ownership of a firm: they indicate the amount of the firm's financing that is not provided by creditors. Equity owners have no assurance of (1) any periodic return, (2) the eventual receipt of the amount they initially paid for their equity securities, or (3) any return at all in case the firm is liquidated. What equity owners do have is a higher expected return, as well as greater risk, in comparison to holders of fixed dollar instruments. As compensation for the uncertainty (risk) involved in their position as residual owners, they have an opportunity to earn quite large returns. More precisely, they expect to receive adequate returns for the risk they assume in ownership, while they also recognize that there are no guarantees.

Other basic distinctions will be referred to later in the chapter when we talk about market organization (in effect, we will be discussing the important characteristic of marketability). For now, however, let us think in terms of the four basic parameters—risk, timing, maturity, and amount of return.

Risk

Risk is an inescapable feature of financial instruments. As was discussed in chapter 6, the proper definition of risk involves the probability that the actual return will differ from the expected or the required return. This means that expected returns on financial instruments should be thought of on the basis of probability distributions and expected values.

There is a relatively high probability that equity securities will not yield what was expected by investors, because the issuer is not obligated to pay specified amounts, and because there is no maturity date. No one can foresee the returns on these claims. Hence equity securities have high risks of uncertain returns, whereas short-term debt securities with known payments and near maturity dates have very low risks. It is this uncertain nature of equity securities that gives rise to great activity in the field of common stocks. Thousands of analysts are employed to estimate the risk of realizing expected returns on these financial instruments.

In discussions of financial instruments, the term *risk* is often used in various ways, making the discussion subject to ambiguity. For example, it is used to refer to the probability of default on an obligation by the issuer. In this sense, Treasury securities have no practical risk, because the likelihood of the U.S. government defaulting on its obligations is virtually nil. Some corporations and municipal government units, however, have defaulted on their fixed dollar commitments. In general, short-term market instruments have very low or virtually no probabilities of default, and long-term instruments have higher probabilities, although these are still not great in many cases.

The concept of risk is also used to refer to the uncertainty of the return if interest rates rise. This is called *interest-rate risk* and refers to the inverse relationship between interest rates and bond prices. If interest rates rise, the prices of fixed dollar claims decline until their yields match those on comparable securities. For example, if you purchased a bond last year for $1,000 when the going interest rate for this type of bond was 7 percent, other investors would not pay you $1,000 for it one year later if interest rates on comparable securities had risen to 8 percent: they could buy comparable new bonds for $1,000 and receive $80 a year in interest payments instead of $70. The price of the old bond must decline until it provides a yield comparable to those on newly issued bonds with the same characteristics. Of course, if fixed dollar assets are held to maturity, there is no loss of principal, except in case of default.

The concept of risk is associated with still other meanings. For example, a *purchasing-power risk* is often associated with fixed dollar instruments (or any fixed dollar asset). Such claims, returning the principal amount years in the future, are exposed to losses of purchasing power, since the value of the dollar seems to decline each year (and has declined rather rapidly in the last few years). Common stocks have often been touted as inflation hedges on the principle that their prices, not being fixed, can rise in an inflationary environment. The experience of recent years, however, has suggested that stocks are not always a good inflation hedge (at least, not on an absolute basis—they may still do better than fixed dollar instruments).

In summary, risk is an integral part of any discussion of financial instruments. It is inescapable—like death and taxes—for anyone dealing in this environment. Most financial instruments are subject to some type of risk at some time and often to several types simultaneously. Most importantly, risk is inseparably intertwined with return, and returns are the ultimate objective of investors. One would do well to remember the general rule that the greater the risk on a financial instrument, the greater the expected return. No other course of action is logical for risk-averse investors—and aversion to risk is assumed throughout economics to characterize the behavior of most individuals.

Timing

Since returns are the reason for investment in financial instruments, the question of when payments are received is of considerable importance. As was discussed in chapter 7, money has a time value: the sooner it is received, the more valuable it is. All rational investors prefer one dollar today to one dollar a year from now, because monies received now can be reinvested to earn compound interest—the longer the period of reinvestment, the greater the final amount from compounding.

Fixed dollar instruments pay interest at stated intervals, with a few exceptions (such as Treasury bills, which are sold at a discount). Corporate bond interest is paid semiannually. Common-stock dividends are paid quarterly. There are many other variations. Potential investors should assess the true return in terms of an effective yield, which recognizes the time value of money.

The timing of returns from financial instruments is very important in calculations of the value of some securities. To compute the intrinsic value of a common stock (i.e., its theoretical price, based on valuation principles), an analyst must estimate future dividends and/or terminal price and must discount this stream at an appropriate rate to reflect risk. In a similar manner, to determine the value of a bond, one must discount the (known) future stream of interest payments and the repayment of principal. The exact number and the timing of payments affect the value because of the time value of money.

Maturity

Maturity is a feature of every fixed dollar instrument, since each such claim is a loan that must eventually be repaid. The time involved varies greatly. Treasury bills have maturities of less than a year. Some bonds, on the other hand, have maturities of 40 years. Common and preferred stocks are perpetual securities with no maturity date.

There is often a "clientele" effect for financial instruments according to their maturities; that is, many purchasers have particular maturities in mind because they need the funds to be repaid at a certain time. For example, a corporation that plans to purchase a $50 million plant and sells bonds to raise the funds knows that it will need the money when the transaction is closed, say, 60 days hence. The firm may therefore invest these funds in a financial instrument (e.g., Treasury bills) with 60 days left to maturity. The firm knows that it will give up a higher return if it invests in safe, liquid, short-maturity assets, but it also realizes that there is a tradeoff between risk and return. To be sure of having its funds in 60 days, the firm must accept a lower return. Alternatively, if it were to invest in higher-yielding corporate bonds for 60 days, it would have to accept the risk that bond prices might drop as a result of a rise in interest rates, which would produce a capital loss.

As a counterexample, consider an insurance company, which receives new premium income monthly, and which can accurately predict its outflows on the basis of mortality tables. It can invest in longer-maturity, higher-yielding assets, such as mortgages or bonds. Furthermore, it can choose to stagger the maturities, so that it is assured of annual inflows from repayment of principal.

These two examples highlight important distinctions between the money market and the capital market.[2] The distinction that is usually made

---

[2]The term *money market* denotes the total market for short-term financial instruments, each of which will be discussed in chapter 11. It has no physical location but consists simply of a network of dealers who make markets in these instruments. This is to be distinguished from the *market for money*, which was discussed in previous chapters with reference to all the demand and supply forces affecting money.

concerns maturity. Instruments maturing in less than a year are generally considered money market instruments, and those with longer maturities are generally considered capital market instruments. The dividing line is somewhat arbitrary, but clearly one of the characteristics of a money market instrument is short maturity with high safety and liquidity—and these factors can usually be assured only for short-term instruments. After all, the probability that adverse circumstances will occur in 30, 60, or 90 days, etc., is much smaller than the probability that they will arise over the life of a 20-year bond; and, perhaps just as importantly, what is likely to happen can be much more easily foreseen for short periods than for long periods. This distinction between maturities is so pervasive that chapter 11 is organized to provide separate treatments of the money market and the capital market.

Amount of Return

Obviously, investors in financial instruments are interested in the amount of return. To discuss this intelligently, we need to learn some basic concepts about financial returns.

Cash is the most liquid of all financial assets. It has no explicit return, but neither does it have a real risk in the sense of the probability that the Treasury will go broke. Although cash is not convertible to gold or silver through the government, other people will presumably continue to accept it. However, it does have an opportunity cost. The holder of cash (currency or coin) passes up the possibility of a return from some other financial asset that does produce a yield.

Treasury bills and most commercial paper are sold on a discount basis. Interest on discount instruments is calculated from the face amount. Purchasers pay less than face value, hold the instrument to maturity, and redeem it at face value. The effective yield therefore exceeds the nominal yield, because the interest payment is earned in relation to the purchase price, which is less than the face value. This difference increases with maturity or with a general rise in rates. Hence yields on discount instruments are not comparable to yields on interest-bearing assets unless an adjustment is made.

In the case of capital market instruments, returns can include both interest or dividends and capital gains or losses. Both must be properly accounted for if true returns are to be determined. A correct measure of the total return is the *holding period yield* (*HPY*), which relates both the interim returns (interest and dividends) and the capital gains or losses to the purchase price. This measure can be used for any financial asset—real estate, money, bonds, savings accounts, or stocks. In general, it can be defined as

$$HPY = \frac{\begin{array}{c}\text{income payments received} \\ \text{during period (in dollars)}\end{array} + \begin{array}{c}\text{capital change over} \\ \text{period (in dollars)}\end{array}}{\text{original investment at beginning of period (in dollars)}} \quad (10\text{--}1)$$

For a bond,

$$HPY_b = \frac{C_t + \Delta P}{P_t} = \frac{C_t}{P_t} + \frac{\Delta P}{P_t} \quad (10\text{--}2)$$

where C_t is the coupon interest payment in dollars, P_t is the price at the beginning of the holding period t, and ΔP is the change in price over that period. For a 9 percent bond purchased for $900, held for one year, and sold at par,

$$HPY = \frac{90 + 100}{900} = .2111 = 21.11\%$$

The total return consists of the coupon interest payment ($90) plus a capital gain ($100), and HPY captures both components.
For a stock,

$$HPY_s = \frac{D_t + \Delta P}{P_t} = \frac{D_t}{P_t} + \frac{\Delta P}{P_t} \quad (10\text{--}3)$$

where D_t represents a flow like C_t, namely, the dividend received during the period. It should be noted that, in the second formulation of equation 10–3, the first term is the well-known dividend yield measure and the second term is the percentage change in stock price. This equation shows clearly why one cannot compare bond yields (for bonds held to maturity) to stock yields, since yield is only one part of the total return from stocks. (For bonds not held to maturity, HPY_b must be calculated anyway.)

The holding period yield measures the total return per dollar of original investment, and it can therefore be used to formulate percentage returns for any type of asset. It allows rational comparisons of the expected return from an asset with its returns in the past and also with the expected returns from other assets for any future period—whether the assets in question are bonds, shares of common stock, or a savings account at a commercial bank.

Holding period yield is the preferred measure of the return from a financial asset. It is not universally applied, however. Traditional methods of comparing returns, such as yield measures, are still used. *Yield* can be defined as the ratio of the cash income received during a designated period to the price of the asset. If the price used is the current price, the result is the *current yield;* returns from assets purchased at any other time at a different price will not be equal to the current yield.

Yield to maturity provides a more correct assessment of the return on bonds than does current yield. This is the percentage yield earned on a bond from acquisition date to maturity date. Yield tables are available to provide data for combinations of purchase price, time to maturity, and stated interest rates. Yield to maturity can also be calculated via an approximation formula.

It is possible to calculate yields on common stocks, primarily a *dividend yield* (dividend divided by price) and an *earnings yield* (earnings divided by price). As was indicated above, the former is only part of the true return from a stock; moreover, the latter is not an accurate measure of stockholder return, because total earnings per share are not usually paid out to stockholders. The holding period yield is the preferred measure of stock returns.

Taxes are another factor that needs to be considered in any discussion of returns, as was seen in chapter 9. Like risk, they are an inescapable part of the financial environment. As long as the government makes tax laws affecting the returns on financial assets, careful consideration must be given to after-tax returns.

Since individuals and institutions are in different tax brackets, ranging from 0 percent in the case of some institutions to 70 percent at the margin for some wealthy individuals, taxes matter greatly. On securities held long enough, profits qualify as long-term capital gains, which are taxed differently than are returns in the form of dividends or interest. State and local government security returns are exempt from federal taxation (and from some state taxation); thus, for example, a 5 percent interest rate on a California state bond, which is not taxable, is not the same thing to an investor as a 5 percent interest rate on a Treasury bond, which is taxable.

In summary, when considering the returns from financial instruments, one must be certain that the calculations are standardized. Measurements must be made on the same calculation basis (discount instruments versus interest-bearing assets), time basis (quarterly, semiannual, annual, etc.), tax basis, and total return basis (HPYs, etc.). Measurements that do not adjust for these factors must be carefully qualified.

TYPES OF FINANCIAL INSTRUMENTS

The major types of financial instruments can now be considered in terms of the four characteristics discussed above—risk, timing, maturity, and amount of return. Not all of the specific instruments will be analyzed here, but they will be discussed in chapter 11.

All financial instruments are claims to a future stream of benefits and, as such, are transferred from one economic unit (the issuer, borrower, demander of funds) to another economic unit (the holder, lender, supplier of funds). What is a financial liability to one economic unit is simultaneously a financial asset to another. Thus, although this discussion about financial instruments will generally be conducted in terms of assets only, it must be remembered that assets represent only one side of the coin.

For purposes of discussion, financial instruments can be categorized in accordance with the distinction presented above.[3] Fixed dollar assets, on the one hand, represent creditors' claims; they pay stated rates of return and, at worst (except in case of bankruptcy), are always redeemable at a specified time in the future. The distinguishing feature of these instruments is that the dollar amount of the claim, payable at maturity, is fixed. Equity assets, on the other hand, represent ownership claims; they do not necessarily pay stated rates of return and have no maturity date. Since the prices of equity assets change continuously across time, their returns are not guaranteed, and therefore considerably more risk is attached to them.

The major types of financial instruments, organized under these two categories, are as follows:

I. Fixed dollar instruments

   A. Short-term
      1. Federal
      2. Private

   B. Long-term
      1. Federal
      2. Municipal
      3. Private

II. Equity instruments

   A. Preferred stock
   B. Common stock

FIXED DOLLAR INSTRUMENTS

Fixed dollar instruments require periodic payments of a fixed amount to the holder, as well as repayment of the principal at maturity. The periodic fixed payments are in the form of interest.

---

[3]Technically, there is another distinction that is pertinent to financial assets—open market and institutional. The former can be freely traded in the marketplace, but the latter are traded in closed or institutional markets. Holders of this latter type must normally deal with the issuing institution. The organization and discussion of financial instruments presented here is based on Charles P. Jones, Donald L. Tuttle, and Cherrill P. Heaton, *Essentials of Modern Investments* (New York: The Ronald Press Company, 1977), Chapter 2 and Henry A. Latané, Donald L. Tuttle, and Charles P. Jones, *Security Analysis and Portfolio Management* (New York; the Ronald Press Company, 1975), Chapter 3.

Short-Term Fixed Dollar Instruments

Numerous fixed dollar instruments are available. Each represents a loan from the economic unit acquiring the claim. In return, the economic unit earns a return until or upon repayment at a specified future time, the maturity date. Each of these instruments can be sold to another economic unit by the original lender (purchaser). The seller simply transfers to the purchaser a piece of paper and the privileges of income and principal repayment that accompany it, in exchange for a mutually agreed upon price. This transaction price can be greater than, less than, or equal to the asset's *par value*, the amount that can be claimed from the issuer when the instrument matures.

Federal. The United States Treasury is the world's largest borrower. The securities it issues are backed by the full faith and credit of the government, and, as a practical matter, there is no risk of default. After all, the government can simply borrow new funds (i.e., engage in refunding) to redeem obligations that are maturing; this is, in fact, how our national debt is serviced. Also, of course, the government has the power to tax to raise funds.

Among short-term instruments, those issued by the federal government are obviously the safest, since the financial risk of possible nonpayment of interest and principal is virtually nonexistent, and since the likelihood of capital losses (if the asset is sold before maturity) is small. The most important instrument of this type is Treasury bills, offered weekly on a discount price basis, with maturities from three months to one year. These are sold at discount (less than face value) and redeemed at face value, and hence they provide a return or yield. Short-term coupon obligations sold by federal agencies such as the Federal National Mortgage Association or the Federal Home Loan Banks are also available, and their safety is considered to be only very slightly less than that of Treasury securities.

Private. Numerous privately issued short-term money market instruments are available on the open market. For example, commercial paper consists of short-term unsecured notes, with maturities from 3 to 270 days, that are issued by companies of strong credit standing that need short-term financing. Prime banker's acceptances are short-term instruments issued by a firm but guaranteed by an accepting bank, and they can be traded in the open market. A third alternative is negotiable certificates of deposit, which are claims on specified amounts of interest-earning time deposits left at commercial banks for a stated period of time. Each of these instruments is discussed in more detail in the next chapter.

Long-Term Fixed Dollar Instruments

Federal. Debt issues with longer terms to maturity can likewise be distinguished by issuer. Federal government issues consist of Treasury notes (totaling $226 billion at the end of 1978) and Treasury bonds (totaling $60 billion at the end of 1978). Federal agency issues have maturities ranging up to 25 years. Roughly $130 billion was outstanding at the end of 1978.

Municipal. Municipal bonds are debt issues of state and local governments. There are two types: general obligations, which pledge the full credit of the issuer, and revenue bonds, which pledge some specified source of revenue, such as bridge or turnpike receipts. Although most are generally considered to be quite safe, a number of municipal bonds defaulted during the 1930s, and others have defaulted over the years. The troubles New York City has had with its municipal financing are well known.

Municipal bonds, which totaled $285 billion at the end of 1978, are unique in that the interest paid is exempt from federal (and in some cases from state) taxes. For example, a 5 percent return for a bond-holder in the 50 percent tax bracket is equivalent to a 10 percent return on a taxable bond.

Private. Private long-term fixed dollar instruments are a very important category of open-market fixed dollar contracts. Corporations have typically raised most of their external funds in the bond market, which is basically an institutional market, since institutional investors own and trade the bulk of corporate bonds.

There are many varieties of private fixed dollar instruments, such as debentures, subordinated debentures, senior mortgages, junior mortgages, and income bonds. The key distinction here is the order of priority with respect to payment and in case of default. Debentures, for example, are unsecured bonds. Mortgages are secured by a pledge of real assets. Income bonds pay interest only if interest is earned.

Characteristics of Fixed Dollar Instruments.

Fixed dollar instruments can have several important features. For example, bonds can be retired systematically by the use of sinking funds or by the issuance of bonds with serial maturities. The former requires specified periodic payments by the issuing company to a trustee who retires the bonds periodically by open-market purchase or by calling them in. Serial issues are basically several small bond issues with various maturities stretching over the life of the longest-maturity bond, so that redemptions occur periodically at set intervals. Municipals are often serial issues, as are long-term privately placed bonds.

Another characteristic of debt issues is the call feature, which allows the issuing firm to recall a bond issue and, in effect, to replace it with a new issue that carries a lower interest rate. If interest rates drop significantly, it is advantageous to the issuer to replace the older bonds (with their higher rates) with new bonds (at the lower rate). Corporations typically pay a call premium per bond of perhaps one year's interest, but this is small compensation for investors who must give up a higher-yielding issue for a lower-yielding one.

Some bonds are also convertible into common stock at the option of the bond-holder. This convertibility feature causes different prices to exist for the bond—one price based on its debt characteristics and the other based on the aggregate market value of the shares of stock into which the bond is convertible. For example, a convertible bond with a par value of $1,000 might be converted into 20 shares of common stock of the firm issuing the bond. If the price of the stock rises above $50, the bond will be valued above $1,000 because of its conversion value.

Bond Discounts and Premiums. Bonds are the most important category of fixed dollar assets, and a very important factor concerning bonds is the current market price in relation to the par value. As has been noted, interest rates are inversely related to bond prices—as interest rates rise (or fall), bond prices decline (or rise). Since investors act on the basis of expected returns and risk, the returns on two fixed dollar instruments with identical risks cannot differ much, if any. Investors would purchase the higher-yielding one and sell the lower-yielding one until the yields were equilibrated.

Premium bonds sell above par because the coupons on such bonds exceed the current market rate for their particular maturity and risk. Discount bonds sell below par because their coupons are lower than the market rate for their particular maturity and risk. Par bonds sell at par because their coupons are equal to the market rate. The following are examples of these three types of bonds, using as illustrations bonds traded on the New York Stock Exchange:

Premium	ATT	8¾s	00	8.6	101½	101	101½
Discount	Pacific Telephone	4⅜s	88	6.1	72	72	72
Par	New York Telephone	8s	83	8.0	100	100	100

The figures represent, in order, the coupon; the year of maturity; the current yield; and the high, the low, and the close for the bond on a given day. (Bond prices are traditionally shown as hundreds, so that 100 represents a price of $1,000, and 90 represents $900, and so forth.)

The American Telephone and Telegraph (AT&T) bond is an 8¾ percent coupon bond, paying $87.50 in interest per year (actually paid in semiannual payments of $43.75 each) and maturing in the year 2000. Since interest rates on our observation date were lower than rates for bonds of this type when they were issued, the price of an AT&T bond was above $1,000. Namely, purchasers paid $1,015 on that date for each of these AT&T bonds; they will receive $1,000 for each bond held to maturity. However, the purchaser also will receive $87.50 in interest each year, whereas interest rates on similar bonds were less than 8¾ percent at the time of purchase. For example, if AT&T had issued a new bond on our observation date to mature in the year 2000, its coupon rate would have been less than 8¾ percent.

The Pacific Telephone bond is a "deep" discount bond, selling at $720 on the observation date. A purchaser who bought it then can redeem it for $1,000 in 1988 but, in the meantime, will be paid annual interest of only $43.75, much below the coupon of a currently issued bond with identical characteristics. The purchaser makes up for the interest deficiency with a capital gain over the period of $1,000 − $720 = $280 per bond. The total yield (return) is similar to what would be received by investors who bought currently issued bonds with high coupons but with little or no capital gains. The Pacific Telephone bond was obviously issued many years ago, when the going rate was much lower than it was on our observation date. As interest rates rose, the price of this bond had to decline, so that its yield would approximate yields on comparable fixed dollar instruments.

For the New York Telephone bond, the going rate for bonds of that risk category (Standard & Poor's rating) and that maturity must have been 8 percent on the observation date. A purchaser who paid $1,000 then for a bond will receive $1,000 at maturity from New York Telephone and will earn an annual coupon of $80, or a yield of 8 percent. The current yield of this bond ($80 divided by the current closing price) is equal to its yield to maturity (explained earlier in the chapter). In comparison, the current yield of the Pacific Telephone bond is 6.08 percent ($43.75 divided by $720), while its yield to maturity is 8.34 percent.[4]

EQUITY INSTRUMENTS

Equity instruments represent *residual claims* with regard to both income and return of principal. This means that stockholders are the last to receive

---

[4]The approximation formula for yield to maturity is

$$\text{yield to maturity} = \frac{C \pm \dfrac{\text{discount or premium}}{\text{years to maturity}}}{\frac{1}{2}(1{,}000 + \text{current market price})}$$

where C is the coupon in dollars, the discount or premium is the difference between the current market price and $1,000, and $1,000 is the par value of the bond; the plus sign is associated with a discount, the negative sign with a premium. For Pacific Telephone, a discount bond currently selling at $720 with a coupon of $43.75, approximate yield to maturity is (as of 1978—i.e., 10 years until maturity),

$$\text{yield to maturity} = \frac{43.75 + \dfrac{280}{10}}{\frac{1}{2}(720 + 1000)}$$

$$= 8.34 \text{ percent}$$

a return on their investment. If the firm suffers adverse circumstances, the stockholders may receive nothing. If the firm prospers, however, the stockholders may receive amounts far in excess of what the bondholders receive, because the latter are limited to a fixed (but prior) claim on the firm.

Equity securities are usually characterized by variable returns. Cash dividends, which are the only direct return received by an investor on common stocks from the firm itself, are paid out of the net income remaining after all other expenses (including bond interest) have been paid. These dividends are declared periodically by the board of directors of the issuing corporation, and they are subject to change, omission in one or more years, or elimination altogether. Since equity securities have no maturity date, holders must look to the marketplace, where they can receive only what a buyer is willing to pay for a security, and this commonly results in capital gains or losses.

Preferred Stock

Preferred stock and common stock are the best-known open-market equity assets. *Preferred* refers to the fact that preferred stockholders receive their dividend before common stockholders receive theirs; they also have priority over common stockholders in the event of liquidation. The preferred dividend is stated either as a percentage of the par value (as is bond interest) or as a fixed dollar amount. The par value of preferred stock is usually $100, and the par value of a bond is virtually always $1,000; therefore the annual dividend on a 9 percent preferred stock is $9 (usually payable at $2.25 quarterly), and the interest payment on a 9 percent bond is $90 (usually payable at $45 semiannually).

Preferred stock is a hybrid security in that it resembles both fixed dollar obligations and equity instruments. For example, the dividend return is fixed, as is the interest payment on a bond, but all dividends, whether preferred or common, must be declared and paid by the issuer's board of directors, and therefore a payment can be skipped if circumstances warrant. However, preferred dividends are typically cumulative, so that all omitted dividends on a company's preferred stock must be paid before dividends can be paid on its common stock.

Owners of preferred stock must sell these securities in the open market to regain their investment. There is no maturity date on these issues. However, many preferred stocks are callable, have sinking funds, or are convertible into common stocks, and hence they often prove not to be perpetual in fact. Preferred stocks dividends are not tax deductible for the issuer as is bond interest.

Common Stock

Common Stock denotes the ownership interest in a company by which a stockholder owns the company in common with the other stockholders. Its dividends are payable only after all other corporate obligations have been met. Thus they represent the residual earnings, and even then they are discretionary: the board of directors can, if it chooses, pay any amount, large or small. Since return of principal on common stock is determined in the open market, the stockholder is subject to capital gains and losses.

Although common stockholders are last in payment priority and in liquidation priority, they do have primary voting control of the business. They elect the board of directors of the firm, which in turn chooses the management. Stockholders have the right to vote on major issues confronting the firm, such as a merger offer or recapitalization. Of course, for most large firms, with millions of shares of stock outstanding, the vast number and the dispersion of owners means that individual stockholders have great difficulty exerting any real influence over management decisions.

It should be noted that stockholders own the net earnings of the firm. The firm, however, usually pays only a percentage of these earnings (in the form of dividends) directly to stockholder and keeps the remainder (retained earnings) for reinvestment purposes. Although the stockholders own these funds, they can receive them only if the price of the stock is bid up as a result of market recognition of the successful investment of funds (which includes the retained earnings). Stockholders can then enjoy a capital gain, since they can sell their shares for more than what they paid for them. The price of the common stock, unlike a fixed dollar asset with a known maturity value, can theoretically be any amount. It can decline to zero or rise to any amount.

AMOUNTS OF FINANCIAL ASSETS

To illustrate the preceding discussion, it is instructive to examine some figures on the actual amounts, not only of these financial instruments, but of all financial assets. This will provide a perspective from which to judge the various markets (such as the money and capital markets, discussed in the next chapter); it will also serve as a basis for the theory of intermediation (which will be discussed in chapter 12).

Table 10–1 shows the amounts, in billions of dollars, of all financial assets and liabilities outstanding at the end of 1975. (Use of 1975 figures will provide a perspective for the discussion in Chapter 7 which also used some 1975 figures—we will, however, also refer to 1978 figures in this discussion). The rows of this matrix represent the various financial assets (which are simultaneously liabilities to their issuers), and the columns show the various sectors of the economy, according to the typical presentation in flow-of-funds accounts. Although floats and discrepancies prevent assets and liabilities for all sectors from being equal (as is shown in the column labelled "All sectors"),[5] the matrix is nevertheless very informative about both the absolute and the relative amounts of financial assets and liabilities, including such institutional assets as time and savings accounts and pension reserves, as well as the specific financial instruments just discussed.

Fixed dollar instruments corresponding to those in the previous discussion are reflected in lines 20 through 27 of the table, which give, for each type of instrument, both the amount outstanding (shown as a liability to the issuing sector) and the amount held by every other sector (shown on the same row as assets for all other sectors).[6] For example, municipal (state and local) governments (line 22) issued $223.8 billion of fixed dollar instruments to finance the activities of governmental units all over the United States. These instruments were held by the various sectors, as is shown in their asset columns. Thus commercial banks, the largest single holder of municipal securities, owned $102.8 billion in 1975. Households are the second largest, with holdings amounting to $74.2 billion in 1975. Presumably, much of these holdings is possessed by individuals in higher tax-brackets because of the exclusion of municipal security income from federal taxes.

Corporate equities are shown on line 18. (The table makes no distinction between common and preferred stock.) Assets are shown at market value, not at book value. The $42.2 billion figure on line 18 under "All sectors" is the redemption value of shares of open-end investment companies (mutual funds), a major institutional equity asset. Investment companies are in business to invest in various financial assets, primarily the securities of other corporations. The equity shares of the investment companies, exactly like any other equity instrument, are owned by investors.

It is interesting to compute a few basic ratios with the figures given in Table 10–1; also, for comparison, some updated figures will be included. Consider the following facts (drawn from the data in the table) as a guide to point out proportions and relations among financial assets and liabilities:

1. Fixed dollar financial instruments constituted about 43 percent of total financial assets in 1975, and 45 percent in 1978.

---

[5]There are other technical reasons why the amount of total assets does not correspond to the amount of total liabilities.

[6]The previous discussion omitted mortgages, the majority of which are claims on individuals, and consumer credit, which is not an open-market instrument. It also omitted bank loans and other loans that are included in lines 20 through 27.

2. Corporate equities amounted to only about 14 percent of total financial assets in 1975. However, we should note that this percentage can vary considerably from year to year because of sharp fluctuations in the stock market. For example, at the ends of 1976, 1977, and 1978, the dollar value of corporate equities was respectively $1060 billion, $997 billion, and $1026 billion.

3. Money, savings deposits, life insurance reserves, and pension fund reserves, which are institutional fixed dollar assets, amounted to about 29 percent of total financial assets in both 1975 and 1978. Therefore financial instruments—fixed dollar and equity—constitute most of the dollar value of all financial assets.

4. Households owned about 41 percent of the total financial assets in 1975 and 1978, which clearly emphasizes the importance of this sector in any discussion of financial assets and liabilities. Households completely dwarf the business sector in this regard and are about twice as large as the next most important holder of financial assets, the private nonbank finance sector (21 percent). As for financial instruments, households owned one-third of the dollar value of those outstanding in 1975 and 1978.

5. The largest issuer of financial liabilities is the private nonbank finance sector (23 percent). This is to be expected from the nature of its operations: institutions in this sector perform an intermediary function, purchasing primary securities on the one hand and issuing indirect securities on the other, as will be explained in chapter 12.[7] The business sector, however, is not far behind, accounting for roughly 20 percent of total liabilities outstanding.

6. The largest issuer of financial instruments—fixed dollar and equity—in 1975 was the business sector, which issued almost half of the total. Business firms issue all the equity securities other than investment company shares. However, households were a close second in the issuance of financial instruments, primarily because of mortgages.

RETURNS AND RISK ON MAJOR FINANCIAL INSTRUMENTS

Having examined the most important types of financial instruments, as well as their absolute and relative significance in terms of amounts out-

---

[7]Note that, for the financial intermediaries—i.e., for the private nonbank finance sector—total financial assets are very close to total liabilities. This is because the function of intermediaries is to do just that—to intermediate. They transform financial claims but hold little in the way of real assets.

TABLE 10–1. Financial Assets and Liabilities, December 31, 1975 (Amounts outstanding in billions of dollars)

Sector / Transaction category	Private domestic nonfinancial sectors								Rest of the world		U.S. Government	
	Households		Business		State and local governments		Total					
	A	L	A	L	A	L	A	L	A	L	A	L
1 Total financial assets	2496.9	....	629.0	....	139.2	....	3265.0	....	247.7	....	122.4	....
2 Total liabilities	....	782.8	....	1109.3	....	240.3	....	2132.4	....	271.0	....	510.8
3 Gold	....	....	....	....	....	....	....	....	38.1	....	....	....
4 SDRs	....	....	....	....	....	....	....	....	8.9	....	2.3	....
5 IMF position	....	....	....	....	....	....	....	....	....	2.2	2.2	....
6 Official foreign exchange	....	....	....	....	....	....	....	....	....	0.1	....	....
7 Treasury currency	....	....	....	....	....	....	....	....	....	....	....	8.7
8 Demand dep. and currency	165.6	....	67.4	....	14.3	....	247.3	....	14.0	....	11.2	....
9 Private domestic	165.6	....	67.4	....	14.3	....	247.3	....	....	....	11.2	....
10 U.S. government	....	....	....	....	....	....	....	....	....	....	....	....
11 Foreign	....	....	....	....	....	....	....	....	14.0	....	11.2	....
12 Time and savings accounts	776.2	....	22.4	....	48.1	....	846.7	....	20.9	....	0.6	....

13	At commercial banks	350.7		22.4		48.1		421.1		20.9		0.6	
14	At savings institutions	425.6						425.6					
15	Life insurance reserves	164.6						164.6					7.7
16	Pension fund reserves	368.6						368.6					41.9
17	Interbank claims									26.7			
18	Corporate equities	630.5						630.5					
19	Credit market instruments	346.8	753.5	85.5	834.4	70.1	229.6	502.4	1817.5	77.5	94.2	88.2	446.3
20	U.S. Treasury secs.	114.3		14.3		30.6		159.2		66.5		7.0	437.3
21	Federal agency secs.	9.1		3.2		22.3		34.6					7.9
22	State and local govt. secs.	74.2		4.5	6.7	4.4	223.8	83.1	230.5				
23	Corp. and fgn. bonds	65.9			254.3			65.9	254.3	2.6	25.6		
24	Mortgages	72.7	508.2		286.8	12.8		85.6	795.0			13.5	1.1
25	Consumer credit		197.3	30.9				30.9	197.3				
26	Bank loans n.e.c.		16.5		198.2			214.7			21.8		
27	Pvt. short-term paper	10.5		32.6	17.8			43.1	17.8	8.4	11.1	67.7	
28	Other loans		31.5		70.6		5.8	4.0	107.9	0.4	35.7		
29	Security credit	4.0	13.7					13.7			0.3		
30	Trade credit		7.9	283.3	234.8	6.6	10.7	283.3	253.4	11.6	14.2	6.4	5.2
31	Taxes payable			13.4	13.4			6.6	13.4			5.3	
32	Miscellaneous	40.5	7.7	170.5	26.7			211.1	34.5	49.5	160.0	6.1	1.2

(continued from pages 296 and 297)

Transaction category	Financial sectors										All sectors		Floats and discrepancies
	Total		Sponsored agencies and mortgage pools		Monetary authority		Commercial banking		Private nonbank finance				
	A	L	A	L	A	L	A	L	A	L	A	L	A
1 Total financial assets	2407.1	.....	127.1	.....	124.7	.....	373.6	.....	1281.6	.....	6042.1	.....	373.3
2 Total liabilities	.....	2291.7	.....	124.9	.....	124.7	.....	826.5	.....	1215.6	.....	5205.9	.....
3 Gold	11.6	.....	.....	.....	11.6	.....	.....	.....	.....	.....	49.7	.....	.....
4 SDRs	.....	.....	.....	.....	.....	.....	.....	.....	.....	.....	11.2	2.2	.....
5 IMF position	.....	.....	.....	.....	.....	.....	.....	.....	.....	.....	2.2	0.1	.....
6 Official foreign exchange	0.1	.....	.....	.....	0.1	.....	.....	.....	.....	.....	0.1	.....	.....
7 Treasury currency	10.6	.....	.....	.....	10.6	.....	.....	.....	.....	.....	10.6	8.7	-1.9
8 Demand dep. and currency	17.8	325.0	0.3	.....	.....	82.5	0.9	242.5	16.7	.....	290.3	325.0	34.7
9 Private domestic	17.8	300.1	0.3	.....	.....	74.3	0.9	225.8	16.7	.....	265.2	300.1	35.0
10 U.S. government	.....	10.9	.....	.....	.....	7.8	.....	3.1	.....	.....	11.2	10.9	-0.3
11 Foreign	.....	14.0	.....	.....	.....	0.5	.....	13.5	.....	.....	14.0	14.0	.....
12 Time and savings accounts	16.4	884.6	.....	.....	.....	.....	.....	455.6	16.4	429.0	884.6	884.6	.....

13	At commercial banks	13.0	455.6	...	...	...	...	455.6	13.0	...	455.6	455.6	
14	At savings institutions	3.4	429.0	...	...	...	...	...	3.4	429.0	429.0	429.0	
15	Life insurance reserves	...	156.9	...	...	...	...	...	...	156.9	164.6	164.6	
16	Pension fund reserves	...	326.7	...	...	...	...	...	...	326.7	368.6	368.6	
17	Interbank claims	58.6	58.6	...	3.9	38.3	20.3	54.7	196.5	...	58.6	58.6	
18	Corporate equities	197.4	42.2	...	...	...	...	0.9	...	42.2	854.7	42.2	
19	Credit market instruments	1958.6	268.7	125.7	95.3	...	33.9	745.4	992.4	120.3	2626.7	2626.7	
20	U.S. Treasury secs.	211.6	...	2.9	87.9	...	...	85.4	35.3	...	437.3	437.3	
21	Federal agency secs.	79.2	112.9	0.4	6.2	...	...	34.5	38.0	...	120.8	120.8	
22	State and local govt. secs.	147.4	...	...	...	...	...	102.8	44.6	...	230.5	230.5	
23	Corp. and fgn. bonds	248.7	37.3	...	...	...	4.5	8.6	240.2	32.8	317.2	317.2	
24	Mortgages	704.2	7.2	87.5	...	...	...	136.5	480.3	7.2	803.3	803.3	
25	Consumer credit	166.4	...	...	...	...	...	90.3	76.1	...	197.3	197.3	
26	Bank loans n.e.c.	277.0	40.5	...	...	...	10.5	277.0	...	29.9	277.0	277.0	
27	Pvt. short-term paper	28.7	51.4	3.0	1.1	...	18.9	10.3	14.4	32.5	80.3	80.3	
28	Other loans	95.3	19.4	31.8	1.6	...	...	14.6	63.5	17.8	163.0	163.0	
29	Security credit	24.6	15.0	...	...	...	...	...	10.1	15.0	29.0	29.0	
30	Trade credit	7.7	...	...	...	...	...	...	7.7	...	308.9	272.8	-36.2
31	Taxes payable	...	2.7	...	...	...	0.6	...	...	2.1	12.0	16.0	4.1
32	Miscellaneous	103.6	211.3	1.2	3.2	3.8	73.6	57.1	42.0	123.5	370.3	406.9	36.6

Source: Board of Governors of the Federal Reserve System, *Flow of Funds Accounts, 1946–75*, December 1976, p. 90.

standing, we now focus on the two parameters that are most important to purchasers of these claims. Although investors have different objectives, they are ultimately interested in returns and in the risk involved therewith. It should be kept in mind that investors buy financial instruments on the basis of expected returns, although returns are subject to uncertainty. Ex ante returns and risk are related, since investors expect larger returns for assuming larger risks—any other expectation would be illogical. Obviously, we cannot foresee what future returns will be. We can, however, examine the historical returns on financial assets. Although expectations are not always realized, the basic risk-return relationship must prevail over long periods of time: that is, more risky assets should exhibit greater returns but also greater variability.

Figure 10–1 shows annual returns on common stocks, corporate bonds, government bonds, and Treasury bills (as well as the rate of inflation) over the period from 1926 through 1976. Both the average return (arithmetic mean) and the compound return (geometric mean) are shown, as is the standard deviation—a measure of variation about the mean return. The distribution of returns is illustrated by bar graphs in the figure. Return as used here is equivalent to the holding period yield discussed earlier. The figure shows that, as would be expected, common stocks had the largest average returns over this 51-year period; also, again as would be expected, they exhibited the greatest variability of return as measured by the standard deviation. Corporate bond returns were less than half as great as those of stocks, but they displayed only one-fourth as much variability. Government bonds returned even less, as would be expected from the fact that they carry no risk of default. However, the standard deviation was actually higher for government bonds than for corporate bonds over this period of time. Treasury bills, being short-term, safe assets, had the smallest returns and risk, again as would be predicted from a knowledge of risk-return relationships for financial assets.

FINANCIAL MARKETS

Financial instruments are bought and sold in several different marketplaces, collectively known as the financial markets, or the securities markets. As was previously noted, an arbitrary distinction can be drawn between the money market (for issues maturing in less than one year) and the capital market (for issues maturing in more than one year or not at all).

The securities markets constitute an apparatus where investors with savings can invest them in newly issued securities or in existing securities.[8] Demanders of funds, on the other hand, can seek to borrow the funds they

---

[8]This discussion is indebted to Latané, Tuttle, and Jones *Security Analysis and Portfolio Management*, pp. 59–62.

Series	Geometric Mean	Arithmetic Mean	Standard Deviation	Distribution
Common Stocks	9.2%	11.6%	22.4%	
Long Term Corporate Bonds	4.1%	4.2%	5.6%	
Long Term Government Bonds	3.4%	3.5%	5.8%	
U.S. Treasury Bills	2.4%	2.4%	2.1%	
Inflation	2.3%	2.4%	4.8%	

−50%　0% +50%

FIGURE 10–1. Average Annual Returns on Selected Financial Assets, 1926–1976.

Source: Roger Ibbotson and Rex Sinquefield, *Stocks, Bonds, Bills, and Inflation: The Past (1926–1976) and the Future (1977–2000)* (Charlottesville, Virginia: Financial Analysts Research Foundation, 1977) p. 10. Reprinted by permission.

need to invest in real assets or carry on their operations. Corporations and governments, as noted in Chapter 7, are the largest demanders of funds. Households are the saving surplus sector of the economy. Either directly, or more importantly through financial intermediaries, households provide funds for the economy. Household saving as a source of loanable funds was considered in Chapter 6.

Securities markets are a very important part of our economic and financial system. They perform several tasks, possibly with different degrees of success. First, securities markets are the framework in which suppliers and demanders of funds, whatever their particular characteristics and needs, can meet. The pool of savings is widespread while the individual borrower's demands for capital are often large. The basic function of securities markets is to collect and channel the pool of savings to the relatively few who need it for productive investment in real assets.

Second, the market should be an efficient allocator of capital, in the sense that those firms that can best use the funds are, in fact, the firms that obtain the funds. Thus, an efficient market allocates funds to the most productive uses. Profitable firms in the early stages of their life cycle (for example, IBM when it was emerging) that need funds to grow to meet market demands and can afford to pay the going rate should be able to raise capital in an efficient market.

Third, securities markets must provide for the orderly and efficient trading of existing securities. Liquidity is very important for investors—they must be able to get their funds back.

Primary Markets

New issues of securities are handled by *primary markets*, which are essential if deficit units are to acquire necessary funds. Good primary markets are essential for our economic system to prosper; for example, economic units wishing to invest in real assets would probably have to do much of the saving to finance such investment—a clearly inefficient process—if good primary markets did not exist.[9]

In recent years, the primary market has largely been a bond market: in 1977, for example, 80 percent of the new security issues was bonds, because debt is cheaper than equity as a source of finance, and because the sale of new equity securities is more expensive than the use of "old" equity (i.e., retained earnings).

Primary issues are often marketed through a middleman called an *investment banker*. An investment banking firm typically buys securities from the issuing corporation and sells them to the general public at a profit. By relieving the issuers from the risk of adverse price fluctuations while the securities are being marketed, investment bankers perform a valuable function in the financial system. The process by which an issue of securities goes from the issuer (seller) to the investors is shown in Figure 10–2.

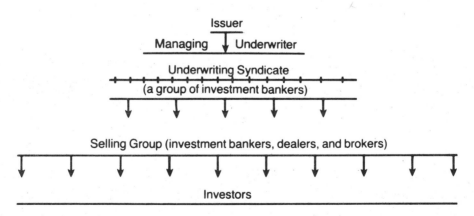

FIGURE 10–2. Issuance of Securities through Investment Bankers.

An investment banker, acting as the *managing underwriter* for a new

---

[9]The discussion in the remainder of this chapter is indebted to Jones, Tuttle, and Heaton, *Essentials of Modern Investments*, Chapter 3.

securities issue, organizes all the details of the sale. To reduce its own risk on a large issue, the investment banker can form an underwriting syndicate consisting of a few major investment banking houses and several dozen participating houses. Once the registration is approved by the Securities and Exchange Commission, the issuance price is fixed and the securities are offered to the public. The selling group consists of the underwriting syndicate and retailing organizations (i.e., dealers and brokers), which handle the actual distribution of the securities to the public. The profits are in the *spread*—the difference between what the investment bankers paid for the issue and what the investors pay for it, with the latter being a function of market conditions at the time of sale.

In recent years, many corporations have placed their new securities issues privately rather than publicly. This means that the issue is sold directly to an institution, so that it bypasses the open market. Life insurance companies and pension funds have been active buyers of private offerings. Any type of security can be privately placed, although such placements usually involve bond issues rather than some other security.

Secondary Markets

Once securities have been sold by the issuer, an efficient mechanism is needed for their resale. Investors will not buy primary securities very readily if they cannot sell them when they choose. Therefore good *secondary markets* are absolutely vital to our economic system. A further benefit of secondary markets accrues to the management of individual corporations. The objective of Managerial Finance is assumed to be shareholder wealth maximization. This can be accomplished by maximizing the current share price of the stock. The price of the stock in a secondary market is readily available for all to see and presumably reflects the actions of management.

Secondary markets can be classified as either negotiated markets or auction markets. The former involve firms who act as dealers buying and selling for their own account; the latter involve an auction or bidding process wherein brokers represent investors and act on their behalf. In effect, dealers are direct participants, owning the securities themselves; brokers are intermediaries who simply represent buyers and sellers.

Negotiated Markets. These markets have no single identifiable physical location but rather are a system of dealers linked together electronically. Dealers make markets in the various securities traded, with the number of dealers per individual security ranging from one or two to many. The over-the-counter market (OTC) is the most prominent negotiated market. The majority of all common stocks (in terms of number of companies), most corporate bonds, and all government bonds are traded in this market; thus, in terms of number of individual securities handled, the OTC market is the largest secondary market. Investors wishing to transact in these securities call their broker who in turn transacts with dealers making a market in the security of interest. Stock X may involve 3 dealers who make a market in this security while Stock Y may involve 30 dealers. The OTC dealers sell their securities for a price agreed to by them and the buyer; i.e., a net price. A broker could buy a security from an OTC dealer and resell it to the investor for a higher price, or a commission could be charged. The OTC dealer profits by the spread between prices paid for securities when bought from customers and prices obtained by selling the securities to other customers. The OTC market has made vast improvements in terms of facilitating trading.

Still another negotiated market is the third market—where exchange-listed securities are traded over the counter. Participants primarily include institutions and firms acting as intermediaries.

The third market developed because the exchanges at one time did not allow discounts on the purchase or sale of large quantities of stock. By offering discounts, third-market firms attracted considerable business for a while. Brokerage fees on exchanges are now negotiable, however, and exchange member firms can engage in some off-board trading activities, which are scheduled to accelerate. It is important to note that the Securities Acts Amendments of 1975 called for a national market system, which will probably be achieved sometime in the 1980s. Therefore the third market, and all current markets for that matter, will most likely change drastically.

Another negotiated market has developed in recent years—the fourth market. Here, institutions trade directly with one another. For perspective, it should be noted that in 1976 institutions accounted for about half to total New York Stock Exchange volume (shares traded).

Auction Markets. The national and regional stock exchanges, officially designated as registered exchanges, are mostly auction markets. The largest and best known of all secondary markets in the world is the New York Stock Exchange (NYSE), a national exchange that accounts for the bulk of the volume traded on all exchanges. The second largest auction market is the American Stock Exchange (ASE), also located in New York City. Nine regional U.S. and Canadian exchanges account for a small percentage of all exchange volume. Their relative sizes can easily be seen in Table 10–2, which shows the volume of shares sold on the NYSE, the ASE, and all other registered exchanges in selected years from 1935 through 1977.[10]

The NYSE is the premier auction market for stocks. Specialists maintain orderly trading in each stock listed on the exchange by continuously offering to buy and sell the stocks for which they are responsible. They can buy or sell for their own accounts or for brokerage firms acting for inves-

---

[10]In terms of the value of shares traded, the NYSE is even more dominant.

TABLE 10–2. Shares Sold on Registered Exchanges

Year	Number of shares (mils.)			Per Cent of Total		
	NYSE	ASE	Other	NYSE	ASE	Other
1935	513.6	84.7	63.6	77.6%	12.8%	9.6%
1940	282.7	47.9	41.4	76.0	12.9	11.1
1950	655.3	114.9	86.9	76.5	13.4	10.1
1955	820.5	243.9	148.0	67.7	20.1	12.2
1961	1,292.3	525.3	192.9	64.3	26.1	9.6
1962	1,186.5	332.6	144.4	71.3	20.0	8.7
1963	1,350.9	336.3	151.4	73.5	18.3	8.2
1964	1,482.3	397.0	165.6	72.5	19.4	8.1
1965	1,809.4	582.2	195.3	69.9	22.5	7.5
1966	2,204.8	730.9	252.2	69.2	22.9	7.9
1967	2,885.8	1,290.2	327.8	64.1	28.6	7.3
1968	3,298.7	1,570.7	442.6	62.1	29.6	8.3
1969	3,173.6	1,341.0	448.8	63.9	27.0	9.0
1970	3,213.1	878.5	444.1	70.8	19.4	9.8
1971	4,265.3	1.049.3	601.1	72.1	17.7	10.2
1972	4,496.2	1,103.2	699.8	71.4	17.5	11.1
1973	4,336.6	740.4	653.2	75.7	12.9	11.4
1974	3,821.9	475.3	541.9	79.0	9.8	11.2
1975	5,056.5	540.9	637.6	81.1	8.7	10.2
1976	5,649.2	637.0	749.5	80.3	9.1	10.7
1977	5,613.3	651.9	758.2	79.9	9.3	10.8

Source: The New York Stock Exchange, *1978 Fact Book*, p. 73 (Reprinted by permission).

tors. Brokers are the middlemen: they represent buyers and sellers as they try to obtain the best possible prices for them. The market value of all stocks listed on the NYSE in 1977 was around $800 billion. It now lists about 1,600 common stocks. Companies that are listed on the NYSE represent only a tiny fraction of all those in the U.S., but they account for a very significant percentage of the total assets and sales and over 80 percent of the net income of all U.S. corporations. This concentration is shown in Table 10–3. The NYSE has dominated in the trading of stocks in this country because it includes those of major companies. The over-the-counter market handles mostly small companies that are not well known or actively traded.

Since August 1976, it has been permissible for securities listed on the NYSE to be traded on the ASE. More and more securities will be traded simultaneously by two or more exchanges in the future. Also, the Securities and Exchange Commission has ruled that the prohibition preventing

TABLE 10-3. Comparison of NYSE Listed Corporations With All U.S. Corporations

Year	Number of Companies			Total Assets			Sales or Revenues			Net Income		
	All U.S.	NYSE	Per Cent	All U.S.	NYSE (bils.)	Per Cent	All U.S.	NYSE (bils.)	Per Cent	All U.S.	NYSE (bils.)	Per Cent
1976	n.a.	1,550	—	n.a.	$2,067	—	n.a.	$1,583	—	n.a.	$82	—
1975	2,022,000	1,531	0.1%	$4,268	1,793	42.0%	$3,198	1,404	43.9%	$84	63	75.0%
1974	1,966,000	1,543	0.1	3,996	1,700	42.5	3,090	1,332	43.1	84	69	82.1
1973	1,905,000	1,536	0.1	3,649	1,491	40.9	2,558	1,072	41.9	72	63	87.5
1972	1,813,000	1,478	0.1	3,257	1,270	39.0	2,171	905	41.7	57	49	86.0
1971	1,733,000	1,399	0.1	2,889	1,125	38.9	1,906	809	42.4	44	42	95.5
1970	1,655,000	1,330	0.1	2,635	1,007	38.2	1,751	734	41.9	33	37	#
1969	1,659,000	1,290	0.1	2,446	887	36.3	1,680	687	40.9	43	39	90.7
1968	1,542,000	1,251	0.1	2,216	737	33.3	1,508	650	43.1	49	37	75.5
1967	1,534,000	1,253	0.1	2,010	625	31.1	1,375	536	39.0	47	33	70.2
1966	1,469,000	1,265	0.1	1,845	571	30.9	1,307	498	38.1	48	34	70.8

Source: The New York Stock Exchange, *1978 Fact Book*, June 1978, p. 35. (Reprinted by permission).

Note: These data were derived from U.S., Treasury Department, Statistics of Income.
Note: n.a. Not Available.
Percentage relationship not meaningful.

NYSE members from making markets in NYSE-listed stocks off the NYSE will be lifted.

One can hardly overestimate the importance of a strong secondary market, where the shares of publicly owned corporations can be traded, since this provides a basis on which to raise additional equity funds, which finance additional growth.

How Secondary Markets Work. The Securities and Exchange Commission, by virtue of legislation passed in 1933 and 1934, has the primary responsibility for regulating the securities industry and assuring the smooth functioning of the exchanges. The Securities Acts Amendments of 1964 imposed the same standards for the over-the-counter market that existed for listed securities. The securities industry also follows self-imposed regulations set by the NYSE and ASE for the registered exchanges and by the National Association of Securities Dealers for the OTC market.

Investors wishing to trade can enter orders to buy or sell at the current bid or asked price (called *market orders*) or at specified prices (called *limit orders*). Limit orders predominate in the over-the-counter market because the price is negotiated; on the auction-markets, however, market orders are frequently placed because of the near-continuous trading of the securities. *Round lots* of 100 shares are standard on exchanges; *odd lots*, or orders for less than 100 shares, carry an additional charge, from 12½¢ to 25¢ per share.

A typical round-lot buy order for Exxon on the NYSE might be executed as follows. The buyer phones a local broker (registered representative) and, after learning the current market price of Exxon, instructs the broker to purchase 100 shares "at the market." The order is transmitted to the broker's New York office, which then relays it to its member partner on the exchange floor, where securities are traded. The partner proceeds to the area where Exxon is traded and asks the specialist there (to whom the NYSE assigns the task of maintaining an orderly market in that stock), "How's Exxon?" Since specialists maintain a record of all limit orders for the stock they are in charge of, they know the current market conditions. (Technically, specialists can quote their own bid and ask prices, since they can buy and sell for their own accounts as well as for brokers.) The current bid and ask quotes given by the specialist for Exxon are good only for 100 shares. The partner, after receiving the current quotes, reveals that there is a purchase order to be filled at the ask price (a sell order would be filled at the lower bid price). The purchaser relays a confirmation, often within minutes, and the trade subsequently appears on the NYSE consolidated tape, which shows all transactions on nine exchanges for NYSE-listed stocks.

Brokers make money from the commissions they charge, which usually are a function of the dollar amount of the transactions; therefore, for a given price of stock, it does not matter to brokers whether a buy order or a sell order is placed. Specialists make money from (1) commissions they charge to brokers for the execution of limit orders; and (2) dealings for their own accounts when there are no offsetting public orders—that is, specialists can purchase stock when other investors want to sell but there are no market orders to buy, and later they can sell this stock at a higher price to the public. They can also sell for their own accounts when investors want to buy but there are no market orders to sell. Since specialists are charged with maintaining an orderly market, they must at times like these go against the trend.

SUMMARY

This chapter has described financial instruments, which represent claims on borrowers for funds obtained. Characteristics of financial instruments include the certainty, timing, duration, and amount of payments to be received. Each of these parameters was considered in some detail.

Financial instruments are of two general types—fixed dollar and equity. Fixed dollar instruments represent claims of creditorship; they pay stated rates of return, and the dollar amount of the claim, payable at maturity, is fixed. Equity instruments, conversely, represent claims of ownership; they do not necessarily pay stated rates of return and have no maturity date. Fixed dollar instruments discussed in the chapter were short-term federal and private and long-term federal, municipal, and private. Equity instruments discussed were preferred and common stocks.

The stocks of all financial assets, including the financial instruments discussed in this chapter, were examined as to their absolute amounts and their positions in relation to each other. Financial instruments account for most of the dollar value of all financial assets, with fixed dollar instruments about three times as important as equity instruments.

During the 51-year period ending in 1976, common stocks had the largest average returns and the greatest variability of return. Corporate bonds returned less but with considerably less risk. Government bonds and Treasury bills returned still less, because of the risk-free nature of the federal government as an issuer of securities.

Financial instruments can be organized into markets. The securities markets in the United States fulfill the very important function of raising and allocating capital to users.

Primary markets involve new issues of securities. Investment bankers are a key component of primary markets; they help issuers to sell their securities to investors. Secondary markets for the trading of existing securities provide liquidity to investors who purchase primary claims. They are either negotiated markets, involving dealers who make a market in various securities, or auction markets, involving brokers who represent both buyers and sellers wishing to transact in securities.

11

The Money and Capital Markets

Financial markets include all the mechanisms for the issuance, trading, and redeeming of claims. We have already established that they are vital for the proper functioning of the economy.

There are numerous ways to classify financial markets, according to the distinctions between institutional markets (in which investors deal directly with institutions) and open markets or between fixed asset markets and equity markets. However, having developed some background for financial instruments, we can now proceed to talk about two basic markets—the money market, which deals with short-term instruments, and the capital markets, which deal with long-term instruments. (Maturity, of course, is a primary characteristic of all financial instruments).

The first section of this chapter explains what the money market is, how it is organized, and who the participants are. Then the various money market instruments are examined. This section concludes with some facts and figures, including amounts outstanding and recent rates.

The second section of this chapter follows the same format to examine the capital market. Taken together, these two sections provide a complete basic coverage of the major forms of financing in this country.

THE MONEY MARKET

The *money market* is a market for short-term claims.[1] The term is used loosely to denote a set of related markets in which similar financial

---

[1]The term *money market* has this common usage among financial analysts. Of course, this usage does not refer to the *market for money* in the Keynesian liquidity preference

instruments are traded. These instruments have short maturities, are very liquid, and are relatively without risk—in short, they are reasonably close substitutes for money.

The primary purpose of the money market in our economy is to optimize the use of financial claims, which means (1) to permit those who need short-term funds to raise them quickly and efficiently by the issuance of financial liabilities; and (2) to provide saving surplus units with a ready outlet for the investment of idle cash, but which also permits quick adjustments of their portfolios of financial assets as the need arises. In effect, the money market gives the issuers of financial claims (borrowers) an orderly method of short-term finance. At the same time, it gives the purchasers of financial claims (lenders) a means to adjust their portfolios and to add to them as new short-term funds are acquired. For example, suppose that a financial institution finds some of its long-term bonds maturing and that, at the same time, it wishes to make a long-term commitment 60 days hence. By temporarily purchasing one or more money market instruments with the bond redemption funds designated for the subsequent long-term commitment, the institution can improve its portfolio position. Simultaneously, with these transactions, deficit units with short-term needs can achieve their desired financing patterns. As we know, the economy benefits by any private financial transactions that speed the flow of saving from surplus units to deficit units.

The money market performs a valuable function for society. It encourages financial activity, since its existence assures borrowers (lenders) of the availability of short-term funds (returns). Thus, if corporations know that they can raise short-term funds if the need arises, they may be more encouraged to invest a larger percentage of their total capital in real assets—and real assets, as we know, are vivtal to the creation of wealth. Lenders, being assured of a relatively safe, liquid, and short-maturity outlet that provides a return on their funds, can seek out the best investment opportunities available without having to worry about opportunity costs on idle funds.[2]

Organization

The money market is not a physical entity in the form of, say, a stock exchange. Rather, it is a network of dealers who are linked to each other

---

theory of interest-rate determination. We have tried to take care to use the latter term to deal with forces affecting the overall supply of and demand for money, and we reserve the term *money market* for the use noted above.

[2]Rightly or wrongly, the money market also plays another role—it provides the Federal Reserve with daily information with which to monitor the flow of the economy and the need for Fed actions. The use of a money supply target, as some economists advocate, would eliminate this role.

by telephone and other communication devices. New York is considered to be the center for money market activity in this country.

Money market dealers are constantly in touch with each other, producing a continuously changing set of price quotes on offers to buy and sell. Dealers, by definition, *take positions* in securities: they buy for and sell from their own accounts. They profit by the spread between their bid and ask prices (and by any resulting price appreciation during the time they hold the securities).[3]

Most money market transactions take place by telephone, as participants are continuously communicating with dealers. The actual mechanics of transactions are handled for the most part by commercial banks, particularly those specializing in money market transactions, by dealers in the various types of money market instruments, and by the Fed. For example, payment for purchased securities is often made with federal funds, which are on deposit in the Federal Reserve banks. These funds can be easily transferred by a telephone call to the appropriate Federal Reserve bank.

Demanders and Suppliers in the Money Market

Participants in the money market can be suppliers or demanders of funds or both. The major participants and the positions they usually assume are listed below.

1. The U.S. Treasury is one of the world's largest borrowers; it is the greatest demander of funds in the money market. Treasury issues constitute the largest single item in the money market.

2. The Federal Reserve, unlike the Treasury, is a major supplier of funds in the money market, as it purchases large quantities of money market instruments, primarily Treasury issues. As we saw in Chapter 5, these purchases and sales are carried out in connection with open-market operations.

3. Commercial banks are both suppliers and demanders of short-term funds. In the former role, they hold large amounts of money market instruments because of their need for liquidity. The latter role has developed recently, as banks have become more aggressive in seeking out funds for investment purposes. Negotiable certificates of deposit are the prime example of a money market instrument designed by banks to raise short-term funds.

4. Nonfinancial corporate business is both a supplier and a demand-

---

[3]Also, since money market dealers are highly leveraged (they are heavy users of borrowed money to finance their positions), they profit if the return on their securities exceeds the cost of their borrowed funds.

er of funds in the money market. Their most important means of short-term financing are trade credit and bank loans, but they do sell commercial paper to raise funds. On the supply side, it is important to remember that, since nonfinancial corporations seek to invest in real assets, they invest in short-term assets only to the extent necessary to carry on the operations of a business. They do hold marketable securities, however, to maintain liquidity and to accumulate temporary funds for subsequent investment in permanent assets. Also, the successful efforts in the last 15 years to manage cash efficiently and to minimize the amount held have resulted in the freeing of funds for short-run investment in return-earning liquid assets.

5. Financial corporations, such as finance companies, are heavy demanders of funds. They typically sell great quantities of commercial paper to finance their operations.

6. Foreign central banks and related financial entities have become increasingly important as suppliers of funds in the money market. Thus, to handle their accumulation of American dollars, foreigners have often chosen to invest in interest-bearing American securities.

Money Market Instruments

Treasury Bills. The dominant money market instrument is Treasury bills. The Treasury has great financing needs, which must be satisfied, and they are met mostly through the issuance of bills. (The average maturity for all government securities has decreased over the years, because short-term financing has increasingly been relied upon.) Also, monetary policy is carried out via open-market operations using Treasury securities. Thus these securities (and particularly bills) occupy a prominent place in the financial system.

Treasury bills are sold weekly by auction in denominations starting at $10,000 and for various maturities of up to 12 months. The Treasury decides the dollar amount of bills it will redeem at maturity, and potential purchasers, having seen these issues advertised, bid on them. That is, this is an auction process, conducted by the Fed on behalf of the Treasury, whereby purchasers bid for the quantities of particular denominations they want. Since Treasury bills are sold at a discount from face value, the prices that are bid determine the yields that will be earned on these securities. The higher the price the purchaser is willing to pay, the lower the return to the purchaser; that is, the Treasury receives more dollars and has to pay a lower cost for its financing. The Treasury accepts the highest bids first and works down to the point that depletes the amount of a particular issue being offered.

The principal purchaser of Treasury bills is the Fed, holding almost 30 percent of all bills at the end of 1978. For subsequent transactions, there is a very good secondary market. Government securities dealers maintain large inventories of the various issues and stand ready to buy and sell on short notice. Keen competition assures an efficient market, in which orders can be filled quickly and price changes are relatively small; therefore, Treasury bills are highly liquid. Treasury bills themselves are virtually without risk, of course, because the government is not going to default on them, and because their short-term nature rules out much risk anyway.

Federally Sponsored Agency Securities. Several governmental agencies issue their own nonguaranteed securities. They include the Federal Home Loan banks, the Federal Land banks, the Bank for Cooperatives, the Federal Intermediate Credit banks, the Federal Home Loan Mortgage Corporation, and the Federal National Mortgage Association.[4] The dollar amount of such issues has grown tremendously in the last few years. Several types of securities are issued, with a wide range of maturities. As the long-term instruments approach maturity, they become short-term instruments in effect—i.e., they become money market instruments. The result is that agency securities can be considered as part of the money market.

The federal government is not legally obligated in case of default on these securities. However, it is widely believed that Congress would not allow any of these agencies to default. Although some of the agencies have now been transformed into private ownership, the prevailing belief is that they are still virtually free of default risk.

Some of these agency securities can be used for collateral by commercial banks borrowing from the Fed. They can also be bought and sold by the Fed in the conduct of open-market operations. The total size of these issues (over $100 billion by the end of 1978) makes both of these actions feasible.

The purchasers of these securities are numerous and include banks, the Fed, savings and loan associations, households, and state and local governments. A good secondary market has developed for these securities. Purchasers can obtain higher yields on them than on Treasury securities with virtually no significant difference in default risk. However, their marketability is still not as good as it is for Treasury bills. Purchasers pay federal tax on gains from these securities but generally do not pay state and local taxes.

Federal Funds. Federal funds are simply deposits at Federal Reserve banks that are owned by commercial banks or, to some extent, by foreign banks. These deposits are, of course, liabilities of the Fed.

------

[4]This discussion abstracts from the Federal agencies themselves, which include the Government National Mortgage Association, the Federal Housing Administration, the Export-Import Book, etc.

Participants in the federal funds market include commercial banks and securities dealers and, to some extent, foreign banks. Most of the activity is accounted for by the banks, particularly by a small group of large banks. Securities dealers require a substantial amount of financing and therefore have developed a wide variety of sources. The large New York banks provide the bulk of dealer financing. An easy way to do this is to obtain bank loans in federal funds.

Most transactions in this market are between banks and are generally conducted to adjust reserve positions. One day-transactions predominate, but they can be extended for longer periods. Larger banks obtain unsecured loans in this manner, while smaller ones typically put up collateral for one day until the loan is repaid.

Federal funds transactions are quick and efficient. In a typical transaction, Bank X borrows from Bank Y for one day. Part of Y's deposit at a Federal Reserve bank is transferred to X's deposit at the Fed. One day later, the transaction is reversed, and, in addition, Bank Y gains an interest payment equal to 1/360 multiplied by the product of the amount borrowed and the going federal funds rate.[5] Both banks gain from this transaction: Y presumably has some excess reserves, on which it would like to earn a return; X presumably has a shortage of reserves, which it would like to correct as easily and cheaply as possible. It can be less costly to acquire reserves in this manner than it is, say, to sell Treasury bills. Beyond this, however, some very aggressive banks sometimes borrow federal funds as one more alternative source of finance. Whatever the reason, the vast majority of all transactions in this market are between banks.[6]

The federal funds market is centered in New York, but it is broad in scope. It is uniquely a secondary market, because deposits already exist for reasons other than lending as federal funds. Transactions can be executed quickly by phone, a characteristic that is associated with the money market in general. The mechanics of transactions are well established now, with many more participants than there were previously. Brokers exist to bring the two sides together.

The growth of the federal funds market is noteworthy. Virtually all of the large major city banks participate. Potential suppliers include any bank with excess reserves. Daily sales of federal funds in early 1979 for all large reporting banks amounted to over $25 billion.

The role of federal funds as an indicator of money market conditions deserves mention. The federal funds rate has been used as an indicator of money market conditions because of the rapidity with which it is adjusted

---

[5]A standard assumption in finance is that there are 360 days in a year.

[6]Government securities dealers also participate in this market to some extent. Dealers keep these balances to facilitate trades in government securities, which are made in federal funds.

in response to open-market operations.[7] When the Fed acts, the money market in New York reacts the quickest. The first adjustments to the action are often in the federal funds market. Thus, the federal funds rate can be used as a measure of the actions of money market banks to adjust their reserve positions. The federal funds rate is extremely volatile, fluctuating widely on any given day.

We should remember that the federal funds market does not really allocate funds from saving surplus units to ultimate borrowers, as do some other money markets. Rather, this market serves to permit banks to shift funds among themselves in order to accomplish necessary daily adjustments in their reserve positions.

Banker's Acceptances. A banker's acceptance is really a hybrid security: it is a debt instrument created by nonfinancial business firms and guaranteed by a bank. Although acceptances have existed for over 50 years and lately have consistently grown in volume, this market is still relatively small. 1978 figures indicate a volume on the order of $33 billion, with perhaps a 50-50 split between international trade and domestic use.

A business firm that needs short-term funds can obtain them (among other ways) in the form of a negotiable and marketable obligation. The firm can issue a *draft* on a bank, which, in effect, is a promise by the bank to honor the draft when it is presented sometime in the future by the holder. The firm must first ascertain that the bank will honor the draft. If the bank agrees, it marks *accepted* on the note (hence, the name banker's acceptance). Since it is then guaranteed by the bank, the draft is negotiable and marketable and can be traded as the situation warrants. Upon maturity, the holder of the acceptance can present it to the bank for payment. The business firm that issued the acceptance must provide the bank with funds (in its demand deposits) to cover the draft. Of course, the bank charges a fee to the firm for this service.[8]

Negotiable Certificates of Deposit. In the early 1960s, a completely new instrument and a new market were created with the birth of negotiable time certificates of deposit (CDs). This innovation demonstrates the great vitality and flexibility of our money markets in adjusting to new conditions. It is one more indication of the depth and strength of our financial markets and their ability to match demanders with suppliers of funds.

CDs were created in 1961 to allow banks to compete for short-term

---

[7]The Fed now issues open-market directions that include a target range for the federal funds rate.

[8]It is interesting to note that, theoretically, a bank could guarantee an unlimited amount of acceptances, since these transactions normally do not involve the use of bank funds. The bank is merely "lending" its name in return for a fee. It is obvious, however, that the bank does take a risk here. Since bank regulators worry about the riskiness of banks, there are limits to the amount of acceptance business that can be done.

funds.[9] As interest rates rose in the late 1950s and early 1960s, firms shifted funds out of demand deposits and into high-yielding money market instruments. To counter this loss of deposits, banks started issuing CDs to these firms. A CD is nothing more than a receipt for a deposit of funds in the bank, which, when presented at maturity, entitles the holder to receive the deposit plus interest. (In effect, a CD represents borrowing by a bank through the issuance of short-term notes.) The creation of this instrument coincided with a rise in the sophistication of firms' cash management practices, which led to the minimizing of noninterest-paying bank balances and the investing of these surplus funds in interest-earning money market securities. By issuing CDs, the banks hoped to retain their existing deposits, which they had rapidly been losing, and to acquire new funds. They achieved considerable success with this maneuver, as can be seen by the growth in CDs. In 1961, they amounted to approximately $3 billion; in 1964, $13 billion; in 1968, $24 billion; in 1970, $26 billion; in 1974, $93 billion; and in 1978, $100 billion.

Negotiable CDs are distinguished by the following characteristics: (1) they are typically short-term, with maturities less than one year; (2) they cannot be redeemed before maturity; (3) they are issued in bearer form—i.e., they are payable to the holder upon maturity—and they can be traded in secondary markets; (4) their denominations vary widely but the minimum is typically $100,000; (5) they are typically sold to corporations, government entities, and institutional investors (such as pension funds); (6) for the period 1976–79, their yields ranged from 2 to ¼ of a percentage point above the yields on Treasury bills with the same maturity.

We should note the distinction between CDs and other time deposits. All time and savings deposits pay interest and are technically (i.e., legally) subject to a waiting period before the bank has to honor a demand for withdrawal. Beyond this, there are differences. (1) Passbook savings deposits (i.e., savings accounts) have no maturity date and, in actual practice, can be drawn out (or added to) anytime. They carry low rates of interest and are typically held by individuals in relatively small amounts (before 1975, corporations were prohibited from having savings accounts). (2) Time certificates of deposit, which can be either negotiable or nonnegotiable, are a different form of time deposit. A receipt must be presented for redemption, and interest is paid from the day of issuance to maturity. Early withdrawal is normally not permitted; it is allowed only with a substantial penalty in the form of interest reduction. These certificates can be purchased by anyone at anytime. Denominations are fixed— e.g., $1,000, $5,000, etc.—and time to maturity varies. (3) A nonnegotiable certificate of deposit cannot be sold before maturity, whereas a negotiable CD can be sold by the original depositor anytime.

---

[9]See G. Walter Woodworth, *The Money Market and Monetary Management* (New York: Harper & Row, Inc.; 1972), pp. 138–141.

We should also note here that in 1978, for the first time, banks and thrift institutions were allowed to offer special "money market time deposits" where the rate of interest is tied to interest rates on Treasury bills. This move was designed to protect the housing industry from the disintermediation effects of rising interest rates. In previous high interest rate periods, such as 1974, depositors withdrew funds from thrift institutions, where interest rates were strictly controlled, and deposited them directly in the money and capital markets.

An important part of the success of CDs has been the development of a good secondary market.[10] If dealers stand ready to repurchase them, liquidity is assured. *Federal Reserve Bulletin* data through early 1979 indicate that rates on large CDs in the secondary market exceed those in the primary market anywhere from a few basis points to ½ of 1 percent. As money market conditions change, rates on the secondary CDs change in line with supply and demand forces. In particular, they are forced into alignment with yields on newly issued money market instruments. In the past, CD rates have been subject to the Federal Reserve's Regulation Q, which limits the interest payable on time deposits. This regulation has had severe effects on the CD market during periods when interest rates rose substantially. For example, in 1969–70, money market rates hit all-time modern highs, but the maximum rates payable on CDs were limited. The result was that CDs could not compete with other instruments, and money flowed out of them (as they matured) and into competing assets that paid higher returns. In effect, through Regulation Q, the government severely damaged the CD market in 1969 (and also in 1966, when the same circumstances occurred). The maximum rates on time deposits in denominations of $100,000 or more were suspended in mid-1973. The Fed has indicated a movement away from Regulation Q as an instrument of monetary policy.

Commercial Paper. Commercial paper is simply promissory notes issued by large firms with high credit standings. It gives firms a way to borrow short-term funds on the open market, and hence it provides an alternative to borrowing from a bank. It is unique to this country: no other financial system has anything similar on a comparable scale.

Commercial paper is unsecured and therefore can only be sold by firms with very high credit ratings. Maturities are from three days to nine months. It is sold on a discount basis in various denominations ranging up to $5,000,000.

Commercial paper can be sold directly or placed by dealers.[11] In the former case, there is a direct transaction between the issuer (borrower) and the purchaser (investor). Large finance companies often sell by this

---

[10]Woodworth, pp. 142–145.
[11]Woodworth, pp. 93–103.

method, because they are continually raising large sums of money. Since these companies finance consumer installment purchases, which can be quite volatile, commercial paper sales timed to meet their needs are attractive to them. Much of the total finance company receivables in this country is now effectively financed by commercial paper, as most large companies of this type now sell it directly.

Directly placed commercial paper can be redeemed at maturity by the bearer. The rate earned by the bearer depends upon the discount from face value and the length of time held. Maturities and denominations are variable, since this paper can be designed to suit the buyer. Rates must, of course, be in line with those on other money market instruments.

The dealer market for commercial paper consists of a few dealers, the firms issuing the paper, and the investors purchasing it. Dealer-placed paper is unsecured and, at maturity, is payable to the bearer at a specified bank. In 1979, about 75 percent of all commercial paper outstanding was issued by financial companies. Only about 20 percent of this financial company paper was dealer placed.

Commercial paper has grown rapidly since 1972 when it amounted to about $35 billion. At the beginning of 1979, the total outstanding was $80 billion.

Borrowers include only the largest and the financially strongest firms, because of the unsecured nature of the obligation. The default rate has been extremely low, a fraction of 1 percent. The most famous case of default involved the Penn Central Transportation Company, which defaulted on its commercial paper in 1970. A short-term crisis resulted in the commercial paper market—buyers refused to purchase—but it quickly subsided, and the market has continued to function well.[12] Commercial paper is rated by Standard & Poor's on a scale from A–1 to D, to assess default risk.

Financial corporations compose the largest single category of borrowers, with nonfinancial companies and commercial banks being the other major borrowers. The real advantage of commercial paper to borrowers is a cost below the prime rate on bank loans (in late 1978, 1 percent lower). However, this lower cost must be balanced against the damage that might be done to a firm's relation with its bank. Banks favor their best customers and probably take note of those who often sell commercial paper to avoid the slightly higher bank rate. For nonfinancial companies, bank loans are still much more important sources of funds than is commercial paper.

---

[12]To avert a crisis where lenders temporarily suspended new purchases of commercial paper after the Penn Central default, the Fed acted to make funds readily available to banks for loans to business firms. Firms that typically sold commercial paper did in fact make heavier use of bank loans.

Nonfinancial corporations are the major purchaser of commercial paper; thus they are a substantial seller and the largest buyers. This simply reflects the fact that, while some firms need funds, some firms have surplus funds to invest. At the beginning of 1979, this sector held about $30 billion of commercial paper. The benefits of commercial paper to investors include safety (because of the high financial quality of the issuers) and a return that typically exceeds the yield on Treasury bills.

There is no secondary market for commercial paper. At best, dealers will help the holder to find a buyer. A member bank, however, may rediscount it at its Federal Reserve bank.

Eurodollars. The term *Eurodollars* refers to dollar-denominated deposits in foreign commercial banks (or in foreign branches of U.S. banks). The Eurodollar market, like the CD market, is a good example of the financial community's response to a changing environment. This market is now about 20 years old and has grown rapidly over the last several years. Although the concept of Eurodollars is complex and often poorly understood, this market is a very important entity, which must be reckoned with because of its effects on the international financial system and on our own.

Eurodollar deposits arise from various sources, ranging from deposits in U.S. banks transferred by individuals or firms into foreign banks[13] to the official dollar deposits included in the holdings of foreign central banks. Actually, anyone with a demand deposit in a U.S. bank can create Eurodollars simply by transferring it to a European bank; upon completion of the transaction, the depositor holds a dollar-denominated claim (paying interest) on a foreign bank, which in turn can lend dollars against this deposit with an American bank. Reasons for the creation of these Eurodollar deposits are numerous; they include ease of transacting abroad and favorable interest-rate differences.[14]

Eurodollar funds involve both deposits and loans. Since a Eurobank must pay interest on the deposits accepted, it invests these funds (subject to reserve requirements). This process can become quite complex. For example, a Eurobank could lend to someone who redeposits in the bank, which would allow further loans. Alternatively, the Eurodollars could be lent to U.S. residents. Since there are various sources of these funds, the possible combinations of events are very complex. However, from our standpoint of studying the money market, we need only think of Eurodollars as a source of short-term funds and/or as a use of short-term funds. As

---

[13]Foreign banks (or foreign branches of U.S. banks) that are willing to accept deposits denominated in dollars are referred to as *Eurobanks*, although the prefix *Euro-* is misleading, because not all banks engaging in this type of transaction are located in Europe.

[14]This discussion is indebted to Geoffrey Wood and Douglas Mudd, "Do Foreigners Control the U.S. Money Supply?", *Review—Federal Reserve Bank of St. Louis*, vol. 59, December 1977, pp. 8–11.

such, they are just another money market instrument, and the Eurodollar market works exactly like a domestic money market.

The Eurodollar market is really a wholesale market, in which the general unit of account is typically large, but there are wide variances to accommodate different types of participants. Maturities vary subject to negotiations. Although London is considered to be the center of activity, the market is truly international in scope, with trading in all major financial cities.

Interest rates for Eurodollars are determined in the marketplace and therefore ultimately reflect demand and supply conditions. There is one set of rates for Eurodollar depositors and another set for borrowers. To attract depositors, Eurobanks generally must offer rates in excess of those available in domestic money markets. These rates must also exceed the yields on alternative short-term financial instruments. For example, the Eurodollar rate has exceeded the CD rate in the United States by amounts ranging from ¼ to about 1 percentage point from 1976 to early 1979 (for 3-month maturities). Rates usually rise with maturity, but the complete term structure can decline—i.e., the yield curve (as explained in chapter 9) can slope downward.

The Eurodollar loan rate is similarly affected by alternatives such as the rate for comparable bank loans in the United States. One advantage of Eurodollars, however, is that they may be available when other sources dry up (such as during a credit squeeze in the United States). During the 1969–70 credit crunch, U.S. banks borrowed Eurodollars (although they paid premium rates to obtain them) because funds in this country were tight. There has been a wide array of borrowers in the Eurodollar markets —commercial banks, business firms, even foreign governments. U.S. borrowers may pay less than they do in this country because of the wholesale nature of Eurodollars, the lesser restrictions, etc. Banks and corporations are important suppliers of Eurodollars.

The Eurodollar market remains a complex but interesting alternative to domestic money markets. U.S. participation will continue to vary with such factors as bank demand for funds to lend and interest rates available on Eurodollars. From the perspective of the United States, it is difficult to predict growth for this market. The Fed has introduced more stringent requirements for Eurodollar borrowings in the last few years. Reserve requirements on Eurodollar borrowings have ranged widely: at one time (1971), the reserve ratio was 20 percent. Tax laws on foreign operations have been tightened. Finally, participation in this complex market requires considerable expertise. For all of these reasons, Eurodollar borrowing has become less attractive to U.S. banks.

Money Market Facts and Figures

Amounts Outstanding. Now that we have discussed the general nature of the money market and the various instruments traded within it, it is appropriate to consider the size and character of this important segment of our financial system. Our objective is to obtain a basic idea of the parameters involved—amounts, rates, and trends—so that the money market can be placed in perspective with other segments of the financial system.

The size and the complexity of the money market transactions make it difficult to obtain strictly comparable figures for all such transactions for a particular point in time. For example, federal funds transactions are very volatile and change hourly. Also, with the complexity of the Eurodollar market, it is impossible to assess its size on a precise basis. Because of these problems, we will provide only a basic sketch of the money market, which is really all that we need.

Tables 11–1 through 11–4 show recent figures for five of the money market instruments previously discussed. The first of these tables includes Treasury bills, one of three components of marketable government debt.[15] In December 1978, bills amounted to $161 billion, or almost 40 percent of marketable government debt and 25 percent of total public debt in the United States. As we noted previously, Treasury bills are the dominant money market instruments. They will continue to occupy the prominent position in our financial system.

Federally sponsored agency securities, depending on their maturity, are either capital market instruments or money market instruments. Those with long maturities become money market instruments as they approach maturity. (Since separate figures according to maturities are not readily available, Table 11–2 shows the total amounts outstanding. These same figures will apply when we talk about these securities as capital market instruments.) The volume of these securities has been increasing as new agencies are created and as the demand for their services increases. The Federal National Mortgage Association alone accounts for almost 40 percent of the total issues outstanding.

The figures reported in Table 11–3 for CDs reflect only large (issued in denominations of $100,000 or more) negotiable time CDs included in time and savings deposits. For large banks in September, 1978, the amount involved was around $91 billion, with New York City banks accounting for about one-third of this volume. Of course, the total figure for all banks and all denominations is larger than what is reported here. The amount of these large negotiable time CDs varies substantially over time. Before the suspension of Regulation Q as it applied to CDs, the amount outstanding was very volatile. As was previously noted, the CD market was severely damaged in the credit squeeze of 1969, when CDs could not compete for funds because of rate restrictions imposed by Regulation Q. Even since the

---

[15]Total gross public debt in the United States ($789 billion in January 1979) consists of marketable debt ($487 billion) and nonmarketable debt ($295 billion), such as savings bonds.

TABLE 11–1. Gross Public Debt, 1974–1978 (in billions of dollars)

	1974	1975	1976	1977	1978				
					May	June	July	Aug.	Sept.
1 Total gross public debt	492.7	576.6	653.5	718.9	741.6	749.0	750.5	764.4	771.5
By type:									
2 Interest-bearing debt	491.6	575.7	652.5	715.2	740.6	748.0	749.5	763.4	767.0
3 *Marketable*	282.9	363.2	421.3	459.9	473.7	477.7	481.0	485.6	485.2
4 Bills	119.7	157.5	164.0	161.1	159.4	159.8	160.1	160.6	160.9
5 Notes	129.8	167.1	216.7	251.8	261.6	265.3	266.6	268.5	267.9
6 Bonds	33.4	38.6	40.6	47.0	52.7	52.6	54.4	56.4	56.4
7 *Nonmarketable*	208.7	212.5	231.2	255.3	266.9	270.3	268.4	227.8	281.8
8 Convertible bonds	2.3	2.3	2.3	2.2	2.2	2.2	2.2	2.2	2.2
9 State and local government series	.6	1.2	4.5	13.9	18.6	20.6	20.8	24.2	24.2
10 Foreign issues	22.8	21.6	22.3	22.2	22.4	21.5	20.8	22.2	21.7
11 Savings bonds and notes	63.8	67.9	72.3	77.0	79.0	79.4	79.7	79.9	80.2
12 Government account series	119.1	119.4	129.7	139.8	144.4	146.4	144.7	149.0	153.3
13 Non-interest-bearing debt	1.1	1.0	1.1	3.7	1.0	1.0	1.0	1.0	4.6

Source: *Federal Reserve Bulletin*, Vol. 64, October 1978, p. A32.

TABLE 11-2. Federally Sponsored Agency Securities, Debt Outstanding, 1975–1978 (in millions of dollars)

	1975	1976	1977	Feb.	March	Apr. 1978	May	June	July
Federally sponsored agencies	78,634	81,429	87,164	89,661	90,676	92,137	95,864	97,256	99,352
Federal home loan banks	18,900	16,811	18,345	19,893	20,007	20,163	22,217	22,306	23,430
Federal Home Loan Mortgage Corporation	1,550	1,690	1,686	1,768	1,768	1,639	1,637	1,937	1,937
Federal National Mortgage Association	29,963	30,565	31,890	32,553	33,350	34,024	35,297	36,404	36,900
Federal land banks	15,000	17,127	19,118	19,350	19,350	19,686	19,686	19,686	20,198
Federal intermediate credit banks	9,254	10,494	11,174	10,958	10,881	10,977	11,081	11,257	11,392
Banks for cooperatives	3,655	4,330	4,434	4,622	4,728	5,046	5,264	4,974	4,788
Student Loan Marketing Association	310	410	515	515	590	600	680	690	705
Other	2	2	2	2	2	2	2	2	2

Source: *Federal Reserve Bulletin*, Vol. 64, October 1978, p. A35.

TABLE 11–3. Large Negotiable Time Certificates of Deposit (in millions of dollars)

	1978
Total:	Sept.
Large banks	**90,977**
New York City	24,595
Banks outside New York City	66,382
Issued to IPC's:	
Large banks	*64,380*
New York City Banks	17,721
Banks outside New York City	46,659
Issued to others:	
Large banks	*26,597*
New York City banks	6,874
Banks outside New York City	19,723

Source: *Federal Reserve Bulletin,* Vol. 64, October 1978, p. A23.

Note: The figures reflect only negotiable time CDs issued in denominations of $100,000 or more and included in time and savings deposits.

freeing of the rate that banks can pay (in mid-1973), the amount of CDs outstanding has varied significantly. In January 1975, for example, large banks reported $92 billion in large negotiable time CDs; in January 1976, they reported $80 billion.

Table 11–4 shows that commercial paper of all issuers amounted to about $74 billion in August 1978. It seems that growth may be somewhat limited in the future, because only firms that are rated the highest financially can issue this unsecured debt, and their numbers are limited. Also, there is no secondary market for dealer-placed paper.

Banker's acceptances (also given in Table 11–4) remain a small item in relation to other money market instruments. In August 1978, the total outstanding amounted to only about $28 billion. However, there did seem to be renewed interest in acceptances in the mid-1970s, and the amount outstanding could grow in the future.

Information on the size of federal funds and Eurodollars will be given more informally than that available in the tables. These instruments do not generally involve as many different market participants as do Treasury bills, CDs, or commercial paper. For large weekly-reporting commercial banks, federal funds sold on September 27, 1978, amounted to about $23 billion. Of this total, about $18 billion was sold to commercial banks. This agrees with the earlier observation that this market primarily serves to permit banks to shift funds among themselves so as to make daily adjustments in their reserve positions.

Eurodollar figures are difficult to obtain. Our best information is that Eurodollar balances in 1979 were approximately $600–700 billion, an amount significantly larger than all foreign deposits with American banks. Figures on the size of this market are often confusing, because both net and gross figures are reported, and because there is some double-counting.

Rates. Money market rates are determined in open markets by the forces of supply and demand. Rates on the various short-term instruments generally move together, because they are affected by many of the same basic phenomena (for example, by a basic easing in the demand for funds). However, the movements are by no means always close, and, for some instruments, they can be very dissimilar. For example, federal funds rates often fluctuate independently of the others.

Money market rates do not contain large default premiums (explained in chapter 9), because these instruments are issued by high-quality borrowers with strong financial positions. Since they are, by definition, short-maturity instruments, the pattern of rates does not reflect increasing returns to compensate for an uncertain future. Of course, these rates may reflect a large premium for inflation, because lenders wish to be compensated for its perceived effects.

Table 11–5 contains some money market rates for selected periods of time for most of the instruments previously discussed. In studying such a table, one should carefully note at least three factors: (1) the size of the absolute returns, which provide a reference point for interest rates in general; (2) the relative returns, i.e., the relationships between the various instruments at any point in time; and (3) the trend of rates over time— money market rates change often, and sometimes drastically. Although the data in the table cover a period of only 3¾ years, the rates fluctuated widely during that time.

Treasury bills, the dominant money market instrument, carry no practical risk of default. As such, they reflect the time value of money and are often used as a proxy for the pure rate of interest; that is, because Treasury bills have short maturities, are highly liquid, and have no practical risk, their rate best reflects the basic cost of borrowing. Since they are auctioned weekly, their rates quickly reflect changing conditions in the marketplace. Table 11–5 shows that the average rate on 3-month bills fluctuated from a low of 4.98 percent in 1976 to a high of 8.02 percent in September 1978.

The federal funds rate is very sensitive to monetary policy and quickly reflects changes in the money markets. It is clearly influenced by short-term effects from the management of bank reserve positions. Because most federal funds transactions are for one-day periods, the amount of funds in existence changes very rapidly as banks continuously assess their reserve positions and requirements. The federal funds rate fluctuates widely but in most cases seems to parallel the rate on 3-month Treasury bills quite closely, as the table shows.

TABLE 11–4. Commercial Paper and Banker's Acceptances Outstanding, 1975–1978 (in millions of dollars)°

Instrument	1975 Dec.	1976 Dec.	1977 Dec.	Feb.	Mar.	Apr.	1978 May	June	July	Aug.
	Commercial paper (seasonally adjusted)									
1 All issuers	48,459	53,025	65,209	65,578	67,476	70,289	71,213	74,536	74,900	73,960
Financial companies:[1]										
Dealer-placed paper:[2]										
2 Total	6,202	7,250	8,871	8,918	8,889	9,670	10,314	10,327	10,617	10,868
3 Bank-related	1,762	1,900	2,132	1,997	1,993	2,078	2,217	2,442	2,633	2,935
Directly-placed paper:[3]										
4 Total	31,374	32,500	40,496	42,238	42,903	44,326	44,664	47,315	46,594	45,519
5 Bank-related	6,892	5,959	7,102	7,718	8,153	7,995	9,258	9,585	10,030	9,634
6 Nonfinancial companies[4]	10,883	13,275	15,842	14,422	15,684	16,293	16,235	16,894	17,689	17,582

Dollar acceptances (not seasonally adjusted)

7 Total	18,727	22,523	25,654	25,411	26,181	26,256	26,714	28,289	27,579	28,319
Held by:										
8 Accepting banks	7,333	10,442	10,434	7,513	7,375	7,091	7,286	7,502	7,244	7,048
9 Own bills	5,899	8,769	8,915	6,583	6,375	6,117	6,365	6,520	6,345	6,131
10 Bills bought	1,435	1,675	1,519	931	1,000	974	921	983	899	917
F.R. Banks:										
11 Own account	1,126	991	954	....	1	....	....	1	....	....
12 Foreign correspondents	293	375	362	456	522	550	679	625	568	633
13 Others	9,975	10,715	13,904	17,442	18,283	18,614	18,749	20,160	19,766	20,638
Based on:										
14 Imports into United States	3,726	4,992	6,532	6,842	6,979	7,108	7,027	7,578	7,415	7,885
15 Exports from United States	4,001	4,818	5,895	5,739	6,034	6,216	6,494	6,906	6,565	6,558
16 All other	11,000	12,713	13,227	13,026	13,168	12,932	13,193	13,805	13,599	13,876

Source: *Federal Reserve Bulletin*, Vol. 64, October 1978, p. A25.

[1] Institutions engaged primarily in activities such as, but not limited to, commercial, savings, and mortgage banking: sales, personal, and mortgage financing; factoring, finance leasing, and other business lending; insurance underwriting; and other investment activities.

[2] Includes all financial company paper sold by dealers in the open market.

[3] As reported by financial companies that place their paper directly with investors.

[4] Includes public utilities and firms engaged primarily in activities such as communications, construction, manufacturing, mining, wholesale and retail trade, transportation, and services.

TABLE 11–5. Selected Money Market Rates, 1975–1978 (averages, per cent per annum)

| Instrument | 1975 | 1976 | 1977 | 1978 | | | | 1978, week ending — | | | | |
				June	July	Aug.	Sept.	Sept. 2	Sept. 9	Sept.16	Sept.23	Sept.30
							Money market rates					
1 Federal funds	5.82	5.05	5.54	7.60	7.81	8.04	8.45	8.28	8.30	8.33	8.36	8.62
Prime commercial paper												
2 90- to 119-day	6.26	5.24	5.54	7.59	7.85	7.83	8.39	7.97	8.18	8.39	8.48	8.56
3 4- to 6-month	6.33	5.35	5.60	7.63	7.91	7.90	8.44	8.03	8.24	8.43	8.51	8.60
4 Finance company paper, directly placed, 3- to 6-month	6.16	5.22	5.49	7.41	7.66	7.65	8.18	7.74	7.98	8.14	8.27	8.37
5 Prime bankers acceptances, 90-day	6.30	5.19	5.59	7.75	8.02	7.98	8.54	8.19	8.31	8.44	8.62	8.82
Large negotiable certificates of deposit												
6 3-month, secondary market	6.43	5.26	5.58	7.82	9.00	8.05	8.61	8.19	8.35	8.44	8.63	8.83
7 3-month, primary market	.....	5.15	5.52	7.68	8.00	7.86	8.42	7.90	8.14	8.38	8.50	8.65
8 Euro-dollar deposits, 3-month	6.97	5.57	6.05	8.33	8.52	8.48	9.12	8.61	8.88	8.85	9.09	9.41
U.S. Government securities												
Bills:												
Market yields:												
9 3-month	5.80	4.98	5.27	6.73	7.01	7.08	7.85	7.50	7.60	7.77	8.02	7.96
10 6-month	6.11	5.26	5.53	7.23	7.44	7.37	7.99	7.65	7.69	7.87	8.10	8.28
11 1-year	6.30	5.52	5.71	7.53	7.79	7.73	8.01	7.86	7.86	7.95	8.08	8.16
Rates on new issue												
12 3-month	5.838	4.989	5.265	6.707	7.074	7.036	7.836	7.323	7.659	7.695	7.884	8.106
13 6-month	6.122	5.266	5.510	7.200	7.471	7.363	7.948	7.550	7.742	7.793	7.979	8.276

Source: *Federal Reserve Bulletin* Vol. 64, October 1978, p. A27.

Commercial paper, unlike Treasury bills, carries some risk of default. Penn Central proved that in 1970, when it defaulted on its commercial paper and went into bankruptcy (which significantly hurt the commercial paper market for a short time). Rates on these instruments are therefore higher than rates on Treasury bills, which is understandable, but they are not always as high as those on CDs, which is not as readily understandable. It is difficult to understand why bank paper is not as sound as corporate paper and must yield higher returns. Rates on commercial paper and on CDs, like the other money market rates, have fluctuated widely to reflect market conditions.

According to the averages in the table, prime banker's acceptances typically, but not always, yield more than commercial paper of comparable maturities. Conversely, they usually yield less than secondary-market CDs.

The three-month Eurodollar deposit rate is also shown in the table. As was noted in the previous discussion, it is higher than the rates for other money market instruments, which contributes to the appeal of Eurodollars to lenders.

Table 11–5 does not contain rates for federally sponsored agency securities. In the past, these yields have averaged only slightly higher than comparable yields on Treasury bills. Since these securities are not explicitly guaranteed by the Treasury, this difference may reflect a premium for risk. Common sense indicates, however, that the real risk of these securities is very small, because it is unreasonable to believe that the federal government would allow them to actually go into default. Another possible explanation for the differential is that these issues are not as well known, and the market for them is not as well established as is the market for Treasury bills. Also, smaller amounts are issued than in the case of Treasury bills.

THE CAPITAL MARKETS

Capital markets, by accepted definition, are markets in which long-term funds are exchanged for long-term claims. Like the money markets, the capital markets include lenders (investors) with excess funds on which they wish to earn a return and borrowers (issuers) who wish to borrow funds for the long term. It is important to remember that, although these markets involve financial claims, the underlying basis for it all is real assets; that is, the returns on real assets generate the demand for funds, which is satisfied in the capital markets and to some extent in the money market.

The capital markets perform a valuable function. All permanent assets and some current assets of business firms, which form the basis for the firms' production, need to be financed by permanent capital, both debt and equity. Firms cannot operate effectively unless they are assured of permanent financing for most of their operations. Our financial system would obviously be very unstable if the business sector continually had to worry about refinancing as short-term debts came to maturity. Investment in real assets is a commitment of funds to assets that are often quite illiquid and that require long periods of time to generate a cash flow equal to the original investment. These assets must be financed primarily through capital market instruments.

At the same time that members of the business sector wish to secure funds for long periods of time, there are a number of investors who wish to purchase, sell, or trade long-term securities. They do this in attempts to maximize their utility, which in effect simply means that they try to maximize returns while they minimize risks. A portfolio of financial assets gives utility through some combination of return and risk, which presumably is optimal to the investor. To continue maximizing their utility as conditions change, holders of long-term financial claims must change their portfolios. Such changes take place within the capital markets.

Organization

Capital markets, exactly like the money market, include primary markets for new issues and secondary markets for existing claims. In the primary markets, borrowers and lenders come to terms for funds, which are invested in real assets and facilitate our economic growth. Here is where the transfer of savings takes place from savers to users. Good primary markets are necessary for our society to grow and to prosper. Existing assets must be replaced as they are exhausted, and new ones must be financed if we are to meet new needs, employ additional resources, and provide employment to a growing number of workers. We must keep in mind the basic facts we learned in chapter 1, namely, that the business sector has financing needs in excess of its savings every year and that it must be financed if we are to create wealth. As was previously noted, primary markets involve investment bankers, among other entities, to facilitate the raising of new funds. They work with borrowers to design attractive claims to be sold in the marketplace, and they then carry through by organizing a distribution network to get the claims into the hands of buyers (investors).

Secondary markets are concerned with the resale of existing claims. They are indispensable to primary markets, since investors would be discouraged from originally purchasing long-term claims if there were not an efficient means for disposing of them when the occasion arose. Thus secondary markets provide liquidity for long-term claims. They receive the bulk of attention in discussions of capital markets, because most of the activity in capital markets involves the trading of existing claims. A given security is issued only once in a primary market—it can be traded endlessly in a secondary market.

The organization of capital markets involves the full range of entities engaged in primary and secondary markets for long-term financial claims. This discussion will focus on federal government debt, federal agency securities, municipal securities, mortgages, bonds, and stocks. Participants transacting these claims include (in the primary markets) governments, underwriters, the Federal Reserve System, securities dealers, banks, and mortgage companies; and (in the secondary markets) the New York Stock Exchange, the American Stock Exchange, the regional exchanges and the over-the-counter market, government agencies, and securities dealers.

Demanders and Suppliers in the Capital Markets

Those who participate in the capital markets can be suppliers or demanders of funds or both. The major participants and the positions they usually assume are listed below. After completing our list of participants, we can look at the specific instruments that are prominent in the capital markets.

1. Financial intermediaries are the main purchasers of capital market assets. Such entities as pension funds grow larger year by year, so that additional funds become available to invest over the long term. Intermediaries now own significant percentages of all capital market assets.

2. Individuals are primarily purchasers—as opposed to issuers—of capital market assets. They save more than they wish to invest in real assets, and they wish to maximize their utility by means of portfolios of financial assets. Thus they purchase stocks, bonds, and government securities of all types. However, they do issue mortgages.

3. Business firms issue the stocks and nongovernmental bonds that exist in the capital markets. They are net borrowers, and the amounts they raise are large.

4. Government's role in the capital markets is basically that of a borrower. Both the federal government and state and local governments raise large amounts through the sale of debt issues in the capital markets, as was discussed in chapter 7. Whereas they may invest short-term idle funds in the money market, they do not contribute to the demand for claims in the capital markets.

Capital Market Instruments

Federal Government Securities. Long-term marketable federal government debt (notes and bonds) amounts to about $325 billion; this is less than half of total public debt, and in relation to other capital market instruments, this figure is not large. Regardless of size, these instruments are relevant to an analysis of the capital markets, because government debt represents the ultimate in liquidity among long-term financial claims. Also, the government continues to raise large amounts of capital.

As we have seen, the Fed acts as fiscal agent for the government and handles the issuance of new securities. Most debt issuance is for the replacement of existing debt—refunding—because the government typically does not reduce the size of the national debt. If additional funds are needed to finance new deficits, the government simply issues more securities, above and beyond those needed in refunding. The Treasury usually coordinates its debt issues with Federal Reserve open-market operations. The Fed generally maintains an "even keel" policy when Treasury financing occurs, but there have been occasions when the Fed did not support a Treasury issue.

There exists a broad and deep market in government securities. It consists of dealers who are linked together in a very efficient network that facilitates quick, easy trading. These dealers, who trade with the open-market desk of the Federal Reserve Bank of New York, are a select group that stand ready to efficiently carry out trading activities. Like all dealers in markets such as these, they buy and sell for their own accounts. Their large inventories of securities must be financed, so that they can maintain liquid positions for both buying and selling. Dealers can and do act to maintain an orderly market—they buy as others sell and sell as others buy—with the result that prices adjust to reflect market conditions without the shock of abrupt fluctuations, which would result if dealers were not well financed.

Both the primary and the secondary markets for government securities are important, and dealers operate in both. They help to bring out a new issue by buying it from the Fed and reselling it. They generally also maintain large inventories in the secondary market, so that buyers can usually find an issue exactly suited to their needs. Inventories do fluctuate, however: they decrease in reponse to higher interest rates, which create greater risk (since prices decline) and add to the cost of financing an inventory.

Federally Sponsored Agency Securities. The last few years have seen a great increase in the issuance of federal government agency securities, which were described in the earlier part of this chapter. It is important to remember that these securities are considered quite safe, because the Treasury is not likely to stand idly by in case of default. Also, remember that some of these agencies are now privately owned, even though they were created by the government. One advantage of setting up these agencies is to take pressure off the Treasury in financing. A disadvantage, according to some observers, is that the government loses control over these agencies.

The primary market here consists of securities dealers or underwriters. Buyers include a variety of groups—banks, foreigners, municipal governments, individuals, savings institutions, and the Fed (since these securities can now be used in open-market operations). Of the seven issuers of these securities identified in the *Federal Reserve Bulletin,* at least four have enough issues outstanding to make reasonable secondary markets.

Mortgages. Many people do not realize that mortgages are the largest category of long-term fixed dollar instruments. Mortgages represent financial claims on real assets (i.e., on property) and property or real estate constitutes real wealth. Total mortgages amounted to about $1170 billion at the start of 1979. Mortgages are therefore important in helping to finance the acquisition of the very substantial part of our society's wealth that is in the form of real estate.

Mortgages arise, of course, as buyers of real estate seek to finance the balance of their purchases beyond the down payment. Mortgages are amortized today (but were not many years ago), so that the borrower periodically repays a part of the principal and interest. In the early years of a contract, most of the payment goes for interest, while, in the latter years, the bulk of it goes to repayment of the principal.

It is difficult to discuss the mortgage market without a lot of terms and details. Only the basics are presented here.

Roughly one-third of all mortgage money now comes from savings and loan associations; mutual savings banks, life insurance companies, and commercial banks supply most of the remainder. There also exist mortgage companies, which originate mortgages and sell them to such investors as financial institutions. All of these institutions deal in varying degrees with both conventional mortgages (issued through a private lender) and insured (FHA) or guaranteed (VA) mortgages. The former are most prominently associated with savings and loan associations, which, as we shall see in chapter 14, are local institutions dealing primarily in mortgages. The latter are backed by the government and carry restrictions on interest rates and the maximum amount that can be loaned. Conventional loans usually yield more than insured or guaranteed loans because of the greater risk involved. Traditionally, savings and loan associations constituted the secondary market for conventional mortgages. Those with excess funds in one area would in effect purchase mortgages from others in areas where the demand for funds exceeded the supply. Currently, however, several agencies create a secondary market for mortgages of both types:

1. The Federal National Mortgage Association (FNMA or Fannie Mae) originated as a government agency to buy mortgages from the mortgage lenders and to help develop a secondary market. It is now a privately owned, profit-seeking company primarily accountable to its stockholders. FNMA obtains mortgages from financial institutions (and thereby provides them with money to invest in other mortgages) and finances these purchases with the

sale of its own bonds in the marketplace. In periods of looser credit, it sells mortgages to institutions.

2. The Government National Mortgage Association (GNMA or Ginnie Mae) took over some of FNMA's activities after it became a private firm, so that the government would still have a role here. GNMA purchases mortgages from financial institutions and either holds them or resells them to FNMA. It also acts as a guarantor of some debt securities sold by financial institutions.

3. The Federal Home Loan Mortgage Company (FHLMC or Freddie Mac) was established in 1970 to buy mortgages from institutions such as savings and loan associations with funds raised in the open market.

4. The MGIC Mortgage Corporation (MGIC or Maggie Mac) was established in 1972 as a private company that sells securities on the open market and handles mortgages on a secondary market basis.

As a result of these agencies, the secondary market for mortgages has developed to its highest level thus far in U.S. financial history. The mortgage market is still not free from shocks, however. It is vulnerable to the drying up of new funds, which occurs periodically and causes a depression of residential construction. For example, the credit crunch of 1969–70 resulted in a drop in the financing of housing, as the corporate bond rate exceeded the yield on mortgages in the secondary market. This is an unusual occurrence; the yield on mortgages generally exceeds the yield on high-grade corporate bonds.

Municipal Securities. Municipal securities are issued by all levels of state and local government and by some special authorities created for particular purposes (such as construction of a bridge or a road). The total number of issues involved here is immense because of the large number of independent government units that exist. Borrowing demand is basically a function of population factors and demands for services. Funds are typically used for capital expenditures.

Municipals have traditionally been full faith and credit securities, so called because they are backed by the taxing power of the government that issued them. However, it has become quite common for governments to issue revenue bonds, which are serviced by revenues from the particular projects they finance (bridges, roads, etc.). Lacking funding from general tax revenue, they are more risky than full faith and credit bonds. Several well-known defaults illustrate the riskiness that characterizes revenue bonds.

The distinguishing characteristic of municipal securities is that the interest paid on them is exempt from federal income tax. Typically, a state does not tax the income on its own issues, although other states do. Because of this tax exclusion factor, municipal securities are somewhat different from other debt issues. For example, their nominal before-tax yields appear low in relation to alternative securities, but what is relevant is the yield after tax. This is a function of the purchaser's marginal tax bracket; those in higher brackets favor municipals, other things being equal.

The primary market for municipal securities involves a competitive bidding process, which supposedly is accountable to the public. Syndicates—i.e., buying groups of investment bankers—are formed to bid for each new issue of bonds. The size of the issue influences the size of the group formed. The syndicate that offers the highest bid to the issuing government receives the bonds and will in turn sell them to the public. The spread between the bid price and the sale price to the public represents the markup, or gross profit, for the selling group.

Most municipals are serial bonds, which mature periodically until final maturity, and this complicates the marketing process, because different buyers want different maturities.[16] This is one reason that it takes longer to sell municipals (often days or weeks) than it does to sell corporate bonds. Considerable advertising has to be done by dealers. Also, the municipal bond market is fragmented so that many small transactions take place in the municipal market. Given the different nature of this segment of the capital markets, it is interesting to note that many consider the issuance process to be efficient, in that margins for underwriters are small.

The secondary market for municipals consists mostly of underwriters, serving as dealers, but there are also some brokers. As with any dealer market, the buy-sell process is one of negotiation. Data are somewhat imprecise about the secondary market, but it is believed that sellers obtain fair prices in relation to new-issue prices. However, the secondary market is not very deep. There are many issues of small amounts, and usually there are only a few dealers for each issue. One should expect yields to be quite volatile in a market such as this, and, in fact, they are.

Corporate Bonds. Corporate bonds are fixed-principal securities (typically $1,000), which have definite maturity dates, and which carry specified coupon interest payments. Business firms borrow money by selling bonds. They use the proceeds for capital expansion and other purposes. Long-term debt borrowings are the most important external source of permanent funds to business firms; historically, they dwarf new common stock sales. This is because of their cheaper cost, resulting from their priority in terms of payment by the firm, and because the interest on bonds is tax deductible (dividends on common stock are not).

Corporate bonds are issued in primary markets either by open-mar-

---

[16]See Roland Robinson and Dwayne Wrightsman, *Financial Markets: The Accumulation and Allocation of Wealth* (New York: McGraw-Hill Book Company, 1974), pp. 268–270.

ket sale via investment bankers or by private placement. A public offering involves working with an investment banker to design an issue that presents an attractive combination of maturity, interest rate, price, and special features to be attached to the bonds. The investment banker handling the transaction usually forms a syndicate of other investment bankers to help market the issue. There are different arrangements that can be made in a situation such as this, but underwriting is common: it involves the purchase and subsequent resale of the bonds by the syndicate. In this procedure, the syndicate assumes the risk of unsuccessful marketing of the issue to the public in return for a chance to earn a price spread. If the offering goes well, the retail end of the syndicate operation can successfully sell the bonds to investors quite quickly (a good issue is often sold out in 60 minutes).

In a private placement, the issuer (seller-borrower) deals directly with the buyer of the bonds. The issue is designed to meet the needs of the two parties. Lenders can bargain for the particular features they most desire, and borrowers are able to bypass the open market and the investment banking process, with all the delay and red tape that involves. However, investment bankers are sometimes used to advise corporations in working out a private placement. The available evidence indicates that the total cost of a private placement is higher than that of a public offering. The reason that private placements are used is that they provide a way for small and often risky companies to sell bonds, which they could not readily do in the open market. Also, the seller avoids registration with the Securities and Exchange Commission and disclosure of considerable data, as is required by law in a public offering. Life insurance companies are often involved as buyers in private placements.

A strong secondary market for corporate bonds does not exist, because it is not needed. Many bonds are privately or directly placed, and they are bought primarily by institutional investors with little need for liquidity, who therefore can hold the issue to maturity. These institutions—for example, pension funds and life insurance companies—invest for the long run, because their future liabilities can be estimated, and because they must seek safety of principal.

A small amount of bond trading is done on the New York Stock Exchange. Much more is done in the over-the-counter market.

Common Stock. New issues of common stock are handled by a rights offering, by investment bankers, or by a combination of the two. A *rights offering* is a process that allows the current stockholders to subscribe to a new issue of stock in proportion to their current holdings; this allows them to maintain their proportionate ownership of the firm. Investment bankers often handle the sale of stock for firms, since they are experts in the legal process needed to bring an issue to market, and since they are able to organize a distribution network. They generally form syndicates to handle particular issues, since this reduces the risk of adverse selling results for any one investment banker.

Most investors simply buy and sell existing claims, so that, for them, dealing in common stocks involves the secondary markets. These allow individuals and institutions to buy and sell all individual common stock issues that are publicly traded, in attempts to maximize their utility from their portfolios. In essence, investors try to maximize their returns from stocks and other financial assets while they minimize their risk. Equity ownership involves substantial risk, because there is no guarantee of return: dividends may or may not be paid, and losses can result from sales of stock.

The stock market is a well-developed component of the capital marketplace in the United States. Firms must have equity financing to exist. Since the bulk of our productive assets are privately owned, a business must be able to raise equity capital in order to support borrowings, and the total pool of these funds finances its assets.[17] Good secondary markets for stocks are vital to the functioning of our economy; without them, investors would have no other feasible and efficient way to liquidate their ownership interest. Also, the secondary markets allow investors to receive part of their total return from equity investments in the form of capital gains. If a firm makes good investment decisions in real assets and prospers thereby, investors will bid up the price of its common stock, since it now represents ownership of a more valuable entity—i.e., it is a claim on an increasing stream of earnings.

Thus the equity market is distinct from the capital markets previously discussed in that it is primarily a secondary market. When we talk about the equity market, we are talking most about the trading of existing stocks. However, it is this very elaborate mechanism that permits the private financial system to continue to operate and to raise new funds: equity capital must be raised along with debt capital, or firms will become too risky. And new stock could not readily be sold unless a good secondary market existed.

The market for common stocks is a dual one, consisting of organized securities exchanges—the New York Stock Exchange, the American Stock Exchange, and the regional exchanges—and the over-the-counter market. The former dominate the equity market in terms of value of stock represented. The latter handles most of the bond transactions in this country, and, although thousands of stocks are traded over the counter, they represent mostly small companies of limited interest to investors. The New York Stock Exchange, which represents only about 2,200 total stock issues (a small percentage of the total), accounts for the bulk of daily trading, both in terms of volume and in terms of market value of the stocks. (The total

---

[17]Actually, most equity capital that is raised is held in the form of retained earnings. These cannot be paid as dividends, but they still belong to the stockholders. Stockholders ultimately "receive" these funds through a higher price for the stock, which is bid up as a reflection of the profitable reinvestment of retained earnings.

market value of IBM stock is equal to the combined market values of hundreds or thousands of issues in the OTC market.) Individuals have been net sellers of stock for the last few years, but they still own the majority of the market value of all common stocks. Institutional investors, however, now account for the bulk of daily trading on the exchanges.

Organized security exchanges involve brokers who represent both buyers and sellers, and who earn a commission for their services. OTC markets involve dealers who, buying and selling for their own accounts, make a market in an issue.

The equity market is a distinctive part of the capital markets for another reason: it involves much uncertainty and does not respond predictably to changing events. The value of a common stock is what the marketplace makes it as a result of demand and supply, which depend on investors' estimates of the uncertain future. No one can predict with any degree of certainty the total return from a stock in any future year. Thus, if an oil company suddenly discovers a new, large pool of oil, the value of its stock should increase substantially. This is a rational change, based on new information, because clearly the oil company is a more valuable property after the discovery than it was before. Investors must try to assess future prospects. Prices reflect what values are expected to be, not what they were last year.

The prices of corporate bonds, on the other hand, change rather predictably in response to changes in interest rates, although most forecasters of interest rates are notorious for being consistently inaccurate. The same is true of any fixed principal security, on which the interest payment stream and the amount of principal to be returned at maturity are known. Thus equity markets respond differently and less predictably to any change in events than do other segments of the capital markets because of the nature of the instrument. There is simply no a priori method of correctly and consistently assessing the reaction of equity markets to events that affect investors' expectations.

Capital Market Facts and Figures

Amounts Outstanding. Just as we did with the money market, we will now take a brief look at the size and character of the market for long-term funds. It is desirable to have a basic knowledge of the amounts of the various capital market instruments and the trends in the way long-term funds are raised. (We will not discuss federally sponsored agency securities here, as the data for them do not distinguish between long-term and short-term issues. The totals were reported in Table 11–2.)

The amounts outstanding of the capital market instruments we have discussed are shown in Table 11–6 for the years 1966–75. The figures for U.S. government securities include only the combined amount of notes and bonds, since these have maturities greater than one year (i.e., Treasury bills are excluded here). Also, note that corporate equities and the value of mutual fund (investment company) shares have been listed separately.

We can see from the table that long-term federal government financing had been quite steady until the sharp jump in 1975. This basically reflects the fact that Treasury bills have been the important source of financing for the Treasury in the last few years. The average maturity of all federal debt has shortened considerably over the years. By the end of 1978, long-term federal debt totaled $326 billion.

The value of outstanding state and local obligations (municipal securities) has continued to climb steadily. By the beginning of 1979, these obligations amounted to $300 billion. This reflects the ever-growing need of state and local governments to finance increased services for their constituents. The greatest attraction of these securities is that their interest is exempt from federal taxes.

Corporate bonds have grown steadily as our capital stock continues to increase. Firms must have funds to expand, and these can come from internal sources (retained earnings and depreciation charges) or from external sources (sales of new bonds, new preferred stock, or new common stock). Because bonds are the cheapest source of external capital, firms have tried to sell bonds whenever possible. The ratio of debt to equity for all manufacturing firms has increased, reaching about a 50-50 balance (on an inflation-adjusted basis), as they have strived to sell cheap debt instead of expensive equity. The stock market has been severely depressed for the last few years; as a result of low prices, firms do not want to sell new common stock if it is possible to avoid it. Corporate and foreign bonds totaled $423 billion at the start of 1979.

Mortgages have also grown steadily over the years, as a reflection of the continuing American dream of home ownership. Housing seems to have been one of the few good inflation hedges of the last few years, and many people have sacrificed to buy in fear that prices will go even higher. As prices have risen, of course, so too has the average amount of mortgage funds needed to finance the purchase of a house. Mortgages totaled $1169 at the beginning of 1979.

The figures for corporate equities reflect market value figures and are thus subject to the sharp changes of the stock market. We need only examine the figures for 1972, 1973, 1974, and 1975 to see the very large fluctuations that take place for these instruments. Most people recognize that equity securities are quite risky and are subject to wide movements in price, which presumably reflect investors' expectations of the future. A share of stock is valued in accordance with the stream of income that is expected to be received on that share in the future. What happened in the past is basically irrelevant! At end of 1978, stocks were valued at over $1000 billion.

It is interesting to note that relatively few new equity securities are

TABLE 11–6. Selected Capital Market Instruments, Amounts Outstanding, 1966–75. (in billions of dollars)

	1966	1967	1968	1969	1970	1971	1972	1973	1974	1975
1 U.S. government securities — long-term	153.4	156.6	161.8	155.3	159.8	169.3	165.6	162.4	163.2	205.7
2 State & local obligations	105.925	113.703	123.219	133.145	144.370	161.881	177.282	193.598	213.219	230.500
3 Corporate & foreign bonds	133.842	149.415	163.677	176.494	201.605	225.685	244.196	257.540	281.094	317.221
4 Mortgages	358.406	382.873	412.527	443.238	473.148	525.656	602.427	682.321	742.522	803.311
5 Investment company shares	34.829	44.701	52.677	48.289	47.618	56.694	59.831	46.519	34.061	42.178
6 Other corporate equities	647.824	823.938	981.352	866.353	859.373	1003.74	1142.24	864.526	608.911	812.482

Source: Board of Governors of the Federal Reserve System, *Flow of Funds Accounts, 1946–75*, December 1976, p. 94.

12

The Theory of Financial Intermediation

This chapter is intended to deepen your understanding of intermediation, with particular attention to the rationale for the existence of financial intermediaries. Following this discussion, chapters 13 and 14 provide a comprehensive review of the specific functions performed by each of the most important intermediaries. Of course, all such units are similar in that they perform functions that concern intermediation; however, as we shall see, the total scope of their activities involves much more than this.

Intermediation is a general term that refers to the practices of economic units that obtain and issue financial claims.[1] That is, any unit that acquires the financial claims of another and simultaneously issues claims on itself is engaging in intermediation. Members of all sectors in the economy—households, business firms, and government units, as well as financial intermediaries—participate in such activity. Intermediation can occur in countless particular ways because of the broad array of claims that exist. Virtually every economic unit practices intermediation, and it is at least possible that no two units do so in exactly the same manner.

Although intermediation is a very general phenomenon, encompassing a broad scope of activities, not every transaction that involves claims is an example of it. For intermediation to occur, two increases must take place for any economic unit: there must be an increase in claims held against some other unit or units and an increase in claims against the gaining economic unit. Conversely, a unit that reduces both its claims on

---

[1]Thomas E. Van Dahm, *Money and Banking: An Introduction to the Financial System* (Lexington, Massachusetts: D. C. Heath and Company, 1975), p. 84.

others and the outstanding claims on itself is engaging in disintermediation.

FINANCIAL INTERMEDIARIES

In broad terms, a financial intermediary is any entity that links ultimate borrowers and ultimate lenders. Saving surplus units provide funds, and these are typically funneled through intermediaries, who borrow them through the sale of indirect securities to savers.[2] By borrowing from saving surplus units (the ultimate lenders), intermediaries are able to lend to financial deficit units (the ultimate borrowers). In effect, intermediaries lend funds by the purchase of direct (primary) securities from financial deficit units and borrow funds by the issuance of indirect securities to saving surplus units. For example, insurance companies often lend to corporations through the purchase of corporate bonds. (This is called a *private placement*, because the corporation, bypassing the open market, places the bonds with the insurance company directly.) In such cases, the insurance company is purchasing primary securities. It obtains the funds to do this from its policyholders, who have purchased insurance policies (indirect securities) and are now paying premiums. Thus the company is an intermediary between an ultimate borrower (the corporation) and the ultimate lenders (households, which provide the bulk of saving in our economy). The insurance company provides services on both sides of the transaction—otherwise, it would have no reason to exist. On the one hand, the policyholders do not wish to lend money to corporations by buying their bonds; rather, they want an indirect security in the form of an insurance policy to protect the family in case of adverse circumstances. On the other hand, the corporation does not wish to solicit buyers for its bonds in the open market; it prefers to deal with one lender in a quick and convenient manner.

Definition

Many economic units act as financial intermediaries in some form at some time. That is, many units borrow and lend funds, break up transactions, etc. For example, a wealthy individual, being a good credit risk, could borrow $100,000 from a group of doctors and then could turn around and lend $10,000 each to 10 other people who are unable to borrow directly from the doctors. This individual would be acting as an intermediary, operating between and linking ultimate lenders and ultimate borrowers. With our broad definition of what constitutes an inter-

---

[2]See Raymond W. Goldsmith, *The Flow of Capital Funds in the Postwar Economy* (New York: National Bureau of Economic Research, 1965), p. 23.

mediary, a large proportion of households, business firms, and government units qualify.

Clearly, our tentative definition is too broad to be useful. The scope of the term *financial intermediary* can be measured if it is reserved for entities whose primary task is to stand between savers and borrowers, so that they are continuously taking in funds from the former and allocating funds to the latter. In addition, since this is their main activity, financial liabilities greatly outweigh net worth in the composition of their total capital. To illustrate this role, Table 12-1 is a consolidated balance sheet for savings and loan associations (S & Ls). It shows that they acquire most of their funds from savers ("Savings capital" in the table denotes depositors' money) and that they supplement this to a small degree with borrowed money. These funds are allocated to investments, primarily mortgages, with investment securities playing some role (mostly to provide liquidity) and miscellaneous assets accounting for the rest. It should be noted from the table that the net worth of these institutions is a relatively small entry, amounting to only about 5.5 percent of all assets and liabilities plus net worth (in August, 1978). Thus savings and loan associations meet our narrowed criteria for functioning as an intermediary—most of their funds (sources) are borrowed and rechanneled into financial assets of various types (uses), and net worth is only a small percentage of their total capital. They simply act as go-betweens, standing between ultimate savers and ultimate users of funds. Financial firms are in fact distinguishable by their high ratio of borrowed funds to owners' equity funds. The average nonfinancial firm, in contrast, generally has more equity than debt.

By narrowing our definition of an intermediary, we have confined our attention to units that exist to borrow and lend continuously and simultaneously, providing a service (and earning a return) as they do so. Most of these institutions stand ready to accept funds at any time and usually are actively seeking uses for the funds acquired, subject to internal and regulatory constraints and to overall environmental factors, such as the tightness of money.

Characteristics of Financial Intermediaries

Figure 12-1 illustrates the basic nature of financial intermediaries in comparison to the other two sectors of interest to us—households (the saving surplus sector) and business firms (the saving deficit sector). No attempt is made to depict exact percentages. The important point to note is simply that there are basic differences in the three sectors with regard to assets (both real and financial) and liabilities (both net worth and total liabilities). These differences are summarized below.

Financial intermediaries are characterized by the fact that most of their assets are financial assets. They hold relatively few real assets. The business sector, in contrast, has for its primary function the holding of real

TABLE 12–1. Consolidated Balance Sheet for Savings and Loan Associations, 1974–August, 1978 (in millions of dollars).

Account	1974	1975	1976	Nov.	Dec.	Feb.	Mar.	Apr.	May	June	July	Aug.
				1977		1978						
1 Assets	**295,545**	**338,233**	**391,907**	**455,644**	**459,282**	**469,726**	**475,320**	**480,986**	**487,091**	**491,616**	**498,341**	**504,348**
2 Mortgages	249,301	278,590	323,005	376,468	381,216	387,644	392,479	397,335	402,356	408,019	412,008	416,801
3 Cash and investment securities[1]	23,251	30,853	35,724	40,522	39,197	41,646	41,870	41,901	42,493	41,553	43,676	44,173
5 Liabilities and net worth	**295,545**	**338,233**	**391,907**	**455,644**	**459,282**	**469,726**	**475,320**	**480,986**	**487,091**	**491,616**	**498,341**	**504,348**
6 Savings capital	242,974	285,743	335,912	381,333	386,875	391,917	399,070	399,628	402,008	408,665	411,740	414,091
7 *Borrowed money*	*24,780*	*20,634*	*19,083*	*25,540*	*27,796*	*28,666*	*29,274*	*31,838*	*32,689*	*34,183*	*35,633*	*37,140*
8 FHLBB	21,508	17,524	15,708	18,275	19,945	20,602	21,030	22,692	23,323	24,875	26,151	27,375
9 Other	3,272	3,110	3,375	7,265	7,851	8,064	8,244	9,146	9,366	9,308	9,482	9,765
10 Loans in process	3,244	5,128	6,840	9,924	9,932	9,924	10,435	10,959	11,408	11,650	11,558	11,430
11 Other	6,105	6,949	8,074	13,846	9,498	13,456	10,511	12,194	14,252	10,081	12,016	13,901
12 Net worth[2]	18,442	19,779	21,998	25,001	25,181	25,763	26,030	26,367	26,734	27,037	27,394	27,786
13 Memo: Mortgage loan commitments outstanding[3]	7,454	10,673	14,826	21,270	19,886	20,625	22,320	23,409	23,951	22,936	22,401	22,032

Source: *Federal Reserve Bulletin*, October 1978, p. A30.

NOTE: *Savings and loan associations:* Estimates by the FHLBB for all associations in the United States. Data are based on monthly reports of Federally insured associations and annual reports of other associations. Even when revised, data for current and preceding year are subject to further revision.

[1] Holdings of stock of the Federal home loan banks are included in "other assets."

[2] Includes net undistributed income, which is accrued by most, but not all, associations.

[3] Excludes figures for loans in process, which are shown as a liability.

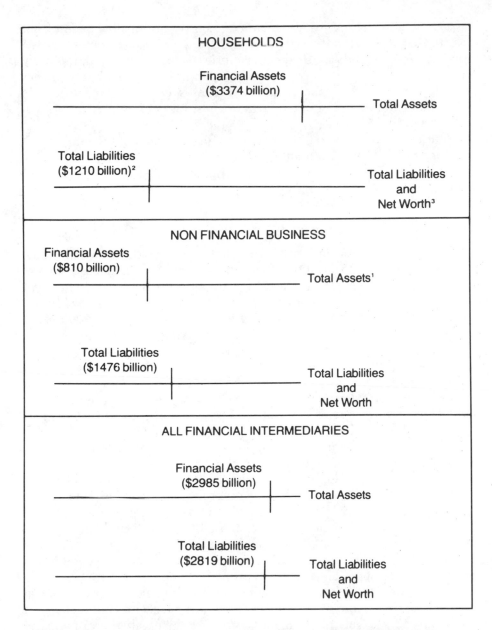

FIGURE 12–1. Financial Assets, Total Liabilities and Implied Net Worth Relationships for Households, Nonfinancial Business, and Financial Intermediaries.

Source: *Flow of Funds 1978 Outstandings* (Preliminary), Board of Governors of the Federal Reserve System, February 1979, pp. 541, 542, 549, 551.
[1]Total assets are used here to imply the sum of financial assets and real assets.
[2]In all cases, dollar amounts are for 1978.
[3]Net worth is the residual between total assets and total liabilities.

assets. Intermediaries are also characterized by the small amount of net worth that appears on the right-hand side of their balance sheets: most of their sources of funds are financial liabilities of various types. In this, they are again unlike the business sector, which generally must rely on net worth more than on financial liabilities. That is, creditors expect the sale of stock or the retention of earnings to constitute more than half of total financing.

Financial intermediaries are also distinguishable from the household sector, which has considerable net worth in relation to total liabilities. Most household assets are in the form of financial assets, as opposed to real assets.

Services Performed by Financial Intermediaries

Why do financial intermediaries exist? Why do other economic units find their services so attractive that a great variety of them exist and are, in fact, very large in terms of assets? After all, a saving surplus unit could lend to an ultimate borrower and generally receive a higher rate of return than what it could receive by lending to an intermediary (for example, in the form of money deposited at a bank or a savings and loan association).

The answer to the question of why these intermediaries exist must surely be that they perform services that both ultimate savers and ultimate borrowers desire. Thus saving surplus units must prefer not to hold claims on ultimate borrowers. Either the primary securities issued by the latter do not have the characteristics that lenders desire (e.g., maturity, liquidity, accessibility), or they are not viewed as providing a favorable risk-return tradeoff. Lenders want specific indirect securities—an insurance policy, a liquid claim that can be withdrawn at any time and that earns interest, etc. Intermediaries supply these indirect claims, which cannot be duplicated by ultimate borrowers. On the other side, ultimate borrowers often benefit from the aggregation process that intermediaries perform: pooling money from many small economic units, they can lend large sums to borrowers more efficiently than could many small savers lending directly.

In effect, then, financial intermediaries perform a transformation function for society: they transform primary claims on ultimate borrowers into indirect claims, issued on themselves to ultimate lenders. Financial intermediation involves changing claims on real assets into indirect claims of diverse kinds. Only financial intermediaries can create the vast array of unique claims desired by a heterogeneous group of saving surplus units. This is their basic appeal—the ability to transform claims on ultimate borrowers into unique claims, tailor-made to meet the desires of ultimate lenders. Financial intermediation involves changing claims on real assets into indirect claims of diverse kinds.

Figure 12–2 indicates, for the prominent financial intermediaries, what indirect securities they issue and what primary securities they pur-

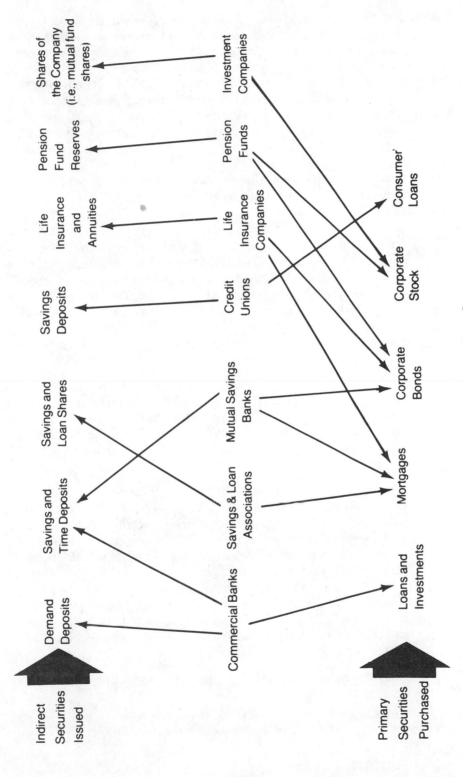

FIGURE 12–2. Prominent Financial Intermediaries — Major Indirect Securities Issued (Sources of Funds) and Primary Securities Purchased (Uses of Funds)

chase. Only the major activities of each are represented. However, as can easily be seen, just these few institutions issue a diverse assortment of indirect securities to meet the needs and the desires of saving surplus units. A checkbook deposit payable on demand is surely quite different from pension fund reserves payable in installments after retirement; stock ownership in an investment company is very different from either of these claims; and so on for the list of securities at the top of the figure. Also, intermediaries purchase a wide range of primary securities, by which they provide financing for a diverse group of individuals and firms needing credit.

Financial intermediaries offer a variety of services besides the transformation function. It is worthwhile to list these in detail, to emphasize the importance of intermediation in our economy.[3]

1. Intermediaries provide an aggregation service: they collect the savings of many individuals and funnel them to ultimate users of saving. This would be an extremely inefficient and costly process, if not impossible, without intermediation. The ability to offer many kinds of indirect securities to savers permits intermediaries to accumulate savings from many individuals, each of whom provides a small fraction of the total. Once these savings are aggregated primary securities issues of virtually any size can be purchased.

2. Intermediaries offer great accessibility (ease) in the borrowing of funds, because even large-scale borrowers can deal with one (or a few) intermediaries, instead of a large number of savers, and still acquire sizable bundles of funds. This is more efficient and less costly than other alternatives—otherwise, intermediaries would not be employed.

3. An important aspect of security transformation is that intermediaries can effectively alter the maturities of primary securities by purchasing them and, in turn, offering indirect securities with various maturities. For example, a life insurance company might purchase 30-year bonds from a corporation, while it issues policies of various lengths (e.g., a term policy of 5 years). Generally, ultimate borrowers want funds for extended periods, but savers want to provide funds for shorter periods. Intermediaries permit both to obtain what they want—a result that would not be possible if the transactions were to take place directly between borrowers and lenders.

4. Intermediaries are specialists, providing a specific service in our

---

[3]This discussion is indebted to James C. Van Horne, *Function and Analysis of Capital Market Rates* (Englewood Cliffs, New Jersey: Prentice-Hall, Inc., 1970), pp. 6–7.

economy. Financial transactions can be quite complex, involving information and paperwork costs that would be oppressive for transactors unfamiliar with established procedures. Intermediaries deal with borrowers continuously and know how to evaluate risks, etc. They are geared to make the financial transactions desired quickly and efficiently, even though these involve many details and considerable red tape. And, of course, intermediaries know how to attract savers and know what financial services they require.

5. Finally, intermediaries reduce the risk that savers face in trying to earn a return on their savings. By spreading this risk among a large number of diverse holdings, financial institutions gain a benefit that simply cannot be achieved on a small scale. It is firmly established in the finance literature that proper diversification of asset holdings pays, and sizable funds are required to diversify adequately. If you were to lend a firm money by buying its bonds, you would be taking a large risk, because your returns would be contingent on the fortunes of that one company. An intermediary, however, knows that any single loss would consume only a small part of its total holdings and would not seriously damage its position. Such a loss is likely to be offset by profitable transactions with other borrowers. An intermediary can continue to function with some losses, whereas individual lenders might not be able to. This idea of risk-reduction through diversification is directly related to portfolio theory, which applies to both individuals and institutions. The basis for this theory and the concept of an efficient portfolio were developed in chapter 6. Here we examine closely one of the key concepts of portfolio theory, the process of diversification.

PORTFOLIO CONCEPTS FOR FINANCIAL INTERMEDIARIES

Portfolio theory involves the study of concepts for the effective management of portfolios. The principles that have been derived are applicable both to individuals and to institutions, i.e., they apply to anyone who manages a portfolio of financial assets. For our purposes here, however, we are ultimately concerned with how portfolio theory is related to the concept of intermediation.

Portfolio Diversification

One of the basic tenets of portfolio theory involves the concept of diversification. A financial intermediary holds many financial assets, which together constitute its portfolio. Since the very act of intermediation involves the transformation of claims, intermediaries must be concerned with their holdings of claims at all times. While trying to earn a return on these financial assets, they are simultaneously assuming a risk. However, if this risk is properly distributed among diverse holdings, it can be reduced in relation to what it otherwise would have been. This applies to both the asset side and the liability side of the financial intermediaries' balance sheet.

Modern portfolio theory has demonstrated that a portfolio of assets is not in all respects simply the summation of the characteristics of the individual asset holdings. The return on a portfolio of financial assets is in fact a weighted average of the returns on the individual assets: each individual return is weighted by the percentage of the total portfolio that the corresponding asset constitutes. Thus, if a portfolio contains 10 assets in equal dollar amounts, the return on the portfolio is equal to the sum of 10 products, i.e., the sum of each of the 10 individual asset returns multiplied by 0.10. The higher (lower) the expected return on each of the individual assets, the higher (lower) the expected return on the portfolio.

This is not true of portfolio risk. One cannot simply add the weighted risks of the individual assets. Portfolio risk is a function of, not only the weighted risk of each individual asset, but also the weighted interrelationships among the assets.

To assess portfolio risk, it is necessary to determine the correlation of returns on the individual assets. If asset returns move together, they are positively related. If they move inversely to each other, they are negatively related. It is possible for there to be no relationship, either positive or negative, between them. Whatever the relationship may be, we can measure it with the correlation coefficient, which ranges in value from $+1$ to -1, with 0 being no relationship. If the returns on two assets display a perfect positive correlation (coefficient of $+1$), as in Figure 12–3(a), and if the return on one changes, then the return on the other also changes in the same direction. A little thought quickly reveals that this is an all-or-nothing situation—the two returns go up together or down together. As asset-holders, we would like to see both go up, but we would not like to see both come down at the same time. To reduce the risk that all the assets in our portfolio might suffer a decline in returns at the same time, we must diversify into several assets. In particular, we must combine assets that do not display perfect positive correlation, i.e., whose correlation coefficient is less than $+1$. If two assets' returns are exactly opposite in their motions, we have the situation depicted in Figure 12–3(b). Finally, if there is no relationship between the movements in the returns of two assets, we have the situation depicted in Figure 12–3(c).

The maximum risk reduction can be attained with a correlation coefficient of -1. Significant risk reduction occurs with a correlation coeffi-

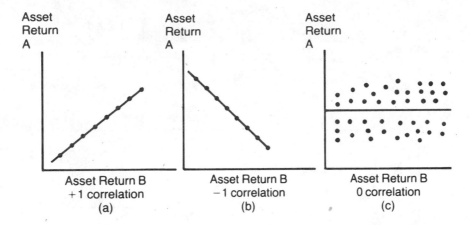

FIGURE 12–3. Positive, Negative, and Zero Correlation of Returns on
Two Assets

cient of 0. Less-than-perfect positive correlation, although still positive, is always preferable to perfect positive correlation and is, in fact, what is typically found in the real world of financial assets. That is, most returns move together, but not perfectly: in a vigorous economy, most financial assets perform well; in a declining economy, most of them perform badly.

The rationale of portfolio diversification, then, is that it combines assets systematically in a manner that reduces risk. If we were certain of any asset's future return, we could hold only that asset and would profit thereby. But, unless we can foresee the future, we must diversify our risk. A savings and loan company that holds only one giant mortgage, say, on a big shopping center, takes the risk that the complex could go bankrupt. A credit union that lends to only one borrower risks everything on the fortunes of that one borrower. And an individual whose entire wealth is placed in one stock takes the risk that this stock could suffer adverse circumstances and cause the loss of part or all of this wealth. Diversification is prudent—it reduces the risk of the unforeseen future. Moreover, it is important to diversify correctly. It is not only the number of separate assets held that reduces a portfolio's risk—the interrelationships among the particular assets also matter greatly. A portfolio of 10 assets, all of which have perfect positive correlation with each other, provides no reduction in risk. For all practical purposes, one might just as well be holding one asset, as far as the risk of the portfolio is concerned.

An intermediary, like any investor, cannot predict the future with perfect accuracy. However, it can reduce its risk through a combination of assets that have return patterns independent of or inverse to each other.

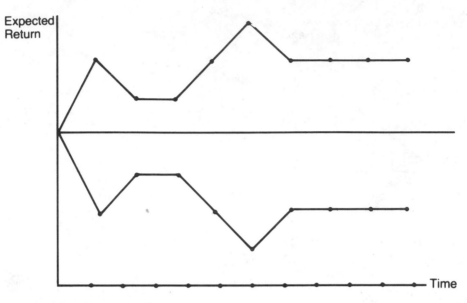

FIGURE 12-4. Completely Offsetting Variation in Expected Returns on Two Assets

For example, consider Figure 12–4, which depicts the variation of expected returns on two assets across time: although each asset separately is risky, the combination of the two eliminates risk, because the variations in expected returns exactly offset each other. We might think of the assets depicted in Figure 12–4 as two loans held by an intermediary. One loan is to a steel mill, which tends to do well when the economy is strong, because then the demand for steel is also strong. The second loan is to a major builder of residential construction, which tends to be (at least, has been in the past) countercyclical to the economy. In effect, the prospects of these two borrowers tend to move inversely to each other. Although each loan is risky by itself, the two taken together interact in such a way that risk is reduced or eliminated. In the normal situation, not all risk can be eliminated by portfolio diversification, but it can be reduced. What is required is the combining of assets whose return patterns are not perfectly positively correlated.

It should be carefully noted that return and risk calculations for a portfolio are independent. The portfolio return is a weighted average of the individual asset returns, whatever their risk and their interrelationships. Portfolio risk, however, depends directly on correlations among returns and on the amount of funds placed in each asset. A proper combination of assets can reduce portfolio risk.

Applying Diversification Concepts to Intermediaries

We have examined the basic nature of financial intermediation, which takes in funds from savers and channels these funds to borrowers. In the process, as an intermediary comes to hold a portfolio of financial assets, the exact nature of which depends upon which intermediary is involved, it should apply diversification theory. At the same time, it may also be able to apply the basic concept to the liability side of its balance sheet; if so, it can achieve some benefit by reducing the risk that has to be assumed in the course of operations. We will examine each of these ideas in turn.

Diversification of Assets. What was said above about the theory of diversification should be obvious to an intermediary: funds must not be concentrated in one or a few assets. Rather, they should be distributed among many, to reduce portfolio risk. Further, the asset holdings must have less than perfect positive correlation with each other if they are to provide the beneficial effects of diversification, since portfolio risk is inversely related to the number of independent or negatively correlated assets in the portfolio.

The nature of intermediaries is such that, to a great extent, their objectives dictate what type of portfolio they hold. For example, a savings and loan association holds mostly mortgages, a life insurance company holds mostly corporate bonds and mortgages, a commercial bank holds mostly loans of various types. Intermediaries therefore cannot simply combine assets that provide the utmost diversification benefits. They are constrained in this by the basic nature of their operations. What they can do, however, is to carefully consider the assets they hold from the perspective of obtaining whatever diversification benefits there are to be obtained. This means that they may wish to place their funds as much as possible in different types of assets, such as Treasury securities, corporate bonds, mortgages, stocks (both common and preferred), and money market assets. Perhaps more importantly, within a category of assets, intermediaries should attempt to find individual positions that are not strongly related in a positive manner—for example, the loans to the steel mill and to the residential construction firm in our general discussion of diversification. Of course, corporate bond holdings and stock holdings should be scattered over a wide selection of industries and companies.

It should be noted that intermediaries are forced by law in many cases to diversify and/or to limit their holdings to various types of assets. Life insurance companies, for example, are closely regulated by state laws as to the types and qualities of assets they can hold. Commercial banks are limited in the amount of money they can lend to any single borrower. Savings and loans associations are effectively constrained to invest primarily in mortgages. These regulations have probably served on balance to safeguard the viability of the intermediaries. However, they do not reflect what is known today about the benefits of portfolio diversification —they often ignore the importance of the interrelationships among assets in the construction of a reduced-risk portfolio. Of course, the law of large numbers assures some reduction of risk as holdings increase. Thus a portfolio of 200 different assets is normally safer than a portfolio of 20 if equal amounts are invested in each asset in both cases. To the extent that regulations prevent concentration in a few assets, then, some safety is assured. On the other hand, it is interesting to note that a portfolio of between 8 and 16 common stocks can provide about 95 percent of the maximum beneficial effects of diversification if they are properly selected on the basis of their interrelationships.[4]

Diversification of Liabilities. Just as financial intermediaries can reduce the risk of loss by diversification of their assets, so can they reduce their risk by diversification of their liabilities and net worth items, i.e., their sources of funds. The concept is the same but the effect is different. By diversifying their liabilities, financial intermediaries reduce the risk of losing a substantial amount of funds in a short time. Such a quick loss could lead to a sudden shrinkage of assets, because the left-hand side of the balance sheet for an intermediary (or for any firm) must equal the right-hand side of the balance sheet—i.e., total uses of funds (assets) must equal total sources of funds (liabilities plus net worth). An unexpected shrinkage of assets could have detrimental effects on an intermediary if it were forced to sell assets at losses. Thus intermediaries obviously desire to reduce their risk of sudden sizable losses of funds.

Some intermediaries, e.g., savings and loan associations and banks, have the bulk of their liabilities in the form of obligations that, in practice, are payable on demand. At the extreme, they could lose very large amounts of their funds very quickly if, for example, there were a run on the institution. This is quite unlikely today, because the fact that accounts are insured for up to $40,000 gives depositors confidence. Apart from runs, intermediaries are still potentially vulnerable to losing some large accounts or to losing a number of accounts at the same time. In these cases, the law of large numbers helps to reduce their risk. By diversifying the claims on themselves across a large number of depositors and sources, the intermediaries reduce their risk of loss. At the same time that some depositors are withdrawing money, others are depositing money; at the same time that an insurance company is paying off on several policies, it is selling new policies, which will generate cash flows from new premium income.

While diversification principles imply that intermediaries should obtain funds from as many different sources as possible and that, ideally,

---

[4]See J. Evans and S. Archer, "Diversification and the Reduction of Dispersion: An Empirical Analysis," *Journal of Finance 23* (December 1968), pp. 761–67.

these sources would be independent of each other, we know that, in practice, intermediaries are restricted to certain types of sources that they can employ. For example, Table 12–1 shows that savings and loans associations obtain funds principally from savings, with a relatively minor volume of funds provided by a combination of net worth, borrowed money, loans in process, and other sources. Within a particular source of funds, such as savings for the savings and loan associations, an intermediary can be highly diversified across a broad spectrum of savers—old, young, rich, poor, etc. Presumably, these sources of funds function independently of each other in many cases, so that the intermediary gains the risk-reducing benefit of diversification. However, not all intermediaries enjoy independence in this respect. A town that is highly dependent on one employer whose business moves cyclically has many depositors who are not so independent of each other. Economic adversity for the firm could result in substantial withdrawals of funds from the intermediary.

THE ROLE OF FINANCIAL INTERMEDIARIES

Scope of Activities

We have now examined the basis for intermediation by financial institutions and the portfolio management principles that are relevant to their actions as intermediaries. At this point, we need to recognize that these institutions do much more than provide intermediation.

As we learned in the early chapters of this text, commercial banks play an important role in the creation of money and in the functioning of our overall payments system (involving check collection, the provision of credit, etc.). Although these roles are closely related to intermediation by banks, bank activities involve more than intermediation. In a similar vein, the issuance of traveler's checks by a savings and loan association has little direct connection with intermediation. As we obtain a more detailed view of the functioning of the most prominent intermediaries, the wide scope of their activities will be apparent. Intermediation, however, remains their prime function.

The Importance of Financial Intermediaries

Having established the meaning of intermediation and described the nature of financial intermediaries in general, we now need to consider just how important they are in our economy. We know that savings must be allocated from those that do the saving to those that wish to invest. We also know that this transfer of funds can take place directly from saver to user or indirectly through financial intermediaries.

Individuals in the form of households are the principal savers in our economy. Most of this saving is done via financial intermediaries, including banks, savings and loan associations, insurance companies, investment companies, pension funds, credit unions, and mutual savings banks. These institutions together form a massive vehicle for the collection and allocation of funds. The indirect claims that they provide span the spectrum of assets that most individuals desire. In turn, intermediaries are able to purchase large quantities of virtually every financial obligation issued by borrowers.

So pervasive is the use of financial intermediaries in our economy that individual savers have relatively little direct involvement in the use of saving. One thing they do, of course, is build on equity in the homes they purchase. A second important direct use of savings is the purchase of common stocks. Individuals still own more common stock than do institutions, but the latter account for more of the daily trading on the exchanges. Also, individuals have been net sellers of stock for several years, so that their relative importance has declined. Nevertheless, they are still the dominant force in the ownership of equity securities. (We should again carefully note that the purchase of stocks does not directly involve financial intermediaries, whereas an individual's participation in a pension fund that owns common stocks does involve them. In fact, purchase of common stock by either individuals or institutions does not directly affect real investment; it simply represents transactions in the secondary markets, where asset-holders trade existing claims.)

To see the importance of financial intermediaries, consider Table 12–2, which lists the direct and indirect sources of funds to the credit markets for the last several years. This table shows, among other information, the total funds advanced in the credit markets to the nonfinancial sectors ($370 billion in 1978, based on mid-year figures); total net advances by public agencies and foreign sources ($83 billion in 1978); and total net advances of private domestic funds ($326.8 billion in 1978).[5] The latter category is broken down into credit market funds advanced by private financial institutions ($307.9 billion in 1978) and direct lending in credit markets ($71.8 billion in 1976).[6] Thus, as we can see from lines 47 and 48, the public support rate in 1978 was only 22.4 percent, and the private financial intermediation rate was 94.2 percent of all funds supplied by the private market.

Table 12–2 also provides information on the relative importance in the financial marketplace of different intermediaries and groups of intermediaries. For example, we can see from lines 20, 21, and 22 the importance of commercial banks, savings institutions, and insurance and pension

---

[5]Agency borrowing (line 11) must be deducted from the sum of the latter two figures to make the latter two figures agree with the total funds advanced figure of $370 billion.

[6]Line 26, credit market borrowing, must be deducted from "credit market funds advanced by private financial institutions" to make this statement true.

funds in advancing funds in the private credit markets. Roughly 77 percent of the total funds advanced in credit markets to nonfinancial sectors (line 1) in 1978 came from these three groupings.

Clearly, ours is an economy in which financial transactions are dominated by intermediaries. Just as clearly, any event that impedes them in raising and supplying funds is potentially very harmful.

A STRUCTURE FOR FINANCIAL INTERMEDIATION

The various financial intermediaries can be categorized according to the basic nature of their operations. This provides a useful organizational framework and a point of reference for the two subsequent chapters, which discuss the various intermediaries. These groupings are intended, not to reflect the relative importance of these institutions to the economy, but simply to rank them according to how close the claims they issue are to money.

The First Level—Commercial Banks

It seems logical to clsssify commercial banks as the most basic, the most obvious, and the most familiar type of financial intermediary. After all, the overwhelming majority of Americans deal with a bank in some respect at some time in their lives. Banks have been more closely studied, discussed, and worried about than any other financial institution. And, as a group, they have been regulated more closely than virtually any other business endeavor in this country, with the possible exception of the utilities.

Banks deserve a unique status in the hierarchy of financial intermediaries primarily because they alone can create money. They provide the bulk of the supply of narrowly defined money (M_1) in the form of demand deposits. One can quickly convert savings deposits at banks into demand deposits. Thus banks are the most basic of the financial institutions with respect to taking funds in and lending them out.

Also, banks constitute the largest single category of financial intermediary, not only in terms of total assets, but also in terms of the most diversified portfolio by type of asset (this latter fact can readily be observed in Table 13–1). Finally, banks transcend domestic boundaries and conduct international operations, directly or indirectly. Most other financial intermediaries have only domestic operations.

The Second Level—The Thrift Institutions

All other intermediaries are, of course, nonbank intermediaries. However, there is a group of institutions that are like banks in some respects, and which in fact compete with banks so aggressively in some

TABLE 12–2. Direct and Indirect Sources of Funds to Credit Markets, 1972–Mid 1978 (in billions of dollars, except as noted; quarterly data are at seasonally adjusted annual rates).

Transaction category, or sector	1972	1973	1974	1975	1976	1977	1977 Q1	Q2	Q3	Q4	1978 Q1	Q2
1 Total funds advanced in credit markets to nonfinancial sectors	165.5	196.1	184.9	198.0	261.7	337.4	303.6	298.4	385.0	362.5	380.9	370.0
By public agencies and foreign:												
2 *Total net advances*	19.8	34.1	52.6	44.3	54.5	85.4	59.2	79.3	81.4	121.8	116.3	83.0
3 U.S. government securities	7.6	9.5	11.9	22.5	26.8	40.2	14.8	39.7	40.8	65.6	48.7	33.9
4 Residential mortgages	7.0	8.2	14.7	16.2	12.8	20.4	23.6	16.3	18.8	23.0	27.2	20.0
5 FHLB advances to S&Ls	*	7.2	6.7	−4.0	−2.0	4.3	2.6	4.3	−.1	10.4	12.8	15.3
6 Other loans and securities	5.1	9.2	19.4	9.5	16.9	20.5	18.2	19.1	21.9	22.8	27.5	13.8
Total advances, by sector												
7 U.S. government	1.8	2.8	9.7	15.1	8.9	11.8	10.3	1.8	17.4	17.8	28.7	8.5
8 Sponsored credit agencies	9.2	21.4	25.6	14.5	20.6	26.9	28.4	24.9	25.7	28.7	39.9	43.6
9 Monetary authorities	.3	9.2	6.2	8.5	9.8	7.1	−5.8	26.1	2.1	6.2	−4.1	30.7
10 Foreign	8.4	0.6	11.2	6.1	15.2	39.5	26.2	26.5	36.2	69.2	51.8	0.3
11 Agency borrowing not included in line 1	8.4	19.9	23.1	13.5	18.6	26.3	27.4	22.6	25.4	29.7	38.8	39.8
Private domestic funds advanced												
12 *Total net advances*	154.1	182.0	155.3	167.3	225.7	278.2	271.8	241.7	328.9	270.4	303.5	326.8
13 U.S. government securities	16.0	18.8	22.4	75.7	61.3	44.1	64.7	20.9	64.8	26.1	56.3	54.5
14 State and local obligations	14.7	14.7	16.5	15.6	19.0	29.2	20.5	38.2	33.0	25.0	22.3	35.8
15 Corporate and foreign bonds	13.1	10.0	20.9	32.8	30.5	22.3	19.6	14.9	31.1	23.6	19.3	21.5
16 Residential mortgages	48.2	48.4	26.9	23.2	52.7	83.2	59.7	90.0	92.0	91.2	75.6	79.8
17 Other mortgages and loans	62.1	97.2	75.4	16.1	60.4	103.7	109.9	82.0	107.9	115.0	142.8	150.6
18 Less: FHLB advances	*	7.2	6.7	−4.0	−2.0	4.3	2.6	4.3	−.1	10.4	12.8	15.3
Private financial intermediation												
19 *Credit market funds advanced by private financial institutions*	149.7	165.4	126.2	119.9	191.2	249.6	239.3	242.9	280.6	235.4	266.6	307.9
20 Commercial banking	70.5	86.5	64.5	27.6	58.0	85.8	85.0	77.1	103.1	77.9	114.2	136.8
21 Savings institutions	48.2	36.9	26.9	52.0	71.4	84.8	85.5	85.1	89.1	79.6	79.1	81.6

#													
22	Insurance and pension funds	17.2	23.9	30.0	41.5	51.7	62.0	58.6	62.0	66.4	61.1	62.7	66.2
23	Other finance	13.9	18.0	4.7	-1.1	10.1	16.9	10.2	18.7	22.0	16.8	10.6	23.3
24	*Sources of funds*	*149.7*	*165.4*	*126.2*	*119.9*	*191.2*	*249.6*	*239.3*	*242.9*	*280.6*	*235.4*	*266.6*	*307.9*
25	Private domestic deposits	100.6	86.6	69.4	90.6	121.5	136.0	140.3	113.7	165.4	124.5	112.3	124.0
26	Credit market borrowing	17.1	36.2	13.0	-2.5	9.6	32.0	31.6	40.3	17.3	38.7	71.1	52.8
27	*Other sources*	32.0	42.5	43.8	31.9	60.1	81.6	67.3	89.0	97.9	72.3	83.2	131.1
28	Foreign funds	4.6	5.8	16.8	0.9	5.1	11.6	-7.6	9.1	20.4	24.4	-2.4	16.4
29	Treasury balances	0.7	-1.0	-5.1	-1.7	-.1	4.3	4.3	-7.9	5.5	15.2	-14.1	12.3
30	Insurance and pension reserves	11.6	18.4	26.0	29.6	34.8	48.0	40.6	50.4	51.9	48.9	47.7	50.1
31	Other, net	15.0	19.4	6.0	3.1	20.3	17.8	30.0	37.4	20.0	-16.2	52.0	52.3

Private domestic nonfinancial investors

#													
32	*Direct lending in credit markets*	*21.5*	*52.8*	*42.2*	*44.9*	*44.1*	*60.6*	*64.1*	*39.1*	*65.6*	*73.6*	*108.0*	*71.8*
33	U.S. government securities	3.9	19.2	17.5	23.0	19.6	24.6	34.3	-6.0	37.8	32.5	51.7	20.7
34	State and local obligations	3.0	5.4	9.3	8.3	6.8	9.1	2.1	14.2	7.3	12.9	4.4	9.6
35	Corporate and foreign bonds	4.4	1.3	4.7	8.0	2.1	1.1	0.9	*	3.5	0.2	-3.5	-2.1
36	Commercial paper	2.9	18.3	2.4	-.8	4.1	9.5	12.7	13.3	.5	11.5	37.2	22.6
37	Other	7.3	8.6	8.2	6.4	11.5	16.2	14.3	17.6	16.5	16.5	18.3	21.0
38	*Deposits and currency*	*105.0*	*90.6*	*75.7*	*96.8*	*128.8*	*144.3*	*146.9*	*118.3*	*182.2*	*129.7*	*123.2*	*133.9*
39	*Time and savings accounts*	*83.8*	*76.1*	*66.7*	*84.8*	*112.2*	*120.1*	*119.6*	*101.5*	*151.4*	*108.0*	*110.5*	*110.5*
40	Large negotiable CDs	7.7	18.1	18.8	-14.1	-14.4	9.3	-13.5	4.8	13.1	32.7	5.4	19.8
41	Other at commercial banks	30.6	29.6	26.1	39.4	58.1	41.7	62.9	27.7	60.0	16.3	52.8	33.6
42	At savings institutions	45.4	28.5	21.8	59.4	68.5	69.1	70.2	69.0	78.3	59.0	52.3	57.0
43	*Money*	*21.2*	*14.4*	*8.9*	*12.0*	*16.6*	*24.2*	*27.3*	*16.8*	*30.8*	*21.7*	*12.7*	*23.5*
44	Demand deposits	16.8	10.5	2.6	5.8	9.3	15.9	20.8	12.2	14.0	16.5	1.8	13.5
45	Currency	4.4	3.9	6.3	6.2	7.3	8.3	6.6	4.6	16.8	5.2	11.0	9.9
46	**Total of credit market instruments, deposits and currency**	**126.5**	**143.4**	**117.8**	**141.6**	**172.9**	**204.9**	**211.1**	**157.3**	**247.8**	**203.3**	**231.3**	**205.7**
47	Public support rate (in percent)	12.0	17.4	28.5	22.4	20.8	25.3	19.5	26.6	21.1	33.6	30.5	22.4
48	Private financial intermediation (in percent)	97.2	90.9	81.3	71.7	84.7	89.7	88.0	100.5	85.3	87.1	87.8	94.2
49	Total foreign funds	13.0	6.4	28.0	7.1	20.3	51.1	18.6	35.6	56.6	93.5	49.4	16.6

Memo: Corporate equities not included above

(continued from pages 362 and 363)

	13.3	8.9	3.4	11.1	11.4	3.8	-1.3	4.7	4.2	7.4	.9	2.1
51 Mutual fund shares	-.5	-1.2	-.7	-.1	-1.0	-1.0	-2.6	1.0	-3.3	.9	*	.4
52 Other equities	13.8	10.1	4.1	11.2	12.4	4.8	1.3	3.7	7.5	6.5	.9	1.8
53 Acquisitions by financial institutions	16.5	13.3	5.8	9.7	12.5	6.2	6.0	6.2	8.0	4.6	-1.5	.4
54 Other net purchases	-3.3	-4.4	-2.4	1.4	-1.1	-2.4	-7.3	-1.5	-3.8	2.8	2.3	1.8

50 Total net issues ....

Source: *Federal Reserve Bulletin*, October 1978, p. A54.

NOTES BY LINE NUMBER.
2. Sum of lines 3–6 or 7–10.
6. Includes farm and commercial mortgages.
11. Credit market funds raised by Federally sponsored credit agencies, and net issues of Federally related mortgage pool securities. Included below in lines 3, 13, and 33.
12. Line 1 less line 2 plus line 11. Also line 19 less line 26 plus line 32. Also sum of lines 27, 32, 39, and 44.
17. Includes farm and commercial mortgages.
25. Sum of lines 39 and 44.
26. Excludes equity issues and investment company shares. Includes line 18.
28. Foreign deposits at commercial banks, bank borrowings from foreign branches, and liabilities of foreign banking agencies to foreign affiliates.
29. Demand deposits at commercial banks.
30. Excludes net investment of these reserves in corporate equities.
31. Mainly retained earnings and net miscellaneous liabilities.
32. Line 12 less line 19 plus line 26.
33–37. Lines 13–17 less amounts acquired by private finance. Line 37 includes mortgages.
45. Mainly an offset to line 9.
46. Lines 32 plus 38, or line 12 less line 27 plus line 45.
47. Line 2/line 1.
48. Line 19/line 12.
49. Sum of lines 10 and 28.
50, 52. Includes issues by financial institutions.
  Note. — Full statements for sectors and transaction types quarterly, and annually for flows and for amounts outstanding, may be obtained from Flow of Funds Section, Division of Research and Statistics, Board of Governors of the Federal Reserve System, Washington, D.C. 20551.

activities that they take business away from the banks. We can call this group the thrift institutions. It includes savings and loan associations, mutual savings banks, and credit unions.

Thrifts raise funds like any other intermediary, by issuing claims on themselves. These claims are very close approximations to a commercial bank's savings deposits. They are generally available to be quickly converted into some component of M_1; traditionally, they had to be converted before they could be spent (NOW accounts have changed this situation).

For years, the thrifts have battled the commercial banks for the surplus savings available (primarily from households). They become more aggressive each year, as they constantly strive to offer one or more services traditionally offered only by commercial banks. Examples include traveler's checks and various unsecured loans. Several attempts have been made to secure demand deposit creation privileges for some of the thrifts and, as we have noted, limited success in this area has been achieved with NOW accounts.

The important point to note here is simply that, although commercial banks are the dominant single group of financial institutions in this country, there is another group of institutions that in many ways are similar to them. They compete in most of the same markets, offer claims very much like those of commercial banks, and make many of the same investments. They do tap, in a very direct and obvious manner, savings of the surplus sectors, and they do this essentially as commercial banks do, by being readily available and offering a needed or desired commodity in the form of interest-bearing deposits. Nevertheless, they are not fully comparable to banks, which have the ability to create money. Also, it seems safe to say that they are not as well known to the average person as banks.

The Third Level—Other Intermediaries

We can identify yet another layer of intermediaries according to the nearness of the sources to the uses (nearness in the sense of where they get their funds and what they do with them). It is easy to think of a commercial bank as a first-level intermediary, taking in deposits from A and loaning these funds to B. Almost everyone knows that a bank is in business to loan money and that it uses other people's money to do this. Not everyone stops to think that an insurance company writes policies for individuals and uses part of the premiums to buy large quantities of corporate bonds or to finance residential and commercial construction. Thus banks issue demand deposits—part of our money supply—so that they are closely involved in our everyday lives, and thrifts issue close substitutes that can be quickly converted into money to be spent. A third group of intermediaries issues claims that are not readily spendable—e.g., life insurance policies—and may acquire funds from some source other than the general public.

This third level includes a direct intermediary—investment companies—and a variety of specialized intermediaries—life insurance companies, property and casualty insurance companies, personal trust funds, pension funds, and finance companies. This list is not exhaustive. In fact, there is such a wide range of specialized intermediaries (in the sense of institutions that borrow by issuing claims on themselves and then lend for varied and often special purposes) that we could not discuss all of them in this text. We will refer only to the more important ones in chapter 14.

SUMMARY

This chapter is designed to develop the concept of intermediation. In general, it refers to the simultaneous acquisition and issuance of claims, which occurs in many ways.

Financial intermediaries loan funds by the purchase of direct (primary) securities from ultimate borrowers (financial deficit units) and borrow funds by the sale of indirect securities to ultimate lenders (financial surplus units). That is, they stand between ultimate savers and ultimate users of funds, and their primary task is to conduct such transactions. They hold few real assets; most of their sources of funds are financial liabilities.

Intermediaries exist because they perform services that both savers and borrowers desire, primarily transformation of claims, but also aggregation, convenience, transformation of maturities, expertise, and reduction in risk.

Portfolio concepts are applicable to financial intermediaries. The principle of diversification is particularly relevant to their attempts to reduce risk. The chapter examined diversification concepts for both assets and liabilities.

Financial intermediaries are pervasive in this economy. In 1978, they provided about 90 percent of all funds supplied by the private market; direct lending accounted for the rest. Commercial banks, savings institutions, and insurance and pension funds supplied about two-thirds of the total funds advanced in credit markets in 1978.

The chapter concluded by categorizing the various financial intermediaries according to the nature of their operations. Commercial banks are the first level of intermediation because of their role as creators of money, and because they are so basic to the economy. The thrifts—savings and loan associations, mutual savings banks, and credit unions—constitute the second level of intermediation. These institutions are in many respects similar to banks and compete aggressively with them. The third level of intermediation consists of all other intermediaries. This is such a diverse group that not all of its members can be discussed. They range from investment companies to pension funds and finance companies. These will be discussed in chapter 14.

13

Banks as Financial Intermediaries

Banks clearly qualify as financial intermediaries. They raise funds primarily through deposits, and they invest or lend these funds, presumably at a profit. They provide services on both sides of the transaction. For example, an individual who desires to have a savings account at a local bank has no desire to lend money to the local manufacturing plant. The bank, however, can accept deposits from many such individuals and lend part of these funds to the plant for constructive purposes. Both sides receive the particular services that they desire. The individual holders of savings accounts have claims on the bank, which in turn has an interest-paying claim on the business firm. The bank intermediates between savers and borrowers who either do not wish to transact directly with each other or would find it relatively expensive to do so.

To examine the role of banks as intermediaries, it is desirable first to look closely at their sources and uses of funds. This will indicate where they obtain their funds and what they do with them, and it will serve as a background when this chapter proceeds to demonstrate how banks operate as financial intermediaries. The knowledge gained in chapter 12 is of direct use in this task. Although banks have some unique characteristics, the general theory of intermediation is certainly applicable to them. The basic nature of banking, some of which was developed in chapter 4, will be reviewed, as will the fundamental operations of banks. Banks must operate within a stringent regulatory environment while they seek to maximize their stockholders' wealth. They face tradeoffs for which they must make difficult decisions.

Banks, like any dynamic and growing entity, have changed considerably over the years and will continue to change. Therefore the chapter concludes with a look at their changing nature as intermediaries. What are the new trends in banking, and how will these trends affect banks as intermediaries? These are important questions that deserve much thought and analysis!

CONSOLIDATED BALANCE SHEET, COMMERCIAL BANKS

To start the analysis, we need to examine the assets and liabilities of the banking system. Summary figures for all insured commercial banks on June 30, 1977, are presented in Table 13–1. We will refer to this table as we work our way through the various sources (the right-hand side of the balance sheet) and uses (the left-hand side of the balance sheet) of bank funds.

Sources of Funds for Commercial Banks

The primary sources of funds for commercial banks are demand deposits and time and savings deposits. The two together constitute 80 percent of total sources, with time and savings deposits dominating demand deposits. Of course, most are subject to fast withdrawal, since savings account withdrawals are typically honored upon demand. Hence banks can be viewed as raising most of their funds from volatile short-term sources. Those who provide the funds are seeking liquidity, convenience, and safety, but not necessarily simultaneously or in that order, so that there is a variety of deposit sources. Each of these sources are examined briefly below.

Demand Deposits. The largest component of our money supply is demand deposits. They are valued for their convenience in carrying out transactions. Most business firms and individuals want to hold demand deposits in order to carry out necessary payment transactions. They know they are holding a safe, convenient, and liquid alternative to currency and coins. From the depression era of the 1930s until the advent of NOW accounts, holders have received no explicit interest on demand deposits. Most now pay service charges on their accounts if they do not meet minimum requirements, defined in terms of average or fixed minimum balances.

Private demand deposits—from individuals, partnerships and corporations—constitute the bulk of total demand deposits (about 77 percent). Of this amount, perhaps one-half belongs to nonfinancial business and perhaps one-third to individuals. Additionally, banks hold some U.S. government deposits, considerably more state and local government deposits, and even some foreign demand deposits. Finally, they hold each other's deposits for a variety of reasons (such as correspondent relations).

Demand deposits are obviously an important source of funds for commercial banks. They arise out of a unique need in the financial sector—asset-holders' demands for specialized assets that can be safely held and conveniently transferred as the need arises. Demand deposits constitute the bulk of our money supply and give us an effective and efficient medium of exchange. By providing this means of transactions in the course of their intermediation activity, banks clearly perform a valuable service for asset-holders. Furthermore, excess amounts that are not needed to satisfy reserve requirements and other liquidity needs are lent to units that can use these funds.

Time and Savings Deposits. Time deposits are the largest single category of funds for commercial banks. They are liquid assets that permit savers to earn interest; however, they cannot be directly used as a medium of exchange. Again, the bank performs a service to asset-holders as it provides them with a way to earn a return in a safe, convenient, and liquid form. Because these depositors have different needs and preferences, there are various forms of time deposits.

The best-known form of time deposit is the passbook savings account. Ownership is evidenced by a passbook, which is used to record deposits and withdrawals. Although banks may legally require a notice of intention to withdraw funds, they do not do so in practice. Thus a passbook savings account is a very liquid asset, paying a relatively small rate of interest, which, for all practical purposes, is guaranteed to be received. Maximum rates payable are limited by Federal Reserve Regulation Q. Individuals and nonprofit organizations own 95 percent of all savings deposits.

Time deposits other than savings accounts total more than the savings deposits—$309 billion versus $216 billion in 1977. These time deposits consist of a wide variety of offerings designed to attract idle cash balances. They can be fixed maturity or renewable, negotiable or non-negotiable, and they have various maturities.

Private time deposits—held by individuals, partnerships, and corporations—constitute the bulk of all time deposits. State and local governments are also a sizable source of funds in this form.

As noted in the previous chapter, as of 1978, there is a new form of savings deposit that promises to be very important in the future. This new form is a money market time deposit of six months maturity whose rate is pegged to the Treasury bill rate. As the Treasury bill rate rises, for example, banks and thrift institutions can pay higher rates on these certificates. This slows down or even eliminates disintermediation whereby depositors withdraw their funds from these institutions and invest them directly in the financial markets. The result of such disintermediation in the past was that the housing market was severely damaged because as interest rates rose, depositors withdrew funds that could have been used for mortgages. Now, the banks and thrift institutions can remain competitive with Treasury bills as interest rates rise.

TABLE 13–1. Commercial Bank Assets and Liabilities as of June 30, 1977 (in millions of dollars)

Asset Account		Liability or Capital Account	
Cash bank balances, items in process	$139,055	Demand deposits	$337,428
Currency and coin	12,729		
Reserves with F.R. banks	25,536		
Demand balances with banks in U.S.	36,269	Time deposits	308,831
Other balances with banks in U.S.	6,128		
Balances with banks in foreign countries	5,018		
Cash items in process of collection	53,375	Savings deposits	215,772
Total securities held — book value	254,052		
U.S. Treasury	101,560		
Other U.S. government agencies	35,827	Total deposits	862,031
States and political subdivisions	110,106		
All other securities	6,452		
Unclassified total	108		
Trading-account securities	7,055	Federal funds purchased and securities	
Bank investment portfolios	246,998	sold under agreements to repurchase	79,167
F.R. stock and corporate stock	1,618		
Federal funds sold and securities		Other liabilities	51,354
resale agreement	44,318		
Other loans, gross	577,689	Total liabilities	992,552
Less: Unearned income on loans	13,610		
Reserves for loan loss	6,553		
Other loans, net	557,525		

Other loans, gross, by category		Subordinated notes and debentures	$ 5,393
Real estate loans	$161,276		
Loans to financial institutions	40,151		
Loans to security brokers and dealers	10,436	Equity capital	
Other loans to purch./carry securities	4,142	Preferred stock	76,397
Loans to farmers — except real estate	25,642	Common stock	77
Commercial and industrial loans	192,715	Surplus	16,719
Loans to individuals	127,701	Undivided profits	30,211
Installment loans	101,424	Other capital reserves	27,608
Single-payment loans to individuals	26,277		1,782
All other loans	15,624		
Total loans and securities, net	857,514		
Direct lease financing	5,169		
Fixed assets — buildings, furniture,			
real estate	20,360		
Investment in unconsolidated subsidiaries	2,634		
Customer acceptances outstanding	12,749		
Other assets	36,862		
TOTAL ASSETS	1,074,343	TOTAL LIABILITIES AND EQUITY CAPITAL	1,074,343

Source: *Federal Reserve Bulletin,* February 1978. pp. A18–19.

Note: Number of banks = 14,718

Nondeposit Sources of Funds. Table 13–1 shows the sources of bank funds other than deposits. All these except equity capital might be labeled *miscellaneous*. These sources include such items as accrued tax liabilities, advances from the Fed, Eurodollar borrowings, federal funds purchased, and securities sold under agreement to repurchase. Miscellaneous sources amounted to about 12 percent of all sources in 1977.

Capital accounts (equity capital) are the remaining important source of funds for banks. They amounted to about 8 percent of all sources in 1977. The capital account, like the owner's equity of a nonfinancial corporation, is the residual between total assets and all liabilities. It is normally composed of funds raised by the sale of stock when the bank was started and retained earnings, i.e., earnings of the bank not paid out to stockholders in the form of dividends. In recent years, banks have sold debentures (long-term debt) to raise funds, and this item is also counted in the capital account (although it is shown separately in Table 13–1).

The capital account represents a buffer for the creditors and the depositors of a bank, since (at least, theoretically) it reflects the amount by which assets exceed liabilities. As is the case with nonfinancial firms, banks must pay creditor claims before the stockholders receive anything, in both the distribution of earnings and the settlement of claims in case of bankruptcy. Other things being equal, depositors and creditors prefer a large buffer between their claims and the means to satisfy these claims. Bank capital accounts are not large in relation to total liabilities or total assets. The 8 percent of total sources that capital accounts constitute for banks is in sharp contrast to the large percentage of total sources that equity constitutes for all manufacturing firms. Of course, the two are not directly comparable because of the different types of operations being conducted. Also, banks have alternative sources of funds to fall back on, such as advances from the Fed.

The ratio of capital accounts to total assets has been trending downward over a long period of time. The current figure of 8 percent is only two-thirds of what it was 45 years ago. It seems reasonable to believe that bank regulators will not permit a further decline in the future.

Uses of Funds for Commercial Banks

As Table 13–1 indicates, bank assets are divided into three broad categories: bank cash balances, securities, and loans. Percentages of total assets for these three in 1977 were 13, 24, and 54, respectively.[1] Within the latter two categories, bank asset portfolios span a relatively broad spectrum. Banks must make decisions involving tradeoffs in deriving their portfolios; that is, they must decide how much to hold in cash balances for

---

[1]Loans, as measured here, exclude federal funds sold, which are a form of loan. Also, securities are measured at book value. Finally, the three percentages do not sum to 100 percent because of other assets, such as fixed assets and miscellaneous assets.

safety, how much to lend, and how much to invest in each of the numerous assets that are available.

Bank Cash Balances. Regulations require banks to hold specified percentages of legal reserves. For member banks, these can be held as vault cash and as deposits at district Federal Reserve banks or branches. The exact percentage that is specified depends upon the classification of the bank, the type of deposit, and the current legal requirements set by the Board of Governors. Nonmember banks are allowed by most states to include deposits at other large banks as legal reserves. Deposits held at the Fed can be used in the check-clearing process, as banks make settlements among themselves for checks that have been written.

Besides legal requirements, normal business practices necessitate the holding of cash balances for transactions purposes. Other things being equal, banks would like to minimize their cash balances because of the opportunity cost of holding cash, which earns no interest. For example, deposits at the Fed do not earn interest. Other things are not equal, of course, because banks are very concerned with safety and therefore with liquidity. As of the 1977 date in Table 13–1, currency and coin amounted to slightly more than 9 percent of bank cash balances, compared to 18 percent for reserves held at the Federal Reserve banks.

A large component (38 percent) of total bank cash balances is involved in cash items in process of collection. These items represent checks being collected; checks deposited at the Federal Reserve banks are transferred to bank reserves according to a fixed schedule.

Finally, banks have traditionally maintained sizable correspondent relations with other banks. In 1977, this item accounted for a substantial portion (34 percent) of total cash balances. Correspondent banks earn returns on at least a portion of the funds deposited with them by other banks. In return, the correspondent banks provide the depositing banks with services not provided by, for example, the Federal Reserve banks (one such service is efficient collection of some checks not easily handled by the Fed). Smaller banks that are not members of the Federal Reserve System use large correspondent banks to collect their checks and to provide them with such services as investment counsel, which they cannot justify providing for themselves. Because of the large number of nonmembers—roughly two-thirds of all commercial banks—the use of large correspondent banks for the provision of services is commonplace.

Securities. Table 13–1 shows that the security investment part of the overall bank portfolio amounted to $254 billion, or 24 percent of total assets, in 1977. The largest category in the investment portfolio was municipal (state and local) securities, an important asset in bank portfolios. Bank purchases (or lack thereof) have very important effects on the municipal market. Municipal securities are distinguishable in that all interest payments are exempt from federal income taxes—an important consideration for all investors because effective (after tax) yields are what matter.

United States Treasury securities accounted for about 9 percent of all bank assets in 1977. Banks held even less by the end of 1978. These securities are held because they are liquid and safe. They can be purchased directly from the Treasury or traded in the secondary markets. Treasury securities constitute the major part of trading account securities.

According to Table 13–1, other investments amounted to only 6 percent of all assets in 1977. Corporate bonds are not a large item and most banks are prohibited from holding common stocks. In the final analysis, bank investment portfolios are comprised mostly of U.S. Treasury, government agency, and state and local securities.

The investment portfolio of a bank is determined by several factors, including liquidity, loan demand, the state of the economy, and the overall risk posture taken by the management of the bank. The risk posture assumed, in turn, depends upon the type of bank (e.g., a large New York City bank versus a small bank in a rural area), the general attitudes of the management and board of directors, the amount of liquidity and bank capital, and the overall skill of the bank personnel in handling the many complex transactions that can occur in banking.

Banks must consider several factors pertinent to their investment portfolios. One factor is the maturity structure of the investments. Obviously, banks could invest for any period of time ranging from very short to very long. Because of the short-term nature of their sources of funds, banks are conscious of investing in long maturity assets. One approach is to evenly space assets of ten or fifteen years maturity so that some cash is available each year. Alternatively, banks could balance off investments having long maturities with additional short-maturity investments.

A second factor that banks must consider is the marketability of their investments. This applies particularly to bonds. As noted in chapter 9, one of the reasons for differentials between bonds is marketability. Because banks may need to raise funds quickly to cover withdrawals, some portion of their bond portfolio must be very marketable. Of course, higher marketability results in lower yields, other things equal. Banks face a trade-off here—liquidity versus return.

As any other investor tries to do, banks attempt to maximize returns while minimizing risk. Banks are particularly sensitive to interest rate risk (as discussed in chapters 9 and 10). If interest rates rise, bond prices will decline. Banks would suffer capital losses if interest rates were to rise subsequent to bond purchases and they had to sell bonds for liquidity reasons. Bonds held to maturity will, of course, return the full par value unless the issuer defaults. Since banks hold high-grade bonds (because of close scrutiny by regulators) default is not a significant worry. Banks could speculate on declining interest rates which would result in capital gains. To do this, they would purchase bonds when interest rates are high and are expected to decline.

It does seem safe to say that bank portfolio managers face some significant constraints as they seek to maximize their investment returns. Unlike insurance companies, they must worry about liquidity and must emphasize the shorter maturities. In the final analysis, banks are greatly constrained in their behavior by the short-term nature of their sources of funds—i.e., demand and time deposits.

Loans. As Table 13–1 indicates, commercial and industrial loans make up the largest single part of the loan portfolio. Banks are the second most important source of short-term funds to the business sector. Corporate business is very important to banks, and most firms borrow funds often from them. These borrowers are generally the best credit risk for banks, and the most credit-worthy firms are able to borrow at the prime rate, which is in the daily media as a popular measure of credit costs.

Real estate loans are the second largest category of loans. About one-half of this amount is in one- to four-family residences. This figure indicates the extent to which banks are competing with savings and loan associations and mutual savings banks in a market where banks had little involvement until recent years.

Loans to individuals, the category most people think of when they think of bank loans, is third in importance. The bulk of these take the form of installment loans to finance such purchases as autos and appliances.

Loans to financial institutions, federal funds lending, and loans to farmers are the other sizable categories of bank loans.

Bank loan policies must reflect other considerations as well as a concern for yields. Liquidity is needed because of the volatility of demand deposits and time deposits and to provide flexibility for making new loans that may provide even higher returns. Banks are in business to lend money. They invest in securities on a residual basis, after providing for loan demands and net withdrawals. Loans typically provide higher returns to banks than do investments because the risk is greater (also, the cost of making loans is higher).

FUNCTIONING AS AN INTERMEDIARY

Having examined financial intermediaries in general (chapter 12) and the sources and uses of funds for banks in particular, we can now consider very precisely the nature of a bank as an intermediary. Although each type of financial intermediary is different and has its own unique problems and opportunities, the basic functioning of intermediaries can be studied through the use of banks as an example. Observations here can therefore be generalized to some degree across the board.

Basic Nature of Banking

Commercial banks are privately owned, profit-seeking institutions. Their most basic characteristic is that they are in the business of assuming risks. Everyone thinks of banks as conservative financial institutions that work aggressively to avoid risk—and, in fact, they do constantly strive to minimize it. Nevertheless, risk is a pervasive element in the everyday life of a bank. Since bankers cannot foresee the future any better than anyone else, they are faced with the risk of loss in their asset holdings and the risk of sudden, unpredictable losses in their sources of funds. More will be said about risk below.

Another fact about the basic nature of banks is that any one of them is predominantly a creature of its own environment; i.e., it serves a particular community, which significantly shapes its operations. A bank in a small western town has a different character than First National City Bank of New York. Within a community, banks can specialize in certain aspects of the banking business. Probably the key determinant of exactly what a bank does within its environment is the bank's management. Thus banks differ by region and community and, in particular, as a result of individual management decisions. They are also significantly affected by existing federal and state regulations, since banking is a heavily regulated industry.

Banking in the United States has traditionally been practiced on a unit basis (i.e., with single-office banks). Branch banking has gained strength over time, although even today it remains a controversial topic. The states decide whether to allow branch banking, for both state-chartered and nationally chartered institutions. Fourteen states now allow no branching, 15 allow limited branching, and 22 allow statewide branching. Nationwide branching is an issue that is still to be resolved, but clearly such a move would significantly affect the banking industry as we know it today.

Mergers have been numerous, and they also affect the basic nature of banks. Mergers are strictly regulated by the Bank Merger Act of 1960. They have decreased over the years.

The formation of bank holding companies has been a significant development in bank organization. A holding company can acquire one or more banks by issuing its own stock (or the stock of various banks). A bank holding company does not perform banking services itself but rather owns banks—an important distinction. In effect, a holding company permits banks to diversify into nonbanking activities, since it is the holding company, and not the bank itself, that operates these nonbanking businesses. Holding companies also allow banks to circumvent branching restrictions, simply by the acquisition of a bank in the forbidden area. It should be noted that the Bank Holding Company Act of 1956 and the subsequent amendments of 1970 provide for regulation of all activities of all bank holding companies. The Federal Reserve has the authority to strictly regulate all significant matters with regard to what the holding companies can actually do.

Fundamental Operations of a Bank

The general nature of any bank is to take in funds on the one hand and to invest them on the other hand. A bank tries to do this in such a way as to optimize the return-risk tradeoff. Constraints are faced in the form of needs for solvency and liquidity.

Raising and Using Funds. It was noted at the outset that banks have a number of sources of funds: demand deposits, time and savings deposits, capital accounts, and miscellaneous sources. Each of these has different characteristics; for example, demand deposits have a significantly larger legal reserve requirement than do time deposits. A simple technique for the bank to follow is to pool all the funds it acquires for allocation.[2] Under this *pool-of-funds approach*, funds are allocated to meet specific needs and objectives, regardless of the source of the funds. However, because of the rapid growth of time deposits (with their lower reserve requirements) in the last 20 years, an alternative approach has been suggested—the *asset-allocation approach*. Under this alternative, banks consider their sources of funds in relation to such factors as legal requirements and rapidity of turnover, and they match different sources with different uses (each source has more than one use).

Traditionally, the first requirement of a bank in allocating funds has been to provide for liquidity. The assets set aside specifically for this have often been referred to as *primary reserves*.[3] The distinguishing characteristic of these funds is that they are available instantly to meet liquidity needs created by, for example, unexpected withdrawals. Primary reserves include vault cash, deposits at other banks or at the Fed, correspondent balances, and cash items in process of collection. These assets do not earn interest, so that the bank immediately faces one of the many tradeoffs that always exist in the financial system. This tradeoff is liquidity versus profitability, since the less funds are held in primary reserves, the more are available to be used in an earning capacity, but they are available at a cost in terms of liquidity needed to meet adverse circumstances.

Next, banks have traditionally allocated funds to *secondary reserves*. These consist of very liquid assets, which can quickly be converted into cash with minimum risk, and which also earn a return. Thus secondary reserves are a back-up for primary reserves: they are assets the bank can fall back upon if the need arises but which, in the meantime, earn a return. Highly liquid investment securities—typically, short-term Treasury securities—make up secondary reserves.

Since loans represent the real profit potential for a bank, and since banks are in business to loan money, funds are next allocated for loans. As

---

[2]The discussion in this section is indebted to Edward Reed, Richard Cotter, Edward Gill, and Richard Smith, *Commercial Banking* (Englewood Cliffs, N.J.: Prentice-Hall, Inc., 1976), pp. 105–111.

[3]The term *primary reserves* does not appear on the balance sheet of a commercial bank.

we saw in Table 13–1, loans represent the largest single part of the asset side of the balance sheet. Here banks face their greatest risk of losses, since some loans will subsequently be in default.

Finally, banks can allocate funds to the investment portfolio in a residual fashion. Investments provide income on reserves that would otherwise be idle, since the bank either cannot or is not willing to lend them because of the risk. Although the investment portfolio earns less than the loan portfolio, it provides greater liquidity and less risk.

The above allocation scheme is essentially that of the pool-of-funds approach. Under an asset-allocation approach, each source of funds (demand deposits, time deposits, etc.) is allocated independently. Capital accounts, for example, are permanent long-term funds that can be safely allocated to long-term loans, capital improvements, etc. Demand deposits, on the other hand, are highly volatile and require the highest legal reserves. They are usually allocated to primary reserves first and then to secondary reserves.

Making a Profit. We can see from the above analysis that banks have the characteristics of financial intermediaries as outlined in chapter 12. First of all, they simultaneously and continuously borrow and lend funds. Every day, money is deposited in most banks by many individuals, and, every day, money is withdrawn from all types of accounts. At the same time, a bank is usually making new loans and investments even as existing loans and securities mature. Banks are often expanding in size, too, which generates new opportunities for the aquisition of assets.

Second, like any other intermediary, banks profit by the spread between the return on the primary securities they purchase and the cost of their indirect securities (plus the cost of their operations). Third, in seeking to profit by this action, banks (like all intermediaries) help to make markets efficient. Borrowers obtain a lower cost than they otherwise could if they had to borrow from less expert lenders, who could less well assume the inherent risk. And savers-lenders benefit by receiving the indirect claims they most desire. After all, virtually every household wants the convenience of a checking account.

Exactly how do banks earn a return from their intermediation actions? On the one hand, their costs consist primarily of personnel costs, interest costs (the cost of all funds), and miscellaneous expenses.[4] Currently, the cost of funds is the largest category, approximating one-half of all expenses. On the other hand, their revenues are derived from loans and investments and from charges for services. Loan revenues approximate two-thirds of all revenues, with investment revenues

---

[4]This discussion is based on 1977 data. See *Annual Report of the Federal Deposit Insurance Corporation 1977*, Federal Deposit Insurance Corporation, Washington, D.C., August 15, 1978, pp. 153–183.

amounting to about one-fourth of the total. Earnings have been around 1 percent of assets. However, banks are highly leveraged, so that the return to invested capital in 1977 was over 12 percent. Leverage involves the use of fixed-cost sources of funds; therefore all net sums beyond the fixed cost accrue to the stockholders. Banks rely on borrowed funds, for which they pay a fixed cost, for more than 90 percent of their total financing. Although their expenses have risen quite sharply over time, their revenues have been rising almost as quickly.

Banks earn a return and remain in business because they can raise funds and employ them profitably. To remain in existence, a bank (or any financial intermediary) must allocate funds from the ultimate saver (lender) to the ultimate borrower at a lesser cost than what could be accomplished in a direct transaction. The intermediary must provide services on both sides of the transaction, and a bank clearly does. It is a fact that individuals who are able to borrow from banks for consumer or personal loans can usually do so more cheaply than they could elsewhere, except possibly from credit unions. It is equally true that (at least until the mid-1970s) demand deposits were only available from commercial banks and that millions of households desired the convenience of a commercial bank.

Adjusting to Regulation: Safety versus Performance. In allocating available funds and in seeking to make a profit, banks face severe regulatory constraints. Furthermore, these constraints actually conflict to some extent and involve a tradeoff between bank safety and optimal bank performance.

Perhaps the first issue to be considered is who does the regulating. A bank can be federally chartered or state-chartered. It can also choose to have the Federal Deposit Insurance Corporation (FDIC) insure its deposits, by which it incurs additional regulatory supervision. Of course, federal charters require membership in the Federal Reserve System, which involves stiff requirements in relation to state regulation (i.e., higher legal reserve requirements and less flexibility in what can be counted as legal reserves). In terms of numbers, most banks are state-chartered, nonmember, insured banks. Regardless of who does the regulating now, the banking environment is much improved—we no longer have bank panics, such as those that occurred in 1873, 1884, 1893, and 1907.

Bank regulatory authorities seek to insure the safety of the individual depositor as well as the safety of the banking system. A loss of confidence in the safety of banks could have a severe effect on our economy—at its worst, it could cause a collapse of the monetary system. Thus regulators have sought to provide a virtually failure-proof banking system.

One way in which regulators have sought to protect the banking system is to prohibit excessive, or cutthroat, competition for depositors and borrowers. It is believed that such competition could result in the failure of weak banks and an attendant loss of confidence; it could also result in excessive extension of credit, which could lead to a financial collapse. Regulations designed to limit competition include the prohibition of interest payments on demand deposits, ceilings on the interest payable on time deposits, reserve requirements (which limit the total volume of credit banks can extend), and limits on the ability of banks to enter particular geographical market areas.

Another type of regulation to insure bank safety has taken the form of limitations on the types and amounts of assets that banks can acquire. For example, they are prohibited from owning common stocks, and the bonds that they hold must be of a certain quality rating; also, there are limits on the size of a loan to any one borrower and on real estate loans in general.

Bank regulation should ideally seek to insure, not only safety, but also optimal competitive performance, which would include the provision of services to users at the lowest cost and the provision of the highest returns to the providers of funds. This ideal cannot be obtained in practice; for example, it would be very difficult even to measure such performance. However, regulators do seek to insure a competitive environment for banks through controls on branch banking, mergers, holding companies, etc.

There is a tradeoff in the dual nature of bank regulations aimed at providing safety and optimal performance. If banks are prohibited from competing too aggressively for deposits (as they are in not being able to pay explicit interest on demand deposits), savers are denied one alternative as they seek to achieve the highest returns on their savings. As another example, to the extent that banks are restricted in their branching activities, customers are denied the convenience, the ease of access, and possibly the differentiated services or costs that these particular banks might provide. Restrictions on the acquisition of assets can prohibit funds from being allocated to the highest-priority uses. Finally, excessive protection of banks can simply subsidize the inefficient and provide excess returns for the efficient.

Perhaps there is too much emphasis on safety. Despite the relatively large number of technical bank failures in 1975 (13) and 1976 (18), the banking business in modern times has the lowest failure rate of any business category in the United States.[5] Furthermore, the insuring of deposits through the FDIC has prevented virtually all losses to depositors from insured banks that fail. (FDIC policy is to reorganize or merge the endangered bank, to try to prevent actual failure. This avoids the actual liquidation process, which would be troublesome to depositors and would tend to reduce confidence in the banking system.)

---

[5]Available empirical evidence suggests that the increase in bank failures in 1975–76 was primarily due to the severe recession. See Carl M. Gambs, "Bank Failures—An Historical Perspective," *Monthly Review*, Federal Reserve Bank of Kansas City, June 1977, pp. 10–20.

A good example of the tradeoff of safety versus competitive performance involves the question of capital adequacy. Bank capital (as measured both by the ratio of equity plus reserves to total assets and by the ratio of equity plus reserves to risk assets) reached a historical low in 1973–74. Current estimates are that banks will need to raise record amounts of capital to function effectively in the future; that is, they cannot acquire assets and fulfill their role as lenders unless they have an adequate capital base to support their other sources of funds. Thus bank regulators face a dilemma. On the one hand, they cannot in good conscience allow the capital ratios to decline any further because of the safety issue involved. On the other hand, current estimates are that banks will need to raise additional external capital by 1980 to finance a continuing growth in assets (which, after all, reflects the credit needs of the economy). If regulators require that banks build up their capital ratios from the recent low point, even more bank capital will need to be raised if the same growth in assets by 1980 is assumed.

One suggested solution to the capital adequacy problem is, first, to broaden the scope of deposit insurance to cover all deposits and, second, to establish for banks a variable fee structure tied to the degree of risk with which they operate (i.e., banks would be charged on a basis that fully compensated for excessive risk, which would reduce the worry over inadequate capital per se).[6] This approach would contribute to resolving the risk-performance tradeoff, since safety for depositors would be maintained, while banks would be permitted to concentrate on their competitive performance.

THE CHANGING NATURE OF BANKS AS INTERMEDIARIES

Having examined both the intermediation process in general and banks as intermediaries in particular, it is instructive to consider the evolving nature of intermediation, with particular reference to banks. Intermediation in the U.S. economy is constantly changing to adapt to new government regulations, the economic climate, the world financial situation, etc.

It is, of course, very desirable for intermediation to be a dynamic process rather than a static one. The job of the financial system is to allocate saving from those who have saved to those who wish to invest in real assets in an amount exceeding their own saving. The job of financial intermediaries, standing between savers and borrowers, is to take in funds from the former and to allocate them to the latter on a continuous basis.

---

[6]See Bruce J. Summers, "Bank Capital Adequacy: Perspectives and Prospects," *Economic Review*, Federal Reserve Bank of Richmond, vol. 63, July-August 1977, pp. 3–8.

As conditions change, so must the intermediaries if they are to do the best possible job. Unfortunately, as will be seen below, banks have sometimes evolved modes of operations that have produced negative effects, some of them quite serious. This section also examines how banks might evolve to meet the needs of the financial system of the future.

Bank Holding Companies

During the 1950s and the 1960s, many mergers took place, as individual banks sought ways to grow. Mergers, however, are subject to close regulation, provided for by the Bank Merger Act of 1960. Merger activity has decreased since then, as the most attractive opportunities were eliminated; also, branch banking regulations have impinged upon merger opportunities (since banks acquired in a merger become branches of the acquiring bank).

As mergers subsided, bank holding companies emerged. A holding company is a form of corporate organization that allows two or more businesses to operate within one controlling framework. In the case of banking, these businesses can be banks themselves, or they can be related firms. The parent company is formed to own the stock of the formerly separate businesses and is owned in turn by the stockholders of the two businesses. For example, Bank X and Bank Y can become a part of XY United if the stockholders of each trade the stock in their bank for shares of XY United itself. XY United can then proceed, subject to regulatory approvals, to acquire a third bank via a stock trade. XY United is an example of a multibank holding company. On the other hand, a one-bank holding company is a corporation that owns the stock of one bank. It might also acquire a firm engaged in a related activity (such as a data processing firm, which sells its services to those who need computer processing, or an insurance company that services the needs of bank borrowers, who are often required to have insured loans) or perhaps even a real estate investment trust (a spectacular phenomenon of the early 1970s, which resulted in even more spectacular failure, as we will see later).

The Bank Holding Company Act of 1956 permits only one-bank holding companies to acquire nonbank businesses, i.e., a holding company that owns only one bank may acquire nonbank firms. Companies that meet these restrictions have, in the past, aggressively diversified into a number of lines. Congress amended the Bank Holding Company Act in 1970 to better regulate one-bank holding companies and prevent conflicts of interest. It is easy to see that a holding company whose bank serves an entire community could exert unfair pressure on potential borrowers (who have no ready alternative) to utilize other services provided by the holding company. To prevent such practices, regulations control the activities in which holding companies can engage. These activities involve credit-card lending, mortgage lending, economic forecasting, issuing insurance (related to credit), data processing, industrial banking, leasing, factoring, forming trust companies, and a few others.

Although the holding company concept was once viewed as a way to achieve great banking success, it is no longer considered to be as good. Bankers argued that diversification was a beneficial activity and that they needed to provide many services to their customers. Also, they needed to guard against adverse circumstances resulting from their being limited to a narrow line of activity when conditions were unfavorable (e.g., bank earnings have traditionally been very closely correlated with interest rates). However, the holding company form of organization has neither stabilized nor contributed significantly to bank earnings. In fact, the non-banking activities of holding companies seem to have generated very small earnings (or none) through the mid-1970s. In 1975, for example, the net income from nonbanking operations amounted to less than 1.2 percent of the parent companies' earnings for the six largest banking companies in the United States.[7] Interestingly enough, many holding companies charge nonbanking expenses, not to the nonbanking subsidiaries themselves, but to the parent; this possibly overstates the earnings that are realized. Other holding companies with profitable nonbank subsidiaries have found that realized earnings on these operations are below expectations. Some bank holding companies have failed, primarily as a result of actions directly attributable to nonbank subsidiaries.

The Federal Reserve in mid-1974 instituted a slowdown of holding companies' activities in an attempt to strengthen the current activities of such companies. In just two years, 1974 and 1975, the Fed rejected 84 applications to form new holding companies (or to expand existing nonbank activities).[8] Presumably, as banks learn of the poor results that other holding companies have experienced, and if this poor performance continues, there will be fewer applications anyway.

In summary, the traditional form of bank intermediation has changed as banks have diversified into nonbank sources. Although holding companies have altered the face of banking forever, this trend has recently slowed down considerably because of problems. However, it may still portend significant changes for the future. For example, some bankers view it as the best way to realize interstate banking.[9]

Banks and REITs

In effect, a trust is very similar to a closed-end investment company, which is formed to invest in securities, and which in turn has a fixed

---

[7]See Edward P. Foldessy, "Holding-Firm Concept Turns Sour for Banks as Profits Fall Short," *The Wall Street Journal*, April 20, 1976, p. 1.

[8]*Ibid.*, p. 33.

[9]*Ibid.*

number of its own shares outstanding (in chapter 14, we discuss the open-end investment company—the mutual fund, which can issue any amount of its own stock to satisfy current investor demand). The Real Estate Investment Trust Act of 1960 made possible the flourishing of real estate investment trusts (REITs), which borrow funds and operate a "portfolio" of real estate activities. Their activities vary widely, depending on the types of REIT; some make construction and development loans, some own and manage property (equity trusts), and still others make long-term loans in the form of mortgages held on buildings of various types (mortgage REITs).

REITs are usually run by a management team that charges a fee—typically expressed as some percentage of assets managed—for its advisory services. The management group is often a bank, an insurance company, or a mortgage company. This connection allows banks (or other managers) to engage in mortgage lending through REITs, which broadens the intermediation function and therefore warrants our attention here.

Let us note here that REITs are part of the evolutionary process of bank intermediation. They represent a new type of intermediary, a good example of how our financial system continues to innovate to meet current needs. After the passage of the REIT Act of 1960, very few trusts were formed. Then, in the late 1960s, many were organized, because the tight money conditions during that time severely hampered real estate financing by conventional means. Roughly half of these REITs were independents, while the rest were sponsored by banks and other institutions. Thus, banks were sponsoring trust companies that specifically concentrated on real estate activities. These REITs were related to banks in several ways: they kept demand deposits at their banks and borrowed money from them; most importantly, the bank-sponsored REITs were managed by subsidiaries of bank holding companies. In some cases, they were simply the vehicle with which banks, by means of the holding company concept, carried out their mortgage activities. Again, bank intermediation had changed its format to accommodate what was viewed at the time as a favorable way to acquire and utilize funds. In effect, a bank-related REIT is an intermediary sponsored by an intermediary—raising funds by an initial equity sale plus subsequent borrowings via commercial paper, bank loans, etc., and using funds specifically for real estate activities. Clearly, this is an example of evolutionary intermediation.

REITs ran into real problems, starting in 1973–74, because of inflation (which hit the construction industry with the double shock of high interest rates and rapidly rising building costs), a decline in stock prices, and a shrinkage in national income. Hardest hit were the mortgage REITs, which depended heavily on the public sale of new equity, on the basis of which they borrowed money to raise funds. Banks had to loan their REIT affiliates billions of dollars, and REITs suddenly found themselves unable to service much of this debt. The losses involved have not been fully clarified, as banks are still trying to work out means of survival for some of the REITs. Banks have accepted lower interest rates on some of the debt, have restructured some of the debt, have stretched out some maturities, have traded debt for real assets held by the trust, or have simply written down (or have written off) some of the loans as losses.[10]

A problem for REITs in the late 1970s and early 1980s is that publicly held subordinated debt matures in those years. It is considered to be almost impossible that the REITs will be able to redeem their debt, so severe has been their collapse. The question is, what will happen to them as this debt matures? Increasingly, banks seem to be leaning to bankruptcy proceedings as the solution that is fairest to everyone, so that there is a good chance that a number of REITs will declare bankruptcy in the years ahead.[11]

The impact on banks of the spectacular decline of some of the REITs has been substantial. Bank-sponsored REITs often had names related to the names of the banks. Since banks are very conscious of their good names, they felt an obligation to do all they could to help the REITs survive.[12] The accommodations that they made were mentioned previously. But banks can do only so much for these trusts, because they could be subject to legal action from their own shareholders if they helped the trusts in a manner deemed unfair to their equity holders. It is said that, at the height of the crisis in 1974–75 banks relied heavily on the Fed to back them in their handling of the REIT problem. Their belief was that, to avoid major bankruptcies and their attendant problems, the Fed would lend to the banks if they needed funds to accommodate the REITs.

In conclusion, we have here an example of a new development in bank intermediation—the sponsoring of bank-related REITs and the massive lending to all REITs—that definitely turned out to be, on balance, a very negative affair, with both large actual losses and large potential losses. Whether this is an isolated example due to a combination of adverse circumstances occurring simultaneously, or whether it is a more pronounced case of unsuccessful innovation (like the case of bank holding companies), only time will tell. Clearly, such ventures do not support the idea that banks should strive to get far afield from the traditional concept of the basic banking unit (with or without branches), providing its basic intermediation function, as has existed for many years.

---

[10]See Philip Geer, "Grim Third Act Starting in Long-Running REIT Drama, *Financier,* May 1977, p. 26.

[11]*Ibid.*

[12]See Charles N. Stabler, "Problem Loans Follow Easy Credit, Causing Headaches for Bankers," *The Wall Street Journal,* August 20, 1975, p. 26.

New Trends in Lending

A good intermediary is one that can change with the times to meet new demands. If existing uses of funds are not adequate to utilize the funds raised and to meet the profit objective that banks have, new uses have to be developed. Of course, as the REIT situation illustrates, there is a potential for danger, in that banks can overdo it. The feeling seems to have been that they could not lose in real estate. Earnings had been good, land and building prices had been rising, everyone was making a lot of money—and yet the bottom fell out on the REITs, and banks suffered greatly.

One recent trend in banking is banks' attraction to second mortgages. Traditionally, this financial instrument was shunned by bankers, because its use implied a weak financial position for the issuer. A slack demand for business loans in 1976–77, however, forced banks to look elsewhere for an earnings outlet, and they developed a new interest in second mortgages.[13]

Second mortgages are secured by real estate, i.e., by an individual borrower's house. The amount of the mortgage can range up to 80 percent of the appraised value of the house minus the first mortgage. Maturities range up to 30 years, and interest rates are typically around 12 percent. Thus banks find second mortgages to be very attractive uses of funds.

Whether second mortgages will become even more important to banks in the future is not known. They certainly constitute a strong recent trend, and the high returns that are available will probably continue to attract more banks that are willing to borrow funds and to intermediate them in this manner. Some states still restrict or prohibit second mortgages, and national banks were prohibited from making them until 1974. However, as homeowners find that the rapidly rising value of their houses is their principal basis for borrowing and that they need larger loans because of inflation, demand should increase, and states will probably ease their restrictions.

New Trends in Demand Deposits

One of the major issues now confronting banks involves what is perhaps their most basic intermediation process—the raising of funds through demand deposits and the subsequent use of these funds in a variety of loans, investments, etc. The outcome of this unsettled issue will profoundly affect banks in terms of the intermediation activities they have traditionally performed.

Until recently, anyone wanting a checking account (demand deposit) had to open it with a commercial bank, which was prohibited by law from paying interest on these funds. Following a 1972 court decision, however, Congress exempted New England financial institutions from this prohibi-

---

[13]See "Second Mortgages Entice the Big Banks," *Business Week,* May 9, 1977, p. 49.

tion; they are allowed to pay what amounts to interest on a particular type of checking account. These so-called NOW accounts (negotiable orders of withdrawal) are offered by all of the thrift institutions, as well as the banks, in New England. Thus aside from paying interest on the funds deposited in NOW accounts, banks must compete with savings and loan associations, mutual savings banks, credit unions, etc., for this form of demand deposit. This is a radical departure from the past, and one that troubles bankers greatly. Table 13–2 shows the status of NOW accounts in New England from their beginning through mid-1977.

NOW-type accounts are expected to grow, because they offer consumers a return on funds that might otherwise remain idle. In late 1978, the Fed and the FDIC implemented an automatic transfer system, whereby banks would automatically transfer customers' funds from savings accounts to checking accounts to cover overdrafts or to maintain some minimum balance. Credit unions can now issue so-called share drafts, which transfer members' funds to another party—this amounts to checking privileges. The American Bankers Association, claiming that share drafts are illegal, sued the National Credit Union Administration on this issue.

There are numerous implications of the trend to competition for checking accounts and the trend to the payment of interest on them. First of all, the evidence to date indicates that bank earnings have been adversely affected in at least some New England states because of the NOW accounts. The impact would perhaps be greater except for the fact that large banks in New England derive only 7 percent of their funds from retail (individual) deposits.[14] However, a recent study predicts that retail deposits will become increasingly important to banks.

A second implication is the effect that this invasion on the traditional turf of bankers will have on membership in the Federal Reserve System. As we know, member banks control the bulk of demand deposits in this country; the Fed, in turn, is able to influence the money supply, and hence economic activity, through its control of member-bank reserves. Some banks, faced with competition from other financial institutions for deposits, and forced to pay interest on these accounts, have dropped out of the system. The savings are often very substantial for banks that drop out.[15] Of course, as more of them do so, the Fed has less direct influence on the money supply. Not only that, but the Fed has no control on the increasing

---

[14]See Neil Ulman, "Banks Vexed by Rivals That Now Pay Interest on Checking Accounts," *The Wall Street Journal,* November 10, 1976, p. 1.

[15]A bank that is trying to offset higher costs could drop out of the Federal Reserve System and be regulated by a particular state that allows some interest-bearing securities to be counted as reserves. Fed membership requires that reserves be held as vault cash or deposits at the Fed (which do not pay interest).

TABLE 13–2. NOW Account Activity in New England

Month Ended	Commercial Banks		Mutual Savings Banks		Savings and Loan Associations	
	Number of Banks offering NOWs	Outstanding balances ($thousands)	Number of MSBs offering NOWs	Outstanding balances ($thousands)	Number of S&Ls offering NOWs	Outstanding balances ($thousands)
September 1972[1]			23	$ 11,094		
December 1972[2]			59	45,272		
December 1973[2]			90	143,254		
December 1974[2]	63	$ 65,249	151	213,661	81	$ 33,666
December 1975[2]	134	358,940	175	386,560	121	93,756
December 1976	242	1,265,262	248	580,596	159	179,622
June 1977	247	1,501,135	250	661,760	158	213,498

Source: J. Lovati, "The Growing Similarity among Financial Institutions," *Review—Federal Reserve Bank of St. Louis*, October 1977, p. 10.

Note: Based on data from The Federal Reserve Bank of Boston.
[1]Massachusetts only
[2]Massachusetts and New Hampshire only.

number of thrift institutions that now offer checking accounts, because they do not keep reserves on deposit at the Fed.

One proposed countermeasure to the problem of declining Fed membership and commercial banks' loss of funds is that both the banks and the Fed should do some "unbundling" in their pricing of services, much as the brokerage industry has done for securities. This means that banks would restructure their costs for services on the basis of their having to pay for demand deposits; until recently, the whole structure of bank costs was based on their not having to pay holders directly for the use of demand deposits. Checking accounts are expensive to service, and banks have traditionally not charged users the true costs of them. Small depositors could find themselves paying more for their checking privileges under the new format than they do now. As for the Fed, it now pays no interest on bank reserves deposited with it. New proposals have suggested that the Fed could pay interest on these deposits but could also charge for the use of its check-clearing facilities. Another solution here could be that thrift institutions also be required to hold reserves at the Fed—a proposal that bankers find appealing.

A third implication of this new trend in banking is perhaps the most obvious: the nature of bank intermediation will change. Banks will have to attract funds from different sources, perhaps by means of a different form of indirect claim than what is now offered. They will emphasize some services that they do not now emphasize, such as clearing services for "checks" issued by thrift institutions; in fact, this is now being done by some banks. The movement to electronic banking may well accelerate. This involves the electronic transfer of money, as opposed to the writing of conventional checks. This movement is already under way, but it is constrained by federal regulations that prohibit branching by federally chartered banks if state laws prohibit it, since electronic equipment in retail outlets is considered a branch bank. Some states, such as Massachusetts, do not consider these outlets to be branches, so that some banks are moving along these lines. Initially, they are offering check verification systems, but such operations can easily be expanded to do much more.

In summary, new innovations in the financial system, such as competition for demand deposits, promise to make significant changes in the traditional operations of banks. They will continue to be intermediaries in the full sense of the word, and they will continue to be important intermediaries, but the intermediation process will clearly be different, involving both new sources and new uses of funds.

SUMMARY

Commercial banks are the largest single category of financial intermediaries as measured by total assets. They clearly affect the financial lives of almost everyone. As such, their nature and their role as intermediaries deserves special attention. This chapter has sought to examine in detail several aspects of banks in this role.

A logical beginning in an examination of banks as intermediaries is an analysis of their sources and uses of funds on an aggregate basis. Demand deposits and time deposits together comprised 80 percent of total sources in 1977; therefore banks raise most of their funds from volatile short-term sources. Nondeposit sources of funds include primarily capital accounts and secondarily such sources as advances from the Fed, Eurodollar borrowings, and federal funds purchased.

Major uses of funds include bank cash balances, loans, and securities. Bank cash balances include vault cash, deposits at Federal Reserve banks and at other commercial banks, and checks in process of collection. Loans comprise more than half of all assets, because banks are in business basically to loan money. Major borrowers include the business sector and individuals who need mortgages or various types of consumer loans. Finally, banks invest in securities to the extent that funds are not needed for loans or net withdrawals. Net returns are generally lower on investments than on loans. The largest category in the investment portfolio is municipal (state and local) securities.

To examine banks' functioning as intermediaries, it is useful to review the basic nature of banking. Banks are in the business of assuming risks. As is the case with any intermediary, they simultaneously take in funds and use funds. They can employ various strategies of asset and liability management. Two approaches available for the allocation of funds are the pool-of-funds approach and the asset-allocation approach. Ultimately, banks must provide for liquidity with primary and secondary reserves and then allocate the remaining funds to loan and investment opportunities (presumably in that order). They profit, like any other intermediary, by the spread between the returns on the assets they obtain and the cost of their funds plus the cost of doing business. Banks do face severe regulatory constraints, which involve tradeoffs between safety and optimal performance.

The nature of bank intermediation has changed and continues to change. Good examples of structural change are the formation of bank holding companies and bank-sponsored real estate investment trusts, neither of which proved to be too successful in many cases. There are new trends in lending, such as banks' interest in second mortgages, and new trends in demand deposits, such as the automatic transfer of savings to checking accounts (in effect, indirectly paying interest on demand deposits) and the move to electronic banking. Clearly, banks will continue to be important intermediaries, but they will be different intermediaries than what they were in the past, with both new sources and new uses of funds.

Appendix 13A

The Uniqueness of Banks

Our discussion of banks as intermediaries should have convinced you that the banking system is important. Just how important it is bears scrutiny, and, in that regard, financial market analysts have long been concerned with assessing the degree of uniqueness of commercial banks. In many respects, banks are like other financial institutions: as we have seen, they accept deposits, which are a safe and accessible haven for the savings of surplus units, and they provide financing for deficit units by the extension of negotiated loans and by investment in securities. In some respects, however, banks are quite different from other financial institutions, and the nature and importance of those differences merits close attention.

TRACE 13A–1.

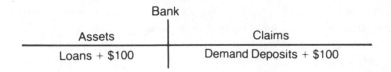

The argument that banks are truly unique in important ways can be understood most easily from the processes of credit creation, by commercial banks on the one hand and by nonbank intermediaries (to be discussed in Chapter 14) on the other. To that end, consider the following illustrations. First, asume that a bank is provided with $100 of excess reserves, which it chooses to lend; hence the bank increases its demand deposit obligations as it increases its loans, as is shown in balance-sheet Trace 13A–1. Note that, as we have shown before, this bank has acquired a financial claim (the loan) by creating a financial claim against itself (the demand deposit). After checks have been drawn against this $100 deposit and have ultimately been deposited elsewhere, the summary balance-sheet adjustments that will have occurred are shown in Trace 13A–2.

TRACE 13A–2.

Banking System			Nonfinancial Public	
Assets	Claims		Assets	Claims
Loans + $100	Demand Deposits + $100		Money + $100	Debt + $100

Overall Financial System	
Assets	Claims
Loans to the nonfinancial public + $100	Demand deposits held by the nonprofessional public + $100

With a fractional reserve system, part of the $100 of excess reserves will now be absorbed in required reserves ($20 with a 20% reserve ratio), and part will remain available to the banking system, which provides a continued increase in the total volume of deposit obligations as banks extend loans (ultimately, this volume is by a multiple of the original $100 of excess reserves).

Contrast these results with the impact on money supply and credit extended of the provision of $100 of *surplus* and lendable reserves to a nonbank intermediary—say, a savings and loan association. Typically, an S & L holds the bulk of its reserve funds on deposit in commercial banks. When the S & L extends a loan, it does so by making out a check to the borrower in the amount of the loan. The borrower can be expected to deposit the check proceeds in a bank account, which can be drawn on, so that deposits are shifted from the S & L to the nonbank public's possession. Trace 13A–3 illustrates the results of this set of transactions for a $100 loan. In this case, the financial institution (the S & L) that had surplus reserves managed to acquire a financial claim (the loan), but, in return, it had to give up another financial claim (money), which constituted its lendable reserves. *This is important, because the lendable reserves lost by one S & L are generally lost to the entire system of S & Ls.* There is little chance that

TRACE 13A–3.

Savings & Loan Association

Assets	Claims
Cash reserves − $100	
Loans + $100	

Banking System

Assets	Claims
	Demand deposits held by the nonfinancial public + $100
	Demand deposits held by the S & L − $100

Nonfinancial Public

Assets	Claims
Money + $100	Debt + $100

Overall Financial System

Assets	Claims
Loans to the nonfinancial public +$100	Demand deposits held by the nonfinancial public + $100

any sizable portion of the funds withdrawn from one S & L will be redeposited in others. Clearly, this makes S & Ls (and, likewise, other nonbank financial intermediaries) different from banks, since the bulk of the reserve funds withdrawn from one lending bank can be expected to be redeposited in other banks. With this background, we can now focus attention on the unique attributes of banks, and we can assess the importance of those attributes.

The Creation of Money

Our balance sheet traces for the commercial bank loan of $100 shows that the publicly held money stock (in the form of demand deposits) increased by $100 as that loan was extended. And, we know that, as the

$100 of new demand deposits are spent and reappear in other banks, a further expansion of the money supply will take place. As long as money is defined narrowly as currency and demand deposits (M_1)), or slightly more broadly (M_2) as currency, demand deposits, and time deposits in commercial banks (exclusive of large CDs), only banks can create claims against themselves that serve as money. Moreover, throughout the system as a whole, they can create those monetary claims in an amount that is a multiple of the reserve base that they are provided.

Whether this unique ability to create what we have labeled monetary claims is important or not is dictated by the importance of money as we have defined it. Most analysts agree that money is important—that changes in the quantity of money cause systematic changes in economic activity, with an increase in the money stock stimulating the economy and a reduction in the money stock slowing economic activity. Hence, the ability of banks to acquire assets by creating money claims against themselves must be judged an important distinction, particularly since the central bank can, by exercising control over the volume of money banks provide, influence the economy.

The Extension of Credit

Banks are unique, too, in their capacity to mobilize reserves in the extension of credit. As the illustration above shows, with $100 of surplus reserves, the S & L system can extend only $100 of new credit, for, with that volume of loans, the S & L system loses the $100 of surplus reserves. Borrowers from the S & L acquire title to demand deposits in commercial banks and can transfer title to those deposits by writing checks, which makes the existing money supply work a bit harder (as it turns over more frequently for financing purchases). But no additional credit creation by banks is generated and, hence, no new money is created.

In contrast, if a commercial bank with $100 of excess reserves lends those reserves, the $100 of new credit (and created money) represents merely the first stage in an expansion process that results in the extension of a volume of credit that is a multiple of the initial excess reserves. Moreover, after the bank credit expansion process (which simultaneously increases the volume of demand deposits), if the public chooses to restore its original proportional mix of demand deposits and savings and loan accounts by making deposits in S & Ls, it provides funds that the S & Ls are apt to lend out. This adds another layer to the tier of credit created on the basis of $100 of excess reserves in a commercial bank.

Undeniably, banks are a potent force in the financial marketplace, as they enjoy capacities that nonbank financial institutions do not possess. The basic reason for banks' unique importance is that their deposit liabilities are money, serving as a medium of exchange for all segments of the economy, *including* nonbank financial institutions, which hold the bulk of their reserves in bank deposits. To the extent that ongoing evolutionary changes in the structure of the financial system change the privileges accorded to nonbank financial intermediaries so that they will function more like commercial banks, the uniqueness of banks will dissipate. But, for the present, banks remain in a class of their own in terms of the clout they yield in financial markets as creators of credit and money.

14

Nonbank Intermediaries

In studying the financial system, we must pay close attention to financial intermediaries other than banks. Although commercial banks are the largest single category of private intermediaries (as measured by total assets), the remaining financial intermediaries are very significant forces in our economy. They influence the economy's growth path by their effect on the amount of saving, and they influence the allocation of that saving to alternative investment uses. Also, they can affect the Fed's ability to influence the economy.

This chapter will continue the classification of intermediaries by levels. The second level to be discussed is the thrifts—savings and loan associations, mutual savings banks, and credit unions—so called because, like banks, they are depository intermediaries; i.e., they generate deposit-like claims that are held by other sectors, principally the household sector. These claims are very liquid, as they are typically payable on demand (or with very short notice) or have short, specified maturities. Because of these features, the thrifts, just like commercial banks, must place more emphasis on liquidity in their portfolio decisions than do other nonbank intermediaries.

The third level to be discussed is all other intermediaries. We will separate these into three groups. Because of its different nature, we will discuss a direct intermediary, investment companies, first.

This third group of nonbank intermediaries to be discussed within our classification system also includes insurance companies, private noninsured pension funds, property and casualty insurance companies, and finance companies. The first two—the insurance companies and the pension funds—are *contractual intermediaries*, reflecting the existence of a special contractual arrangement between the institution and the recipients of its services. A life insurance policy, for example, is a contract, guaranteeing certain payoffs in exchange for specified premiums. The remaining two members of this category will simply be called *other specialized intermediaries.*[1]

Relative Sizes of Nonbank Intermediaries

To gauge the relative sizes (as measured by total assets) of these nonbank intermediaries, both in comparison to each other and to commercial banks, consider Table 14–1. Note, again, that commercial banks dominate every other intermediary or group of intermediaries. For example, the assets of the thrifts combined amount to only about 64 percent of those of commercial banks. The other intermediaries are a little larger, but their assets still amount to only about 76 percent of those of commercial banks. Finally, the table shows that direct intermediary assets are only a very small fraction of bank assets.

As for the institutions within the three nonbank groups distinguished in the table, savings and loan associations are the largest (but are still less than half the size of banks), and life insurance companies are the second largest, being about one-third the size of banks. There is a considerable drop to the third largest nonbank intermediary listed here, the private noninsured pension funds.

THE THRIFTS

The relative importance of commercial banks versus the three types of thrifts in terms of savings accounts for 1966 and 1976 is shown in Figure 14–1.[2] The rapid growth of banks is clearly shown. However, the thrift

---

[1]REITs could be included here as one of the other specialized intermediaries. Since they were considered in some detail in the previous chapter, and since they are really quite small in terms of total assets, they are omitted.

[2]To the extent that any claims are similar to, say, a commercial bank's savings deposits, their issuance qualifies as a thrift activity. Although it is not an intermediary in the normal sense, the government conducts activities that, in this regard, are similar to those of the thrifts. Savings bonds represent a way in which the government taps household savings through the issuance of claims on itself. These programs originated out of the necessity to help finance the tremendous costs of World War II. Today, the issuance of savings bonds continues to raise funds, as they provide the purchaser (the bond-holder) with a virtually risk-free asset that can be quickly liquidated and that pays a clearly defined rate of interest while the bond is held. Savings bonds totaled $80 billion in 1978.

Savings bonds are not marketable and can be transferred only at death. They can be redeemed at financial institutions. There are two basic types of savings bonds, E bonds and H bonds. The former are sold at discount, the latter at par value. E bond denominations run as small as $50; for H bonds, the minimum is $500. Holders of E bonds earn interest if they

TABLE 14–1. Total Financial Assets of Commercial Banks and Nonbank Financial Intermediaries, Preliminary Year-end 1978 (in billions dollars)

Commercial banks	1151
THRIFTS	
Savings and loan associations	524
Mutual savings banks	159
Credit unions	58
Total	741
DIRECT INTERMEDIARIES	
Open-end investment companies	44
Closed-end investment companies[1]	3
Total	47
OTHER INTERMEDIARIES	
Life insurance companies	378
Private noninsured pension funds	208
Property and casualty insurance companies	126
Finance companies	146
Total	858

Source: Board of Governors of the Federal Reserve System, *Flow of Funds 1978 Outstandings (Preliminary), February 1979.*

[1] As of June 30, 1977.

intermediaries now control significant amounts of savings accounts and also are growing rapidly. For example, credit unions are growing at a faster rate than are banks, as can be seen in the figure. These trends reinforce the suspicion that, in the future, the relative proportions of savings accounts held by banks and by thrifts will be quite different from what they are now. At the end of this section, we will examine the growing similarity between banks and thrifts and will see how traditional relationships between them are changing rapidly.

hold them to maturity, which has been shortened from time to time to increase the yield. They now yield 6 percent if held five years and five months. Rates on both are generally similar to those offered by other savings-type claims, so that savings bonds provide a ready alternative to bank and thrift claims. Some savers feel more comfortable knowing that the federal government provides the backing for these bonds, and hence they view them as superior to claims offered by institutions. Sales amounted to $8 billion in 1978.

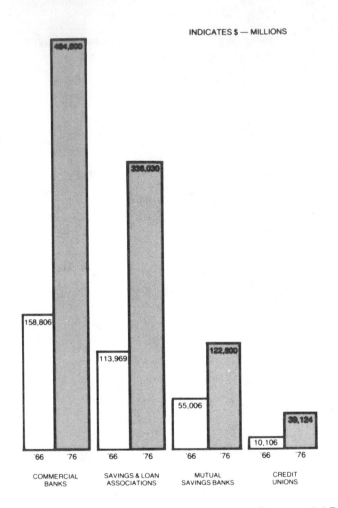

INDICATES $ — MILLIONS

484,800

336,030

158,806

113,969

122,800

55,006

38,124

10,106

'66   '76   '66   '76   '66   '76   '66   '76

COMMERCIAL
BANKS

SAVINGS & LOAN
ASSOCIATIONS

MUTUAL
SAVINGS BANKS

CREDIT
UNIONS

FIGURE 14–1. Savings Accounts in Commercial Banks and Thrifts, 1966 and 1976

(Source: *CUNA Yearbook 1977,* Credit Union National Association, Inc., Madison, Wisconsin, 1977, p. 5.)

Savings and Loan Associations

Savings and loan associations (S & Ls) originated to provide mortgage funds to potential house buyers who had no access to alternative credit sources.[3] Members of these mutual associations provided a savings pool

---

[3]In the past, S & Ls have often been referred to as *building and loan associations.*

from which funds were lent. The concept was eventually generalized in that the public was invited to participate. Savings and loan associations provided the bulk of the funds to build many of the towns that were settled in the westward development of the United States.

These institutions are now chartered by both the federal government and the state governments. Those that are federally chartered must belong to the Federal Savings and Loan Insurance Corporation (which is comparable to the Federal Deposit Insurance Corporation for commercial banks). Most S & Ls are owned by their depositors (i.e., they are mutuals), although there do exist some state-chartered stock S & Ls.[4]

S & Ls are managed by a board of directors elected by the depositors. Earnings are distributed quarterly, semiannually, or annually. Depositors receive interest, and shareholders (in stock associations) receive dividends. Of course, savers can withdraw funds easily—in the case of regular passbook accounts, at virtually any time.

S & Ls offer savers several alternative financial claims—regular passbook accounts, 90-day-notice accounts, savings certificates of various sizes and maturities, and special accounts (such as Christmas clubs). A recent innovation offered by some Northeastern S & Ls is NOW accounts, which were discussed in the previous chapter; these pay interest but allow the holder to write negotiable orders of withdrawal, which are, in effect, checks.

S & Ls operate as transformers of claims. Their sources of funds (their liabilities) are the deposits of savers. Their uses of funds (their assets) are the financial claims that they purchase from other sectors. They provide a service that is valuable to both sides of the market—otherwise, they would cease to exist. Imagine, for example, how inefficient it would be to try to borrow 30-year mortgage money from various sources, each of which lent only a fraction of the needed amount. Also, each of the individual lenders would assume considerable risk unless they diversified their holdings, which would be quite difficult unless each had considerable funds to invest. Since S & Ls own huge portfolios of mortgages, the overall risk that they assume is greatly reduced.

Mortgages constitute over 80 percent of the assets of S & Ls (refer to Table 12–1 for a consolidated balance sheet). These institutions are the dominant force in the mortgage market. They handle close to 50 percent of the home mortgages that are made; for example, at year-end 1978 S & Ls held $355 billion of the $758 billion of home mortgages.

---

[4]Since 1969, holders of savings deposit accounts in mutual S & Ls have been considered creditors with full voting rights and other privileges of shareholders. In stock associations, which are owned by regular stockholders, savers do not have ownership rights and privileges.

S & Ls must maintain liquidity because of the demand aspect—namely, withdrawal—of their sources of funds (i.e., their liabilities). To achieve liquidity, they hold cash and investment securities that are easily convertible into cash; also, members of the Federal Home Loan Bank System (FHLBS) can borrow funds in much the same way that commercial banks borrow from the Fed. The FHLBS sets the percentage of savings accounts and short-term borrowings that must be held in liquid assets. In April, 1978, the percentage was cut from 7.0 percent to 6.5 percent; this reduction is estimated to have freed an additional $2 billion for mortgage lending.

Mortgage monies have been very volatile in the past. For example, in the credit crunches of 1969 and 1973, investors withdrew funds from S & Ls to invest in alternatives that paid higher rates (i.e., disintermediation occurred). Mortgage rates soared for those who were still able to obtain mortgage funds. S & Ls now contend that they are less vulnerable to such drastic losses of funds, primarily because new regulations allow them to issue certificates of deposit with maturities ranging up to six years; additionally, S & Ls can now offer money market time deposits whose yields are tied to the current yield on Treasury bills. Also, since 1975, S & Ls can sell bonds that are secured by mortgages, and this provides additional funds to offset withdrawals. The continuing development of a secondary market for mortgages means that S & Ls can resell mortgages they hold, to raise additional funds. Finally, a new investment device, conventional mortgage pass-through certificates (called "*Connie Macs*"), issued by banks and S & Ls, provide buyers with income from a pro rata share of a pool of mortgages assembled by the issuers.

Mutual Savings Banks

Mutual savings banks (MSBs) are examples of a financial institution created out of humanitarian motives. In the early nineteenth century, a few citizens organized the first such bank in Philadelphia, to encourage workers to be thrifty and to provide them with a safe, income-yielding outlet for small amounts of savings. Such banks are governed by a board of trustees, usually at no pay. They are closely regulated by the various states. Day-to-day operations are directed by managers chosen by the trustees. All mutual savings banks are chartered and supervised by state governments and are owned by and operated for their depositors.

The approximately 500 MSBs have changed very little in the last 50 years. They are centered in the northeastern part of the United States, with a few scattered in six other, widely separated states. MSBs are by far the largest deposit intermediaries in terms of average assets per institution, averaging roughly four times the size of commercial banks and S & Ls.

Just as in the case of S & Ls, mutual savings banks' sources of funds (their liabilities) consist primarily of deposits from savers and secondarily of surplus, undivided profits, other minor capital accounts, and miscellaneous sources. Perhaps more than any other institution, they serve small savers. Their depositors do not wish to risk their funds directly in equities, bonds, mortgages, etc.; they would rather deposit small amounts of savings periodically, earn a return, and know that their savings are both safe and liquid. As for the banks' uses of funds (their liabilities), a mortgage borrower desiring funds wants to go to one source that is quick, efficient, and knowledgeable.

Mutual savings banks offer several ways to save, including passbook accounts, special-purpose accounts (such as Christmas clubs), and NOW accounts. Most of their funds are in passbook accounts, but current growth is in other deposit sources. MSBs are regulated as to the maximum interest rates they can pay, just as are S & Ls and commercial banks.

Their liabilities, consisting almost entirely of savings deposits, are very stable, because the typical saver deposits funds periodically over a long period of time. Also, limits on the size of individual deposits make it unlikely that large amounts would be withdrawn at any one time.

Because of the stability of their liabilities, MSBs can invest heavily in long-term mortgages; at year-end 1978, mortgages constituted about 60 percent of their assets. They also hold substantial amounts of corporate and agency bonds. To maintain their safety, much of the remainder of their assets is liquid holdings that can easily and quickly be converted to cash to meet withdrawal demands. Generally, MSBs must conform to guidelines laid out by state regulatory authorities, which specify the types and the amounts of assets that can be held.

Like other financial institutions, mutual savings banks are changing. They either now offer or will eventually offer a wide range of financial services to their depositors—checking accounts, credit cards, financial counseling, cash-dispensing machines operating 24 hours a day, etc. They are expanding their consumer loan activities, and some now serve as trustees for individual retirement plans. Table 14–2 shows the wide range of services of mutual savings banks in mid-1976, with the percentage of banks offering each service.

All of these trends reflect the dynamic nature of our economy and the fact that financial intermediaries must and do adapt to changing times. Yesterday's needs and services can become obsolete. If our economy is to continue to function soundly, and if financial intermediaries are to survive competitively, they must do everything possible to accommodate both savers and borrowers. The trends mentioned above indicate that even basically conservative institutions, such as MSBs, are making quite extensive changes to meet new conditions.

Credit Unions

Credit unions are a relatively new phenomenon, but, until recently, they have been quite similar to other deposit institutions. Savers deposit

TABLE 14–2. Selected Services Offered by Mutual Savings Banks

June 30, 1976

	Number of Mutual Savings Banks	Percent of Total
Automated teller facilities	59	12.4%
Checking accounts[1]	222	46.7
Club accounts	411	86.5
Collateral loans	410	86.3
Credit cards	79	16.6
Educational loans	376	79.2
Home improvement loans	447	94.1
24-hour cash dispensing	48	10.1
Individual Retirement Accounts[1]	379	79.8
Money orders	455	95.8
NOW accounts (interest bearing)[1]	254	53.5
Passbook loans	469	98.7
Pay-by-phone[2]	14	2.9
Payroll deductions	281	59.2
Personal loans[3]	369	77.7
Personal trust services	51	10.7
Point-of-sale services	7	1.5
Safe deposit boxes	378	79.6
Savings Bank Life Insurance	325	68.4
Savings payment plan	94	19.8
School savings	119	25.1
Self-employed retirement savings (Keogh)[1]	259	54.5
Travelers checks	453	95.4
Total number of mutual savings banks	475	

Source: Jean Lovati, "The Growing Similarity among Financial Institutions," *Review — Federal Reserve Bank of St. Louis,* October 1977, p. 10.

[1] As of December 31, 1976.
[2] As of June 1977.
[3] Includes overdraft loans.

funds (technically, they purchase shares) and acquire claims on credit unions, which in turn primarily purchase the claims of the household sector by making loans to it. Savers who belong to a credit union are supposed to have a common bond, i.e., they represent an identifiable group, such as the employees of a particular state or the military personnel of a particular military installation. A credit union lends only to members who have purchased shares.

Credit unions operate as nonprofit institutions. Each is separately organized and financed. If federally chartered, they are supervised by the National Credit Union Administration, which also administers a national credit union insurance fund for all federally chartered unions and for some state-chartered ones. More than 90 percent of all credit unions (through 51 member leagues) belong to the Credit Union National Association, the largest credit union service organization.

Credit unions specialize in lending to households, with about 76 percent of their assets devoted to consumer loans. They compete with other lenders that serve the same market—banks, retailers, and finance companies, but particularly commercial banks. Between 1970 and 1976, consumer loans grew at an average annual rate of 16 percent faster than banks. Such loans can be made at lower interest rates, because the fixed costs on them are lower as a result of the non-profit aspect of credit unions and such factors as cheaper payment collection costs (e.g., payroll deduction by the employer).

Credit unions maintain liquidity by holding demand and time deposits and government securities, just as do S & Ls and MSBs. Another source of funds to credit unions is new shareholders. Savings of members grew rapidly from 1970 to 1977 (over 16 percent a year on average), which provided new liquidity.

Credit unions now emphasize two objectives, both of which are of a service nature. First, they pay high interest rates to members for their savings—for example, during the last half of 1976, the North Carolina State Employees Credit Union paid 7 percent on savings accounts that are withdrawable on demand. This is a very high rate for accounts of this type, and no bank or S & L can come close to it on ordinary passbook accounts. Second, they provide loans at low rates to borrowers, who are also members, and credit unions are now striving to offer new services demanded by their members (e.g., share drafts and credit cards). Their overall objective is to serve all members to the maximum extent possible. Being a nonprofit institution, a credit union can do both—pay higher rates to savers and provide loans to borrowers at lower costs than what alternative institutions offer. Thus the spread between sources of funds and uses of funds can be and is quite small.

Credit unions are expanding their services and are the fastest-growing type of financial institution in the United States. Table 14–3 illustrates their rapid growth over a 30-year period. There are now more than 23,000 credit unions, involving over 30 million people, in the United States. Savings approximated $53 billion by the end of 1978, and loans to members were about $49 billion (total assets amounted to about $58 billion). Here again is a good example of what an intermediary does: it takes in funds on the one hand (in this case, members' savings) and invests them on the other hand (loans to members). The latter is a high percentage of the former, with the difference being mostly reserves for liquidity and safety and some investment in facilities. This arrangement facilitates an efficient, resourceful, and useful transformation process.

Credit union growth is largely attributable (on the source side) to the higher rates paid on savings and (on the use side) to the lower rates charged on loans in relation to the rates of banks or finance companies. The cheaper cost of loans from credit unions is illustrated by the changing proportion of auto loans and installment credit supplied by various sources of funds, which is shown in Table 14–4. Growth is also increasingly attributable to the expanding services being offered, including many that were once thought of only as bank services. Credit unions now offer what amounts to demand deposits in the form of *share drafts*, which can be paid to third parties through the credit union's account at a commercial bank. As a result of legislation passed in 1977, credit unions can now make mortgages with maturities up to 30 years and home improvement loans with maturities up to 15 years. Furthermore, in 1976, one of the leading bank credit cards, VISA, changed its membership rules to include credit unions, and a few of them have been approved to issue such cards. Credit unions are aggressively offering and advertising multiple services and are seeking legislation that will enable them to (1) offer trust, estate, and similar services and (2) offer members other types of deposits, such as certificates of deposit.

The Growing Similarity among Deposit Institutions

After our discussion of the largest deposit institutions, commercial banks, in chapter 13, and the nonbank deposit institutions in the first part of this chapter, it is now worthwhile to consider the relationships among these institutions. How are they alike, and how are they different? What new trends are taking place that will cause changes in both their overall operations and their relationships with each other?[5]

It is obvious from previous discussion that commercial banks, savings and loan associations, mutual savings banks, and credit unions perform a number of similar functions. Acting as intermediaries, they allocate savings to borrowers. Although each has its own identifiable characteristics, this group of institutions has become more alike in a number of ways. To examine this growing similarity in more detail, we will focus first on their assets and then on their liabilities.

The changes now occurring in asset composition for the nonbank

---

[5]The discussion in this section draws heavily from Jean Lovati, "The Growing Similarity among Financial Institutions," *Review—Federal Reserve Bank of St. Louis*, October 1977, pp. 2–11.

Table 14–3. United States Credit Union Operations, Selected Years, 1945–77

Year	Number of Credit Unions	Number of Members	Savings (Shares & Deposits) ($ Millions)	Loans Outstanding ($ Millions)	Reserves ($ Millions)	Assets ($ Millions)
1977p	22,385	36,309,367	$46,644	$40,361	$2,540	$53,169
1976	22,615	33,760,396	39,150	34,280	2,280	45,013
1975	22,769	31,435,417	33,108	28,221	1,997	37,964
1974	22,964	29,502,615	27,566	24,434	1,782	31,953
1973	22,999	27,488,416	24,669	21,771	1,572	28,418
1972	23,115	25,753,543	21,628	18,675	1,400	24,609
1971	23,284	24,094,257	18,367	16,164	1,246	21,134
1970	23,699	22,797,193	15,492	14,108	1,190	17,960
1969	23,876	21,591,369	13,699	12,956	1,004	15,900
1968	23,406	20,264,487	12,324	11,284	861	14,210
1967	23,049	19,070,072	11,126	9,877	779	12,775
1966	22,686	17,897,351	10,106	9,093	682	11,606
1965	22,119	16,753,106	9,249	8,095	590	10,552
1964	21,944	15,623,336	8,242	7,046	510	9,361
1963	21,512	14,586,988	7,166	6,171	441	8,131
1962	21,021	13,762,047	6,331	5,477	381	7,186
1961	20,612	12,882,793	5,636	4,818	326	6,383
1960	20,456	12,037,533	4,975	4,377	272	5,653
1955	16,201	8,153,641	2,447	1,934	110	2,743
1950	10,591	4,610,278	850	680	52	1,005
1945	8,683	2,842,989	369	128	24	435

Source: *Credit Unions: Progress for People,* 1978 Yearbook, Credit Union National Association, back cover. *CUNA Yearbook 1977,* p. 25.

Table 14–4. Auto Loans and Installment Credit by Selected Lenders for Selected Years, 1966–76.

Installment Credit by Selected Lenders

	1966	1971	1972	1973	1974	1975	1976
Commercial banks	40.40%	46.04%	46.96%	49.09%	48.82%	48.52%	48.07%
Finance companies	33.65	25.96	25.20	24.18	23.30	22.62	22.32
Credit unions	10.65	13.27	13.28	13.39	14.23	15.63	17.15
Retailers	13.94	12.71	12.52	11.19	11.54	11.09	10.10
Misc. lenders	1.36	2.02	2.04	2.15	2.11	2.14	2.36

Share of Auto Loan Market by Selected Lenders

	1966	1971	1976
Banks	55.57%	59.70%	58.37%
Finance companies	32.36	24.74	21.59
Credit unions	12.07	15.56	20.04

Source: *CUNA Yearbook 1977,* Credit Union National Association, Inc., Madison, Wisconsin, pp. 5–6.

deposit institutions reflect their attempts to stabilize their deposit sources of funds. The instability is a result of two factors. First, deposits fluctuate because of disintermediation, whereby investors shift out of savings accounts and into other instruments when current short-term interest rates exceed the rates (imposed by regulatory authorities) that these institutions are allowed to pay.[6] Second, these nonbank institutions suffer from the problem of financing long-term assets (i.e., mortgages) with short-term liabilities (i.e., deposits). Their asset portfolios change only slightly each year as a result of mortgages being replaced. Therefore earnings usually fail to rise enough to offset increases in short-term rates, which causes an earnings squeeze. In response to these conditions, nonbank deposit institutions have altered the composition of their assets in several ways.

1. They emphasize shorter-term assets in their portfolios. Table 14–5 shows the distribution of assets for commercial banks and for thrifts and their annual rates of change for the periods from 1960 to 1970 and from 1970 to 1976. Clearly, investment securities, which usually have shorter maturities than mortgages, are growing in importance.

2. They emphasize the development of consumer loans, an action that often requires new regulatory powers. These developments include overdraft checking privileges and bank credit card services.

3. They emphasize variable-rate home mortgages, on which the interest rate is related to a cost-of-funds index. This type of mortgage allows these institutions to adjust more quickly to changes in interest rates.

Changes are also taking place in the deposit (liability) composition of the nonbank institutions.

1. Negotiable Orders of Withdrawal (NOW), started in 1972, are available in various forms from mutual savings banks, savings and loan associations, and commercial banks in all the New England states and from credit unions in 46 states. Although such accounts are currently restricted, changes have been proposed to make them available in all states.

---

[6]Commercial banks are not as vulnerable in this regard, because they have multiple sources of funds, which are more stable.

TABLE 14–5. Distribution of Assets for Commercial Banks and Thrift Institutions

	1960	1970	1976	Annual Rates of Change 1960–1970	Annual Rates of Change 1970–1976
	($millions)	($millions)	($millions)		
Commercial banks[1]					
Business loans	$43,132	$112,215	$177,128	10.0%	7.9%
Mortgages	28,694	73,053	149,276	9.8	12.7
Consumer loans	26,377	66,006	118,051	9.6	10.2
U.S. Treasury and agency securities	60,423	61,617	136,729	0.2	14.2
State & local securities	17,337	69,390	104,374	14.9	7.0
Other assets	80,360	194,070	318,462	9.2	8.6
Total	256,323	576,351	1,004,020	8.4	9.7
Savings & loan associations					
Mortgages	$60,070	$150,331	$323,130	9.6%	13.6%
Investment securities[2]	4,595	13,020	35,660	11.0	18.3
Other assets	6,811	12,832	33,209	6.5	17.2
Total	71,476	176,183	391,999	9.4	14.3

				8.0%	5.9%
Mutual savings banks					
Mortgages	$26,701	$ 57,775	$ 81,630	8.0%	5.9%
U.S. government securities	6,243	3,151	5,840	−6.6	10.8
State & local securities	672	197	2,417	−11.6	51.9
Corporate and other securities	5,076	12,876	33,793	9.8	17.5
Other assets	1,878	4,996	11,131	10.3	14.3
Total	40,571	78,995	134,811	6.9	9.3
Credit unions					
Loans outstanding	$ 4,402	$ 14,152	$ 34,293	12.4%	15.9%
Other assets	1,257	3,798	10,542	11.7	18.6
Total	5,659	17,950	44,835	12.2	16.5

Source: Jean Lovati, "The Growing Similarity among Financial Institutions," *Review — Federal Reserve Bank of St. Louis*, October 1977, p. 3.

¹Insured banks.
²Includes cash.

2. Remote service units (RSUs), which are electronic terminals, allow depositors of thrift institutions to conduct numerous transactions quickly—withdrawing cash, making loan payments, or transferring funds from one account to another. RSUs have been located in many places for convenience. Such services differ little from demand deposits except that they pay explicit interest.

In summary, commercial banks, savings and loan associations, mutual savings banks, and credit unions are becoming more similar. The asset portfolios of these institutions are becoming more alike in that all now contain more short-term assets and all are concentrating more on consumer loans of various types. On the liabilities side, commercial banks no longer are the sole provider of demand deposits. All of the nonbank deposit institutions feature some kind of demand deposit service. Competition among these institutions is increasing, and their specialized activities are becoming more generalized. Regulations that once forced or encouraged specialization are being broken down. Table 14–6 traces the significant institutional changes since 1970 that have promoted competition among these institutions.

OTHER INTERMEDIARIES

The last level in our classification system is called simply other intermediaries. They are unlike the banks and thrifts because their sources of funds are not largely deposits of various types. We will consider them by groups, starting with a direct intermediary, investment companies. Two of these other intermediaries, insurance companies and pension funds, can be classified as contractual institutions. The remaining two, property and casualty insurance companies and finance companies, will be labelled other specialized intermediaries and discussed last.

In effect, a direct intermediary clearly and directly acts on behalf of its owners in whatever actions it takes. In the case of an investment company, the owners benefit from the diversification that they achieve when they buy shares in a large portfolio and from the full-time management that their portfolio receives.

Investment Companies

Investment companies are one of the best-known nonbank intermediaries.[7] Virtually everyone who is seriously interested in common

---

[7]This discussion is indebted to Charles P. Jones, Donald L. Tuttle, and Cherrill P. Heaton, *Essentials of Modern Investments* (New York: The Ronald Press Company, 1977), pp. 339–342.

stocks has heard of mutual funds (i.e., open-end investment companies, the dominant type of such intermediaries). Their activities are widely reported in the popular media. Fund salesmen are widespread, and mutual fund ads proliferate in many magazines, both financial and nonfinancial. The funds are required to issue reports describing their activities in considerable detail. They are regulated under the Investment Company Act of 1940.

Investment companies are called *open-end companies* if the number of shares that they themselves issue is not fixed; that is, these companies stand ready to redeem shares from existing stockholders at any time (shares must be sold back to the company). Also, depending upon demand, any number of new shares can be sold. Purchases and sales occur at net asset value per share, which is the total market value of a fund's portfolio (less any liabilities) divided by the number of shares outstanding of the investment company itself (in the case of sales, a commission is added). Thus a mutual fund—an open-end investment company—has an open-end capitalization subject to the forces of supply and demand.

There is a second type of investment company, called the *closed-end company*. Their shares are traded in the open market, just as are shares of any other publicly owned company. Also, like any other publicly traded share of stock, the value of a closed-end share is whatever investors are currently willing to pay. Current market price per share can be greater than, less than, or the same as net asset value per share. If it is greater, the shares are said to be selling *at a premium;* if it is less, they are said to be selling *at a discount.* Current market price and net asset value are almost always different.

Investment companies assess their owners (investors) for operating expenses, which include the management's fee. Buyers of load funds also pay an initial sales charge (*load charge*), and this cost (often from 7 percent to 9 percent of the amount invested) reduces the net invested by the buyer. However, there are a number of *no-load funds*, whose sales are conducted by mail, so that they do not charge a sales fee. Since the typical sales commission is 8½ percent, it is easy to see why no-load funds have increased in popularity: at the time of purchase, the buyer "gains" 8½ percent of an investment, in relation to what it would cost if it were purchased through a load fund. No-load funds now account for a sizable portion of mutual fund assets. The trend clearly favors them, and dozens of load funds have switched to being no-loads in the last few years. Empirical evidence shows that, on average, load funds do not outperform no-load funds (in fact, some evidence shows that they perform worse).[8]

---

[8]See, for example, Robert S. Carlson, "Aggregate Performance of Mutual Funds, 1948–67," *Journal of Financial and Quantitative Analysis,* March 1970, pp. 1–32.

Table 14–6. Selected Regulatory and Institutional Changes for Commercial Banks and Other Financial Institutions, 1970–77

DATE	COMMERCIAL BANKS	OTHER FINANCIAL INSTITUTIONS
September 1970		Savings and loan associations (S & Ls) are permitted to make preauthorized nonnegotiable transfers from savings accounts for household-related expenses.
June 1972		Massachusetts mutual savings banks (MSBs) begin to offer Negotiable Order of Withdrawal (NOW) accounts.
September 1972		New Hampshire MSBs begin to offer NOW accounts.
January 1974	All depository institutions in Massachusetts and New Hampshire (except credit unions) are authorized by Congressional actions to offer NOW accounts. This action limited interest-bearing negotiable deposits to these two states. Thus, interest-bearing negotiable transfer accounts at banks begin on an experimental basis.	
January 1974		Nebraska S & L begins Point-of-Sale (POS) electronic funds transfer system. First Federal S & L of Lincoln, Nebraska places an electronic terminal in a "Hinky Dinky Supermarket." The terminal allows customers of the S & L to pay for groceries, make deposits to, or withdrawals from their savings accounts.
April 1974	State of Washington enacts legislation which allows state-chartered commercial banks, MSBs, S & Ls to establish any number of automated facilities throughout the state, provided that those operating these facilities share the cost and operations of the terminals when asked to do so by the state authorities. Commercial banks are required to share facilities with other commercial banks and have the option of sharing them with thrift institutions. Thrifts are permitted, but not required to share facilities.	
May 1974		Experimental 24-hour electronic facility opens on a shared basis by 15 Washington MSBs and S & Ls.
June 1974		New York state bank regulation permits MSB to offer non-interest bearing NOW accounts (NINOWs).
August 1974		Administrator of the National Credit Union Administration grants 3 Federal credit unions temporary authority to

September 1974	begin offering share drafts. These 3 credit unions were joined by 2 state credit unions in a 6-month pilot program (launched October 1974.)	
December 1974	Pennsylvania Attorney General rules MSB may legally offer a form of negotiable order of withdrawal account. Federal Home Loan Bank Board (FHLBB) adopts a regulation which gives depositors traveling more than 50 miles from their homes access to their savings account balances through any other federally-insured S & L by means of a Travelers Convenience Withdrawal (wire or telephone access).	Comptroller of the Currency's interpretive ruling permits national banks to operate Customer-Bank Communications Terminals (CBCTs).
January 1975	California state-chartered S & L offers Variable Rate Mortgages (VRMs). Minnesota MSB introduces Pay-By-Phone service.	
April 1975	FHLBB adopts two regulations: 1). Authorized Federal S & Ls to offer their customers bill-paying service from interest-bearing savings accounts. 2). Allows Federal S & L service corporations and companies to make consumer loans (limited to states which allow such activity and subject to state restrictions).	Commercial banks are authorized to make transfers from a customer's savings account to a demand deposit account upon telephone order from the customer.
May 1975		CBCT operated exclusively by a national bank is subjected to a 50-mile geographical restriction unless CBCT is available to be shared with one or more deposit institutions. A national bank may use a CBCT established and operated by some other institution and may participate in a statewide EFTS system.
June 1975		Oregon governor signs into law legislation which allows the state's only MSB to offer checking accounts.

Table 14–6. (continued)

DATE	COMMERCIAL BANKS	OTHER FINANCIAL INSTITUTIONS
June 31, 1975	U.S. District Court Judge Robinson rules CBCTs authorized for national banks by the Comptroller of the Currency are illegal and must be shut down. (About 72 CBCTs, owned by national banks, have been installed in various parts of the country under the interpretive ruling issued by Comptroller December 12, 1974). Robinson's decision directly attacks the December 12, 1974 interpretation, calling the terminals branches, both as defined by the U.S. Supreme Court in its 1969 Plant City case and as construed by Congress when it passed the McFadden Act in 1928.	
September 1975	Commercial banks are authorized to make pre-authorized nonnegotiable transfers from a customer's saving account for any purpose. Previously (since 1962), such transfers were limited to mortgage-related payments.	Massachusetts MSB introduces VRM program.
October 1975		State legislation permits state-chartered thrift institutions in Maine to offer personal checking accounts.
November 1975	Federal Reserve amends definition of savings deposits in Regulations D and Q to permit business savings accounts, up to $150,000, at member banks.	
December 1975		State legislation permits thrift institutions in Connecticut to offer personal checking accounts.

While the authority to offer share drafts was still officially temporary, additional credit unions begin to offer share draft accounts following the end of the 6-month pilot program initiated in Fall 1974. |

January 1976	As of the year end, 222 credit unions (roughly 1 percent) in 44 states have been approved to offer share drafts to their shareholders.
	Federal Reserve System adopts a policy for automated check clearing systems (ACHs) to offer their services on a nondiscriminatory basis to all types of financial institutions.
	Illinois S & Ls begin offering noninterest bearing NOW accounts.
February 1976	Congress authorizes all depository institutions in New England to offer interest-paying NOW accounts (effective March 1, 1976).
	New York governor signs legislation permitting checking accounts, including over-draft privileges, at state-chartered MSBs and S & Ls.
May 1976	U.S. Court of Appeals for the District of Columbia upholds earlier ruling by the U.S. District Court for the District of Columbia that national banks' CBCTs are branches under the McFadden Act.
October 4, 1976	U.S. Supreme Court lets stand ruling that CBCTs are bank branches.
February 14, 1977	Iowa statewide electronic banking system begins operating and represents the nation's first shared statewide network, encompassing a broad range of large and small banks in Iowa. (At last count, the system had 33 participating banks; 92 merchant terminals operate through a switch or central computer.)
April 1977	All but 15 of the nation's 470 MSBs have either NOW accounts, traditional checking accounts, or a combination of the two.
	Legislation enacted to expand credit union lending authority, including authority to make 30-year mortgage loans.

Source: Jean Lovati, "The Growing Similarity among Financial Institutions," *Review — Federal Reserve Bank of St. Louis, October 1977, pp. 6"7.*

Investment companies blossomed and grew in the 1920s, did poorly from the early 1930s to the end of World War II, and then grew rapidly once more until the early 1970s. The closed-end form predominated at first but lost favor during the depression because of excessive leverage—i.e., the use of fixed-cost financing, such as debt securities on which interest must be paid—which often resulted in bankruptcy. Open-end funds completely dominate today.

Open-end investment company assets have grown rapidly since 1950. Although growth has been very rapid, however, it peaked in 1972, when, for the first time, more mutual fund shares were cashed in than were bought. Total assets have not recovered to the record set in that year and at the end of 1978, as shown in Table 14–1, amounted to about $44 billion.[9]

An investment company's portfolio depends on its stated objective, which must be broadly stated and adhered to by law. Classifications of mutual funds include common stock funds, which can be subdivided into maximum capital gain, growth, growth and income, and specialized; balanced; income; bonds and preferred stock; money market; and tax-free exchange. Approximately one-half of total mutual fund assets are in the form of common stock growth and growth and income funds. Mutual funds, on average, are very large, with over 40 percent of their total assets held in funds of $500 million or more.

Although exact portfolio composition depends upon a company's objective, on average 85 percent of the funds' assets are invested in common stocks, with perhaps one-half the remainder in corporate bonds and one-half in liquid assets (cash or government securities). Thus we have here an example of direct intermediation. Mutual funds raise their capital by the sale of shares of stock, and they invest these funds, primarily in a portfolio of the stocks of other companies. Individual investors can buy a life insurance policy only from an insurance company, but they can buy common stocks directly either from the issuing company (in a primary offering) or on the secondary market (this is the usual method); or, alternatively, they can buy shares in a mutual fund and thereby own a pro rata share of the portfolio of common stocks owned by the mutual fund. In effect, individuals can construct a portfolio for themselves or can simply buy a portfolio by the purchase of shares in a mutual fund.

This direct intermediary is different from virtually all other intermediaries we consider in this chapter, because transactions here involve no new primary securities. Investment companies deal with secondary markets and securities that already exist. Other intermediaries help to finance the economy through the purchase of primary securities, as hap-

---

[9]At mid-1978, open-end investment company assets amounted to over $49 billion. See *Federal Reserve Bulletin*, October 1978, p. A37.

pens when a savings and loan association or a mutual savings bank purchases a mortgage on a new house or when a credit union or a bank purchases a new IOU. However, the existence of mutual funds enhances the tapping of the total pool of savings, since they create another alternative for savers. Further, they enhance the efficiency of the secondary market for equities, and any action in this respect also improves the efficiency of the primary market for equities.

Contractual Savings Institutions

Contractual savings institutions, such as life insurance companies and pension funds, are identifiable both by their well-defined obligations and by their large and stable intake of funds. Liquidity is not as important for these intermediaries as it is for banks or the thrifts. They can estimate quite accurately their obligations, which change slowly from year to year and are based on actuarial considerations. Having estimated the outflows, these intermediaries are usually prepared to meet them, since they receive massive inflows of new funds through the collection of insurance premiums and pension contributions. In fact, investing their funds can be a significant problem to contractual savings institutions because of the tremendous amounts that flow in each month.

Contractual savings institutions represent another example of specialization by a financial intermediary to service a distinct need. Owners of life insurance policies do not want a claim on a bank or a credit union, etc. They want a secondary claim on an insurance company that will provide funds to their estate in the event of their death. Pension fund participants want a claim in the form of a stream of retirement income. It is efficient for an insurance company or a pension fund to pool the monthly (or quarterly, etc.) contributions of millions of individuals, diversify their risks, and tailor exactly the claim that each contract-holder desires. Simultaneously, it is efficient for these intermediaries to purchase large amounts of primary claims in the form of corporate bonds, equities, mortgages, etc. Borrowers can efficiently raise the money they want, and intermediaries can, in effect, channel the savings of millions of individuals into the financial markets. Clearly, this is a prime example of the transformation of claims and securities in a manner that is beneficial to savers and borrowers and that also earns returns for intermediaries, which accrue to the benefit of their participants.

Life Insurance Companies. Life insurance companies are the third largest institutional investor (based on total assets). Of the $30 billion increase in total assets in 1977, $2.6 billion represented a net loss in the valuation of assets already held and $32.7 billion was new funds. The life insurance companies supplied $29 billion in net investments in financial markets in 1977, to rank fifth among the major domestic institutional sources of funds.[10]

Life insurance companies incur future obligations in exchange for stated premium payments.[11] These payments are invested to earn at least enough to meet future contractual obligations. Actually, the rate of return earned (both current and projected) determines the amount of the premium payments that are charged to policyholders.

Life insurance companies are conservative investors, regulated closely by state regulators who emphasize safety of principal. Since companies licensed in New York dominate the industry, New York statutes form the basis for regulation across the country. For the most part, insurance companies are prohibited from owning common stocks (except for separate accounts) whose aggregate value exceeds 10 percent of assets (at cost) or 100 percent of surplus (whichever is less).

Although they are basically conservative, life insurance companies have gradually assumed a more aggressive posture. Like most of the other institutional investors, life insurance companies have become more concerned with performance, i.e., with maximum returns for the level of risk assumed. Also, the separate accounts maintained for pension plans and variable annuities are growing rapidly and can be invested entirely in common stocks since these funds are kept separate from other insurance company assets.

Over the period from 1967 to 1977, assets of U.S. life insurance companies almost doubled ($178 billion to $352 billion). The percentage of assets in government securities rose slightly from 6.2 percent to 6.7 percent, but the percentage in common stock increased more than 50 percent (to 9.6 percent). The percentage in mortgages dropped to 27.5 percent, and the percentage in corporate bonds rose slightly (to 39.2 percent). These latter two categories continue to account for the largest proportion of life insurance company investments, amounting to about 67 percent of assets by year-end 1977.

A large proportion of the assets of life insurance companies are invested in bonds and mortgages because of their conservative nature and their fixed obligations. Since most of their liabilities are long-term, they can take a buy-and-hold approach. Price fluctuations and marketability are not primary considerations because the timing of their cash outflows is actuarially predictable.

Insurance companies are an important intermediary in the financing

---

[10]All of these statistics are available in *Life Insurance Fact Book 1978*, a publication of the American Council of Life Insurance, 1850 K Street, N.W., Washington, D.C., p. 68.

[11]This discussion, and that of pension funds to follow, is indebted to Jones, Tuttle, and Heaton, pp. 335–338, 342–345 and to Henry A. Latané, Donald L. Tuttle, and Charles P. Jones, *Security Analysis and Portfolio Management* (New York: The Ronald Press Company, 1975), pp. 528–533, 537–545.

of real assets. They own over one-half of all corporate bonds outstanding, many of which are acquired in the form of private placements, whereby corporations sell their bonds directly to an insurance company. The insurance companies are able to negotiate on the terms of the bond and may therefore obtain a higher interest rate than that available in the open market. Corporate bonds were heavily purchased in 1977 and 1978, and amounted to about $160 billion at the beginning of 1979.

Mortgages remain an important category of assets because their yields are often higher than yields available from corporate bonds (even allowing for higher expenses). Mortgages were the second largest acquisition in 1977 and 1978, and amounted to over $105 billion at the beginning of 1979.

Insurance companies have traditionally minimized their investment in equities because of investment philosophies that centered on the ability to meet specific dollar liabilities. The growth in variable annuities and in equity funding of pension plans has caused a change in this situation.

Pension Funds. Pension funds (corporate trust funds) are one of the largest and most rapidly growing of the institutional investors. A retirement program, set up by an employer, represents funds designed to provide future retirement payments. The employer can make all of the contributions or can require that the employee pay part. There are two types of plans. An *insured pension fund* is a contract with an insurance company to provide retirement payments in return for the premium payments. A *private noninsured pension plan* involves the payment of company contributions to a trustee which invests the contributions and makes benefit payments. Trustee arrangements range from complete discretion for the trustee to very little discretion, in which case the trustee acts as a custodial agent.

Life insurance companies manage insured plans. A wide range of people and organizations manage private noninsured pension funds, including bank trust departments, other trustees (such as investment advisory firms), and perhaps even the employers. Banks still manage most noninsured pension funds, but, in this, they are subject to stiff competition. Independent investment counselors, brokerage houses, and open-end investment companies have all acquired new business at the expense of banks and insurance companies.

Private pension fund managers have shifted from fixed-income securities to stocks, and back again, in their pension fund investments. There is intense competition by investment management organizations to manage pension funds, which often leads to equity investments, but strict legislation in the form of The Employee Retirement Income Security Act of 1974 (ERISA) leads managers to favor more conservative investments. The traditional view of pension fund management was that they should earn specified amounts in order to meet future fixed liabilities. The modern (pre-ERISA) view is that future payouts are not predictable and therefore managers should maximize long-run returns consistent with cash flows, liquidity, and legal constraints. This shift in philosophy helps to explain the sharp shift to common stocks and the associated decline in corporate bonds and U.S. government securities up to the passing of ERISA. Since then there has been a small shift to fixed-income securities. Some pension fund managers have moved toward an active portfolio policy in an attempt to achieve better performance. The average portfolio turnover rate for the private noninsured pension funds increased dramatically in the late 1960s and early 1970s.

Other Specialized Intermediaries

Property and Casualty Insurance Companies. Property and casualty insurance companies provide financial protection against a wide range of risks, including fire, wind, hail, theft, auto damage, accident, and health. They can be organized as mutual companies, stock companies, cooperative nonprofit associations, or "domestic Lloyds" (which resemble the arrangements of Lloyds of London). They are, in fact, quite often stock companies.

These companies provide important services by the issuance of specialized contingent claims that most individuals want or must have. Their premium inflows may or may not offset their outflows in the form of claims and expenses. What they earn from their investments can help offset their expenses and provide a return.

Property and casualty insurance companies are not in the same category as life insurance companies and pension funds, because their obligations are not as easily forecasted, i.e., their payoffs are not as predictable as deaths (which are based on quite accurate actuarial tables). Liquidity needs are greater because of this uncertainty. To compensate for higher risks as a result of inflation or calamities, they seek larger returns through such investment as stocks. Thus they maintain greater liquidity than life insurance companies and take more risks in their investment activity.

In particular, these companies invest their funds with safety of principal and maximum income as their dual (and conflicting) objectives.[12] Bonds account for about half their assets, with common stocks constituting perhaps another 30 percent. Small amounts of mortgages, preferred stocks, etc., are held. The nature of their business—less predictable payments for claims than life insurance companies—means that they must be more liquid and invest for a somewhat shorter term than life insurance companies do. There is a wide range of investment portfolios among the property and casualty insurers because of the broad scope of their activities and because of their different forms of organization.

---

[12]This discussion is based on Federal Reserve Bank of Richmond, *Nonbank Financial Institutions,* October 1975, pp. 18–24.

Property and casualty insurers obtain their funds from two basic sources—premiums and investment income. Of course, any funds on hand are invested, generating additional sources. Also, premium income is large simply because of the volume of insurance in effect for all of the activities covered by these companies.

These companies typically have a net worth—labeled *earned surplus* —constituting perhaps one-third or two-fifths of their total liabilities. Preferred stock and bonds are generally not used to raise funds. Other liabilities include unearned premiums (collected premiums covering the unexpired part of a policy in force) and claim reserves (estimates of claim values currently pending plus an estimated amount).

Finance Companies. Finance companies have traditionally been classified into categories such as personal finance, business finance, etc., but these distinctions are no longer clear because of the mixed business that each typically does. For our purposes, finance companies range from local one-office enterprises to conglomerate companies with branches in many cities. Acting as specialized intermediaries, they provide services by raising funds and investing them in financial assets.

Finance companies raise their funds by the sale of commercial paper, by the tapping of the long-term debt markets, by borrowings from commercial banks, and from other miscellaneous sources. In 1978, corporate bonds and commercial paper amounted to $100 billion of their total liabilities of $142 billion.

Finance companies are primarily in the receivables business, and they compete very strongly for consumer installment business. In particular, household loans (consumer credit) are the largest single category of assets ($67 billion outstanding at the end of 1978). This category includes financing for autos and other durable goods and for personal loans. Loans to business run a close second and include loans to dealers in durable goods, financing for equipment used in business, leasing, and financing that provides working capital ($63 billion outstanding in 1978).

The regulation of these companies is of some interest. States often regulate finance company loans to consumers with regard to maximum interest rates and maturity of loans. However, there are few regulations on business loans. In a sense, the specialty of finance companies is their diversity, in such fields as commercial leasing and mobile-home financing, and their willingness to assume greater risks than other lenders do. It is often believed, with considerable justification, that borrowers who cannot otherwise obtain financing turn to finance companies. Of course, in return for assuming these greater risks, they charge higher interest rates.

There has been a declining trend in the number of finance companies because of mergers and liquidations. Also, there is very heavy concentration of business in a relatively small number of companies. Given an increase of almost $100 billion in total financial assets between 1967 and 1978, the smaller number of companies was growing significantly in average size. Along with the decline in the number of firms is the trend toward diversity in their lending activities.

In summary, finance companies are specialized intermediaries with regard to the risk they assume. Although they compete aggressively with banks and credit unions for consumer loans, they provide loan services to high-risk borrowers that other institutions cannot or will not handle. They represent a good example of the depth and the diversity of our financial markets, in the sense that we have many different intermediaries that provide a wide spectrum of lending activities while they attract funds from many different sources. In the next few years, finance companies will probably become even more aggressive in servicing new (for them) areas of need, such as business lending involving such specialties as leasing.

SUMMARY

This chapter explained and analyzed the nonbank intermediaries. The discussion centered on two groups of them—the thrift group, and other nonbank intermediaries. In terms of assets, banks dominate each of these groups.

Thrifts are depository institutions that are very similar to banks. They include savings and loan associations, mutual savings banks, and credit unions. Their sources of funds are primarily deposits, and their uses of funds include primarily mortgages in the case of savings and loan associations and mutual savings banks and consumer loans in the case of credit unions.

Asset growth for savings and loan associations and credit unions has been more rapid than that for banks since 1960, and credit unions have grown very rapidly in the 1970s. Actually, banks and thrifts are becoming more similar in their activities. There is a trend to shorter-term assets in the portfolios of thrifts, just as commercial banks emphasize short-term assets. There is also an increasing emphasis on consumer loans as competition among all of these institutions grows. Finally, all of the thrifts now provide some kind of demand deposit service, which was formerly the exclusive domain of commercial banks.

A direct intermediary conducts the same type of activities that its beneficiaries could provide for themselves directly. This category consists of investment companies, which hold portfolios of securities for their owners. Open-end companies (mutual funds) continuously buy and sell shares of themselves to the public; closed-end companies have a fixed number of shares outstanding, which are traded on some secondary market. Open-end companies predominate, and they grew rapidly through 1972. Such companies still represent one of the most popular ways for individuals to invest in securities.

The remaining nonbank intermediaries can be subdivided into contractual savings institutions and other specialized intermediaries. This group is larger than the thrifts, but not as large as commercial banks.

Contractual savings institutions include life insurance companies and pension funds. Both have well-defined obligations and large inflows of funds. Liquidity is not a problem for these intermediaries, as it is for banks and thrifts. In the past, life insurance companies have been very conservative, holding primarily mortgages and corporate bonds. They are now changing their philosophies so as to be more aggressive. Pension funds have also been conservative in the past, but they have gradually shifted from fixed-income securities to stocks.

Other specialized intermediaries include property and casualty insurance companies and finance companies. The former has liabilities that cannot be forecasted as easily as those of life insurance companies and pension funds. Such companies tend to emphasize liquidity because of the uncertainty involved. Funds are obtained from premiums and investment income. Finally, finance companies lend heavily to households and businesses. They obtain funds by selling their own paper in the money market, by selling bonds, and by borrowing from banks. Finance companies are distinguishable in that they lend to high-risk borrowers that other institutions cannot or will not service.

PART 5

The Financial System and the Economy

We have now completed a very comprehensive review of the most important components of the U.S. economy. Chapter 2 provided a brief review of the functioning of an important segment of the *real* sector of the economy—the market for goods and services—in which the economy's equilibrium levels of output, income, consumption and saving, investment, and government usage of resources are determined. Since chapter 2, we have focused our attention on money and on the financial markets, in which interest rates and the volumes of loanable funds flowing from surplus units to deficit units are determined. Chapter 8 showed that the forces that determine the general level of interest rates can be viewed as exerting their influence in the market for money or, equivalently, in the "bond" market, which represents all markets for income-yielding securities. Chapters 10 through 14 concentrated on the specialized instruments and institutions that make up the financial marketplace.

We are now ready to construct a comprehensive *macroeconomic* view of the economy. Such a view will take account of the interactions between money, financial markets, and the real sector of the economy. To attain the goal of visualizing the functioning of the overall economic system, it is necessary to sacrifice some detail. As an illustration of this sacrifice, we will no longer be involved in tracing the flow of saving through the intricate intermediation system—consisting of banks, thrift institutions, life insurance companies, pension funds, brokerage houses, and so on—which connects savers with the ultimate users of saving. Instead, we will restrict attention to such variables as the overall volume of saving, the general level of interest rates, and total expenditures in the economy as a whole. As a payoff for our sacrifice of detail, we will be able to identify the factors that result in the major maladies economic systems suffer from—such as excessive unemployment, anemic economic growth, and inflation; we will explain how those ills arise, and we will review the government policy actions that might be undertaken to relieve them.

Chapter 15 provides the basis for an analysis of the macroeconomy by construction of the most widely accepted simple macroeconomic model of a basically free market economy. Chapter 16 then refines that model with the addition of a market for labor services and applies the full model to account for the inflation and unemployment problems that developed economies suffer. The modern-day problem of "stagflation"—of inflation combined with a sluggish economy—is discussed in this chapter, and various possible policy actions for dealing with macroeconomic problems are examined. Chapter 17 provides extensive coverage of the real-world application of monetary and fiscal policies; it highlights the difficulties that emerge in their application and the disagreements that exist over the proper conduct of stabilization policy. Finally, Chapter 18 reviews the modern efforts to construct econometric models of complete economic systems and draws attention to the international linkages that a student of money, financial markets, and the real economy needs to be aware of.

15

Combining Money, Financial Markets, and the Real Economy

To take account of the systematic interactions of money, financial markets, and the real sectors of the economy, it is necessary to view income, employment, interest rates, the supply of money, the flow of credit, and the volumes of consumption, saving, and investment as simultaneously determined. For economywide, or *general, equilibrium*, all markets (i.e., the markets for money, bonds, goods and services, and labor) must be in equilibrium. If any one market is in disequilibrium, at least one other market must also be in disequilibrium; this reflects the interdependence of all markets.

The standard approach to combining the markets for goods and services (the commodity market) with the market for money, so that interactions between the two can be analyzed, involves construction of what is known as the *IS-LM* model. The main task of this chapter is to construct and apply that model to illustrate the manner in which a number of factors can be viewed as influencing the economy.

In its basic form, this model provides a simple view of the linkages between the markets for commodities and for money (and, by implication, for interest-bearing securities). It illuminates the major forces that influence output in the commodity market by altering aggregate demand, and those that influence interest rates by changing the supply of or the demand for money (and, by implication, securities). Moreover, the *IS-LM* framework is flexible enough to accommodate most of the complications we might want to introduce in the interest of realism.

The *IS-LM* model constructed in this chapter represents an economy with three sectors: the household, business, and government sectors. The household sector earns income, which it consumes and saves. The business sector produces final goods and services, generates income for households in the production process, and invests in physical assets to maintain and expand its capital stock. The government sector collects taxes and spends to provide government services. The foreign sector will be ignored in the formal development of the *IS-LM* model, as its inclusion would only complicate our discussion and would not contribute to an understanding of the interactions between money, financial markets, and the commodity markets. It is also noteworthy that the *IS-LM* model will be constructed on the assumption that the price level is constant. The implications of this convenient but unrealistic assumption and the consequences of relaxing it will be explained once we have completed our development of the model.

A GRAPHICAL REPRESENTATION OF WHAT WE KNOW

Figure 15–1 graphically portrays the component parts of the economy, which we have already analyzed, and which will be incorporated in the *IS-LM* model. Part (a) of that figure represents the market for money as it was developed in chapter 8. The money supply schedule (M/P) is shown with a positive slope, reflecting the increase in bank credit as interest rates rise and the possible public shift from currency to time deposits (which raises bank reserves) that higher interest rates might stimulate. The position of the money supply schedule depends on the volume of monetary base provided by the Fed and on the factors that determine the value of the money multiplier—notably, the reserve requirements imposed by the Fed and the portfolio mix of currency, demand deposits, and time deposits that the nonbank public chooses to hold. Remember that the money supply schedule is shifted rightward by such events as an increase in the monetary base, a reduction in reserve requirements, or a move out of currency and into time or demand deposits (it is shifted leftward, of course, by the contrary events).

The demand for money (M_D/P) is inversely related to interest rates; this reflects the interest-sensitivity of transactions-precautionary and/or speculative money demand. You should note that the money demand schedule flattens out at low interest rates and becomes steeper at high interest rates. The degree of interest-elasticity is important in determining how commodity and financial markets react to any disturbance, as will be shown later in this chapter.

The position of the money demand function depends crucially on the level of real output. By changing transactions-precautionary demand for money, an increase in real output shifts the money demand schedule rightward; a fall in output shifts it leftward.

Interest rate i_0 is shown to equate the real value of money in circulation with the real value of the demand for money. Of course, that interest

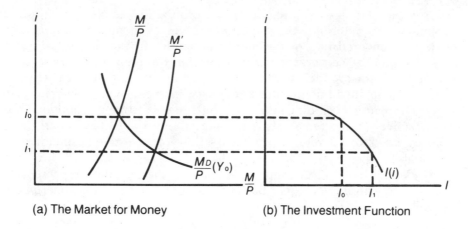

(a) The Market for Money   (b) The Investment Function

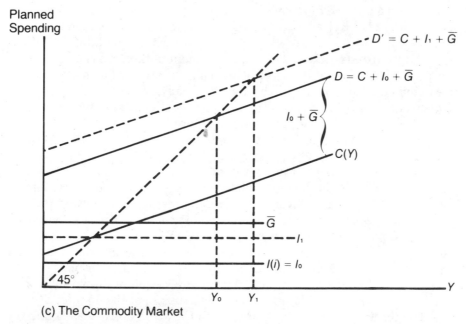

(c) The Commodity Market

FIGURE 15–1. A Two-Market Macroeconomic Model

rate must also permit the "bond" market (in which loanable funds are supplied and demanded) to be cleared if we are to have systemwide, or general, equilibrium.

Part (b) of Figure 15–1 provides a function representing business investment. That schedule portrays a negative relationship between the interest rate and investment (I), as the interest rate represents the opportunity cost of investing in real assets rather than financial assets. Businesses' expectations with regard to the profitability of the future use of capital assets determine the position of the investment schedule. If they expect a lowered rate of business profitability in the future (say, as a result of energy conservation legislation that threatens to raise the costs of doing business), the investment schedule shifts leftward, to reflect a reduction in investment outlays at every interest rate. Conversely, an improvement in business confidence shifts the investment schedule rightward. Given the expectations that determine the schedule in part (b) of the figure, interest rate i_0 provides a flow of investment spending in amount I_0.

Finally, part (c) of Figure 15–1 shows the schedule representing household consumption (C), business investment (I_0), and government purchases (G), which combine to constitute the aggregate demand for goods and services. As was argued in chapter 6, planned consumption outlays are a positive function of the after-tax, or disposable, income available to households. Hence, as total output or income (Y) rises in the economy, with only a part of the increase absorbed in additional taxes, consumption outlays rise as shown. Investment outlays are represented in part (c) of the figure at the level I_0, which is determined along the investment schedule in part (b) of the figure. Finally, government outlays are shown at the constant level $\bar{G}$. This constancy reflects the assumptions that the level of government spending is determined as a policy decision, ultimately made by the Congress, and that government outlays do not respond automatically to changes in output.

Vertically summing the consumption, investment, and government spending schedules in the figure yields an aggregate demand schedule ($D = C + I_0 + \bar{G}$). Along this schedule are the real values of output that the household, business, and government sectors combined plan to purchase, at every possible level of output and income. The level of planned spending is of fundamental importance, of course, because planned purchases must be equal to output if the economy is to be in equilibrium.

Identifying the output level that provides equilibrium in the market for goods and services is a simple task with the aid of the 45° identity line constructed in part (c) of the figure. With the same dollar scale along the horizontal and vertical axes of that graph, perpendicular lines drawn from the axes to any point on the 45° line indicate identical dollar values on both axes. Thus the value of total planned spending is obviously equal to the value of output at output level Y_0. With planned spending just matching output, there are no unplanned and unwanted changes in business inventories, which would serve as a signal that the business sector was producing too much or too little. Hence output level Y_0 is an equilibrium position in the commodity market—an observation that can easily be made with aid of the 45° identity line.

In contrast, if output were less than Y_0, planned spending would exceed output, so that there would be an unplanned and unwanted shrinkage of inventories. The business sector would read this as a signal that it was producing too little and, if possible, it would increase production. Hence output levels below Y_0 cannot provide commodity market equilibrium with aggregate demand at the level represented by schedule D. Comparable reasoning indicates that output levels above Y_0 also fail to provide commodity market equilibrium. At these higher output levels, planned spending would be less than output, which would result in an unplanned and unwanted expansion of inventories. The business sector would take this to be an indication that output was too large and would cut back on production.

If the state of expectations that determines the investment demand schedule and the money demand schedule corresponds to output level Y_0 in the commodity market, Figure 15–1 provides a completely satisfactory graphical representation of a simple model of the macroeconomy in general equilibrium. However, this graphical summary of the component parts of the macroeconomy is not as satisfactory for assessments of the full response of the economic system to any of the shocks it must endure. To illustrate that claim, suppose that equilibrium (at i_0, I_0, Y_0) were disturbed by a central bank purchase of securities that increases the supply of money. Were the real money supply schedule to shift to M'/P, the interest rate would have to fall to level i_1 for equilibrium to be maintained in the market for money. At that lower interest rate, the equilibrium volume of investment would be increased to I_1, and that increase in planned investment would raise equilibrium income to level Y_1. However, with income increased, the demand for money would be increased, raising the equilibrium interest rate at least part of the way back toward its initial level. In turn, with the interest rate raised, investment would be reduced, leading to a lower equilibrium level of income and hence a reduced demand for money and a lowered interest rate, and so it goes *ad infinitum*. Since developments in the commodity market cause adjustments in the market for money, and these in turn have feedback effects on the commodity market, the task of searching out the new equilibrium values of income and the interest rate could be quite tedious if we had to rely on the graphical summary in Figure 15–1. However, thanks to the efforts of a British economist named John Hicks,[1] what we already know about the macroeconomy can be presented in a far more convenient format. That format is the *IS-LM* model.

---

[1] See J. R. Hicks, "Mr. Keynes and the 'Classics': A Suggested Interpretation," *Econometrica* 5 (April 1937): 147–59.

COMMODITY MARKET EQUILIBRIUM—THE *IS* SCHEDULE

Our first task in the construction of the *IS-LM* model is to derive a commodity market equilibrium schedule. This schedule shows all the combinations of interest rates (which influence investment) and income levels (which influence consumption) that provide commodity market equilibrium.

As was discussed earlier, in a closed economy with a government that taxes and spends, total planned expenditures consist of planned consumption, investment, and government purchases. Equilibrium in the commodity market requires that planned spending be equal to current output. With consumption a function of disposable income, taxes a function of total income, investment a function of interest rates, and government spending determined by Congress and given (at $\bar{G}$), total planned spending (D) is

$$D = C + I + G$$
or
$$D = C(Y - T(Y)) + I(i) + \bar{G}$$

Equilibrium income, which prevails when planned spending is equal to income and output, is

$$Y = D$$
or
$$Y = C(Y - T(Y)) + I(i) + \bar{G}$$

The graphical representation of this equilibrium equation, which was provided in part (c) of Figure 15–1, is repeated for easy reference in part (a) of Figure 15–2, showing a commodity market initially in equilibrium at income level Y_0. Of course, this income level corresponds to the particular interest rate (i_0) and the investment flow that is forthcoming at that interest rate. The combination interest rate and income level (i_0, Y_0), which provides our initial commodity market equilibrium, is plotted as point *A* in part (b) of Figure 15–2.

Now, consider the effects of a reduction in the interest rate. Since investment is an inverse function of the interest rate, equation 15–1 shows clearly that a fall in the interest rate, by increasing planned investment, raises aggregate demand. The influence on aggregate demand of an interest-rate reduction is illustrated in part (a) of Figure 15–2 by the new aggregate demand schedule, labeled D', which corresponds to the reduced interest rate i_1. That schedule also shows that the increase in aggregate demand raises equilibrium income to level Y_1. The new combination interest rate and income level (i_1, Y_1), which again provides commodity market equilibrium, is plotted as point *B* in part (b) of Figure 15–2.

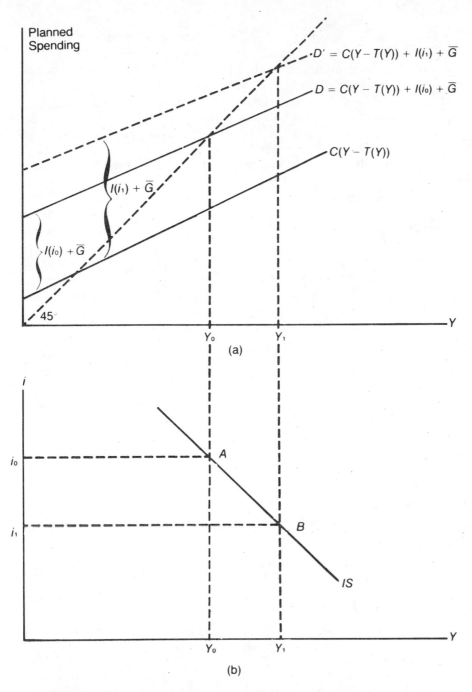

FIGURE 15–2. Combination Interest Rate and Income Level for Commodity Market Equilibrium

Further declines in the interest rate would give additional stimulus to investment spending and thus would raise aggregate demand farther, so that an increase in output would be required for commodity market equilibrium to be maintained. Therefore the schedule showing all the combinations of i and Y that yield equilibrium in the commodity market— the so-called *IS* schedule—slopes downward from left to right.[2]

The steepness, or slope, of the *IS* schedule depends upon the strength of investment's response to interest-rate changes and of consumption's response to income changes. The more investment (and hence aggregate demand) are altered by a change in the interest rate, the more income must change to restore equilibrium, and consequently the *IS* curve becomes flatter. Likewise, the more strongly consumption responds to income changes, the flatter the *IS* schedule is. In the face of a fall in the interest rate, which raises investment spending, aggregate demand exceeds output, which therefore must expand to restore equilibrium. As output grows, however, consumption increases, which further raises aggregate demand. The more strongly consumption responds to output increases, the larger the output expansion must be to restore equilibrium after an interest-rate decline, and hence the *IS* schedule is flatter.

---

[2]If there is no change in the tax structure, disposable income varies with total income, so that the equilibrium condition for our commodity market can be rewritten as

$$Y = C(Y) + I(i) + \bar{G}$$

or

$$Y - C(Y) = I(i) + \bar{G}$$

Since total income is exhausted by taxes plus consumption and private saving, or

$$Y = T(Y) + C(Y) + S(Y)$$

it follows that

$$Y - C(Y) = S(Y) + T(Y)$$

Hence equilibrium requires that

$$S(Y) + T(Y) = I(i) + \bar{G}$$

where S is private saving and T is tax revenues. Combining government spending and tax collection, this equation becomes

$$S(Y) + [T(Y) - \bar{G}] = I(i)$$

The term in brackets is the government surplus, or government "saving." This equation shows that, for commodity market equilibrium, total saving (private plus government) must be equal to investment, that is, $I = S$, and hence the *IS* label on the commodity market equilibrium schedule.

Shifts in the *IS* Schedule

The *IS* schedule plotted in Figure 15–2 is valid only for the particular consumption, investment, government spending, and tax schedules used in its construction. Should any one of these schedules shift, the entire *IS* curve would be shifted.

An improvement in businesses' expectations about future conditions might shift the investment schedule outward, reflecting a larger investment flow at any interest rate. Such an increase raises aggregate demand, so that a higher level of output is required to provide commodity market equilibrium. Since these arguments hold for any interest rate (such as i_0 in Figure 15–3), an outward shift of the investment demand schedule produces a rightward shift of the *IS* schedule, as is shown in that figure. Conversely, an autonomous reduction in investment, which reduces aggregate demand at every interest rate, produces a leftward shift of the *IS* schedule.

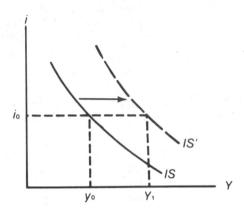

FIGURE 15–3. Shifts in the *IS* Schedule

Shifts in the schedules for consumption or government spending have similar effects. An autonomous increase in either consumption or government purchases results in a higher level of aggregate demand at every interest rate, which produces a rightward shift in the *IS* curve. An autonomous reduction in consumption or government spending, which reduces aggregate demand at every interest rate, shifts the *IS* curve leftward.

Finally, changes in the tax schedule imposed by the government shift the *IS* curve. With an autonomous increase in tax collections, society's disposable income is reduced. Society responds by reducing its consumption, which lowers aggregate demand. An increase in taxes, then, reduces aggregate demand at any interest level and hence shifts the *IS* curve leftward. A tax cut, by raising disposable income, stimulates consumption and therefore raises aggregate demand at any interest level, so that the *IS* schedule is shifted rightward.

In brief, the *IS* schedule represents all the possible combinations of an interest rate and a level of income or output that can yield commodity market equilibrium. Its position and slope depend on the positions and slopes of the consumption, investment, government spending, and tax schedules from which it is constructed. By itself, the *IS* schedule cannot reveal which combination of *i* and *Y* will prevail as the overall, or general, equilibrium combination.

FINANCIAL MARKET EQUILIBRIUM— THE *LM* CURVE

For general equilibrium, it is necessary that we have equilibrium in the financial marketplace as well as in the commodity market. Maintaining the practice employed in chapter 8's discussion of interest rates, in which all financial assets are grouped into two categories, money and interest-bearing assets (bonds), we know that the requirements for financial market equilibrium can be usefully treated if we focus on either the bond market or the market for money. Tradition dictates that we emphasize the market for money, which is in equilibrium if the real value of the money supply is equal to the demand for real money balances.

The equations that represent the real supply of and demand for money balances are, respectively,

$$\frac{M_S}{P} = \frac{M_S}{P}(i) \qquad \frac{\Delta(M_S/P)}{\Delta i} > 0 \qquad \text{(15–2)}$$

and

$$\frac{M_D}{P} = M(i, Y), \qquad \frac{\Delta(M_D/P)}{\Delta Y} > 0 \quad \text{and} \quad \frac{\Delta(M_D/P)}{\Delta i} < 0. \qquad \text{(15–3)}$$

That is, the real supply of money is a positive function of the interest rate, and the demand for real money balances is positively related to real output and negatively related to the interest rate. Thus the equilibrium condition for the market for money is

$$\frac{M_S}{P}(i) = M(i, Y) \qquad \text{(15–4)}$$

Part (a) of Figure 15–4 combines money supply and demand schedules of the form we have described, for which the market-clearing, equilibrium interest rate is i_0. Of course, this interest rate corresponds to the particular income level (Y_0) that determines the initial money demand curve, $\frac{M_D}{P}(i, Y_0)$, in Figure 15–4. Point *C* in part (b) of Figure 15–4 shows the income and interest rate combination (i_0, Y_0) that has provided equilibrium in our market for money. This, of course, is one point on the equilibrium schedule we are constructing for that market.

Now, suppose that the level of real income should rise from Y_0 to some higher level Y_1. A rise in real income (output) increases the real money balances needed for transactions-precautionary purposes, which shifts the entire money demand schedule outward, as is shown in part (a) of Figure 15–4. This shift reflects an excess demand for money (excess supply of bonds), which forces the interest rate upward. With the interest-rate increase, the supply of money grows and the demand for money is diminished until the market for money (and the market for interest-bearing securities) is cleared at interest rate i_1.

Point D in part (b) of Figure 15–4 shows the interest rate and income combination (i_1, Y_1) that provides our new equilibrium in the market for money. With any further increase in real output, money demand is again increased, pushing the interest rate upward. Clearly, the schedule showing the combination of interest rates and output levels that provide equilibrium in the market for money slopes upward, to reflect a positive link between income and the interest rate. That schedule, which is drawn through points C and D in the figure, is labeled the LM schedule (since, at equilibrium, *liquid* money demand, L, is equal to money supply, M).

The slope of the LM schedule reflects the responsiveness of money supply to interest-rate movements and of money demand to changes in both the interest rate and the level of real output. The stronger is the response of money demand to any output changes, the larger is the resulting gap between money supply and demand, which must be closed by an interest-rate adjustment. Hence the larger is the interest-rate change that is required to reestablish equilibrium in the market for money, and the steeper is the LM schedule. On the other hand, the larger are the interest-sensitivities of money supply and demand, the smaller is the interest-rate adjustment that is required to maintain equilibrium in the face of a given change in output, and the smaller is the slope of the LM schedule.

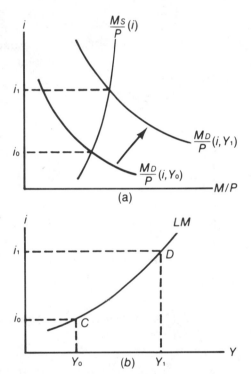

FIGURE 15–4. Combination Interest Rates and Income Levels for Equilibrium in the Market for Money

Shifts in the *LM* Schedule

The *LM* schedule shifts in response to changes in the underlying money supply or money demand functions. From an initial position of equilibrium in the market for money (represented by points A and a in Figure 15–5), a Federal Reserve purchase of securities, which raises the monetary base, shifts the money supply schedule outward, e.g., to M'/P, which creates an excess supply of money (X_S) at the original combination interest rate and income level (i_0, Y_0). For the additional real money balances to be willingly absorbed, there must be an increase in output to level Y' (which would raise transactions-precautionary demand to clear the market for money at point B), a reduction in the interest rate to level i' (which would raise speculative demand and possibly transactions-precautionary demand to clear the market for money at point C), or a combination of both. That is, the *LM* schedule, showing the combination interest rate and income level that equates money supply and money demand, is shifted rightward by an autonomous increase in the money supply, as illustrated in Figure 15–5.

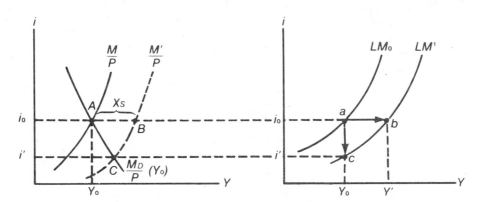

FIGURE 15–5. A Shift in the *LM* Schedule from a Money Supply Increase

Conversely, an autonomous reduction in the money supply requires a leftward shift of the *LM* curve, as a higher interest rate, a lower output level, or a combination of both is then required to equate money supply and money demand.

An autonomous increase in the demand for money (as might occur through an increase in precautionary demand, if society begins to view the future with more uncertainty) results in an excess demand for money. There is some interest-rate increase that, by increasing the supply of money and reducing the quantity of money demanded, would reestablish equilibrium in the market for money. Some decline in output (to reduce transactions-precautionary demand) or a combination of an output decline and an interest-rate increase would produce the same result. Thus an autonomous increase in the demand for money shifts the *LM* curve leftward. Comparable reasoning shows that a shrinkage in money demand (e.g., from the spread of credit-card usage) shifts the *LM* curve rightward.

Clearly, the shape and position of the *LM* schedule depends on the shapes and positions of the underlying money supply and money demand schedules; a shift in either of those shifts the *LM* curve. As was the case with the *IS* curve, although the *LM* curve shows all the combinations of i and Y that can yield an equilibrium in the money market, it cannot tell us which combination will prevail if there is general equilibrium.

GENERAL EQUILIBRIUM

General equilibrium requires simultaneous equilibrium in both the commodity market and the market for money. By combining the equilibrium schedules for these markets (the *IS* and *LM* curves), as in Figure 15–6, we can see that only one combination of i and Y (in this case, i_0 and Y_0) can simultaneously clear both markets. That is, given the money supply and demand schedules that underlie the *LM* curve and the consumption, investment, government spending, and tax schedules that underlie the *IS* curve, the only possible equilibrium values of i and Y are the combination at the *IS-LM* intersection. At any other combination of an interest rate and an income level, the commodity market, the market for money, or both are in disequilibrium. If, for example, the level of income should rise (say, to Y_1), the rate of interest determined in the market for money (i_1) would exceed the interest rate (i_2) that is necessary to stimulate sufficient investment to make Y_1 the equilibrium level of income in the commodity market. Thus there would be excess supply in the commodity market, which would force output and income downward. If income should ever fall below Y_0, the interest rate in the market for money would fall below the level that would restrict investment to a volume small enough to produce equilibrium in the commodity market. That is, planned investment would exceed planned saving, and income would rise. A brief summary of the *IS-LM* model developed above is provided for your review and reference in the following inset.

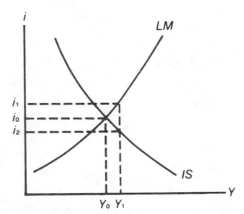

FIGURE 15–6. General Equilibrium: *IS* and *LM* Combined

SUMMARY OF THE *IS-LM* MODEL

1. The Commodity Market

Equilibrium requires that output be equal to aggregate demand. That is,

$$Y = C + I + G$$

or

$$Y = C(Y - T(Y)) + I(i) + \bar{G}$$

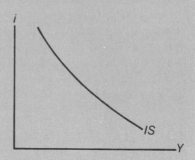

In this equation, consumption is a positive function of disposable income—total income, Y, minus taxes, $T(Y)$—investment is an inverse function of the interest rate, and government spending is a given at a level determined by government decision. A decline in the interest rate raises investment, so that an increase in output is required to maintain equilibrium. Hence the *IS* curve slopes downward from left to right. The *IS* curve is shifted rightward (leftward) by any autonomous increase (decrease) in spending or by a tax cut (increase).

2. The Money Market

Equilibrium requires equality of money supply and demand. That is,

$$M_S/P = M_D/P$$

or

$$\frac{M_S}{P}(i) = \frac{M_D}{P}(i,Y)$$

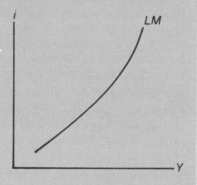

In this equation, money supply is a positive function of the interest rate, and money demand is positively related to output and inversely related to the interest rate. A rise in output increases the demand for money, which creates an excess demand; this requires a rise in interest rates to reduce money demand and raise money supply until supply and demand are equated. The *LM* curve is shifted rightward (leftward) by an increase (reduction) in money supply or a decline (rise) in money demand.

3. General Equilibrium

General equilibrium occurs at the combination interest rate and income level that provides equilibrium in both the commodity market and the market for money. In this model, the price level (P), government purchases (G), and the tax schedule are *exogenous*—that is, they are determined outside the model. Income (Y), the interest rate (i), and all the other variables that depend on these are determined within the model, or *endogenously.* These other variables are consumption saving, investment, the real supply of and demand for money, the nominal money supply, and total tax revenues.

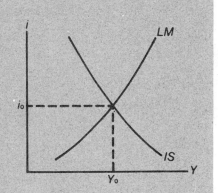

Using the Model

We now have a simple macroeconomic model which can be used to trace the impact of various economic disturbances on an array of important economic variables. In particular, we can introduce shocks into the system (changes in money supply or money demand, changes in consumption, changes in investment, or changes in the government budget) and trace the impact of those shocks on income (output), the interest rate, consumption (saving), investment, and the supply of and the demand for money.

Shifts in the LM Schedule. To illustrate the use of the simple *IS-LM* model, suppose that general equilibrium is disturbed by an autonomous increase in the money supply. According to our analysis, an increase in the money supply, which immediately creates an excess supply of money (an excess demand for bonds), reduces the interest rate and stimulates investment spending. In Figure 15–7, the increase in the money supply is represented by a rightward shift of the *LM* schedule (from *LM* to *LM'*), so that equilibrium is restored at a reduced interest rate (i_1) and a higher income level (Y_1). Since consumption and saving are positive functions of income, the values of both of these variables are greater in the new equilibrium. Transactions demand for money also increases, due to the increase in income. The lower interest rate results in a higher level of investment spending and a further increase in the demand for money, particularly the speculative demand for money. What would be the impact of a reduction in money supply?

Any event that shifts the money demand schedule requires an economywide adjustment. Consider, as an example of such a shift, a spread of the use of credit cards for the financing of purchases, which reduces the demand for money. This disturbance produces an excess supply of money at the original combination interest rate and income level, so that the *LM* schedule shifts rightward (also illustrated in Figure 15–7). The restoration of equilibrium requires a reduced interest rate and an increased level of income. Of course, the reduced interest rate raises investment spending, to provide the higher level of aggregate demand for goods and services. With the higher income level, consumption, saving, and the government's tax revenues are increased, too. Finally, with the reduced interest rate, the real value of the money supply is reduced.

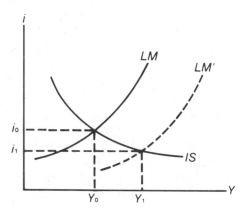

FIGURE 15–7. A Change in General Equilibrium from a Shift in the *LM* Curve

Shifts in the IS Schedule. Equilibrium is also disturbed by events that shift the *IS* schedule. Suppose that the initial equilibrium at (i_0, Y_0) in Figure 15–8 is disturbed by an autonomous increase in investment as business decision-makers become more optimistic. This disturbance shifts the *IS* curve rightward, to a position like that of IS_1, which shows that an increase in investment provides higher equilibrium values of both the interest rate and income (i_1 and Y_1). At the same time, the volumes of real money balances supplied and demanded are increased, and consumption, saving, and tax collections increase (with income).

Why does the equilibrium level of income not increase by the full amount of the horizontally measured shift in the *IS* curve (that is, by $Y_0 - Y_2$)? The reason is simply that the interest rate rises as income rises, which tends to reduce the amount of investment spending. In our example, the increase in investment spending initiates an expansion in output. However, as output and income rise, transactions-precautionary demand for money rises, which creates an excess demand for money (an excess supply of bonds). This results in an interest-rate increase that *damps out* some investment, which causes the expansion in output to be smaller. This feedback phenomenon, which vividly illustrates the importance of interactions between the commodity market and the market for money, can be labeled the *monetary dampener*. It acts as an automatic stabilizer on the economy, as it makes the response of output to any shock to the economy smaller than it otherwise would be.

Like an increase in investment demand, an autonomous increase in consumption spending shifts the *IS* curve rightward—both income and the interest rate are forced upward. Once again, the increased interest rate discourages investment, so that income rises by less than it would without the monetary dampener. You can determine for yourself what changes occur in the other variables in the *IS-LM* model. With that task completed, you should review this section; reverse the shocks that are imposed on the economy and work out the resulting changes in output, the interest rate, and the other variables in the *IS-LM* model.

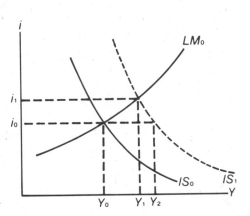

FIGURE 15–8. A Change in General Equilibrium from a Shift in the *IS* Curve

Government Budget Changes

The government, by changing its expenditures level or by altering taxes, can cause the *IS* schedule to shift. Through such budgetary changes, it can exert some control over the economy's equilibrium position. The budgetary changes that the government might deliberately institute to influence economic activity are referred to as *fiscal policy* actions.

Suppose that, with the *IS-LM* model in general equilibrium at position (i_0, Y_0) (as in Figure 15–8), the government increases its spending. This increase in spending shifts the *IS* curve rightward (as to IS_1 in that figure), which raises the equilibrium level of income to Y_1 and the equilibrium interest rate to i_1. The increase in income results in a rise in consumption, saving, and transactions demand for money, while the rise in the interest rate tends to reduce investment (the monetary dampener effect). With the interest rate increased, the real supply of money is increased, and, overall, the demand for money must be increased (through the rise in income) even though the opportunity cost of holding money has risen. Trace the effects of a decrease in government spending on your own.

Clearly, if the government wishes to change the level of income by the use of fiscal policy—that is, through discretionary changes in government spending and/or tax collections—it can do so. In addition, as we already know, the government can use monetary policy—alterations in the quantity of money held by the public—to alter the economy's equilibrium position. The effects of money supply changes are those spelled out beginning on page 440: an increase in the money stock raises income and reduces the interest rate. Monetary and fiscal policies can also be used together to pursue the government's policy goals. For a particular income target, the equilibrium level of the other variables (the interest rate, consumption, investment, and so on) differ with the particular mix of monetary and fiscal policy actions. For example, pursuit of an increased output level through an increase in government spending crowds out some private investment as interest rates rise. In contrast, the same income target might be achieved by an increase in the money supply to stimulate investment while government spending stays constant.

Elasticities and the Strength of Monetary and Fiscal Policies

When the *IS* and *LM* schedules were constructed earlier in the chapter, we argued that the slopes of those schedules are determined by the sensitivities to interest rate and/or income changes of money supply and money demand (in the case of the *LM* schedule) and of consumption and investment (in the case of the *IS* schedule). The sizes of those sensitivities (or interest- and income-elasticities) crucially influence the strength of monetary and fiscal policies, as can be shown by appropriate adjustments in the slopes of the *IS* and *LM* schedules to reflect different elasticities. Reflecting the prominent attention that has been focused on the properties of the *LM* schedule in both theoretical and policy-oriented debates, our major concern will be that curve.

The Liquidity Trap. Our development of the liquidity preference theory of money demand indicated that the speculative demand for money is negatively related to the interest rate. A reduction in the market rate of interest, it was argued, convinces more wealth-holders that the market rate is below normal and will rise (bond prices will fall) in the future. To avoid an expected capital loss, then, more wealth-holders demand speculative money balances, which raises the speculative demand for money. However, suppose that the interest rate falls to a level so low (perhaps to 1 percent, in a deep depression of the sort that prevailed when Keynes espoused the liquidity preference theory) that everyone becomes convinced it can go no lower—so low that everyone expects higher interest rates in the future. In this case, no one would be willing to swap money for bonds, no matter how large one's money balances should become. In effect, the speculative demand for money and hence the total money demand function would be perfectly interest-elastic at this low interest rate, as society would willingly hoard unlimited volumes of money rather than exchange money for bonds, which are expected to fall in value. This possibility was suggested by Keynes and was labeled the *liquidity trap.*

Should a liquidity trap occur during a period of depressed economic activity, monetary policy would be powerless to stimulate the economy, as is illustrated in Figure 15–9. With the economy at the depressed position represented by interest rate i_{LT} and income level Y_0, an increase in the money supply would shift the *LM* curve rightward (as to *LM'*). However, since no one is willing to exchange money for bonds (an exchange that would push bond prices upward and interest rates downward), the additional money balances are just hoarded, and the interest rate remains unchanged at i_{LT}. With no interest-rate reduction, the monetary policy action fails to stimulate investment, and equilibrium output remains at level Y_0.

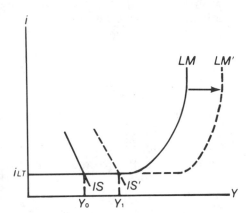

FIGURE 15–9. Monetary and Fiscal Policy in a Liquidty Trap

While monetary policy is powerless in a liquidity trap, fiscal policy can be quite potent. Consider, for example, an increase in government spending or a tax cut that shifts the *IS* curve in Figure 15–9 from *IS* to *IS'*. In this case, output could increase by the full amount of the horizontally measured rightward shift of the *IS* curve. There is no monetary dampener effect, as the increase in spending is readily financed out of idle, surplus, hoarded money balances. On the basis of an assumption that money demand is highly interest-elastic, some of the most ardent supporters of Keynesian analysis have favored fiscal policy for stimulation of the economy and have dismissed monetary policy as weak and ineffective.

In reality, there probably is no liquidity trap at any positive interest rate, and Keynes himself never claimed to have observed an actual liquidity trap. Still, these arguments highlight the importance of the money demand sensitivities that influence the slope of the *LM* curve. Most notably, the more interest-elastic the demand for money and the associated *LM* curve are, the weaker monetary policy is, and the stronger fiscal policy is.

The Classical Region. The fact that there could be an interest rate so low as to convince everyone that rates must be higher in the future suggests that there should also be an interest rate so high as to convince everyone that rates will be lower (bond prices higher) in the future. In this case, *all* wealth-holders would want to hold their speculative wealth in securities, none in speculative money balances. Hence the speculative demand for money would be zero at or above this elevated interest rate.

Since Keynes' concept of speculative demand for money serves as the major distinction between his analysis of the market for money and that of his classical predecessors, the classical view of money demand is relevant if interest rates are high enough to eliminate the speculative demand. According to the simplest classical analysis, the demand for money (for transactions-precautionary purposes) depends basically on the level of output. It could be treated as exhibiting very little, if any, sensitivity to interest-rate changes.[3] In turn, the Fed was treated as possessing complete control over the money supply, with no significant interest-sensitivity of the money stock.

Earlier in this chapter, it was argued that the *LM* schedule is more interest-elastic (flatter), as money supply and money demand are more interest-elastic. If both money supply and money demand respond only weakly to interest-rate changes, the *LM* schedule must be very steeply sloped. Indeed, if neither money supply nor demand are at all sensitive to interest rates, the *LM* curve is exactly vertical at the output level that equates money supply and demand: no interest-rate change would be capable of directly disturbing the equality of money supply and money demand.

Figure 15–10 represents an economy faced with a vertical *LM* schedule above interest rate i_c. Within the vertical segment of the *LM* curve, monetary policy is quite potent. An increase in the money supply shifts the *LM* curve rightward (as to *LM'*), and income expands by an amount equivalent to the value of the horizontally measured shift in the *LM* curve.

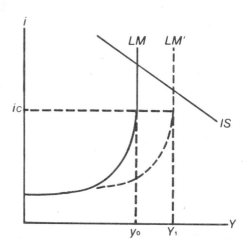

FIGURE 15–10. Monetary Policy in the Classical Region

---

[3]More accurately, classical analysis generally recognized that money demand exhibits some interest-sensitivity. But changes in the money supply, once they had their full effect on the economy, were thought to leave interest rates at their original level, so that no attention had to be paid to the interest-sensitivity of money demand.

According to the classical economists and their modern followers, the exact link between money and economic activity is best viewed through an identity known as the *equation of exchange*. With M the nominal money stock, P the general price level, Y the volume of real output, and V a measure called *velocity*, the equation of exchange is

$$MV = PY$$

Velocity, V, simply measures the number of times per period that the average dollar of money balances is used to buy final goods and services. The product MV, then, is just total spending on final goods and services. With a money supply of \$100 million and a velocity of 3, total spending on final goods and services is \$300 million per period. The product PY, the average price per unit of output times the volume of output, is just total receipts from the sale of final goods and services. Of course, total spending and total receipts must be the same.

Rearranging the equation of exchange to read $(M/P) \cdot V = Y$ suggests that, for a given value of velocity, the existing real money supply is adequate to purchase one particular volume of real output (such as output level Y_0 in Figure 15–10 for a given real money stock M_S/P). With velocity unchanged, an increase in the real money stock corresponds to an increase in output of $\Delta Y = V \cdot \Delta(M/P)$. That is, the increase in income resulting from an enlargement of the money supply (as is illustrated in Figure 15–10) is proportional to the increase in the real money stock.[4] Hence, if the average dollar is used three times per year to buy final goods and services, and if the real money supply is increased by \$10 million, the real value of output that is purchased (with velocity unchanged) rises by \$30 million.

Velocity, according to the classical economists, is ultimately determined by society's tastes (its preference for holding command over goods and services in the form of money) and by the institutional structure that dictates the technical conditions under which purchases of goods and services can be made. Such factors as the extent of usage of credit and the average time period between income payments influence the average volume of money balances held to finance transactions, and the less money needed to finance a given volume of purchases, the higher velocity must be.

Since tastes for liquidity and institutional factors are likely to change only slowly over time, the classical economists could treat velocity as a constant in the face of money supply changes. Thus a change in the real money stock could be expected to correspond to an equal proportional change in output.

Fiscal Policy in the Classical Region—The Crowding-Out Effect. Figure 15–11 shows that, with a rightward shift of the *IS* schedule, there

---

[4]Remember that we are holding the price level constant in this chapter.

is an increase in the interest rate but no change in the equilibrium level of output if the *LM* curve is vertical. The *IS* curve is shifted rightward by an autonomous increase in any spending schedule (consumption, investment, or government spending, in our model). To illustrate why such shifts in spending have no influence on equilibrium output, consider an increase in government spending, which we usually would view as an expansionary fiscal policy action.

With an increase in government spending, aggregate demand is increased (as to level Y' in Figure 15–11). However, with any increase in spending, the demand for money for transactions purposes is also increased, which results in an excess demand for money. Society could try to enlarge its money balances through security sales, but, if neither money supply nor money demand is interest-sensitive, the interest rate could rise without limit and not directly equate money supply and money demand. As the interest rate rises, investment spending shrinks, and that reduces the total demand for money. With a large enough rise in the interest rate (as to i_1), investment is reduced by the full amount of the increase in government spending, so that aggregate demand is reduced to its original level (Y_0), and the economy's equilibrium position is left unchanged.

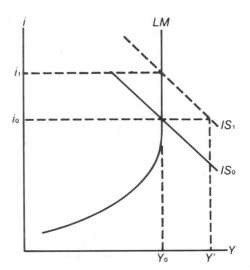

FIGURE 15–11. Shifts in the *IS* Schedule with a Vertical *LM* Curve

In this case, the increase in government spending has *crowded out* an exactly equal volume of investment.[5] In like fashion, a tax cut, which raises consumption, shifts the *IS* curve rightward. However, once again, there is no change in total income, as the autonomous rise in consumption that the tax cut generated crowds out an equal volume of investment

---

[5]Of course, if consumption is negatively related to the interest rate, consumption as well as investment is crowded out, and the combined reduction in those variables matches the increase in government spending.

spending. Clearly, with a vertical *LM* schedule, fiscal policy actions are useless for influencing the overall level of economic activity, since they only cause changes in the composition of output.

This view, that changes in government spending merely alter the composition of output but leave the overall level of economic activity unchanged, is currently voiced by a group of economists who are most often called *monetarists*. Led by Milton Friedman, this group of modern-day supporters of classical theses places emphasis on money as the agent that wields the dominant influence on the level of income. There are other schemes, such as the assumption that competitive pressures in the economy are adequate to always maintain full employment, that result in a crowding-out effect. At full employment, an increase in government purchases of output must displace some other part of aggregate demand. However, the vertical *LM* schedule, which prevails if both money supply and demand are insensitive to interest-rate changes, vividly demonstrates one rationale for monetarist arguments that monetary policy is powerful while fiscal policy is impotent, without the assumption that the economy always operates at full employment.

The preceding discussion has demonstrated that, in determining the potency of monetary and fiscal policies, the income- and interest-elasticities of the functions incorporated in the *IS-LM* model can have crucial significance. The horizontal (liquidity trap) *LM* schedule provided an assessment of the relative strength of monetary and fiscal policy, which is diametrically opposed to the assessment provided by the vertical (classical) *LM* schedule. Now, although the *LM* schedule can become more interest-elastic at low interest rates and less interest-elastic at high interest rates, relatively few economists believe that the real-world economy is characterized by the polar cases of a flat or a vertical *LM* schedule. Most economists would agree that both monetary policy actions and fiscal policy actions can be employed to influence economic activity. Hence an upward-sloping *LM* schedule is representative of the manner in which most analysts view the functioning of the macroeconomy.

Alternative Views of the Macroeconomy

There are, of course, some economists who strongly believe that the demand for money is highly interest-elastic, so that small interest-rate changes can correspond to large changes in the velocity of turnover of money with little change in output and employment. In policy discussions, these economists must favor fiscal actions for economic stabilization instead of money supply changes, and hence the label *fiscalists* is sometimes attached to them.

Monetarists, who generally contend that money supply changes are the prime mover of economic activity, are much more vocal than their fiscalist counterparts. As such, they have succeeded in attracting widespread popular attention focused on money supply changes.

These competing camps, as well as the dominant core of economists who believe that both monetary and fiscal actions have important macroeconomic consequences, can continue to coexist, because no generally accepted statistical test is able to verify the properties of the economic system (e.g., the interest-elasticity of money demand) that correspond to a particular camp's claims. In the meantime, ever more sophisticated theoretical arguments are advanced in support of particular views of the roles of monetary and fiscal policies.

As an example of the theoretical innovations that occur in the debate over policy, there is a recently emerged view of the application of monetary and fiscal policies, which, as a logical extension of classical reasoning, presumes that society enjoys completely *rational expectations* with regard to economic developments. In turn, rational expectations play the pernicious role of preventing *either* monetary policy actions or fiscal policy actions from influencing the level of real variables such as employment and output.

A cornerstone of classical economic reasoning has always been that markets, including the labor market, function like competitive auction markets. In such cases, competitive forces provide market-clearing equilibrium automatically. Thus, according to the classicals, the labor market contains forces that guarantee full employment once sufficient time has elapsed. Faith in the market solution for unemployment, then, has always allowed adherents to classical analysis to conclude that government intervention, in the form of fiscal and/or monetary policy actions, is unnecessary to deal with problems like unemployment. In like fashion, according to classical analysis, real competitive forces dictate the values of all other real variables, including output (which is a function of employment), the *real* interest rate, and so on. Fiscal policy actions, then, affect only the composition of full-employment output, and changes in the money supply change only the price level. However, classical theory maintains that these conclusions hold only in the long run, over a period of time adequate for market forces to provide market-clearing equilibrium in every market.

Now, the advocates of the rational expectations theory have voiced the much stronger claim that classical conclusions hold even in the short run. Although there is no need for us to become involved in the complexities of this theory, it is useful to note that it rests on two propositions. First, just as it is assumed that the public takes account of all currently available information on a firm's future earnings when it bids for shares of stock (and therefore stock prices reflect the best information available), so it is contended that any significant policy move (e.g., to deal with a problem like unemployment) is fully anticipated and adjusted for by the time it is taken. Thus the policy action will have no impact when it is taken. The second and corollary proposition is that only policy moves that are unexpected can affect the real economy (just as only new and unanticipated information influences a stock's price).

If policy-makers' actions are predictable (e.g., the Fed can be expected to increase the rate of money supply growth when unemployment rises and to lower the growth rate when inflation accelerates), they are fully adjusted to before they are imposed, so that only unsystematic, or *random*, policy actions can influence the real economy. Random policy actions, of course, make little contribution toward stabilization of the economy. Therefore the rational expectations thesis concludes that neither monetary nor fiscal policy can be employed to counteract business fluctuations.

Needless to say, the rational expectations arguments are controversial and are fully accepted by only a small contingent of economists and financial analysts. However, the controversy over this theory vividly illustrates ongoing efforts to develop models that better explain the complex reality of our actual economic system. At present, no alternative has displaced the *IS-LM* model as the most commonly employed apparatus for explaining macroeconomic events. That fact is clearly reflected in the next section of this chapter, though the need for possible refinements in that apparatus are also indicated.

More on the Transmission of Monetary Policy

In the basic *IS-LM* model developed earlier, monetary policy actions are transmitted to aggregate demand for goods and services through interest rate changes that alter investment demand. On both theoretical and empirical grounds, there are reasons to believe that money supply changes can alter aggregate demand through other channels as well. In recent years, tests with one of the prominent statistical models of the U.S. economy have indicated that money supply increases can prompt an increase in stock prices, which raises the wealth that society perceives itself to possess. In turn, this apparent increase in wealth can raise consumption and hence overall aggregate demand.

Another channel for the transmission of monetary policy has been emphasized by supporters of classical arguments since Keynesian analysis became popularized in the second half of the 1930s. In this case, an expansionary monetary policy is viewed as increasing the real value of money balances held—a component of wealth—and a part of this increase in wealth is used to buy real goods and services, so that it directly increases aggregate demand. Empirical tests indicate that the *spillover* of increases in real balances into direct purchases of consumer goods exerts at best a weak influence on aggregate demand. Hence this channel for the transmission of monetary policy is mainly of theoretical interest. Still, it is clear that money supply changes can influence aggregate demand through linkages other than that between the interest rate and investment. Different analysts emphasize different links. Some analysts pay heed to changes in yields on more than one asset when the money supply changes, and yield changes can be viewed as resulting in responses in more than one component of aggregate demand. Ignoring the empirically minor effect of real balances on consumption, Warren Smith has provided the following concise summary of the manner in which money supply changes are viewed as affecting the economy. According to Smith,[5]

> Monetary policy induces portfolio adjustments which . . . affect income and employment. A purchase of, say, Treasury bills by the Federal Reserve will directly lower the yield on bills and, by a process of arbitrage involving a chain of portfolio substitutions will exert downward pressure on interest rates on financial assets generally. . . .
>
> With the expected yield on a unit of real capital initially unchanged, the decline in the yields on financial assets, and the more favorable terms on which new debt can be issued, the balance sheets of households and businesses will be thrown out of equilibrium. The adjustment toward a new equilibrium will take the form of a sale of existing financial assets and the issuance of new debt to acquire real capital and claims thereto. . . . This stock adjustment approach is readily applicable, with some variations to suit the circumstances, to the demands for a wide variety of both business and consumer capital—including plant and equipment, inventories, residental construction, and consumer durable goods.

Although the simple *IS-LM* model lacks the rich detail that a more elaborate representation of macroeconomic response to policy actions provides, it incorporates the linkage between portfolio adjustment and real asset purchase that is common to most macroeconomic analyses, even the most elaborate. Hence, buttressed by the details of individual market adjustments that other chapters of this text have provided, the *IS-LM* model can serve as a useful guide to the broad forces that impinge on interest rates and the level of economic activity.

MONETARY EFFECTS OF THE FEDERAL GOVERNMENT BUDGET

The *IS-LM* model provides a vehicle for a simple assessment of the effects of monetary and fiscal policy actions. In that model, money supply

---

[5]Adapted from Warren L. Smith, "A Neo-Keynesian View of Monetary Policy," *Controlling Monetary Aggregates* (Boston: Federal Reserve Bank of Boston, 1969), pp. 106–107.

changes produce shifts in the *LM* curve with no significant impact on the *IS* schedule, while fiscal actions (changes in government spending, tax levies, or both) shift the *IS* curve with no impact on the monetary base and therefore with none on the *LM* schedule. The standard operational methods by which the Fed alters the money supply provide *pure* monetary policy actions (shifts in the *LM* curve without effects on the *IS* curve), but fiscal actions can and often do have an accompanying effect on the monetary base and hence on the position of the *LM* curve. It is important to know the conditions under which fiscal actions result in shifts in the *LM* schedule—a *mixed* fiscal and monetary policy—and the conditions under which changes in the government budget constitute *pure* fiscal actions.

The potential monetary significance of the government's budget activities is easy to illustrate. Suppose that the government makes an expenditure of $1,000 for the monthly pay of a congressional aide. That payment is made with a Treasury check, drawn on an account the Treasury maintains at the Fed. In turn, the congressional aide takes that check to his or her own bank for deposit or for conversion to currency. Whether the aide deposits it in a checking account or cashes it, the monetary base will be increased by $1,000 when the recipient bank has the check cleared through the Fed and receives $1,000 credit in its reserve account, and, correspondingly, the money supply is increased (the *LM* schedule is shifted rightward). Of course, the Treasury must finance this $1,000 expenditure, and the manner in which it provides that financing determines whether the monetary effect of the expenditure is offset (so that the expenditure is a pure fiscal action) or not.

When the Treasury collects tax revenues and transfers them to its Fed account, whether it collects in currency or in checks drawn on checking accounts in commercial banks, the monetary base is reduced by the amount of tax collections. Consequently, the effects on the monetary base (and on the *LM* curve) of a $1,000 government expenditure are offset if the expenditure is tax-financed; a tax-financed fiscal operation is a pure fiscal operation.

Similarly, if the government finances an expenditure program by the sale of government bonds to the public, the fiscal operation is pure. In this case, the public swaps money for bonds, which reduces the monetary base (through a reduction in currency holdings in bank reserves) by the amount of government revenues. The matching government expenditure just restores the monetary base, which leaves the *LM* schedule unchanged. Hence a government budget action that results in a deficit that is financed by bond sales to the public is a pure fiscal policy action. Likewise, a budget change that results in a budget surplus (which otherwise would reduce the monetary base) is a pure fiscal policy action if that surplus is used to retire publicly held bonds.

The Treasury can finance a deficit by borrowing from (selling bonds to) the Fed. In this case, there is no offset to the monetary effect of the expenditure. Thus a government budget change that results in a deficit financed by bond sales to the Fed raises the monetary base and shifts the *LM* curve rightward in each period that the deficit persists. A budget change involving such financing then constitutes a mixed monetary-fiscal operation. The fiscal action is, of course, reinforced by the accompanying monetary expansion. On a comparable basis, a fiscal action that results in a budget surplus is a mixed policy (shifting the *LM* curve leftward each period that the surplus persists) if the surplus is used to retire bonds held by the central bank or if it is just held idle in the account that the Treasury holds in the Fed.

SUMMARY

This chapter provided a simple but useful model of the economy that takes account of the interactions between financial markets and the markets for goods and services. That model ignored some of the detailed information on the behavior of consumption, various components of investment demand, and yields on alternative financial assets that we explored in earlier chapters. In addition, there are alternative models of the macroeconomy that are favored by some analysts. Still, the *IS-LM* model serves as a useful framework for assessment of the economy's responses to a wide array of disturbances and, for that reason, is the most widely employed apparatus for analyzing macroeconomic problems.

Probably the most important limitation on the *IS-LM* model constructed in this chapter is the requirement that the price level remains constant as the equilibrium level of output changes. By implication, this restriction indicates that we have ignored the supply side of the market for goods and services. The elimination of that omission, which is the initial task of chapter 16, will allow us to deal explicitly with inflation and unemployment problems.

16

Aggregate Demand, Aggregate Supply, and the Problems of Unemployment and Inflation

Chapter 15 developed the *IS-LM* apparatus, which integrates the markets for commodities and for financial assets. That model was then refined and applied to assessments of the impact on the macroeconomy of a number of disturbances that can impinge on the commodity and financial markets. Its obvious usefulness in that application is, of course, what accounts for the prominence of the *IS-LM* model in modern macroeconomic analysis. Still, the analysis conducted in chapter 15 was restricted in that the general price level was assumed to be constant, no matter what changes occurred in the equilibrium level of output.

A primary task of this chapter is the development of a more realistic explanation of the relationship between the general price level and the supply of real goods and services. Explaining the link between output and the general price level requires a representation of the market in which labor's services are bought and sold. With the addition of a labor market to our *IS-LM* model, we will be able to analyze the interactions that take place between the labor market and the commodity and financial markets. Thus the resulting *complete* macroeconomic model will permit us to explain what influences the level of unemployment. The addition of a labor market will also permit relaxation of the assumption of a constant price level, so that price-level changes can be taken into account within our aggregate model.

THE LABOR MARKET AND AGGREGATE OUTPUT

The maintenance of full employment and price stability are the foremost concerns of economic policy-makers. The forces that determine the level

457

of employment must do so by their influence on the market for labor services. In addition, it is often argued that forces that originate in the labor market can cause inflation. Most certainly, a model intended to explain the functioning of the aggregate economy cannot be complete unless it includes a labor market, comprised of a supply of and a demand for labor's services.

The Production Function and Labor Demand

Focusing on the *technical* link between employment and output will permit us to explain how the quantity of labor demanded is determined. To begin with, the volume of output that an economy can provide is determined by the quantity and quality of productive factors (land, labor, and capital) that are combined in production. That is, the economy's production function at any point in time takes the form $Y = Y(A,K,N)$, where Y is output, which is positively related to the quantities of land (A), capital (K), and hours of labor services (N) employed. For short-run analysis, the quantity of land and capital employed in the production process can be assumed to remain constant, so that output can change only if there is a change in the quantity of labor that producing firms employ. As they employ more labor, with a fixed stock of other factor inputs, the volume of real output increases, as is shown in the top half of Figure 16–1. Thus, in the short run, output is a positive function of labor employment, or $Y = Y(N)$ with $\Delta Y/\Delta N > 0$. The downward concavity of the short-run aggregate production function reflects the presence of diminishing returns—although output rises as employment rises, it is assumed that the output growth takes place at a decreasing rate, as the fixed factors of production (land and capital) are spread out over more and more hours of labor input. Eventually, output would attain a maximum value and then would begin to fall if enough labor were crowded into employment with the fixed stock of plants and equipment.

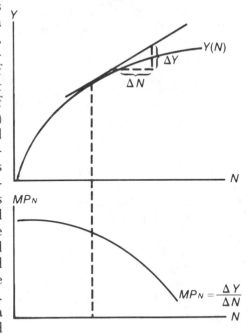

FIGURE 16–1. The Production Function and the Marginal Product of Labor

The *marginal product* of labor, the extra output provided by a unit addition of labor input, is simply the slope of the aggregate production function ($\Delta Y/\Delta N$ in Figure 16–1). By inspection of the production function in Figure 16–1, we can see that the assumption of diminishing returns requires the marginal product of labor to fall as employment increases.

We can now explain what determines the quantity of labor input that individual firms hire, and we can use that information to explain the aggregate demand for labor. For simplicity, the argument will be developed for firms that operate in competitive markets. As a firm increases the quantity of labor employed, it increases output by $(\Delta Y/\Delta N)\Delta N$, the marginal product of labor times the increase in employment. Since competitive firms face a given product price level, the dollar revenue increase from extra labor input is $\Delta R = (P \cdot \Delta Y/\Delta N)\Delta N$, the *value* of labor's marginal product times the increase in employment. Of course, with more labor employed, a firm's total costs are increased. The extra dollar costs faced by a firm employing ΔN additional units of labor is just $\Delta C = W \cdot \Delta N$, the market-determined money wage rate times the increase in employment. A profit-maximizing firm will always increase its labor input as long as the increase adds more to revenue than to cost. Thus, for equilibrium, employment must be increased until the extra revenue generated by the last increment of labor employment just covers the cost to the firm of employing that last increment—that is, until $\Delta R = \Delta C$. If, in equilibrium, *marginal revenue* (ΔR) must equal *marginal cost* (ΔC), then

$$P \cdot \frac{\Delta Y}{\Delta N} \cdot \Delta N = W \cdot \Delta N$$

or, by cancellation of the common ΔN terms,

$$P \cdot \frac{\Delta Y}{\Delta N} = W$$

where, once again, $P \cdot \Delta Y/\Delta N$ is the value of labor's marginal product and W is the money wage. Rearrangement of this equality provides the expression

$$\frac{\Delta Y}{\Delta N} = \frac{W}{P}$$

In this expression, $\Delta Y/\Delta N$ is the marginal product of labor and W/P is the *real wage* of labor. The specific prevailing values of the money wage and price level determine the real wage. Any competitive firm strives to employ the particular volume of labor that equates the marginal product of labor with the real wage. Should the real wage fall, either through a fall in money wages *or through a rise in the price level*, firms would find it profitable to increase the volume of labor employed. For the collection of all firms, this implies the aggregate labor demand function in Figure 16–2, which is nothing more than the aggregate marginal product of labor schedule from Figure 16–1. According to this schedule, at real wage $(W/P)_0$, the business sector will employ N_0 units of labor. Should the real wage be reduced to $(W/P)_1$, the business sector would find it profitable to increase employment, for, at that wage rate, the marginal product of labor exceeds the real wage of labor for every level of employment less than N_1. Thus business firms' profits would be increased by adding to employment until level N_1 is established.

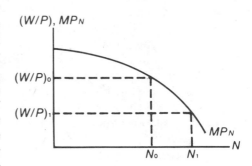

FIGURE 16–2. The Real Wage and the Level of Employment

Labor Supply

To have a complete model of the labor market, we need a schedule showing what determines the number of hours of labor that would be supplied to the business sector at every wage rate. On the assumption that labor rationally chooses the number of hours it wishes to work and the number of hours of leisure it wants each period, it is the *real* wage that dictates how labor divides its time between those alternative uses. Since the real wage is the opportunity cost of leisure, we generally can expect that an increase in the real wage prompts labor to forego leisure and offer more hours of work to employers, as is reflected in the labor supply schedule in Figure 16–3.

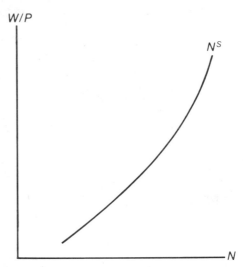

FIGURE 16–3. Aggregate Labor Supply

Labor Market Equilibrium

Combining the labor supply and demand schedules, as in the lower portion of Figure 16–4, shows that there is only one real wage rate $(W/P)_f$

that clears the labor market. At that real wage, labor is selling all the hours of services it wishes, and employers are purchasing all the hours they want. Thus employment level N_f represents full employment in that, at that level, there is no *involuntary* unemployment. Of course, there can be a significant amount of measured unemployment at this point (perhaps from 4 to 6 percent of the labor force) because of workers changing jobs (voluntarily or involuntarily); because of new entrants into the labor force who must search out an acceptable job slot (who are counted as unemployed while searching); and because of those who voluntarily choose to be unemployed (in many cases, subsidized by unemployment compensation, welfare payments, or other transfers), although they claim to be seeking work and would accept employment at some higher wage. All of these forms of unemployment (which may be labeled *search*, or *frictional*, unemployment) are usually viewed as voluntary and not subject to treatment with the monetary and fiscal tools that the government uses to alter aggregate demand for output.

Figure 16–4 combines our labor market model with the aggregate production function to show that the full employment level of labor use results in a particular full employment output level (Y_f). In contrast, if the real wage were somehow raised to a level above the market-clearing level, as to $(W/P)_1$, and held there, a significant amount of involuntary unemployment (excess supply of labor) would exist, with a correspondingly reduced level of real output (Y_1). At this higher real wage, business firms are simply unwilling to employ the volume of labor services being offered. In fact, firms would employ only N_1 units of labor, while N_2 units would be willingly supplied. Hence, as Figure 16–4 shows clearly, depressed levels of employment and of production go hand-in-hand.

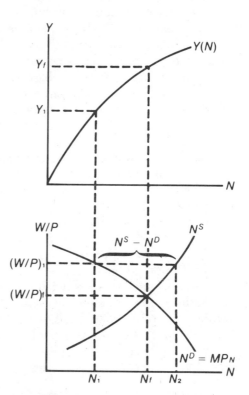

FIGURE 16–4. The Labor Market and Output

Now, if the labor market were a frictionless, competitive market in which there were no restrictions on wage movements, in the face of an excess supply of labor (such as at real wage $(W/P)_1$), money wages would be bid down, lowering the real wage as long as prices did not fall by the same proportion. With a decline in the real wage, the volume of labor demanded would expand, while labor supply would shrink, tending to restore full employment. This is the manner in which classical economic analysis viewed the functioning of the labor market, as was indicated in chapter 5. As we will see a bit later, this view of labor markets is retained in the analysis of the *neoclassical monetarists*. However, the actual labor market can be afflicted with substantial imperfections, which prevent it from functioning like a competitive auction market, and modern Keynesian analysis treats money wages as sticky downward because of such imperfections. Minimum wage laws and long-term labor contracts might place floors under money wages, so that they can't decline no matter how much involuntary unemployment develops. Moreover, even wages that are not fixed by such institutional restrictions exhibit a great deal of inertia in periods of decreased economic activity: they adjust downward very slowly even in the face of substantial involuntary unemployment. This is usually explained as the result of imperfect information available to workers; accurate information on the general level of wages and prices becomes available to them only after a protracted time period.

Workers are assumed to base their money wage demands on what they perceive to be the prevailing level of money wage offers and on what they believe to be the prevailing general price level, but the only directly observable information that is available to a worker is the money wage that his or her employer is offering. If something happens to lower the general price level, firms would continue employing the same labor force only with a correspondingly reduced money wage (holding the real wage constant). However, until workers discover that prices in general are declining (or rising by less than what was predicted) and that money wage offers in general have been reduced, they might refuse to accept reduced money wage offers. Individual workers, offered reduced money wages, may rationally refuse to accept such offers, on the basis of the imperfect (and now obsolete) information available to them, and accept unemployment instead, to seek another job at what they expect to be a better wage. Money wages, then, would decline only when, through the market search process, workers generate the information that money wage offers in general have declined and that prices have declined. With that information, job-seekers would revise their wage requirements, permitting money wages to decline. The time required for this learning process to take place can be quite long.[1]

With money wages very slow to decline even in the face of substantial unemployment, short-run macroeconomic analysis generally proceeds

---

[1]Research in recent years suggests that wage demands of unemployed workers fall very slowly, perhaps at a 0.27 percent monthly rate. See Charles Holt, "Job Search, Phillips Wage Relation and Union Influence," in Edmund Phelps et al., *Microeconomic Foundations of Employment and Inflation Theory* (New York: Norton, 1970), pp. 96–101.

as if money wages were completely rigid in the downard direction. As a consequence, real wage reductions that can stimulate employment and production must come from increases in the general price level.

PRICES AND OUTPUT—AGGREGATE SUPPLY

With the recognition that price changes can alter real wages and hence the levels of employment and real output, we are ready to depict the aggregate supply schedule for our economy. Like any supply schedule, this function shows the quantity of output supplied at an array of possible price levels. Consider an economy that is initially at rest with labor suffering a significant amount of involuntary unemployment. This situation is represented in Figure 16–5 with money wage W_0 and general price level P_0 (real wage W_0/P_0), prompting firms to employ N_0 units of labor, producing Y_0 units of real output. Note that, by representing one optimal combination of price and output quantity, point A in part (c) of Figure 16–5 is one point on the economy's aggregate supply schedule.

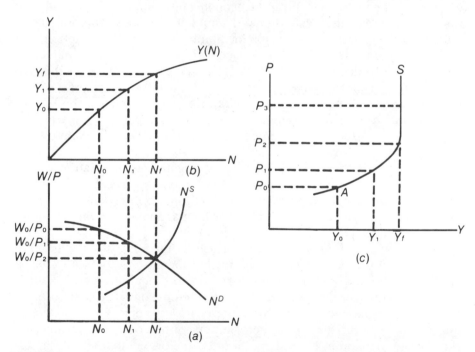

FIGURE 16–5. Prices and Output — The Aggregate Supply Schedule

Now, with an unemployment level that is viewed as excessive, the government might attempt to raise employment and output through a monetary policy action (increasing the money supply), a fiscal policy action (reducing taxes or increasing government outlays), or through a combined monetary-fiscal action. (Respectively, these would result in rightward shifts in the *IS* schedule, the *LM* schedule, or both. Each stimulative action would increase aggregate demand for goods and services until it exceeded output level Y_0, at which point, with an excess demand for goods and services, the general price level would rise. An increase in prices to level P_1 would reduce the real wage (to W_0/P_1), and firms would increase employment to level N_1. With N_1 units of labor employed, aggregate output supplied would be Y_1, so that the price-quantity combination (P_1, Y_1) represents another point on the economy's aggregate supply schedule.

With any further increase in aggregate demand, no matter what its source, prices again would be pulled upward, further reducing the real wage. Suppose prices should rise to a level (P_2) that reduces real wages to level W_0/P_2 in Figure 16–5. At that point, labor is fully employed (there is only search, or frictional, unemployment) with a corresponding full employment output level Y_f. On the economy's aggregate supply schedule, we are at point (P_2, Y_f). With the economy now at full employment, any further increase in aggregate demand would only increase the price level with no further lasting expansion of employment and production. An increase in demand that lifted prices to level P_3, with no change in money wages, would reduce the real wage. However, any reduction in the real wage below the market-clearing level (W_0/P_2) results in an excess demand for labor and, as firms bid competitively for labor's services, the money wage would rise until no excess demand for labor persists. Clearly, the aggregate supply schedule becomes vertical at the full employment output level.

In summary, the supply side of the aggregate economy can be represented in the short run by the labor market and an aggregate production function linking employment to output; that function expresses a positive link between employment and output as long as some involuntary unemployment exists. Once the economy has reached full employment, the aggregate supply schedule becomes vertical, as any increases in aggregate demand raise prices but produce no further increases in output.[2] Over a longer time horizon, the volumes of capital and other factors that labor is combined with may change, and the state of technology may change. Such developments would shift the aggregate supply schedule. Any improvement in the quality of factor inputs employed in the production process, an increase in the volume of other factors combined with labor,

---

[2]Note that, if competitive forces always maintain full employment, the aggregate supply schedule is always vertical at the full employment level.

or an increase in the supply of labor itself, shifts the aggregate supply schedule rightward, as you can prove by repeating the derivation above and adjusting the schedule for aggregate production and the schedules for labor demand (marginal product of labor) or labor supply as necessary. Conversely, the aggregate supply schedule is shifted leftward by a shrinkage of the labor force or by any change in the quality or the quantity of factors employed with labor that results in a reduction in labor's productivity. For example, an oil embargo by the Organization of Petroleum Exporting Countries (OPEC), which would reduce the flow of oil imports used in U.S. production by around 10 million barrels daily, would shift the aggregate supply schedule leftward.

AGGREGATE DEMAND

In chapter 15, we developed the *IS-LM* model, which combines the commodity and financial markets, and then used that model to explain how disturbances in either of those markets could be expected to influence the aggregate economy. However, our analysis assumed that any adjustments in output that were required for reestablishing equilibrium took place with no change in the price level. That is, the supply of real output was assumed to respond completely passively to changes in demand, with no price adjustments. As such, the *IS-LM* model shows us only how *aggregate demand* is altered by disturbances in the commodity and financial markets. For a full representation of the macroeconomy, we must combine the demand-side model of the economy (the *IS-LM* model) with the supply-side model developed above.

Part (a) of Figure 16–6 represents an *IS-LM* model of an economy that is originally in equilibrium at interest rate i_0 and aggregate demand level Y_0. Of course, corresponding to this equilibrium must be some prevailing stable price level P_0, which is plotted in part (b) of that figure. (Recall that a particular price level is necessary to dictate the real value of the money stock and, with money demand, to determine the position of the *LM* curve.) Now, suppose that the general price level should fall from P_0 to the lower level P_1. How will aggregate demand respond? In the *IS-LM* analysis in chapter 15, we argued that a price change alters the real value of the money stock (which shifts the *LM* curve) and hence influences interest yields. In turn, interest-rate changes influence the demand for real goods and services. The price decline introduced in Figure 16–6 increases the real value of the money stock, shifting the *LM* schedule rightward to LM_1. As the *IS-LM* model indicates, then, with a price decline raising the real value of the money stock, society experiences a portfolio disequilibrium, since it holds more money than is desired at prevailing interest yields. By attempting to exchange excess money balances for securities, society drives interest yields down (as to i_1), which stimulates investment and hence overall demand for goods and services (as to Y_1).

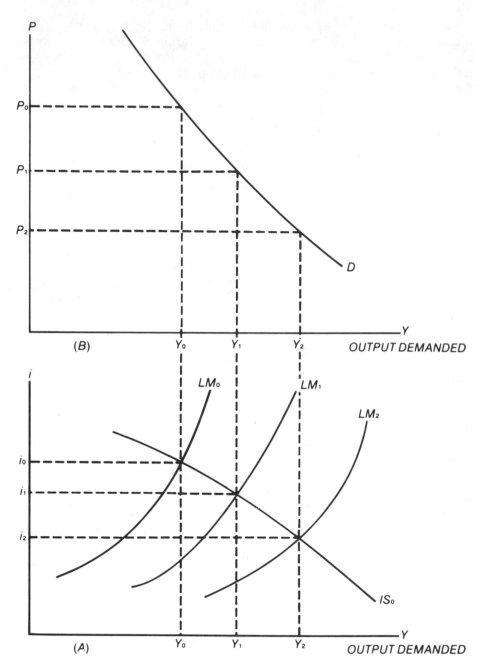

FIGURE 16–6. Prices and Output Demanded — The Aggregate Demand Schedule

Any further decline in the price level (as to P_2) would further increase the real money stock, which accordingly would reduce interest yields (as to i_2) and would increase aggregate demand (as to Y_2). Clearly, the economy's aggregate demand schedule, linking the general price level to the volume of real goods and services demanded, slopes downward from left to right, as is illustrated in part (b) of figure 16–6. Of course, the position of the aggregate demand schedule is dictated by the positions of the underlying *IS* and *LM* schedules.

Except for a change in the price level that moves us *along* the aggregate demand schedule, any event that shifts the *IS* or the *LM* schedule also shifts the aggregate demand schedule. For example, Figure 16–7 shows that, at any prevailing price level, an increase in the nominal money stock increases the real money supply (shifting the *LM* schedule rightward, as from LM_0 to LM_1), which drives interest rates downward and raises aggregate demand—i.e., it shifts the aggregate demand schedule rightward, as to position D', since demand is now higher than before at any price level. An automonous reduction in the demand for money, which results, say, from the spread of electronic fund transfers, would have the same effect on aggregate demand. Conversely, a reduction in the nominal money stock or an automonous increase in the demand for money, both of which shift the *LM* curve leftward, also would shift the aggregate demand schedule leftward.

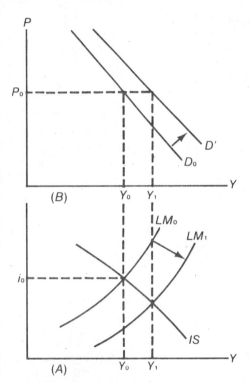

FIGURE 16–7. A Shift in Aggregate Demand from a Money Supply Increase

At any arbitrarily selected price level, an increase in government spending (which shifts the *IS* schedule rightward) increases aggregate demand—i.e., it shifts the aggregate demand schedule rightward. Likewise, aggregate demand is increased (the *IS* schedule is shifted outward) by an autonomous increase in consumption or investment or by a tax cut that raises consumption. In symmetrical fashion, the aggregate demand schedule is shifted leftward by an autonomous reduction in spending (consumption, investment, or government spending) or by a tax increase that reduces consumption spending.

APPLYING THE AGGREGATE MODEL—RECESSION AND UNEMPLOYMENT

In Figure 16–8, the aggregate supply schedule from Figure 16–5 is combined with the aggregate demand schedule from figure 16–6 to provide a complete representation of a macroeconomy. This economy is represented as being in full employment equilibrium (output level Y_f, corresponding to the vertical segment of the supply schedule) with the general price level stable at P_0. The adjustments that are required to provide an equilibrium of the sort represented in Figure 16–8, adjustments in which prices as well as real output are now endogenous, can be readily illustrated as the aggregate supply and demand model is applied to the analysis of real-world problems.

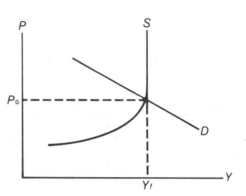

FIGURE 16–8. Aggregate Supply and Aggregate Demand Combined

Economic Contraction

Figure 16–9 uses the aggregate model to represent an economy initially at full employment equilibrium, producing an output level (Y_f) of $203.6 billion and with the price level (P_0) that is assigned an index value of 1.00. Now, suppose that a collapse in confidence in the economy's future prompts a cutback in business investment and household consumption. Such reductions in aggregate demand for goods and services would shift the demand schedule leftward to a position like that of D' in Figure 16–9. This economy is no longer in equilibrium, for, at price level $P_0 = 1$, the supply of real goods and services (Y_f) far exceeds the demand for them (Y'). The general price level must decline and, as it does, adjustments in both the supply of and the demand for goods and services take place to reestablish equilibrium.

Consider, first, the supply side of the economy (which consists of the labor market and the aggregate production function). With prices falling, labor's real wage (W/P) is rising, which prompts business firms to reduce the volume of labor employed and hence reduces the supply of output—

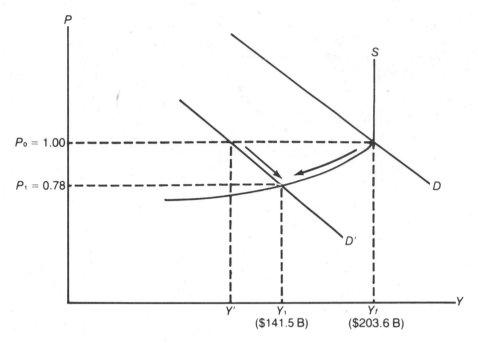

FIGURE 16–9. An Economic Contraction

i.e., we move back along the supply schedule in Figure 16–9 from (Y_f, P_0) toward a position of reduced price and output.

At the same time, on the demand side of the economy, the price decline increases the real money supply, which drives interest rates downward, to stimulate investment and hence overall demand for output—i.e., we move down and out along demand schedule D' from (Y', P_0) toward a position of lower price and larger output demand. Shrinking supply and growing demand have to meet somewhere between Y_f and Y', as at output level Y_1, ending the adjustment, for with the volume of output supplied equal to the volume demanded, the impetus for a change in the general price level is removed.

Thus the contraction in demand has driven the economy into a depression situation with both the output level and the price level lowered. Our analysis also indicates that, in the new equilibrium, real wages are higher but employment lower (unemployment higher) than before and that interest yields are also lower than before. Of course, with real income reduced, consumption is reduced, as are transactions money balances, since a larger part of the money supply is now allocated to speculative hoards.

The numerical values for real output and prices in Figure 16–9 indicate the actual U.S. experience during the Great Depression. From a high in 1929 of $203.6 billion (in terms of 1958 dollars), real GNP in the United States fell by roughly 31 percent to a low of $141.5 billion in 1933. At the same time, the general price level declined by more than one-fifth, and the unemployment rate rose dramatically from 3.2 percent of the labor force in 1929 to 24.9 percent—one of every four workers—in 1933.

In the post–World War II era, contractions have not been as severe. The unemployment rate remained below 7 percent during the recessions of 1958, 1961, and 1971. During the recession of 1974–75, the worst contraction our economy has faced since the Great Depression, it rose to 8.5 percent of the labor force in 1975, before it gradually shrank as economic expansion resumed in 1976 and continued through 1977 and 1978.

Recovery from Recession

If money wages don't decline to stimulate employment, some means for increasing aggregate demand is essential if the economy is to recover from a depressed state. Our analysis has indicated that, generally, either fiscal or monetary policy actions can be relied upon to increase aggregate demand and hence to stimulate employment and production.

With the initially depressed output level Y_1 in Figure 16–10 and the corresponding price level P_1, a Federal Reserve–engineered increase in the money supply, a congressionally mandated increase in government outlays, or a cut in government tax collections would shift the aggregate demand schedule outward (as to D'), to create an excess demand ($Y' - Y_1$) for output. In response to demand, the general price level rises.

With an increased price level, the real wage is reduced, which prompts an increase in employment and in the supply of output. Also, the price increase reduces the real money supply, which drives up interest yields and reduces aggregate demand. Equilibrium would be restored, with employment and output, consumption, saving, transactions money holdings, and prices all increased. Unemployment would be reduced, and so would the real wage. Changes in the interest rate, investment, and speculative money hoards would be dictated by the particular form of stimulative policy action the government employs, but our analysis suggests that both fiscal and monetary policy are effective in altering the level of economic activity. With appropriately sized policy actions, the economy could be returned just to full employment equilibrium.

INFLATION

Inflation, which can be defined as a sustained *rise* in the general price level, is something of which U.S. citizens have become acutely aware in the past decade. As did other inflationary periods, our recent experience has prompted efforts to identify *villains,* who are at fault in causing inflation. Business leaders accuse unionized labor of forcing firms to pay higher

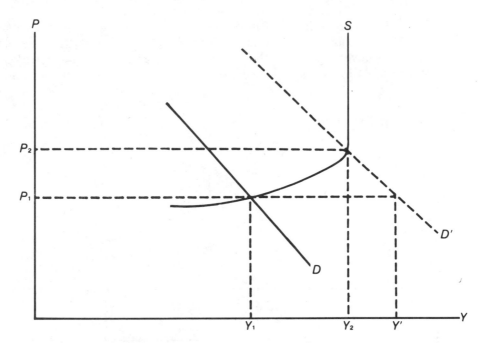

FIGURE 16–10. An Economic Expansion

wages driving up production costs and hence prices. Labor accuses greedy, profit-seeking management of engaging in unwarranted price increases. And every group seems to save some blame for government mismanagement of the economy.

Our immediate task is to attempt to explain how inflation can occur (and thus to identify the villains). After identifying the possible causes of inflation, we can review the stabilization policy options available to government.

Demand-Pull Inflation

Demand pull, or *excess-demand, inflation* is a rising price level that results from aggregate demand exceeding the volume of output. This variety of inflation has frequently been described as the result of "too many dollars chasing too few goods."

Figure 16–11 uses aggregate supply and demand schedules to represent an economy originally in equilibrium at output level Y_0 and price level P_0. With an increase in aggregate demand, which shifts the aggregate demand schedule to position D_1, there is an excess demand for real goods and services ($Y_1 - Y_0$) at the original price level. This excess demand *pulls* prices upward. As we have already shown, the rising price level increases output and reduces demand until equilibrium is restored—i.e., until output supplied and output demanded match, as at output level Y_f with the new, higher price level P_1. While the price increase that ultimately restores equilibrium is proceeding, the economy is experiencing a demand-pull inflation.

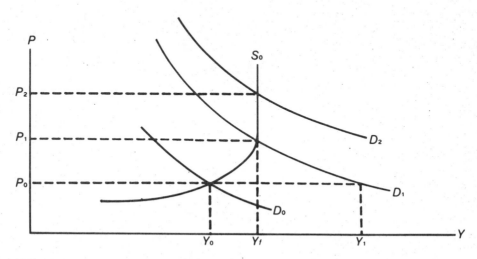

FIGURE 16–11. Shifts in Aggregate Demand and Inflation

Now, at the new equilibrium position (Y_f, P_1), suppose that aggregate demand once again increases, shifting the aggregate demand schedule to position D_2. In this case, the economy is already operating at its capacity output position, so that the increase in aggregate demand will raise the price level (to P_2) with no increase in output. While the adjustment to a new equilibrium is taking place, the economy is experiencing a demand-pull inflation, but, once the price level rises to P_2, the inflation halts. For a pure demand pull inflation to persist indefinitely, demand would have to continue shifting upward. This would require a continuing automonous (1) increase in spending (C, I, or G), (2) reduction in taxes, (3) increase in the money stock, or (4) reduction in the demand for money. Moreover, if the LM schedule becomes interest-inelastic at elevated interest rates, the continuing increase in aggregate spending that is needed to maintain a persistent demand pull inflation would ultimately have to be fueled by a growth in the supply of money.

Cost-Push, or Seller's, Inflation

While economic analysis traditionally has emphasized the role of demand pressure on the price level, in the post–World War II period there has been widespread interest in theories that focus on the role of aggregate supply in the inflation process. The simultaneous appearance of both inflation and excessive unemployment in the postwar period suggests, as we shall see, that inflation can stem from a leftward or an upward shift of the aggregate supply curve. A rise in prices that stems from such a shift, labeled *cost-push*, or *seller's*, inflation, has usually been attributed to sellers of labor services or products who raise their prices when there is no generalized excess demand for labor or output.

   With an upward shift of the aggregate supply curve, the business sector will continue supplying any selected volume of real output, only at a higher price level. In Figure 16–12, our aggregate model is reproduced, with the economy initially at full employment equilibrium with output Y_f and price level P_0. An upward shift in the aggregate supply function to position S_1 creates excess demand for output $(Y_f - Y_2)$ at the original price level (P_0), and, as usual, the general price level rises with excess demand. As the price level rises, reducing the real value of the money supply and raising the interest rate, aggregate demand shrinks along the original demand schedule (D_0); and, as the real wage declines, supply grows along the new supply schedule (S_1). Thus the rising price level closes the gap between supply and demand, to allow the restoration of equilibrium at an increased price level (P_1) and a reduced output level (Y_1). Of course, with output reduced, employment is reduced. Clearly, cost-push inflation not only can accompany unemployment but can, in fact, cause it. Figure 16–12 shows that, should the aggregate supply schedule continue shifting leftward, the price level would continue rising and output would continue falling.

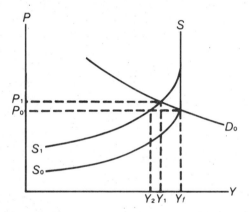

FIGURE 16–12. An Upward Shift of the Aggregate Supply Curve — Cost-Push Inflation

Shifts in the Supply Curve

   To explain why the aggregate supply curve might shift upward, the standard cost-push inflation theories have relied on the possession and exploitation of monopoly power. According to the supporters of the cost-push explanation of inflation, the monopoly power that causes inflation can reside in the hands of organized labor or big business.

If organized labor uses its market power to acquire an inflationary boost in wages, the result is viewed in cost-push terms as a *wage-push inflation*. Still, not all wage increases are inflationary. Should labor bargain successfully for a 4-percent increase in money wages over a 1-year period, and should labor productivity increase by 4 percent during that period, the wage increase would not be inflationary. In that case, firms' labor costs per unit of output would be unaffected—they could employ the same number of workers and pay them 4 percent more, but those workers would be making a 4 percent larger contribution to physical output, which would leave unit labor costs unaffected. Hence an unchanged volume of employment could be maintained with a money wage increase that just matches the growth in labor productivity, yet the higher wage would require no increase in the price level. However, a money wage increase that exceeds the proportionate increase in labor's productivity does raise the labor cost of producing. In this case, an unchanged level of employment would remain optimal for profit-motivated firms only if prices were increased. Hence, if wages increase at a rate that exceeds the rate of growth of labor productivity, the aggregate supply curve is shifted upward.

A *profit-push inflation* is the result of business firms' using any monopoly power they enjoy in product markets to directly raise product prices. With firms charging higher prices on any volume of output in order to enjoy greater profit margins, the aggregate supply curve is shifted upward. No matter whether labor or business firms are held responsible for an upward shift in the aggregate supply schedule, as prices rise, a cost-push inflation occurs.

Dealing With Demand-Pull and Cost-Push Inflation

Curing an inflation that results purely from demand pressure would be quite simple. In that case, inflation occurs only because aggregate demand exceeds supply: all that is necessary to stop it is a reduction in demand until the dollar value of demand equals the dollar value of supply at the existing price level. The prevention of demand-pull inflation requires only that demand grow at the same rate as supply. As we know, the necessary tools for controlling aggregate demand are available. Both restrictive monetary policy, causing a reduction in the money stock or in its rate of growth, and restrictive fiscal policy, causing a shift toward a smaller deficit or larger surplus, are able to effectively combat the pure demand-pull inflationary forces in our model.

Unfortunately, as a practical matter, a number of difficulties (often essentially political, rather than economic) stand in the path of a program to abate inflation. A reduction in government spending can require cutbacks in programs that have high social priorities; a restrictive monetary policy can raise interest rates to distastefully high levels; and tax increases are always unpopular measures. We will have more to say about these difficulties later. But, practical difficulties aside, it is easy to see that treating a pure demand-pull inflation would be simple in comparison to curing a cost-push inflation. As has already been indicated, from a position of full employment and stable prices, the appearance of cost-push pressures shifts the aggregate supply curve upward, which results in both a higher price level and a higher unemployment level. Cost-push pressures are shown to shift the aggregate supply curve from position S_0 to S_1 in Figure 16–13. If increased unemployment is deemed unacceptable, fiscal and/or monetary policy actions must be undertaken to maintain full employment. However, to maintain full employment, the demand schedule has to be shifted to D_1, which results in a further rise in the price level to P_2. With prices increased, those who are responsible for the initial cost-push pressures might be expected to push again, for higher (wage or profit) returns, which would continue the inflationary process. If, via permissive monetary and fiscal policies, government allows aggregate demand to grow as rapidly as necessary to maintain full employment in the face of a cost-push inflation, it would be ratifying or validating the uses (or abuses) of market power, which were responsible for the inflation, rather than allowing the inflation process to terminate itself.

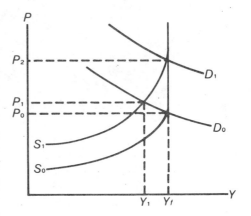

FIGURE 16–13. Policy Choices in a Cost-Push Inflation

If, however, the government chooses not to allow any increase in aggregate demand, the result is no more satisfying. If demand is maintained at level D_0 while cost-push pressures force the supply schedule upward, there will be some increase in the price level together with an increase in the unemployment level. The longer cost-push pressures are maintained in our model (that is, the further upward the supply schedule is pushed), the greater the resulting sacrifice in employment and sales. Presumably, there is some level of excess capacity that would induce the possessors of monopoly power to stop the actions (attempted wage or profit boosts) that result in greater excess capacity. Thus restrictive monetary and fiscal policies could stop or prevent a cost-push inflation. However, the employment cost of that policy stance could be deemed a heavy charge to pay for price stability.

Now, whether the cost-push explanation of inflation is tenable or not is a matter of considerable debate among economists. All would agree that firms with monopoly power will charge higher prices than competitive firms and that organized labor might succeed in winning a higher wage than unorganized labor. But *higher* prices and wages are not the same thing as *rising* prices and wages, and it is the latter that is the essence of inflation. Other things being constant, a firm with monopoly power that continues increasing its product prices will eventually reduce its profits as sales fall. In the same vein, a union that continues raising its workers' wages will, at the same time, be reducing the demand for those workers, so that excessive wage increases will leave the workers worse off than before. Hence standard economic theory argues that cost-push inflation requires irrational behavior and is unlikely to be a problem in reality. The supporters of cost-push theories argue that the "other things" that are assumed constant in standard economic analysis are, in fact, influenced by wage and price increases, so that the possessors of monopoly power can benefit from a push for a bigger share of the economy's output. We cannot settle the debate over the validity of the cost-push thesis, but the experience of recent years, in which both the unemployment rate and the inflation rate have been high and at times have risen together, argues forcefully that shifts in the aggregate supply schedule can play an important role in the inflationary process. Indeed, to fully understand the events of recent years, we must explore some nontraditional views of the forces that can shift the aggregate supply schedule, resulting in an active and pernicious role for aggregate supply in real-world inflation processess.

Contemporary Supply Shocks and Inflation

In 1974, the Middle Eastern oil producers who dominate the Organization of Petroleum Exporting Countries (OPEC) used the market power that they possess as a cartel to quadruple world oil prices. As the largest highly industrialized country in the world, the United States is the world's largest consumer of oil, and a sizable proportion of the oil used in U.S. production consists of imported oil. With the sharp increase in prices charged by the OPEC countries, U.S. firms could profitably continue producing any particular volume of real output only if their higher costs were covered by higher prices. Moreover, with oil imports *relatively* more expensive, producers could try to economize on the volume of oil used with other inputs in the production process, which reduced the productivity of those other inputs and consequently restricted the economy's full employment capacity to produce. Thus the aggregate supply schedule for the United States was shifted upward and leftward, as is shown in Figure

16–14.[3] The result, reflected in the events of 1974 and 1975, was a shrinkage in output and employment and a rise in the general price level. In 1974, the United States was already experiencing an inflation at what appears to have been a steady-state rate of roughly 6 percent annually. The rise in prices required by the oil price increase was merely super-imposed on this inflation process, so that the inflation rate was pushed upward. At the same time, major crop failures at home and abroad (another leftward shift of the aggregate supply schedule) were putting additional upward pressure on prices so the United States suffered an unheard-of "double-digit" inflation rate of over 11% annually as measured by the consumer price index for 1974. There remains little doubt that a supply-side disturbance can have significant inflationary con-sequences.

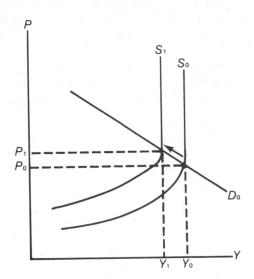

FIGURE 16–14. The Impact of the Increase in World Oil Prices

Although it is hard to conceive of another basic production material that rivals petroleum in its breadth and volume of usage, autonomous price increases on any basic material input, which shift the aggregate supply schedule upward and leftward, prompt a price increase. In addition, there are numerous government activities that can prompt an increase in pro-duction costs and hence in prices. For example, the aggregate supply curve would be shifted upward by pollution abatement laws that required firms to modify their plants or their manufacturing processes in ways that lower efficiency and add to costs. Likewise, safety regulations applied to the workplace can raise production costs and thereby shift the aggregate supply curve upward. The rise in prices prompted by any of these special factors would be superimposed on (and therefore would accelerate) any ongoing inflation.

---

[3]According to our representation (developed in this chapter) of the supply side of the economy in terms of the labor market and the production function, a cutback in the use of oil gives labor less of *other productive factors* (notably, oil) to work with. This rotates the aggregate supply function in a clockwise direction and shifts the labor demand function (the marginal product of labor) downward, so that any chosen output level is willingly supplied (if at all) only at a higher price.

As with any other source of cost-push pressure on the price level, the special factors that affect aggregate supply confront policy makers with a dilemma. With no policy response to an upward shift in the aggregate supply curve, prices would rise and output would contract. To avoid the price increase, restrictive fiscal or monetary actions that accentuate the contraction would be required. On the other hand, stimulative policies, aimed at cushioning the contraction caused by the supply shift, would result in an even larger one-shot increase in prices. There is no easy escape from the dilemma.

Expectations and Inflation

The price level changes that we have considered so far have tacitly been allowed to occur when no inflation (or no change in the inflation rate) is anticipated. Consequently, inflation has involved shifts in the aggregate supply schedule only when some special event occurred. But, once inflation is under way, no matter how it was initiated, society comes to expect future price increases and makes adjustments (including anticipatory wage and price increases) that shift the aggregate supply schedule upward. In actual inflations, then, even those initiated by excess demand, the supply side of the economy is an active participant, as the aggregate supply schedule shifts up systematically in response to anticipated price increases. The traditional distinction between demand-pull inflation and cost-push inflation has little relevance in such an inflation process.

To illustrate the systematic and ultimately pernicious role that the supply side of the economy can play in an inflation, consider an economy that is initially in equilibrium at the full employment output level and with the price level stable, as at (Y_f, P_0) in Figure 16–15. Recall that, at full employment, some 4 percent or 5 percent of the labor force is frictionally (or search) unemployed, since a typical job-seeker takes a finite calendar period (often several weeks) to locate and acquire an acceptable job.

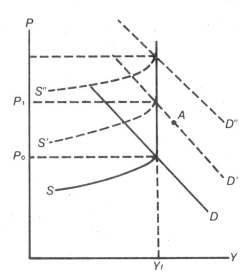

FIGURE 16–15. The Inflation Process when Inflation is Anticipated

Now, consider an increase in aggregate demand from any source, as is represented by the shift from demand schedule D to D' in Figure 16–15. The resulting excess demand for goods and services at price level P_0 causes prices to rise, which prompts firms to seek added employees in order to raise production. As firms compete for extra workers in the labor market, money wages also increase.

As was suggested earlier in this chapter, labor must engage in job-seeking activities with imperfect information, and workers' perceptions of wage levels and prices can become obsolete in the face of abrupt changes in economic conditions. After the rise in aggregate demand, if job-seekers fail to perceive that the economy is now subject to inflationary pressure (in contrast to previous conditions), they will view the higher wage offers they are receiving as isolated examples of good luck and will quickly accept job offers. Thus the average duration of unemployment spells will be shortened, and measured unemployment can actually shrink below the *natural unemployment rate,* i.e., the rate (commonly viewed as being between 4 percent and 5 percent) that persists under conditions of full employment. Correspondingly, output can temporarily rise above the full employment level (Y_f), as at position A in Figure 16–15. At this point, the economy is operating off the aggregate supply schedule that prevails when there is full information on the general price level and wage offers.

As an inflation of the sort initiated above persists, workers will realize that prices have risen and that the higher money wage offers they are receiving are not isolated instances of good fortune, but part of a general rise in money wages. And, as their perception of the real purchasing power provided by their money wages becomes more accurate, they will require that money wages be increased in proportion to prices if they are to work the same amount as before, producing the same output as before. Of course, an increase in money wages—a cost of production—shifts the aggregate supply curve upward. In fact, after an inflationary increase in aggregate demand, if workers and firms come to correctly perceive the price increase that the demand shift will cause and act on that correct information, the aggregate supply curve will be shifted upward precisely in proportion to the rise in aggregate demand. Representing this full adjustment, aggregate demand and supply schedules D' and S' in Figure 16–15 show the economy back in full employment equilibrium, with the real wage unchanged (money wages and prices having risen in exact proportion), and with unemployment back to the natural rate.

Moreover, if the inflation experienced in the time period we have just traced convinces society that prices will rise by a like proportion in the next period, the wage and profit margin adjustments that labor and firms require in the next period to offset anticipated inflation will again shift the aggregate supply curve upward (as to S'' in Figure 16–15). As long as demand continues to grow in step with the rising nominal value of output, inflation could continue at a steady-state rate that matches the anticipated rate, whether that is 5 percent, 10 percent, or any other particular rate. Of course, each period's experience with inflation at the anticipated rate would confirm society's expectations and hence would prompt a comparable upward shift in the aggregate supply schedule in the next period, as wages and profit margins are adjusted to compensate for the expected shrinkage in the purchasing power of money.

Stopping the Inflation Process

Clearly, in the wage-price spiral traced above, the supply side of the economy is an active participant. If we now analyze the results of a government effort to stop an entrenched and anticipated inflation by means of restrictive monetary and fiscal actions, we will discover that the aggregate supply schedule plays a pernicious role: it guarantees that the adjustment from inflation to price stability is slow and painful.

To stop an ongoing inflation, the government must slow the rate of growth of aggregate demand and thereby create an excess supply of goods and services (lowering prices or slowing their rate of increase). However, with imperfect (and, after a cutback in demand, outmoded) information, workers would continue pushing up money wage demands at a rate based on past inflation. In Figure 16–16, an economy's aggregate supply schedule is shown to shift upward (from S_0 to S_1) even while aggregate demand is held constant at D_0. The result, as the figure shows, is a rise in prices (although it is smaller than what would occur if aggregate demand were allowed to rise in step with supply), which is accompanied by declines in output and, correspondingly, in employment. Thus unemployment is seen to increase even while inflation persists. As long as labor pushes for further

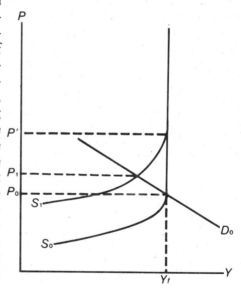

FIGURE 16–16. Restricting Demand with Rising Supply

wage increases to compensate for expected inflation, the aggregate supply schedule will continue to shift upward, raising prices. And, as long as aggregate demand is so restricted as to be inadequate to clear the commodity market of full employment output, there will be a slowing of the inflation rate. Experience eventually provides society with better information (in particular with information that the inflation rate is slowing, so that smaller inflation-motivated adjustments in wages are acceptable), and then the rise in the aggregate supply schedule can slow down, further reducing the inflation rate. If aggregate demand is restricted long enough, inflation can be halted completely with the anticipated inflation rate reduced to zero. However, since inflationary expectations are adjusted downward only slowly by information-generating experience, the elimination of inflation is a painful process, involving a protracted period of inflation combined with depressed levels of employment and output. *"Stagflation"*—referring to a combination of economic stagnation or depression with inflation—is a term that has frequently been employed to describe economic conditions in the 1970s, as the United States has struggled to halt a well-entrenched inflation.

Unemployment and Inflation—The Phillips Curve

In analyzing the inflation episode above, we saw that the actual unemployment rate might be reduced below the natural rate (output raised above the full employment level), at least temporarily, by acceleration of the inflation rate, which fools workers into shortening the duration of spells of search unemployment, as they quickly accept seemingly attractive job offers. Once labor acquired the information that the price level had risen, prompting generalized increases in money wage offers, unemployment would be adjusted back to the natural rate, with output reduced correspondingly. It is possible, however, that labor might not fully perceive the extent of price increases in any meaningful long-run period, so that the unemployment rate might be permanently reduced by the higher wage offers that an increase in the inflation rate provides. Alternatively, an inflation-induced "temporary" increase in employment (which can occur only with imperfect information), to the extent that it gives workers job experience, can make those workers more valuable (and hence better paid) or more willing to remain employed at any wage. As a consequence, employment becomes more attractive in relation to search-unemployment, and the natural rate of unemployment is reduced. The actual link between unemployment and inflation, which dictates whether there is or is not a tradeoff between the two, has been the subject of an intensive debate that began in the late 1950s.

In 1958, A. W. Phillips published the results of an empirical probe of the link between inflation rates and unemployment rates in Britain.[4]

---

[4]A. W. Phillips, "The Relationship between Unemployment and the Rate of Change of Money Wage Rates in the United Kingdom, 1861–1957," *Economica*, new series 25 (November 1958): 283–99. As indicated in the title, Phillips's original investigation was

Following Phillips's lead, economists in other countries were soon generating a large body of evidence on the empirical link between unemployment rates and inflation rates. Reflecting this tradition, Figure 16–17 provides a schedule, called a *Phillips curve*, relating U.S. unemployment rates and inflation rates for an extended period beginning in 1960. The observations in that figure fit our plotted Phillips curve quite well—until the end of the 1960s (we will return shortly to consider this point). And what that plotted Phillips curve appears to show is that full employment and price stability are inconsistent goals—that there is a tradeoff between unemployment and inflation. To have limited inflation to, say, 1 percent or 1½ percent annually in the 1960s, it appears that an unemployment rate between 5½ percent and 6 percent would have to have been accepted. To achieve the full-employment goal of 4 percent unemployment, which was sought in the 1960s, the Phillips curve plot suggests that an inflation rate of some 3 percent annually would have been required. In the early 1960s, the Phillips curve was often viewed in this vein, as representing a "menu of policy choices." With proper attention to the social costs of both unemployment and inflation, policy-makers were to choose, from the unemployment-inflation combinations that the Phillips curve showed were available, the one combination that would maximize social welfare.

Unfortunately, as is shown by the data points from 1970 on, the Phillips curve cannot be counted on to represent a *stable* relationship between unemployment and inflation rates. Every observation in Figure 16–17 from 1970 onward lies well above our plotted Phillips curve: every unemployment rate since the end of the 1960s has corresponded to a more rapid inflation rate. It appears that the mildness and the brevity of inflation episodes in the early and middle 1960s, which provided the Phillips curve observations in Figure 16–17, failed to alter society's inflationary expectations. However, with the fairly rapid and sustained inflation that the United States began to experience in the late 1960s, inflation came to be anticipated, and we should expect the wage and profit margin adjustments that are made in anticipation of inflation to shift the Phillips curve outward.

This systematic shift in the Phillips curve implies that the curve cannot be treated as a stable policy menu. A policy of deliberate accelera-

---

concerned with the link between unemployment and the rate of wage inflation, not with unemployment versus the rate of change of prices in general. However, the shift to the latter concern is simple and straightforward, and the label *Phillips curve* is generally applied to both relationships. A follow-up study, which emphasized the link between unemployment and price change on the basis of U.S. data, was provided in P. Samuelson and R. Solow, "Analytical Aspects of Anti-Inflation Policy," *American Economic Review 1* (May 1960): 177–94.

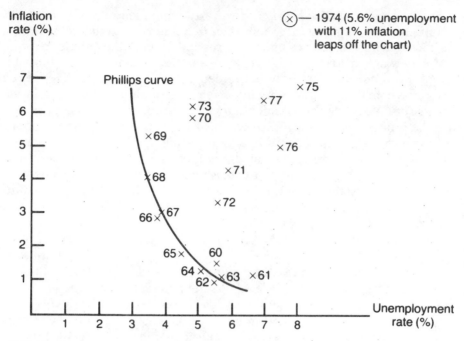

FIGURE 16-17. Unemployment and Inflation, 1960 – 1977

tion of inflation to reduce the unemployment rate, once the increase in the inflation rate has been recognized and built into expectations, will result in the shifting of the Phillips curve upward and rightward, to make the apparent tradeoff between unemployment and inflation less attractive than before.

Indeed, a large contingent of economists believe that the apparent Phillips curve tradeoff is a transitory phenomenon that results simply from imperfect information—from labor's recognizing a general increase in both money wages and prices only after a substantial lag. Dismissing any other reason for a tradeoff between unemployment and inflation, these economists argue that, in the long-run, past price level changes will be fully perceived and ongoing inflation fully anticipated (i.e., that there is complete information on the levels of wages and prices). At that time, corresponding to the steady-state inflation in the episode reviewed above, unemployment must be at the natural rate, represented by the vertical schedule in Figure 16–18. As before, this natural rate of unemployment reflects, by and large, the search unemployment that corresponds to equilibrium in the labor market. With full information, labor bargains for a real wage and adjusts its money wage for every price level change without delay; in the process, full employment is maintained in the labor market.

With an initial equilibrium at full employment, as at point A in Figure

16–18, where there is already a steady-state inflation rate of some 2 percent annually, suppose that there is an increase in aggregate demand. As a consequence, the rate of inflation rises and exceeds the anticipated rate. Money wage increases will accelerate as firms compete for labor, but wages will not rise as rapidly (in percentage terms) as prices. Hence real wages will fall while labor, with imperfect information, thinks its real wage has risen. We are back on familiar ground! The unanticipated acceleration in the inflation rate manages to reduce unemployment, at least temporarily. Figure 16–18 shows a shrinkage in unemployment from 4½ percent (point A), assumed to represent the natural rate of unemployment, to 3 percent (point B) as the inflation rate is raised from 2 percent to 5 percent. By accelerating the inflation rate, we have generated a simple Phillips curve, which shows the apparent tradeoff between inflation and unemployment. However, as was argued earlier, this tradeoff is likely to be temporary. When labor recognizes that prices have risen and perceives the general nature of the increase in money wage offers, it will raise its money wage requirements and will gradually push its real wage back up toward the full employment level. As the real wage rises (money wages rising more rapidly than prices), unemployment grows (to the levels corresponding to points C, D, and so on) even as inflation continues. *If* price adjustments are fully perceived in the long run (so that any inflation becomes perfectly anticipated), and *if* the additional employment induced by the acceleration of inflation fails to provide valuable skills or tastes for employment (which would lower the natural rate of unemployment), unemployment will return to the original level (as at point E) with a steady-state, pure inflation continuing after the adjustment is complete.

After the level of unemployment has returned to the original natural rate of 4½ percent, if the government decides to renew its efforts to reduce unemployment through expansionary monetary or fiscal policy actions, inflation will accelerate again. Reducing unemployment to the 3 percent range would require a movement along a new Phillips curve (such as EF). Even then, unemployment could be held below the natural rate only as long as labor had imperfect information. The natural rate theory implies that there is no long-run tradeoff between inflation and unemployment. According to this theory, policies aimed at reducing unemployment below the natural rate will succeed only in raising the inflation rate in the end. Broadening our perspective outside the boundaries of Phillips curve analysis, we should recall that any change in the anticipated rate of inflation has important financial ramifications. Notably, an increase in the anticipated inflation rate results in an increase in nominal yields on financial claims by the percentage of change in the expected inflation rate. In addition, efforts will be made to economize on the use of money, which pays no interest, and these involve a loss of some of the productive services that money yields to society.

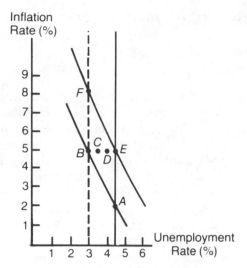

FIGURE 16–18. Dynamic Responses
to Inflation and the
Phillips Curve

An Unsatisfactory Reconciliation

Whether the long-run Phillips curve is merely a vertical line at the natural rate of unemployment or whether (because of a persistent money illusion or because of on-the-job learning) there is some long-run tradeoff between inflation and unemployment is an empirical question that has not been adequately answered. The nature of the economy's dynamic responses to changes in the inflation rate is currently the subject of intense research. Nonetheless, what we already know about the Phillips curve has important policy implications. For example, it is clear that inflation cannot be curbed quickly without significant increases in the level of unemployment. Indeed, if it has persisted for a time period sufficient to permit inflationary expectations to become well imbedded, the inflation will have a great deal of momentum, and a quite extended period of excessive unemployment can be required to restore price stability. The least costly way to achieve price stability is clearly to prevent any significant inflation from persisting long enough to engender a wide spread of inflationary psychology. Moreover, since inflationary expectations raise the short-run Phillips curve, so that the long-run tradeoff between inflation and unemployment is less favorable, if it exists at all, the government should proceed with caution as it considers the purchase of very low unemployment rates through the application of expansionary and inflationary fiscal and monetary policy actions. The short-run Phillips curve cannot be treated as a simple menu of policy choices.

Wage-Price Controls

Probably no other action so clearly reveals the frustration of policymakers, from the inability of the economy to enjoy simultaneously both high employment and price stability, than their well-intentioned efforts to improve economic conditions by direct intervention in the market processes that determine wages and prices. Most recently, in August 1971, the United States adopted a wage-price freeze, which was followed by multiple phases of controlled adjustments in wages and prices. Those controls, which were allowed to lapse in 1973, were imposed to help end the persistent inflation that began in the mid-1960s.

The rationale for wage-price controls differs with the explanation of inflation. Many of their advocates believe that the inflation of the 1970s has resulted from the use of monopoly power by labor unions and large corporations to push up wages and prices—that is, that we have been suffering from cost-push inflation. They contend that, if controls are employed to prevent the further use of that market power, cost-push pressures on the price level can be relieved.

In our discussion of cost-push inflation theories earlier in this chapter, we confronted the view that cost-push forces are incompatible with optimizing behavior by organized labor and by business firms. We cannot settle the debate over the realism of the cost-push explanation of inflation. However, a number of economists, including Arthur Burns, chairman of the Federal Reserve Board from the early 1970s until 1978, have contended that wage-price controls can be useful in curbing inflation, even when inflation is not the result of attempts by big business or organized labor to exploit monopoly power to boost prices and wages. We have seen that, once a demand-pull inflation is under way, if labor and employees adapt their expectations to that experience (so that the aggregate supply curve is shifted upward in anticipation of further price increases), inflation can continue unabated long after the economy has been purged of excess demand. Further, since well-established inflationary expectations are slow to adjust, a restrictive aggregate demand policy can slow the inflation rate only with a lengthy adjustment period during which unemployment is substantially increased. If expectations could somehow be altered more rapidly, the adjustment period, during which the economy suffers the twin evils of inflation and excessive unemployment, could be shortened. If, in conjunction with a restrictive demand policy, government should announce in the most convincing possible way that inflation was going to be stopped, and if it backed up that claim by the application of strict wage-price controls, expectations might adjust far more rapidly than if reliance were placed solely on restrictive monetary and fiscal policy. Where expectations of inflation have become embedded in long-lived contracts, the inflationary wage and price increases that those contracts provide can be circumvented, at least in part, with the application of wage-price controls.

To the extent that wage-price controls, by modifying inflation expectations, could shorten the adjustment period required to lower the inflation rate to the target level, they might serve as a valuable supplement to tools for controlling aggregate demand. However, they should never be looked upon as a substitute for proper control of aggregate demand. If applied during a period when aggregate demand is excessive, those controls can only repress the officially measured symptoms (price increases) of excess demand. More important in that case are the well-known side effects of holding prices below market-clearing levels.

Figure 16–19 shows a market in which controls hold the official product price (P_c) below the market-clearing level (P_{eq}). Price cannot serve its normal rationing function here, since, at the legal ceiling price, the quantity supplied (Q_c) falls far short of the quantity demanded (Q_d).

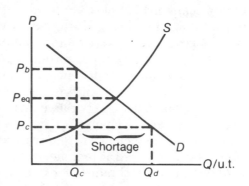

FIGURE 16–19. A Market with Price Controls

If wage-price controls were imposed when there is generalized excess demand, many individual product markets (like the one in Figure 16–19) would suffer shortages. With shortages at the legal price level, waiting lines and waiting lists would form to ration the short supplies. Black markets would develop, as enterprising intermediaries would attempt to profit from the shortages. Figure 16–19, shows that, with supply restricted to output level Q_c by the price ceiling (in effect, the supply schedule becomes vertical above P_c at output level Q_c), society would be willing to pay a black market price of up to P_b and would still take the full quantity that producers were willing to supply. This price ceiling would reward law-breakers while providing society with a reduced quantity of the price-controlled product.

Product quality is also likely to deteriorate as producers seek to escape the lid on prices. By reducing quality (fewer nuts in the candy bar, thinner chrome plating on auto parts, lighter-weight paper in books, and so on), producers can permit the increase in effective prices that market forces call for. With a host of techniques available for circumventing official price ceilings, effective prices cannot be strictly constrained for an extended time period—at least, not without an army-sized network of enforcement agents, which would be intolerably costly (even with public cooperation spurred by patriotism, the price control program deployed in World War II required a staff of 60,000!).

Wage controls are equally difficult to enforce. With excess demand in the labor market at the legal wage rate, nonwage benefits to labor (a company car, more stock options, longer paid vacations, and so on) rise to attract the volume of labor services that firms want to hire. These alternative forms of labor compensation contribute to employers' costs (and thus required product prices) just as wages do.

Experience in a number of countries has shown that people can always find ways to circumvent price constraints that attempt to hold prices below market-clearing levels for long time periods. Most economists, rather than being disturbed by that experience, find it pleasing! Why? A government cannot impose controls on the general price (or wage) level but must apply them to individual prices. If those controls were effective over an extended period, then the price signals that a market economy depends on to shift resources in concert with changes in society's wants would not be operative: with individual prices controlled, relative prices cannot change to induce changes in the composition of production. The social loss from resource misallocation induced by price controls is minimized if techniques for maintaining relative flexibility in effective prices (techniques for circumventing controls) can be devised.

Since circumvention is the likely result of an extended application of wage-price controls, and since a costly distortion of resource usage is likely in the long run if circumvention does not occur, it would seem that controls should be employed strictly only for short periods (perhaps 6 months or 1 year). To reinforce that claim, if monetary and fiscal policy have eliminated excess demand from the economy, controls need be employed only long enough for expectations to be remolded. If controls have any effect on expectations, that effect is probably generated over a relatively short time period. Of course, if monetary and fiscal policy actions permit the reappearance of excess demand while controls remain in force, little good (and perhaps much harm) can result from continued enforcement of those controls.

SUMMARY

At the beginning of this chapter, we combined a model of the supply side of the economy, comprised of the labor market and the aggregate production function, with the *IS-LM* analysis of the factors that affect aggregate demand. The resulting complete macroeconomic model permitted us to explain how output and employment can fall below their full employment levels. In addition, that model provided for determination of the general price level.

Economic contractions were shown to stem from deficient aggregate demand. To avoid recessions or to combat a contraction that is already under way, increases in aggregate demand may be required. Our aggregate model showed that either monetary or fiscal policy actions could raise aggregate demand, with full employment equilibrium easily restored in our static model of the economy if the proper doses of stimulative policy actions are administered.

In our efforts to explain inflation, we reviewed the two dominant explanations for rising prices, the demand-pull and cost-push theses. Demand-pull inflation, the result of excess demand for output, was shown to be self-limiting unless the government pursues fiscal and/or monetary policy actions that result in a continuing inflationary growth of aggregate demand. Preventing demand-pull inflation requires that aggregate demand be allowed to grow only as rapidly as aggregate supply grows.

Cost-push, or seller's, inflation results when the domestic possessors of monopoly power use that power in a way that shifts the aggregate supply curve upward or when some external shock shifts the supply curve upward. This shift raises the price level and reduces employment and output. Our model suggested that cost-push inflation also leads to its own end, increasing the unemployment rate and reducing total sales, unless the government should validate cost-push efforts through an expansionary monetary and fiscal policy posture aimed at the maintenance of full employment.

Whether demand-pull forces or cost-push forces should be held responsible for the initiation of serious episodes of inflation is an issue we were not able to settle. However, we showed that the supply side of the economy plays an active role in the maintenance of actual inflations, even after the elimination of any excess demand for goods and services, as workers and firms adjust their wages and prices upward in anticipation of continued inflation. Hence it is costly to stop an inflation that is expected to continue, as this requires an increased unemployment rate during a typically protracted adjustment period. Given the importance of the link between the inflation rate and the unemployment rate, we focused attention on the nature of that link—the subject of a large and growing Phillips curve literature. We looked at both the short-run and the long-run properties of the Phillips curve, we had to leave unanswered the important question of whether there is a long-run tradeoff between unemployment and inflation. However, what is known about the Phillips curve indicates that the least costly method of achieving price stability is to prevent any inflation from persisting long enough to generate a wide spread of inflationary expectations. Since an increase in the expected inflation rate shifts the short-run Phillips curve upward, so that the long-run tradeoff between inflation and unemployment is made less attractive, if it exists at all, the government should proceed with caution in any attempt to purchase very low unemployment rates through inflationary fiscal and monetary policy actions.

Finally, as an addition to the standard stabilization tools with which we are already familiar—monetary and fiscal policy—we briefly reviewed the use of wage-price controls. We observed that the failure of traditional monetary and fiscal policies to simultaneously achieve full employment and price stability has prompted a number of countries, including the United States, to adopt various forms of wage-price control policies. It was argued that those policies are not likely to be beneficial on balance except when they are applied for short periods during efforts to "disinflate" an economy suffering from an ongoing inflation. We must hope that such applications stimulate expectations of a lower rate of inflation in the future. If expectations are so affected, disinflation can be accomplished more quickly and with a lower cost in unemployment than would be the case if such controls were not adopted.

17

The Application of Monetary and Fiscal Policy

Chapters 15 and 16 developed models that represent the rudiments of mainstream, modern, macroeconomic reasoning. The models depicted in those chapters evolved from Keynesian theory, and they remain best suited to Keynesian-style analysis of the functioning of the macroeconomy. Nonetheless, the basic analytical framework developed in those chapters can be directly employed to depict the anti-Keynesian arguments of the monetarists. Since Keynesians and monetarists form the main competing schools of thought on macroeconomic issues, a brief review of their views on the functioning of the macroeconomy will be helpful. Next, this chapter will discuss controversies over the application of stabilization policy; the major disagreements between those camps on the appropriate use of monetary and fiscal policy will be explored. This chapter will then review some problems in the application of stabilization policy, which are generally acknowledged by economists of all persuasions, or which at least are not central to the Keynesian-monetarist disagreements. Finally, the chapter will be completed with a discussion of the operating targets that are employed in the conduct of monetary policy.

THE KEYNESIAN VIEW

In the Keynesian view, an economic system can be at rest either with full employment or with less than full employment. Because of imperfections that prevent wage and price adjustments, particularly in the labor market, there is no automatic tendency for an economy at rest below full employment to return to full employment in an acceptable time interval. Hence an active government involvement in *stabilization policy* is necessary for the economy to function optimally. The level of aggregate demand, which can be controlled through monetary policy and/or fiscal policy, is the key determinant of employment and production.

The Transmission of Monetary Policy

If the central bank seeks to increase the money supply through a purchase of government securities (an open-market purchase), security prices are driven upward and yields downward. With government security yields less attractive, a part of the increased money supply is used to purchase other financial assets, including corporate bonds, which causes their prices to rise and their yields to fall. Hence the portfolio disequilibrium created by the central bank's purchase of government securities results in a continuing set of revisions in asset demands until interest yields have changed throughout the spectrum of financial assets. Also, the reduced yields on financial assets in general lead to increased demand for real assets, particularly business capital assets. Hence an open-market purchase of government securities affects the macroeconomy by means of lowering interest rates in general so as to stimulate investment spending, which raises aggregate demand. The increase in aggregate demand prompts an increase in employment and in output, with an accompanying rise in prices if the economy was operating below capacity prior to the open-market purchase. If the economy is already at full employment, the predominant effect of an increase in money supply is an increase in the general price level. According to this Keynesian portrayal of the channels through which it has its effects, monetary policy is stronger as money demand is less interest-elastic and as real investment is more interest-elastic.

Fiscal Policy

In the Keynesian model, fiscal policy—a change in government spending or tax collections—directly affects aggregate demand. Hence an increase in government spending or a cut in taxes directly raises aggregate demand and thereby induces a rise (depending upon the economy's initial position) in employment, output, and/or prices. Of course, with an increase in spending, the demand for money (for transactions purposes) is increased, so that interest rates rise with a stimulative fiscal policy action. However, a rise in interest rates causes investment to be reduced, so that aggregate demand does not rise as strongly as it would if the financial market did not have this feedback effect on investment spending. The more interest-elastic is the demand for money, the smaller is the interest rate-increase that results from a growth in transactions demand for money, and hence the more powerful is fiscal policy.

THE MONETARIST VIEW

Monetarist analysis rests heavily on the belief that the private sector of the economy is fundamentally competitive and that the market imperfections that produce wage or price rigidities in Keynesian analysis are imaginary. If some shock causes output and employment to fall below the full employment level, any resulting excess supply of labor pushes nominal wages and hence real wages downward, which prompts an increase in employment and output. That is, there are automatic forces that tend to restore full employment equilibrium. With an economic system that is inherently stable, there is no need for the government to attempt to practice a stabilization policy through monetary and fiscal actions. Indeed, according to many monetarists, government attempts to stabilize the economy often have the opposite effect.

Monetary Policy in the Monetarist World

Monetarism, like Keynesian analysis, views an increase in the money supply as a source of portfolio disequilibrium, which has its effect on the real sector of the economy by alteration of the relative yields on and hence the demands for different assets. However, there are important differences in the particular links that monetarists and Keynesians rely on to explain the transmission of monetary policy's force.

In Keynesian analysis, money and financial assets are viewed as close substitutes, while money and real assets are viewed as poor substitutes. As such, an excess supply of money is believed to have a direct effect only on the demand for nonmonetary financial assets. Money supply changes influence the demand for real assets (primarily business capital) only by means of changing the interest yields on financial assets. Moreover, Keynesian analysis contends that the demand for money is not always a stable function of income and interest rates—e.g., the precautionary demand for money might change abruptly in light of political events. When the money demand fucntion is unstable, money supply changes do not have a predictable influence on aggregate demand or therefore on employment, output, and prices.

Monetarists contend that money is a substitute for both financial assets and real assets (consumer durables and business capital). Thus an increase that produces an excess money supply directly causes an increase in the demand for real assets as well as the demand for financial assets. The increase in consumption and investment demand for real assets occurs no matter how small the decline in interest rates that is created by the increase in money supply. In addition, monetarists believe that money demand is a quite stable function of a limited number of readily identifiable variables (notably, wealth or permanent income, interest rates, and the expected inflation rate), so that the effects of monetary policy actions can be reliably predicted. Since, in the view of monetarists, the economy tends automatically to maintain full employment equilibrium, the major consequence of the changes in aggregate demand that money supply changes generate is an adjustment in the price level. In the long run, the rate of inflation is viewed as being determined by and directly proportional to the rate of monetary expansion, but changes in the money supply exert only transitory influences on employment, output, and other real variables. In turn, since nominal interest rates rise and fall in step with the inflation rate, a change in the rate of monetary expansion can cause interest rates to change in the same direction. E.g., by accelerating inflation and raising the anticipated rate of future inflation, an increase in the rate of money supply growth (which initially lowers interest rates) can be expected to result eventually in a rise in interest rates.

Fiscal Policy in the Monetarist World—Crowding Out

In the monetarist model, fiscal policy has no significant macroeconomic role, for a number of reasons. First, if the economy is inherently stable at full employment—i.e., if the aggregate supply schedule is a vertical line at full employment—there is no stabilization function for fiscal policy to play. An increase in government spending might raise aggregate demand, but, beginning at full employment, an increase in demand results in an excess demand for real goods and services, which bids up prices. A price increase, by reducing the real money supply, drives up interest rates and reduces spending on real assets (notably, business investment) until aggregate demand is returned to the full employment level. In this case, the increase in government spending simply crowds out an equal amount of private investment purchases, so that the total real demand for goods and services is left unaffected. A cut in personal income taxes stimulates consumption, but, as is the case with an increase in government spending, this leads to a sequence of adjustments that crowds out an amount of investment purchases equal to the increase in consumption. Real demand, output, and employment remain unchanged. At full employment, the main impact of fiscal policy actions is on the allocation of resources, as they are shifted between investment use and government or consumption use, with the specific shift dictated by the fiscal action that is undertaken.

The full employment exercise above is instructive, but it fails to capture the entire thrust of the monetarist indictment of fiscal policy, since the monetarists claim that fiscal policy is very weak is not restricted to full employment situations. What are the conditions under which the more powerful monetarist claims are valid? On the basis of a simple and already familiar argument, fiscal policy actions will crowd out an approximately equal volume of private spending, to leave aggregate demand unaltered, even when there is substantial unemployment, if money supply and demand exhibit no significant interest-sensitivity—i.e., in the vertical segment of the *LM* schedule. In this case, an increase in government spending (which shifts the *IS* curve rightward) raises the market interest rate until it chokes off a volume of private spending (investment) approximately equal to the original increase in government spending. While monetarists would find this proposition agreeable, a monetarist's explanation would sound a bit different from the Keynesian account.

In analyzing the effect of an increase in government spending, monetarists pay close attention to the technique used to finance that spending. Their description would proceed as follows: If an increase in government spending is financed by bond sales to the public (a pure fiscal policy), the public's portfolio of assets is being transformed, with a higher proportion being held in bonds. Society must be enticed into accepting that revision of its portfolio by an increase in the reward for holding bonds, the interest rate. Of course, an increase in the interest rate reduces investment, and, if saving shows little or no sensitivity to interest-rate changes, all of the funds borrowed by government must come from a reduction in private investment, so that the government's new bond issue replaces private issue. Hence the increase in government spending can crowd out an approximately equal volume of private (investment) spending.

Similar arguments can be made about the impact of tax changes. If the government cuts taxes and sells bonds to the public to provide financing for its unchanged level of spending, society again must accept an increase in the proportion of its portfolio that is held in bonds. The interest-rate increase required for public acceptance of the portfolio revision crowds out investment; once again, total spending is left virtually unchanged.

In contrast, if the financing needs created by an increase in government spending or a decrease in taxes are accommodated by a new money issue, real income rises. In this case, however, the monetarists would attribute the income growth to the swelling of the money stock: money supply is the prime mover of economic activity, which directly influences the demand for consumer durables as well as the demand for (and hence the yields on) financial assets.

More sophisticated explanations of crowding out can be concocted from consideration of the particular means used to finance government outlays and on the assumption that society's demands for consumption goods and money are positively related to wealth (including the wealth held in the form of government bonds). However, the development of more sophisticated models of the crowding-out phenomenon contributes nothing further to an understanding of the reasons for differences in the policy recommendations of Keynesians and monetarists, so that our analytical discussion of the strength of fiscal policy is complete. You should remain aware, however, that a number of different explanations for the crowding-out phenomenon are possible.[1] Of course, whether fiscal policy really is impotent or not is ultimately an empirical question. At present, no empirical tests that have been devised have provided convincing evidence in support of either Keynesian or monetarist claims, and therefore disagreement over the proper role of fiscal policy continues.

THE BASIC CONTRAST IN POLICY VIEWS

With the differences that exist in the manner in which Keynesians and monetarists view the functioning of the economy, it is no wonder that disagreements arise over the roles of monetary and fiscal policies. Since Keynesians believe the economy can often be persistently stuck at positions not characterized by full employment and price stability, they believe that the government must play an active role to stabilize the economy. In the modern Keynesian model of the economy, both monetary and fiscal policy actions can exert a powerful influence. Hence, with sufficient information on the economy's responsiveness, Keynesian analysis concludes that either fiscal policy or monetary policy can be employed in the pursuit of stability. For a monetarist, fiscal policy actions have no substantive macroeconomic effects and hence are not usable for stabilization of the economy. Money supply changes do have a potent effect on aggregate demand, according to the monetarists. However, since they believe that competitive forces in the economy are adequate to maintain full employment, there is no need to attempt to use money supply changes to deal with the transitory, short-run problem of excessive unemployment.

In the long run, according to monetarist analysis, prices are proportional to the money stock. With no short-run role for monetary policy and with price stability a desirable goal, monetarists conclude that the money supply ought to be allowed to grow at a steady rate—many would say, at the rate at which the economy's production capacity grows, to provide an adequate money supply for the purchase of an expanding volume of real output, but without a monetary expansion that could fuel inflation.

LAGS AND STABILIZATION POLICY

In a static and frictionless world, in which economic adjustments occur timelessly, the effectiveness of stabilization policy actions would rest exclusively on the strength of impact of those actions. However, in a dynamic world, in which output, employment, and prices can fluctuate in a sporadic cycle, and in which the implementation of policy actions and the emergence of their influence take time, more than strength of impact is in-

---

[1]For a more complete discussion of the theoretical distinction between Keynesians and monetarists, see J. C. Poindexter, *Macroeconomics* (Hinsdale, Ill.: Dryden Press, 1976), chapter 10.

volved in the determination of the effectiveness of a policy action. The timing of a stabilization policy's influence on aggregate demand is also crucial.

Figure 17–1 shows an idealized *business cycle* (the solid line) in which output peaks at time t_0, declines, and then begins to rise once more. If an expansionary policy action could begin to stimulate aggregate demand immediately after the contraction in output begins (at t_0), the severity of the contraction might be sharply reduced, so that the time path of output might look more like the broken-line in the figure. Unfortunately, there generally is a substantial lag between the point in time when the need arises for an expansionary (or contractionary) policy action and the time when that action is exerting a significant influence on aggregate demand.

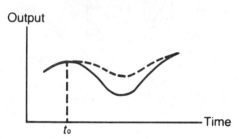

Output

Time

t_0

FIGURE 17–1. Smoothing the Business Cycle

Recognition Administrative and Operational Lags

Our idealized business cycle is reproduced in Figure 17–2. Once again, at time t_0, the need for a stimulative policy action arises. However, policy-makers may not immediately recognize that need. Data on output, employment, and so on are available only at discrete time intervals. For example, figures on gross national product, a basic yardstick of the economy's vigor, are available only at quarterly intervals. To be sure, other important data series, including price indexes and unemployment rates, are available at more frequent intervals. However, one or two monthly observations do not provide clear-cut evidence of a major change in economic developments, and this is what policy-makers need for revising their policy stance. Thus a *recognition lag*, which can last several months, must be endured before stabilization authorities become convinced that a need for policy action has arisen. That lag is represented by the time lapse between t_0 and t_1 in Figure 17–2.

The solution for recognition lag is better forecasting, and a great deal of effort has been expended toward that end. As an aid in the forecasting of economic developments, several available data series, including new orders for machinery and equipment, hiring rates, and even stock market prices, appear to be *leading indicators* of economic activity. Over the business cycle, these data series tend to hit both peaks and troughs earlier than overall economic activity does. Data series on consumer buying intentions and business investment plans are also an aid to forecasters, and,

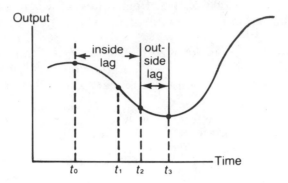

FIGURE 17–2. Lags in Stabilization Policy

increasingly, econometric models are being relied on to predict future developments. Experience shows, though, that in spite of our best efforts. Forecasting is an uncertain affair. In 1929, a prominent group of economic forecasters predicted economic recovery within a year! As an aftermath to World War II, many economists predicted a major recession; in fact, postwar economic activity turned out to be excessively buoyant. In October 1974, President Ford called for a tax increase to combat a continuing inflation, but an abrupt increase in unemployment before the end of the year signaled the need for economic stimulus; by January, in his State of the Union address, Ford reversed his stand and called for a tax reduction. Early in 1977, President Carter called for a stimulative tax rebate and then, shortly thereafter, dropped that request in light of economic developments.

Clearly, economic forecasting remains a somewhat uncertain affair. To have confidence that they are responding to significant changes that are lasting rather than temporary, policy-makers generally must wait for the accumulation of several months of evidence that a turning point in economic conditions has been passed. According to John Kareken and Robert Solow, who investigated the history of stabilization policy, the length of the recognition lag has averaged five months.[2]

A second lag, the *administrative lag*, is the interval between the recognition of the need for policy action and the time when such an action is undertaken. That lag is represented by the time interval between t_1 and t_2 in Figure 17–2. There is no reason to expect the recognition lag to be

[2]John Kareken and Robert Solow, "Lags in Monetary Policy," in *Stabilization Policies*, prepared for the Commission on Money and Credit (Englewood Cliffs, N.J.: Prentice-Hall, 1963). Also see M. J. Hamburger, "The Lag in the Effect of Monetary Policy: A Survey of Recent Literature," *Monthly Review*, Federal Reserve Bank of New York, December 1971.

different for fiscal and monetary policy. The Federal Reserve board, the Treasury, and the Council of Economic Advisors all have the same data series available for their evaluations of the economy's path. Also, these groups are in continuous contact with one another, sharing their projections on economic developments. In stark contrast, there are good reasons to expect the administrative lag to be much longer for fiscal policy than it is for monetary policy.

Having recognized the need for a monetary policy action, the Fed must determine how to administer it and what size of action is needed. Since policy decisions are made by a compact group (the Open Market Committee), which meets at least monthly, the time interval required to formulate a monetary policy action is usually brief. In turn, the implementation of policy decisions (involving open-market operations, changes in the discount rate, or changes in reserve requirements) proceeds with little delay. Thus the administrative lag is quite short for monetary policy.

In contrast, the administrative lag for fiscal policy is usually much more extended. Once the need for a fiscal policy action is recognized, a budget proposal must be formulated, and both houses of Congress must consider and approve the proposed legislation before any policy action may be taken. Proposals to change the level of tax collections for stabilization purposes invite efforts to "reform" the tax system. Mixing tax reform with a change in the level of taxes is sure to slow tax legislation.

Proposals to change the level of government spending require decisions on what government programs will be expanded or contracted and consideration of what states or districts will be affected by the spending changes. With changes in either taxes or spending, the processes of bargaining and debate in congressional decision-making can consume large chunks of time. Still, there are times when, with the need for a fiscal action appearing clear-cut, fiscal policy decisions can be made relatively quickly. Illustratively, in 1975, a tax reduction was implemented with an administrative lag of just two months. Such an experience, however, is exceptional.

The recognition lag and the administrative lag combined are frequently referred to as the *inside lag* from t_0 to t_2—the time interval between the emergence of a need for policy and the administration of a policy action. After a policy action has been administered but before it has its effect on aggregate demand, there is a sizable *operational*, or *outside*, *lag*. To stimulate the economy with monetary policy, the Fed is apt to use open-market operations to increase the monetary base. The commercial banking system must then transform this increase in the monetary base, by means of the credit-expansion process, into an increase in the money supply. It takes time for a general increase in available credit and the full accompanying decline in interest rates to materialize. When that has been accomplished, spending plans will be adjusted, but, again, time delays are involved. Decisions to undertake a factory expansion, to construct an apartment complex, or even to contract for a new home are not made overnight. Once investment decisions are made, contracts must be formalized (typically, this requires an evaluation period by the capital goods suppliers and, often, the submission of competing bids) before those decisions begin to affect production.

The operational lag is represented by the time interval between t_2 and t_3 in Figure 17–2, with an expansionary policy's major impact on output distributed over an interval of time after t_3. Although the operational, or outside, lag is generally conceded to be far more important than the inside lag in delaying the effective application of monetary policy, there is no clear evidence on the length of the outside lag. Milton Friedman argues, though, that this lag is both long and variable. Empirical studies have revealed a diverse assortment of values, ranging from one or two months to three years, for a monetary policy action to begin to exert a significant effect on the economy.

It is possible for the outside lag to be less troublesome for fiscal policy than for monetary policy. A personal income tax change can alter disposable income with little delay: a change in witholding rates will be reflected in the next paycheck. Of course, as our analysis of consumption behavior demonstrated, the size of the consumption response to an income tax change depends crucially on whether the public perceives that change to be temporary or permanent. A 10 percent tax reduction or a tax rebate that is explicitly temporary may have little impact on aggregate demand, even though disposable income can be quickly altered by such a tax change.

In contrast, fiscal legislation that calls for an altered level of expenditures on public works projects directly changes aggregate demand but with a longer lag. An increase in public works projects requires a planning period, the issuance of contracts, and so on. Cutbacks in public works expenditures are inefficient (should projects be left unfinished?) and often are not politically feasible. To relieve partly the extended outside lag, it has been suggested that the government maintain an inventory of carefully preplanned projects; the funding for these "off-the-shelf" projects could be increased or decreased as required for stabilization of the economy.

Changes in the corporate tax rate or in the size of the investment tax credit also suffer from significant lags, since they function by prompting revisions in investment commitments. Government expenditure on labor however, could be changed quite quickly.

Just how quickly or slowly do changes in taxes and government spending affect the economy? Although the precise timing of impact of such changes cannot be assesed with certainty, modern research with empirical models of the aggregate economy suggests that tax and expenditure changes each have some effect on equilibrium output within the first quarter after the policy action and that, within one year, each strongly affects economic activity. The most comprehensive econometric models (the Brookings Institution model, the Wharton School model, and the Federal Reserve–MIT–Penn model) exhibit general agreement on the strength and timing of fiscal policy actions. For example, the consensus from these models is that a $1 billion increase in government spending can be expected to raise GNP by $1 to $1½ billion within the quarter in which government spending rises and by some $2½ to $3 billion after two years.

In summary, fiscal policy appears to have a shorter outside lag than monetary policy, which favors its use as a stabilization weapon. However, this advantage can be outweighed by the extended administrative lag from which fiscal policy often suffers. The implications for stabilization policy of an extended and possibly variable lag are clear-cut: actions intended to stabilize the economy frequently may prove to be destabilizing instead. Figure 17–2 illustrates that possiblity. In that figure an expansionary policy, aimed at combatting the contraction that began at time t_0, does not begin to exert its expansionary effect on aggregate demand until t_3, when the contraction has ended on its own and output is already expanding. A stimulative policy that began to exert its influence at that point could produce an excessively strong, prolonged expansion and hence would favor the development of a needless inflation. On the other hand, if a restrictive policy action is undertaken to stifle an expansion that is judged to be excessive, output may have already peaked with contraction underway by the time that restrictive policy has its effect on aggregate demand. The policy would then reinforce the contraction and would threaten to cause a deep and prolonged recession.

Rules versus Discretion

Recognizing the potential of policy actions for destabilization, critics of government efforts to control the macroeconomy have long favored the abandonment of countercyclical stabilization policy and the adoption of simple rules for government conduct. A focal point of the debate over the government's role has been the manner of providing monetary growth to accomodate an economy that expands over time. The particular issue that emerges, concerning the conduct of monetary policy, is whether the central bank should have a free hand in determining the growth rate of the money supply, as it now does, or whether the rate of monetary expansion should be dictated by a simple rule. The majority of economists favor continuation of the discretionary implementation of monetary policy, but a vocal minority, led by Milton Friedman, support establishment of a requirement that the Fed engineer a steady growth of the money supply at an annual rate approximating the long-run growth rate of real productive capacity (something between 3 percent and 4 percent annually).[3]

---

[3]See, for example, Milton Friedman, *A Program for Monetary Stability* (New York: Fordham University Press, 1959), p. 91. Friedman has argued in support of a much lower rate

That expansion rate, it is claimed, would provide the growing money stock needed to keep step with the financial requirements of an expanding economy.

A part of the debate over rules versus discretion in the conduct of monetary policy stems directly from differences in empirical judgement on the ability of the Fed, with its staff of professional economists, to predict the impact of monetary policy actions. Proponents of simple rules for monetary expansion argue, like Friedman, that the lags in monetary policy's impact are long and variable (and thus hard to predict). As we have just seen, the result of such lags, in combination with a limited ability to forecast movements in economic activity, is that policy actions can frequently be destabilizing. Looking at the historical record on movements in the money supply and movements in nominal output, supporters of simple monetary rules find enough episodes of closely related, sometimes violent movements in those two variables to convince themselves that, on balance, discretionary monetary policy has been destabilizing and is likely to continue to be destabilizing in the future. This conclusion assumes, of course, a dominant role for money as an exogenous determinant of the level of economic activity—as the cause of the observed movements in output.

Advocates of discretion emphasize the endogenous nature of the money supply: they point out that closely related movements (violent or not) in nominal income and in money would be observed if the money supply responds passively to money income changes (thus interest-rate changes) generated by real forces or by shifts in money demand. They contend that to constrain the growth rate of the money supply would often be destabilizing, since the monetary authority could not respond to an excessive expansion or contraction originating in the real sectors of the economy or stemming from an autonomous change in money demand. As a simple illustration of their concern, if a bond-financed increase in government spending (say, for a military engagement) overstimulated the economy, adherence to a simple rule would prevent the monetary authorities from imposing a policy restrictive enough to prevent inflation. Implicit in that concern are the beliefs that, first, the monetary authority can administer discretionary policy wisely and, second, the impact of monetary policy can be predicted accurately enough that the Fed can contribute to economic stability.

We should explicitly recognize that a second difference in judgement also plays a prominent role in the rules-versus-discretion debate. Advocates of a monetary rule typically take the classical position that the

---

of monetary expansion in *The Optimum Quantity of Money and Other Essays* (Chicago: Aldine, 1969), pp. 1–50; also see his "The Role of Monetary Policy," *American Economic Review*, Vol. 58, March 1968, pp. 1–17.

economy is *inherently stable*. They attribute a large part of the responsibility for observed fluctuations in nominal output to monetary mismanagement (which would be eliminated with a monetary rule). With an inherently stable economy, little stability is gained and much can be lost through the well-intentioned but inadvertently misguided use of discretionary monetary policy.

On similar grounds, it is sometimes argued that, to the extent that budgetary changes have a significant influence on aggregate demand, an activist fiscal policy is likely to be destabilizing. Hence, it is argued, fiscal actions should not be undertaken in an effort to "fine-tune" the macroeconomy but only to influence the allocation of resources between government and private use.

Supporters of discretionary policy, monetary or fiscal, believe that sizable expansions and contractions can arise from sources other than government mismanagement and that the self-equilibrating forces in the economy are often unacceptably slow. Thus they contend that discretionary stabilization policy, properly applied, can significantly improve the economy's performance. While conceding that policy actions have at times been destabilizing, proponents of discretion argue that our understanding of macroeconomic forces and our forecasting ability has improved dramatically in recent years, so that policy errors now occur less frequently. In their view, the rather favorable performance of the U.S. economy in the post–World War II period is attributed to the generally skillful use of discretionary stabilization policy, and they anticipate an even better performance from such policy with the growth of knowledge in the future.

To close our discussion of the rules-versus-discretion issue, it is worth noting that supporters of monetary rules frequently are politically conservative (classical, or nineteenth-century, liberals). They judge governmental intervention in human affairs to be at best inefficient and at worst threatening to freedom. As a consequence, if government functions must be tolerated as necessary evils, they believe government should be strictly constrained. The advocates of discretion frequently are modern liberals. They typically have more faith in the ability of government agencies to administer their assigned tasks skillfully and fairly, and they generally do not feel threatened by active government involvement in economic affairs.

ADDITIONAL PROBLEMS IN THE APPLICATION OF MONETARY POLICY

In addition to problems of timing, there are a number of other limitations on the use of monetary policy for stabilizing the economy and, given our primary concern with monetary and financial matters, we should be aware of these limitations.

The Uneven Incidence of Monetary Policy

It is often argued that monetary policy actions have a quite uneven impact on different groups within society. Perhaps most notably, as was argued in chapter 14, a restrictive monetary policy that raises market interest rates can reduce the flow of funds into the home mortgage market to a trickle, and this deals chrushing blows to the home construction industry.

As we know, the extreme interest-sensitivity of the construction industry has existed because (1) there are institutional restrictions on interest rates and (2) there is a difference in the maturity structure of the assets and the liabilities of the financial institutions that provide the bulk of funds to the mortgage market. The federal government imposes ceilings on the interest rates that can be charged on VA-guaranteed and FHA-insured mortgage loans. In addition, many states enforce *usury laws*, which limit the interest charge that can be levied on mortgage loans. When yields on alternative securities rise to levels that are more attractive than the interest that ceilings permit on mortgage loans, we should expect a reduction in the flow of funds to the mortgage market.

More importantly, the specialized financial intermediaries that channel the bulk of funds to the mortgage market face limits (ceilings set by Regulation Q) on the interest yields they can offer on deposits. As yields on money market instruments have risen above the levels that these intermediaries can legally offer, depositors have shifted their funds out of the intermediaries and directly into securities—i.e., disintermediation has occurred—and this reduces the availability of mortgage funds. The highly volatile response that the home construction industry has exhibited to credit market changes is easy to see. As Table 17–1 shows, in the three most recent periods of stringent monetary policy (1966, 1969, and 1974), housing starts plummeted. They dropped from the level of the previous year by more than 20 percent in 1966 and by some 3 percent in 1969, in spite of sizable government support of the mortgage market. In 1974, when the U.S. economy was confronting its deepest recession since the 1930s,

TABLE 17–1. New Housing Starts (in thousands of units)

Year	Housing Starts
1965	1,473
1966	1,165
1967	1,292
1968	1,508
1969	1,467
1970	1,434
1971	2,052
1972	2,357
1973	2,045
1974	1,338
1975	1,160
1976	1,540
1977	1,986
1978	2,019

Source: *Federal Reserve Bulletin,* various issues.

housing starts slumped by 35 percent, and the decline continued through 1975.

These figures illustrate vividly the frustrations of (1) potential new home purchasers who cannot find mortgage funds and (2) home builders, many of whom are driven into bankruptcy, as they are unable to sell the new dwellings they produce. To reduce the pressure that restrictive monetary policy imposes on the housing industry, the interest-rate ceilings that serve to exaggerate the interest-sensitivity of money flows into that industry could be relaxed. In fact, since 1969, some moves have been made in that direction as we have discussed in previous chapters. An alternative, which the government has chosen to emphasize until very recently is the funding of federally sponsored credit agencies, which support the mortgage market directly through purchases of mortgages and indirectly through loans to mortgage-granting intermediaries.[4]

On their own, intermediaries that provide mortgage funds have taken steps to increase their ability to attract funds and to extend credit during periods of high interest rates. The average maturities of their obligations has been lengthened, notably through the increased reliance on time certificates but also by the occasional issuance of long-term debentures. On the assets side of their balance sheets, these institutions have sought additional flexibility through the issuance of variable-rate mortgages. With interest charges that rise with the general level of interest rates, mortgage lenders can compete for funds by raising the yields they offer on deposits. In addition, many of these institutions have purchased an array of government securities and government agency securities, in attempts to shorten the maturity structure of their assets.

Despite the innovations that have been introduced to reduce the sensitivity of home construction to interest-rate changes, the evidence from 1974 suggests that disintermediation remains a serious problem for mortgage lenders. With interest rates again rising strongly in early 1978, the problem has continued and a tendency for deposits to leave financial intermediaries has emerged. Fear of another episode of disintermediation and construction cutbacks has prompted the agencies that regulate financial intermediaries to alter the restrictions those institutions face and to

---

[4]As was explained in chapter 11, the federal agencies that provide support for the mortgage market are the Federal Home Loan Bank Board (FHLB), the Federal National Mortgage Association (FNMA, often referred to as "Fannie Mae"), the Federal Home Loan Mortgage Corporation (FHLMC), and, less directly, the Government National Mortgage Association (GNMA, often called "Ginnie Mae"). During 1969, the federally sponsored credit agencies provided over 40 percent of the funds borrowed to finance housing. For a more detailed treatment of the activities of these credit agencies, see Phillip H. Davidson, "Structure of the Residential Mortgage Market," *Monthly Review*, Federal Reserve Bank of Richmond, September 1972. Also, see the Federal Reserve staff study, "Ways to Moderate Fluctuations in Housing Construction," *Federal Reserve Bulletin*, March 1972, pp. 215–25.

allow the issuance of money market certificates which offer yields greater than those available on Treasury bills. By the end of 1978, intermediaries appeared to have avoided a serious episode of disintermediation, with the new money market certificates doubtlessly playing an important role in maintaining credit flows.

While the housing industry is the one sector of the economy that has been most strongly affected by changed credit conditions, it is not the only one that feels this influence. State and local governments are often subject to legislative and administrative regulations that impose ceilings on the interest rates they can pay on bond debt. As a consequence, when interest rates are high, bond financing of the construction of roads, schools, parks, and so on can become impossible, even if the citizenry is willing to pay the prevailing rate for the funds required for such projects. The impact of high interest rates is vividly apparent in survey data on the cutback in long-term state and local borrowing during two recent periods when rates were high.[5] In 1966, such borrowing was reduced by approximately 20 percent of planned levels; in fiscal 1970 (from July 1969 to June 1970), the cutback was about 28 percent.

It is frequently argued that small businesses are also particularly sensitive to altered credit conditions. Large businesses, it is claimed, have ready access to national credit markets and can borrow funds either from banks or by direct sale of their own security issues. Thus, under restrictive credit conditions, banks might feel it necessary to meet the needs of their large business customers first and to limit the funds they make available to small businesses, which have no easy alternative to bank borrowing. This set of arguments is hard to assess empirically, as are similar arguments that restrictive monetary policies impose a greater burden on lower-income groups than on others. However, the point is well taken that the fear (realistic or not) that a restrictive monetary policy imposes a particularly harsh burden on specific sectors of the economy can foster a reluctance to aggressively employ monetary restraint, particularly if the highly interest-responsive sectors are deemed socially worthy and politically powerful (as are the housing industry and state and local governments).

Compliance with the Treasury

Historically, the conduct of monetary policy has also been seriously restricted through the Fed's efforts to serve the desires of the U.S. Treasury. With high interest rates, the interest cost to the Treasury of issuing

---

[5]See Paul F. McGouldrick and John E. Peterson, "Monetary Restraint and Borrowing and Capital Spending by Large State and Local Governments in 1966," *Federal Reserve Bulletin*, July 1968, pp. 552–81. Also, see John E. Peterson, "Response of State and Local Governments to Varying Credit Conditions," *Federal Reserve Bulletin*, March 1971, pp. 209–32.

new government debt is elevated. However, the interest cost of newly issued government debt can be held down, that is, the interest rate is *pegged,* if the Fed is willing to support bond prices and is standing ready to buy any volume of bonds offered at the support price. Of course, the Fed's bond purchases add reserves to the banking system and thereby provide the base for an expansion of the money supply.

To aid the Treasury in its efforts to bond-finance a massive volume of expenditures at a low interest cost during World War II, the Fed pegged the interest rate at its prewar (depression) level—the yield on short-term Treasury bills was held down to just ⅜ of 1 percent, and the yield on long-term bonds was held at 2½ percent. By the end of the war, this support policy had provided the Fed with a massive portfolio of government securities and, in turn, had pumped a large volume of high-powered money into the economy. Still, the Fed continued supporting government bond prices in the postwar period, although short-term rates were permitted to rise a bit. Of course, with the interest rate pegged, the Fed had no discretionary monetary control power: it had abdicated that power in order to ease the Treasury's borrowing task.

With the war ended, the voluntary restriction on the Fed's independent power became increasingly disagreeable, as the need for stabilization policy regained priority. With U.S. entry into the Korean War in mid-1950, strong inflationary pressures evoked a pressing need for restrictive monetary policy. In March 1951, the Treasury and the Federal Reserve reached an accord, which freed the Fed from responsibility for pegging the interest rate and permitted it to resume the independent, active use of monetary policy for stabilization purposes.

Nonetheless, the conduct of monetary policy has not been completely freed from Treasury influence. As part of its accord with the Treasury (issued on March 4, 1951), the Fed agreed to support the "successful financing of the government's (financial) requirements" and to "maintain orderly conditions" in the government securities market.

Financial Market Stability and Monetary Control

A concern with erratic movements in prices and yields on government securities—with a *disorderly* market—is most evident when the Treasury is engaged in marketing a new security issue. The appearance on the market of a large, new issue tends to depress government security prices abruptly and hence would raise interest yields in step. To prevent the security issue from failing to be fully subscribed at face value, and to avoid the abrupt increase in interest yields on government securities that would otherwise occur, the Fed can maintain an "even keel" policy. That is, to support bond prices, it can serve as a buyer of last resort, when the Treasury markets its new issue. Since the Treasury frequently appears in the securities market to finance current deficits and to refinance outstanding debt, an even keel policy must be folllowed in frequent periods.

Other factors besides Treasury debt issues can cause swings in interest rates. The Fed judges any abrupt changes in interest rates to be undesirable, because, in addition to threatening the success of the Treasury's financing operations, they increase uncertainty and can cause inefficient, temporary shifts of resources from one use to another. Hence the Fed attempts to stabilize interest rates on a short-term basis, without regard for the source of instability.

To accomplish this, the Fed must abdicate control of the supply of money, as was indicated before. Hence, under such a policy, the money supply responds elastically to changes in money demand. However, as we also know, not all changes in money demand are random or seasonal. Some are the result of changes in the level of economic activity of the sort that must be offset if the country's macroeconomic goals are to be achieved. Unfortunately, except in the case of stable seasonal variations in money demand, there is no way the Fed can distinguish changes in money demand that should be accommodated by a change in the money supply because of their random nature from changes that reflect unwanted changes in economic activity and therefore should be met with an offsetting adjustment in the money supply and interest rates. There is some latitude for the Fed to accommodate daily or weekly shocks to the market for money while it still gives prime consideration over a longer time horizon (such as a quarter) to the achievement of changes in monetary aggregates and interest rates that are judged necessary for aggregate stabilization purposes. However, the Fed must be on guard against the widely recognized possibility that successive "special situations" might require a money supply response that cumulatively forces the money stock and interest rates away from the paths needed for aggregate stabilization purposes. The existence of random disturbances in the market for money, to which the Fed must respond, clearly complicates its control task.

Near-Monies and Monetary Policy

Chapter 3 considered alternative definitions of the demand for money and indicated the broad support that exists for a narrow definition. However, it was recognized that many assets have some of the attributes of money narrowly defined. Those assets include time deposits in commercial banks; deposit liabilities of mutual savings banks, credit unions, and savings and loan associations; and even short-term government securities. All of these are highly liquid—they are easily converted into "money" (M_1) at low cost. Serving as stores of value while they earn interest income, these *near-monies* can be close substitutes for money per se in financial portfolios.

In the postwar period, there was a far more rapid growth in the volume of near-monies than in the money stock itself, as wealth-holders substituted interest-yielding assets for money. In the long run, the increased availability of highly liquid money-substitutes certainly played a prominent role in the observed postwar decline in the volume of money balances demanded (increase in velocity) at any income level. The growing importance of near-monies has another implication, however, that is potentially far more important for the effectiveness of monetary policy. In summary form, some economists have contended that, since the monetary authorities directly control only commercial bank reserves and deposits, their power to influence the economy is reduced as money holdings become a relatively smaller share of financial portfolios. This argument can easily be expanded to show exactly how the existence of near-monies can weaken a restrictive monetary policy.

In the interest of slowing economic activity, the central bank can restrict the growth of reserves and, correspondingly, the money supply. We have also argued so far that, with a restriction in money supply growth, interest rates rise, which reduces aggregate demand. However, with a rise in interest rates, near-monies are made more attractive, so that wealth-holders may willingly exchange money for interest-yielding securities, and this provides the business-supporting credit that commercial banks are not able to extend. Business activity is permitted to continue at an elevated level, even though the money supply has been restricted, as the increase in interest rates induces an increase in velocity (a reduction in money demand). The restrictive effect of monetary policy appears to be blunted as each of a reduced number of dollars is used more intensely.[6]

Monetary policy cannot be completely emasculated, since some interest-rate increase, which reduces planned spending, is required to induce the substitution of near-monies for money itself. However, to the extent that the presence of near-monies, which are *close* substitutes for money itself, increases the interest-elasticity of money demand (velocity), the strength of monetary policy is reduced.

The theoretical arguments we have reviewed are appealing, and, in the late 1950s and early 1960s, they evoked some substantial concern over the efficacy of monetary policy. From the mid-1960s until just recently, that concern faded, as empirical studies of money demand indicated repeatedly that it is a stable (and hence predictable) function of the interest rate. As such, even if near-monies increase the interest-sensitivity of money demand, the monetary authorities can still conduct monetary policy effectively. The Fed must simply adjust the monetary base to compensate for any systematic shift from money to near-monies as interest

---

[6]The propositions outlined briefly in this section are most fully developed in J. G. Gurley and E. S. Shaw, "Financial Aspects of Economic Development," *American Economic Review* 45 (September 1955): 515–38; and in J. G. Gurley and E. S. Shaw, *Money in a Theory of Finance* (Washington, D.C.: The Brookings Institution, 1960). Also see Lawrence Ritter, "Income Velocity and Anti-Inflationary Monetary Policy," *American Economic Review* 49 (March 1959): 120–29.

rates rise. The economic slowdowns associated with recent periods of monetary stringency (1966, 1969–1970, 1974) were looked upon as ample proof that monetary policy actions continue to exert a powerful and predictable influence on economic activity.

This comfortable conclusion has been partially shaken, however, by our experience since 1974. Money demand functions fitted to pre-1974 data have predicted consistently and significantly greater demands than actual money holdings have been for the period from 1974 to the present. It remains to be determined whether this observed downward shift in money demand (increase in velocity) is to be explained on the basis of financial market innovations (NOW accounts, telephone and remote teller transfers of funds from savings to draft accounts, etc.) by which M_1 money as it is currently measured has become a closer substitute for other assets, or whether some other explanation is appropriate. What is clear is that, by making shifts in money demand more likely to occur, the presence of close substitutes for money complicates the Fed's task of predicting the economy's response to alternative paths of monetary expansion.

OPERATING TARGETS IN THE CONDUCT OF MONETARY POLICY

If stabilization policy actions immediately produced effects on their *ultimate targets*—e.g., on the value of nominal output—policy would be simpler to conduct. A policy posture that failed to produce the desired value for nominal income could be made more stimulative or more restrictive if its effects were immediately observable. Unfortunately, as we have explained in detail, the timing of such effects involves a lag that is extended and variable in length. Hence policy actions must be undertaken on the basis of predicted future responses to those actions. Some uncertainty in the conduct of stabilization policy arises from an inability to observe quickly how a policy action will influence an ultimate target variable (like nominal income); this is further compounded by uncertainty with regard to the strength of impact of policy actions.

In spite of these uncertainties, stabilization policies must be implemented, and policy-makers must formulate strategies to conduct them. To help circumvent the extended lag between a policy action and the economy's full response to that action they focus attention on the control of one or more *intermediate targets*. Particular variables are chosen as intermediate targets because they are believed to be stably related to ultimate targets (i.e., to the variables that stabilization policy is aimed at controlling) and because they respond quickly to policy actions, so that policy-makers can monitor the influence of their actions.

For intermediate targets in the conduct of monetary policy, the logical choices are interest rates and monetary aggregates. Keynesians, who believe that money supply changes influence the economy by means of altering interest rates and thus real investment, have typically favored the interest rate as an intermediate target of monetary control. Monetarists, who argue that money supply changes influence spending more directly, whether interest rates change or not, favor monetary aggregates as intermediate targets.

Interest Rates as Targets

During the 1960s, policy-makers were optimistic that countercyclical stabilization policy could be successful. There was an active effort to offset any deviation of the economy from what was viewed as its best expansion path. During that period, monetary policy actions generally focused on altering interest rates to control the economy; they allowed the supply of money to change as much as was needed to achieve selected interest-rate goals. However, beginning in the mid-1960s, an inflation emerged, making observed interest rates (which reflect inflationary expectations) unreliable indicators of the tightness or ease of monetary policy. That inflation also called into question the practice of allowing monetary aggregates to change in whatever manner was needed to achieve a selected interest-rate goal, since inflations can persist only if they are fueled by monetary expansion. Further, the combination of a rapid and persistent inflation with a serious recession, which began in 1969, caused a substantial decline of confidence in stabilization policy's ability to fine-tune the economy.

Increased Attention to Monetary Aggregates as Targets

With a widespread belief that, over the long run, there is a stable relationship between the amount of money in circulation and the nominal value of output, and with a reduced confidence in stabilization policy's ability to iron out every wrinkle in the economy's expansion path, monetary policy in the 1970s has placed much more reliance on monetary aggregates as intermediate targets and has focused on steadier growth of these aggregates than what we have had in the past. Under the current strategy for monetary policy-making, the Federal Open Market Committee (FOMC) periodically specifies desired growth rates for monetary aggregates (notably, M_1 and M_2) for the next year. These growth targets are publicly announced in quarterly testimony before a congressional banking committee.

At its monthly meetings, the FOMC compares the actual growth of the monetary aggregates with their desired long-run growth paths. On the basis of this comparison, and in light of the current state of the economy, the FOMC specifies short-run *tolerance ranges* for the growth rates of the aggregates over a two-month period. These tolerance ranges are selected to be consistent with achievement of the long-term goals for monetary growth, but they also can accommodate any temporary deviations from those paths that events might warrant.

Once the short-run tolerance ranges are set, the FOMC specifies a federal funds rate range (normally, from 50 to 100 basis points in width), which it believes to be consistent with short-run growth rates for monetary aggregates that fall within the specified tolerance ranges. Any subsequent deviation of the actual two-month monetary growth rate from the tolerance ranges is likely to lead to a change in the federal funds rate. Open-market operations are then undertaken, altering the reserves provided to the commercial banking system. The change in the reserve base results in pressures in the federal funds market, which generate a new federal funds rate believed to be consistent with desired monetary expansion rates.

Instructions for the conduct of monetary policy, which set long-term and two-month tolerance ranges for monetary expansion and a rate range for federal funds, are forwarded from the FOMC to the Federal Reserve Bank of New York. The form of these instructions is well illustrated by the following passages of a policy directive from October 1977:

> It is the policy of the Federal Reserve Open Market Committee to foster bank reserve and other financial conditions that will encourage continued economic expansion and help resist inflationary pressures, while contributing to a sustainable pattern of international transactions.
>
> Growth of M-1, M-2, and M-3 within the ranges of 4 to 6½ percent, 6½ to 9 percent, and 8 to 10½ percent, respectively, from the third quarter of 1977 to the third quarter of 1978 appears to be consistent with these objectives. . . .
>
> . . . the committee seeks to maintain the weekly-average Federal funds rate at about 6½ percent, so long as M-1 and M-2 appear to be growing over the October-November period at annual rates within ranges of 3 to 8 percent and 5½ to 9 percent, respectively. If . . . it appears that growth rates over the 2-month period are approaching or moving beyond the limits of the indicated ranges, the operational objective for the weekly-average Federal funds rate should be modified in an orderly fashion within a range of 6¼ to 6¾ percent.[7]

The nature of the FOMC policy directive allows the open-market account

---

[7]*Federal Reserve Bulletin*, December 1977, pp. 1073–74. FOMC directives are published, with a roughly three-month delay, in the *Federal Reserve Bulletin*.

manager to engage in security purchases and sales in a manner that prevents abrupt and erratic short-term variations in interest rates but that also, over a longer time horizon, provides changes in the reserve base consistently with long-run targets for monetary expansion. Because of its efforts to smooth the time path of interest rates, and because of numerous slippages between a monetary policy action and the resulting change in monetary aggregates, money supply growth rates often fall outside the prescribed tolerance ranges for several weeks. Over a longer time horizon, however, the Fed can control the money stock with substantial precision, so that, on a yearly average, it comes close to hitting any target growth rate it selects for monetary aggregates. Of course, since the Fed does not directly control money demand, the achievement of a particular long-run growth rate in the money supply requires the Fed to allow interest rates to seek their own level over the long haul. It is not at all clear that the Fed is willing to do so.

SUMMARY

This chapter has provided a overview of the real-world application of stabilization policy, with a particular interest in monetary policy. Our discussion has recognized the existence of uncertainties and, indeed, outright disagreements between competing groups of economists over the strength and the timing of effects of monetary and fiscal policies. Monetarists view money as the prime mover of economic activity, and they discount the macroeconomic influence of fiscal policy. Modern Keynesians believe that both monetary policies and fiscal policies normally have powerful effects but that the strength of each varies according to economic conditions.

Stabilization policy is complicated by uncertainties over the strength and the timing of responses to policy actions, together with our lack of ability to predict those events (like an oil embargo) that disturb the economy. The application of monetary policy is further complicated by concerns over the uneven incidence of monetary policy actions, by the appearance and popularization of near-monies, and by a responsibility to smooth movements in interest rates on a short-term basis. Few economists would claim that a policy-maker's task should be easy, although most monetarists conclude that the economy would be well served if policy-makers were replaced by a simple rule or set of rules for monetary expansion.

For better or worse, stabilization policy continues to be practiced. In the day-to-day application of monetary policy, to reduce the uncertainty over the impact of policy actions, the Fed could choose either interest rates or monetary aggregates as an intermediate target of policy. It appears that in the 1960s, little attention was paid to monetary aggregates, as monetary policy focused on influencing the economy by means of altering interest rates. In the 1970s, although few would claim that interest rates are being ignored, a great deal more attention has been focused on monetary aggregates. Of course, the changes in monetary aggregates and in interest yields that result from stabilization actions impinge on each and on every one of the specialized financial markets we have studied in this text. You should now be able to assess the likely impact in financial markets of shocks that arise in the real or the financial sectors of the economy.

18

International and Other Considerations

The preceding chapters have described and analyzed the financial system in this country and its links to the real sector of the economy. In the process, we have considered the need for a specialized financial structure, the creation of money, the banking system, the role of the Federal Reserve System and the U.S. government, the demand for and the supply of loanable funds and the determination of interest rates, financial instruments and the markets in which they trade, the intermediation process and its participants, and the interactions between the financial system and the real economy—i.e., we constructed a macroeconomic model of the financial and the real sectors, generated aggregate demand and aggregate supply relationships, and used them to analyze unemployment, inflation, and the application of monetary and fiscal policies. Each of these topics has been covered in sufficient detail that a good understanding of the nature and importance of each has been obtained. One important topic, which has appeared intermittently in the discussion up to this point, merits direct attention to provide a complete picture of the parameters involved in our financial system. It is the topic of international relationships. The first half of this chapter analyzes the basics of international trade and finance.

After the completion of our analysis of the entire aggregate economic system, it is appropriate to consider forecasting models. We would like, not only to better understand the economy, but also to be able to make some forecasts of its future direction. The econometric models of the aggregate economy that are currently being used are valuable for both of these purposes; they will be considered in the second half of this chapter.

INTERNATIONAL CONSIDERATIONS

Thus far in this text, we have concentrated our attention mainly on the domestic economy: we have focused on the money transactions, the financial institutions, and real sector of the domestic economic system. However, the United States does not operate in a vacuum but rather is an intricate part of the international economy. The real and financial sectors of our economy are affected by rest-of-world transactions, and we in turn have profound effects on the world economy. It is therefore appropriate for us, concentrating as we have up to now on financial issues, to conclude our analysis with a brief consideration of international financial transactions and markets.

Structure of the International Financial System

We started our analysis of the U.S. financial system with a study of money—what it is, what it does, and how a monetized system operates. It is logical to begin our discussion of the international financial system the same way. A major role of money internationally, as in the domestic economy, is to provide an efficient means of exchange. There is an international exchange of goods and services, just as there is a domestic exchange. Money facilitates this exchange and permits specialization in production; it thereby enhances world productivity. International payments need to be made as expediently as possible. For this to occur, a well-functioning international financial structure is required. Some principal parts of the international monetary system are commercial banks; foreign exchange markets, including dealers; governments—central banks; and international monetary institutions, primarily the International Monetary Fund. Let us consider each of these parts in turn.

Commercial Banks. It is interesting to note that commercial banks are at the center of the international framework, just as they are in our own monetary economy. This is a result of the fact that, as is the case with domestic payments, the most efficient way to make international payments is to transfer claims on banks.

Recall the vast network of domestic banking relationships, which includes intrastate branches (where they are permitted), correspondent relations, and transfers through accounts maintained at the Fed. Similarly, there are banking office networks within countries and a complex of myriad relationships among various countries' banks. The international economy is linked together directly by banks setting up offices or subsidiaries abroad (which are hooked into the collection systems of the various countries) indirectly by correspondent relationships on an international scope (through which banks in various countries provide services for each other) and by governments. Thus the financial world is heavily dependent upon commercial banks.

Individuals or firms in various countries can transact with each other in several ways, with exchanges based on the receiver's currency, the payer's currency, or some third currency used by both parties. For example, French tourists in the United States could purchase dollars in order to transact freely in this economy. A U.S. firm could sell goods in France for francs and convert them to dollars. In either case, francs would be supplied to the foreign exchange market. When a U.S. firm sells to a French firm and requires payment in dollars, the U.S. firm presents a draft to the bank of the French buyer. This bank must purchase dollars in one of the money markets to pay the U.S. firm, and this purchase supplies francs to the foreign exchange market. Finally, two foreign countries could agree to transact with each other on the basis of U.S. dollars.

Foreign Exchange Markets. *Foreign exchange* refers to the cash claims of all countries against the currency of a particular country. Foreign exchange markets, therefore, include the total mechanism available by which the claims on various world currencies are handled. It is really an over-the-counter market, linking together currency dealers and brokers around the world. Participants include commercial banks involved in foreign exchange, specialized foreign exchange brokers, and central banks. Because of the importance of international trade and commerce, almost every country has facilities for exchanges of domestic currency for those of other countries.

Foreign exchange markets primarily transact in claims against banks, since banks are at the center of international transactions; of course, some coins and paper money are traded. Transactions in any of these items can be for immediate delivery to settle current claims. Transactions can also involve a delivery scheduled for some designated time in the future (i.e., it is a foward market). The latter market is heavily used for hedging, which is a method of reducing risk; it is an attempt to protect against losses that arise from changes in the prices or values of foreign currencies. For example, an American manufacturer exporting goods to Japan can hedge against the payment, which is to be received in the future—say, in 60 days. To do this, the exporter sells Japanese yen in the forward market for delivery in 60 days. Then, if the value of the yen fell 3 percent in relation to the dollar during the 60-day period (which would reduce the value of the payment to be received), the exporter would probably gain 3 percent in dollars in the forward market; on the settlement date, the exporter could purchase yen for less than the contracted price to sell yen. Those wishing to hedge future payments, along with speculators and governments, are the major participants in the forward market.

Prices on the foreign exchange markets represent rates of exchange of one national money for another. As in any market, prices in the foreign exchange market (i.e., exchange rates) are governed by the forces of supply and demand.

Central Banks. Central banks have traditionally been involved in international transactions because they were responsible for the international reserves of their country. In earlier times, these transactions often involved the purchase or the sale of gold to prevent changes in the exchange rate. Modern transactions are like the 1978 announcement by the Fed that it (along with the Treasury) would take actions on the foreign exchange markets to prevent a fall in the international value of the dollar. This intervention meant the buying of dollars in conjunction with the U.S Exchange Stabilization Fund.[1]

Obviously, the role of the central bank in international affairs goes beyond the management of foreign exchange reserves. It must integrate international actions and policies with those of the domestic economy. For example, if international considerations dictated it, the central bank (through its monetary policy) could force a rise in interest rates in order to affect capital flows. Also, trade deficit considerations may be tied in with the problem of domestic inflation.

International Monetary Institutions. International monetary cooperation is desirable, and international monetary institutions play a key role in this regard. The most important of these is the International Monetary Fund (IMF), an outgrowth of the famous Bretton Woods conference, held near the end of World War II. Virtually all noncommunist nations are now members of the fund and subscribe to its capital in accordance with a quota formula based on national income, reserves, and trade. Thus the IMF is basically a large fund consisting of international currencies.

The International Monetary Fund serves the world community by providing credit facilities, by trying to bring order to exchange rates, by providing international liquidity to members who need help with their deficits, and by trying to coordinate economic policies among the various countries. One well-known creation of the IMF is special drawing rights (SDRs), or "paper gold."[2] SDRs, created in 1969, were a new type of international monetary reserve, which were designed to substitute for the traditional methods of international payment, gold or major currencies. They were created as bookkeeping entries and, in effect, were given to all IMF members wishing them. SDRs were intended as transfers between central banks as a means of settlement for balance-of-payments deficits. The IMF was to guarantee the value of an SDR in terms of a fixed amount of gold.

SDRs were intended and are now generally accepted as an international reserve asset. They were devised to meet increases in the demand for reserves—a useful idea in a world of expanding trade; that is, an

---

[1]See Anatol B. Balbach, "The Mechanics of Intervention in Exchange Markets," *Review—Federal Reserve Bank of St. Louis*, February 1978, pp. 2–7.

[2]This discussion of SDRs draws heavily on Douglas R. Mudd, "International Reserves and the Role of Special Drawing Rights," *Review—Federal Reserve Bank of St. Louis*, January 1978, pp. 9–14.

international medium of exchange, which can be increased as the need arises to finance international trade, in addition to the standard payment methods, is potentially very desirable. However, the original plan envisioned an end to the U.S. balance of payments deficit, with SDRs becoming the principal reserve asset. Changes in the supply of SDRs could be voted by members, so that total reserves would be independent of any particular country's actions. The success of SDRs depended upon a significant reduction in gold and in dollars as reserve assets. Also, SDRs were introduced when fixed exchange rates prevailed. Continuing U.S. deficits in the 1970s led to the holding of massive amounts of dollars by foreign central banks, a loss of confidence in the ability of the United States to maintain the dollar at a fixed value, a shift by foreign central banks from dollars into gold and other currencies, and a movement toward relatively flexible exchange rates. Thus SDRs were basically rendered irrelevant, because U.S. deficits in the 1970s caused foreign currency holdings (primarily dollars) to become the largest component of international reserves balances.

SDRs have had a minor impact on total international reserves. Starting at 3 percent in 1970, they constituted 6 percent of total reserves by 1972, but no more have been allocated since then. The dollar amount in existence is about $9.3 billion. Since international reserves have risen continuously since 1972, SDRs represent a decreasing percentage, approximating 4 percent in 1976. Table 18–1 shows the growth and composition of international reserves from 1969 through 1976. Gold has decreased sharply in importance; SDRs have remained a small factor, as have countries' reserve positions with the IMF; and currency (foreign exchange) reserves have more than quintupled. The latter accounted for 85 percent of the increase in international liquidity over that period.

In summary, there is a complete operating structure for the international economy. As for international transactions per se, there are two important aspects that need to be considered: the balance of payments and the international rate of exchange of money.

The Balance of Payments

In trading with each other, countries sell both goods and services and transfer financial claims back and forth. The balance of payments constitutes a record of these many international transactions.

Let us consider the U.S. balance of payments. It is a yearly record of purchases from and sales to foreigners; it includes products (and services) and capital assets. The balance of payments accounts are like a corporate balance sheet in that both sides must balance.

A deficit in our balance of payments arises when our expenditures and transfers abroad exceed our sales abroad less transfers and investments from abroad. To finance a deficit, the United States has to borrow

TABLE 18–1. The Growth and Composition of International Reserves, 1969–1976 (End of Period)

	1969	1970	1971	1972	1973	1974	1975	1976
Total Reserves ($ million)	78,670	93,247	133,797	159,077	183,655	220,581	277,404	254,845
Annual Change (percent)	—	+48.53	+43.49	+18.89	+15.45	+20.11	+3.15	+12.07
Gold ($ million)	38,916	36,992	38,990	38,653	42,953	43,531	41,562	41,109
Annual Change (percent)	—	–4.94	+5.40	–0.86	+11.12	+1.35	–4.52	–1.09
Share of Total Reserves (percent)	49.47	39.67	29.14	24.30	23.39	19.73	18.28	16.13
SDRs ($ million)	0	3,124	6,379	9,430	10,624	10,845	10,260	10,057
Annual Change (percent)	—	—	+104.19	+47.83	+12.66	+2.08	–5.39	–1.98
Share of Total Reserves (percent)	—	3.35	4.77	5.93	5.78	4.92	4.51	3.95
Reserve Position in Fund ($ million)	6,726	7,697	6,895	6,867	7,441	10,828	14,778	20,606
Annual Change (percent)	—	+14.44	–10.42	–0.41	+8.36	+45.52	+36.48	+39.44
Share of Total Reserves (percent)	8.55	8.25	5.15	4.32	4.05	4.91	6.50	8.09
Currency Reserves ($ million)	33,028	45,434	81,534	104,126	122,636	155,377	160,804	183,073
Annual Change (percent)	—	+37.56	+79.46	+27.71	+17.78	+26.70	+3.57	+13.85
Share of Total Reserves (percent)	41.98	48.72	60.94	65.46	66.78	70.44	70.71	71.84

Source: Jane Little, "The Euro-Currency Market and the Growth of International Reserves," "New England Economic Review, Federal Reserve Bank of Boston, May–June 1977, p. 12.

from foreign sources or from international agencies, or it has to give up previously earned foreign exchange (or, in the past, gold). Surpluses involve the contrary: the U.S. accumulates exchange (and, in the past, gold) and owes less in liabilities. These definitions are general, and various countries define deficits and surpluses differently.[3]

The balance of payments accounts include the following components: the current account, which shows the amount of goods and services bought and sold, as well as transfer payments; the capital account, which shows both private and government capital transactions; changes in liquid private capital; reserve assets, including gold; and miscellaneous items. The U.S. balance of payments for 1974 is shown in Table 18–2, along with a set of explanations of the various categories contained in the accounts.

Typically, analyses of the balance of payments concern either the current account or the capital account separately. Technically, however, all accounts should be considered simultaneously, because most of the items are closely related. For example, direct U.S. investment abroad (a capital account entry) is related to the return of profits from abroad (a current account entry, as profits are counted as income earned from the current provision of productive services).

Given our emphasis throughout this text on the interdependence of different sectors of the economy, it is interesting to consider the relation between the balance of payments and the domestic economy. According

---

TABLE 18–2. U.S. Balance of Payments, 1974

Summary Explanations of U.S. Balance
of Payments
(To be used in conjunction with Table 18–2.)

The U.S. balance of payments is a summary record of all international transactions by the Government, business, and private U.S. residents occurring during a specified period of time.

As a series of accounts and as a measure of economic behavior, balance of payments transactions are grouped into seven categories: merchandise trade, services, transfer payments, long-term capital, short-term private capital, miscellaneous, and liquid private capital. We successively add the net balances of the above categories in order to obtain:

    Merchandise Trade Balance
    Goods and Services Balance
    Current Account Balance
    Basic Balance

---

[3]Actually, in the United States, there are two definitions of deficit (surplus). One is the *official settlement* basis, which involves only official holdings of exchange or official borrowing. The alternative is the *liquidity* basis, under which a deficit includes private borrowings abroad. The two measures can show substantially different figures.

Net Liquidity Balance

Official Settlements Balance

Below the dashed line there are two additional categories, U.S. liabilities to foreign official holders and U.S. reserve assets. These serve to finance the transactions recorded above the dashed line.

There are interrelationships between these accounts. For example, the credit entry associated with an export of goods could result from the debit entry of a private bank loan, a Government grant, a private grant, or an increase in U.S. holdings of foreign currency or gold.

Merchandise Trade: Exports and imports are a measure of physical goods which cross U.S. boundaries. The receipt of dollars for exports is recorded as a plus and the payments for imports are recorded as a minus in this account.

Services: Included in this account are the receipt of earnings on U.S. investments abroad and the payments of earnings on foreign investments in the U.S. Sales of military equipment to foreigners and purchases from foreigners for both military equipment and for U.S. military stations abroad are also included in this category.

Transfer Payments: Private transfers represent gifts and similar payments by Americans to foreign residents. Government transfers represent payments associated with foreign assistance programs and may be utilized by foreign governments to finance trade with the United States.

Long-term Capital: Long-term private capital records all changes in U.S. private assets and liabilities to foreigners, both real and financial. Private U.S. purchases of foreign assets are recorded as payments of dollars to foreigners, and private foreign purchases of U.S. assets are recorded as receipts of dollars from foreigners. Government capital transactions represent long-term loans of the U.S. Government to foreign governments.

Short-term Private Capital: Nonliquid liabilities refers to capital inflows, such as loans by foreign banks to U.S. corporations, and nonliquid claims refers to capital outflows, such as U.S. bank loans to foreigners. These items represent trade financing and cash items in the process of collection which have maturities of less than three months. The distinction between short-term private capital and liquid private capital is that the transactions recorded in the former account are considered not readily transferable.

Miscellaneous: Allocations of special drawing rights (SDRs) represent the receipt of the U.S. share of supplemental reserve assets issued by the International Monetary Fund. SDRs are recorded here when they are initially received by the United States. The category errors and omissions is the statistical discrepancy between allspecifically identifiable receipts and payments. It is believed to be largely unrecorded short-term private capital movements.

Liquid Private Capital: This account records changes in U.S. short-term liabilities to foreigners, and changes in U.S. short-term claims reported by U.S. banks on foreigners.

NOTE: For analytical purposes the dashed line below the official settlements balance could be moved. For example, if this line were placed under one of the balances above, then all transactions below that line would serve as financing, or offsetting, items for the balance above.

U.S. Balance of Payments, 1974p (Billions of Dollars)	Net Balance	Cumulative Net Balance
Merchandise Trade:		
Exports	+ 97.1	
Imports	−103.0	
Merchandise Trade Balance	− 5.9	− 5.9
Services:		
Military Receipts	+ 3.0	
Military Payments	− 5.1	
Income on U.S. Investments Abroad	+ 29.9	
Payments for Foreign Investments in U.S.	− 16.7	
Receipts from Travel & Transportation	+ 10.2	
Payments for Travel & Transportation	− 12.7	
Other Services (net)	+ 0.3	
Balance on Services	+ 9.1	
Goods and Services Balance		+ 3.2
Transfer Payments:		
Private	− 1.1	
Government	− 6.1	
Balance on Transfer Payments	− 7.2	
Current Account Balance		− 4.0
Long-term Capital:		
Direct Investment Receipts	− 2.3	
Direct Investment Payments	− 6.8	
Portfolio Investment Receipts	+ 1.2	
Portfolio Investment Payments	− 2.0	
Government Loans(net)	+ 1.0	
Other Long-term (net)	− 2.4	
Balance on Long-term Capital	− 6.7	
Basic Balance		−10.6
Short-term Private Capital:		
Nonliquid Liabilities	+ 1.7	
Nonliquid Claims	− 14.7	
Balance on Short-term Private Capital	−13.0	
Miscellaneous:		
Allocation of Special Drawing Rights (SDR)		
Errors and Omissions	− 5.2	
Balances on Miscellaneous Items	− 5.2	
Net Liquidity Balance		−18.3

Liquid Private Capital:

    Liabilities to Foreigners .... + 15.7

    Claims on Foreigners .... − 5.5

        Balance on Liquid Private Capital .   + 10.3

Official Settlements Balance ....   − 8.1

The Official Settlements Balance

    is Financed by Changes in:

    U.S. Liabilities to Foreign

        Official Holders:

    Liquid Liabilities .... + 8.3

    Readily Marketable

        Liabilities .... + 0.6

    Special Liabilities .... + 0.7

        Balance on Liabilities to

            Foreign Official Holders .....   + 9.5

    U.S. Reserve Assets:

    Gold 0.0

    Special Drawing Rights .... − 0.2

    Convertible Currencies 0.0

    IMF Gold Tranche .... − 1.3

        Balance on Reserve Assets ...   − 1.4

Total Financing of Official

    Settlements Balance ....   + 8.1

Source: Donald Kemp, "Balance of Payments Concepts — What Do They Really Mean?" *Review*, Federal Reserve Bank of St. Louis 57, (July 1975), p. 18.

Note: For analytical purposes the dashed line below the official settlements balance could be moved. For example, if this line were placed under one of the balances above, then all transactions below that line would serve as financing, or offsetting, items for the balance above.

Note: Figures may not add because of rounding.

*There was no SDR allocation for 1974.

P — Preliminary

to the monetarist view, surpluses and deficits result from disequilibrium in the demand for and the supply of money. In this case, however, money balances have to be adjusted internationally, not just nationally. Consider the following illustration:

Suppose, for example, that the domestic monetary authorities increase the money supply in country j, which leads to an increase in the demand for goods, services, and securities in that country. Any such increase in domestic demand will result in a tendency for prices of domestic real and financial assets in country j to rise, in the short run, relative to those in foreign markets. As a result, spending units in country j will simultaneously reduce their purchases of domestic real and financial assets in favor of foreign assets while domestic suppliers of these assets will seek to sell more at home and less abroad. At the same time, foreign spending units will decrease their purchases of the assets of country j and foreign suppliers will attempt to sell more of their own assets in country j. All of these factors work in favor of an increase in the demand for imports and a decrease in the demand for exports in country j.[4]

The International Rate of Exchange

The rate of exchange of money between countries is important because it plays a major role in the dictating of the basis on which trade can take place for a country. Thus the conditions under which trade takes place between the United States and the rest of the world depend upon the price levels of both and upon the rate of exchange between the dollar and each of the other currencies. This rate of exchange is set in the foreign exchange market, which was discussed above. However, we have not yet discussed an issue that is one of the major controversies of international economics—fixed exchange rates versus floating exchange rates. We will outline this issue below.

Fixed exchange rates involve governmental agreements to maintain a fixed rate of exchange between their currencies. Floating exchange rates are determined by the forces of supply and demand for foreign exchange. Advocates of the former policy argue that, under floating rates, changes are largely a result of speculation, which can be destabilizing. Some even believe that such speculation can disrupt international trade by means of increasing the risk involved in international transactions. Advocates of floating rates argue that exchange rates change as a result of fundamental economic factors and that speculation is a stabilizing force because it dampens fluctuations. Hence, supporters of that view contend that the growth of international trade is encouraged rather than hampered by floating rates.

Which view is correct? The answer to this question is not immediately available. However, some empirical evidence for the period from 1970 through 1976 indicates that exchange-rate changes have not resulted from destabilization due to speculation.[5] (This evidence covers periods before and after generalized floating, which began in March 1973.)

What does determine exchange-rate changes? One theory of exchange rates indicates that the major factor is relative inflationary pres-

---

[4]Donald Kemp, "Balance of Payments Concepts—What Do They Really Mean?" *Review*, Federal Reserve Bank of St. Louis 57 (July 1975): 15.

[5]See Donald Kemp, "The U.S. Dollar in International Markets: Mid-1970 to Mid-1976," *Review*, Federal Reserve Bank of St. Louis 58 (August 1976): 7–14.

sures in various countries. This relationship becomes better established over longer time horizons. The empirical study cited above indicates that there is a strong inverse relationship, especially in the long run, between movements in exchange rates and relative inflationary pressures.

The exchange rate does affect balance of payments equilibrium, because it affects the current account balance (and possibly the capital account balance). If a deficit exists, a country can choose to lower its official exchange rate—i.e., to devalue its currency. Conversely, a surplus can lead to an upward valuation of its money.

There is often great concern in a system of floating rates that depreciation of the currency of a particular country causes inflation in that country. A counterargument is that currency depreciations are the result, not the cause, of inflationary pressures: depreciation is a result of imbalances in the demand for and the supply of money, and such imbalances must be resolved.

Finally, exactly which type of system does prevail today in the world economy? Since the early 1970s, the trend in a growing number of countries has been to allow the forces of supply and demand in the foreign exchange market to determine the international values of domestic currencies. However, central banks often intervene to adjust daily changes in the relative values of their currencies; they do this by buying or selling the currency in foreign exchange markets. In addition, over 100 smaller countries peg their currencies. This current system could be called a *managed floating exchange-rate* system. Relative values of various currencies can, therefore, vary from what they would be if exchange rates were allowed to "float cleanly."

Some International Concerns for the U.S. Economy

Having considered the basic framework of the international financial system, we will now outline some current international issues that affect the U.S. financial system. We have continuously argued that the U.S. financial system is a highly integrated complex of people, instruments, institutions, markets, and government and that one cannot properly analyze one aspect of this complex in isolation—ultimately, all interrelationships should be considered because of the feedbacks to and from each component. Therefore we now need to go one last step and at least briefly consider international forces that impact significantly on our financial system.

The Flow of Capital. We have established above, through discussion of the balance of payments, that countries are linked together in terms of goods and services traded—the current account—and in terms of the transfer of financial claims—the capital account. The latter consideration is important. For example, some observers believe that the fall in the value of the dollar in the late 1970s was largely due to oil imports by the United States; however, capital movements are a source of both supply and demand for dollars on the foreign exchange market. The facts are that capital inflows in 1977 offset almost half of the U.S. balance-of-trade deficit with those countries that export oil. Thus international capital flows are extremely important to our financial and real sectors, because they represent additions to or subtractions from the pool of domestic saving. Such flows can also conflict with government policies. In the late 1960s, for example, the Fed instituted a restrictive monetary policy, which resulted in a very tight money situation for commercial banks. One response by the banks to a restricted ability to lend was to bring in record amounts of Eurodollars to use for the extension of credit in the United States (at very high interest rates), which thus offset to some extent the Federal Reserve monetary policy.

Foreign investors, like any other rational investors, seek to maximize their welfare. If they perceive U.S. securities to offer attractive opportunities, funds flow into our money and capital markets. This results in an increase of loanable funds in the United States and, other things being equal, can lower interest rates. Such a lowering of the interest rate can have effects on the real economy, as was discussed earlier.

Loanable funds, subject to constraints, will be allocated to the most promising opportunities on the basis of expected return and risk, not only in this country, but throughout the world. Thus most knowledgable investors—and this certainly includes the U.S. institutions that control so much of the economy's funds—seek out the best opportunities anywhere. Commercial banks have foreign branches, and several foreign stock exchanges are well known here. Significant return differentials in various countries will attract capital flows until an equilibrium is achieved. Of course, these international flows are not perfectly efficient in the sense that funds flow to the most promising opportunities. There are constraints, not the least of which are political uncertainties (e.g., consider the Iranian situation in 1979) and imperfect information on the various opportunities that are available in the world economy at various points in time.

International capital flows can affect the monetary policy of a country, which can in turn affect both the financial and the real sectors of the economy. For example, the Fed could adopt a monetary posture to influence interest rates with the objective of affecting international capital flows and ultimately the balance of payments through the capital account.

OPEC—A Major World Force. A major force currently affecting international capital flows is the Organization of Petroleum Exporting Countries (OPEC), the world oil cartel. The very large amounts of funds that it generated from oil sales resulted in massive increases in the OPEC current account surplus and correspondingly massive current account deficits in other countries. These funds have had to be recycled in such a way as to minimize the impact on other countries, including the United States—and, in fact, this has been done quite successfully, on balance. OPEC countries have made very large purchases from other countries in the mid-1970s. However, as is clear from President Carter's constant call to battle in 1977 to save energy and thereby to decrease money flowing to the oil producers, OPEC revenues are still enormous and are growing. The potential problem with this aggregate deficit is that the successful recycling might come to an abrupt end for political reasons, and this could sharply affect multinational capital flows. In turn, a shock to the international credit structure could have significant influences on the U.S. financial system.

The Arab countries have now accumulated massive amounts of financial capital that can be moved around the world. They have invested very substantial amounts in countries like England and the United States. Such actions are a good demonstration of the importance of international capital flows, because they have resulted in the supply of large amounts of funds to financial markets in these two countries and quite likely have held interest rates below the level they would otherwise have reached in the mid-1970s. Table 18–3 shows the estimated disposition of OPEC surpluses for the period from 1974 through 1976.

Commercial Banks and the Third World. The oil crises of the mid-1970s also played a major part in another potential problem for the U.S. financial system as a result of international relationships. Third world countries had to borrow heavily in the mid-1970s to finance their oil imports. Because of a price boom in basic commodities during that period, they appeared to be better credit risks than they really were.[6] These countries actively sought bank loans during that period (banks impose fewer restrictions on the use of funds than do international aid and development loan agencies); and, at the time, banks had excess funds to lend, because domestic loan demand had contracted, since the U.S. economy was suffering its deepest recession since the 1930s. In this setting, American bank loans to third world countries rose very sharply (by tens of billions of dollars) during the mid-1970s. The safety of some of these loans has been called into question.

The net result of this situation is that some major U.S. commercial banks have found themselves with large amounts of very shaky assets. Any sizable defaults could have repercussions on our own economy, because bank lending might have to contract to make up for losses, and the integrity of the banking system—which is essential to faith in our domestic money—could be impaired. The ultimate risk here is the possibility of a collapse of some banks. The question of adequacy of bank capital—discussed in Chapter 13—is relevant here.

In summary, the U.S. financial system—and its constituents—may have to feel the negative impact of bank transactions in the international

---

[6]This discussion is indebted to Cheryl Payer, "Third World Loans Might Make Our Banks Beggars," *Business and Society Review* 20 (Winter, 1976–77) pp. 56–60.

TABLE 18–3. Estimated Disposition of OPEC Surpluses (in billions of dollars)

		1974	1975	1976
I.	In United States	12.0	10.0	11.6
	A. Short-term assets[1]	9.3	0.3	0.3
	B. Treasury bonds and notes	0.2	2.0	4.1
	C. Other deposits and securities[2]	1.3	4.0	3.4
	D. Direct investment	0.3	1.0	−0.5
	E. Other[3]	0.9	2.7	4.3
II.	In United Kingdom	7.2	0.2	−1.2
	A. Liquid sterling assets[4]	5.3	0	−2.4
	B. Other loans and investments	1.9	0.2	1.2
III.	In Euro-currency Markets	24.5	9.1	10.3
	A. United Kingdom	13.8	4.1	5.8
	B. Other centers (est.)[5]	10.7	5.0	4.5
IV.	International Institutions	3.3	3.5	1.5
	A. IBRD bonds	1.5	0.9	0.5
	B. IMF Oil Facility	1.8	2.6	2.0
V.	Total Identified Above	47.0	22.8	22.2
VI.	All Other (Residual)	10.6	9.8	20.2
VII.	Total = Investable Surplus	57.6	32.6	42.4
VIII.	OPEC Grant Aid	2.4	2.4	1.6
IX.	Surplus on Goods and Services[6]	60.0	35.0	44.0

Source: Norman S. Fieleke, "Trade with the Oil-Exporting Countries," *New England Economic Review,* Federal Reserve Bank of Boston, May-June 1977, p.8.

[1]Principally Treasury bills, repurchase agreements, bank deposits and CDs.
[2]Long-term bank deposits, corporate and Federal agency bonds, and equities.
[3]Real estate, prepayments of imports, debt repayment, and miscellaneous investments.
[4]Treasury bills and bonds, bank and other deposits.
[5]Including domestic-currency bank deposits in centers other than the United Kingdom and United States.
[6]With oil receipts on a cash basis.

arena. Clearly, worrying only about domestic loans and domestic default risk is inadequate.

Eurodollars. In chapter 11, we discussed Eurodollars as a money market instrument. Eurodollars are dollar-denominated deposits in foreign commercial banks. The development of the Eurodollar market is a good example of the financial system's quick response to changing conditions. Eurodollars are a significant innovation in the international payments mechanism, and therefore, by extension, they can substantially affect related financial markets.

Any individual or institution—Americans, foreigners, governments, etc.—holding a U.S. bank deposit is a potential creator of Eurodollars.

Therefore a very large potential supply of Eurodollars exists at any time. The demand for Eurodollar loans is also potentially large; it ranges from demands by banks to those of importers and governments. Eurodollars are clearly a major international currency now.

Eurodollars are, in effect, a currency among banks, because they can move among banks, and they often do move before they are lent to someone else. There is a Eurodollar expansion process. Just as in the case discussed in chapter 4, Eurodollar deposits can undergo a multiple expansion, with the maximum expansion depending upon leakages in the system. Because of the movement of Eurodollars among banks, a default by any one of them could have harmful effects on others.

The tie-ins of Eurodollars with the U.S. financial system are multiple. They have been used domestically by U.S. banks when Regulation Q limited deposit rates, so that banks substituted international for domestic borrowing. Also, Eurodollars have encouraged international capital flows, because they are a convenient way to invest in countries with high interest rates. This makes the U.S. economy a more integrated part of a world economy: high interest rates on Eurodollars in a foreign country can cause money to be switched from U.S. banks to the foreign banks.

Summary

In the analysis of our financial system, with its various institutions and markets, international relationships are potentially significant and should be recognized. The international economy is much like our domestic economy. First of all, there is an exchange of goods that is similar to what happens on a local basis. Secondly, commercial banks are a key part of the international structure, just as they are a key part of the U.S. financial system. The other main parts are the foreign exchange markets (including dealers), central banks, and international monetary institutions.

The balance of payments is an annual record of international transactions among countries. The current account shows the amount of goods and services bought and sold; the capital account shows both private and government capital transactions. Deficits and surpluses indicate differences between expenditures and receipts for a country.

The rate of exchange of money between countries is set in the foreign exchange market. A major controversy here is the issue of fixed exchange rates versus floating exchange rates. With fixed rates, the governments involved establish the rate of exchange, while, with floating rates, supply and demand forces determine the exchange rate. There is no established answer as to which system is better. Generalized floating started in 1973.

Some international concerns for the United States include international capital flows, OPEC, commercial bank loans to the third world, and Eurodollars. In the final analysis, all of these factors have to be assessed at some point in order to deal with the U.S. financial system.

MODELING THE FINANCIAL SYSTEM

One of the major tasks of many economists is to make forecasts of the economy for some subsequent period (typically, a year). Such forecasts are clearly of value in the making of plans and the setting of goals for the future and in current preparations for subsequent problems. For example, if investment spending is expected to be sluggish as the economy recovers, an investment tax credit might be considered as a stimulus to investment. It is particularly important to attempt to anticipate this sort of problem because of the lag in getting stabilization policies into action. Alternatively, suppose that banks are expected to squeeze the ratio of free reserves to total reserves in response to a predicted rise in short-term interest rates. The Fed presumably takes this and many other factors into account in the formulation of future monetary policy.

It should be obvious from the preceding chapters that much economic and financial data on the U.S. economy is available. Fortunately, economic reasoning can be augmented with statistical analysis to employ available data in assessments of various theories of the functioning of the economy. Models that are found to have merit in their explanations of economic fluctuations can also be used to forecast the economy's future path. These procedures involve the practice of *econometrics*, which involves the formulation of economic theories as mathematical models whose parameters are estimated statistically.

In this section, we will briefly review the major econometric models that have recently been constructed. They represent a logical extension of our previous efforts to understand the economy and of our attempts to put this understanding to good uses. These models vividly demonstrate the interlocking nature of our financial system, a point stressed throughout this text.

Background for Econometric Models

Large-scale econometric models of the U.S. economy evolved from the work of Jan Tinbergen in 1939. Currently, there are several well-known models that are being used, including the Federal Reserve–MIT–Penn model; the Department of Commerce model; the Wharton School model; the Brookings Institution model; the Chase Econometrics Associates model; and a model developed by Data Resources Incorporated.[7]

How is an econometric model of the U.S. economy constructed? First, a theoretical model of the economy is required. Then, behavioral functions

---

[7]This is a nonexhaustive list. For a good discussion of several of these models, from which the following discussion has benefitted, see William R. Hosek and Frank Zahn, *Monetary Theory, Policy* and *Financial Markets* (New York: McGraw-Hill Book Company, Inc., 1977), Chapter 12.

in the model chosen (e.g., consumption, investment, and money demand functions) are fitted to historical data. The large-scale econometric models currently in existence usually require many equations to obtain detailed subsector predictions on such aggregate measures as consumption and investment. In effect, for each component variable that is analyzed, a separate explanatory equation is generally needed. Also, additional equations may be required to achieve stable regression equations to explain particular variables—e.g., consumption can be broken down into spending on services, spending on nondurable goods, and spending on durables. The regression equations that are needed (and any related identities) constitute a set of simultaneous equations that can be used for predictive purposes. The largest models now in use contain several hundred equations.

We will briefly examine four of the principal econometric models currently in use in the United States. Their details are complex and require serious specialized study. Our purpose is simply to see generally how they model the economy. In particular, we want to note how each represents the financial sector, because that has been our primary interest throughout this text. As does the simple *IS-LM* model, large-scale models capture and reflect the paths through which changes in the financial sector are transmitted to the real sector. This is important for a grasp of the implications of concepts developed earlier, and it is important for an understanding of the interrelatedness of the entire economy; it illustrates the need to study the financial and real sectors together. After reviewing the models themselves, we will consider some evidence on their success.

The Brookings Institution Model. The oldest of the large models now being used is the Brookings Institution model. It has been revised many times and, in fact, is currently revised as needed. It can contain hundreds of equations (depending upon the version).

The Brookings model is basically a Keynesian model, having its foundations in the *IS-LM* framework developed in chapter 15; that is, the *IS-LM* framework forms the bond between the financial sector and the real sector, and output and employment are determined primarily from the demand side.

Consumption, the largest component of aggregate demand, responds only gradually to changes in income; most of current income changes go into saving (consistent with the permanent-income and the life-cycle consumption models). Consumption is also positively related to liquid assets, as it is in monetarist models, but aggregate demand is not primarily determined by monetary variables.

Investment, as would be expected in a Keynesian-style model, is a prominent and volatile determinant of aggregate demand. Business investment is positively related to expected production capacity needs and, through a complex cost-of-capital relationship, is inversely related to interest rates. Investment in residential structures is particularly sensitive to financial market conditions; it is influenced by both the long-term interest rate and the extent of credit rationing (reflecting the disintermediation problem).

Changes in the level of government spending, which is determined exogenously by congressional action, also have a powerful effect in this model. The foreign sector has a much less prominent influence on aggregate demand; the net demand from abroad responds (1) positively to a growth in world trade, (2) negatively to a rise in the U.S. price level in relation to foreign prices, and (3) negatively to an expansion in domestic income, since that raises import purchases.

The remaining part of the model represents the financial sector. The model separates the demand for money into demands for demand deposits and for time deposits, and it relates the supply of money to free reserves. In the liquidity preference framework, the demand for and the supply of money determine short-term interest-rate levels, and changes in the short-term interest rate influence other yields—notably, the time deposit rate and long-term rates. An expectations model of the sort discussed in chapter 9 is used to relate the short-term rate to a long-term rate. Unborrowed reserves (i.e., the sum of free reserves and required reserves) are the primary policy vehicle by which the Fed, generally through open-market operations, can influence the financial sector and hence the real sector of the economy. In turn, since the demand for money is positively related to GNP, changes in the real sector are transmitted to the financial sector in *IS-LM* fashion.

In summary, then, the Brookings model is closely associated with traditional *IS-LM* analysis. Output is significantly affected by current investment expenditures, the principal components of which are residential construction and business investment, and by changes in the government budget. The investment variables are in turn influenced by changes in short-term and long-term interest rates, with the latter, in turn, a function of the former.

The Federal Reserve–MIT–Penn Model. Another basically Keynesian model, but with variations, is the Federal Reserve–MIT–Penn (FRMP) model (formerly, the Federal Reserve Board—MIT model). Consumption is composed of the services provided by stocks of durable goods plus expenditures on nondurable goods and on services. (This model distinguishes between services yielded by durable goods and expenditures on durable goods.) The consumption variable is related to current and past income. The FRMP model, employing a consumption function drawn from the life-cycle theory, links household wealth to aggregate consumption. As a result of this linkage, monetary policy changes play a very important role in this model, as money supply changes alter yields on, and the capitalized value of, equity claims, which in turn alters consumption. This model also assesses a credit rationing effect, unlike the Brookings model.

As for investment, the neoclassical theory of the firm is used as the basis for plant and equipment equations, but allowances are made for such factors as lags in the formation of expectations and technological changes. Interest rates and tax effects are considered by means of the impact they have on investment returns. Equations are included to try to separate builders and owners of housing from users, in order to try to predict housing starts. Municipal government spending (and taxes) is endogenous in the model.

On the financial side, the behavior of financial markets is described, given GNP and some variables determined by Fed policy. Unborrowed bank reserves are exogenous and are related to deposits, reserve requirements, and free reserves. The Treasury bill rate is determined as the money market interest rate and is used to estimate various other short-term rates and the long-term interest rate; the latter, in turn, is used to estimate dividend yields on stocks (which are substitutes for bonds), which, as a capitalization rate, can be used to estimate the market value of stocks.

The FRMP model has several paths by which the monetary sector can affect the real sector of the economy. In general, the financial sector impacts upon the real sector by means of affecting investment expenditures through interest rates. Thus the model is basically Keynesian.

The Wharton School Model. The Wharton School model is quite similar to the FRMP model with regard to the financial sector. Equations for money demand and money supply are estimated, and interest rates are determined. However, consumption changes in this model are a function of changes in liquid assets rather than total wealth. The degree of credit availability is also a factor influencing consumption in the Wharton model.

Like the FRMP model, the Wharton model has several paths by which monetary policy (financial changes) affects spending in the real sector. Again, this is basically a Keynesian model, because interest rates are the primary means of transmission from the financial sector to the real sector (by means of affecting investment spending). Both models differ from the straightforward Keynesian analysis, however, by their considerations of wealth effects in their respective ways.

The St. Louis Federal Reserve Model. The three models discussed above are all basically Keynesian, varying only in degree of departure from basic Keynesian concepts. A completely different approach, representing monetarist reasoning, underlies the St. Louis Federal Reserve model. In this approach, money supply plays the dominant role in the determination of money GNP. A flow diagram of this model is shown in Figure 18–1.

This model assumes that there are multiple channels through which monetary factors influence GNP, but it doesn't spell out what those channels are or test the importance of alternative channels. Fiscal variables, which are treated as exogenous, are included as possible determinants of GNP, but, in statistical tests with the model, they have no measured lasting influence on nominal income (if unaccompanied by changes in money).

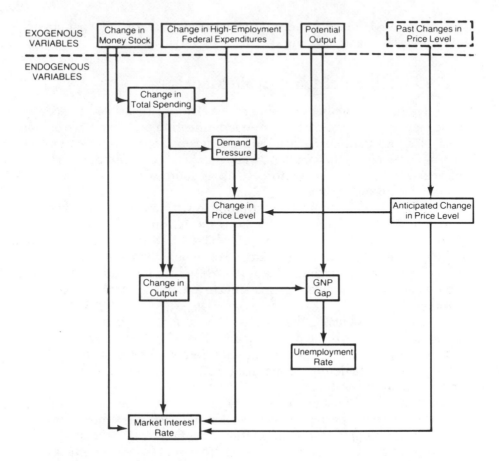

FIGURE 18–1. Flow Diagram of the St. Louis Federal Reserve Model

Source: Leonall C. Andersen and Keith M. Carlson, "A Monetarist Model for Economic Stabilization," *Review–Federal Reserve Bank of St. Louis,* April 1970, p. 10.

The St. Louis model actually has no financial sector as such, but it corresponds to the models considered previously in that money can be assumed to affect GNP. Total spending is a function of both monetary and fiscal actions. Money supply is viewed as an exogenous variable that is determined by Fed actions. Because of this exogeneity, there is no feedback link from interest rates to money supply. Also, although the model determines an interest rate, that rate has no direct effect on spending, output, and prices. In summary, the St. Louis model is a monetarist model, although there are no specified channels by which monetary changes impact on the real sector. The model has no formal theoretical basis, like the *IS-LM* framework, which consists of a set of structural equations that can be derived. Actually, the St. Louis model is very small: it contains only eight equations and only three exogenous variables.[8]

Limitations of Large-Scale Models

There are a number of problems associated with large-scale econometric models. First, there could be an identification problem if two or more variables in a particular equation are logically dependent (i.e., endogenous). To overcome this problem, which has been recognized for a number of years, there have been efforts to apply more sophisticated statistical techniques to the models.

Some observers see a second problem with respect to the very size and complexity of the models themselves. It is argued that the vast detail of the models results in a greater probability of misspecifications, so that they produce inaccurate estimates. Too much disaggregation may be superfluous. However, the St. Louis model—which is a model of few equations—has been criticized for inadequate specification of the economic structure.

Another problem is the choice of the monetary variable to be used in the model. What is the proper financial variable to use in assessing the financial sector where interest rates are determined? Does this variable change because of defensive or dynamic actions, or because of some action independent of the Fed?

Perhaps the most important criticism of large-scale models is simply that they have not performed very well in forecasting—although they are valuable for an understanding of the structure of the economy. Small models can and do forecast as well. There is some evidence available on the results of these models, which we can now examine.

Performance of Large-Scale Econometric Models

How well have these models performed? According to some recent empirical evidence, they have not done too well.

The first question that might be asked is, How well have the models spotted turning points in the economy? Victor Zarnowitz, Charlotte Boschan, and Geoffrey H. Moore have studied this question for the 1969 versions of the Wharton model, the Office of Business Economics model,

---

[8]See Leonall C. Andersen and Keith M. Carlson, "A Monetarist Model for Economic Stabilization," *Review–Federal Reserve Bank of St. Louis* 52 (April, 1970), p. 9 for a list of equations and variables. The main equation expresses changes in money income as a function of dollar changes in both money stock and high-employment Federal expenditures (each on a current and a lagged basis); the monetary changes are found to exert a statistically significant influence on total spending relative to those of fiscal actions.

and the FRMP model.[9] The historical forecasts of these models, on average, were correct two-thirds of the time when the economy either peaked or bottomed out. However, in general, these models predicted turning points too soon (these observations are based on 1957–61 data). As would be expected, the possibility of calling the turn improved as the forecast period approached the turning point (one quarter ahead).

How well have these three models fared in predicting the sizes of peaks and troughs? A weakness of large-scale models is their tendency to smooth out business cycles, and these models are no exception (again using 1957–61 data). The models underestimated both peaks and troughs but again improved as the forecast starting point approached the turn. The models did better, on average, for contractions than for expansions.

This evidence indicates that the models need to be improved. Nariman Behravesh suggests two ways in which this can be done: (1) a prediction can be adjusted to correct for previous errors, and the forecaster's judgment can be interjected; (2) the model itself can be improved.[10]

Another study has been done to shed some light on an issue mentioned above—large-scale models versus small-scale models. An example of the latter is a business anticipations survey, which is a survey by the Department of Commerce of business's intentions to invest in nonresidential fixed investment in the next year. Can the large-scale econometric models, with their equations representing investment, make better forecasts of investment than the anticipations survey? According to some research done by Herman Liebling, Peter Bidwell, and Karen Hall, the answer is no.[11] They examined the forecast record for fixed investment for three of the best-known models for the years 1973, 1974, and 1975. The models were those of Chase Econometric Associates, Data Resources Incorporated, and the Wharton School. Their study indicates that the advantages of large models were not demonstrated by the results for those years: "The performance of the anticipatory surveys of the Department of Commerce continued to show a margin of superiority."[12] Further, they found that forecasted quarterly changes showed significant errors for all three years, which indicates that such forecasts are quite unreliable as guides for policy-makers.

---

[9]See Victor Zarnowitz, Charlotte Boschan, and Geoffrey H. Moore, "Business Cycle Analysis of Econometric Model Simulation," in B. G. Hickman, ed., *Econometric Models of Cycical Behavior* (New York: National Bureau of Economic Research, 1972), pp. 311–541. This article is discussed in Nariman Behravesh, "Forecasting the Economy with Mathematical Models: Is It Worth the Effort?" *Business Review*, Federal Reserve Bank of Philadelphia, July-August 1975, pp. 15–25. The discussion here draws heavily on the latter article.

[10]Behravesh, p. 25.

[11]Herman Liebling, Peter Bidwell, and Karen Hall, "The Recent Performance of Anticipation Surveys and Econometric Model Projections of Investment Spending in the United States," *Journal of Business* 49 (October 1976), pp. 451–77.

[12]*Ibid.*, p. 451.

In summary, there is and always will be a continuing need to improve the large-scale models. Their structures need to be continuously updated to accommodate changes in the structure of the economy. These models will always involve "art" as well as science, since the judgement of the modelers is necessary to introduce refinements, corrections, and changes.

A CONCLUDING NOTE

Having discussed the international financial system and the econometric models of the U.S. economy, we have now completed our original objective—an analysis of money, financial markets, and the economy. It should be apparent at this point that the financial and the real sector of the economy form a completely interrelated structure: each of the many parts goes together to form a cohesive whole, and each part functions in relation to the whole. As a consequence, the financial system cannot be analyzed and understood in isolation but must be considered in relation to the complete economic system.

An analysis of the functioning of the financial system logically begins with a review of the basic functions of the economy and the role of money and financial markets in that system. It is easy to demonstrate the need for a good monetary system and for specialization in the exchange of financial instruments. Money and the monetary role of the banking system should follow because of the importance of money to the financial system. The Federal Reserve is a crucial link in monetary control in the United States. The next major concern in a progression through the financial system is nonmonetary financial transactions. The demand for and the supply of loanable funds determines interest rates. The next broad topic to consider is the institutional structure of the financial system, subdivided by instruments, by markets, and by financial institutions. Wealth is created by investment in real assets, and the financial claims handled within the institutional structure help to finance these real assets. The last issue in an analysis of the financial system is the development of the linkages between it and the real macroeconomy. Such a framework includes consideration of inflation, unemployment, and the application of monetary and fiscal policy.

The preceding summary traces the topics on money, the financial system, and the economy developed in this text. As was noted above, the serious observer of the financial system must eventually go beyond a study of the various parts of the system and must start to think in terms of an integrated and closely-knit economy, which, although it is extremely complex, can be analyzed successfully from several standpoints, because all of its parts are interdependent. It is inadequate to think only in terms of money and banking principles, because other important and related concepts are thus slighted. It is also inadequate to think only in terms of macroeconomics, because this tends to overemphasize the real sector of the economy. Finally, it is inadequate to think only in terms of corporate finance and investments, because the real macroeconomy is thereby ignored, and there are a number of issues here that impact on financial considerations (inflation is a painfully obvious example). What you must do in your future efforts to project economic and financial developments is to analyze events from the perspective of an integrated system of money, financial markets, and the real sector of the economy.

Index

Note: Page references to figures or tables are indicated by italics.